IQ
MINDBENDERS

IQ MINDBENDERS

Over 1000 brainteasing puzzles to test your logical and lateral faculties to the limit

ARCTURUS

ARCTURUS
This edition published in 2009 by Arcturus Publishing Limited
26/27 Bickels Yard, 151–153 Bermondsey Street,
London SE1 3HA

ISBN: 978-1-84837-168-2

Printed in Malaysia

IQ MINDBENDERS

Meticulously compiled from some of the most devious puzzles you are ever likely to encounter, *IQ Mindbenders* has been designed to stretch your mental faculties while leaving you with a glow of satisfaction. Some puzzles will require mathematical ability, others a facility for recognizing abstract patterns, but all are supremely logical and can be solved with the right approach.

If you have a sharp mind, some of the answers to these puzzles will jump straight out of the page at you. However, others will require a bit more thought. Try not to rush for an answer straight away – have faith in your abilities and all will become clear – and don't feel tempted to have a peek at the answer page too soon. If you feel completely stumped by one particular puzzle, then move on and come back to it later – coming up with the solution to a later puzzle just might give you the inspiration you need!

But the idea of this book is not about right and wrong answers, it's about exercising your mind and flexing your mental muscles. So sit back, relax your body and let your brain take the strain – it's all a matter of logic.

Multiplication Table

	1	2	3	4	5	6	7	8	9	10	11	12
1	1	2	3	4	5	6	7	8	9	10	11	12
2	2	4	6	8	10	12	14	16	18	20	22	24
3	3	6	9	12	15	18	21	24	27	30	33	36
4	4	8	12	16	20	24	28	32	36	40	44	48
5	5	10	15	20	25	30	35	40	45	50	55	60
6	6	12	18	24	30	36	42	48	54	60	66	72
7	7	14	21	28	35	42	49	56	63	70	77	84
8	8	16	24	32	40	48	56	64	72	80	88	96
9	9	18	27	36	45	54	63	72	81	90	99	108
10	10	20	30	40	50	60	70	80	90	100	110	120
11	11	22	33	44	55	66	77	88	99	110	121	132
12	12	24	36	48	60	72	84	96	108	120	132	144

	Cube Numbers	Square Numbers
1	1	1
2	8	4
3	27	9
4	64	16
5	125	25
6	216	36
7	343	49
8	512	64
9	729	81
10	1000	100
11	1331	121
12	1728	144
13	2197	169
14	2744	196
15	3375	225
16	4096	256
17	4913	289
18	5832	324
19	6859	361
20	8000	400

Numerical Values

1	A	26
2	B	25
3	C	24
4	D	23
5	E	22
6	F	21
7	G	20
8	H	19
9	I	18
10	J	17
11	K	16
12	L	15
13	M	14
14	N	13
15	O	12
16	P	11
17	Q	10
18	R	9
19	S	8
20	T	7
21	U	6
22	V	5
23	W	4
24	X	3
25	Y	2
26	Z	1

Prime Numbers
2
3
5
7
11
13
17
19
23
29

1 PUZZLE

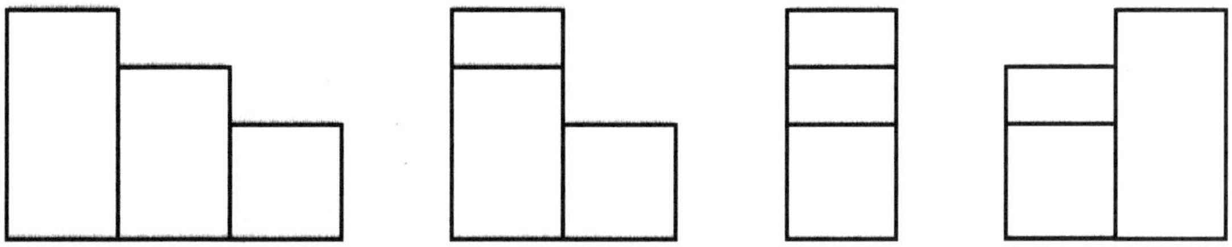

What comes next?

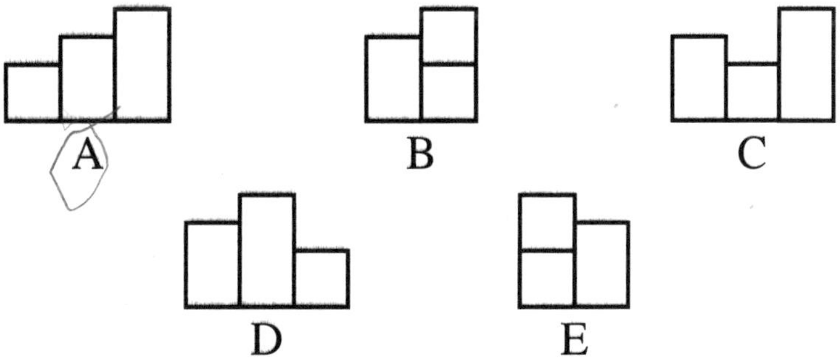

2 PUZZLE

How many minutes before 12 noon is it if 72 minutes ago it was twice as many minutes past 9.00am?

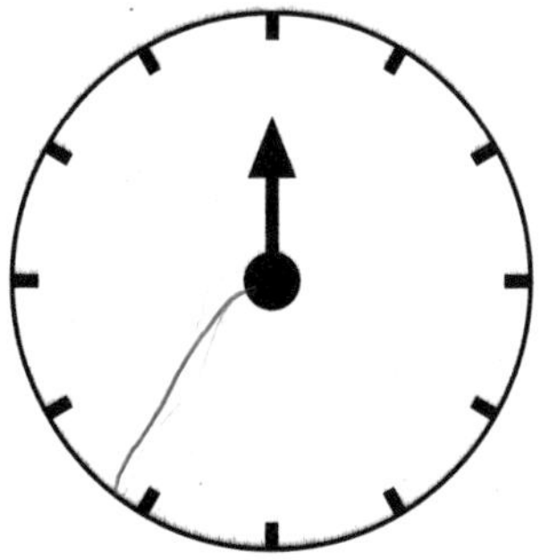

3 PUZZLE

What number should replace the question mark?

4	5	1
2	?	5
4	2	4

PUZZLE 4

Frank has half as many again as Sally who has half again as many again as Mary. Altogether they have 209.

How many has each?

Frank has 99
Sally has 66
Mary has 44

PUZZLE 5

What comes next in this sequence?

346
289
134
628
?

PUZZLE 6

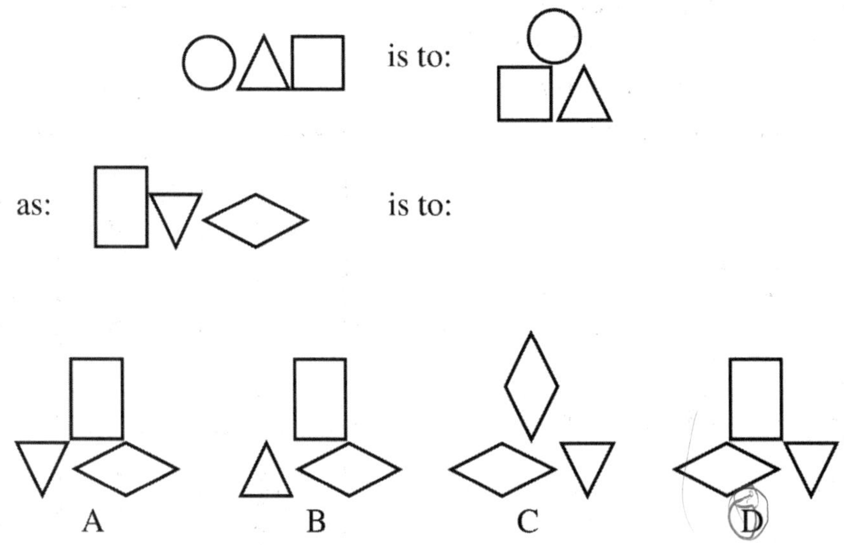

7 PUZZLE

What should replace the question mark?

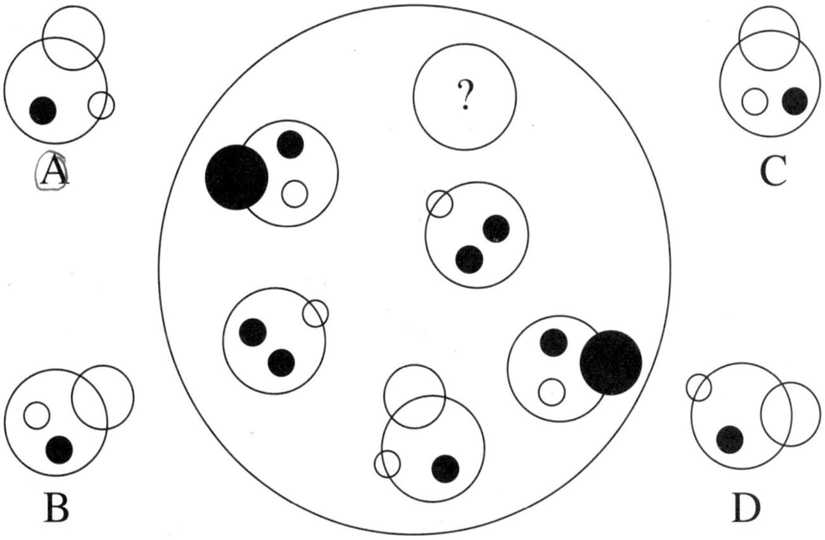

8 PUZZLE

SUNDAY
MONDAY
TUESDAY
WEDNESDAY
THURSDAY
FRIDAY
SATURDAY

What day comes two days after the day immediately before the day three days after the day immediately before the day which comes two days after Sunday?

9 PUZZLE

What number should replace the question mark?

7	8	9
4	6	8
1	?	7

PUZZLE 10

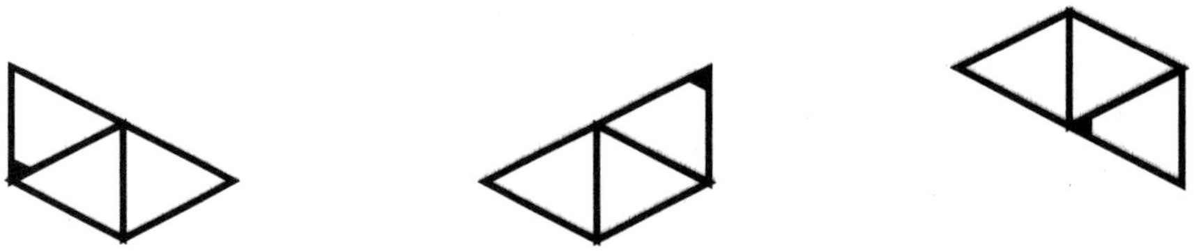

What comes next?

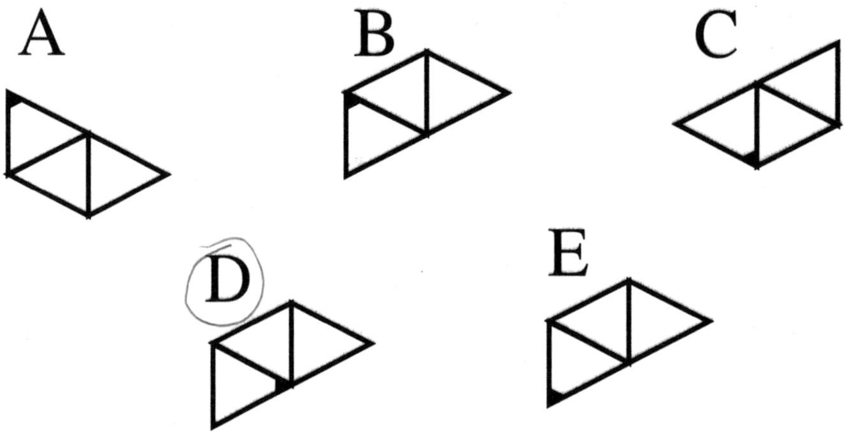

PUZZLE 11

What number should replace the question mark?

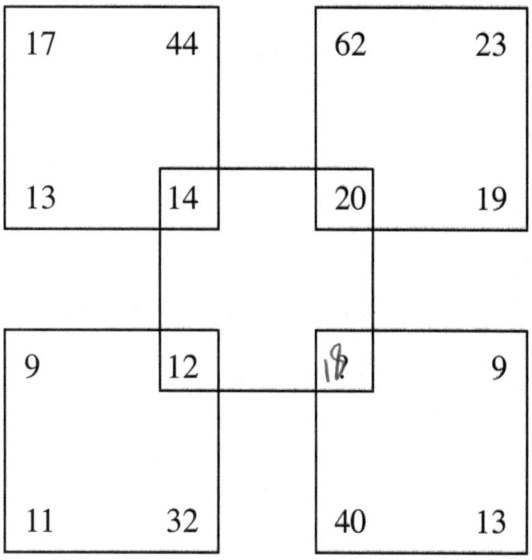

PUZZLE 12

What number should replace the question mark?

7	6	5	23
9	2	8	7
6	14	2	22
4	8	7	?

13 PUZZLE

Each line and symbol which appears in the four outer circles, below, is transferred to the centre circle according to these rules: If a line or symbol occurs in the outer circles: once: it is transferred twice: it is possibly transferred 3 times: it is transferred 4 times: it is not transferred. Which of the circles A, B, C, D or E, should appear at the centre of the diagram, below?

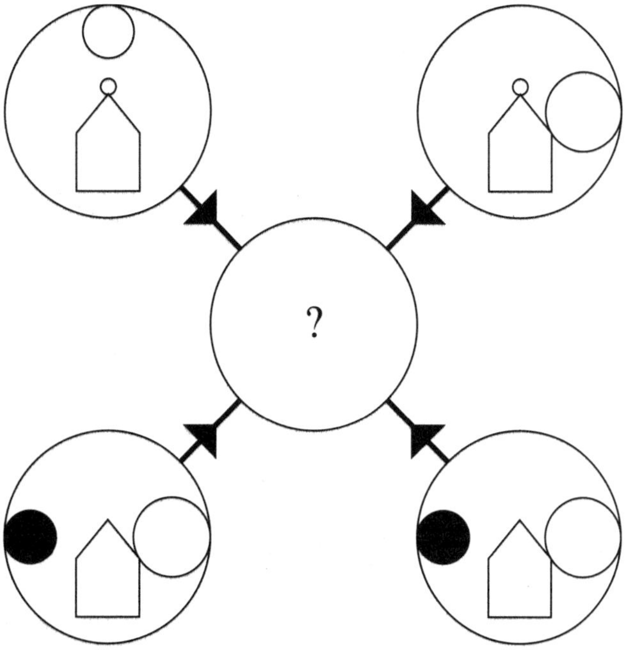

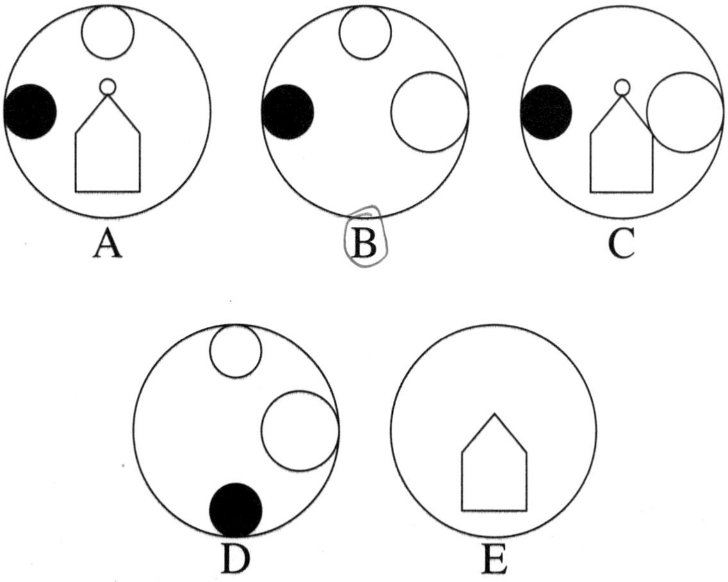

LEVEL 1

LEVEL 1

14 PUZZLE

1	7	9	8	2	0	6

is to:

9	6	0	2	1	7	8

as:

9	8	2	6	0	1	7

is to:

1	8	7	0	9	6	2

0	2	1	8	7	9	6

7	2	1	6	0	9	8

6	8	7	1	9	2	0

15 PUZZLE

Which wave A, B, C or D replaces the question mark?

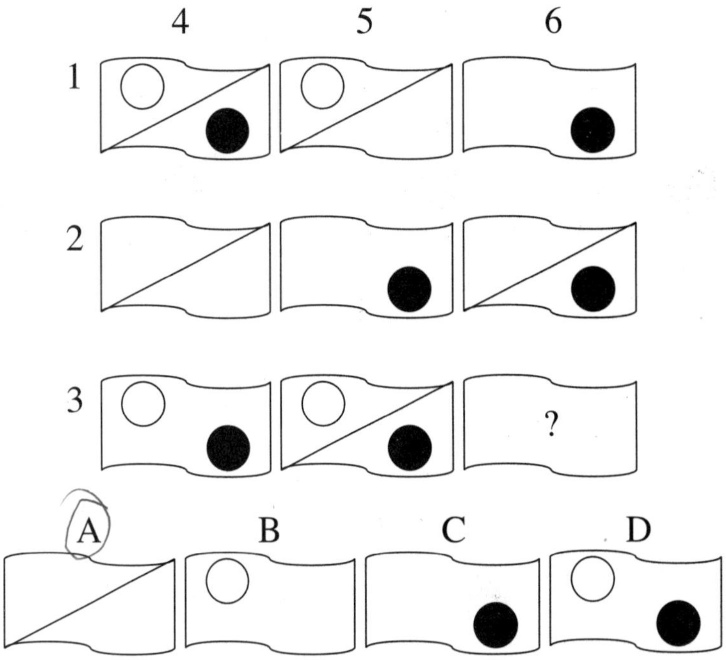

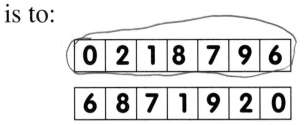

16 PUZZLE

Which circle A, B, C, or D should replace the question mark?

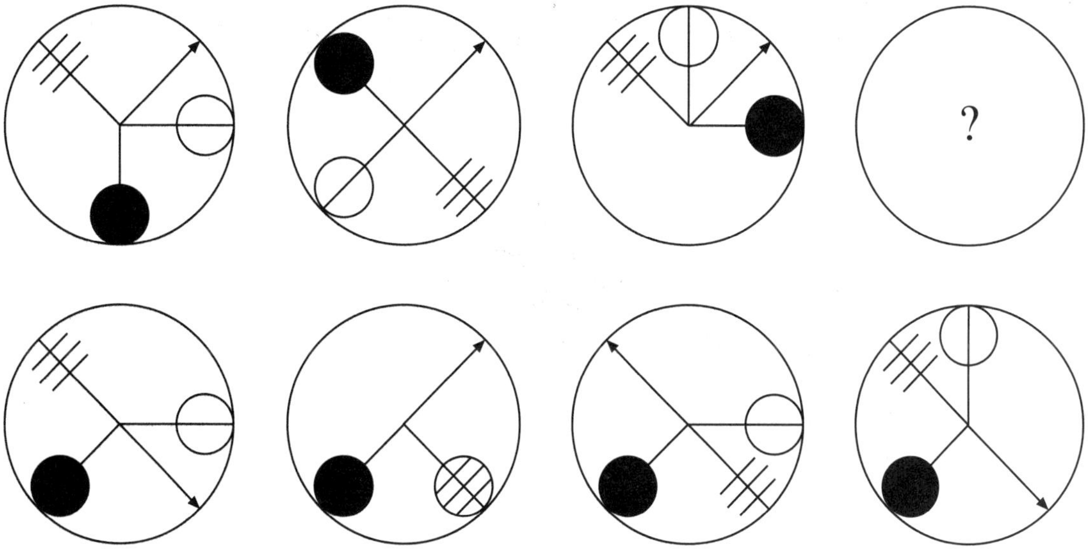

A B C D

17 PUZZLE

Which word is the same or closest in meaning to TORPID?

(a) TORPEDO LIKE
(b) MAGIC
(c) SLUGGISH
(d) ANCIENT
(e) KIND

18 PUZZLE

What is 75% of one half of 52^2?

19 PUZZLE

Which circle is nearest in content to A?

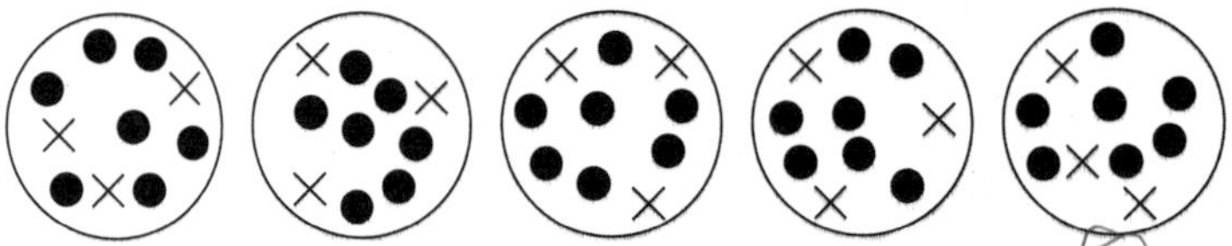

20 PUZZLE

What number should replace the question mark?

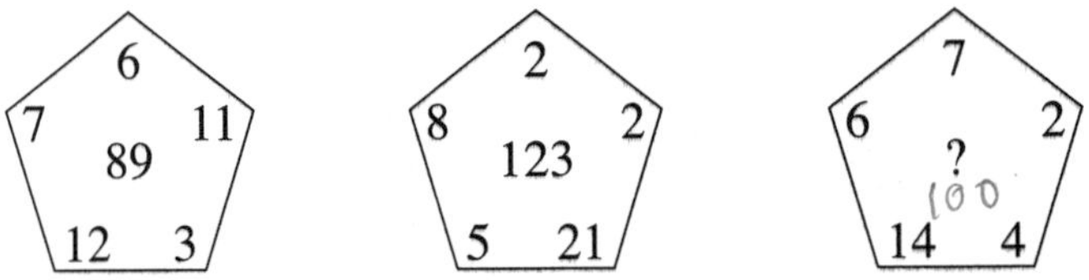

21 PUZZLE

Which one is the odd one out?

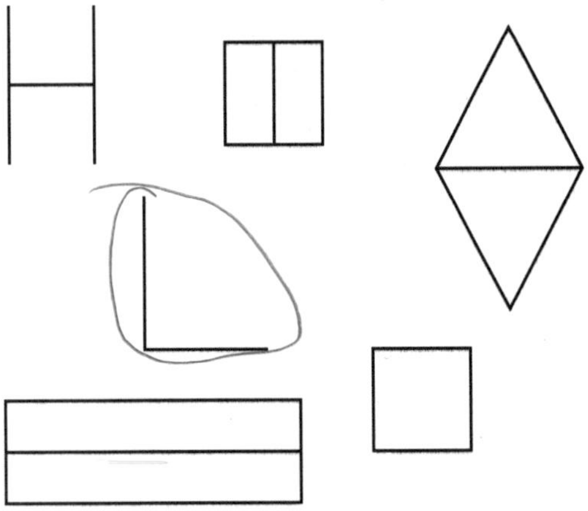

22 PUZZLE

Simplify

16 - 20 x 2 + 40 ÷ 8 + 19 = x

23 PUZZLE

Which word is the same
or closest in meaning to TENUITY?

(a) SOUNDLESS
(b) ACIDITY
(c) LICENCE
(d) BOLDNESS
(e) SLENDERNESS

24 PUZZLE

Each of the nine squares in the grid marked A1 to C3, should incorporate all the lines and symbols which are shown in the squares of the same letter and number above and to the left. For example, B2 should incorporate all the lines and symbols that are in 2 and B. One of the squares is incorrect. Which one is it?

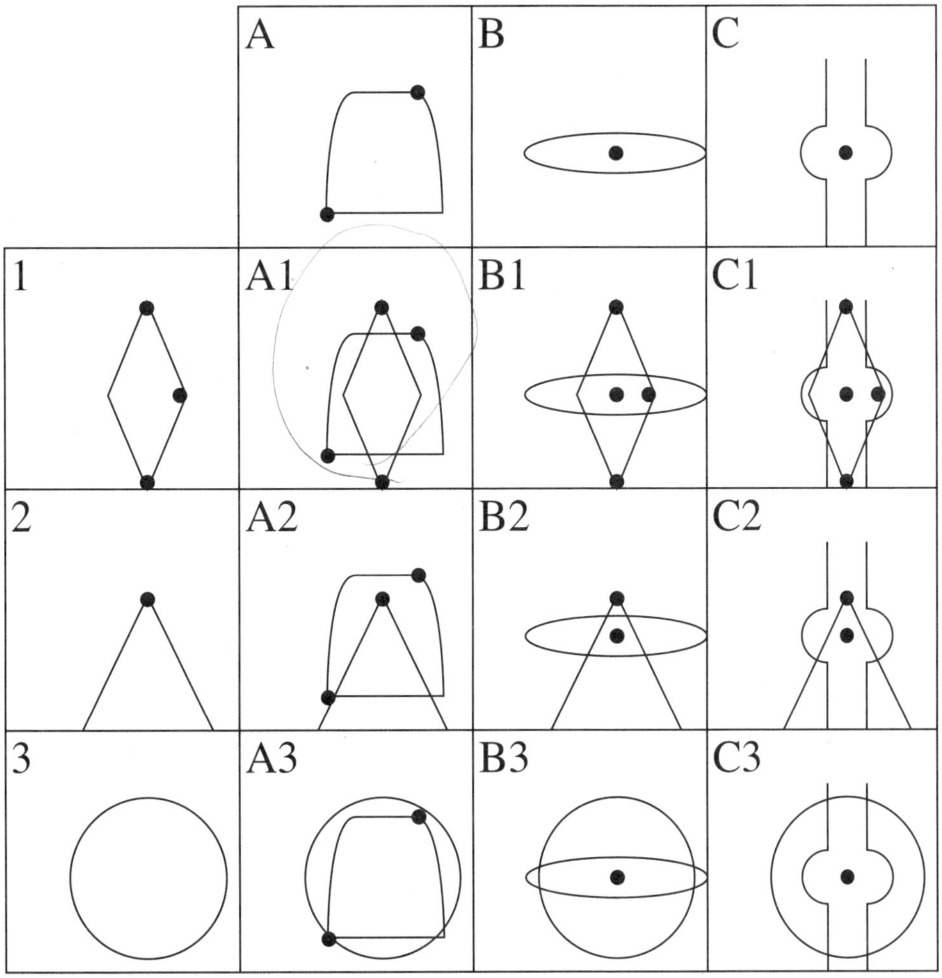

25 PUZZLE

What does PETTIFOGGING mean?

(a) LOSING DIRECTION
(b) AGGRESSIVENESS
(c) QUIBBLING
(d) GETTING LOST

LEVEL

1

26 PUZZLE

Which number replaces the blank and completes the sequence?

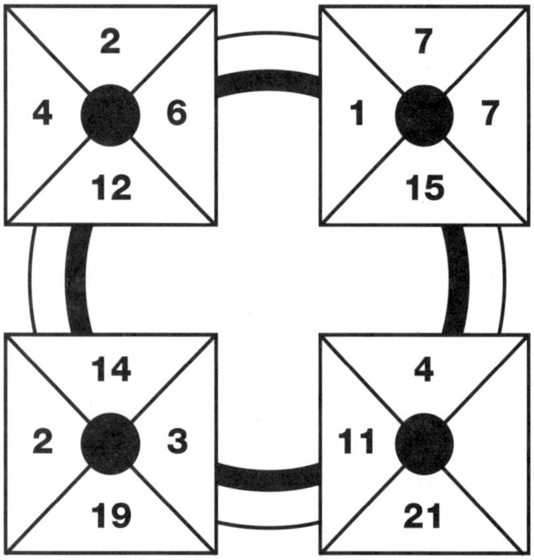

27 PUZZLE

Which letter replaces the blank and completes the puzzle?

B	Q	O
F	P	J
U	X	

28 PUZZLE

Which number is missing from the chain?

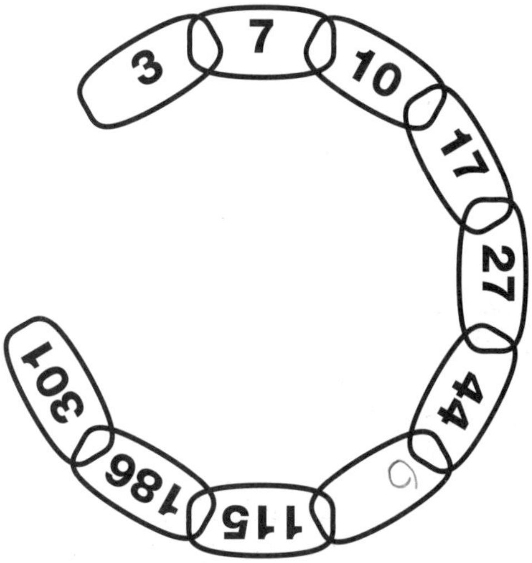

29 PUZZLE

Which number goes in the empty box?

2	3	9
7	6	2
16	11	12
25	20	

30 PUZZLE

Which letter completes the third circle?

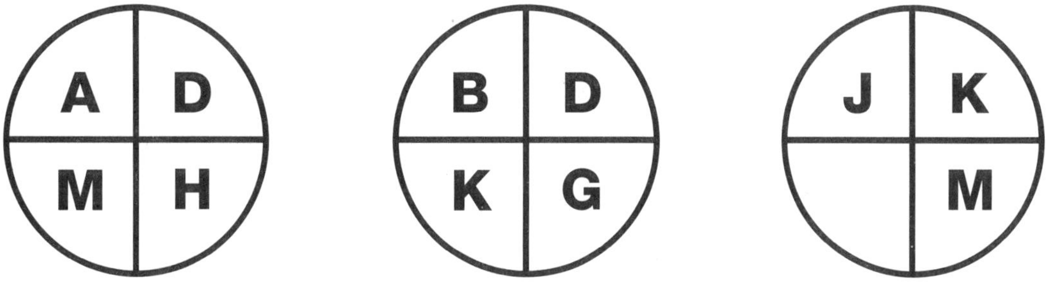

31 PUZZLE

Which number goes in the empty box?

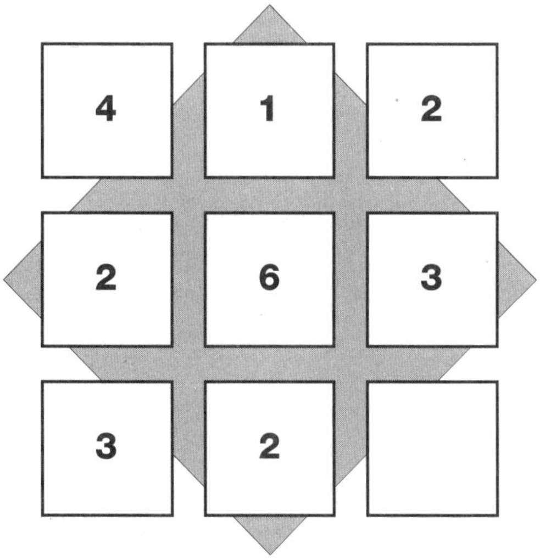

32 PUZZLE

Remove three matches to leave just three squares.

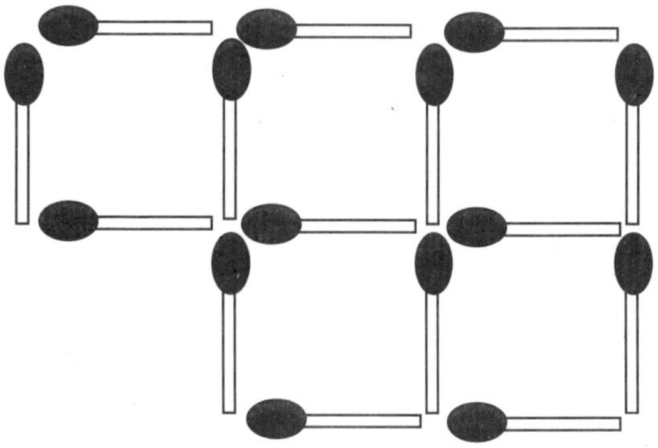

33 PUZZLE

Which letter follows next?

LEVEL 1

PUZZLE 34

Which letter goes in the empty square?

B	G	F
J	L	O
L	S	

PUZZLE 35

Following a logical pattern, complete this puzzle.

5	3	8
4	9	13

2	7	9
3	1	4

3	6	9
7	1	

PUZZLE 36

Which number replaces the blank and completes the sequence?

7	2	9
	3	12
12	4	16

PUZZLE 37

Which number is missing?

3	9	3
5	7	1
7	1	

PUZZLE 38

Which number replaces the blank and completes the sequence?

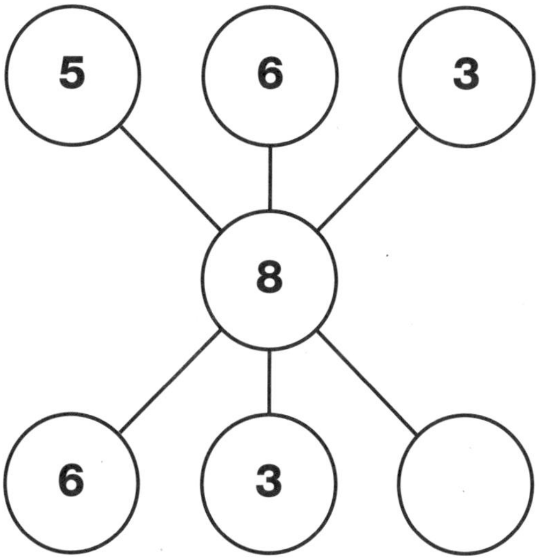

PUZZLE 39

Which number is missing from this sequence?

9	4	1
6	6	2
1	9	

PUZZLE 40

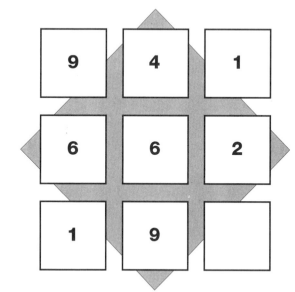

Draw the face in the empty box which continues this pattern.

PUZZLE 41

Which number goes in the empty circle?

2	4	12
3	1	8
4		18

42 PUZZLE

Which number completes the puzzle?

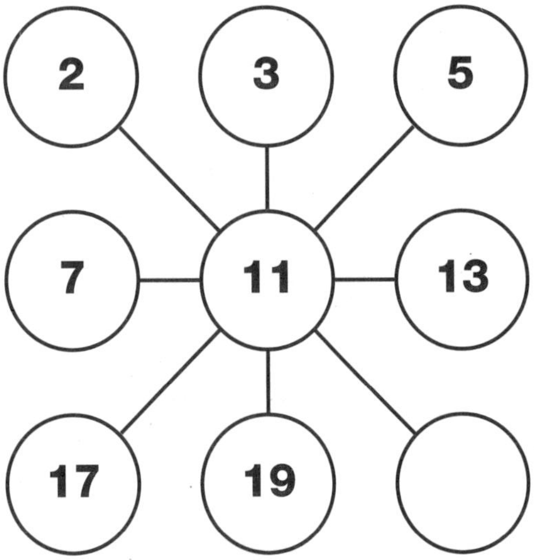

43 PUZZLE

Which number replaces the question mark in the bottom square?

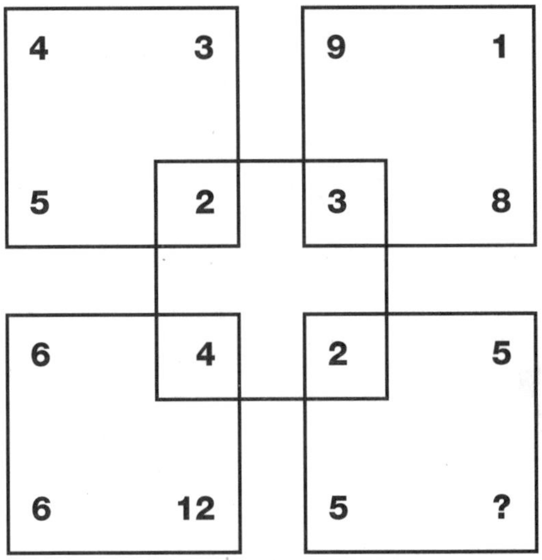

44 PUZZLE

Which letter is the odd one out in each shape?

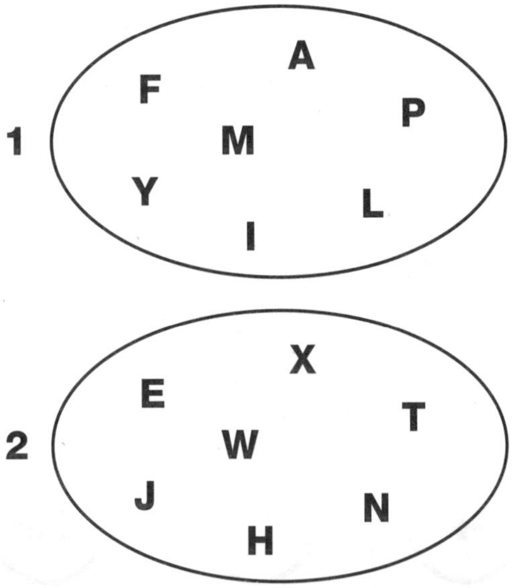

45 PUZZLE

Which number is missing from the empty segment?

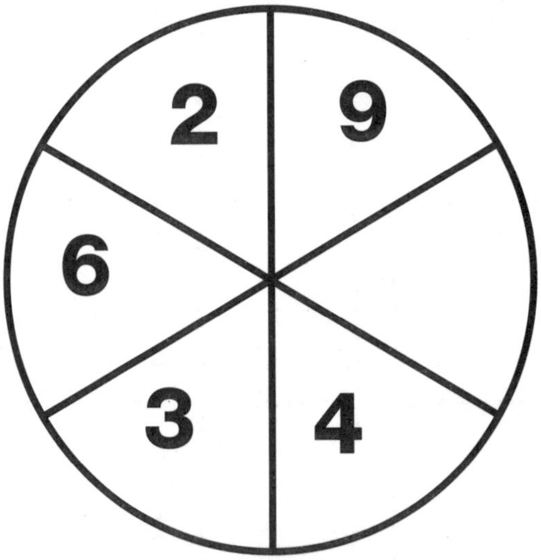

46 PUZZLE

What is missing from the last grid?

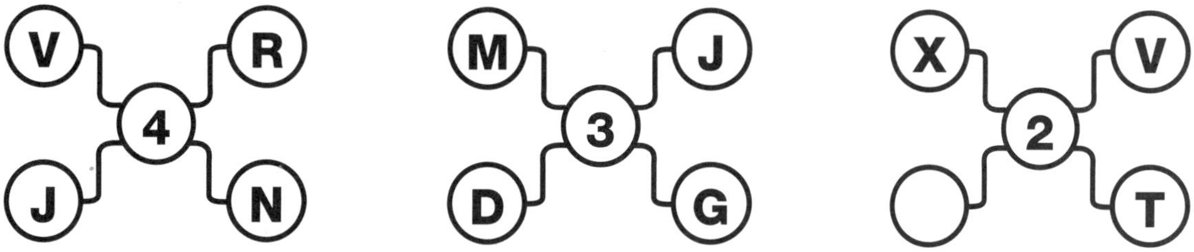

47 PUZZLE

Can you work out which letter is missing?

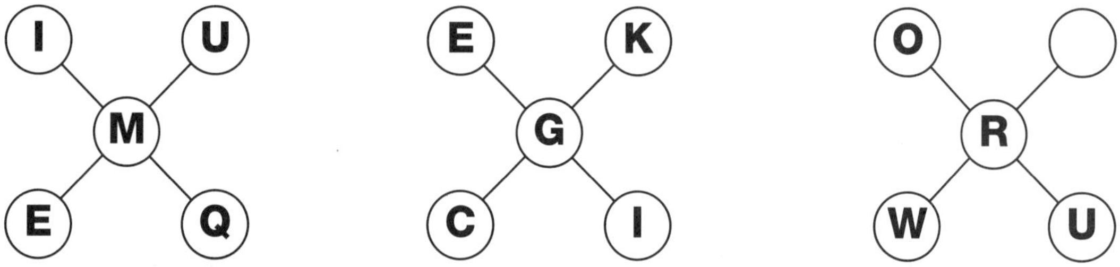

48 PUZZLE

Enter the correct number into the empty square.

4	9	20
8	5	14
10	3	

49 PUZZLE

Following a logical pattern, complete this puzzle.

1	5	7	13
15	5	4	6
3	8	2	13
12	5	2	

PUZZLE 50

By following this series of cogs attached to the float, can you work out if the flood warning works correctly?

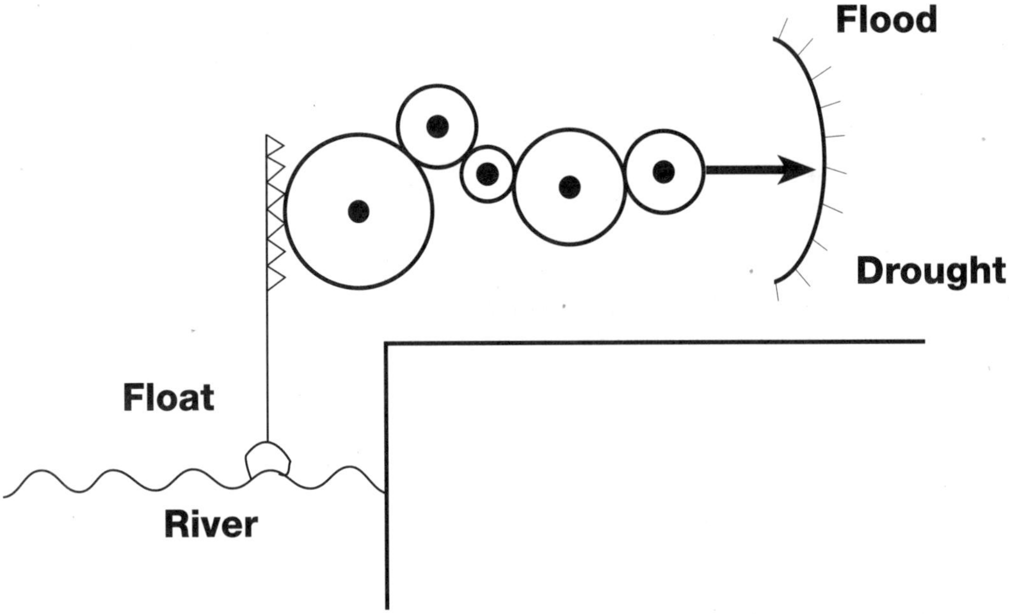

PUZZLE 51

Which letter replaces the blank and completes the sequence?

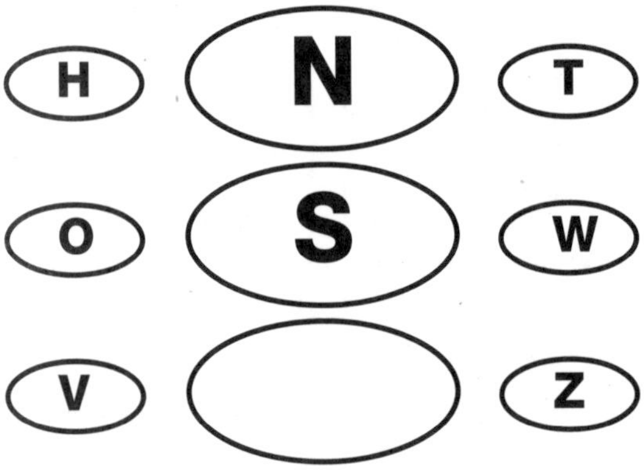

PUZZLE 52

What is missing from the empty segment of the wheel?

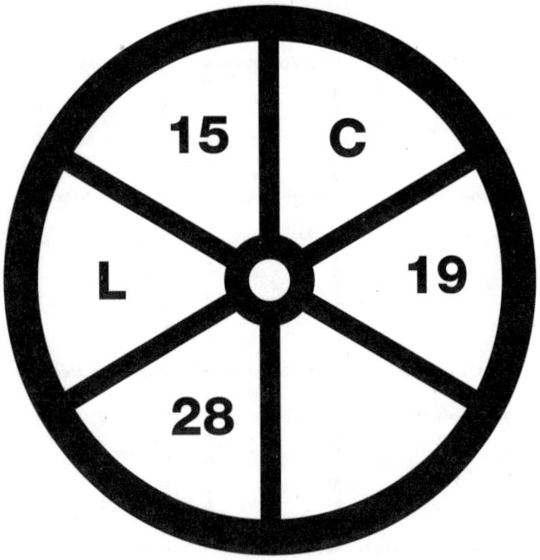

53 PUZZLE

Which playing card completes the sequence?

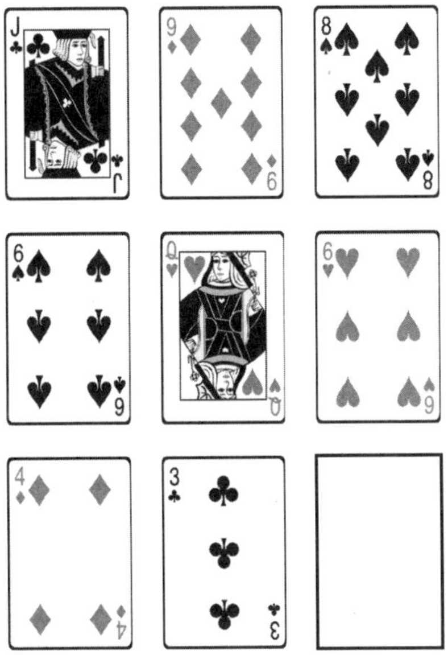

54 PUZZLE

Which two letters are missing?

A	W
C	U
G	Q
I	O
K	M

55 PUZZLE

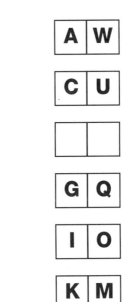

Draw the dot in the correct segment of the last circle.

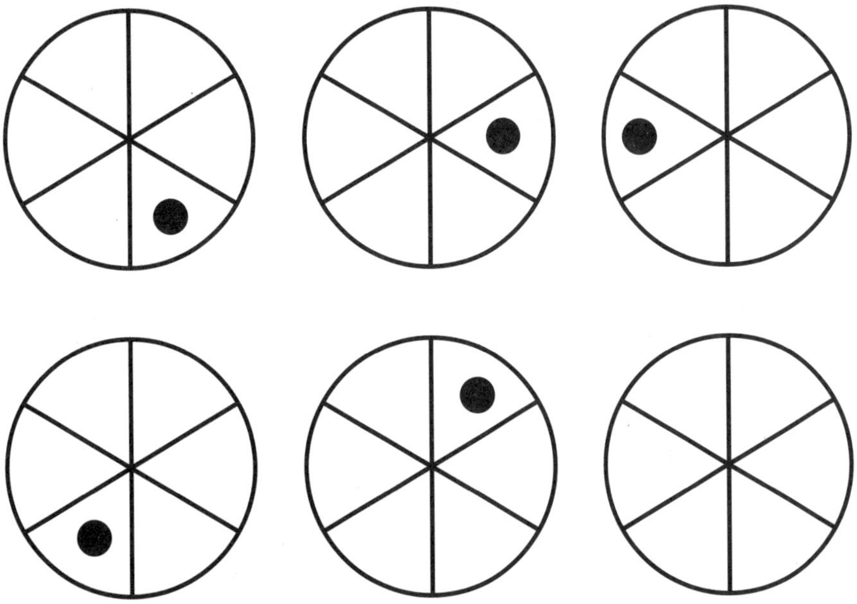

56 PUZZLE

Which number is missing from the third circle?

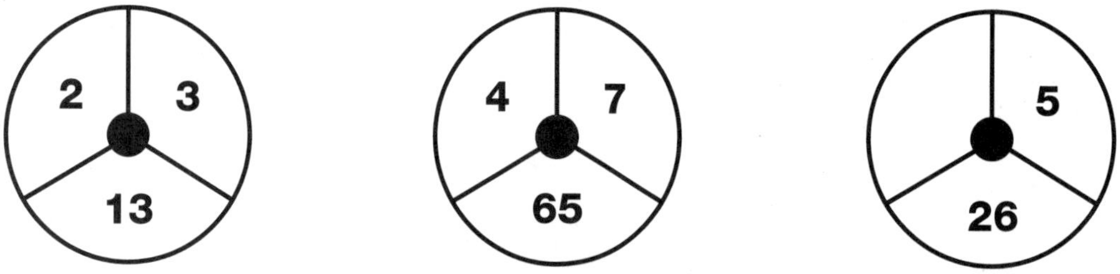

57 PUZZLE

Complete the last star.

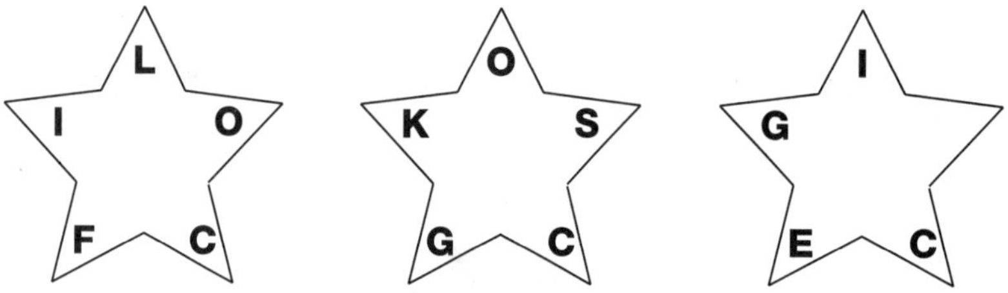

58 PUZZLE

Which two letters will complete this puzzle?

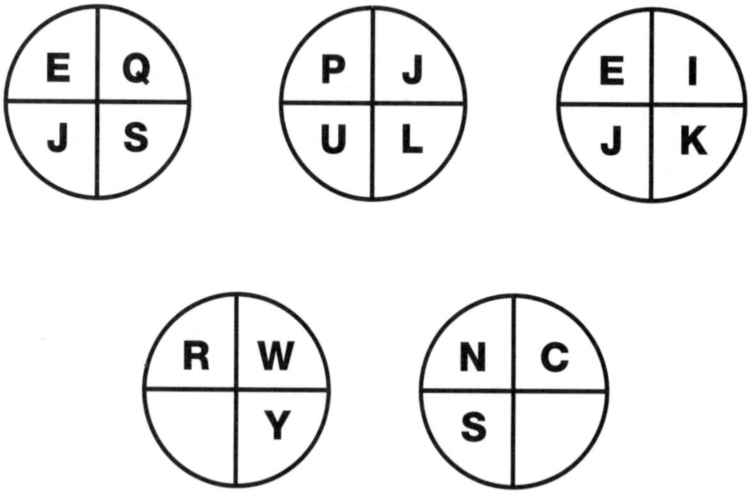

PUZZLE 59

Which number is missing?

3	5	2
6	11	5
2	9	

PUZZLE 60

Which number fits into the empty link?

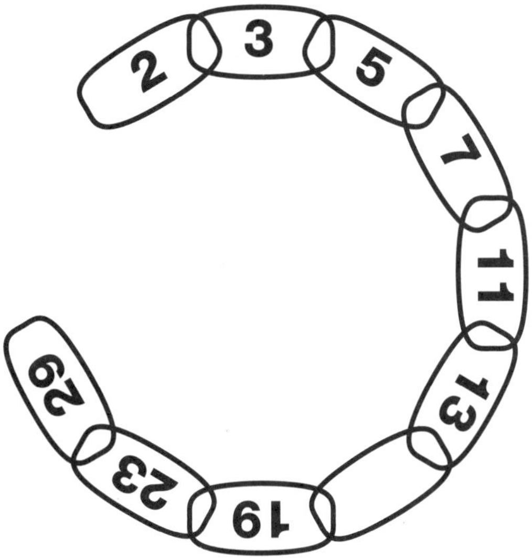

PUZZLE 61

Which letter completes the sequence?

K	Q	F
R	Y	G
M	B	K
O	E	

PUZZLE 62

Which number goes in the centre?

6	9	11
21		12
18	17	15

1 PUZZLE

Which number is missing?

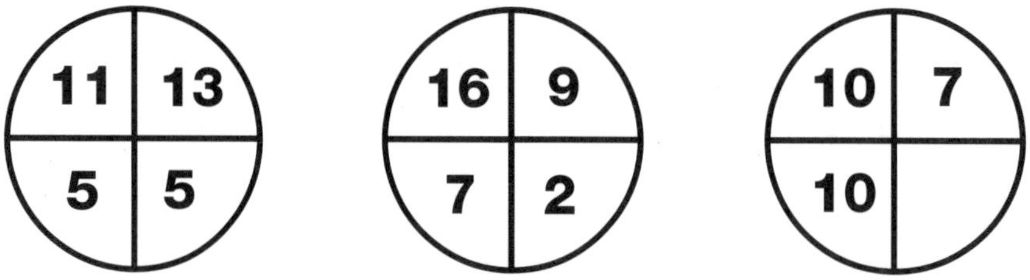

2 PUZZLE

Which letter goes in the empty segment?

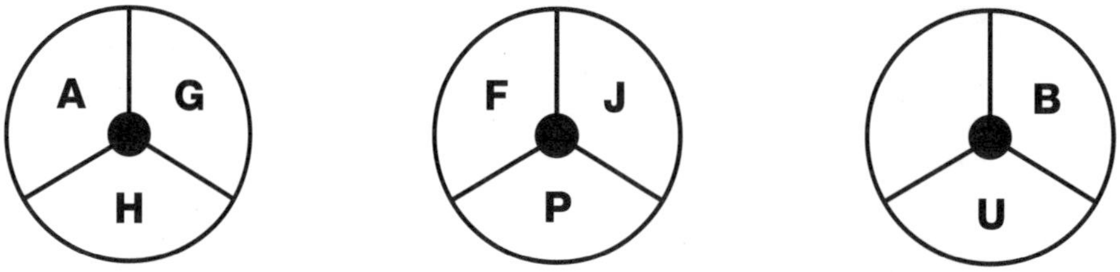

3 PUZZLE

Which letter replaces the blank and completes the sequence?

4 PUZZLE

Which letter completes this puzzle?

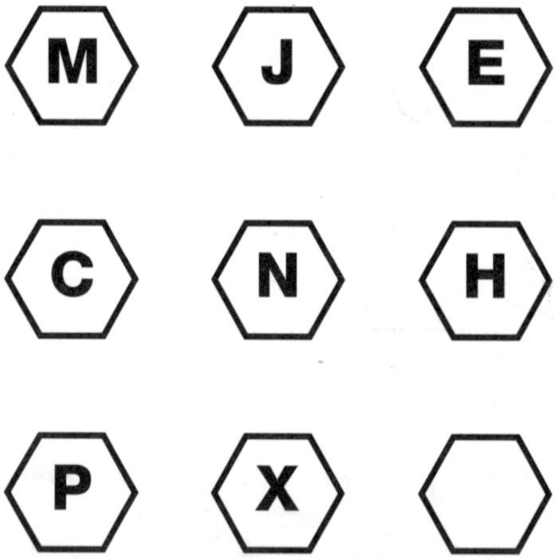

5 PUZZLE

Which is the missing segment?

A

B

C

D

E

6 PUZZLE

Fill the grid with the letters ABCDE so that the same letter does not appear in the same horizontal, vertical or diagonal line.

A				
				B
			C	
		D		
	E			

7 PUZZLE

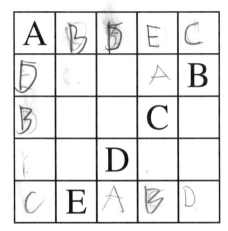

You have accidentally left the plug out of the bath and are attempting to fill the bath with both taps full on. The hot tap takes 5 minutes to fill the bath and the cold tap 4 minutes, and the water empties through the plug-hole in 20 minutes.

In how many minutes will the bath be filled?

LEVEL 2

PUZZLE 8

How many circles appear below?

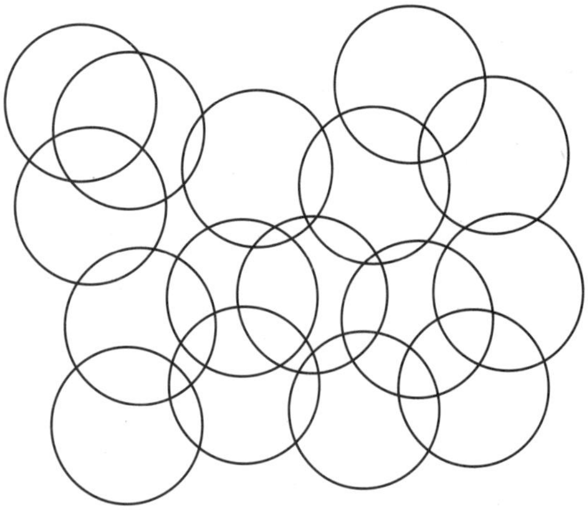

PUZZLE 9

What letter comes next?

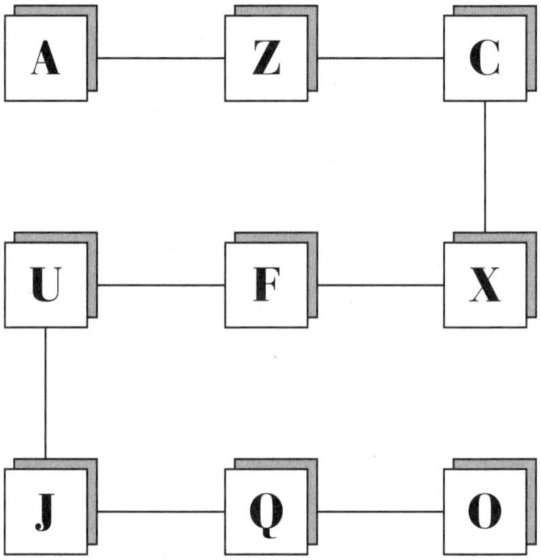

PUZZLE 10

7321 is to **143**

and

8642 is to **3212**

therefore

5126 is to **?**

PUZZLE 11

Which number is the odd one out?

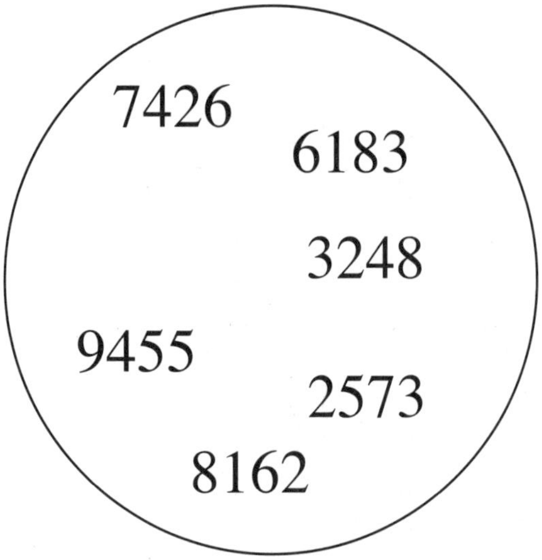

12 PUZZLE

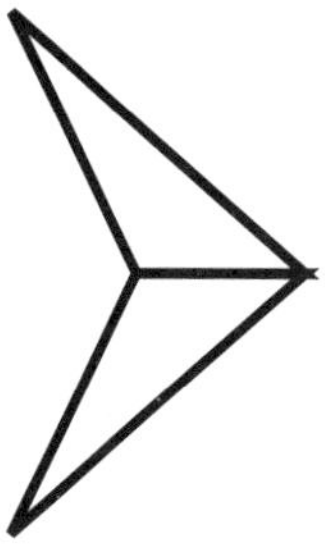

is to:

as:

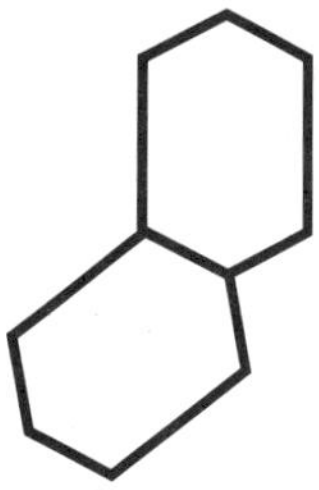

is to:

A

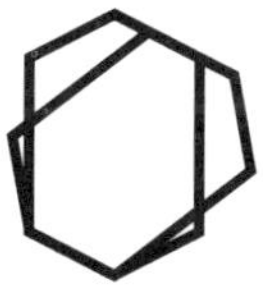

B

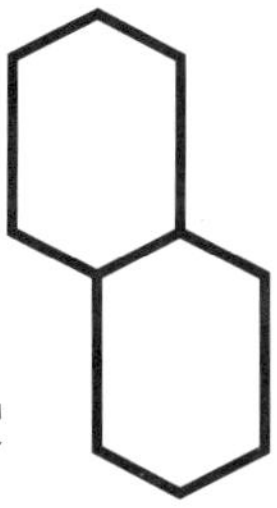

C

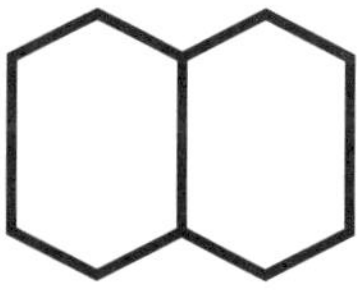

D

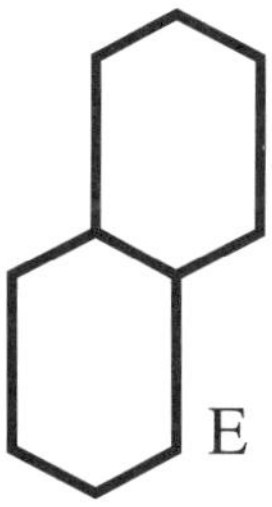

E

13 PUZZLE

What number should replace the question mark?

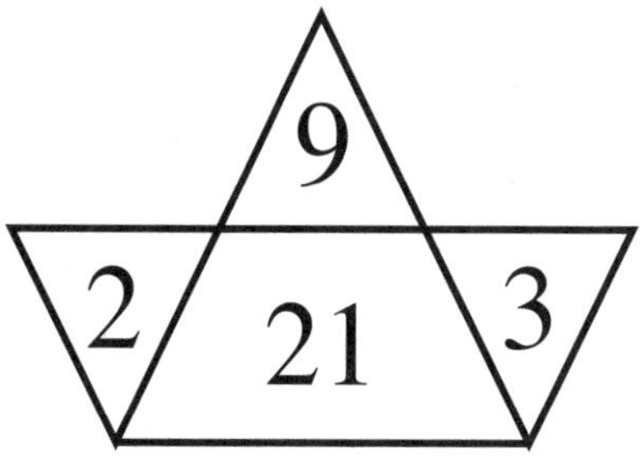

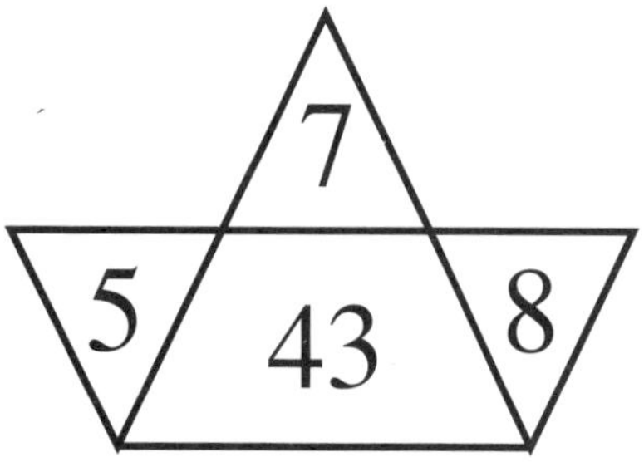

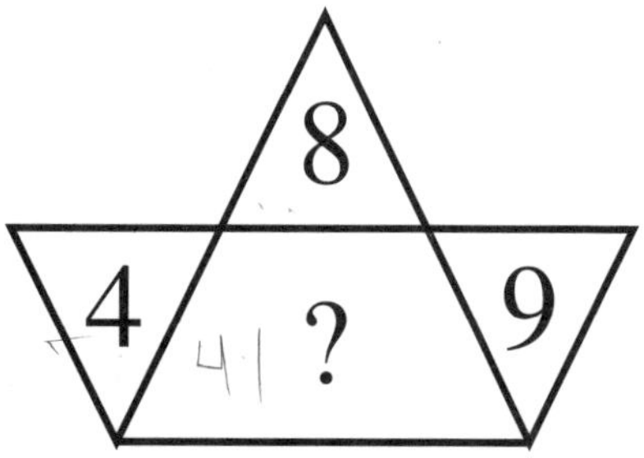

14 PUZZLE

When the left hand pattern is folded to form a cube, which 3 of the following can be produced?

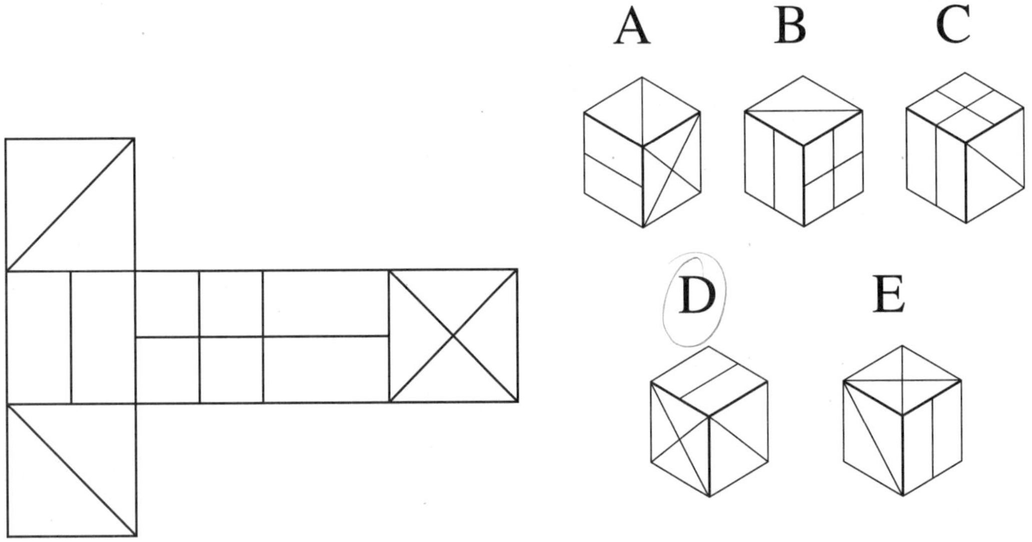

15 PUZZLE

Which circle would continue the sequence?

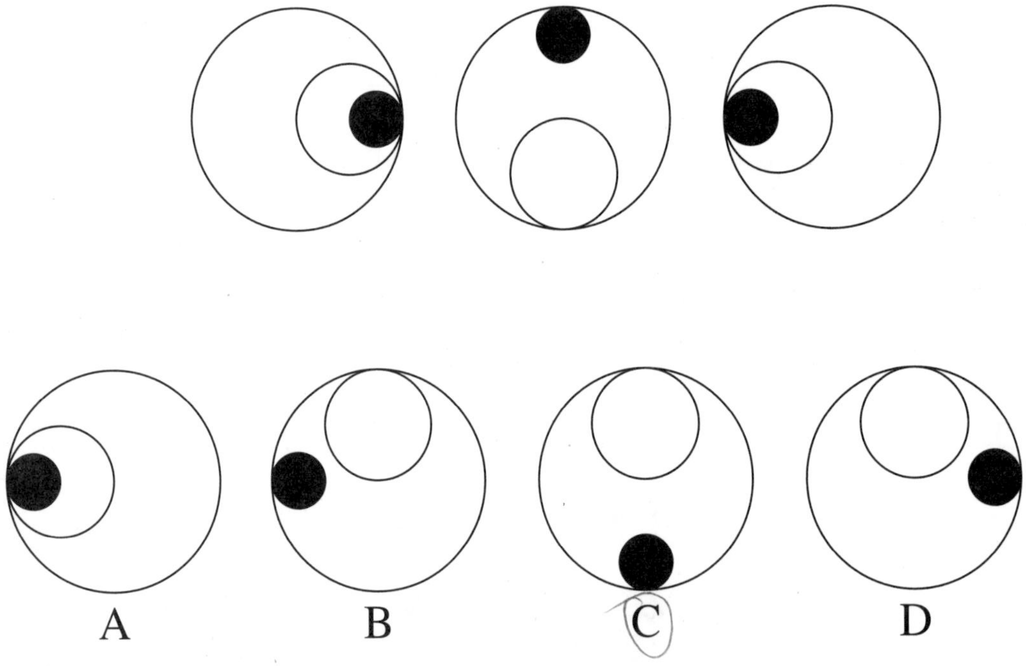

16
PUZZLE

Each line and symbol which appears in the four outer circles, below, is transferred to the centre circle according to these rules: If a line or symbol occurs in the outer circles: once: it is transferred twice: it is possibly transferred 3 times: it is transferred 4 times: it is not transferred. Which of the circles A, B, C, D or E, should appear at the centre of the diagram, below?

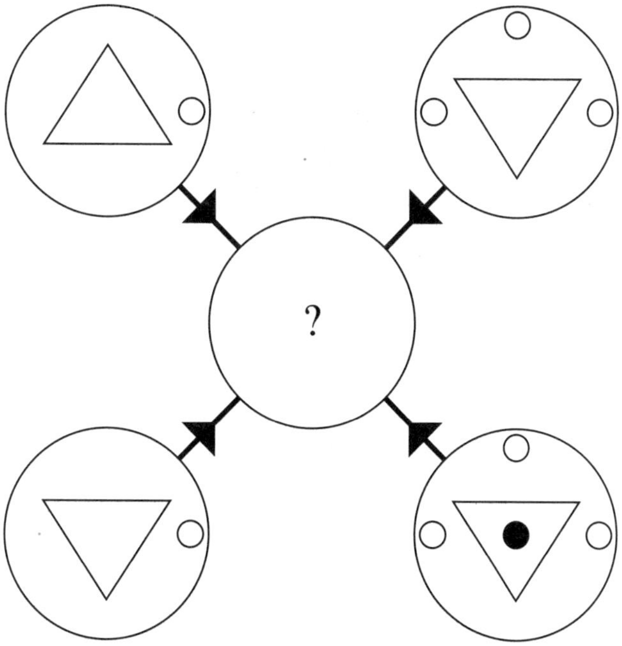

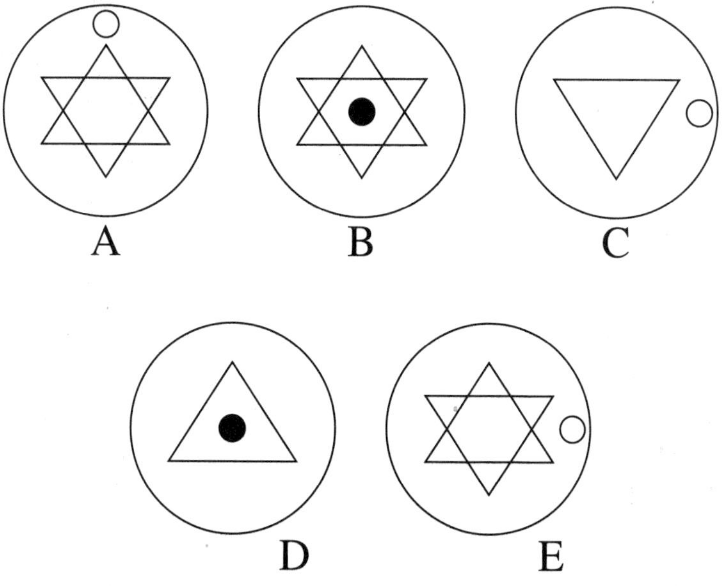

17 PUZZLE

What is the total of the numbers on the reverse side of these dice?

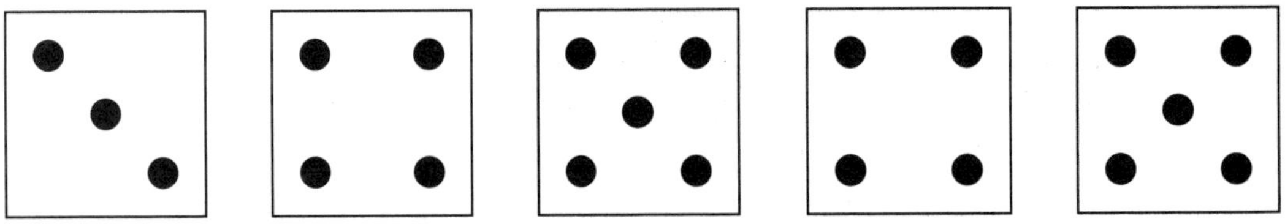

18 PUZZLE

Which number should replace the question mark?

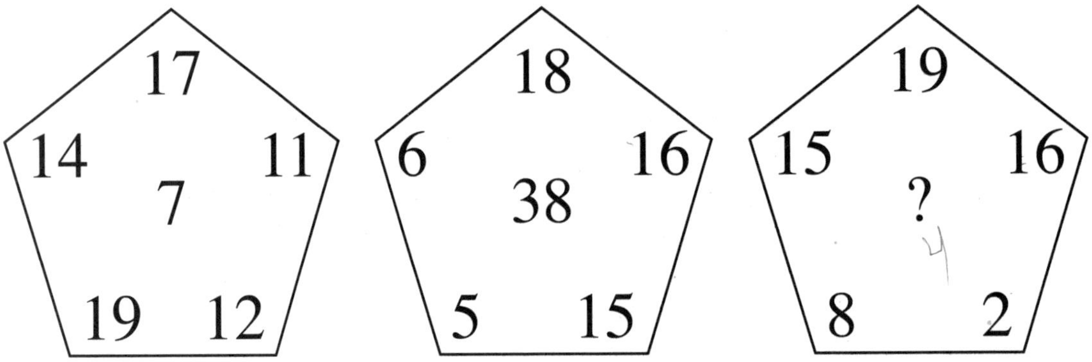

19 PUZZLE

Which word means the same or is closest in meaning to PASTICHE?

(a) ASSEMBLAGE
(b) ARTISTIC LICENCE
(c) NEEDLEWORK
(d) MEDLEY
(e) DEVOTION

20 PUZZLE

Which word means the same as NUGATORY?

SOUR
LISSOM
HARSH
FUTILE
KEEN
SWEET

21
PUZZLE

Which circle should replace the question mark – A, B, C, D or E?

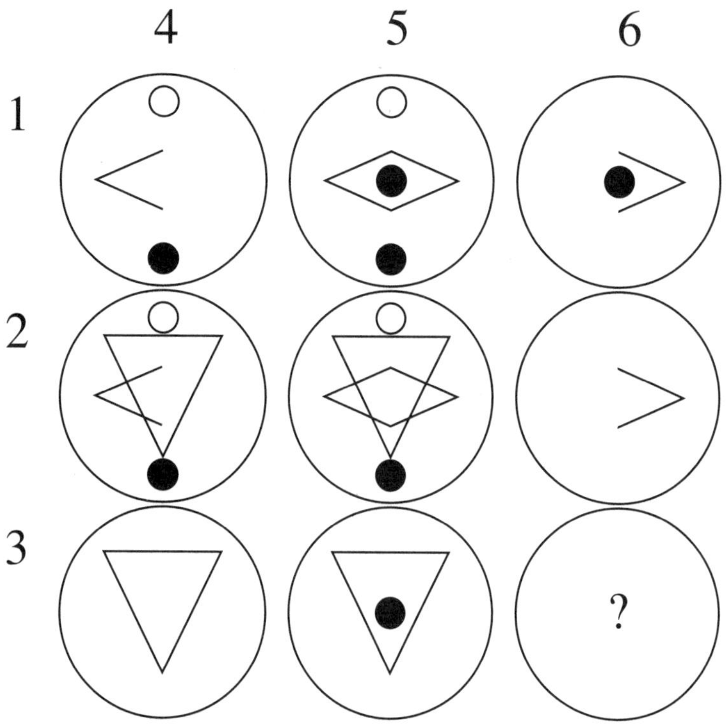

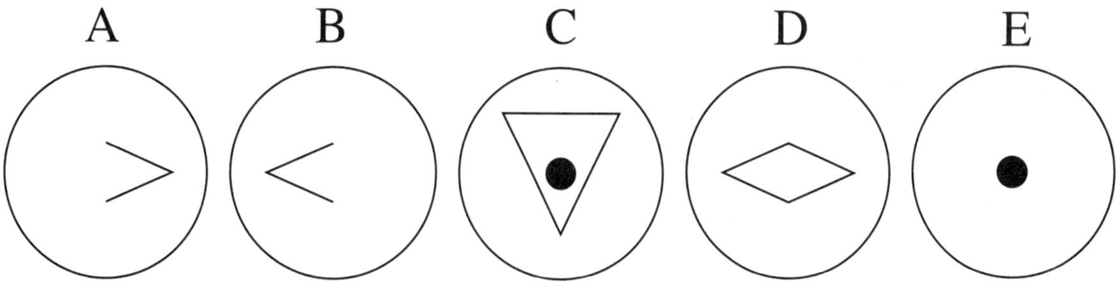

22
PUZZLE

Starting at midnight, snow fell 1½" every 6 hours.
If there was already 2¼" of snow at midnight,
what was the thickness of the snow at 9.00am ?

23 PUZZLE

Place a word in the brackets which means the same as the two words outside the brackets.

TAUNT (. . . . .) EAT GREEDILY

24 PUZZLE

Which is the odd one out?

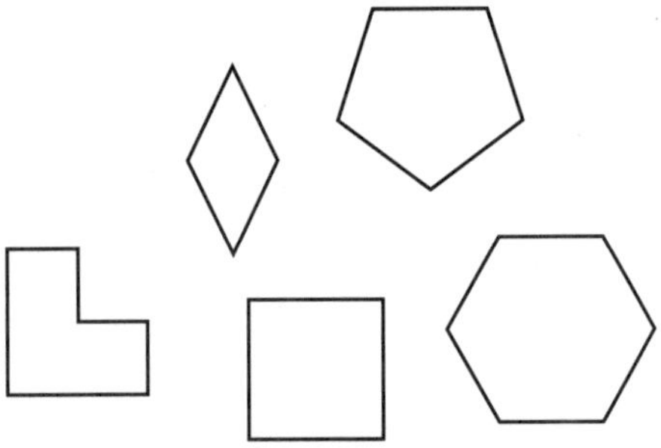

25 PUZZLE

Each of the nine squares in the grid marked A1 to C3, should incorporate all the lines and symbols which are shown in the squares of the same letter and number immediately above and to the left. For example, B2 should incorporate all the lines and symbols that are in 2 and B. One of the squares is incorrect. Which one is it?

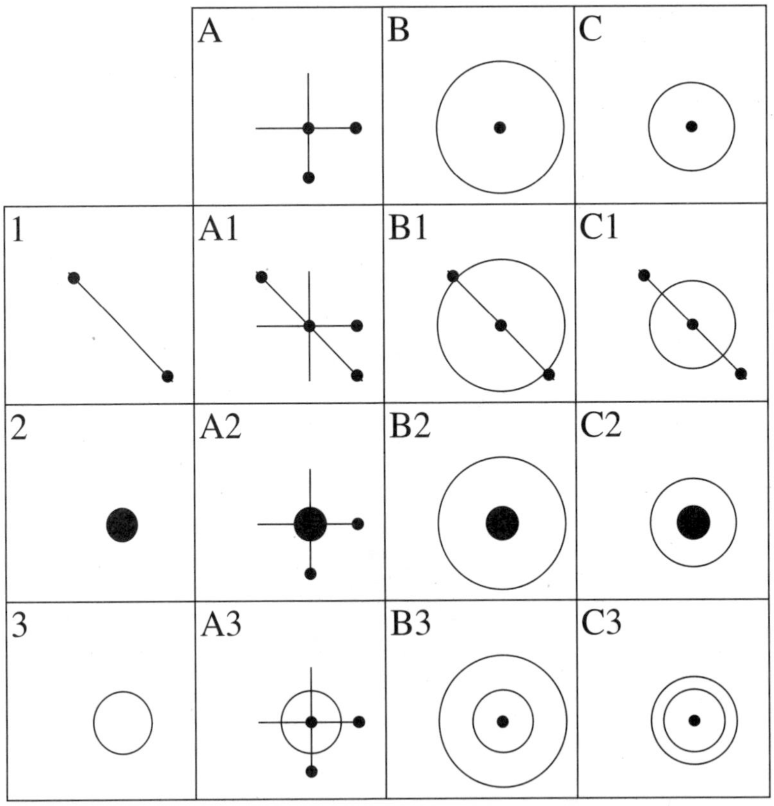

26 PUZZLE

Each symbol ♡ ♧ ♢ ♤ has a value. Which symbol should replace the ? to make the totals correct?

♡	♤	♧	♧	28
♡	♢	♢	♢	26
♡	♤	♤	♧	21
♡	♧	♧	?	32
44	15	22	26	

27 PUZZLE

Simplify

$$\frac{9}{72} \div \frac{36}{144} \div \frac{12}{36}$$

28 PUZZLE

You have 13 diamond cards.

A 2 3 4 5 6 7 8 9
10 J Q K

What are the chances of drawing out K Q J 10 in that order?

29 PUZZLE

The answer is 12. Why?

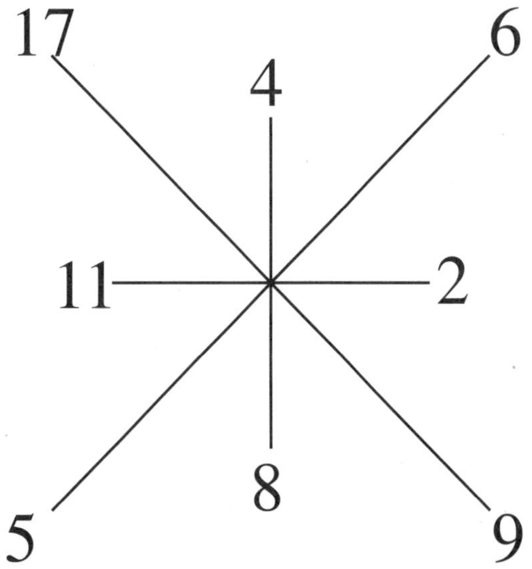

LEVEL 2

LEVEL 2

30 PUZZLE

Remove two matches to leave just four squares.

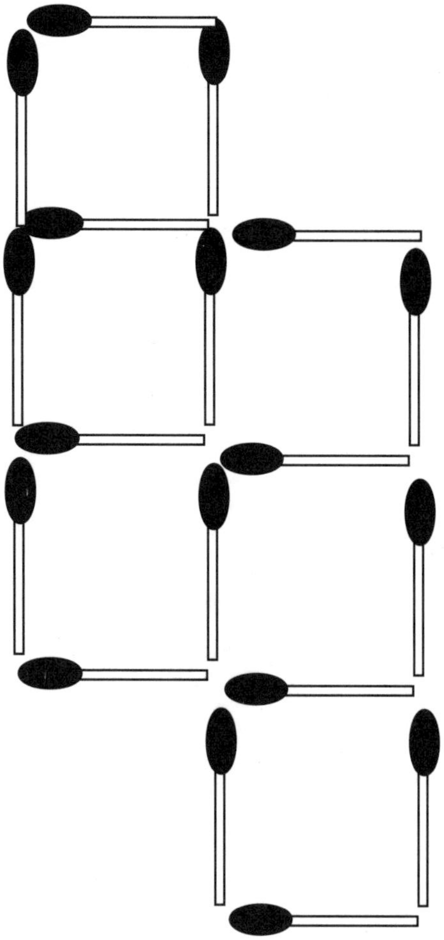

31 PUZZLE

If the bottom cog is turned anticlockwise will the flag at the top be raised or lowered?

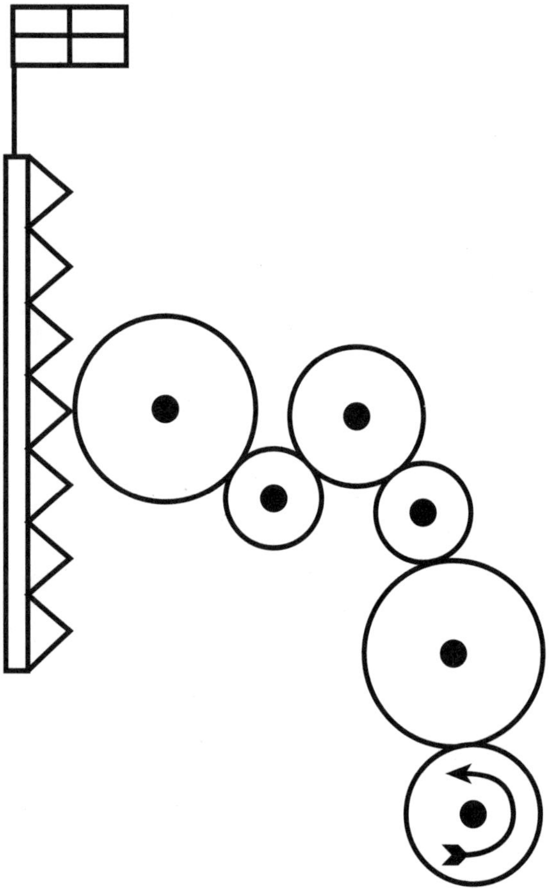

32 PUZZLE

Which number continues this sequence?

18	**20**	**24**	**32**	

33 PUZZLE

Which number will complete this teaser?

10	8	6
3	7	11
2		4

34 PUZZLE

Which letter goes into the last square of the bottom grid?

B	H	J
K	F	Q

T	A	U
G	H	O

L	N	Z
R	C	

35 PUZZLE

Which number is missing from the box?

8	3	4
1	5	
6	7	2

36 PUZZLE

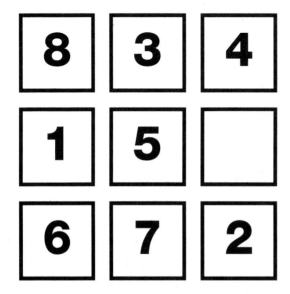

Fill in the final box to complete the sequence.

D	W

2	7

U	L

3	3

G	O

2	

PUZZLE 37

Which letter is missing from the last star?

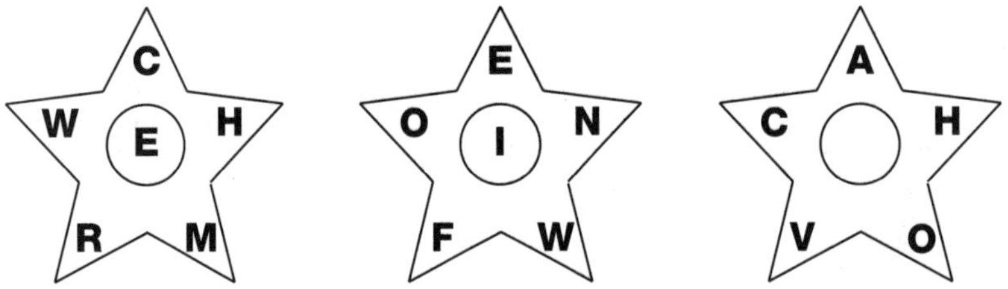

PUZZLE 38

Which letter replaces the blank and completes the sequence?

- **D**
- **P**
- **B**
- **N**
- (blank)

PUZZLE 39

Which letter goes in the empty circle?

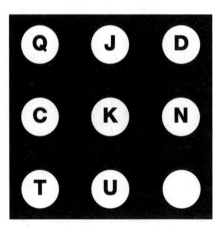

Q	**J**	**D**
C	**K**	**N**
T	**U**	

PUZZLE 40

Which number completes the last triangle?

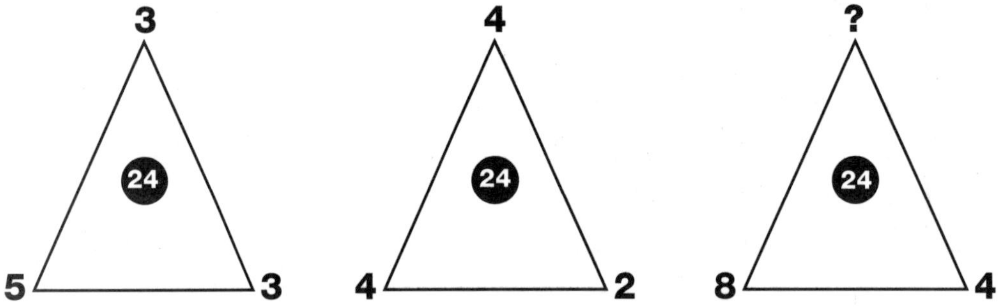

41 PUZZLE

Following a logical sequence, can you complete this puzzle?

5	13	4
6	10	2

3	19	8
6	20	

42 PUZZLE

Which letter replaces the question mark?

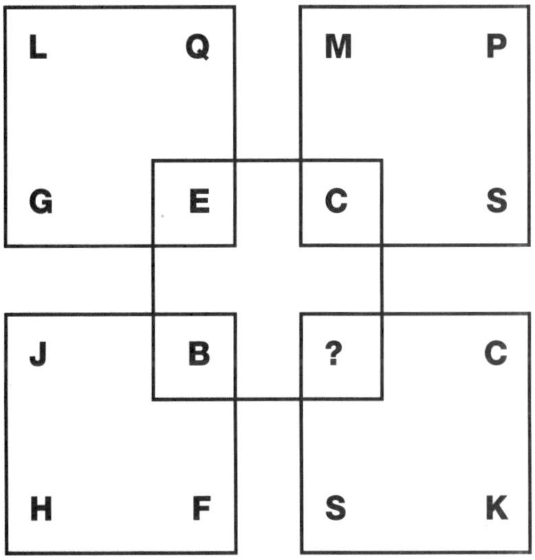

43 PUZZLE

Fill in the empty box.

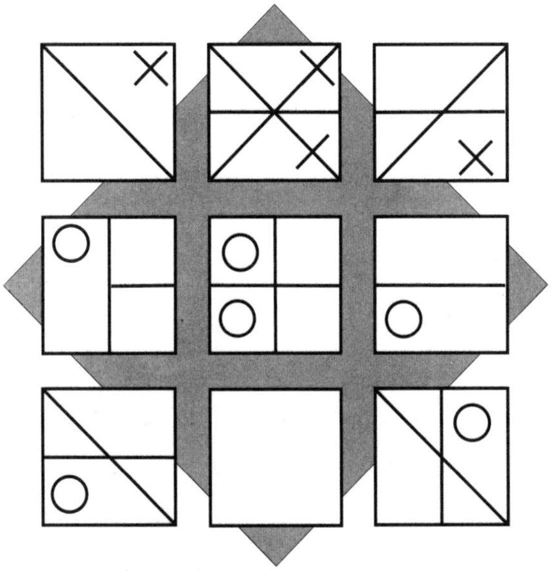

44 PUZZLE

Which number completes this sequence?

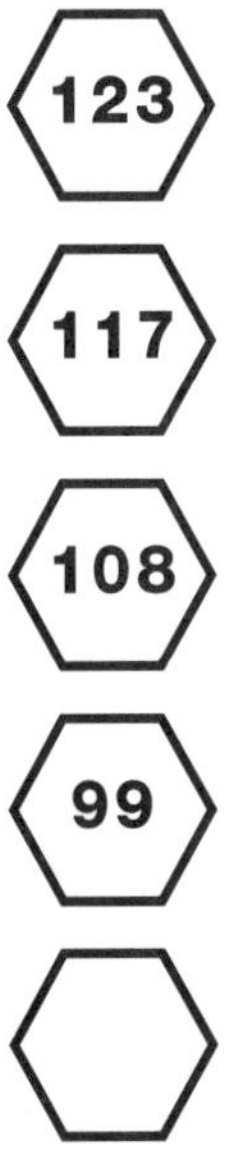

LEVEL 2

45 PUZZLE

Which of the four squares at the bottom completes the pattern?

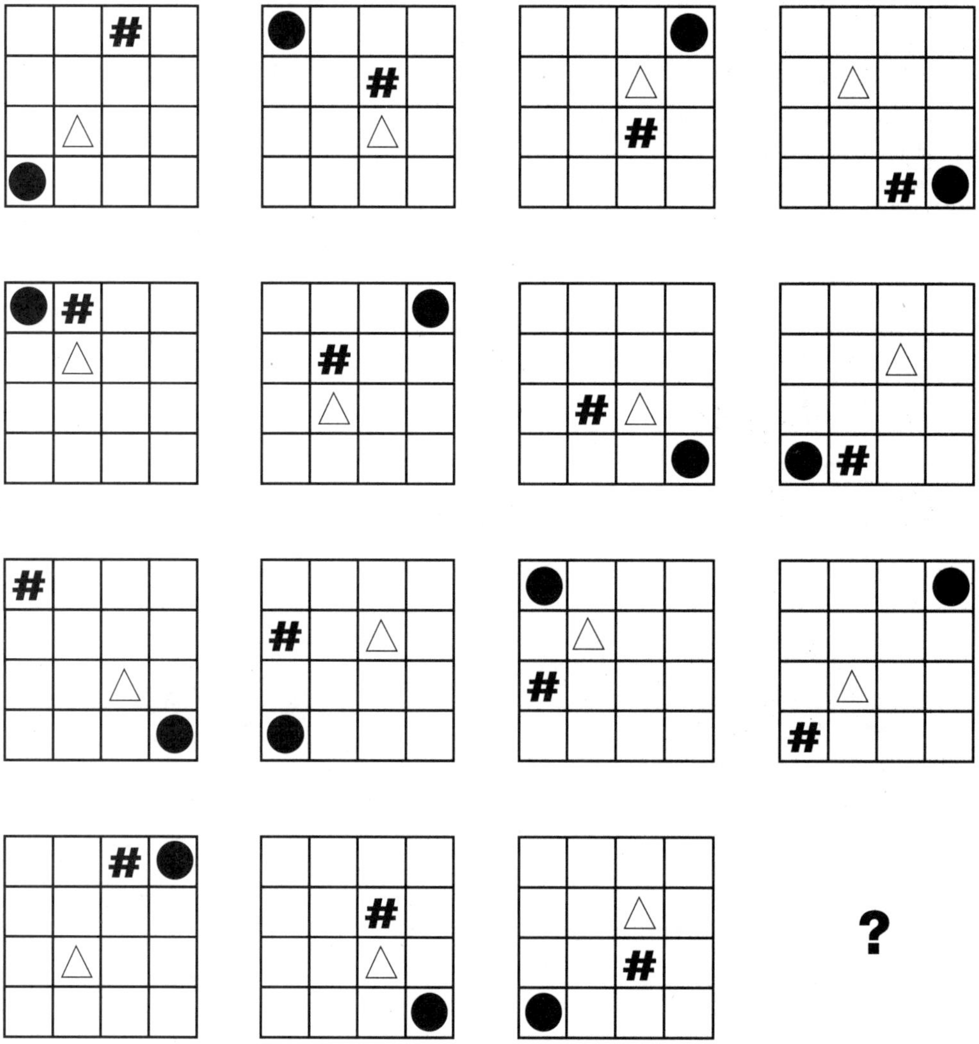

A

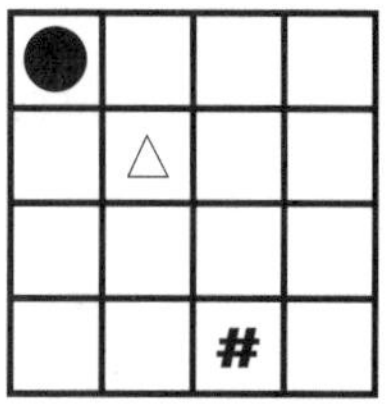

B

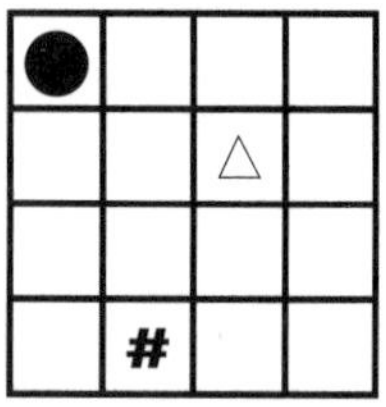

C

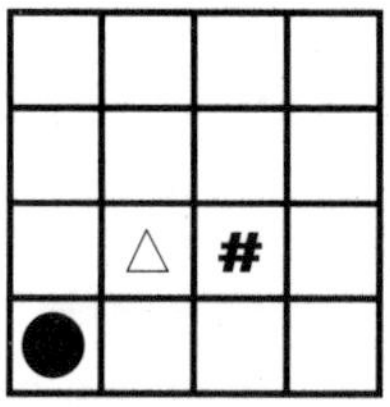

D

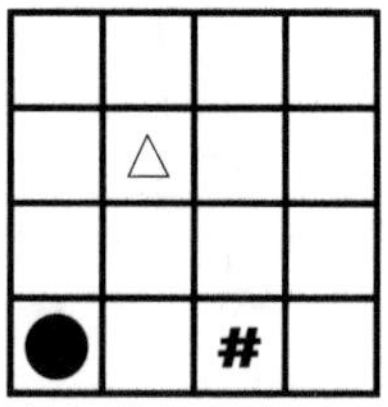

46 PUZZLE

Which number completes this puzzle?

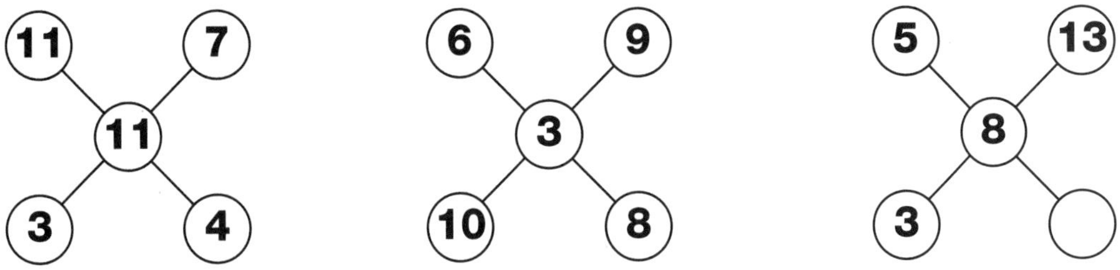

47 PUZZLE

Which pattern completes the grid?

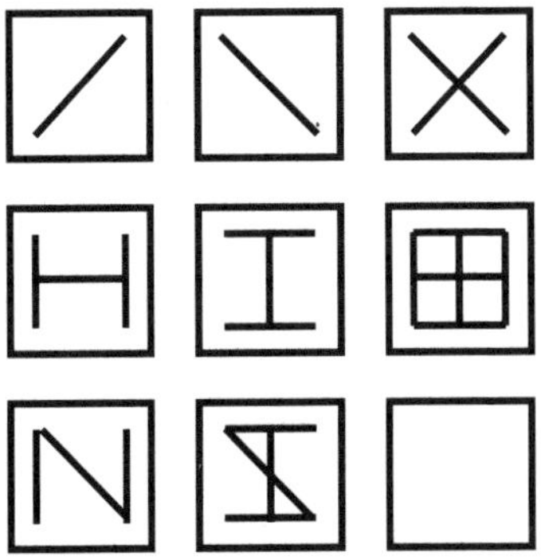

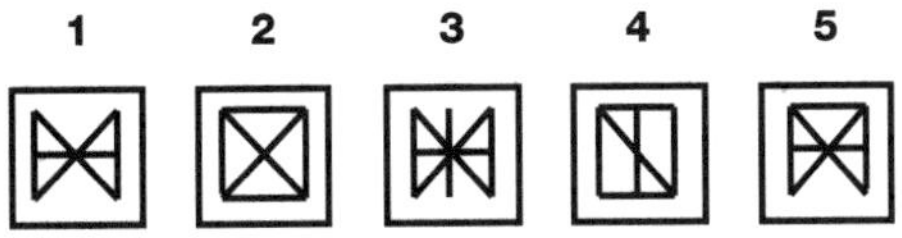

48 PUZZLE

Which number is missing?

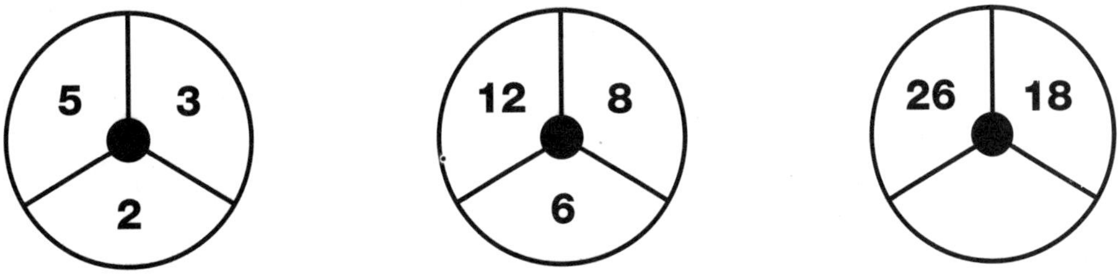

PUZZLE 49

Using every number between 1 and 9, fill in the spaces on this triangle so that the numbers on each side add up to 20.

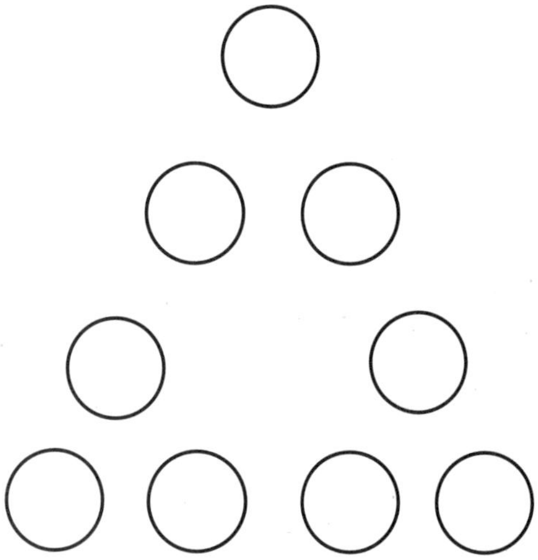

PUZZLE 50

Which number is missing?

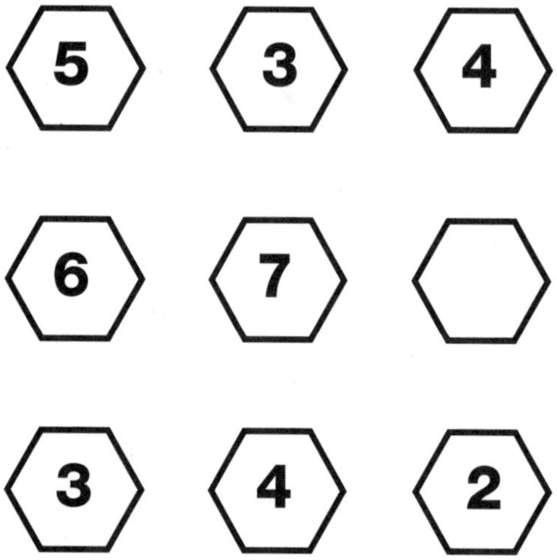

PUZZLE 51

Which number is missing from the third wheel?

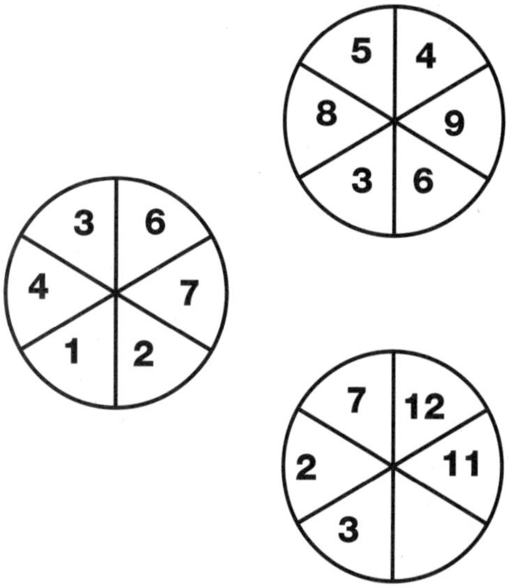

PUZZLE 52

Which number goes in the empty segment?

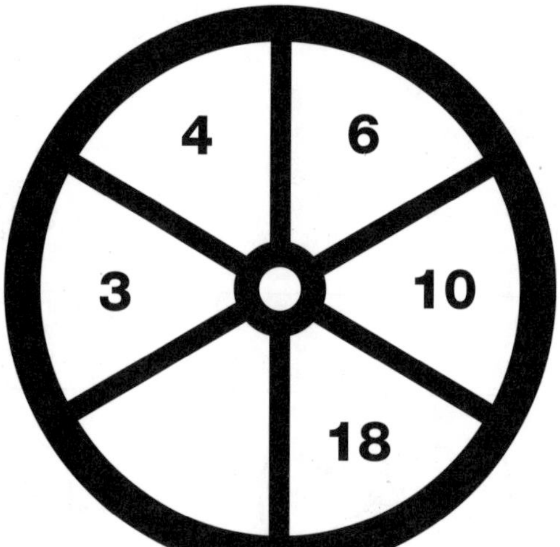

53 PUZZLE

Sean caught a prize fish last weekend. He was going to measure it but realized that his ruler was not long enough. He was able to measure the head and discovered that it was 9cm long, he then measured the tail and found that it was the length of the head plus half the length of the body. If the body was the length of the head plus the tail, what is the total length of the fish?

54 PUZZLE

Which number completes the chain?

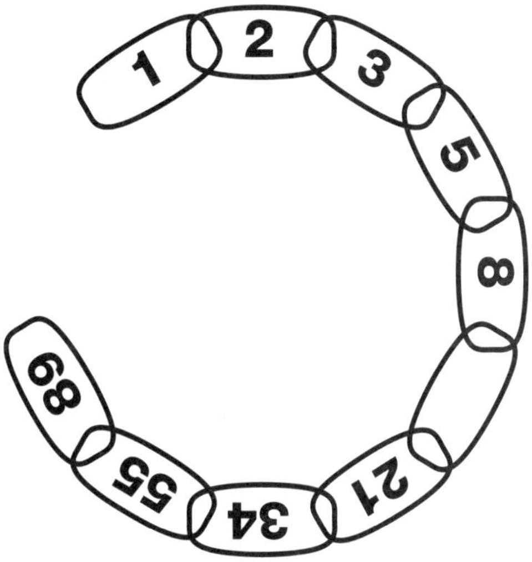

55 PUZZLE

Which letter replaces the blank and completes the sequence?

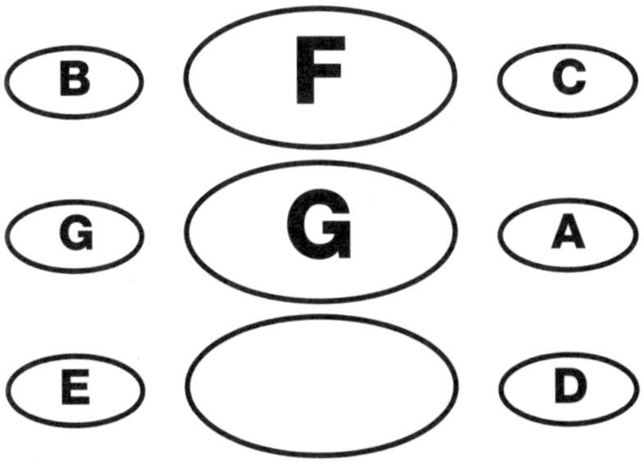

56 PUZZLE

Which number logically goes in the centre of this puzzle?

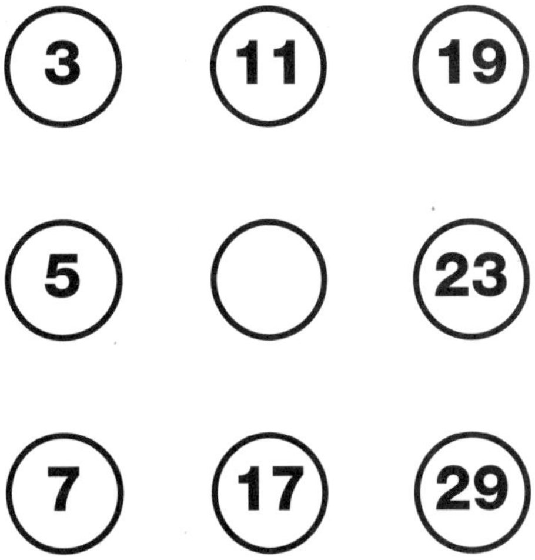

LEVEL 2

57 PUZZLE

Which of the bottom six grids completes this pattern?

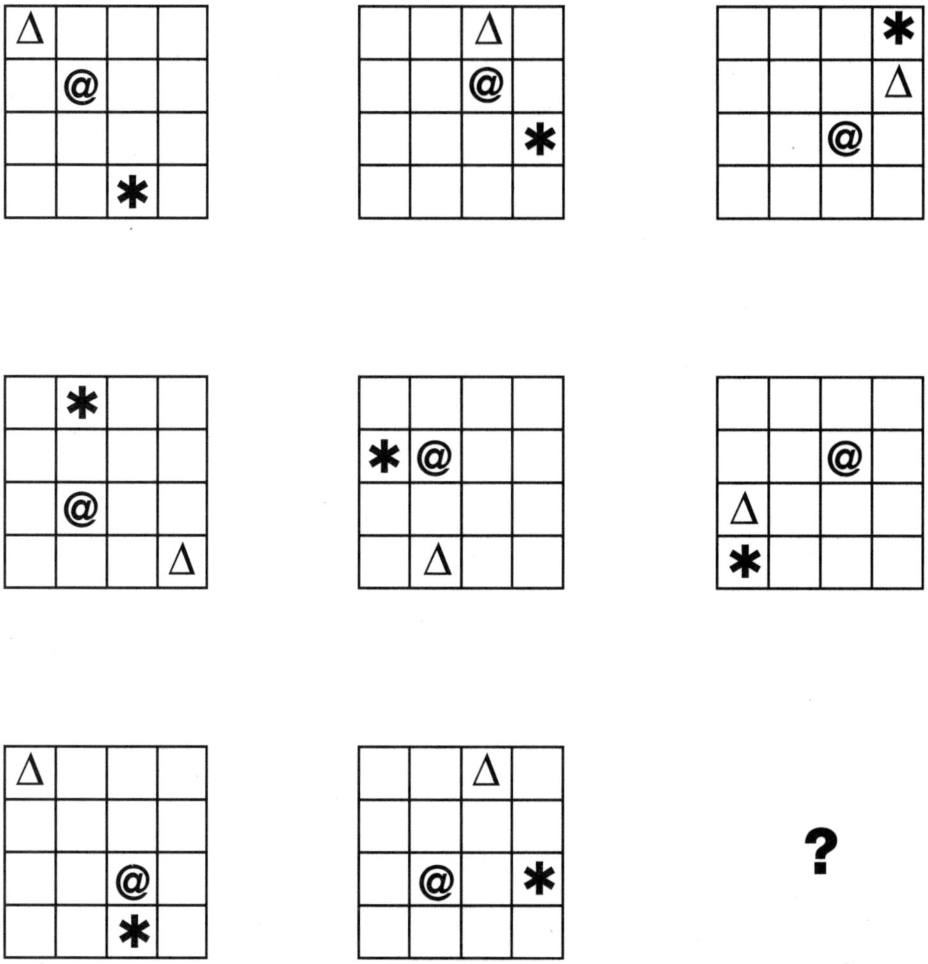

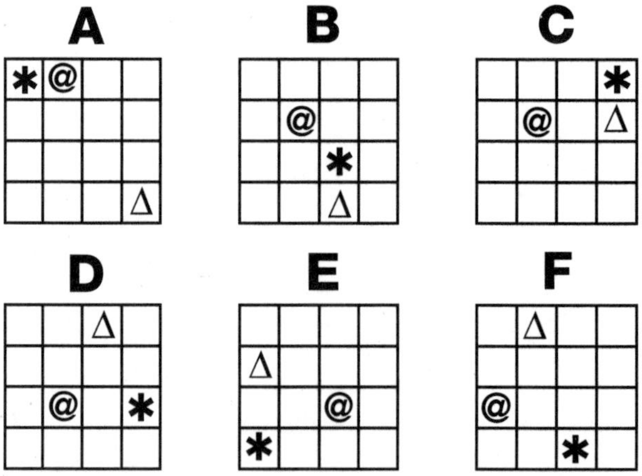

1 PUZZLE

When the left hand pattern is folded to form a cube, which is the only one of the following that cannot be produced?

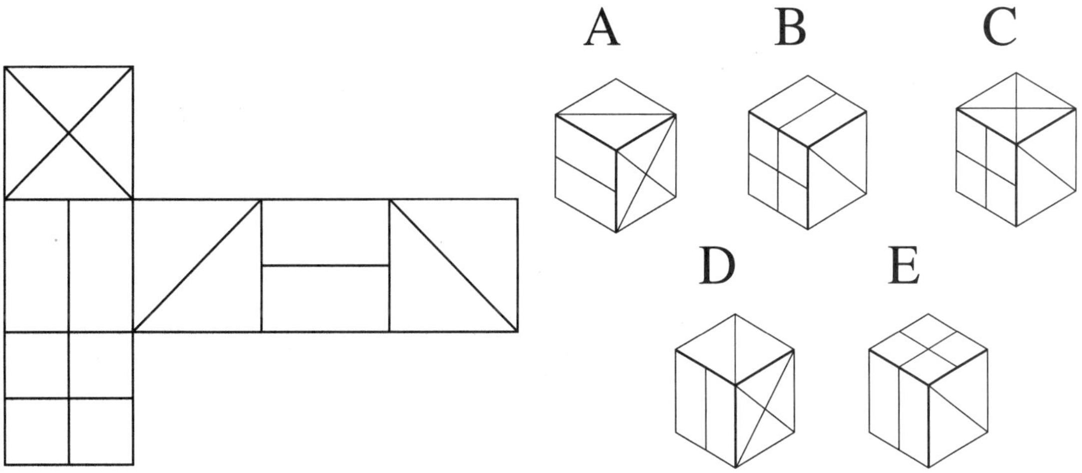

2 PUZZLE

What comes next in the sequence below?

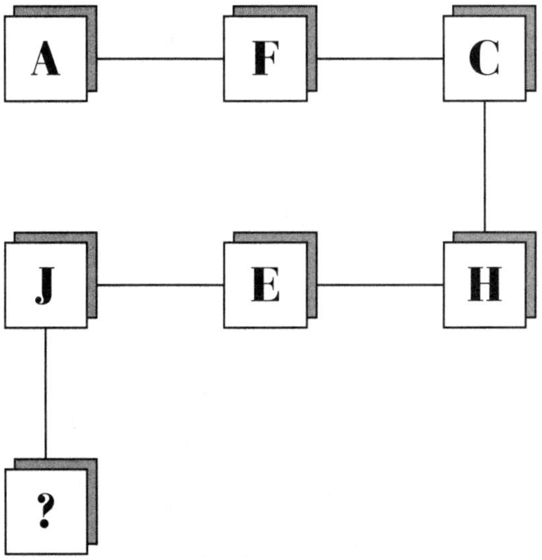

3 PUZZLE

What number is three places away from itself plus 3, two places away from itself multiplied by 4, three places away from itself less 2, two places away from itself plus 8 and three places away from itself less 1?

52	24	30	9	16
5	3	21	12	2
18	45	4	36	7
13	11	8	16	50
40	6	10	15	1

LEVEL 3

4 PUZZLE

You have a range of weights available from 1-10 units. They are all single weights. Which one should you use to balance the scale and where should you place it?

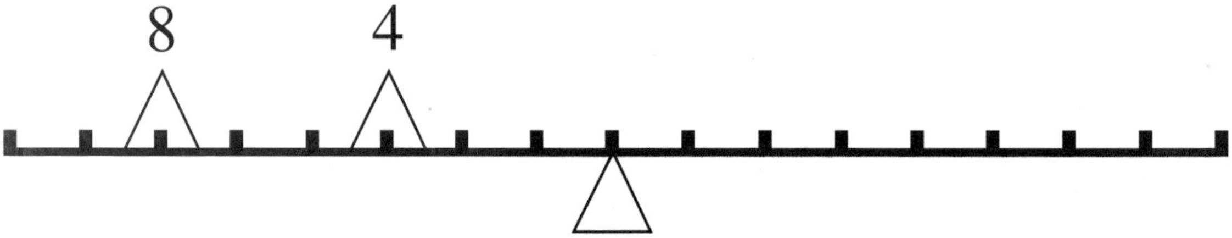

5 PUZZLE

Which is the odd one out?

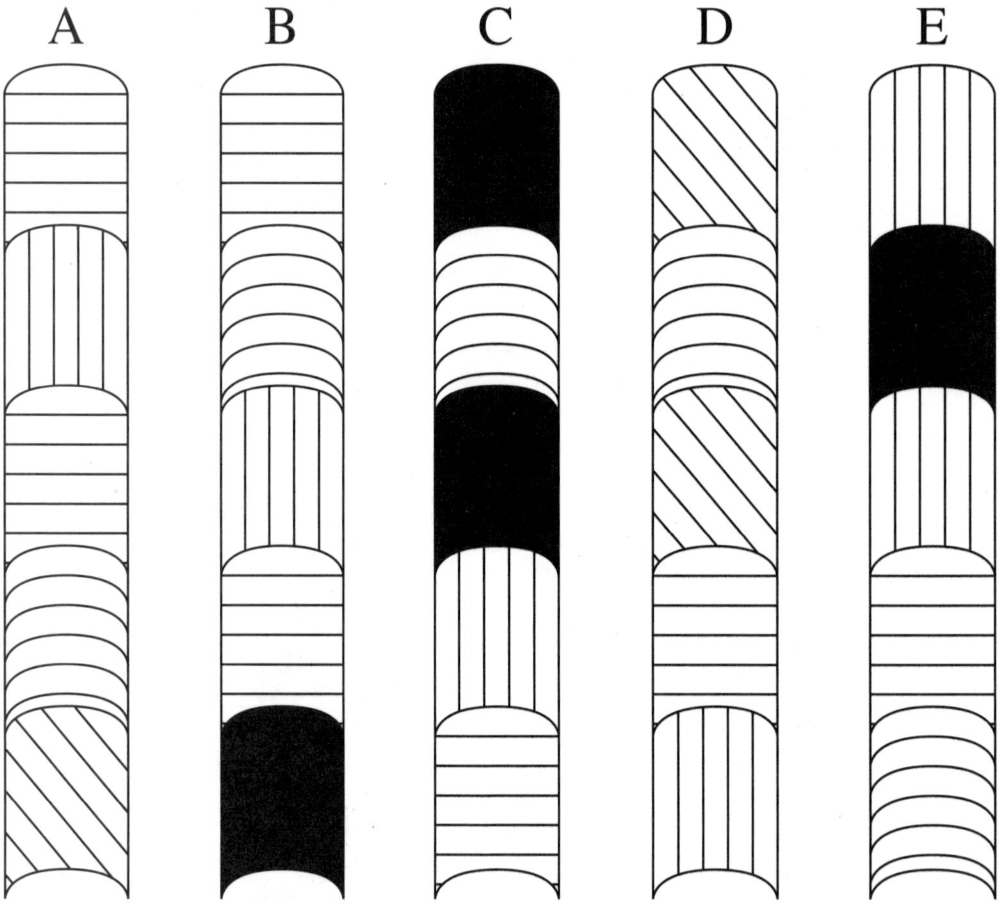

PUZZLE 6

In a game of 6 players lasting for 40 minutes, there are 4 reserves. They substitute each player, so that all players, including reserves, are on the pitch for the same length of time. How long is each player on the pitch?

PUZZLE 7

What comes next?

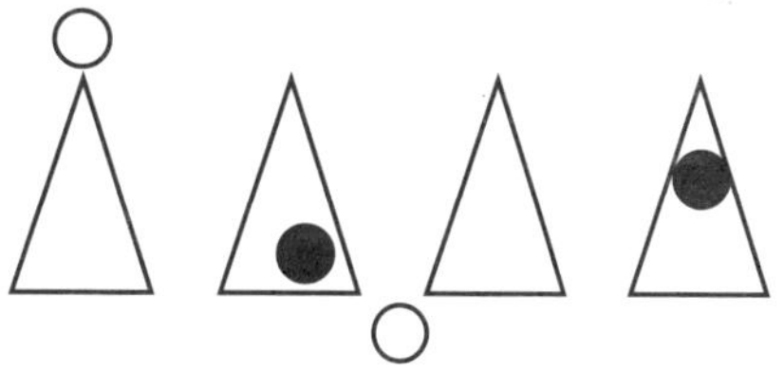

A B C D E

PUZZLE 8

What number should replace the question mark?

17	14	5	16
12			1
?			11
21	9	17	19

PUZZLE 9

What number should replace the question mark?

63

69

78

85

90

?

LEVEL 3

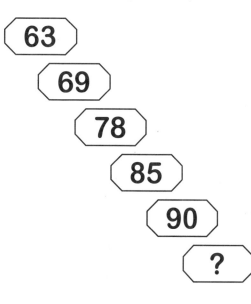

10 PUZZLE

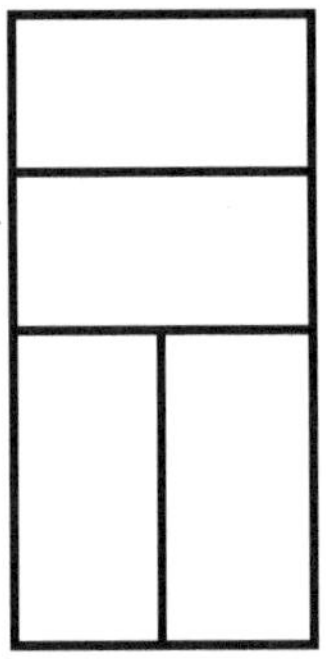

is to:

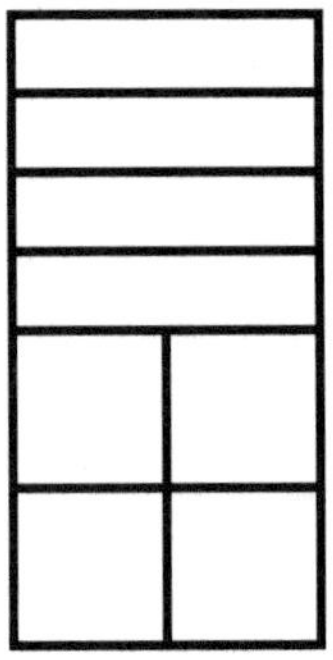

as:

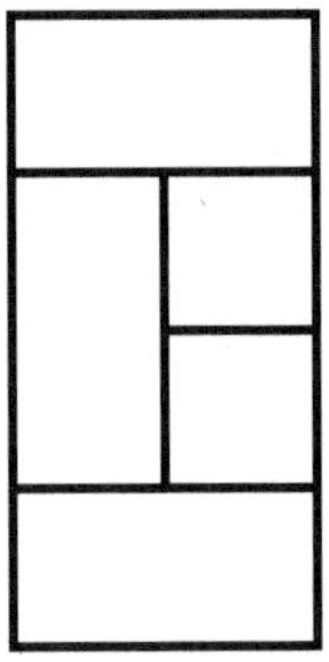

is to:

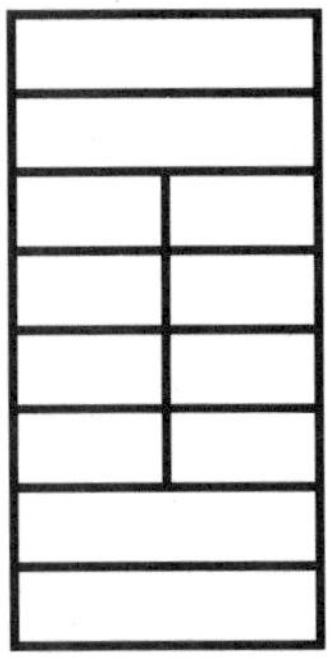

A

B

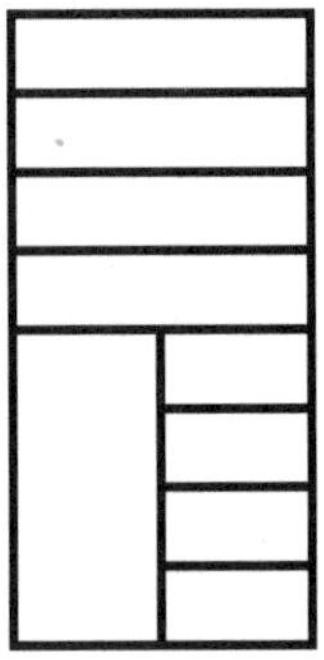

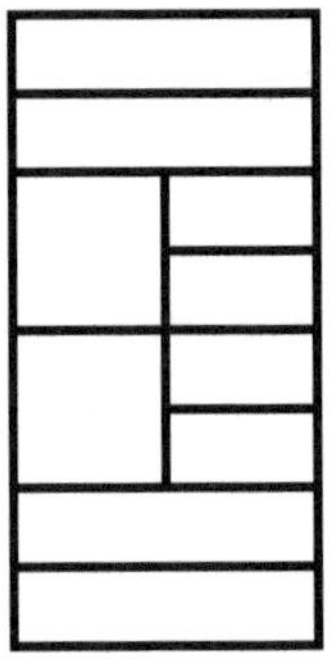

C

D

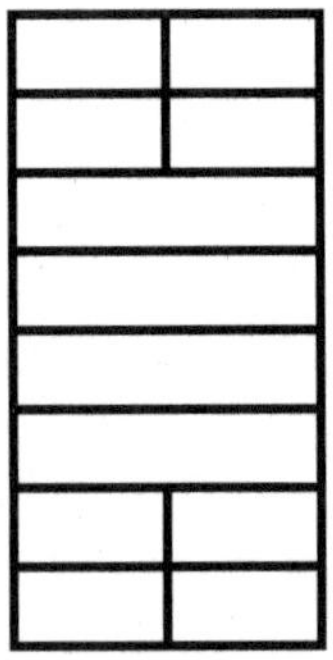

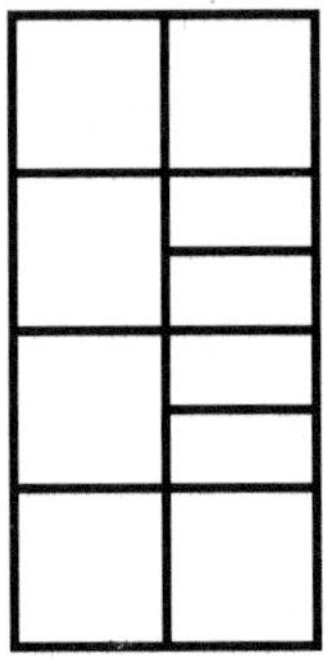

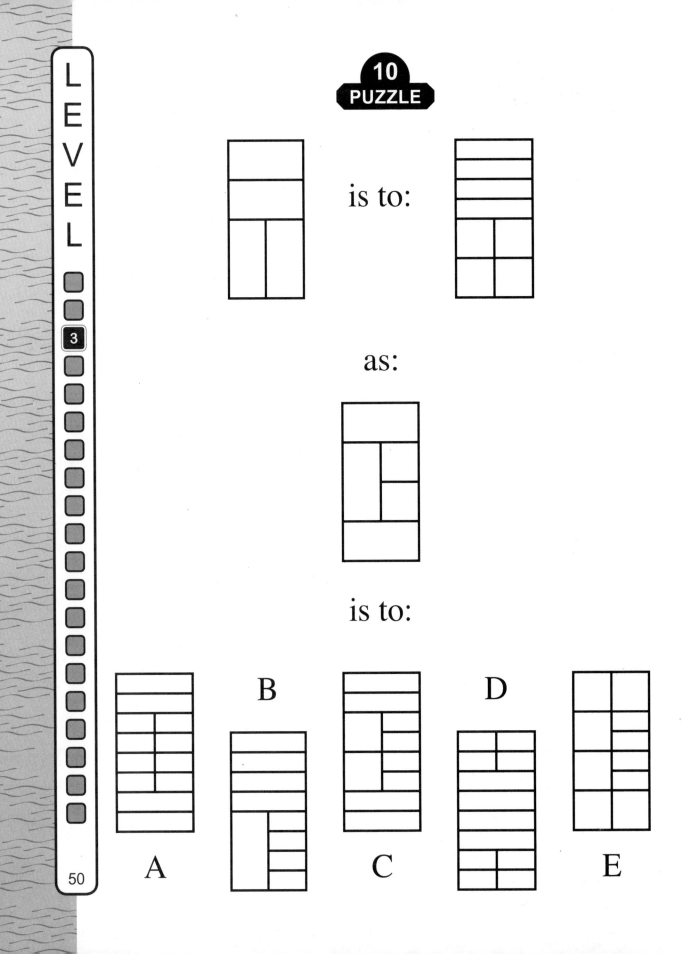

E

11 PUZZLE

Which has the greatest total degrees in their angles, and by how much?

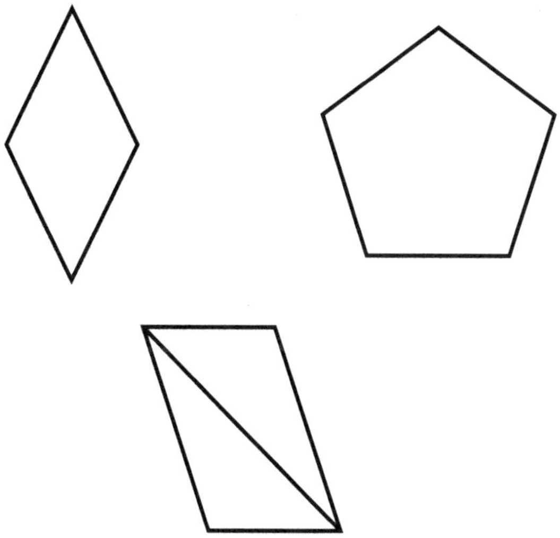

12 PUZZLE

Find the value for A, B, C and D.

C	C	A	D	=22
C	D	D	A	=20
A	A	D	D	=32
C	B	B	A	=30
=24	=25	=23	=32	

13 PUZZLE

Which of these is not a musical instrument?

(a) CLARION
(b) PICCOLO
(c) CLAVECIN
(d) CANTAR
(e) OCARINA

14 PUZZLE

Which numbers will replace the question marks?

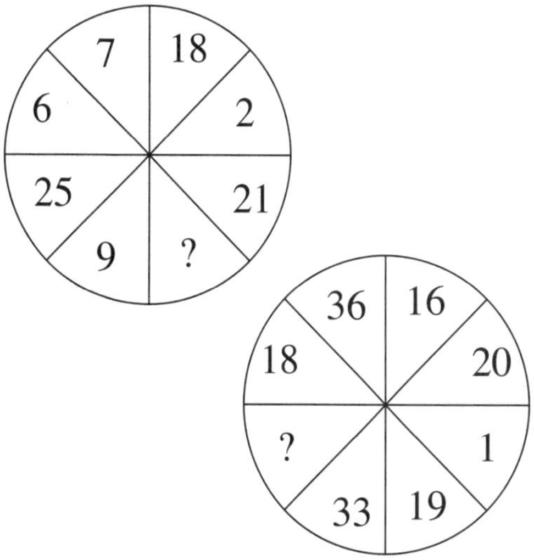

15 PUZZLE

Each line and symbol which appears in the four outer circles, below, is transferred to the centre circle according to these rules: If a line or symbol occurs in the outer circles: once: it is transferred twice: it is possibly transferred 3 times: it is transferred 4 times: it is not transferred. Which of the circles A, B, C, D or E, should appear at the centre of the diagram, below?

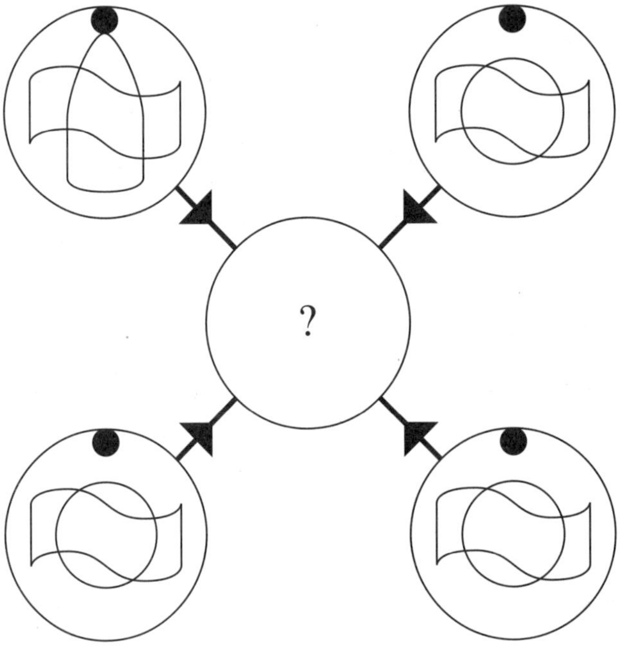

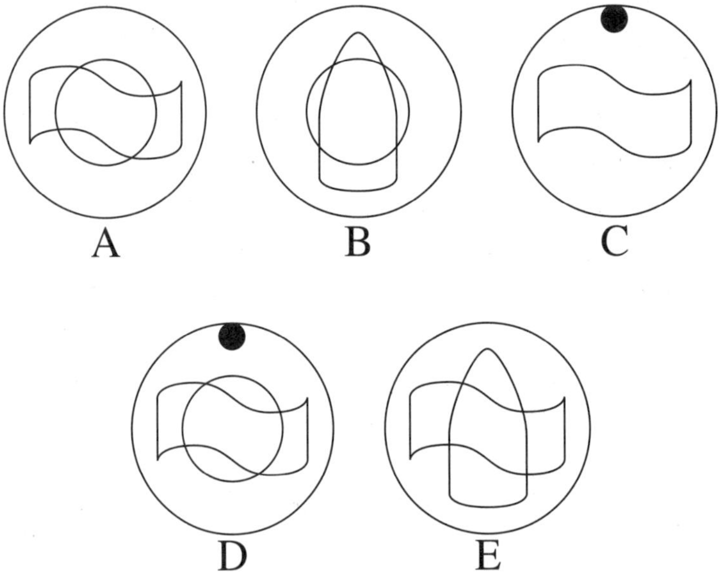

LEVEL 3

16 PUZZLE

What replaces the question mark?

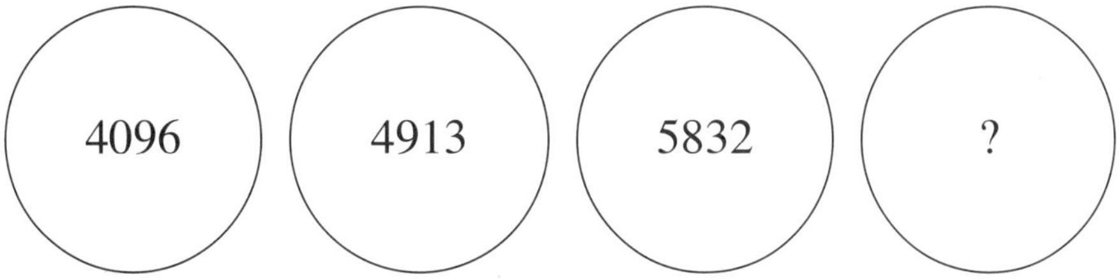

17 PUZZLE

What number should replace the question mark?

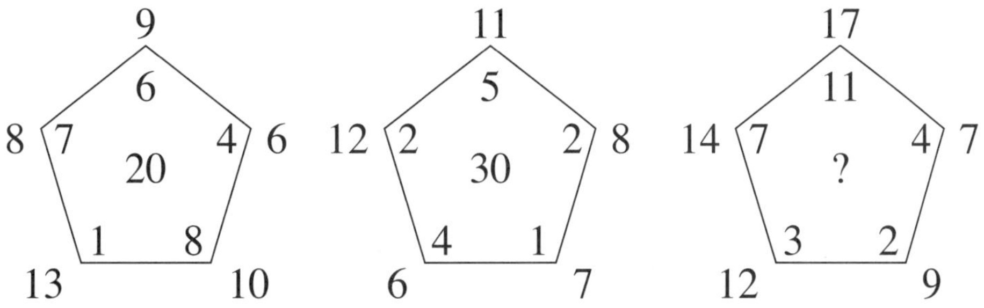

18 PUZZLE

The answer is 156, why?

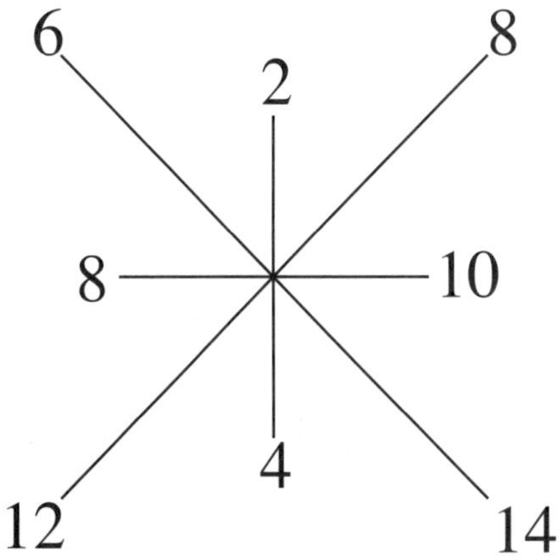

19 PUZZLE

Simplify

$(89^2) - (88^2)$

(a) 176
(b) 177
(c) 178
(d) 179
(e) 180

LEVEL 3

PUZZLE 20

Which should replace the question mark – A, B, C or D?

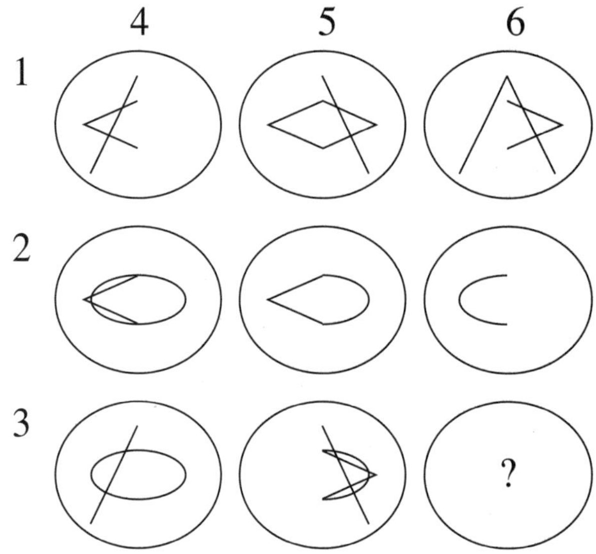

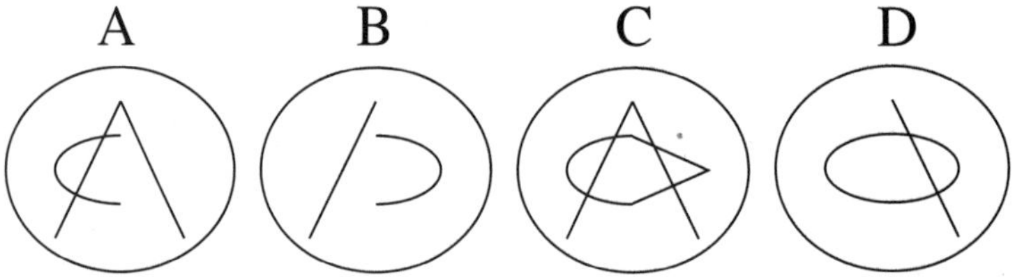

PUZZLE 21

What number should go under the letter E?

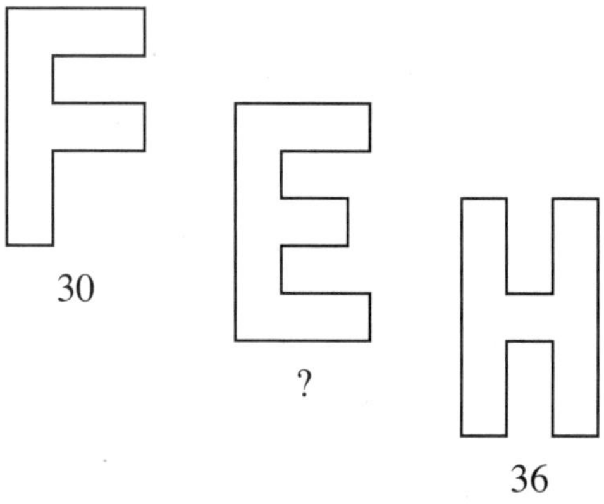

PUZZLE 22

Which word has the same or closest meaning to PALPABLE?

(a) LIKENESS
(b) THROBBING
(c) CRUSHED
(d) CLEVER
(e) OBVIOUS

23 PUZZLE

Each of the nine squares in the grid marked A1 to C3, should incorporate all the lines and symbols which are shown in the squares of the same letter and number immediately above and to the left. For example, B2 should incorporate all the lines and symbols that are in 2 and B. One of the squares is incorrect. Which one is it?

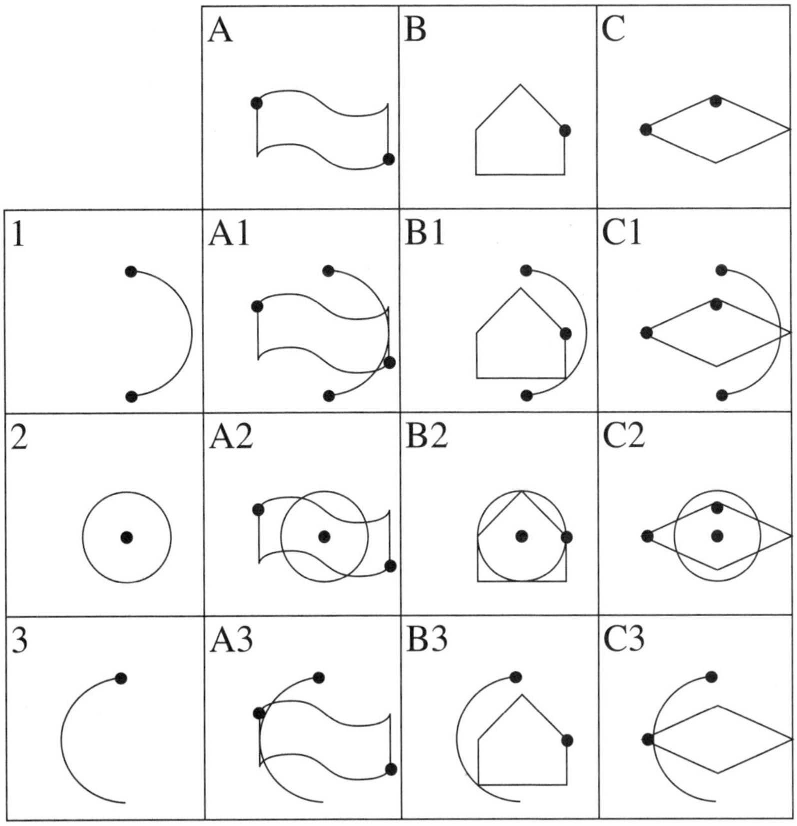

24 PUZZLE

The average of two numbers is 41½
The average of three numbers is 72
What is the third number?

25 PUZZLE

The price of one pair of socks is $3.50
The price of a pack of 6 pairs is $19.50

By what percentage are the socks cheaper when you buy a pack of 6?

26 PUZZLE

Which letter tops the third triangle?

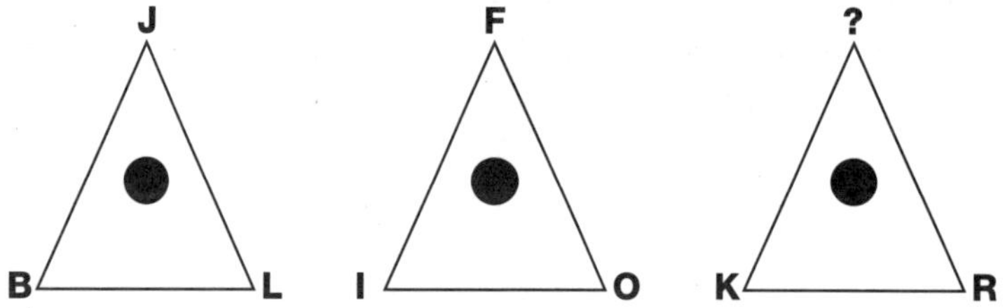

27 PUZZLE

Which number goes in the third star?

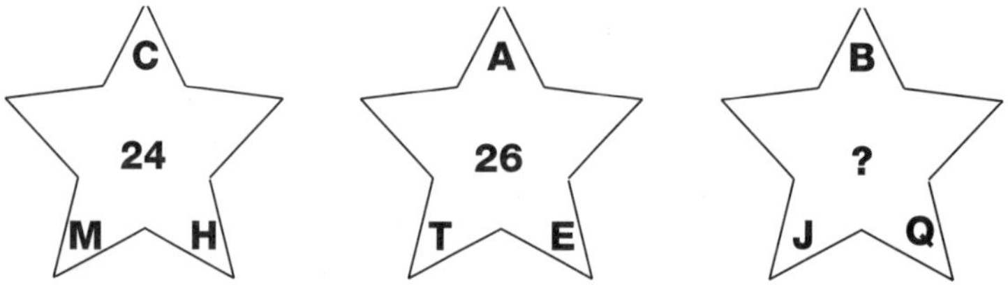

28 PUZZLE

Which letter replaces the blank and completes the sequence?

B	A
C	E
D	F
G	H
J	I
O	

29 PUZZLE

If two painters can complete two rooms in two hours, how many painters would it take to do 18 rooms in 6 hours?

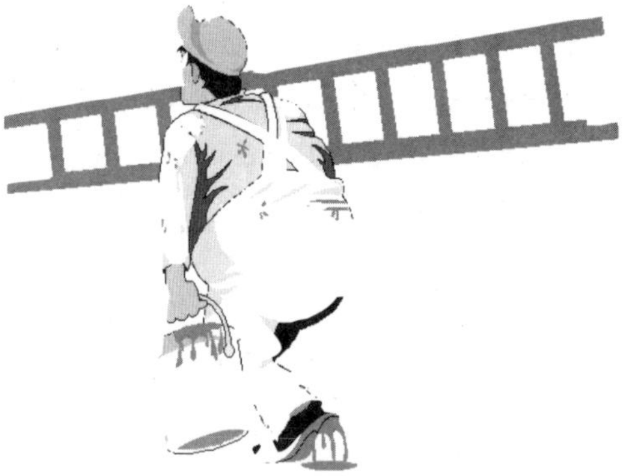

30 PUZZLE

Which letter goes in the empty segment?

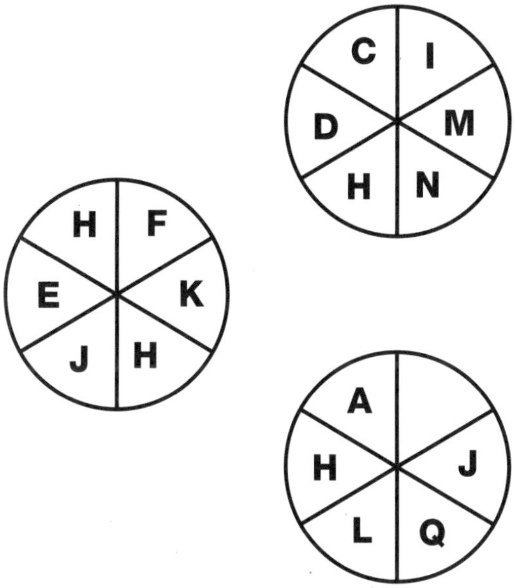

31 PUZZLE

Which number links all these?

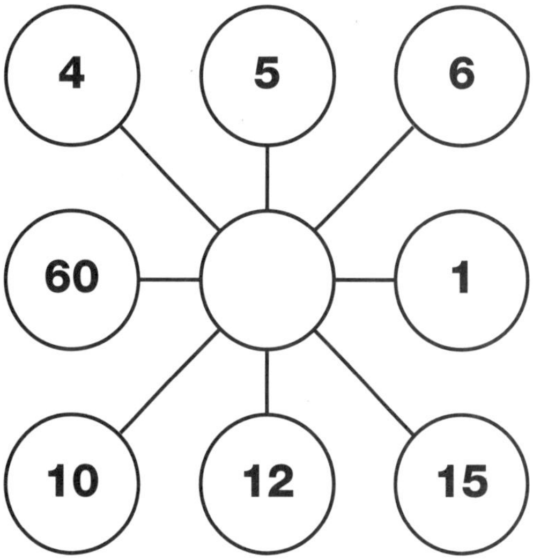

32 PUZZLE

Which number logically finishes this puzzle?

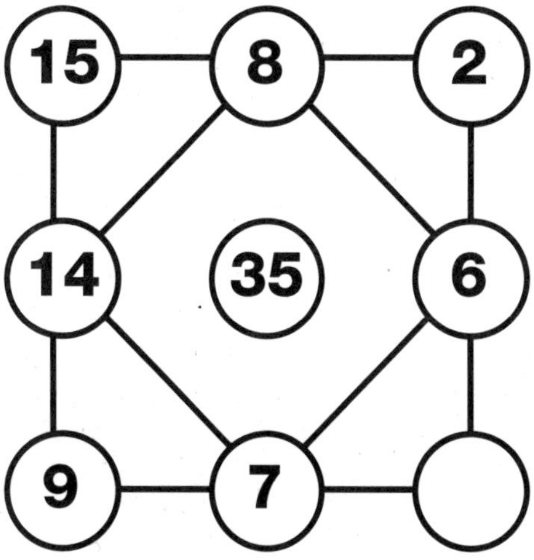

33 PUZZLE

Which number replaces the question mark?

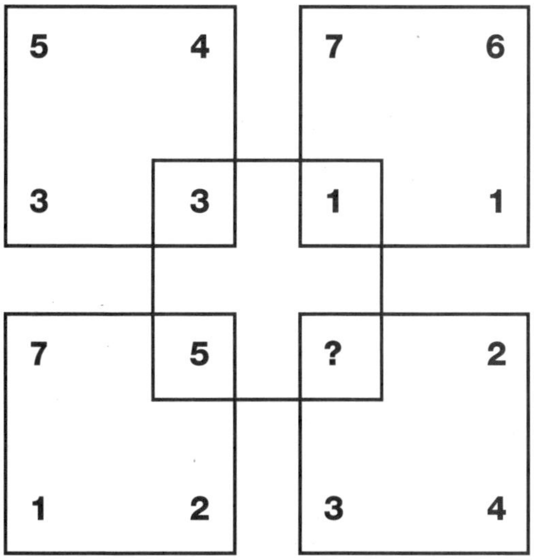

PUZZLE 34

Which number goes in the empty circle?

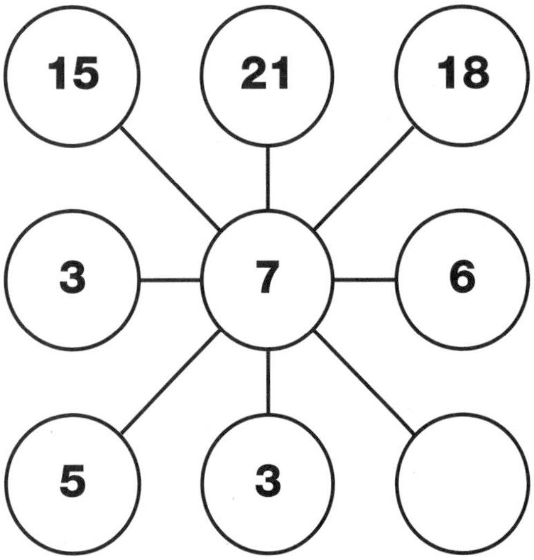

PUZZLE 35

Which number completes this sequence?

2	5
7	3
10	4
14	6
20	8
28	

PUZZLE 36

Which number finishes this grid?

2	6	3
5	3	3
7	2	

PUZZLE 37

Which letter replaces the blank and completes the sequence?

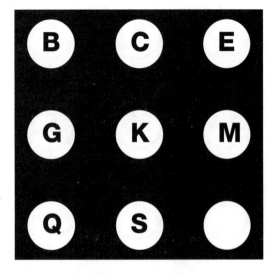

B	C	E
G	K	M
Q	S	

38 PUZZLE

Which playing card is missing?

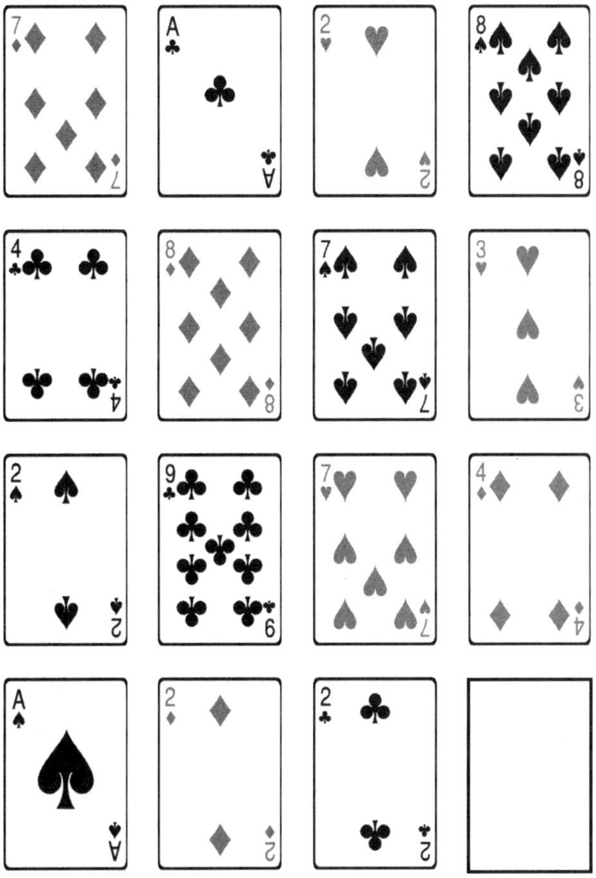

39 PUZZLE

Which character is missing from the point in the last star?

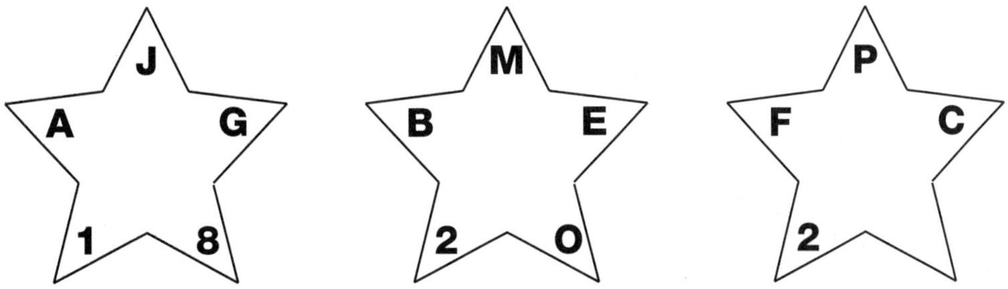

LEVEL 3

PUZZLE 40

Which letter goes in the final link to complete the chain?

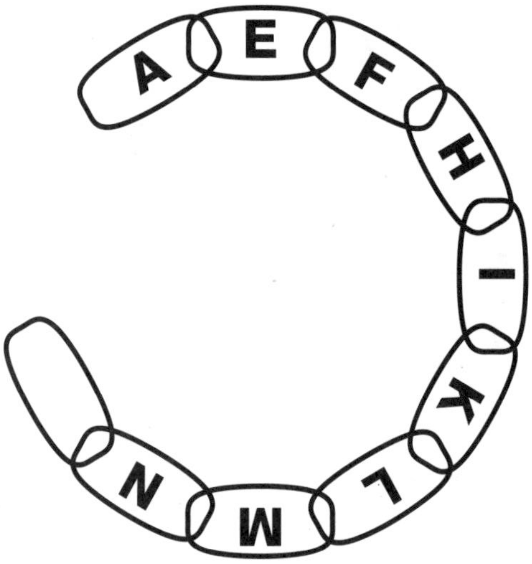

PUZZLE 41

Which number finishes this puzzle?

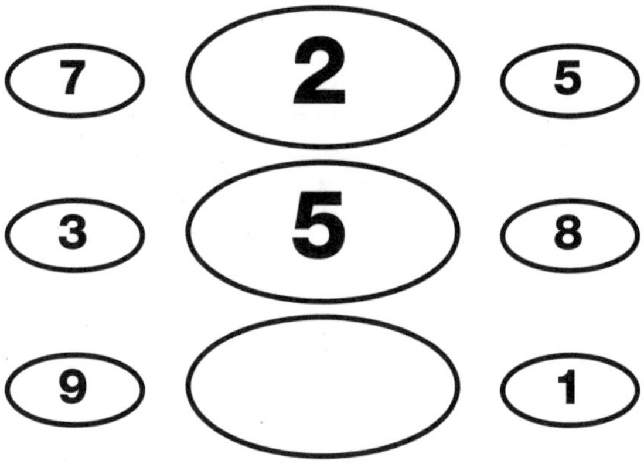

PUZZLE 42

Which number goes in the empty segment?

PUZZLE 43

Which letter replaces the blank and completes the sequence?

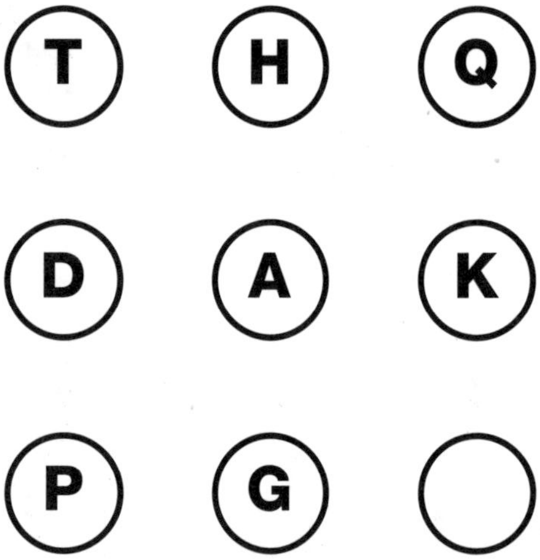

44 PUZZLE

Which number goes in the middle of the last triangle?

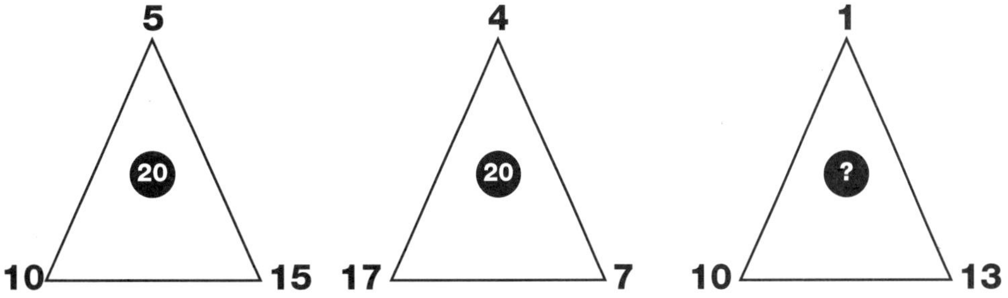

45 PUZZLE

Which number completes the chain?

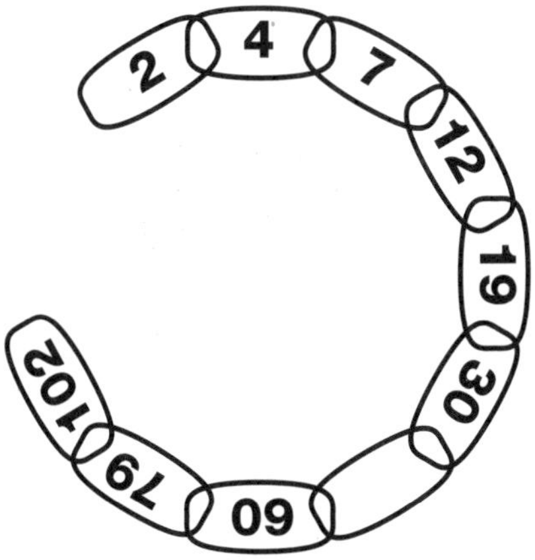

46 PUZZLE

Which letter replaces the blank and completes the wheel?

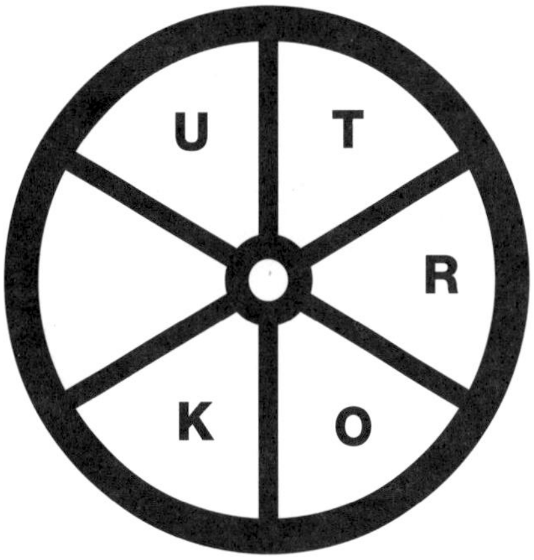

47 PUZZLE

Which number goes in the blank segment of the last circle?

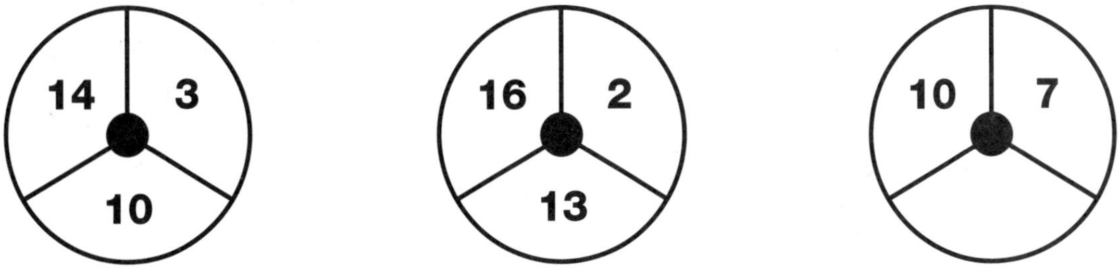

LEVEL 3

48 PUZZLE

Which number goes in the empty circle?

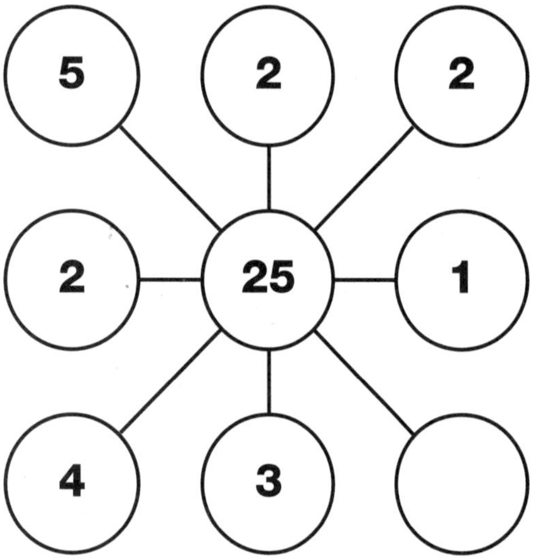

49 PUZZLE

Which character logically completes this sequence?

B	A
2	8
J	N
2	3
Q	K
3	

50 PUZZLE

Which letter goes in the empty segment?

51 PUZZLE

Which number will finish this grid?

5	8	12
7	12	18
3	4	

52 PUZZLE

Which number does not fit in this sequence?

1 - 2 - 3 - 6 - 7 - 8 - 14 - 15 - 30

53 PUZZLE

Which number is the odd one out in each shape?

A

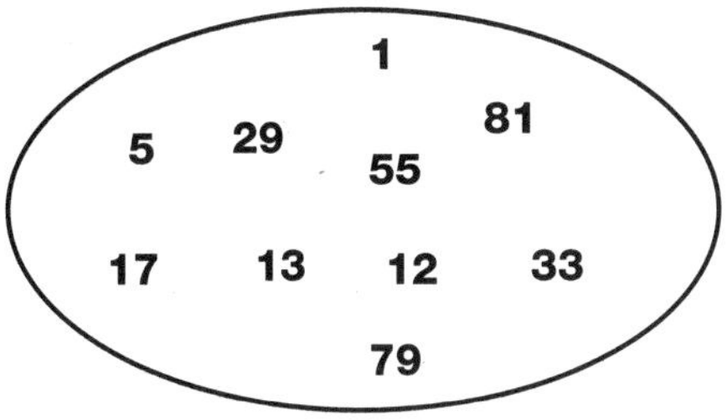

B

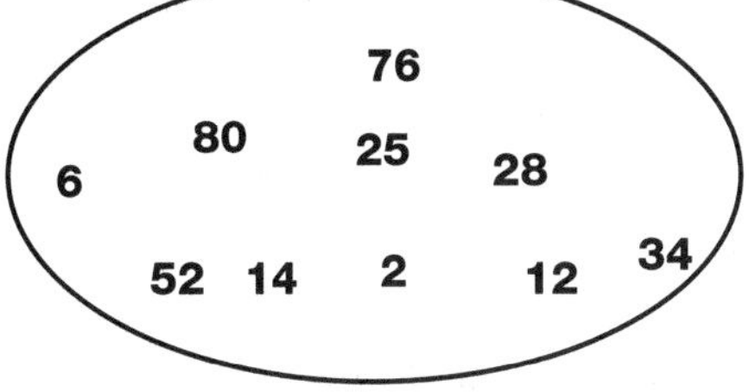

54 PUZZLE

Which number is missing from the puzzle?

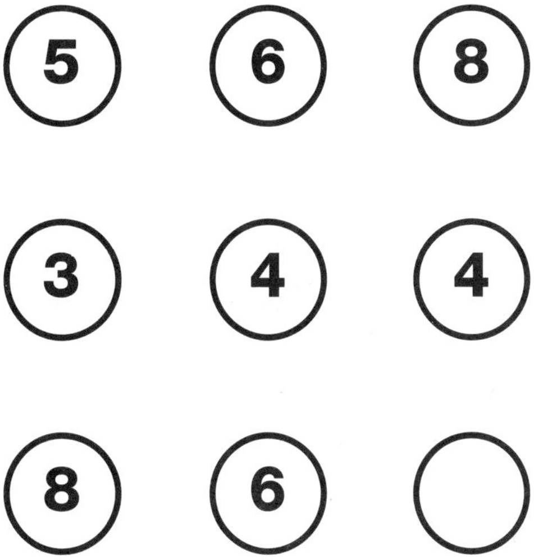

55 PUZZLE

Which number is missing in the last grid?

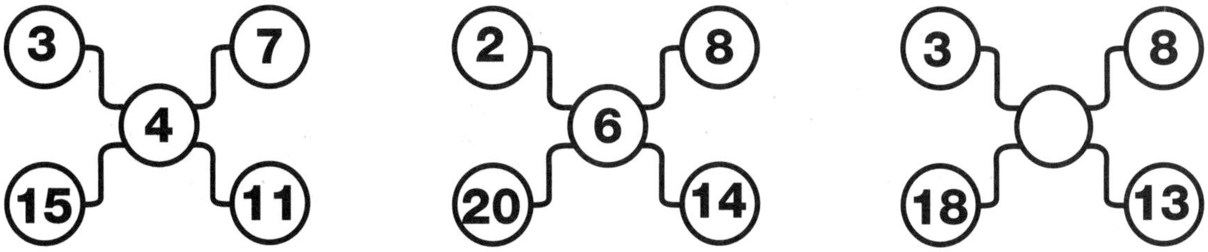

LEVEL 3

56 PUZZLE

Which letter replaces the blank and completes the sequence?

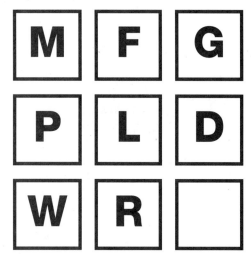

M	F	G
P	L	D
W	R	

57 PUZZLE

Which letter goes in the empty circle and completes this puzzle?

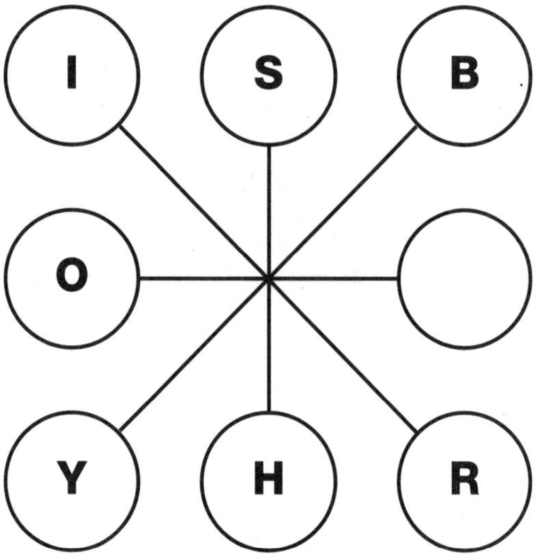

58 PUZZLE

Jacob is 12 years old.
He is 3 times as old as his brother.
How old will Jacob be when he is twice as old?

59 PUZZLE

Which number goes in the empty segment and completes the wheel?

60 PUZZLE

Which number goes in the empty square?

J	F	N
8	4	0

B	G	P
2	2	4

O	D	I
5	4	

61 PUZZLE

Which number goes in the empty circle and finishes the puzzle?

4	6	2
7	8	1
1	4	

62 PUZZLE

Which character is missing from this puzzle?

B	I
W	P

D	J
V	P

A	F
P	K

J	N
V	R

N	
W	T

1 PUZZLE

What heptagon below has most in common with the heptagon above?

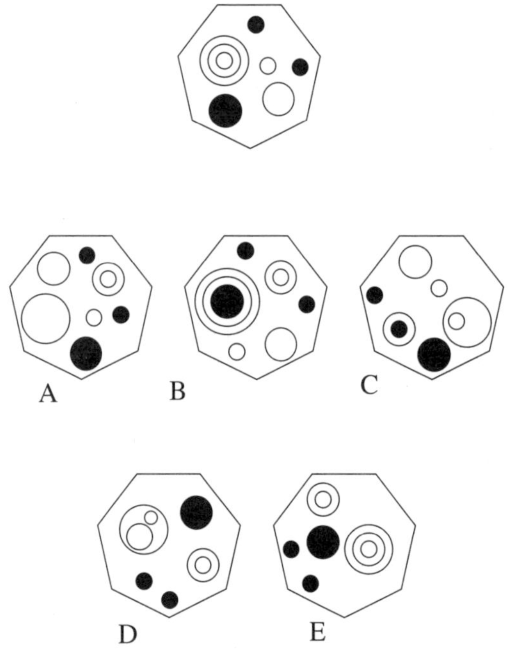

2 PUZZLE

SUNDAY
MONDAY
TUESDAY
WEDNESDAY
THURSDAY
FRIDAY
SATURDAY

What day immediately follows the day three days before the day immediately before the day two days after the day immediately before Thursday?

3 PUZZLE

What number should replace the question mark?

1.5

4.5

13.5

16.5

?

4 PUZZLE

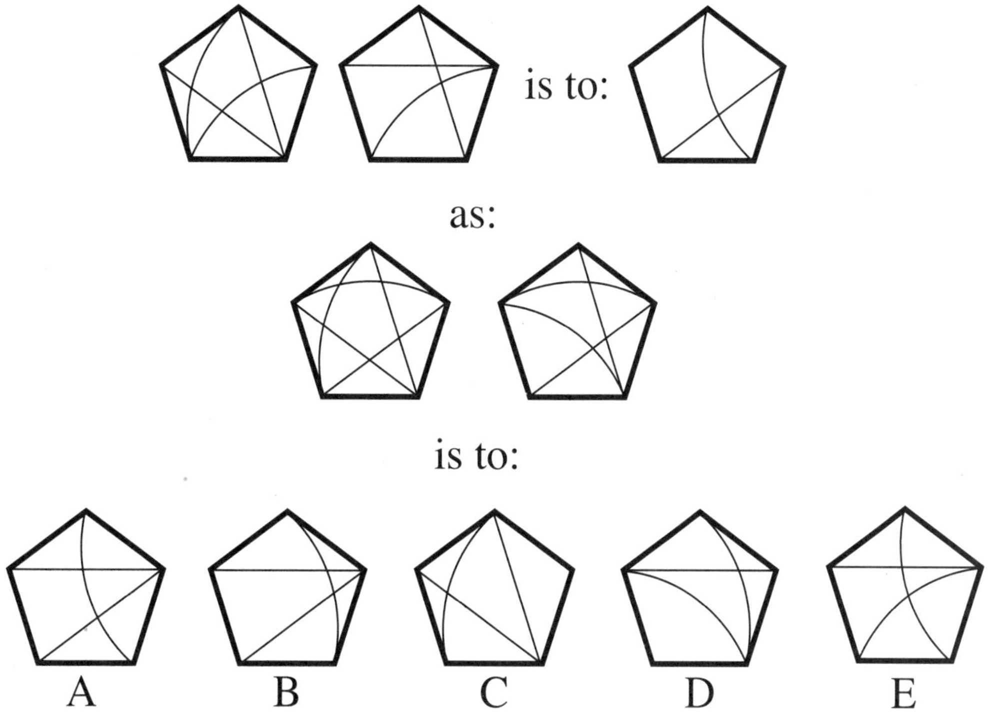

5 PUZZLE

What number should replace the question marks?

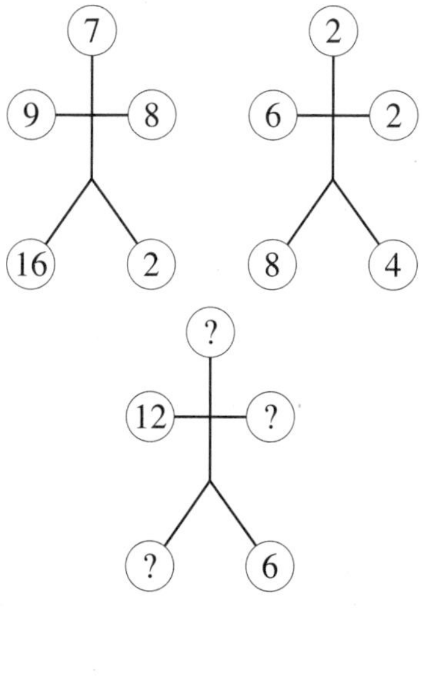

6 PUZZLE

A car travels 40 miles in the same time as another car travelling 20 mph faster covers 60 miles. How long does the journey take?

7 PUZZLE

What should replace the circle with the question mark?

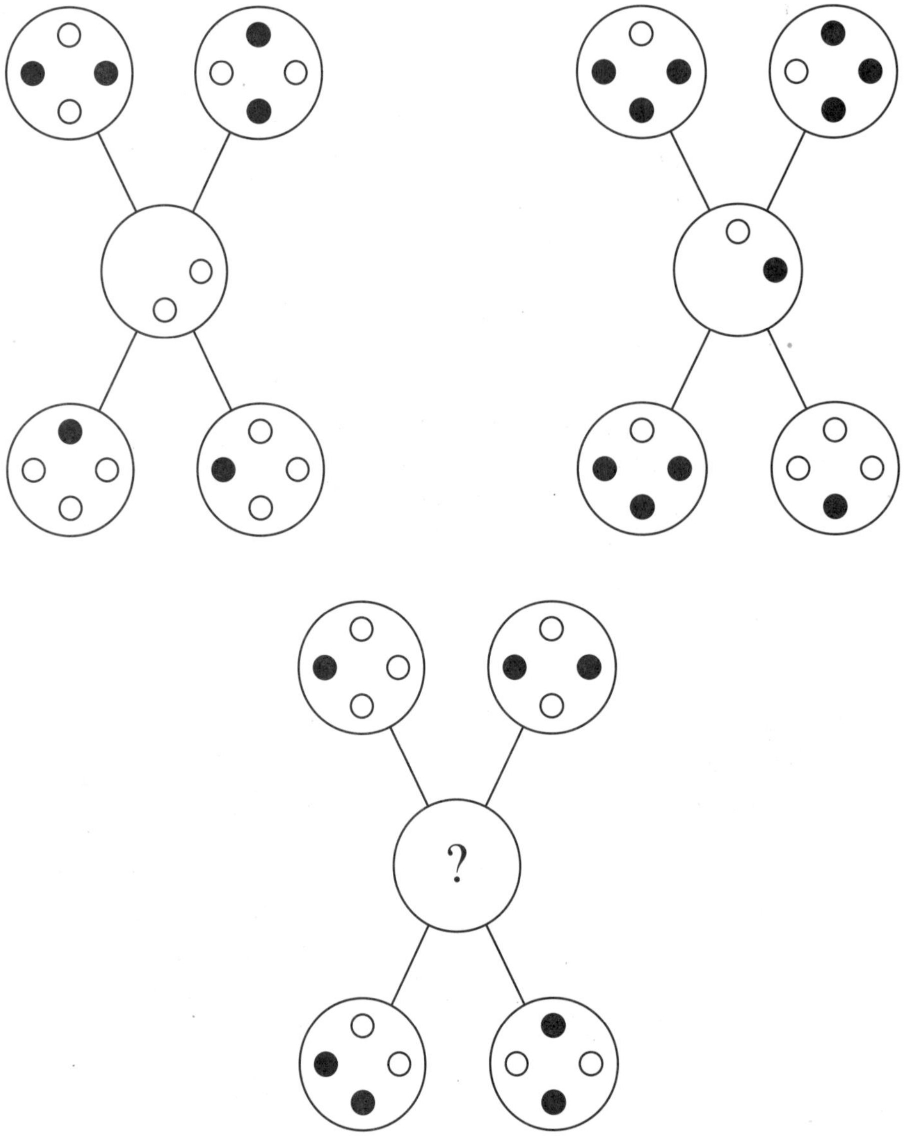

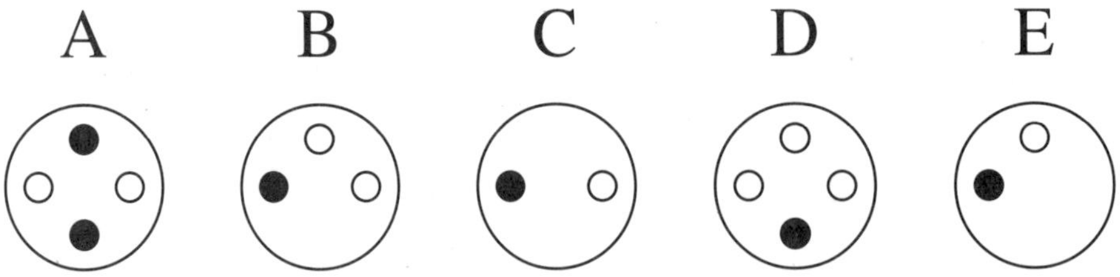

PUZZLE 8

What number should replace the question mark?

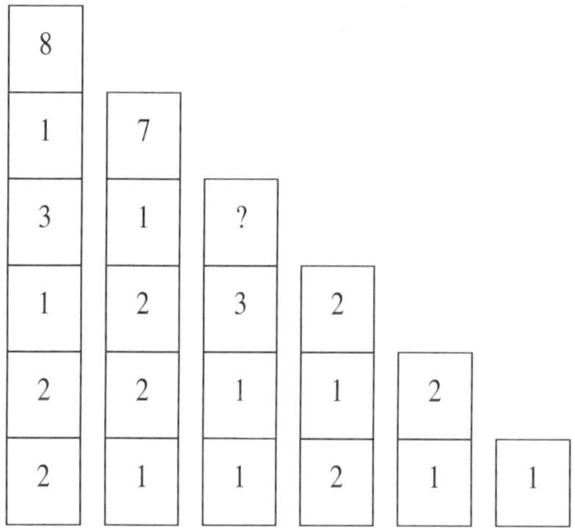

PUZZLE 9

All widgets are round. Everything round has a hole in the middle. Some things that are round have a handle. Therefore:

1. All widgets have a hole in the middle

2. Everything with a handle is a widget

3. Neither of the above is true

4. Both the above are true

PUZZLE 10

Which is the missing tile?

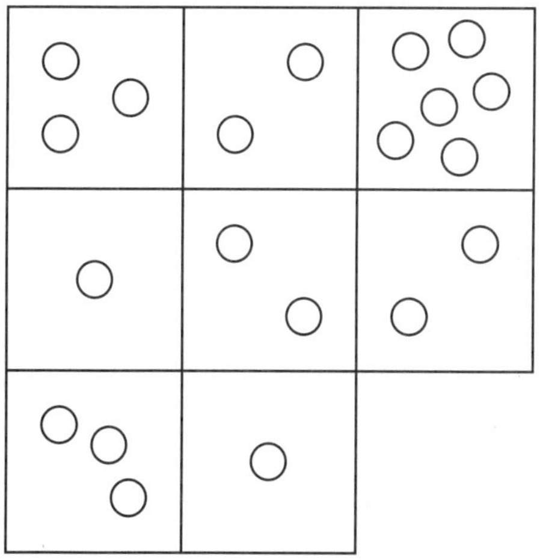

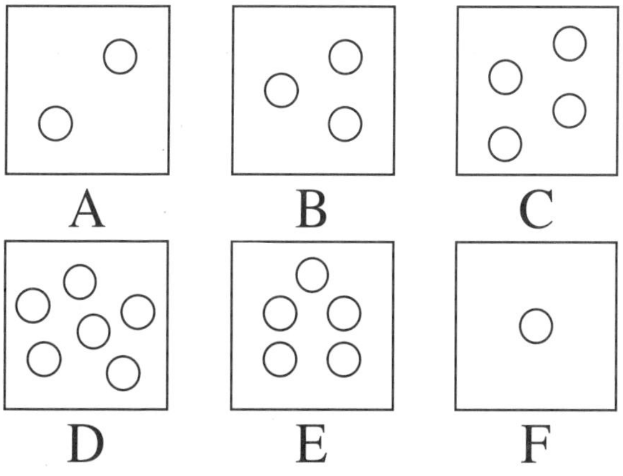

11 PUZZLE

Each line and symbol which appears in the four outer circles below, is transferred to the centre circle according to these rules: If a line or symbol occurs in the outer circles once: it is transferred twice: it is possibly transferred 3 times: it is transferred 4 times: it is not transferred. Which of the circles A, B, C, D or E, should appear at the centre of the diagram, below?

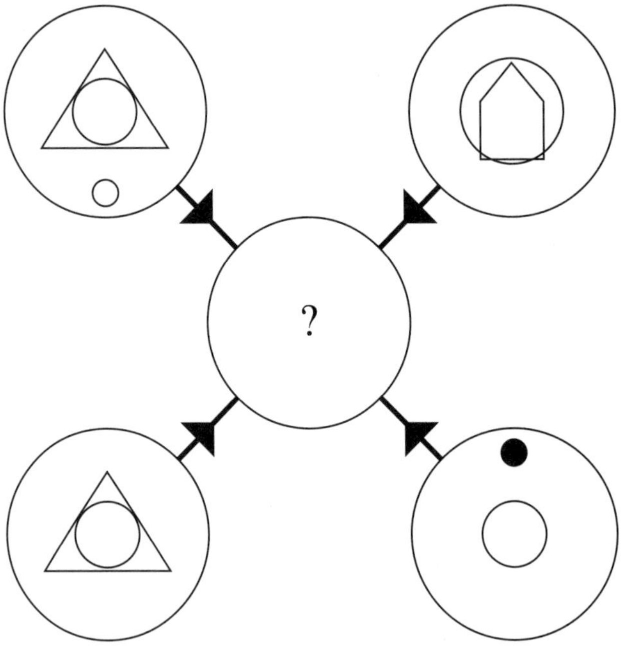

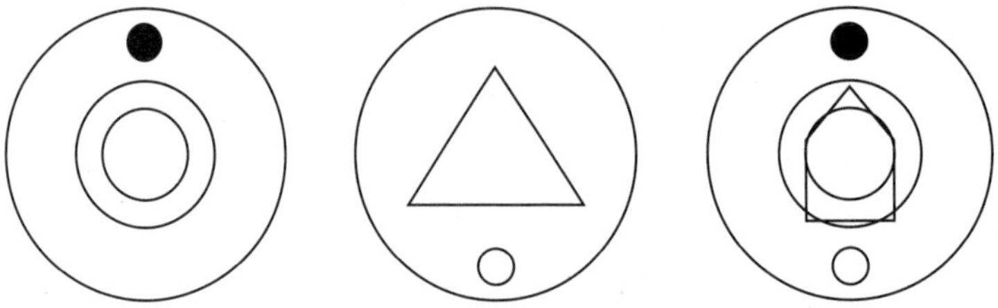

A B C

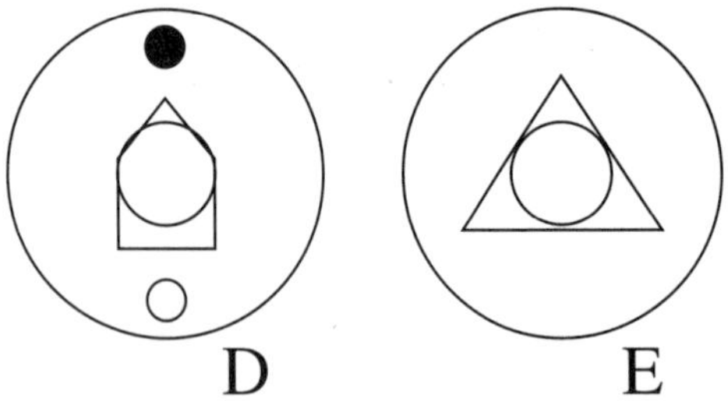

D E

PUZZLE 12

Which letter should replace the question mark?

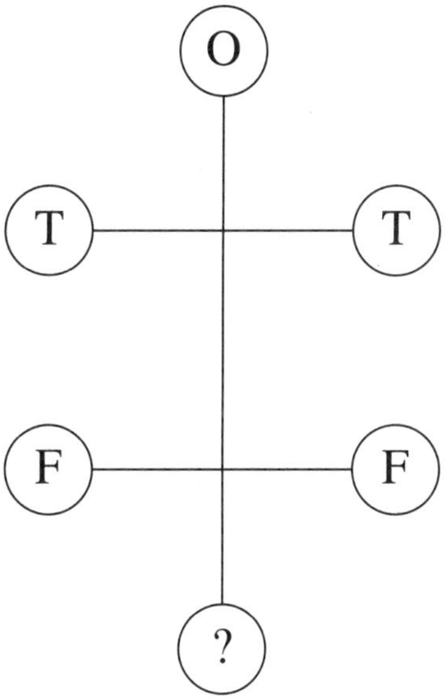

PUZZLE 13

Which is the odd one out?

(a) HESSIAN
(b) MARCASITE
(c) TAFFETA
(d) CORDUROY
(e) ORGANDIE

PUZZLE 14

Which words means the same as FETTER?

MANACLE
BLANCHE
SURPRISE
LARGER
SECONDARY
STEAL

PUZZLE 15

Which is the odd one out?

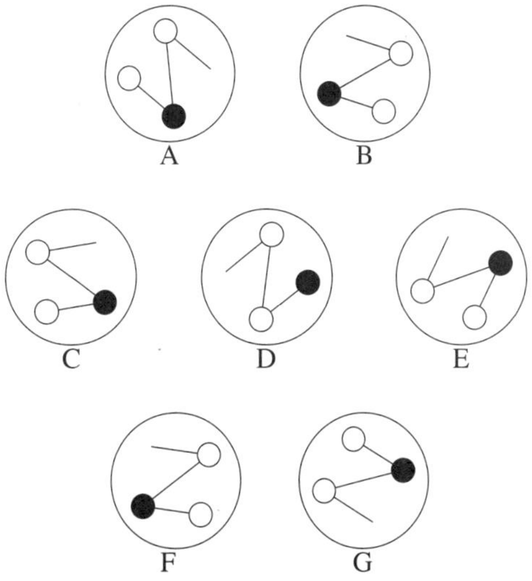

LEVEL

4

16 PUZZLE

What should the time be on Clock D?

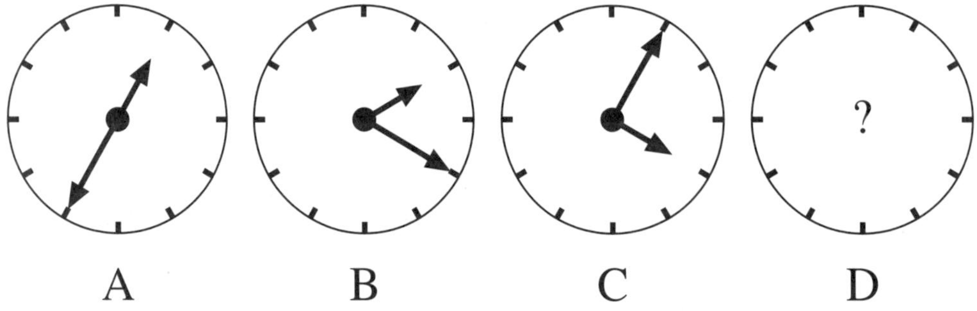

17 PUZZLE

What number should replace the question mark?

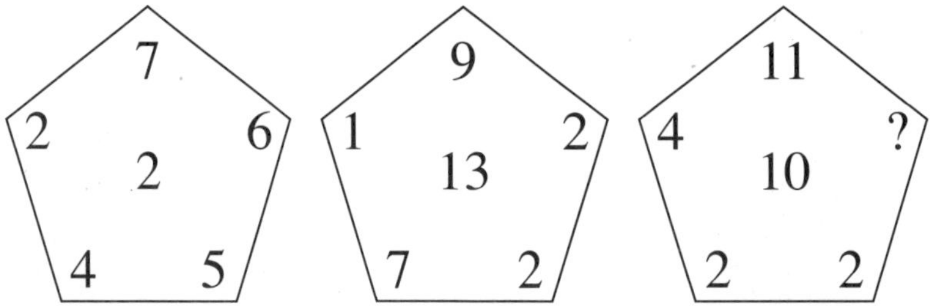

18 PUZZLE

How many times must the large cog revolve before all of the cogs are in their original position?

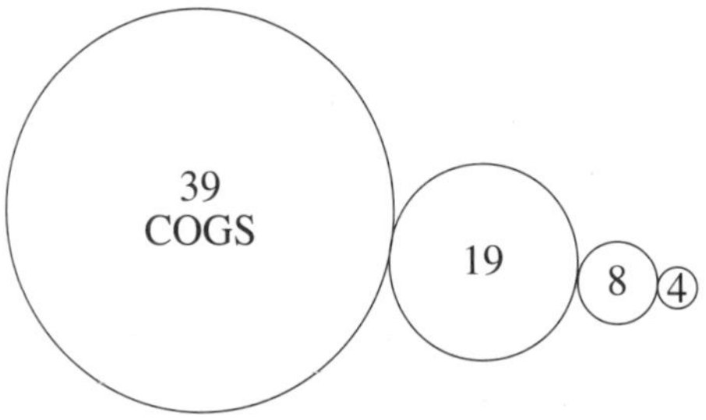

19 PUZZLE

Which number should replace the question mark?

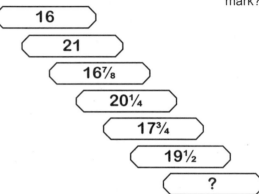

16

21

16⅞

20¼

17¾

19½

?

20 PUZZLE

Each of the nine squares in the grid marked A1 to C3, should incorporate all the lines and symbols which are shown in the squares of the same letter and number immediately above and to the left. For example, B2 should incorporate all the lines and symbols that are in 2 and B. One of the squares is incorrect. Which one is it?

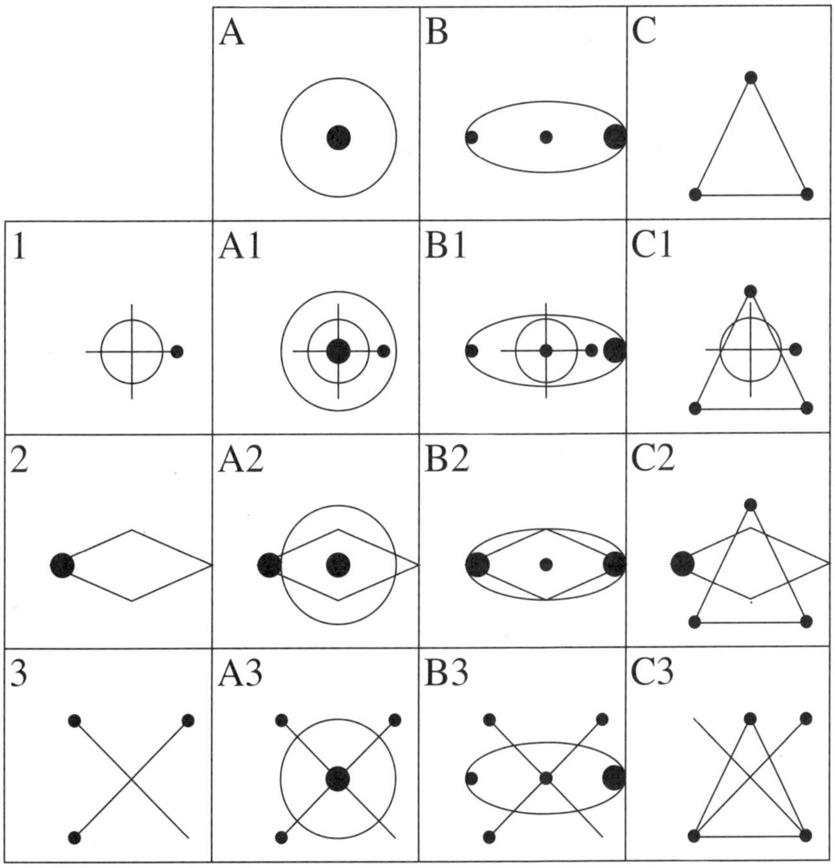

21 PUZZLE

What is a PASHA?

(a) A DOG
(b) A TREE
(c) A TURKISH TITLE
(d) A DISH
(e) A BOAT

22 PUZZLE

Which number comes next to a definite rule?

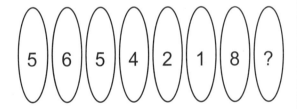

5 6 5 4 2 1 8 ?

23 PUZZLE

Which hexagon should replace the question mark - A, B, C, D or E?

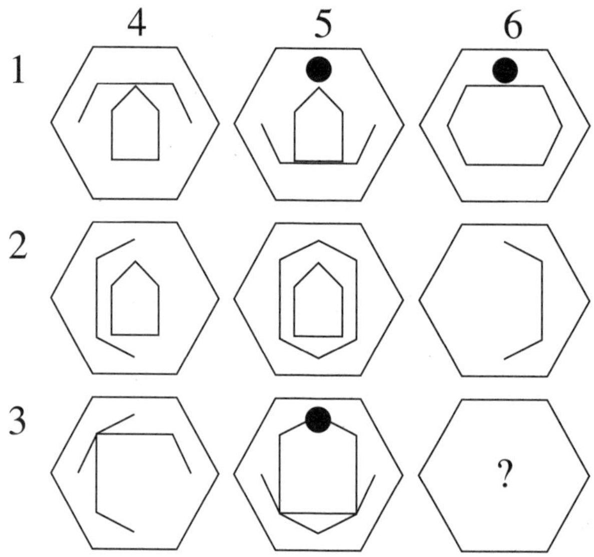

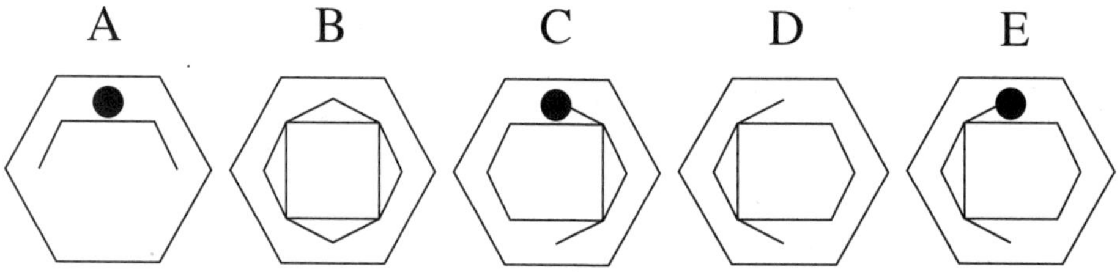

24 PUZZLE

Which is the odd one out?

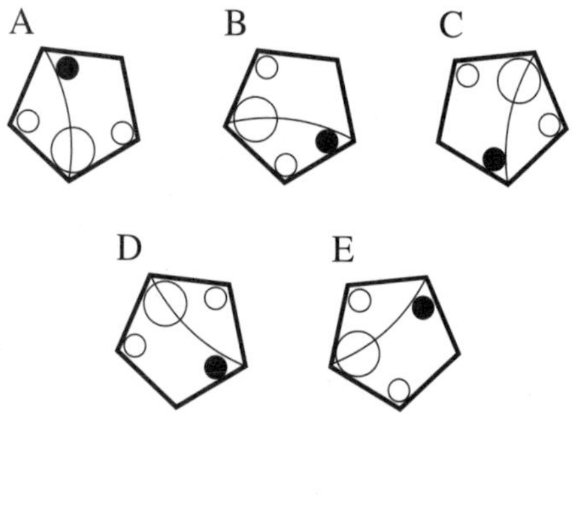

25 PUZZLE

Simplify

$$\frac{22}{\frac{2}{3} - \frac{1}{2}}$$

26 PUZZLE

Which letter replaces the blank and completes the sequence?

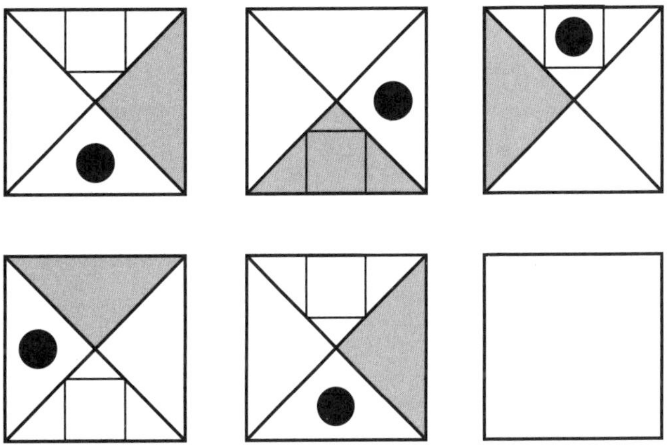

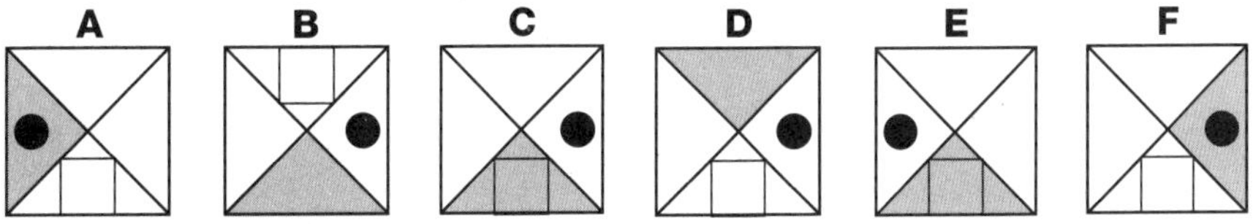

27 PUZZLE

Which number goes in the empty square?

3	7	10
4	11	15
6	4	

28 PUZZLE

Which number completes the sequence?

G	M
2	0
N	T
3	4
U	B
2	

29 PUZZLE

Draw the correct pattern in the empty box to complete the pattern.

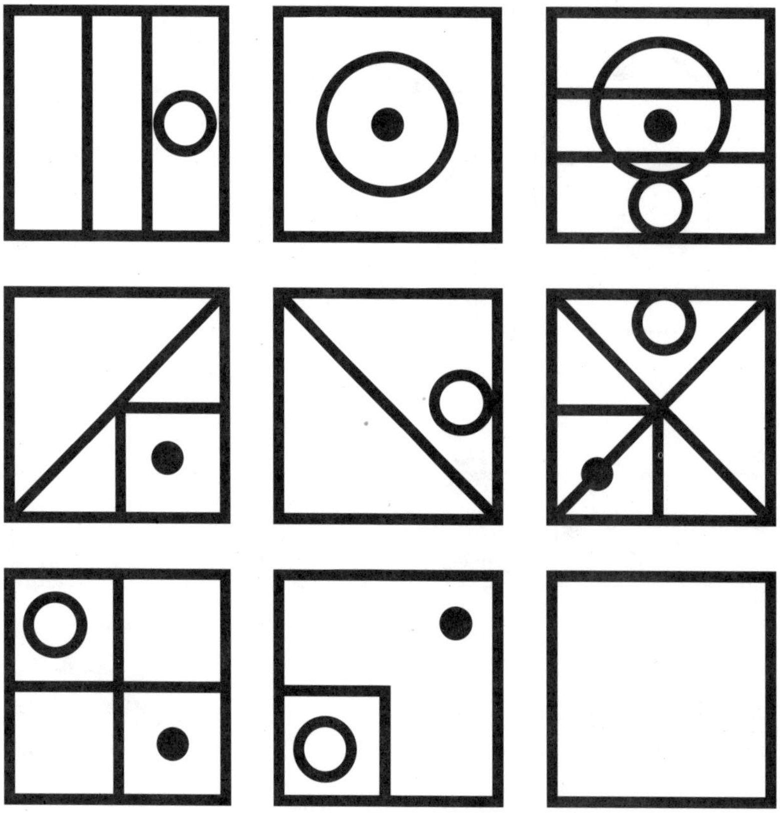

30 PUZZLE

Which number goes in the empty circle?

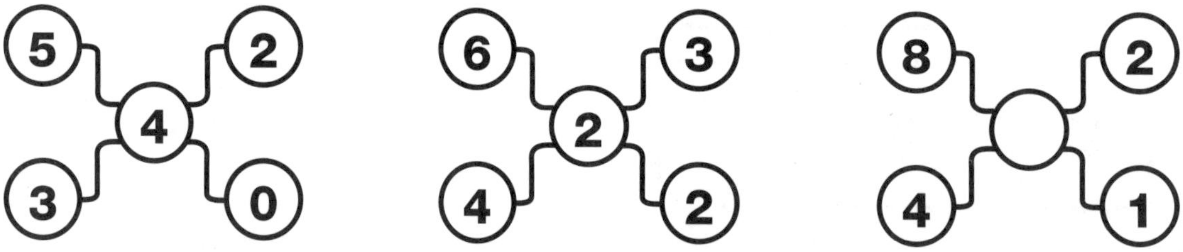

31 PUZZLE

Which letter replaces the blank and completes the sequence?

S	Z	F
K	T	K
B	R	

32 PUZZLE

If the price of a dress was cut by 20% for a sale, by what percentage of the sale price must it be increased by to resell it at the original price?

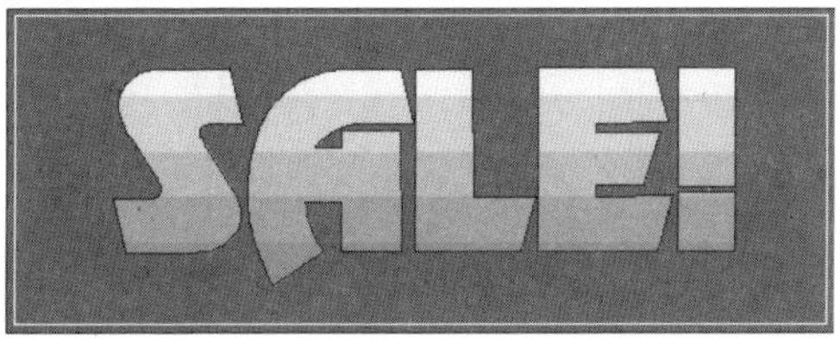

33 PUZZLE

Which number goes at the bottom to start the sequence?

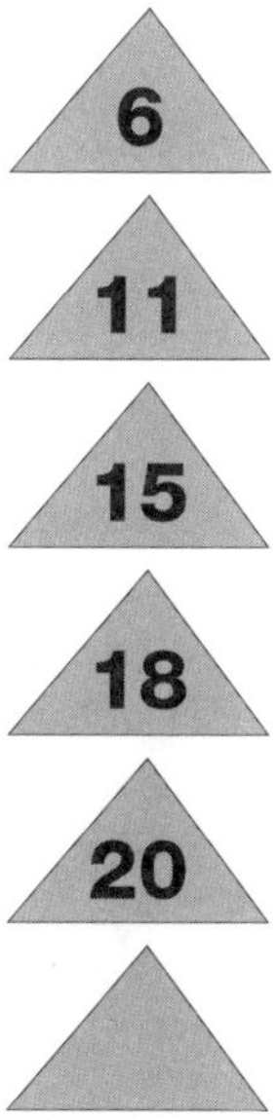

34 PUZZLE

Which characters complete this grid?

J	Q
1	0
P	K
1	6
T	G

35 PUZZLE

Which of the bottom numbers goes in the centre circle?

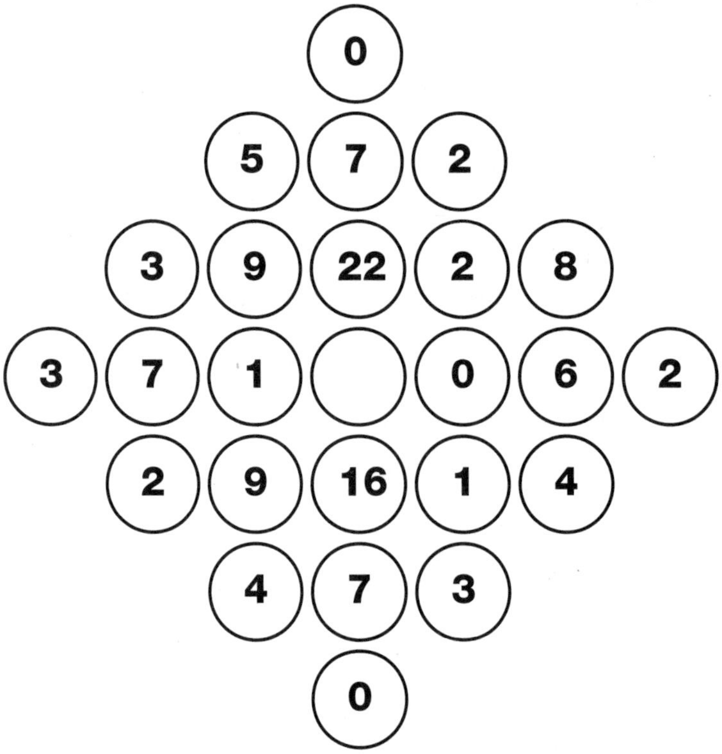

13 15 17 19 21 23 25 27

36 PUZZLE

Which letter finishes off the third triangle?

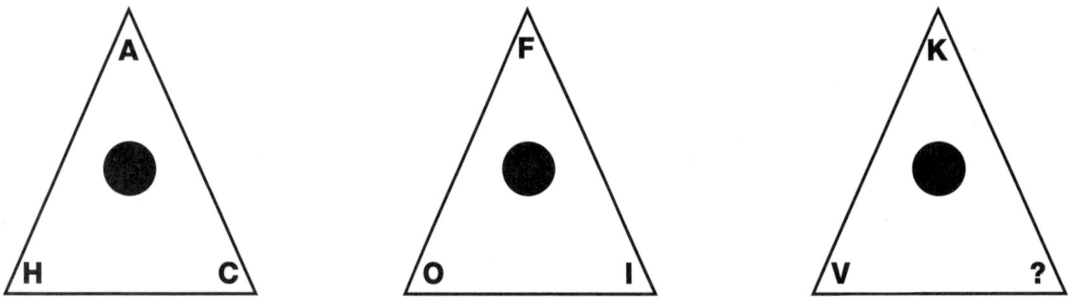

PUZZLE 37

Which number is missing from the bottom grid?

4	15	6
7	27	11

6	33	16
3	12	

PUZZLE 38

Which letter logically completes the last box of letters?

H	X	O
Q	A	J

Z	R	K
F	N	U

S	G	D
A	M	

PUZZLE 39

Which number goes in the empty segment?

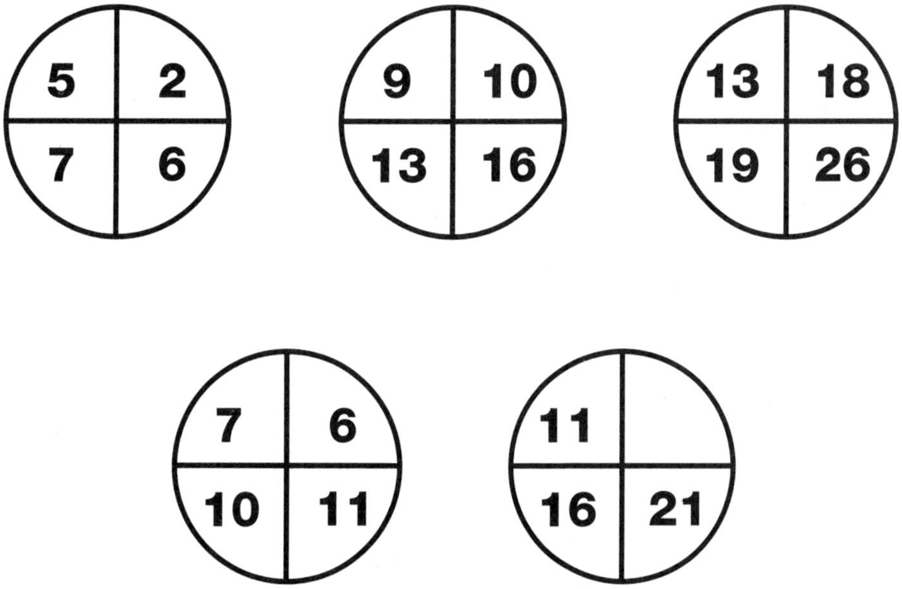

40 PUZZLE

Which letter replaces the blank and completes the third wheel?

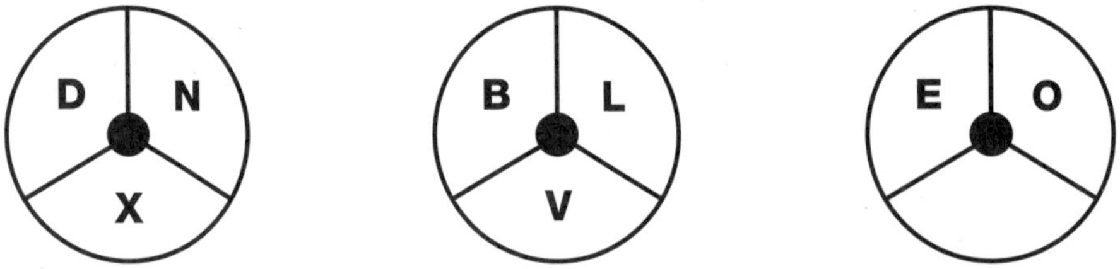

41 PUZZLE

Which number replaces the blank and completes the sequence?

4	5	6	10
4	3	3	2
4	5	6	0
11	7	6	

42 PUZZLE

George has a square plot of land, but the corner of his house takes up a quarter of the available space as the picture shows. He wants to divide the remaining space into four equal plots, of the same area and basic shape. It was difficult to do as the plots were not arranged in the most practical way but can you work out how George managed it?

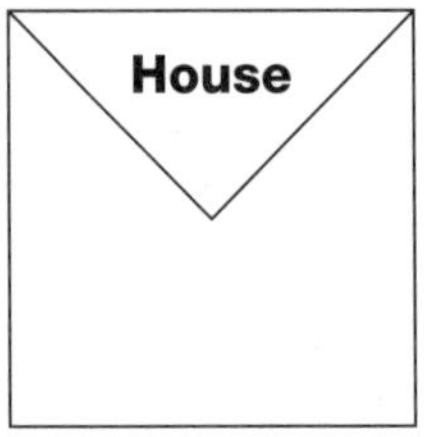

43 PUZZLE

Which letter replaces the blank and completes the sequence?

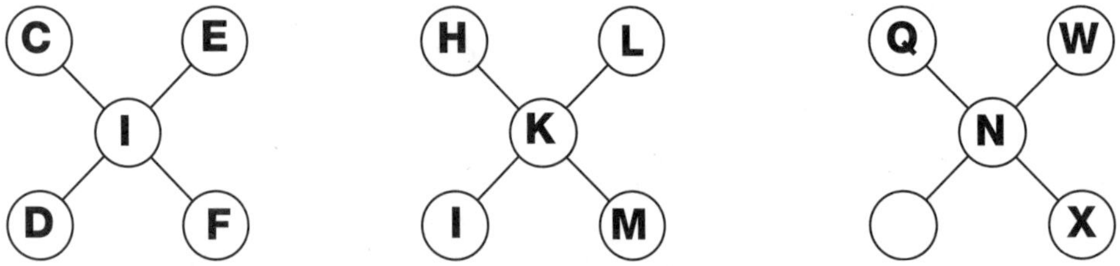

44 PUZZLE

Which number is missing from the last triangle?

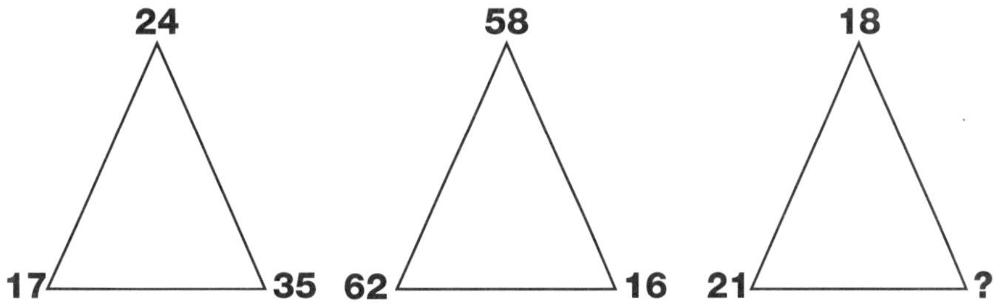

45 PUZZLE

Which number replaces the question mark?

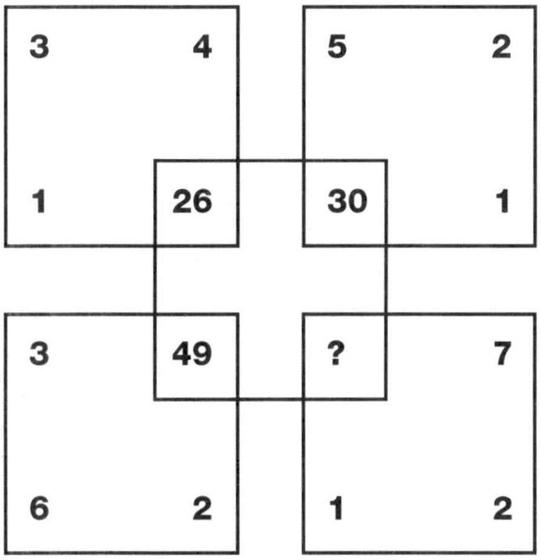

46 PUZZLE

Which playing card is missing from this puzzle?

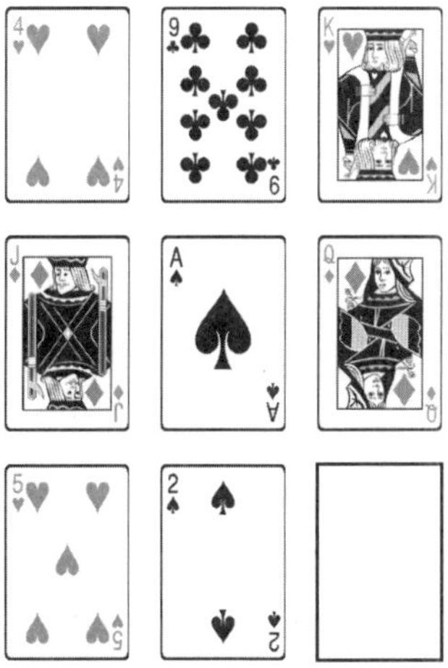

47 PUZZLE

Which letter replaces the question mark and completes the sequence?

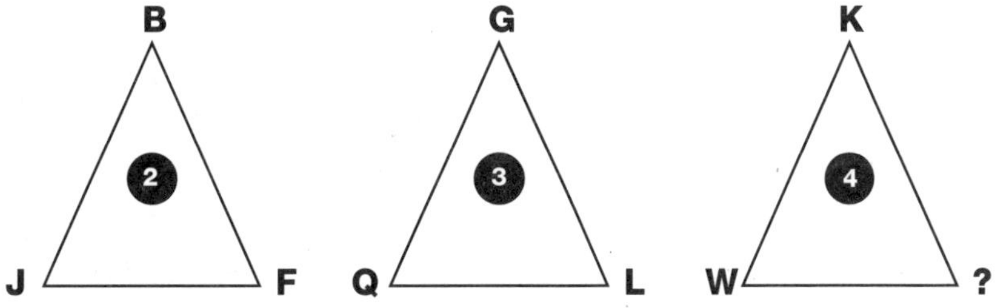

LEVEL 4

PUZZLE 48

If it takes 2 garage mechanics 3 hours to repair 6 cars, how many mechanics would it take to repair 22 cars in 5 hours?

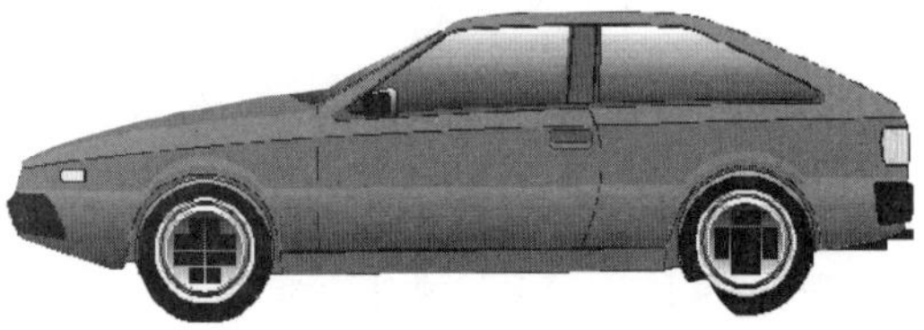

PUZZLE 49

What is the fewest number of matches that need to be moved in order to make the fish swim in the opposite direction?

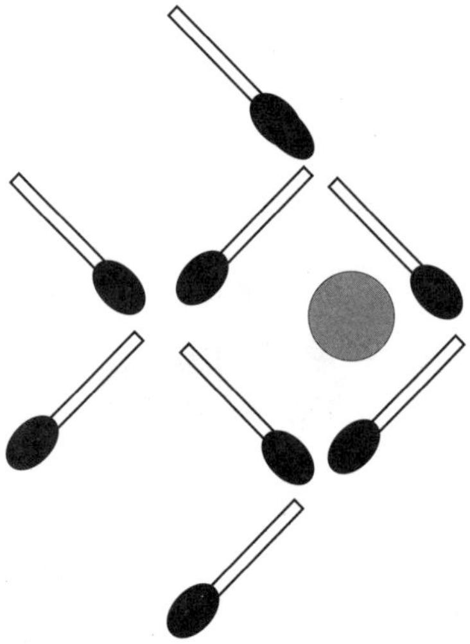

PUZZLE 50

Which number should appear at the bottom of this pile?

PUZZLE 51

Which number goes in the empty segment?

52 PUZZLE

Which number is missing?

3	4	7	2	9	3
2	2	1	9	1	6
5	6	9	2	0	9

1	7	8	6	3	2
4	3	2	8	1	1
6	1	1	4	4	

53 PUZZLE

Move just 4 matches to make 3 equilateral triangles.

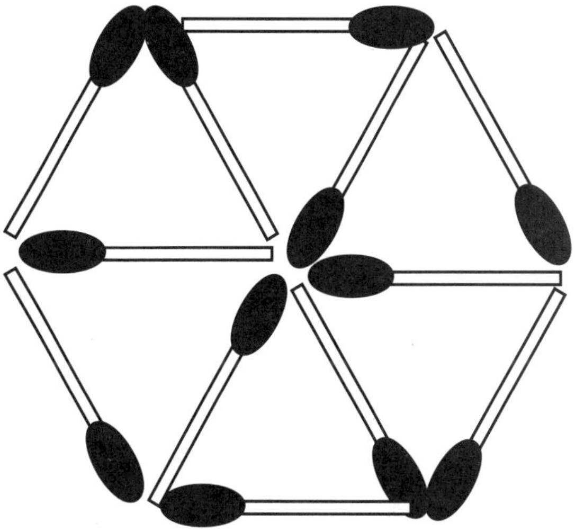

54 PUZZLE

Which letter is missing from the web?

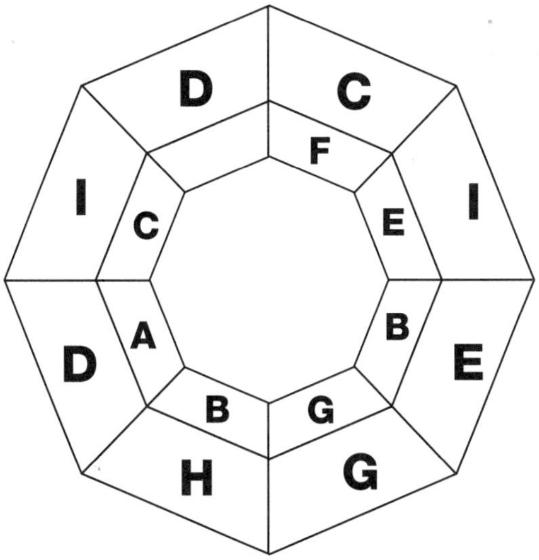

55 PUZZLE

Which letter is the odd one out in each shape?

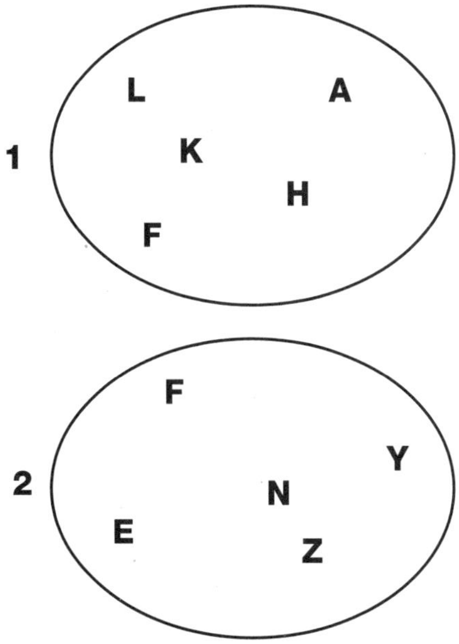

1 PUZZLE

Which is the missing piece?

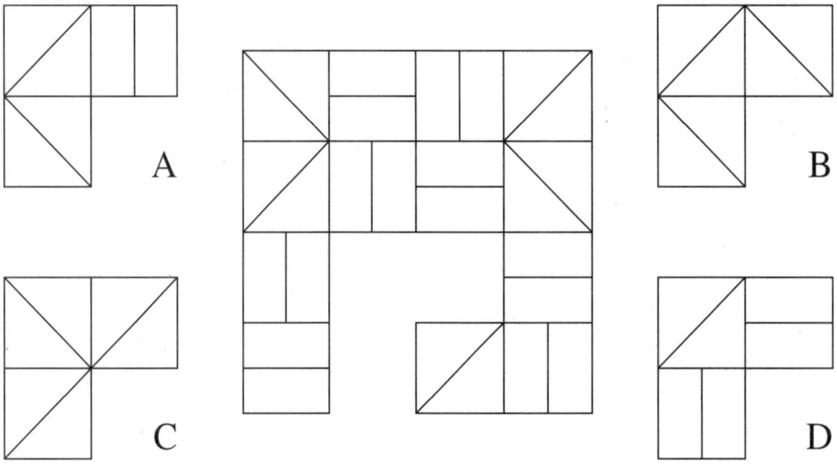

2 PUZZLE

E H L is to **VSO**

as

J K S is to **?**

3 PUZZLE

Which option on the right hand side completes the set below?

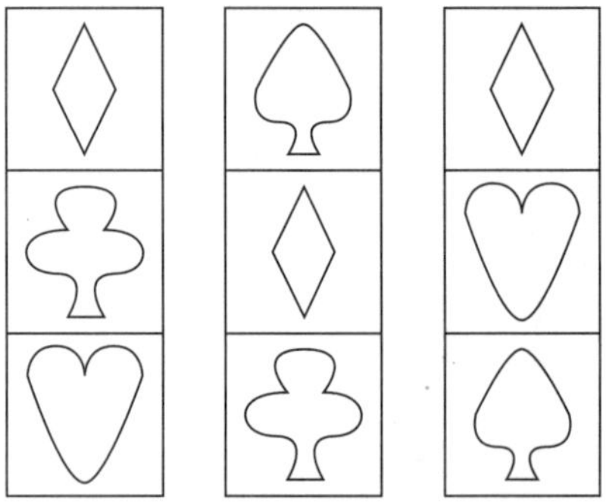

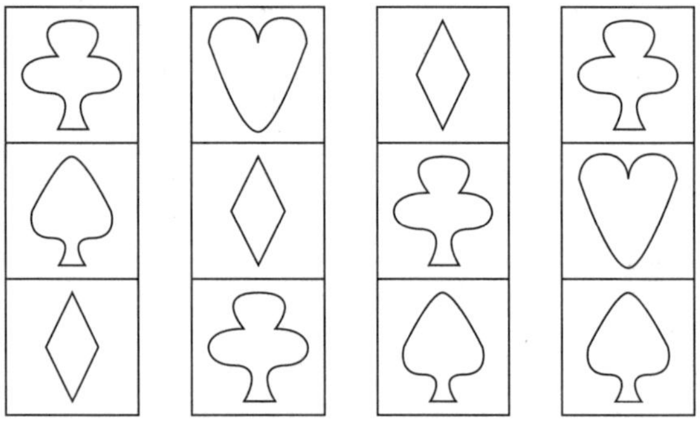

A B C D

4 PUZZLE

What comes next?

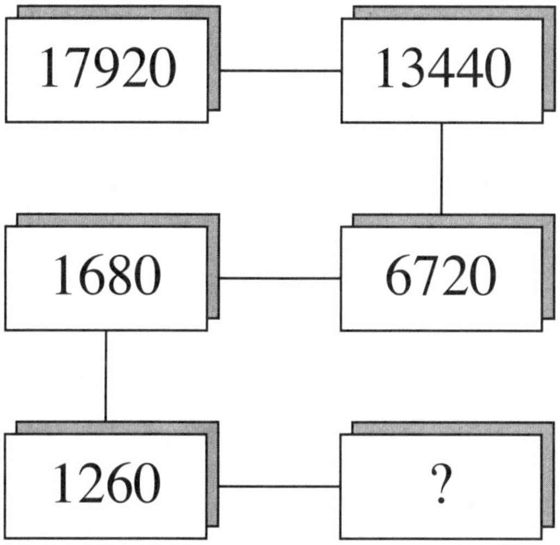

5 PUZZLE

What number should replace the question mark?

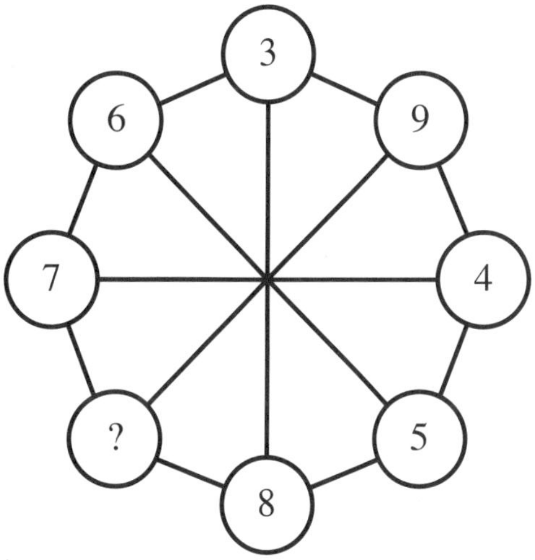

6 PUZZLE

What letter should replace the question mark?

T	
V	R
X	P
Z	N
B	?
D	J
F	H

7 PUZZLE

Which is the odd one out?

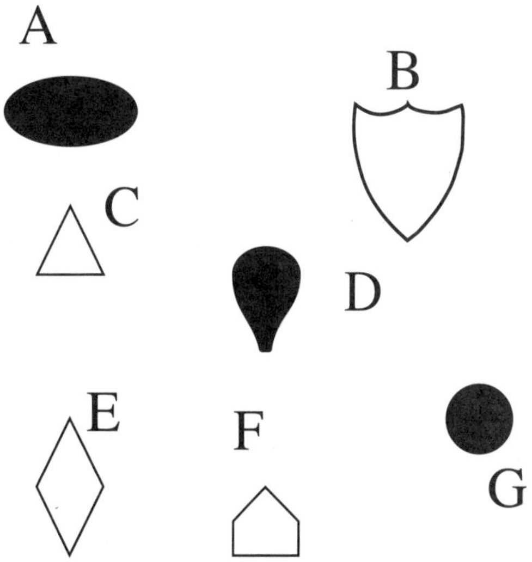

LEVEL 5

8 PUZZLE

What number should replace the question mark?

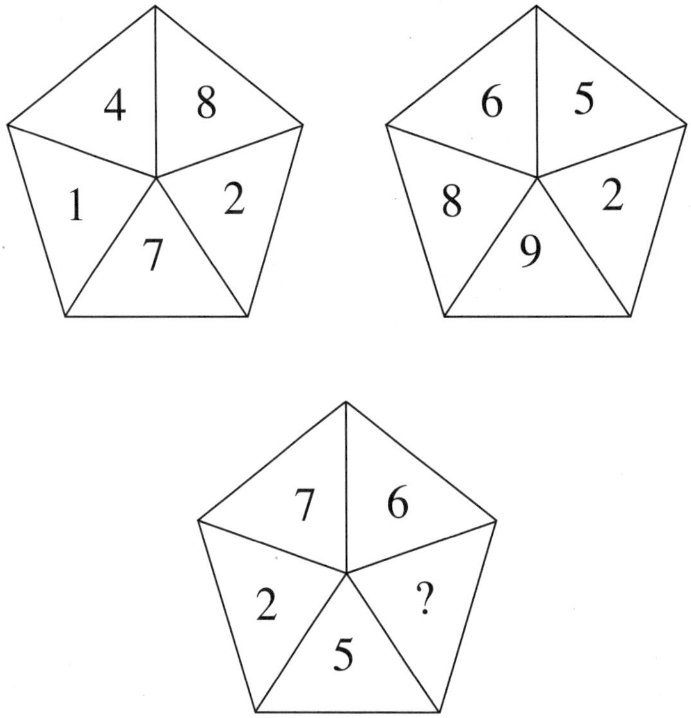

9 PUZZLE

Tanya can swim faster than Jack but slower than Sally. Harry usually swims faster than Jack, sometimes swims faster than Tanya, but never swims faster than Sally. Who is the slowest swimmer?

10 PUZZLE

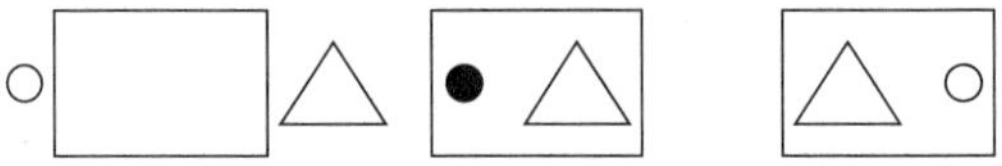

What comes next?

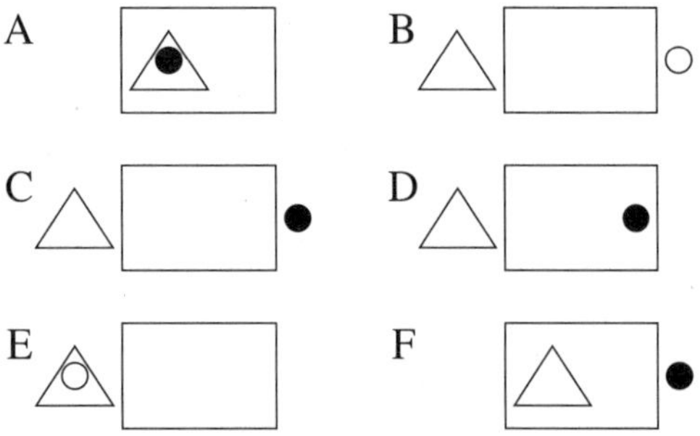

11 PUZZLE

Each line and symbol which appears in the four outer circles, below, is transferred to the centre circle according to these rules: If a line or symbol occurs in the outer circles: once: it is transferred twice: it is possibly transferred 3 times: it is transferred 4 times: it is not transferred. Which of the circles A, B, C, D or E, should appear at the centre of the diagram, below?

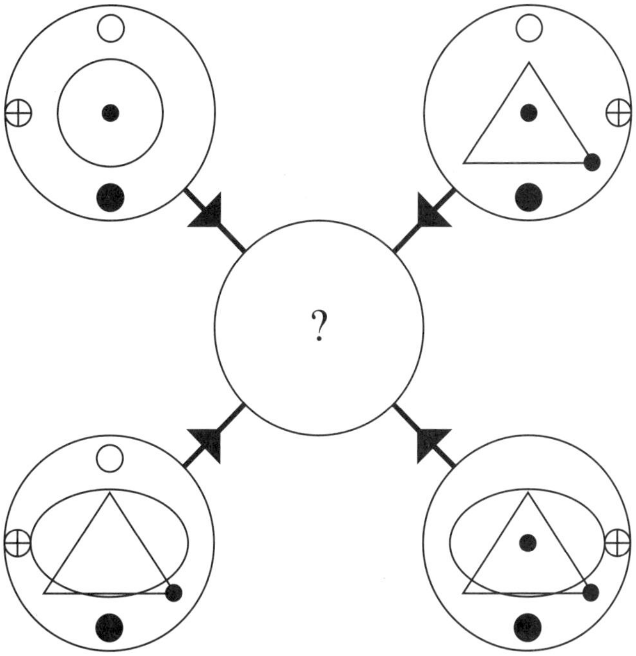

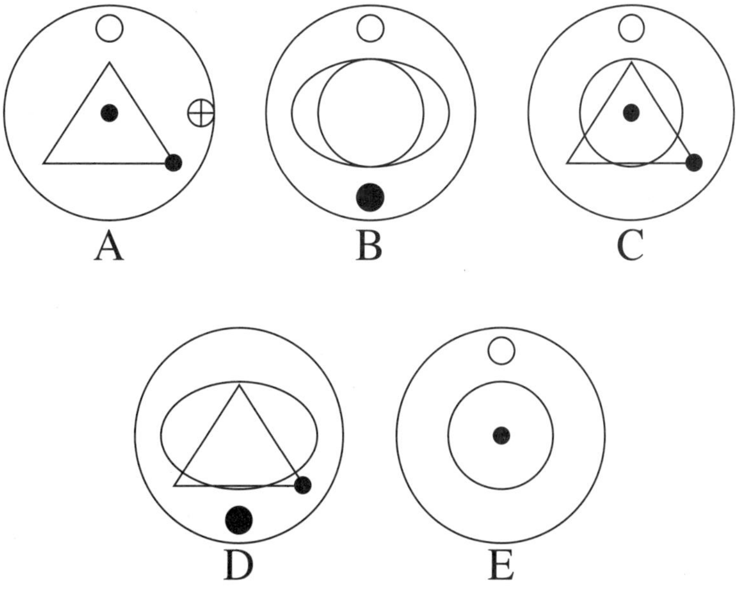

12 PUZZLE

What number should replace the question mark?

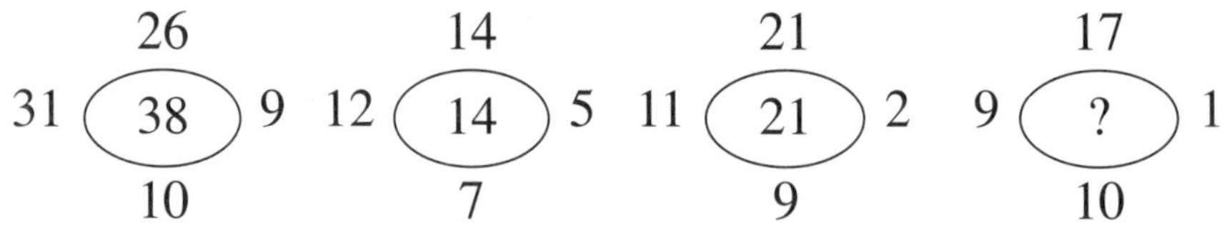

13 PUZZLE

What number should replace the question mark?

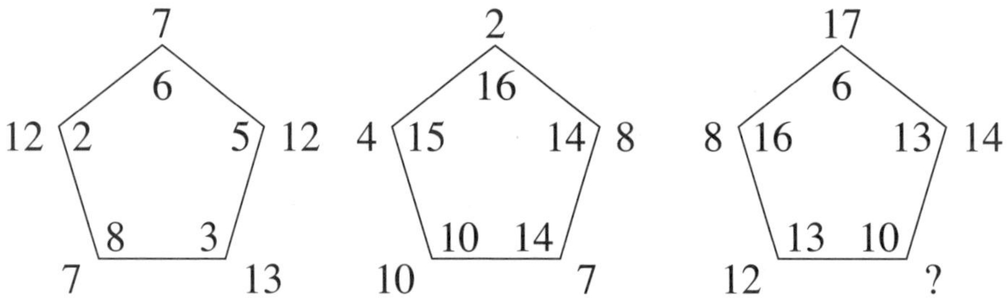

14 PUZZLE

Which hexagon A, B, C or D replaces the question mark?

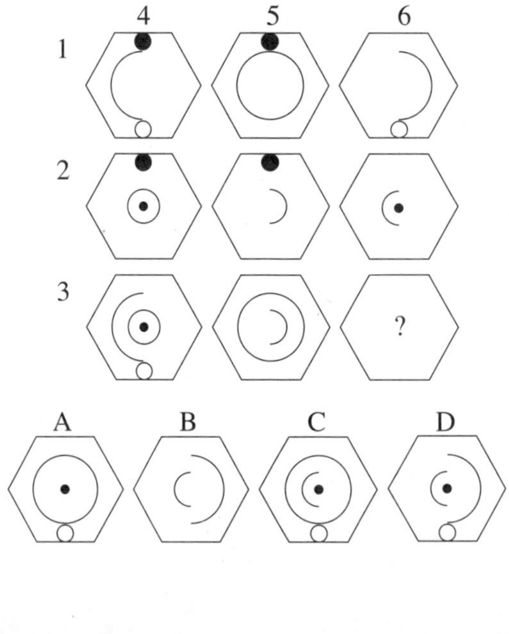

15 PUZZLE

Which circle should replace the question mark?

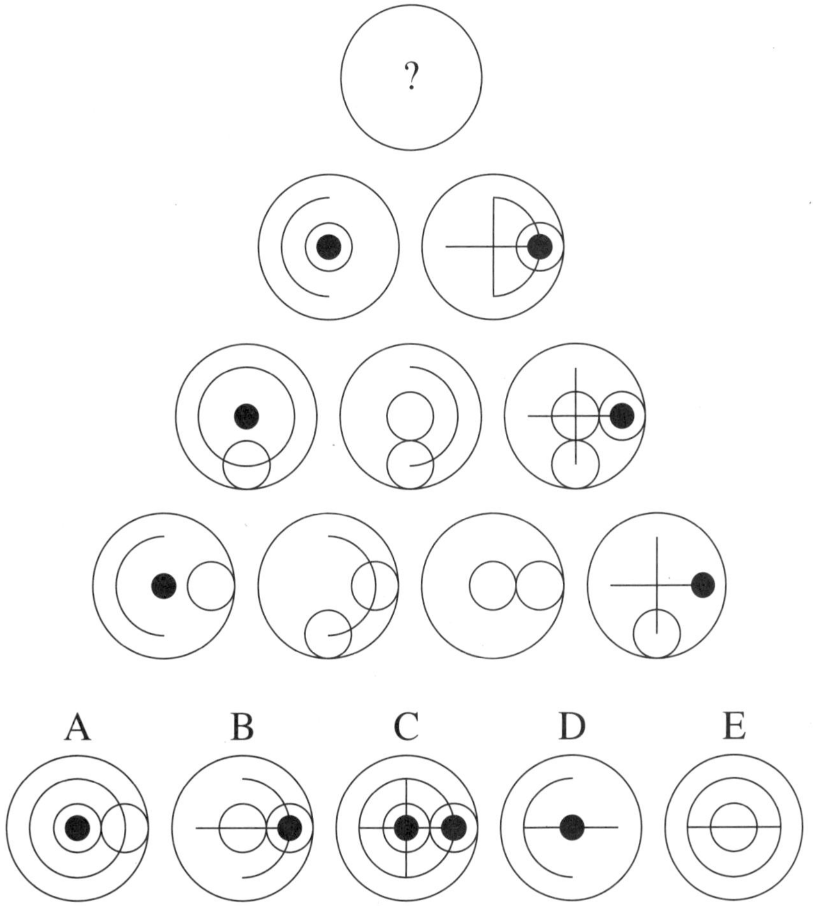

16 PUZZLE

Which word means the opposite of FASHIONABLE?

PIOUS, RETROUSSE, DENIGRATED, REPULSION, SANGUINE, DEMODED, FURBISHED

17 PUZZLE

Which is the odd one out?

PAVANE, ELANCE, FARANDOLE, GALLIARD, CHARLESTON

18 PUZZLE

Which of these is the odd one out?

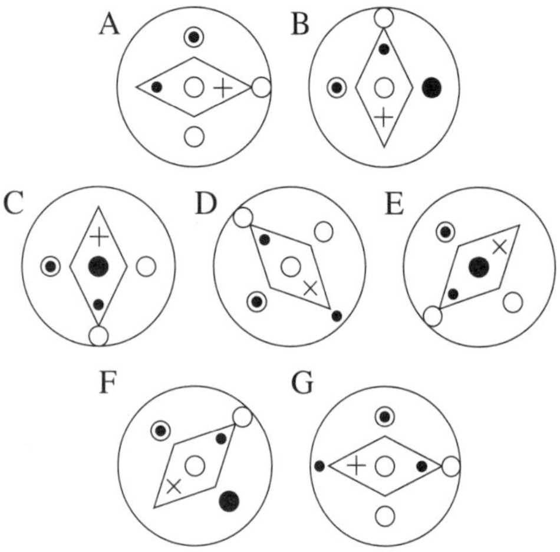

19 PUZZLE

How many revolutions must the largest cog make in order to bring the cogs back to their original positions?

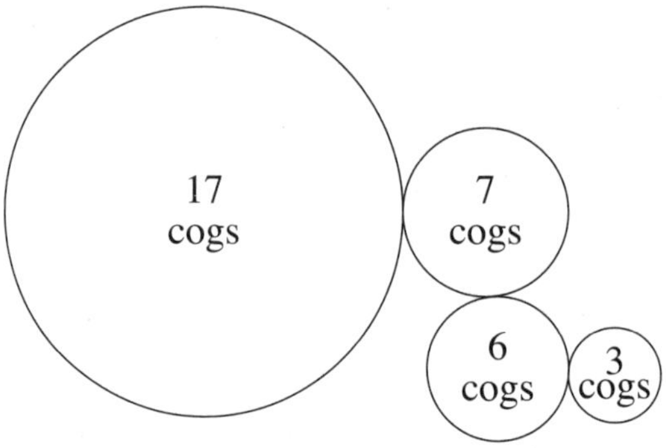

20 PUZZLE

if  is to: 

then 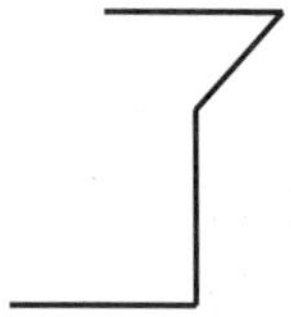 is to:

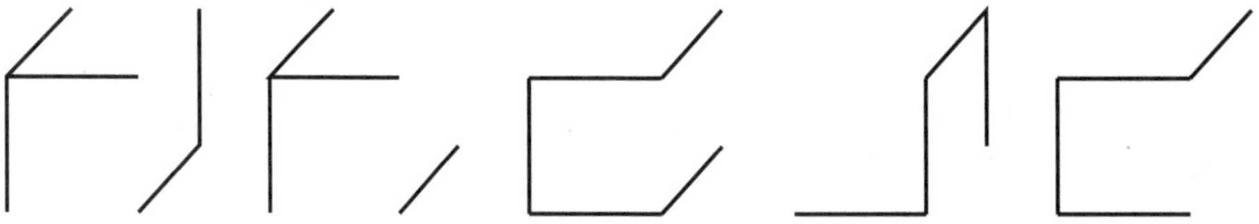

A B C D E

21 PUZZLE

What number should replace the question mark?

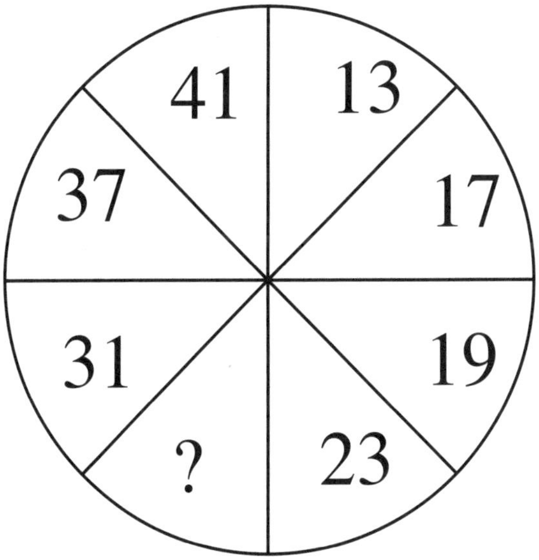

22 PUZZLE

What number should replace the question mark?

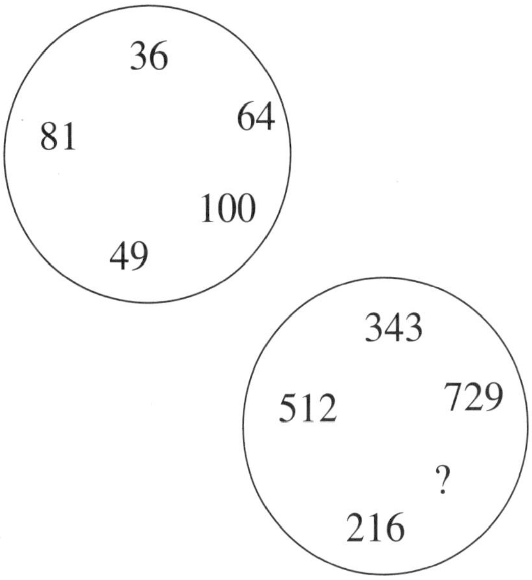

23 PUZZLE

What is a CHALDRON?

(a) A DISH
(b) A JEWEL
(c) A COAL MEASURE
(d) A MINERAL
(e) A CARD GAME

24 PUZZLE

Which of the following is always part of CANNELONI?

(a) PASTA
(b) TRIPE
(c) HONEY
(d) BREAD
(e) ICE CREAM

LEVEL 5

25 PUZZLE

What circle should replace the question mark?

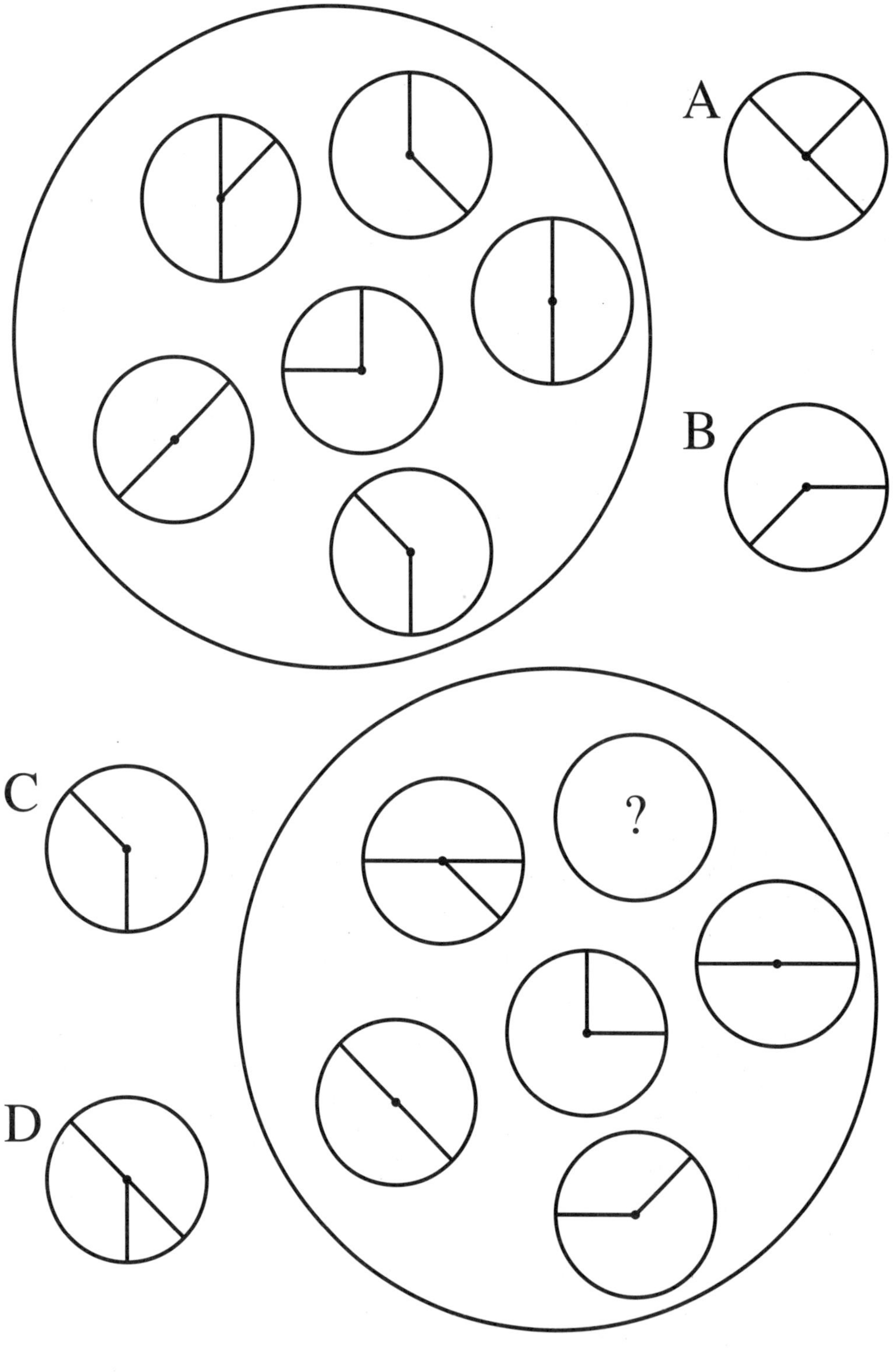

26 PUZZLE

Gill's puppy was growing fast. In the first five days since she got it, the puppy had eaten 100 dog biscuits. If each day it had eaten 6 more than the previous day, how many biscuits had it eaten on the first day?

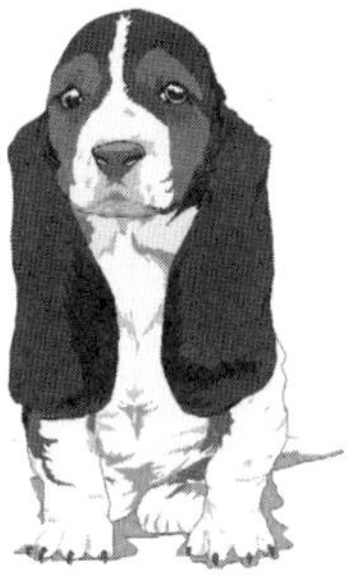

27 PUZZLE

Which two numbers continue this sequence?

1 - 10 - 3 - 9 - 5 - 8 - 7 - 7 - 9 - 6 - ? - ?

28 PUZZLE

Which number follows on from these three?

2	5	26	

29 PUZZLE

Which letter goes in the middle of the third triangle?

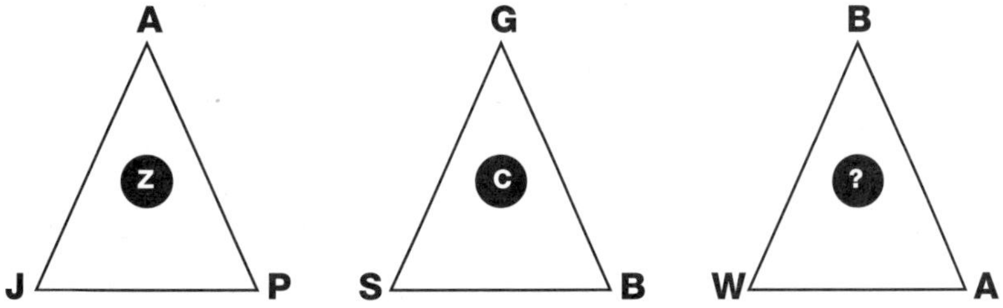

LEVEL 5

30 PUZZLE

Which number continues this sequence?

6	10	18	34	

31 PUZZLE

Which number is missing from the last puzzle?

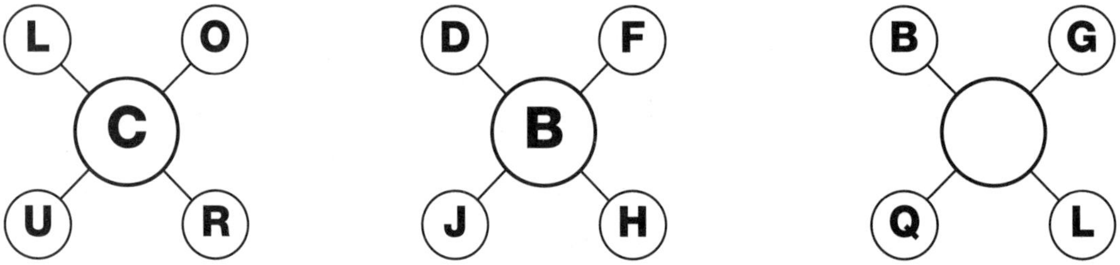

32 PUZZLE

Which number replaces the blank and completes the sequence?

1	1
2	1
3	2
5	3
8	5
	8

33 PUZZLE

Which letter is missing from the empty segment?

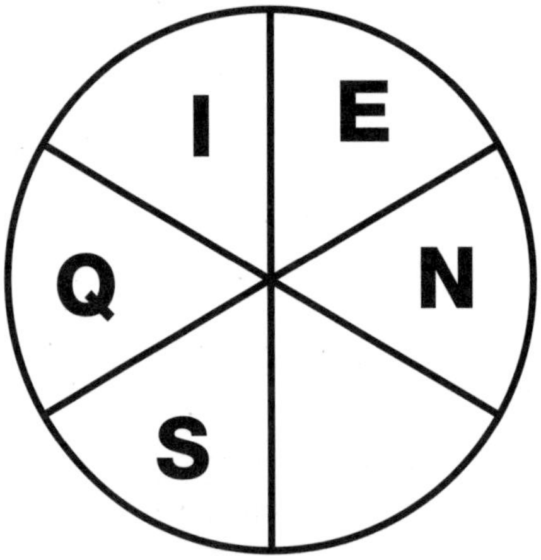

34 PUZZLE

Which number goes in the blank link and completes the chain?

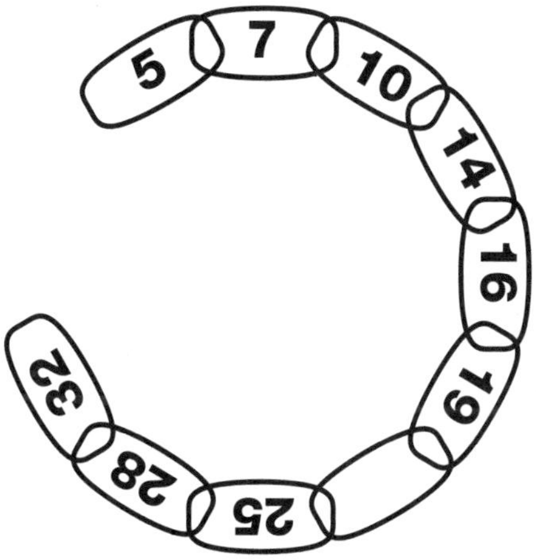

35 PUZZLE

Which number replaces the question mark?

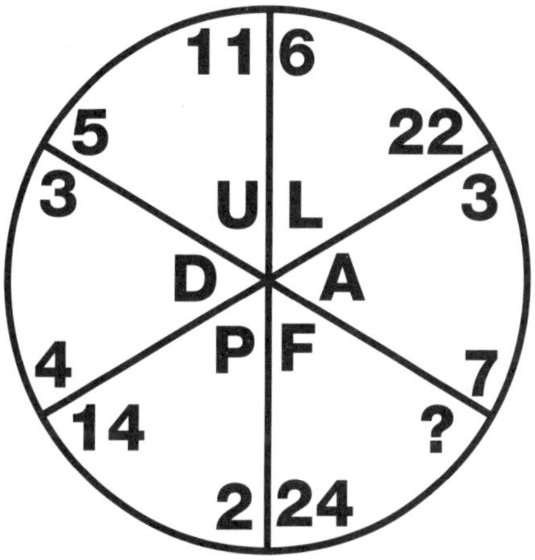

36 PUZZLE

Which letter is missing?

B	D	G
D	O	K
T	A	P
K	C	

37 PUZZLE

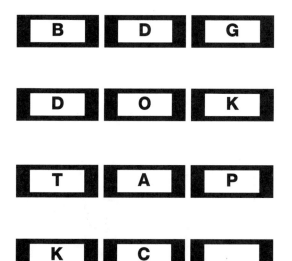

Alex is crossing the desert with his dog, Lucky. He starts off with a full water bottle and drinks one third of the contents during the first day. He then lets Lucky drink half of what is left. The next day, Alex drinks a quarter of what has been saved from the previous day. What fraction of the original amount did he save for Lucky?

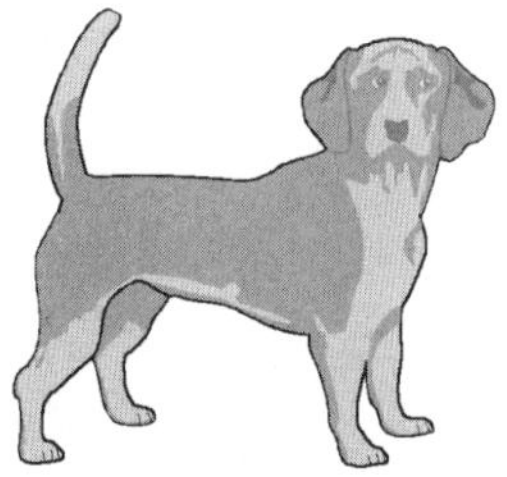

LEVEL

5

PUZZLE 38

Which number continues this sequence?

1	8	16	25	

PUZZLE 39

Which number fills the empty circle?

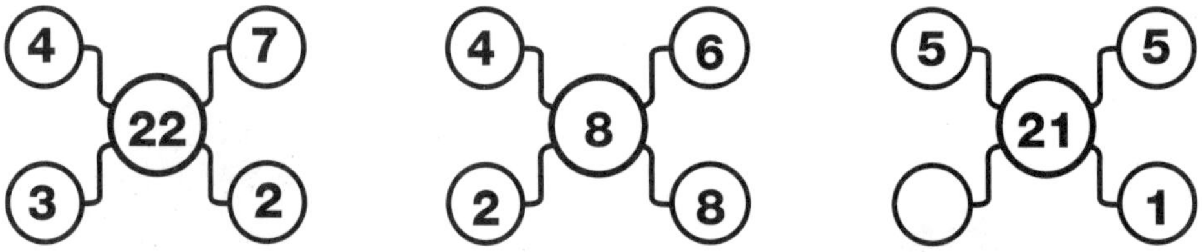

PUZZLE 40

Here is a set of cogs connected via drive belts.
If the top left cog is turned clockwise will all the cogs turn freely?

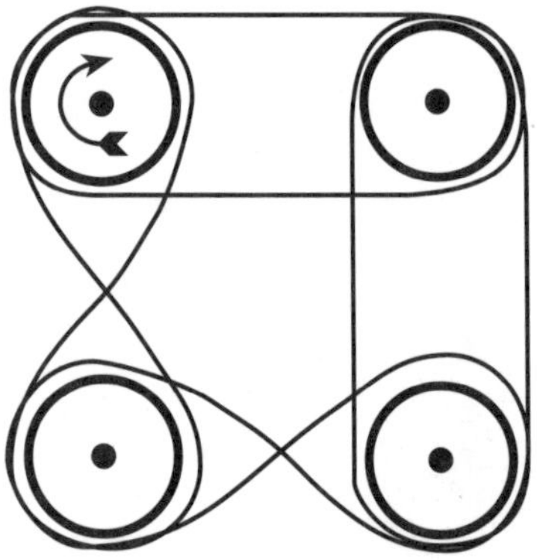

PUZZLE 41

Which number goes in the empty square?

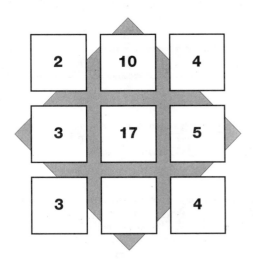

2	10	4
3	17	5
3		4

42 PUZZLE

Which number fills the empty segment?

43 PUZZLE

Which of the bottom squares fits logically with the pattern?

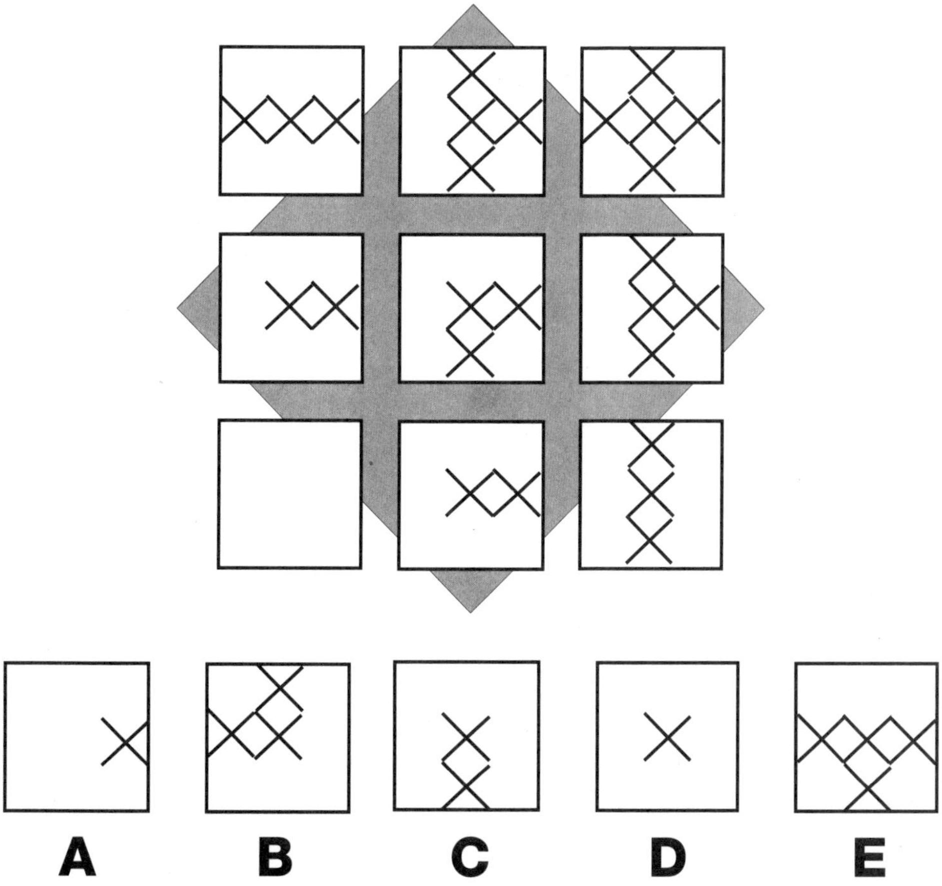

44 PUZZLE

Which watch fits on the end of this sequence?

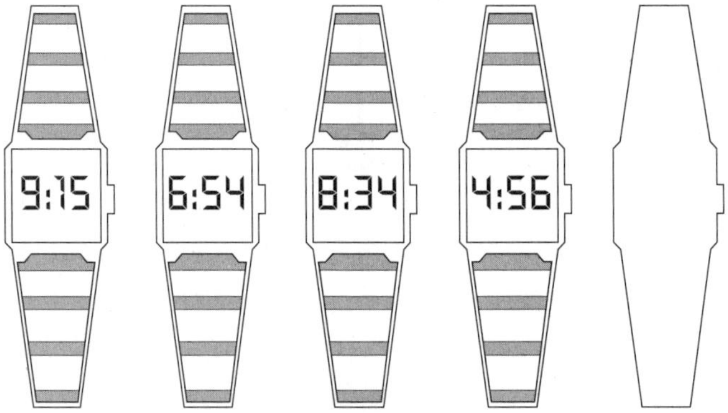

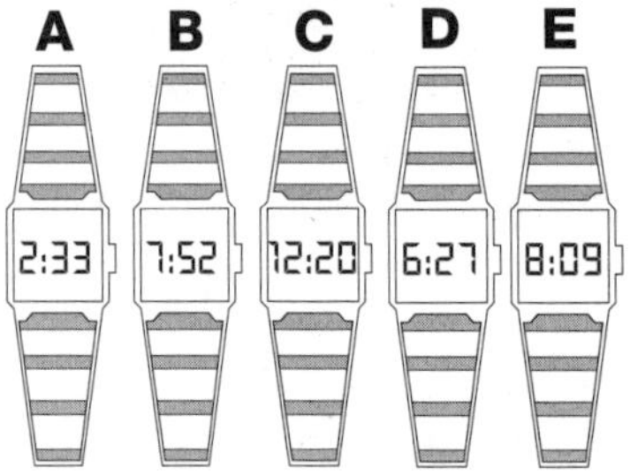

45 PUZZLE

Which number fills the gap in the last circle?

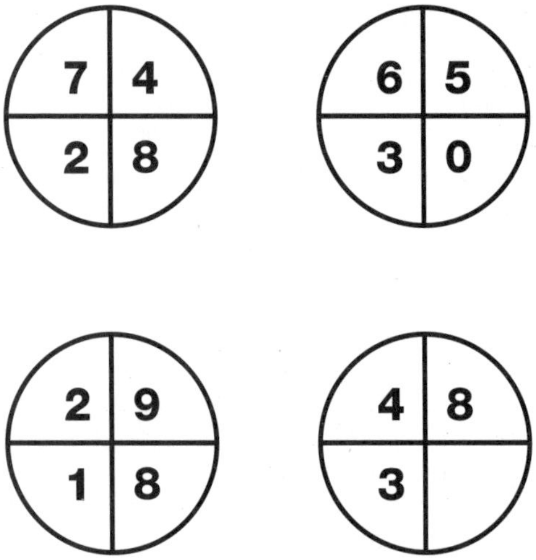

46 PUZZLE

Which number completes this puzzle?

2	8
4	9
3	7
6	9
6	8
3	

PUZZLE 47

Which of the bottom shapes fits on the end of the top line?

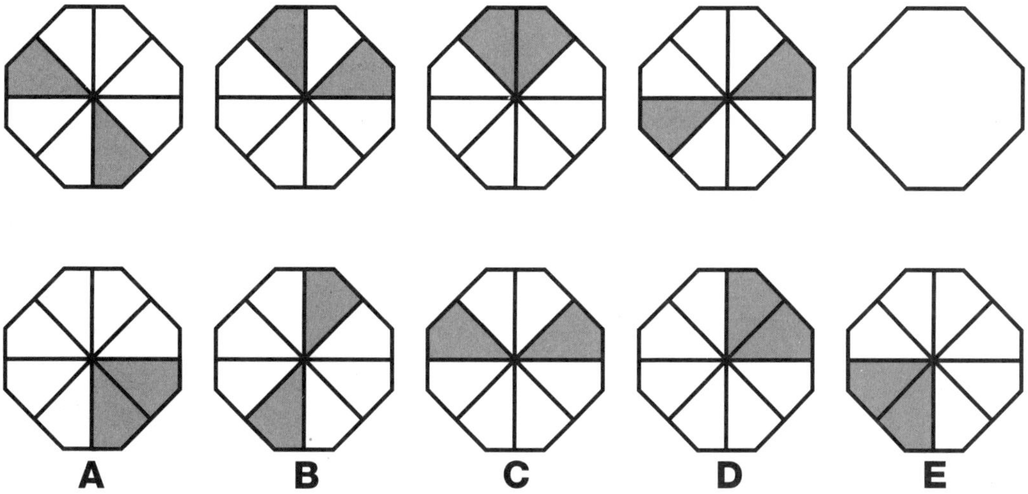

PUZZLE 48

Fill in the empty segment to complete the puzzle.

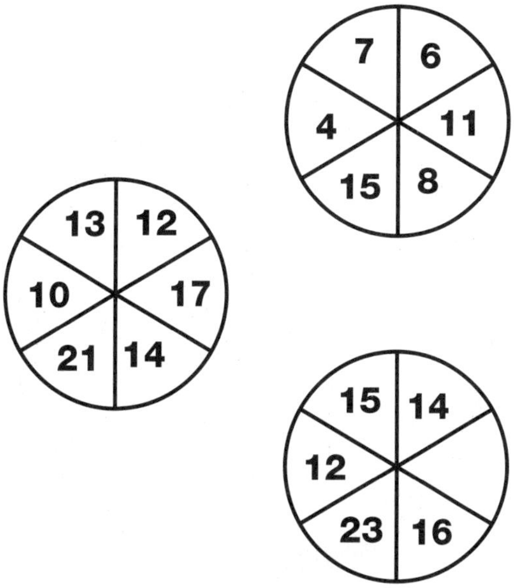

PUZZLE 49

Which number is missing?

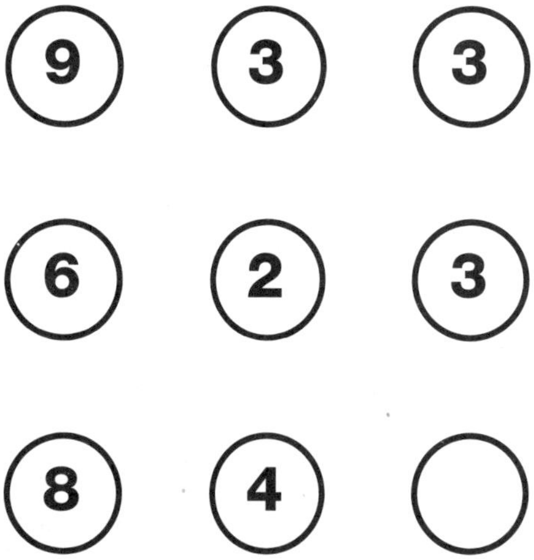

LEVEL 5

50 PUZZLE

Draw the correct symbols in the empty box.

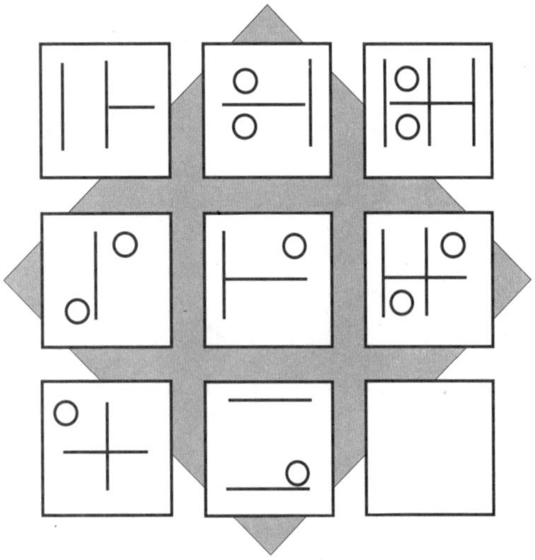

51 PUZZLE

Which number replaces the blank and completes the sequence?

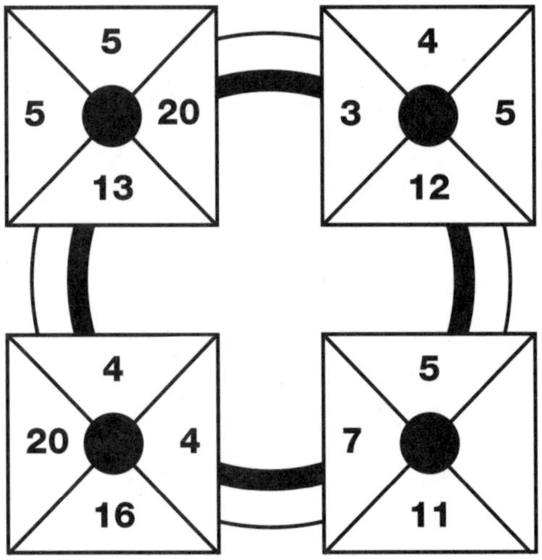

52 PUZZLE

Which number is missing from the empty box?

2	11	20
4	9	32
7	8	49
4	10	

53 PUZZLE

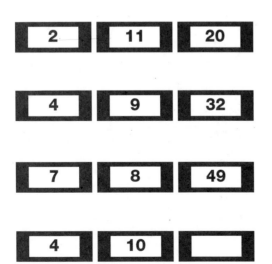

Which letter should be entered into the empty segment?

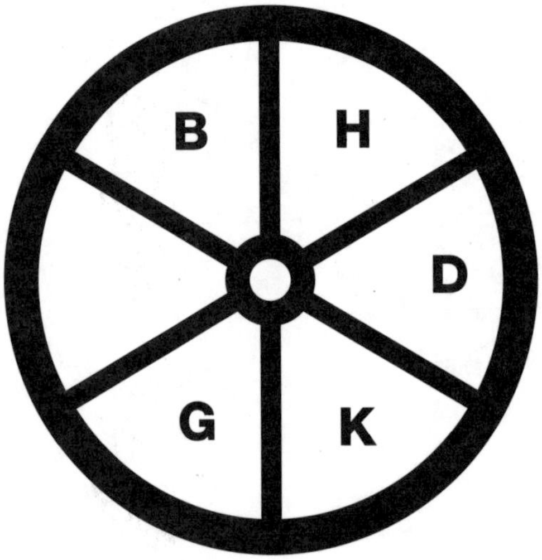

54 PUZZLE

Which letter replaces the blank and completes the sequence?

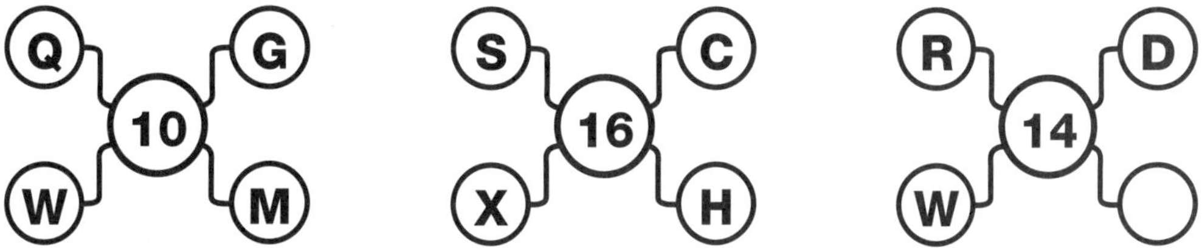

55 PUZZLE

Which number goes in the empty segment?

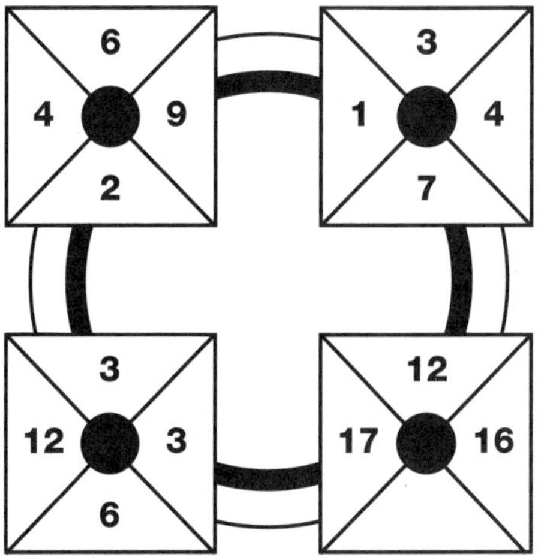

56 PUZZLE

Which number should be written in the empty circle?

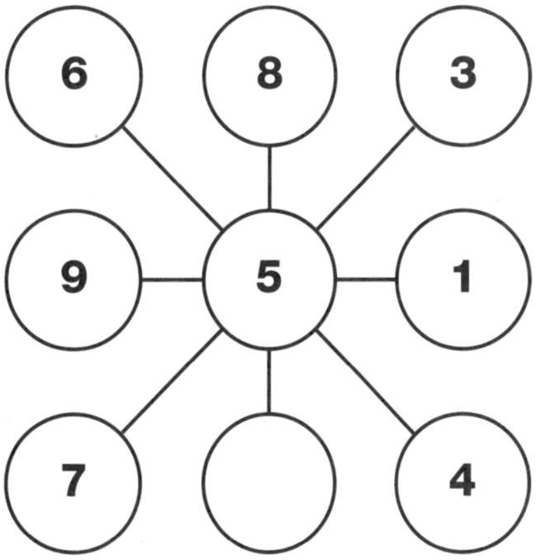

57 PUZZLE

Which number completes the middle star?

LEVEL

5

1 PUZZLE

 is to: 

as:

is to:

A 

B 

C 

D 

E 

2 PUZZLE

The die is rolled one face to square 2 and so on, one face at a time to squares 3 - 4 - 5 - 6. Which number will appear on the top face in square 6?

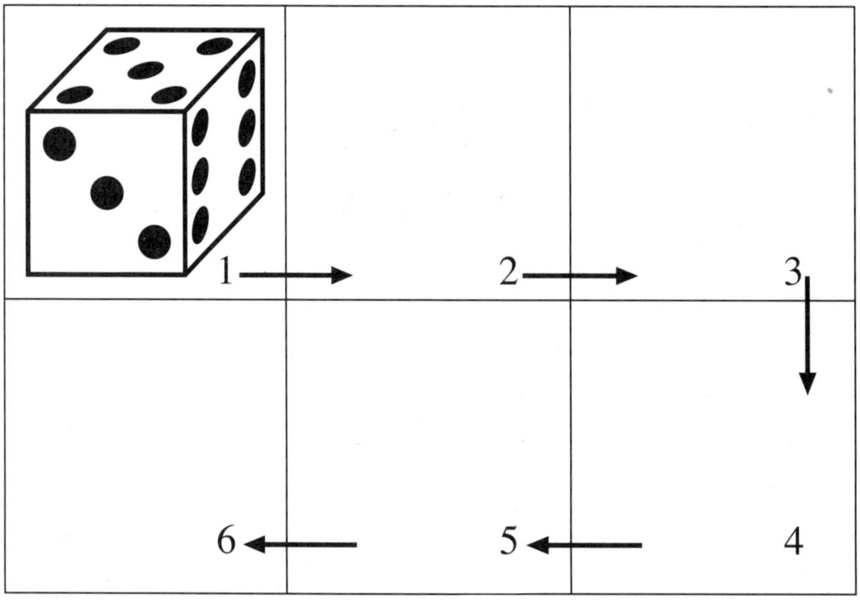

3 PUZZLE

What comes next?

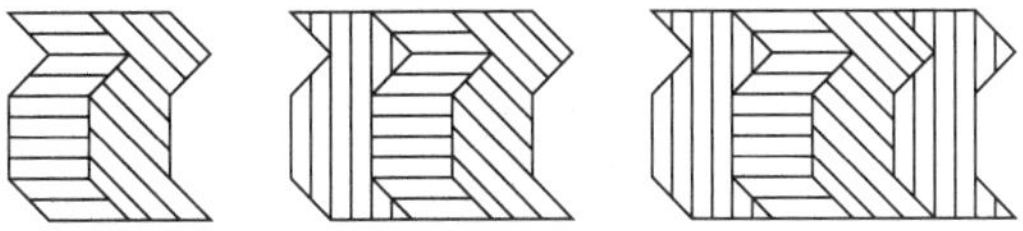

A

B

C

D

E

F

4 PUZZLE

Josie has $600 to spend. She spends three fifths of the $600 on clothes, 0.45 of the remainder at a beauty salon and writes out a cheque for $150 for a new watch.

What is her financial situation at the end of the day?

5 PUZZLE

What number should replace the question mark?

2	7
1	6

7	8
5	?

5	1
4	2

6 PUZZLE

What number should replace the question mark?

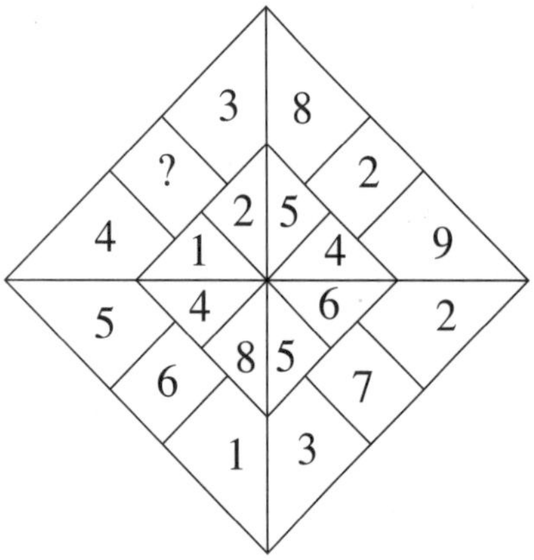

7 PUZZLE

A C F H K M ?
What letter comes next?

8 PUZZLE

What is the meaning of
PANNIER?

(a) A GOLD MINER'S PAN
(b) A WOK
(c) A CLIMBING TOOL
(d) A BASKET

9 PUZZLE

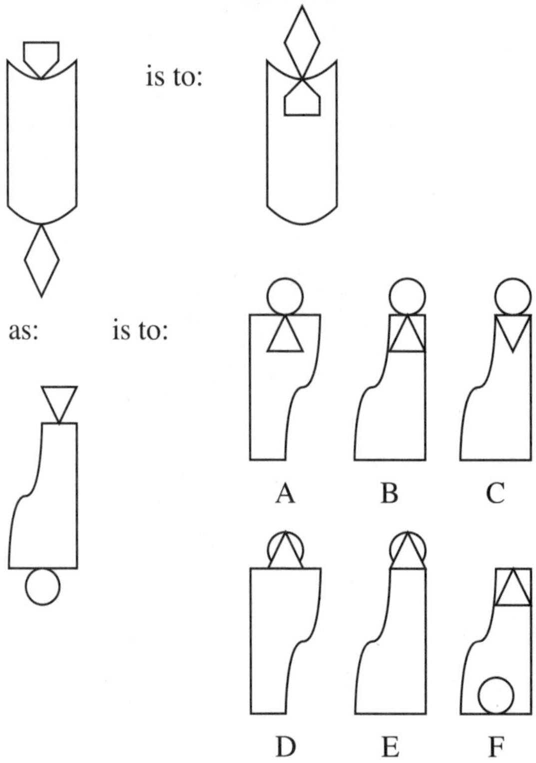

10 PUZZLE

What number should replace the question mark?

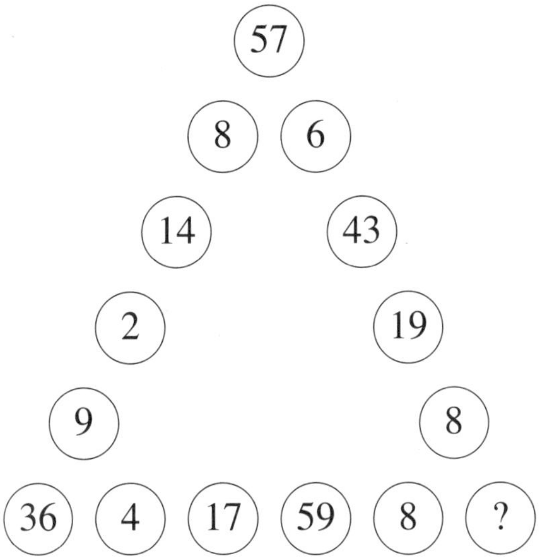

11 PUZZLE

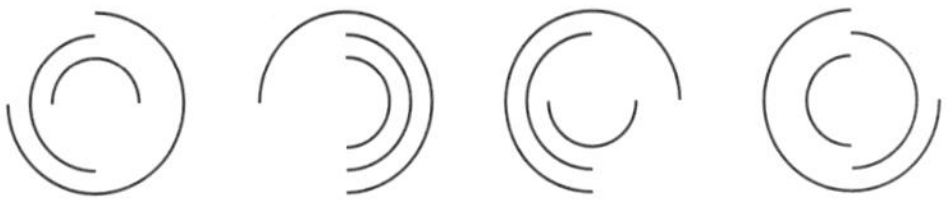

What comes next in the above sequence?

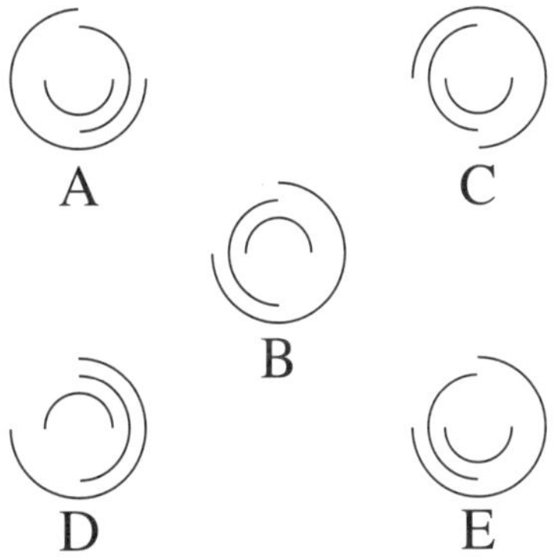

12 PUZZLE

Which is the odd one out?

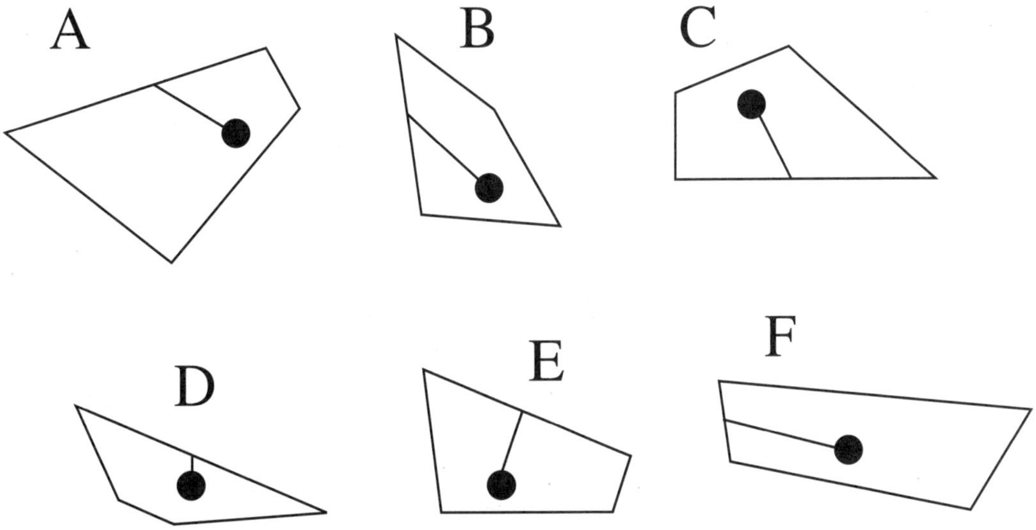

13 PUZZLE

Which is the odd one out?

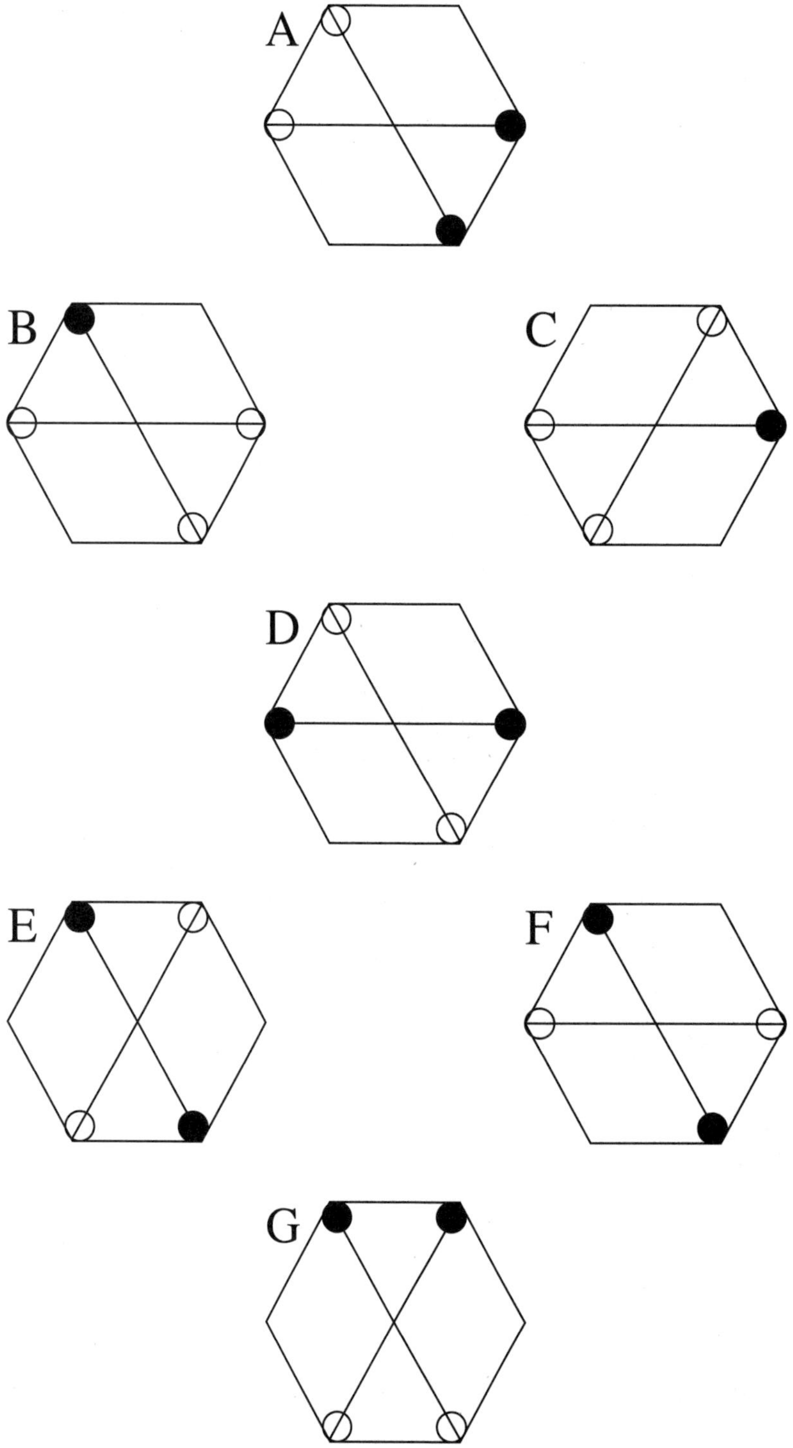

14 PUZZLE

What number should replace the question mark?

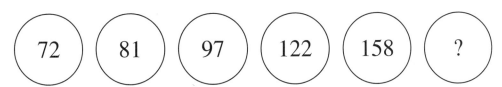

72	81	97	122	158	?

15 PUZZLE

What number should replace the question mark?

16		8	6		7	1		4	7		8
7	22	2	18	27	9	19	25	3	26	?	12
19		10	24		5	29		17	17		10

16 PUZZLE

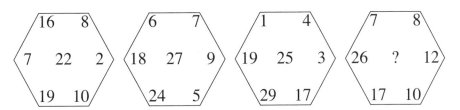

Which hexagon should replace the question mark – A, B, C, D or E?

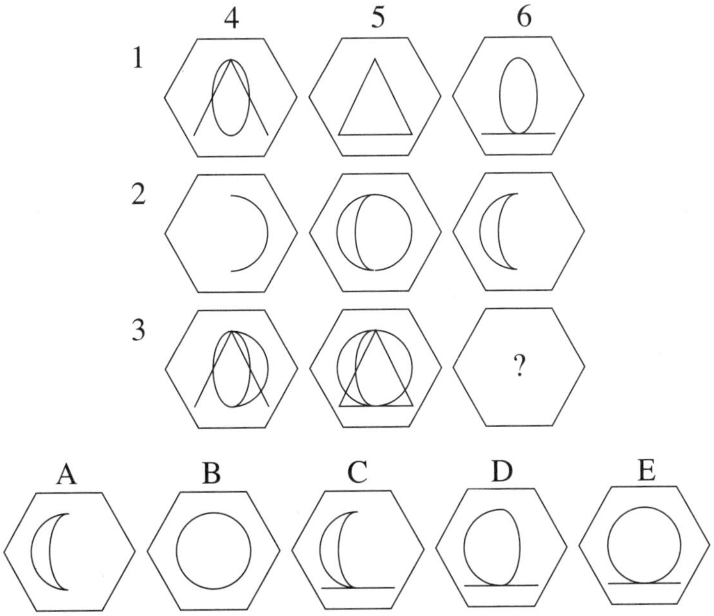

17 PUZZLE

Which is the odd one out?

(a) TIERCEL
(b) REEBOK
(c) LEVERET
(d) MEERKAT
(e) DROMEDARY

18 PUZZLE

Choose the next shape from

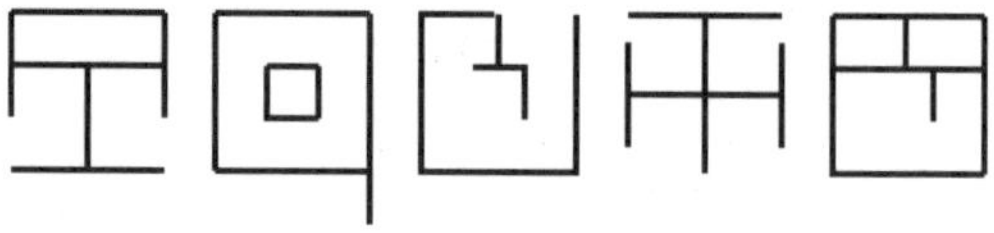

A B C D E

19 PUZZLE

Which is the odd one out?

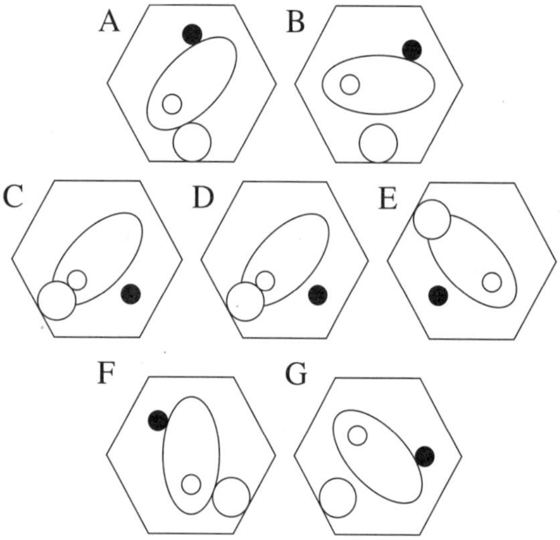

20 PUZZLE

Which is the odd one out?

(a) PAVANE
(b) MAZURKA
(c) RIGADOON
(d) CHARNECO
(e) FANDANGO

21 PUZZLE

If the temperature rises 15% from x F to 103½ °F, what was the previous temperature?

22 PUZZLE

What is a KNOUT?

(a) A KNOT
(b) A PLANT
(c) A PIG'S SNOUT
(d) A CLOAK
(e) A WHIP

23 PUZZLE

Which number should replace the question mark?

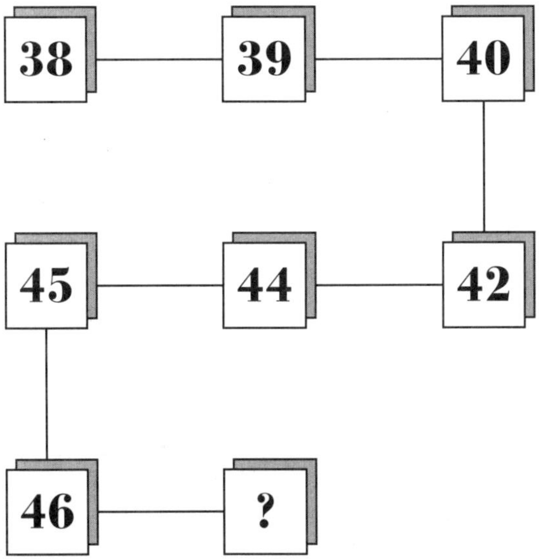

24 PUZZLE

What weight should be placed at the question mark in order to balance the scales?

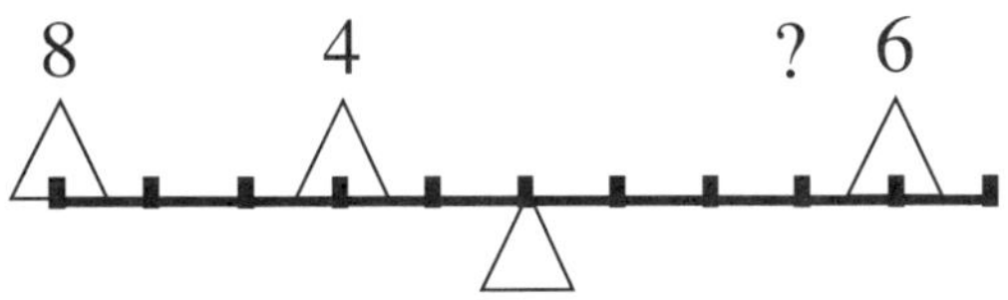

25 PUZZLE

Which circle should replace the question mark?

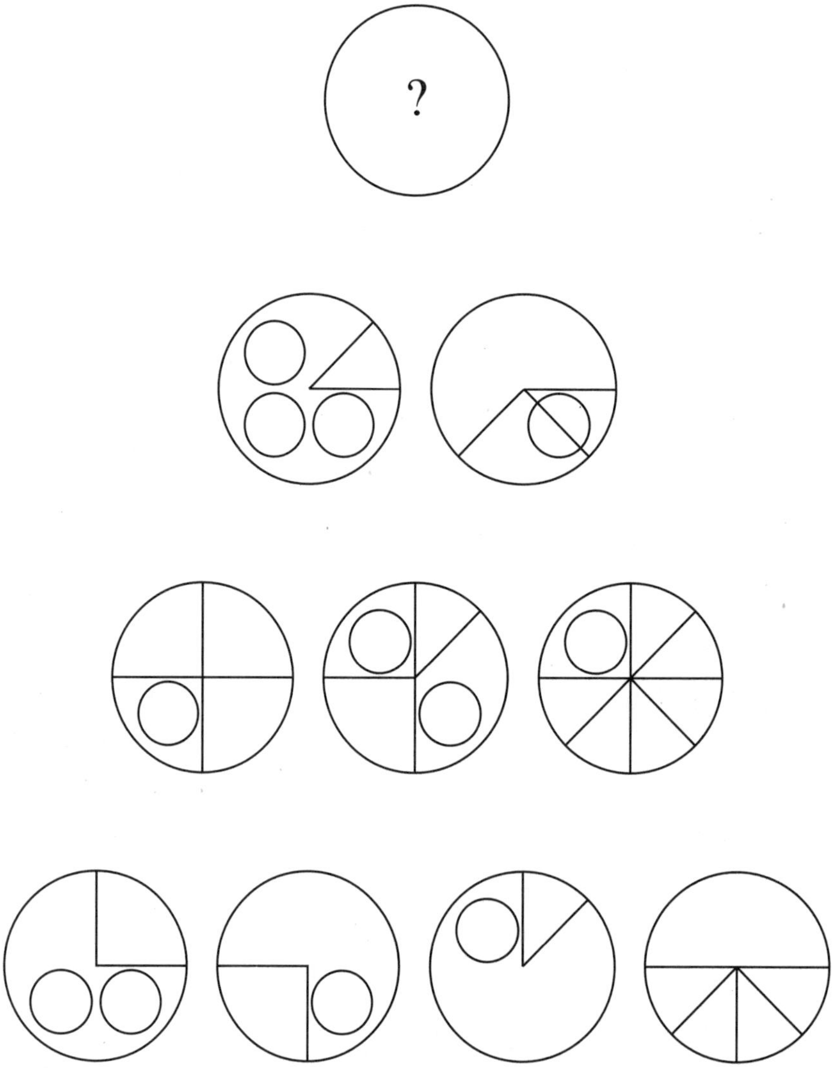

A B C D E

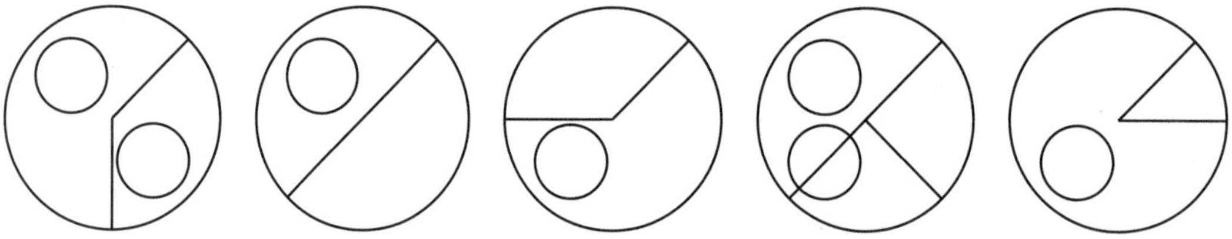

26 PUZZLE

Which number completes this puzzle?

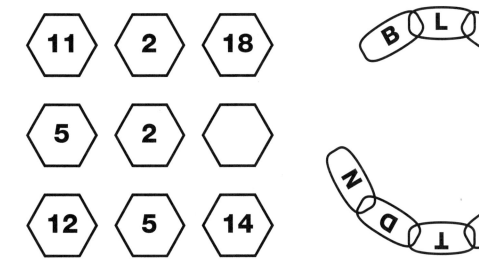

11	2	18
5	2	
12	5	14

27 PUZZLE

Fill in the missing letter to complete the chain.

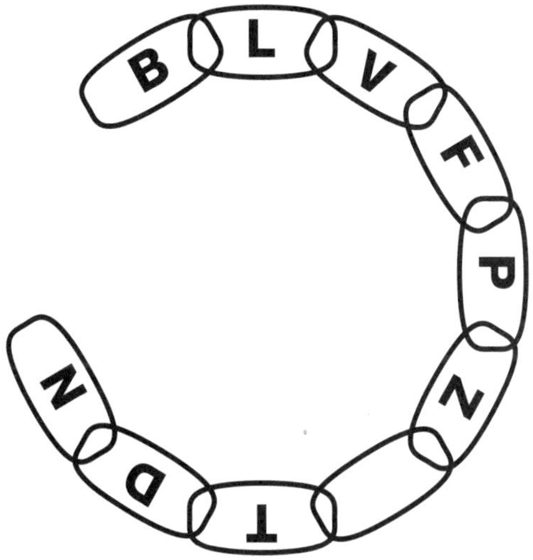

28 PUZZLE

Which number is missing?

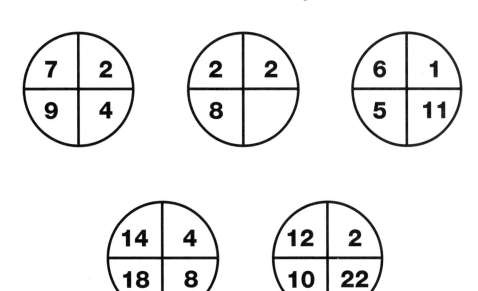

7	2
9	4

2	2
8	

6	1
5	11

14	4
18	8

12	2
10	22

LEVEL 6

LEVEL 6

29 PUZZLE

Which number is missing from the empty segment?

30 PUZZLE

These 12 matches are arranged to give 4 equal areas. Can you rearrange the matches to give 6 equal areas, without adding, removing or breaking any matches?

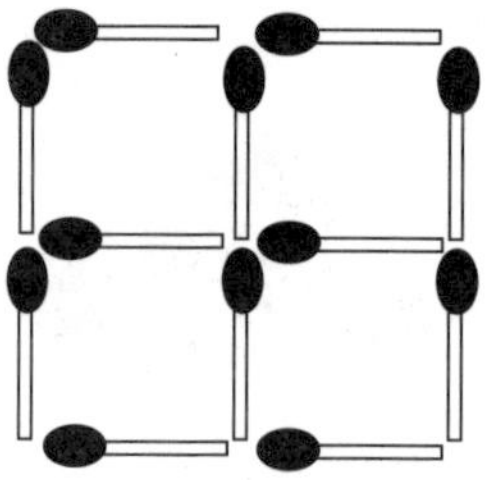

31 PUZZLE

Which letter should be added to the empty segment?

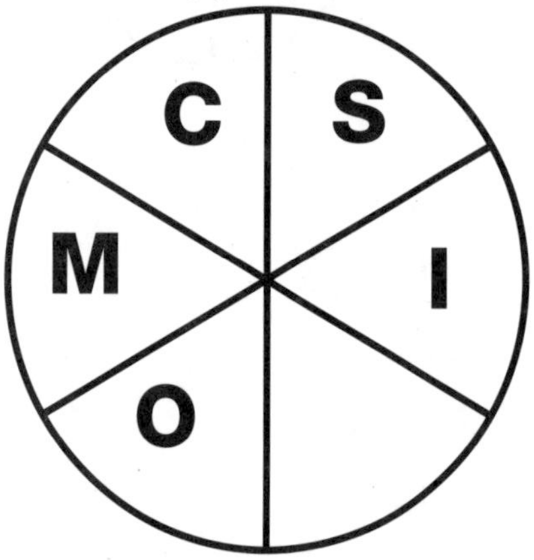

32 PUZZLE

Which number finishes this grid?

5	7	6	8
10	4	6	6
5	7	10	4
12	4	4	

PUZZLE 33

Which number is missing?

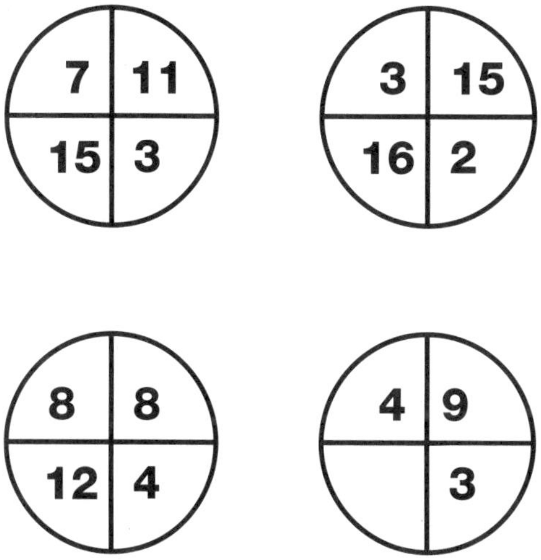

PUZZLE 34

Which number is needed to complete the wheel?

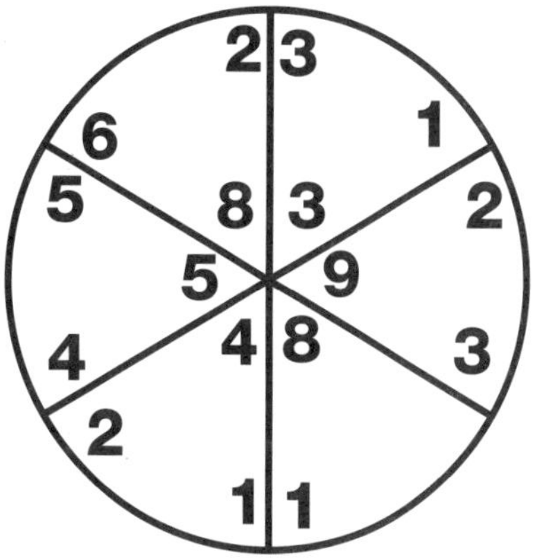

PUZZLE 35

Enter every number between 1 and 8 inclusive in this grid so that no two consecutive numbers are in adjacent squares.

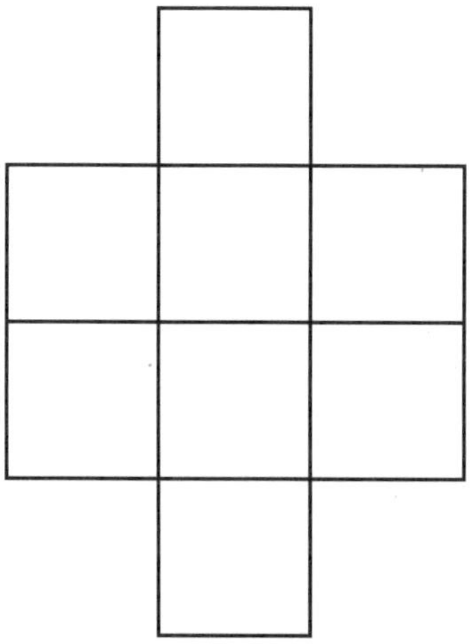

PUZZLE 36

Which letter replaces the blank and completes the sequence?

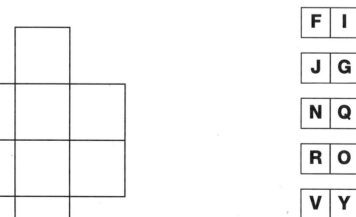

F	I
J	G
N	Q
R	O
V	Y
Z	

LEVEL 6

37 PUZZLE

Which letter should be placed in the empty square?

B	G	L	Q
J	N	R	V
K	N	Q	T
R	T	V	

38 PUZZLE

Which number is missing from this wheel?

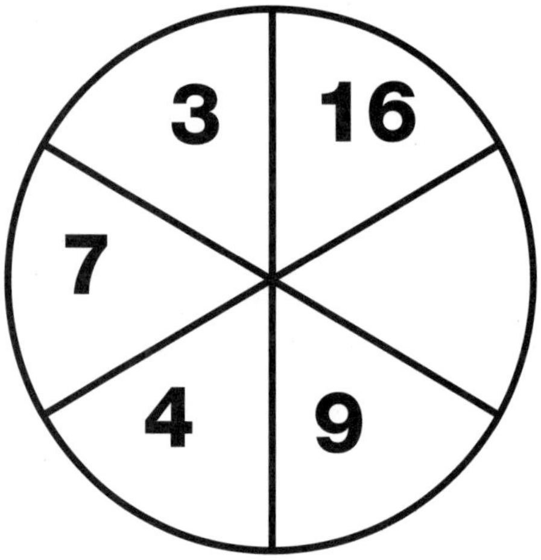

39 PUZZLE

Enter the correct numbers in the blank segments and complete this puzzle.

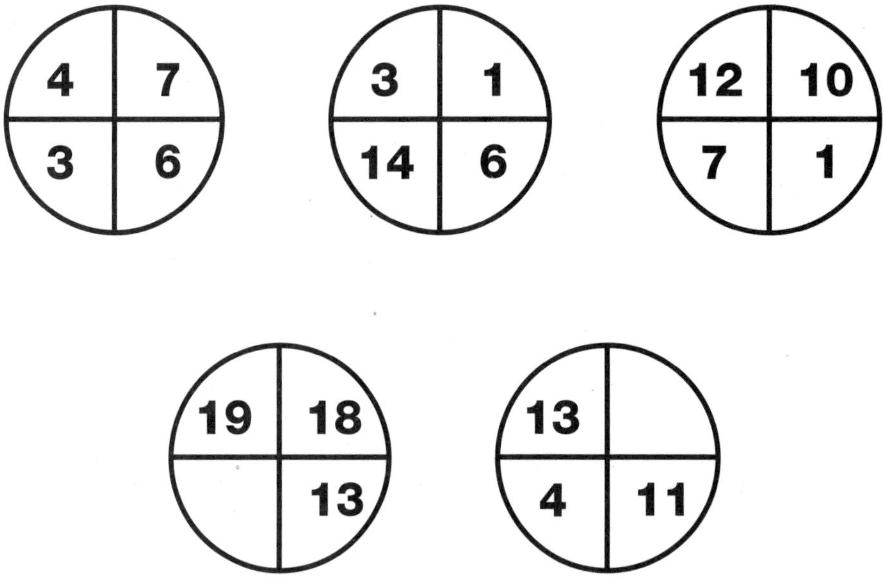

PUZZLE 40

Which number is needed to complete the third grid?

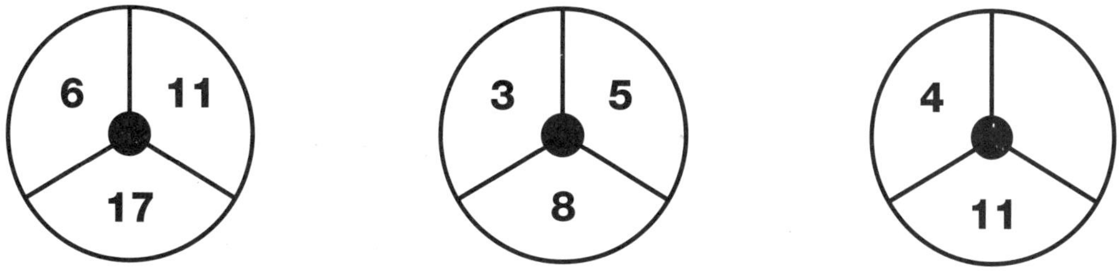

PUZZLE 41

Which number is the odd one out in each shape?

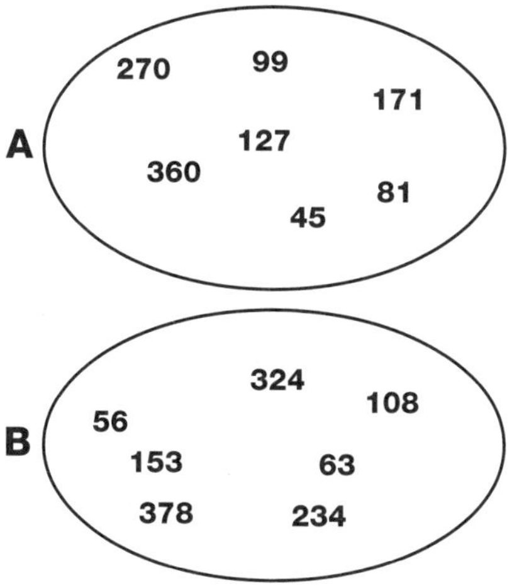

PUZZLE 42

Which number needs to added to the last oval?

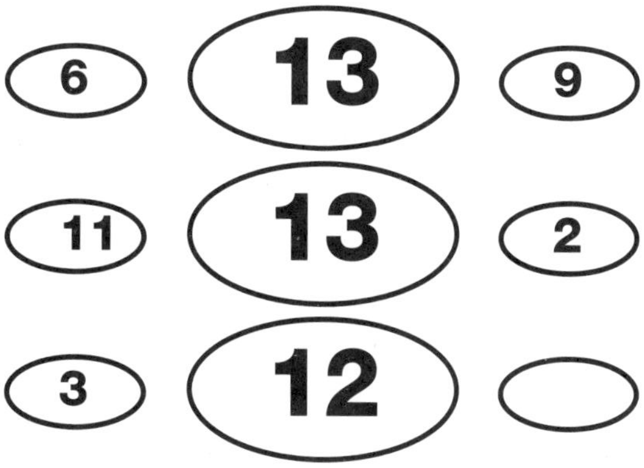

PUZZLE 43

Which number is missing from the last triangle?

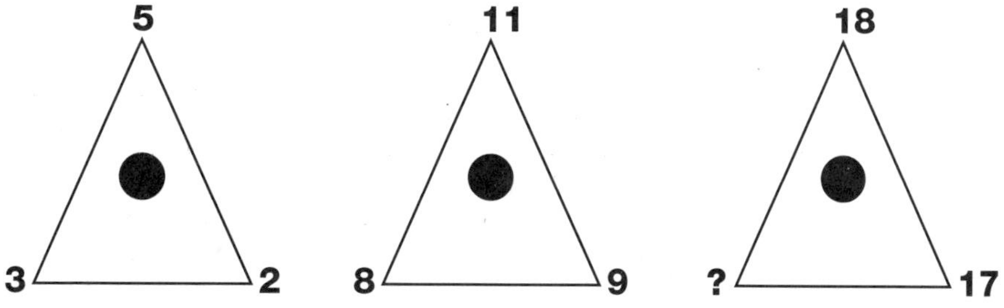

LEVEL 6

44 PUZZLE

Which letter replaces the blank and completes the sequence?

A	G	L
P	S	U

B	I	O
T	X	A

D	L	S
Y	D	

45 PUZZLE

Which number is missing?

1	3

3	4

4	7

7	11

11	18

18	

46 PUZZLE

Which character is needed to fill the blank segment?

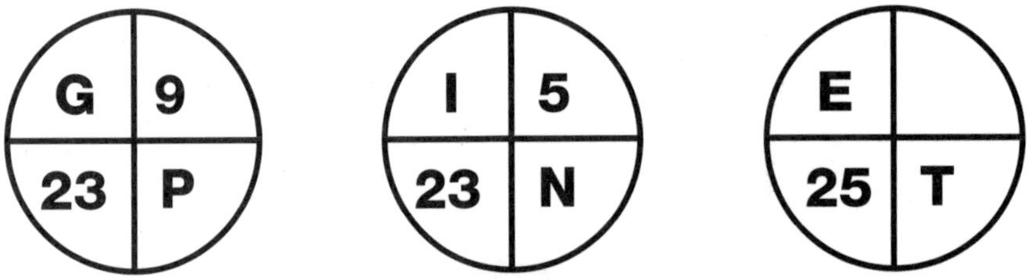

47 PUZZLE

Which number is missing from the last grid?

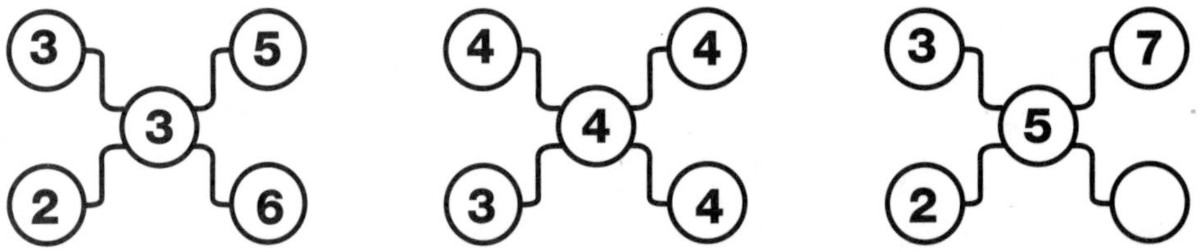

48 PUZZLE

Which number is missing from the final ellipse?

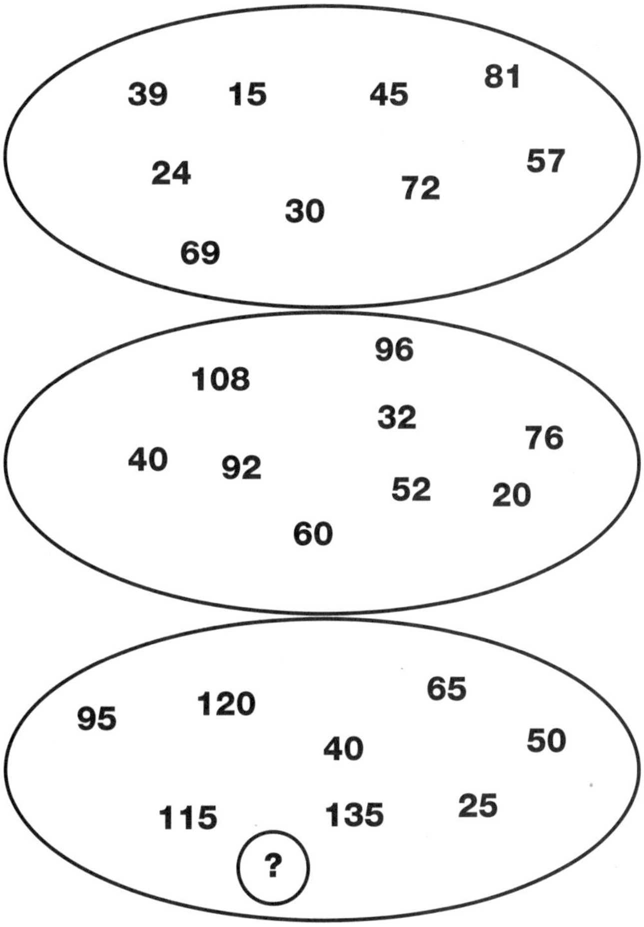

49 PUZZLE

Fill in the missing letter.

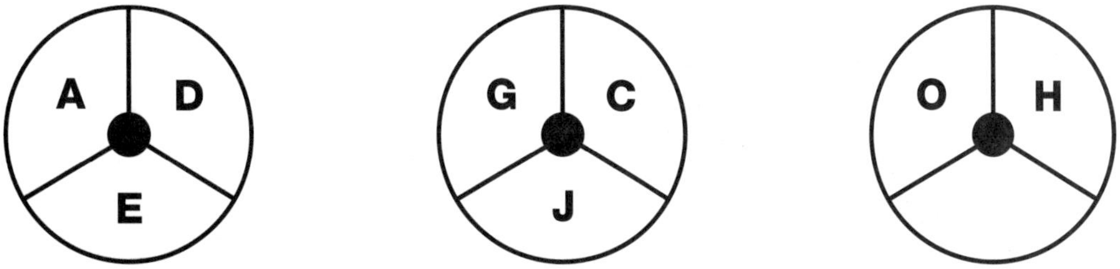

LEVEL

6

PUZZLE 50

Which letter is missing from the bottom circle?

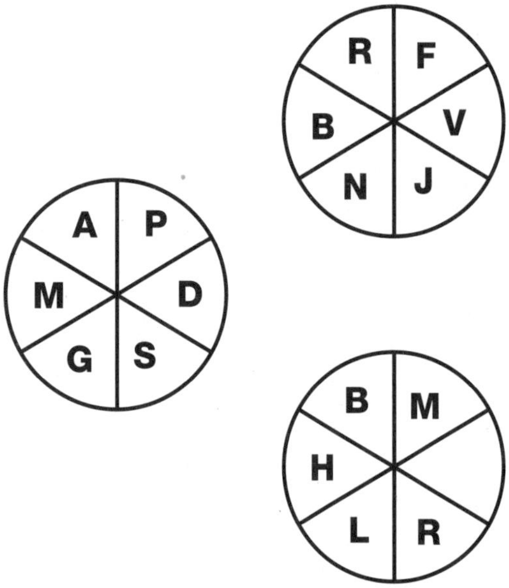

PUZZLE 51

What goes in the empty circle?

X	2	L
R	3	F
P	4	

PUZZLE 52

Which number is missing from this wheel?

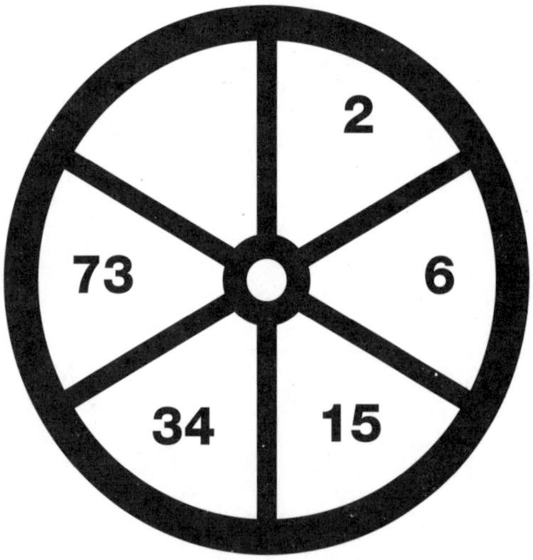

PUZZLE 53

Enter the missing number to complete this grid.

5	21	2
4	20	6
8	55	

54 PUZZLE

Which of the bottom grids logically goes in the centre of this puzzle?

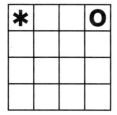

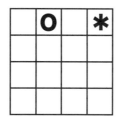

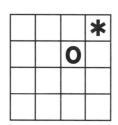

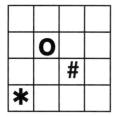

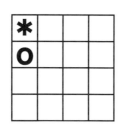

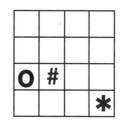

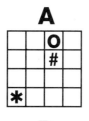

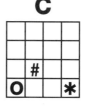

O			
	#		
			*

	O		*

		O	
	#		
*			

*			O

			*
		O	

	O		
		#	
*			

*			
O			

O	#		
			*

A

		O	
		#	
*			

B

		#	O
			*

C

		#	
O			*

D

			O
		#	
			*

E

O	#		
*			

F

*			
		#	O

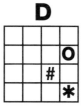

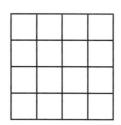

1 PUZZLE

Which is the odd one out?

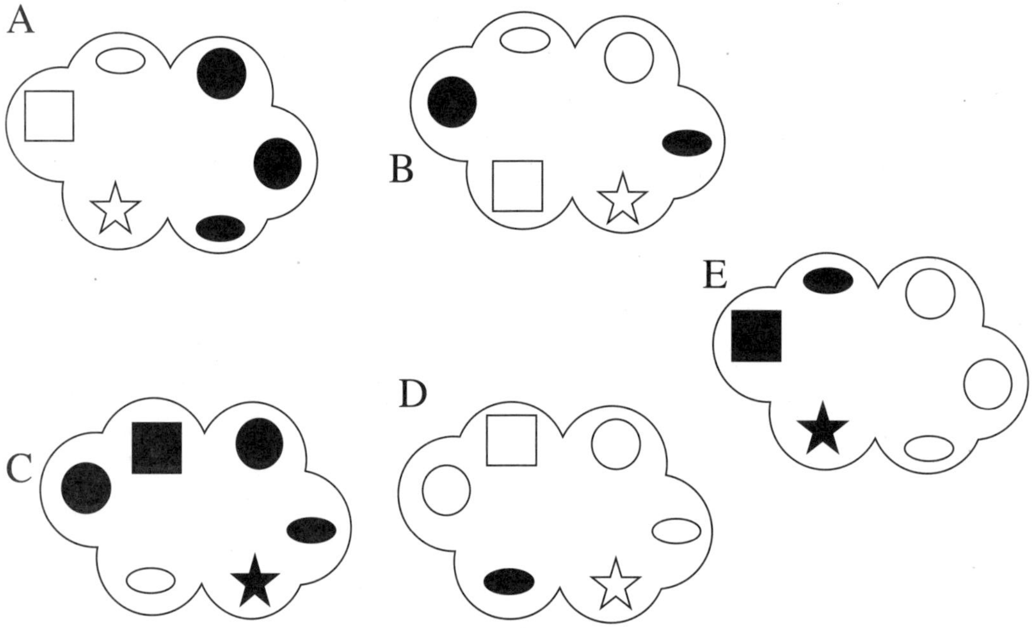

2 PUZZLE

Insert the numbers into the circles so that the sum of all the numbers in the circles directly connected to each circle equals the total as given in the list below.

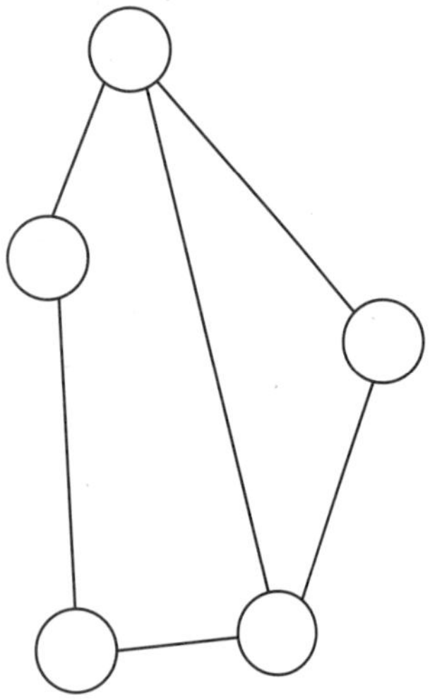

1=8
2=12
3=7
4=5
5=3

for example:

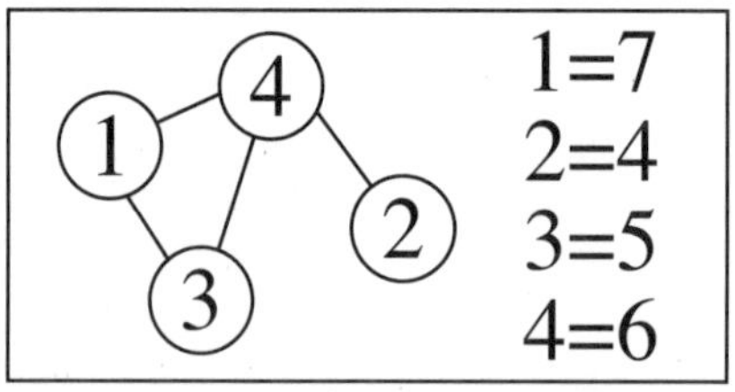

3 PUZZLE

Which is the odd one out?

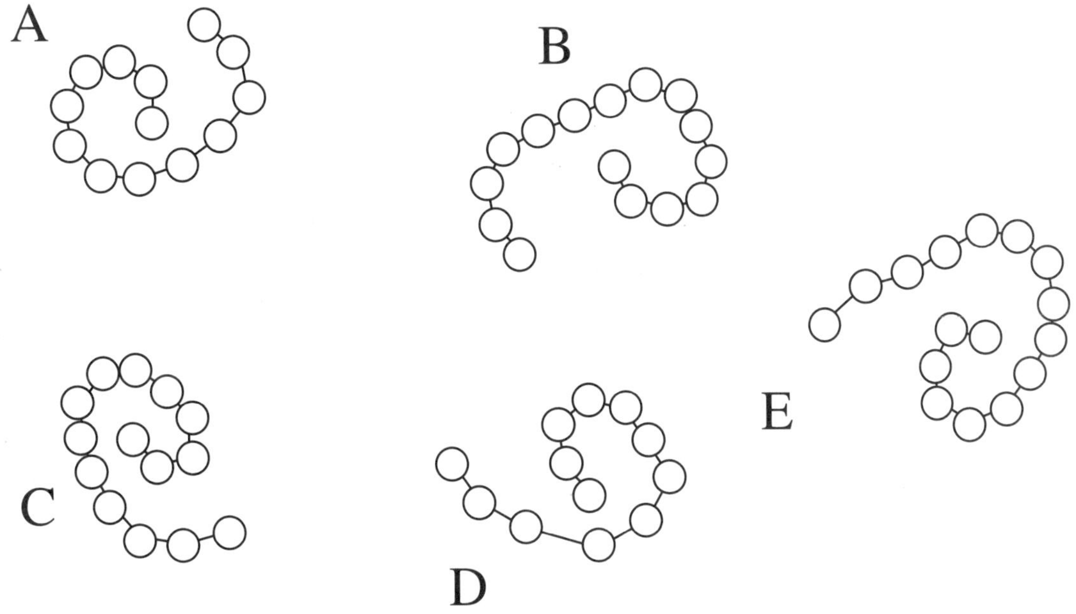

4 PUZZLE

Which set of letters is the odd one out?

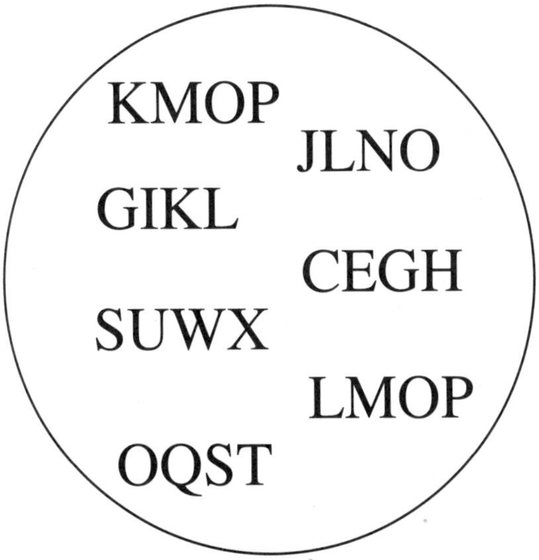

5 PUZZLE

What number should replace the question mark?

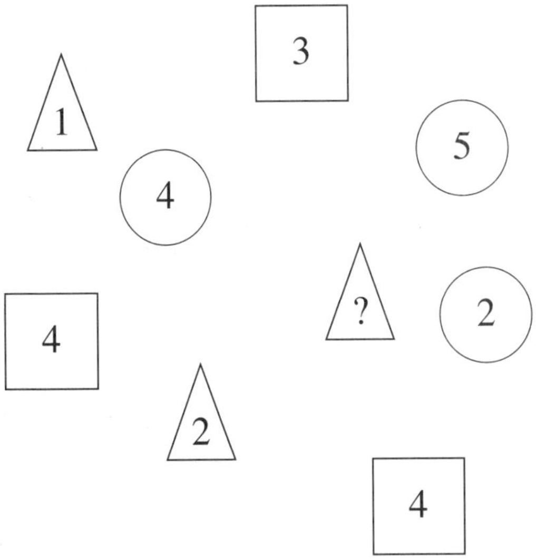

6 PUZZLE

Divide 600 by one quarter and add 15. What is the answer?

7 PUZZLE

The cost of hiring a private rail carriage is shared equally by all the passengers who all paid an exact number of dollars which was less than $100. The carriage has seats for 50 passengers and the total bill amounts to $1887. How many seats were not occupied?

8 PUZZLE

What number should replace the question mark?

1	3	3	5	?
0	2	2	4	?
2	1	4	3	?

9 PUZZLE

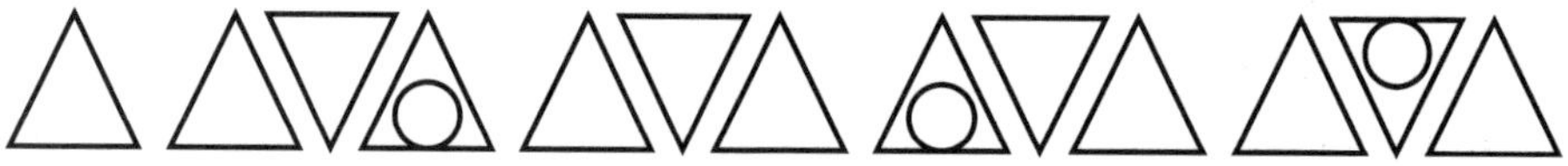

What comes next?

A B C D

10 PUZZLE

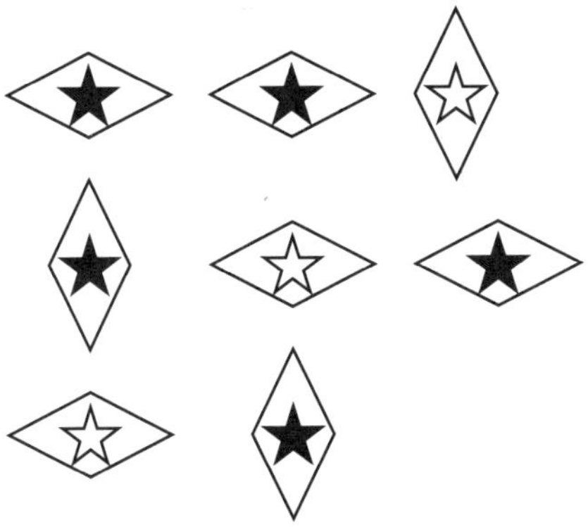

Which is the missing diamond?

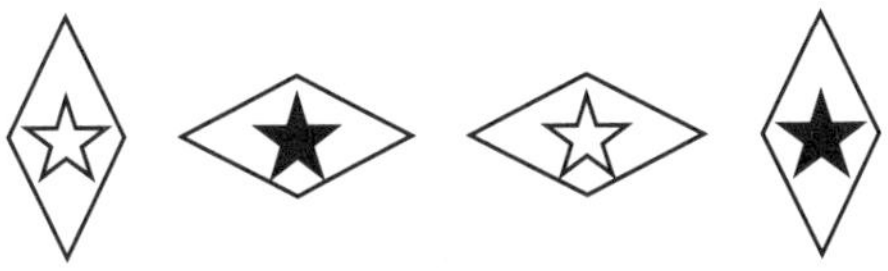

A B C D

11 PUZZLE

Which of these is the odd one out?

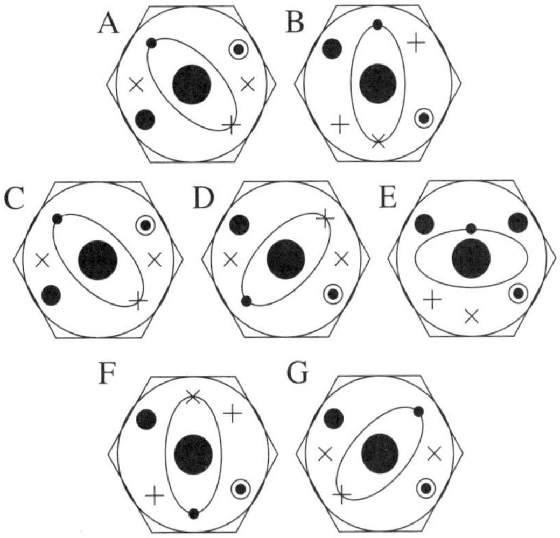

12 PUZZLE

What number should replace the question mark?

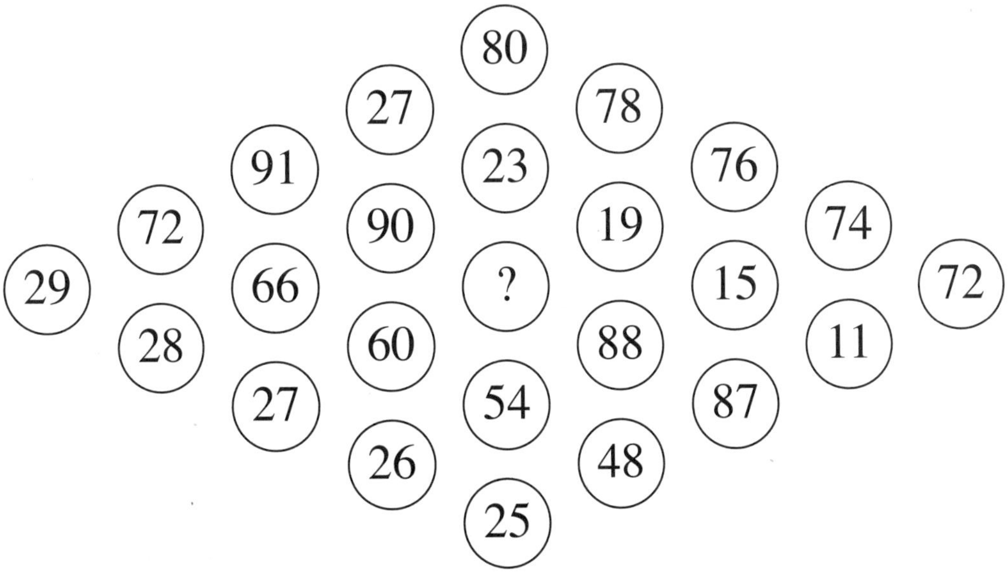

13 PUZZLE

Each line and symbol which appears in the four outer circles, below, is transferred to the centre circle according to these rules: If a line or symbol occurs in the outer circles: once: it is transferred twice: it is possibly transferred 3 times: it is transferred 4 times: it is not transferred. Which of the circles A, B, C, D or E, should appear at the centre of the diagram, below?

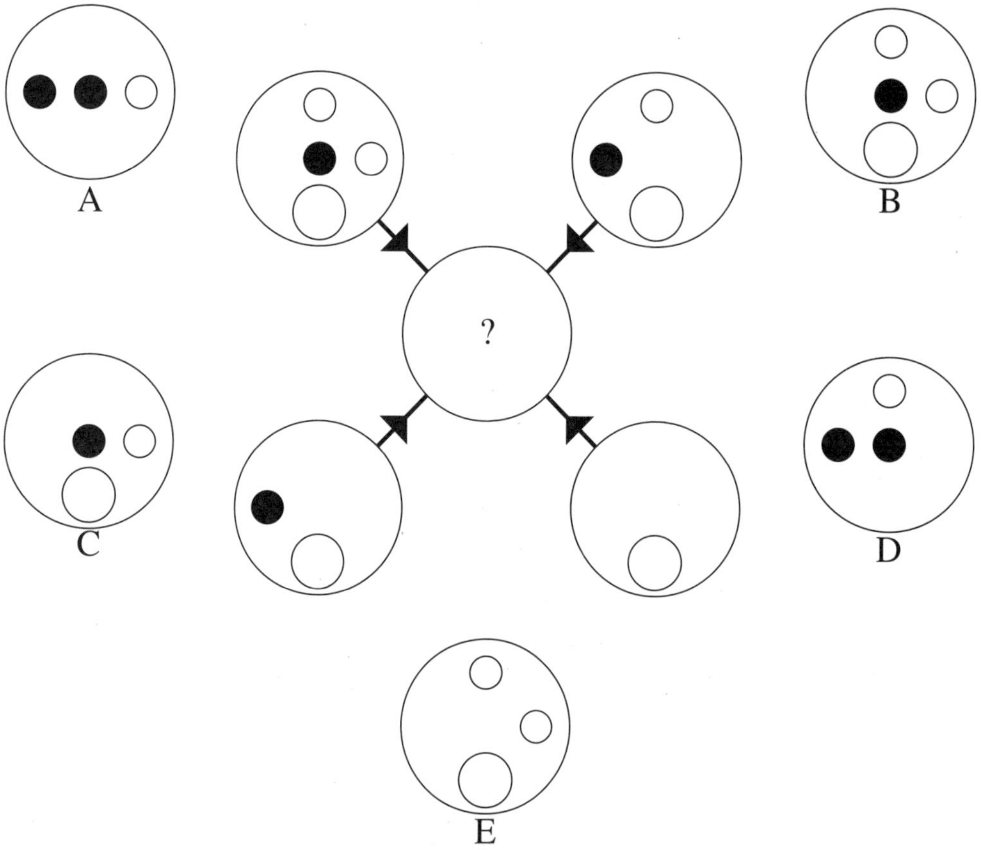

14 PUZZLE

What number should replace the question mark?

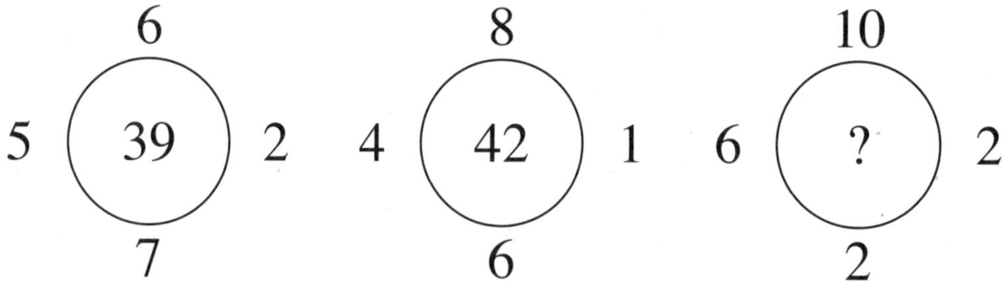

15 PUZZLE

Each of the nine squares in the grid marked A1 to C3, should incorporate all the lines and symbols which are shown in the squares of the same letter and number immediately above and to the left. For example, B2 should incorporate all the lines and symbols that are in 2 and B. One of the squares is incorrect. Which one is it?

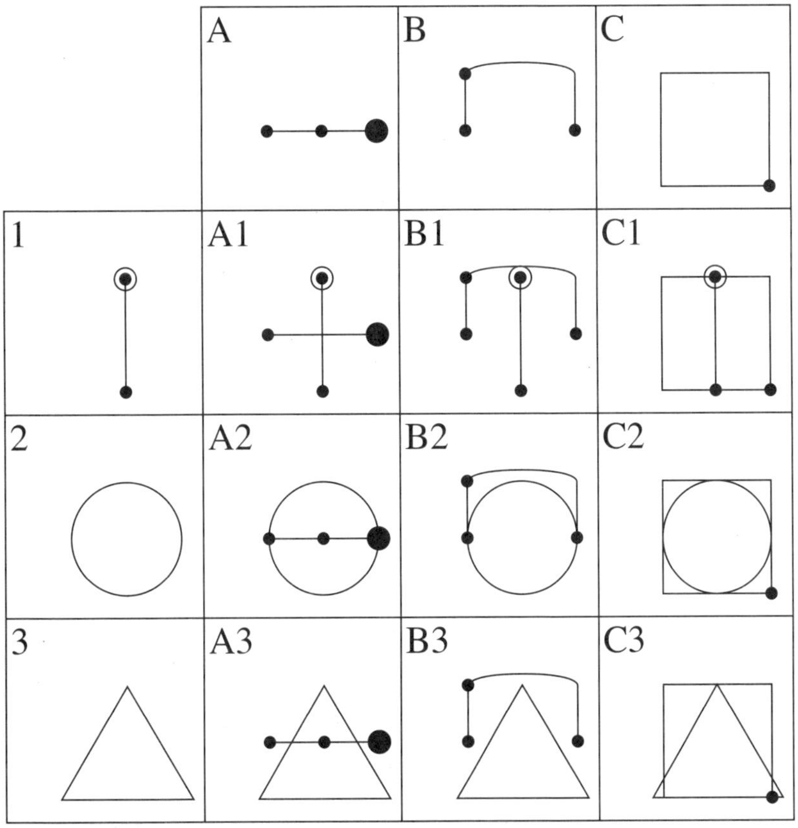

16 PUZZLE

What number should replace the question mark?

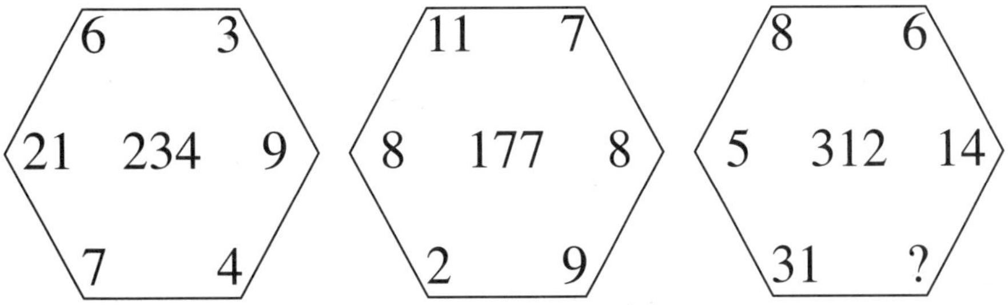

17 PUZZLE

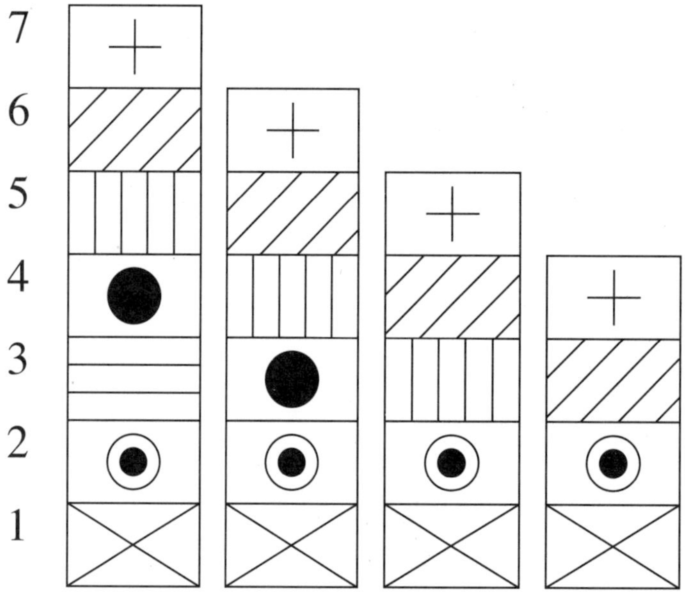

Which option below continues the above sequence?

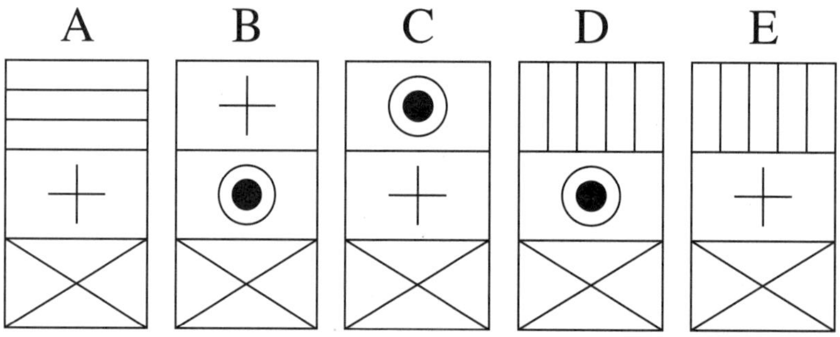

18 PUZZLE

Which letter should replace the question mark?

19 PUZZLE

The combined age of ALAN & BERTIE is 43. The combined age of ALAN & CHARLIE is 55. The combined age of BERTIE & CHARLIE is 66.

How old are ALAN, BERTIE & CHARLIE?

20 PUZZLE

Which two words mean the same?

PONIARD	CAUCUS
PITCH	PILLORY
SORREL	DAGGER
STAMEN	BLOSSOM

21 PUZZLE

Simplify

$$\frac{46}{27} \div \frac{92}{9} =$$

22 PUZZLE

At the dog show the dogs' numbers were

CORGI 11	TERRIER 15
WHIPPET 17	ALSATIAN ?

What was the Alsatian's number?

23 PUZZLE

How many KG should be placed at question mark to balance the scale?

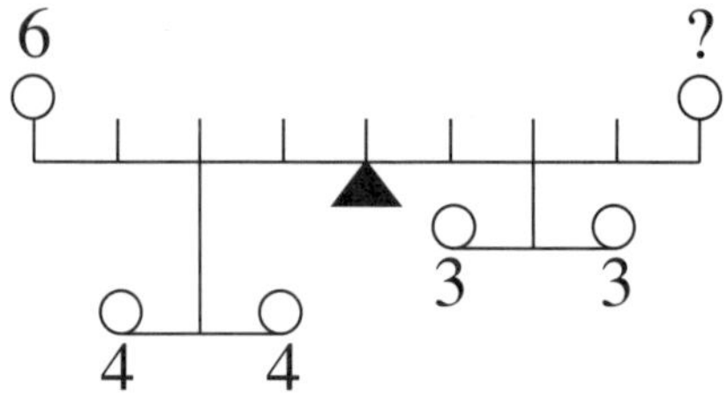

24 PUZZLE

A hundred eggs are in a crate, if you draw out 2, and there are 6 bad eggs in the crate, what are your chances of drawing out 2 bad eggs?

25 PUZZLE

At a school outing
81% of the boys had lost a shoe
82% of the boys had lost a sock
77% of the boys had lost a handkerchief
and 68% of the boys had lost a hat

What percentage at least must have lost all 4 items?

PUZZLE 26

Which number needs to be added to complete the last wheel?

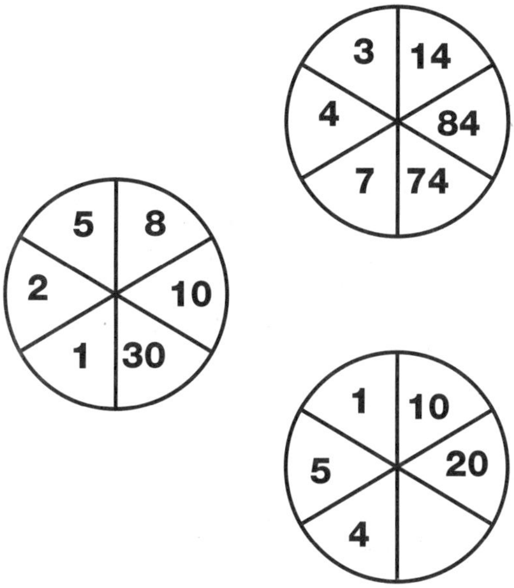

PUZZLE 27

Which number continues this sequence?

PUZZLE 28

Which letter goes in the empty link?

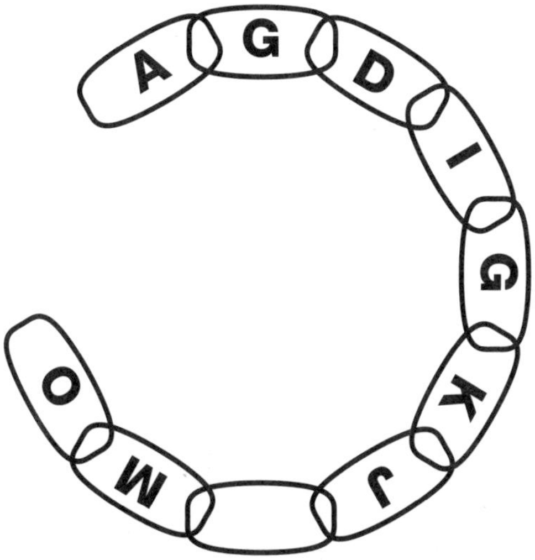

PUZZLE 29

Which number is missing?

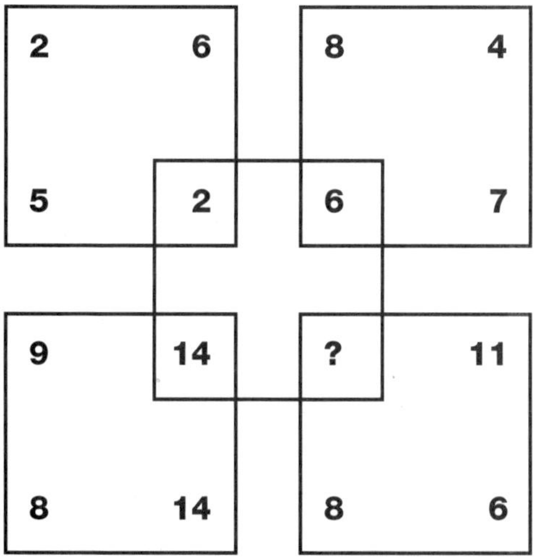

30 PUZZLE

Which domino will complete the third row?

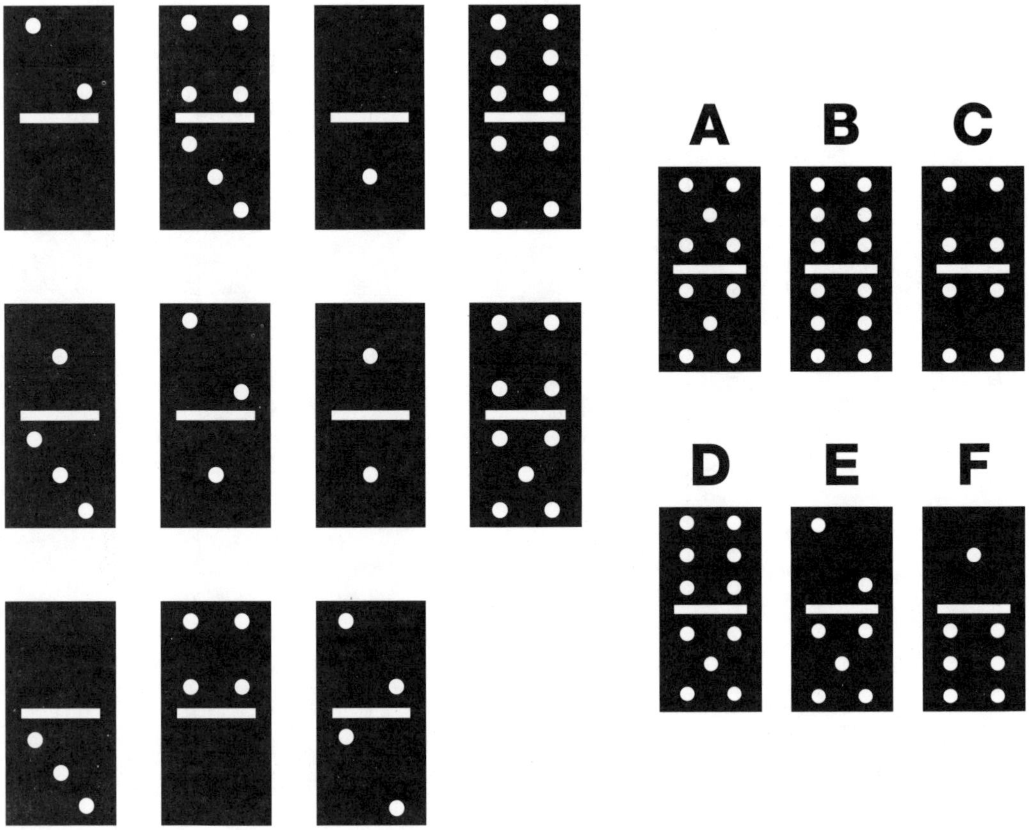

31 PUZZLE

Which letter tops the third triangle?

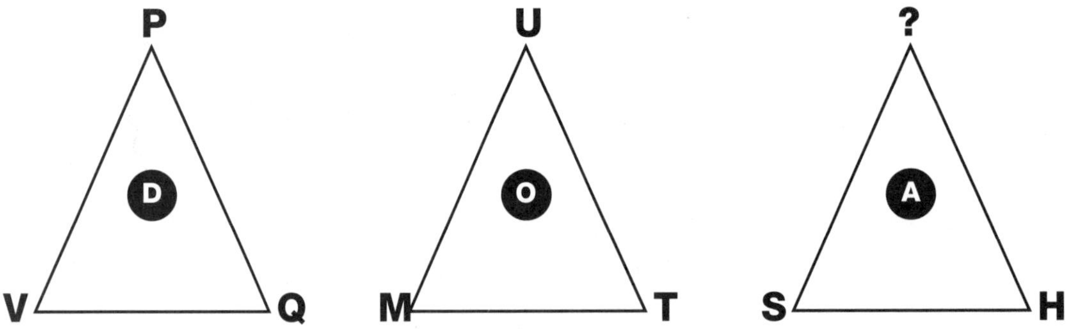

PUZZLE 32

Which number is missing from the grid?

6	2	5
10	3	16
18	6	60
34	15	

PUZZLE 33

Which number goes in the empty circle?

7	13	9
8	5	3
4	8	

PUZZLE 34

Which number is needed to complete the puzzle?

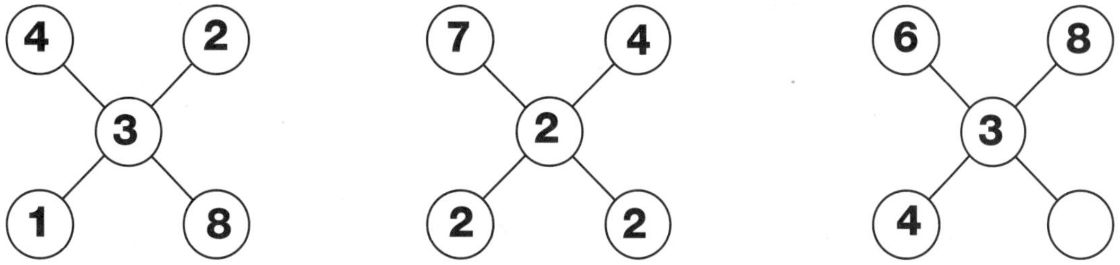

PUZZLE 35

Fill in the blank circle.

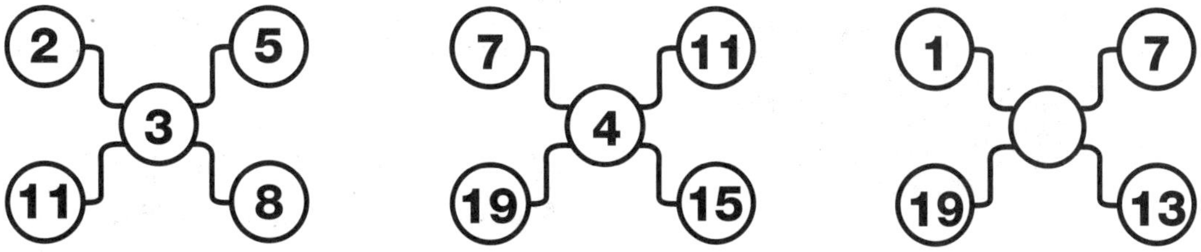

LEVEL 7

LEVEL 7

PUZZLE 36

Which number completes this puzzle?

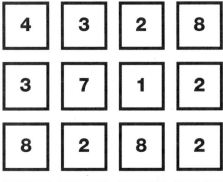

4	3	2	8
3	7	1	2
8	2	8	2
1	2	5	

PUZZLE 37

Which number is missing?

3	11	4
7	13	2
4	23	

PUZZLE 38

Which letter is the odd one out in each ellipse?

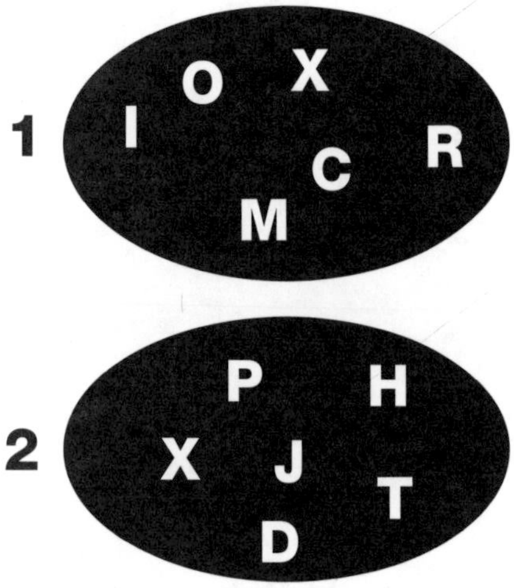

PUZZLE 39

Which number goes in the empty box?

46	85	12
13	48	71
81	54	63
61		53

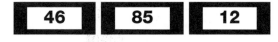

40 PUZZLE

Which playing card is missing from this pattern?

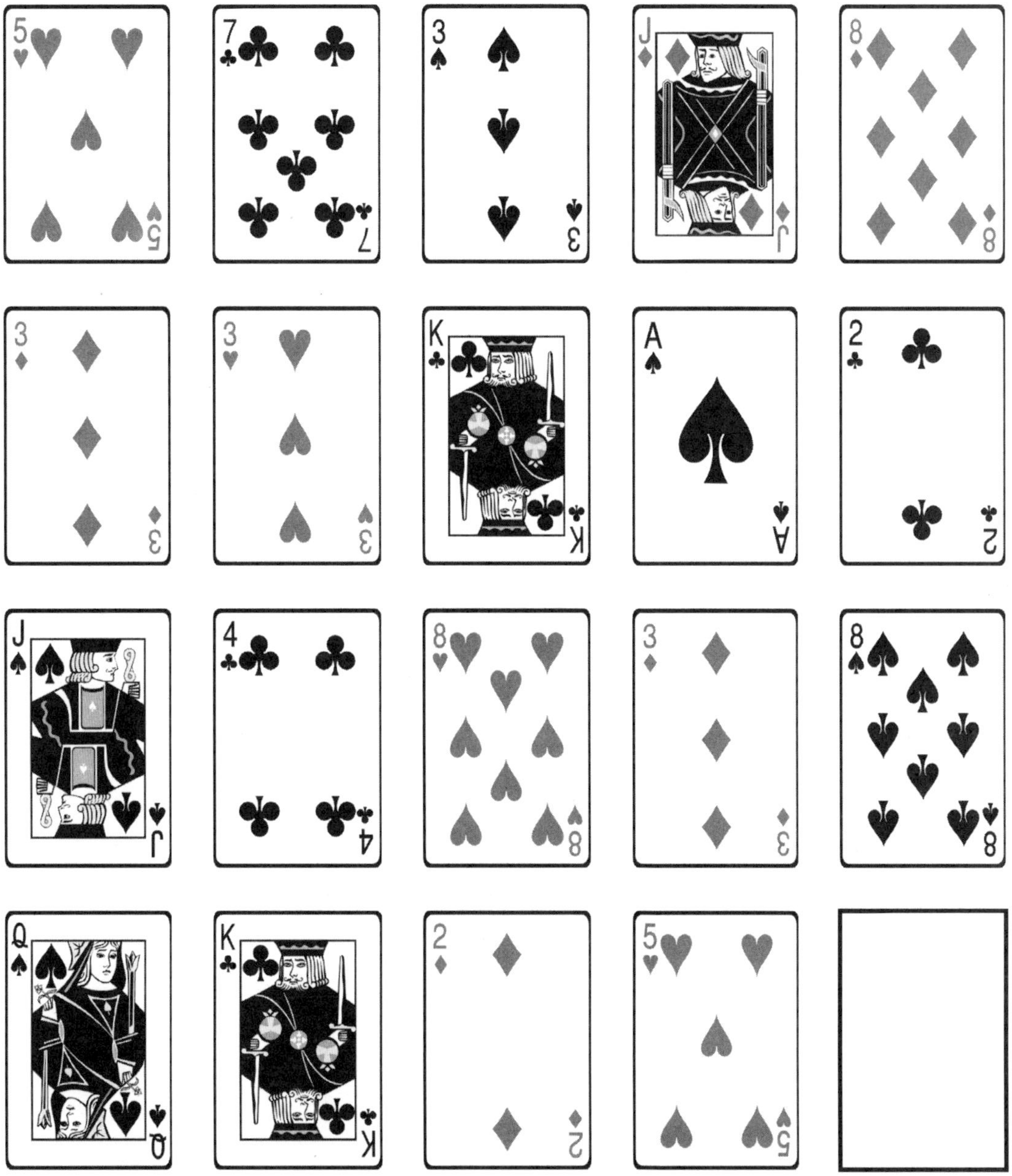

41 PUZZLE

Which number needs to go in the blank segment?

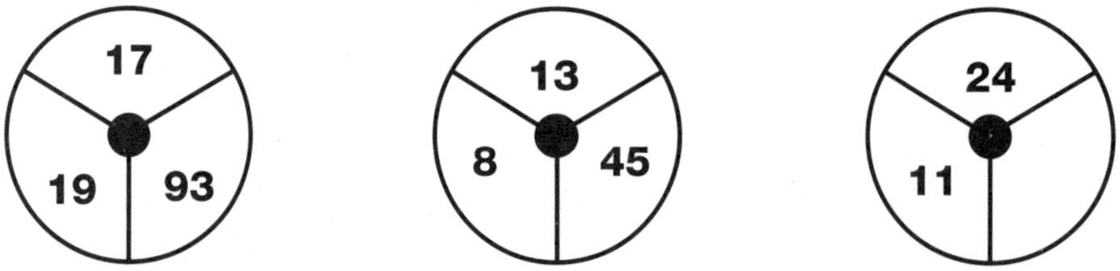

42 PUZZLE

Which number finishes the sequence?

43 PUZZLE

Which letter replaces the blank and completes the puzzle?

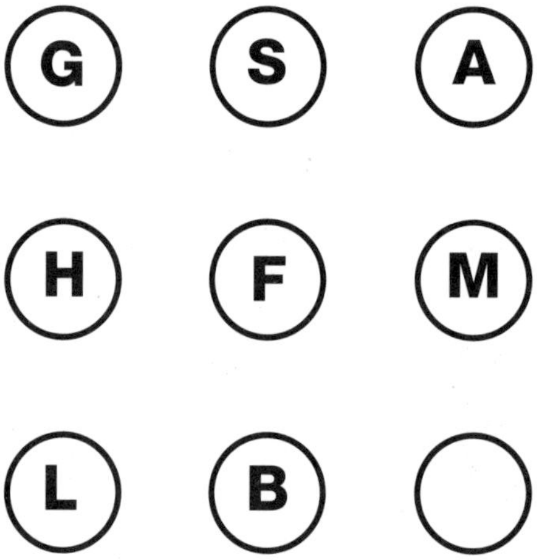

44 PUZZLE

Which letter needs to go in the blank circle?

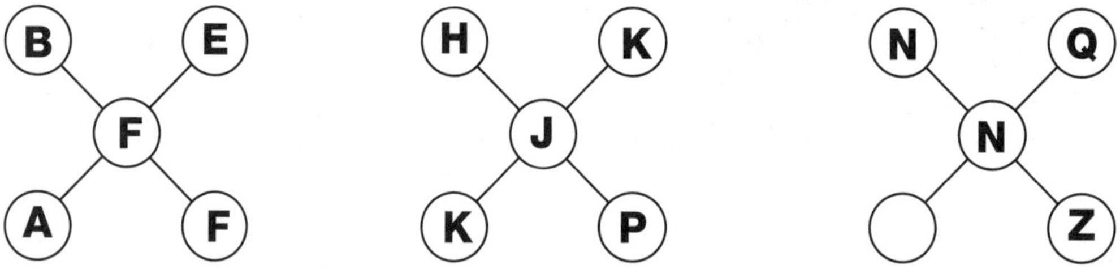

PUZZLE 45

Fill in the empty box with the correct letter.

H	C	N
26	15	20
R	L	

PUZZLE 46

Which number is needed to finish this puzzle?

4
2
9
7
14

PUZZLE 47

Which letter goes in the empty circle?

B	F	H
O	G	V
Y	A	

PUZZLE 48

Which number goes in the empty box and finishes the grid?

5	2	3
12	6	6

4	2	3
8	8	13

6	5	11
18	6	

PUZZLE 49

Which number goes in the blank segment?

PUZZLE 50

Which letter completes the sequence?

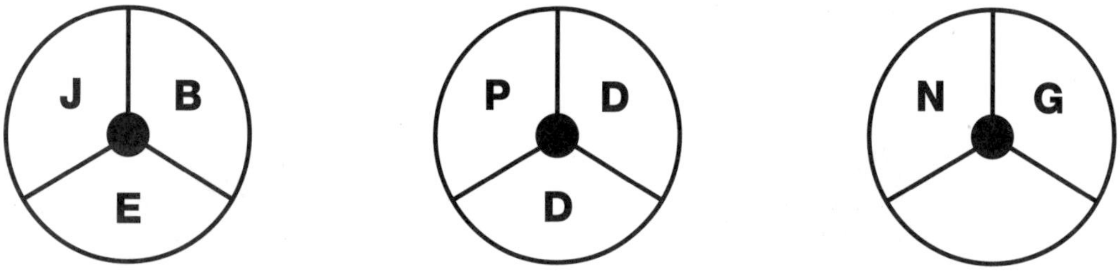

PUZZLE 51

Which number goes in the empty segment?

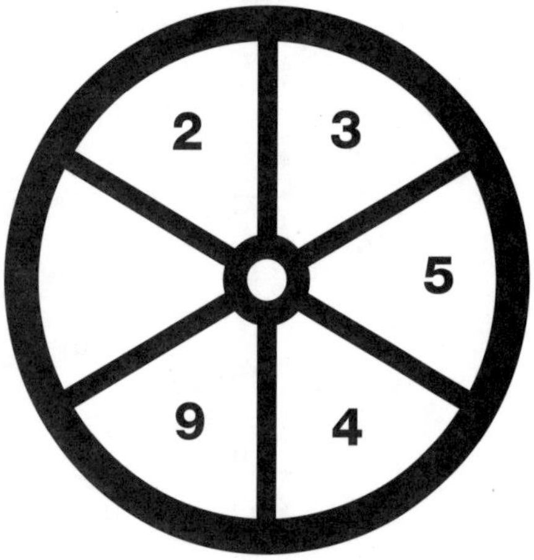

PUZZLE 52

Which number should be added to the empty circle?

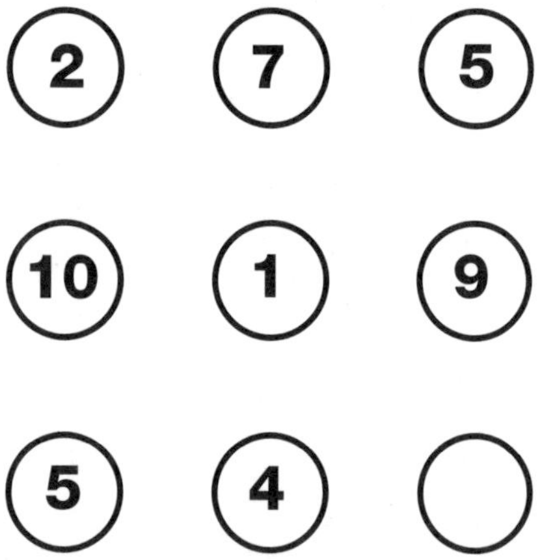

53 PUZZLE

Which letter replaces the blank and completes the sequence?

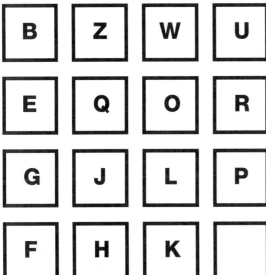

B	Z	W	U
E	Q	O	R
G	J	L	P
F	H	K	

54 PUZZLE

Can you finish this sequence?

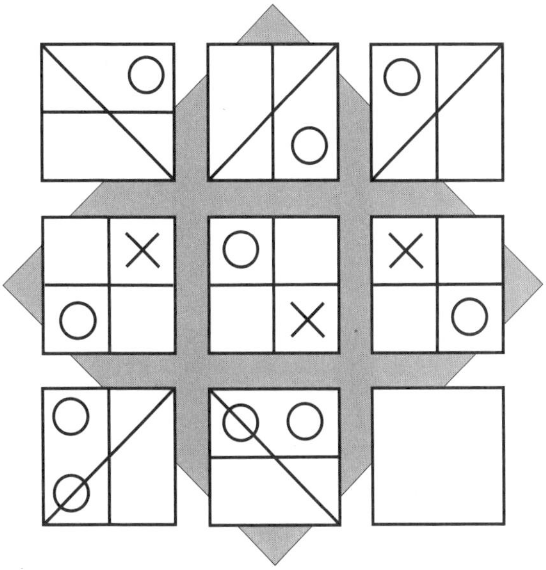

55 PUZZLE

What goes in the empty box?

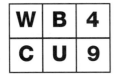

W	B	4
C	U	9

N	L	5
S	F	1

Z	Q	7
T	I	

56 PUZZLE

Which letter is missing?

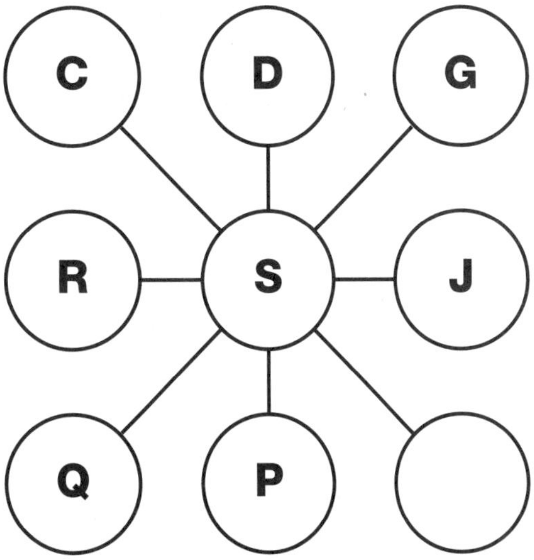

[redacted] PUZZLE

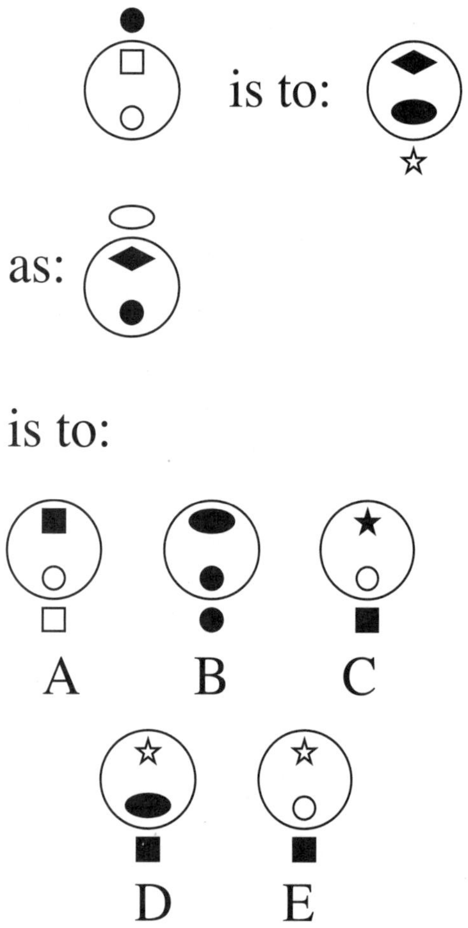

[redacted] PUZZLE

What should replace the question marks?

HF	86	SU
?	?	TX

3 PUZZLE

4 9 6 2 3 4 7 8 2 1 9 6 4 3 2

Multiply by 7 the number of odd numbers which are immediately followed by an even number in the list above.

What is the answer?

4 PUZZLE

Which is the odd one out?

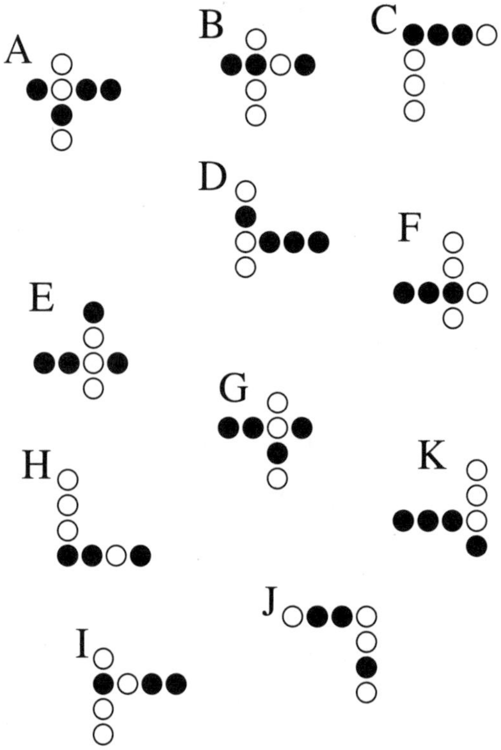

5 PUZZLE

Which is the missing shield?

A B C

6 PUZZLE

What comes next?

2

4

6

9

12

15

19

?

7 PUZZLE

What number should replace the question mark?

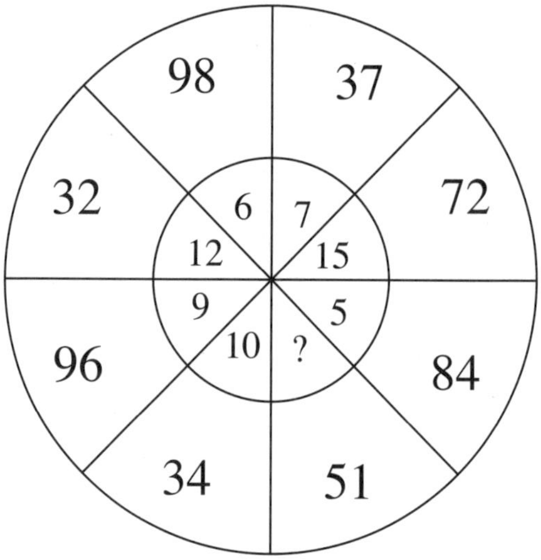

8 PUZZLE

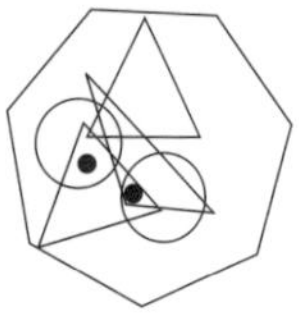

To which heptagon below can a dot be added so that both dots then meet the same conditions as in the heptagon above?

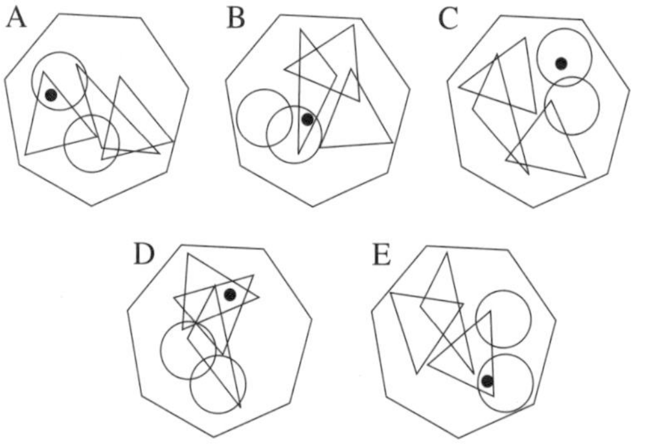

9 PUZZLE

Find the starting point and visit each square once only to reach the treasure marked T.
1N 2W = 1 North, 2 West

2S 2E	1S 1W	1W 1S
2E 1N	T	1S 1W
1N 2E	2N 1W	2N 1W

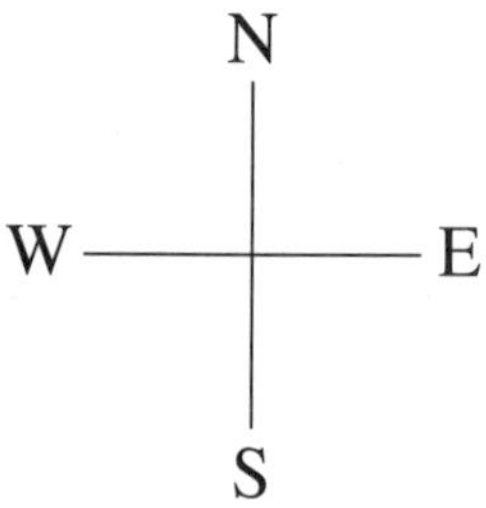

10 PUZZLE

What comes next?

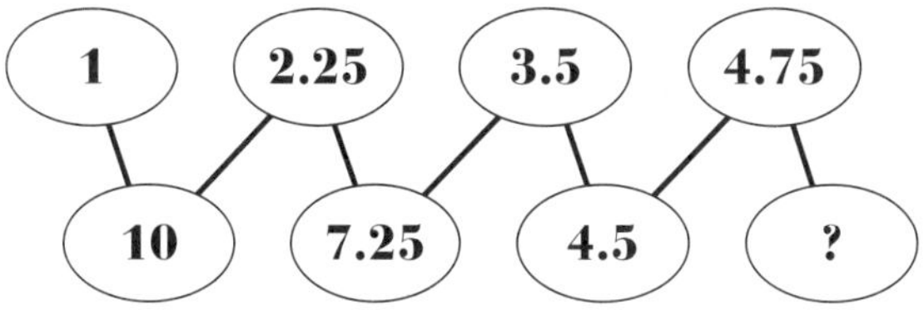

11 PUZZLE

How many squares are there in this figure?

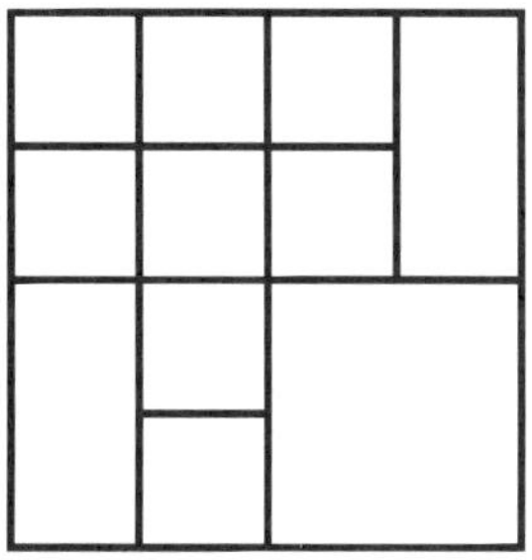

12 PUZZLE

Each of the nine squares in the grid marked A1 to C3, should incorporate all the lines and symbols which are shown in the squares of the same letter and number immediately above and to the left. For example, B2 should incorporate all the lines and symbols that are in 2 and B. One of the squares is incorrect. Which one is it?

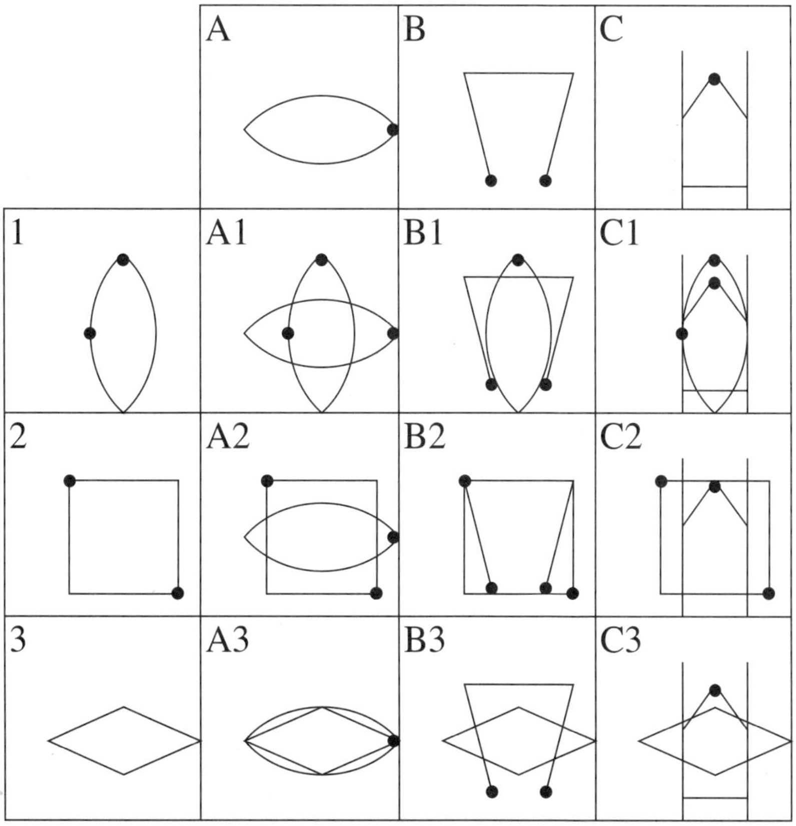

PUZZLE 13

What number should replace the question mark?

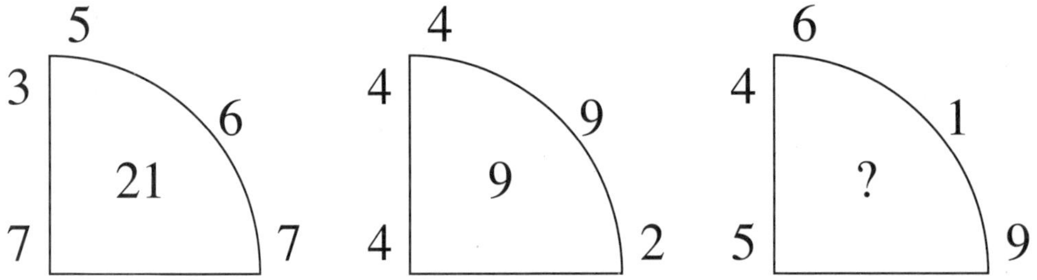

PUZZLE 14

What number should replace the question mark?

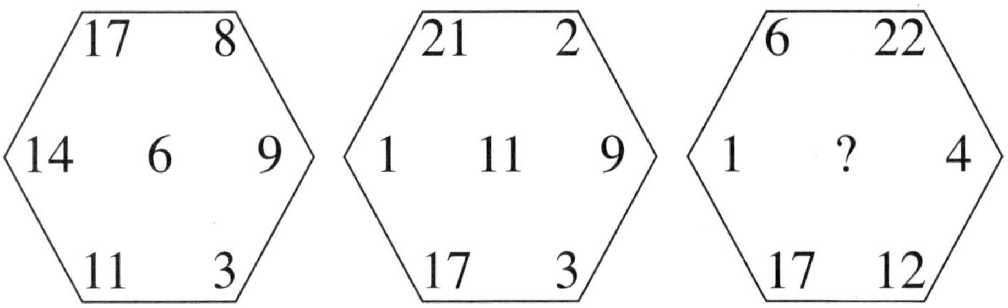

PUZZLE 15

What number should replace the question mark?

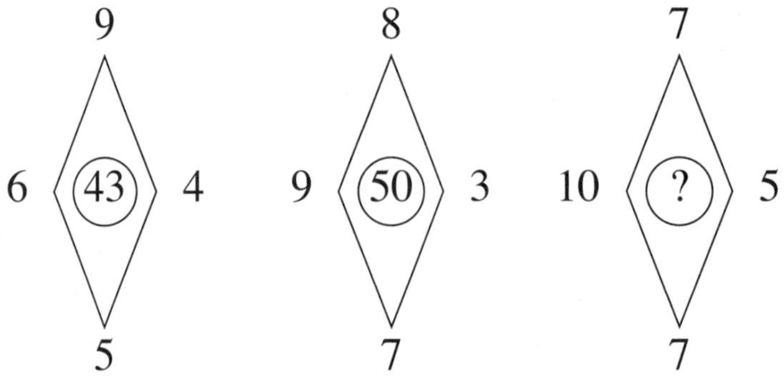

16 PUZZLE

Which square will replace the question mark?

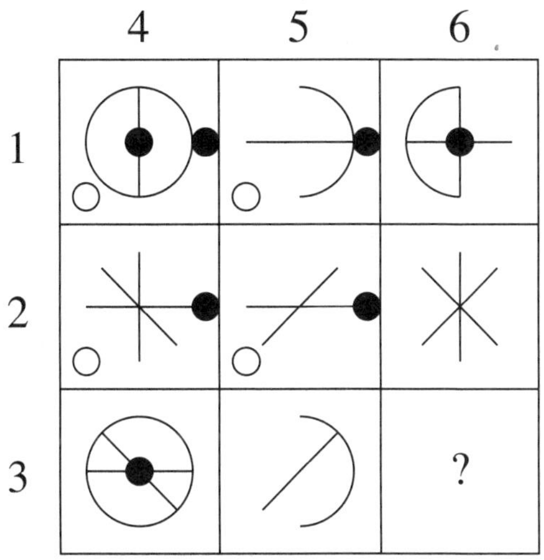

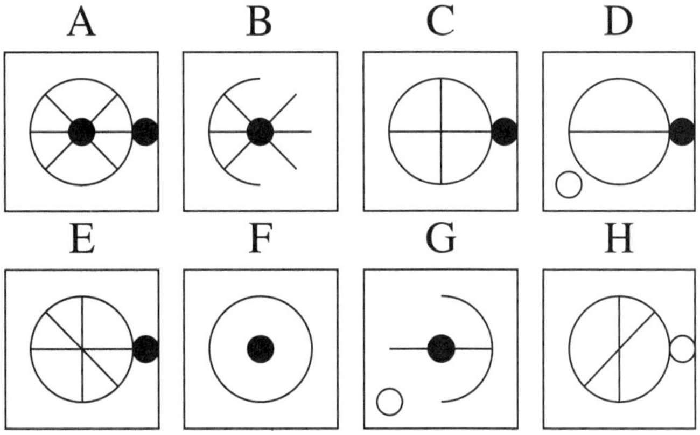

17 PUZZLE

Find the weight to balance the scales.

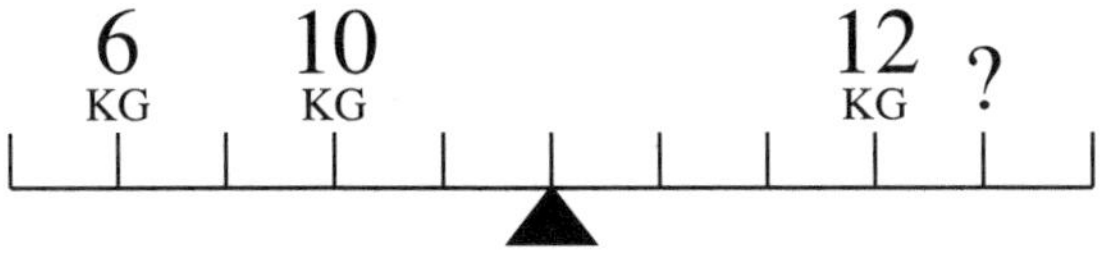

18 PUZZLE

There are two brothers
and two sisters.
In 10 years they will
total 100 in their ages.
How much will the
total be in 7 years?

LEVEL 8

19 PUZZLE

Each line and symbol which appears in the four outer circles, below, is transferred to the centre circle according to these rules: If a line or symbol occurs in the outer circles: once: it is transferred twice: it is possibly transferred 3 times: it is transferred 4 times: it is not transferred. Which of the circles A, B, C, D or E, should appear at the centre of the diagram, below?

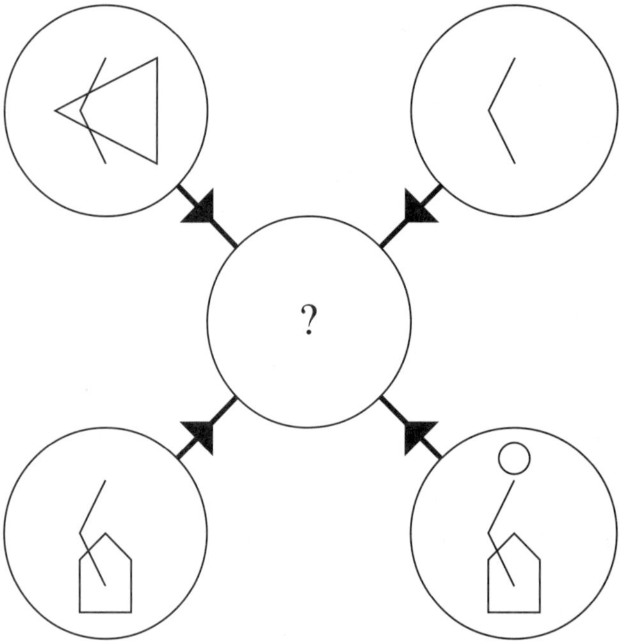

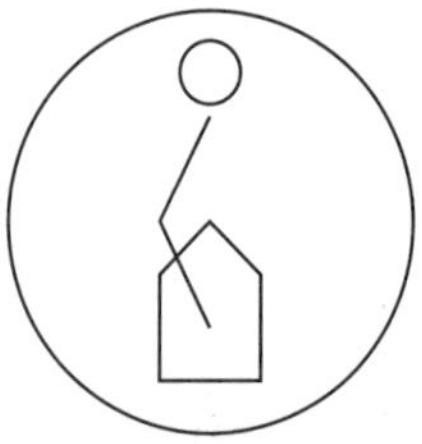

A

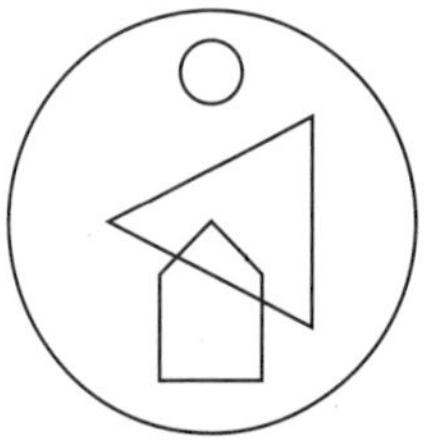

B

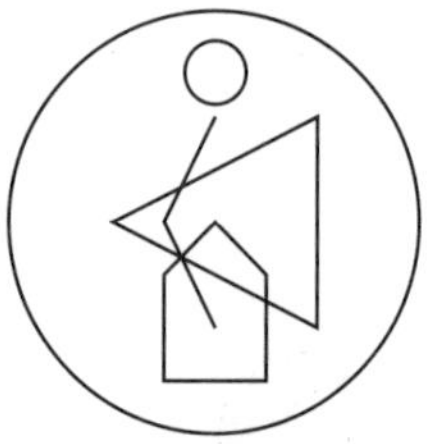

C

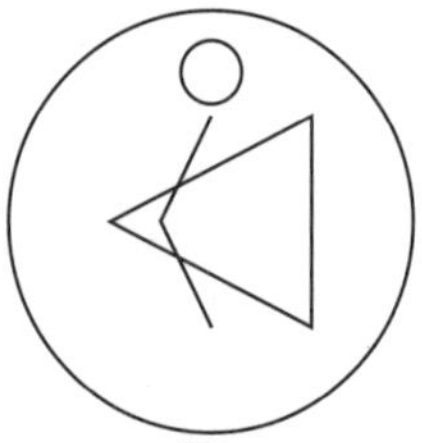

D

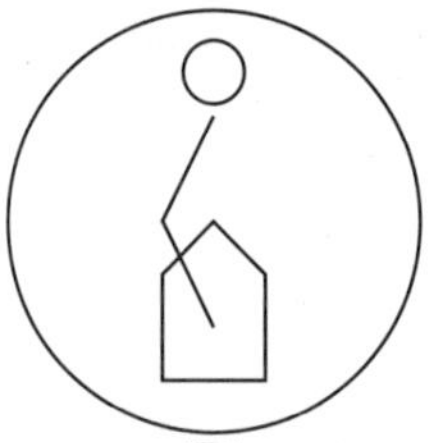

E

20 PUZZLE

Which is the odd one out?

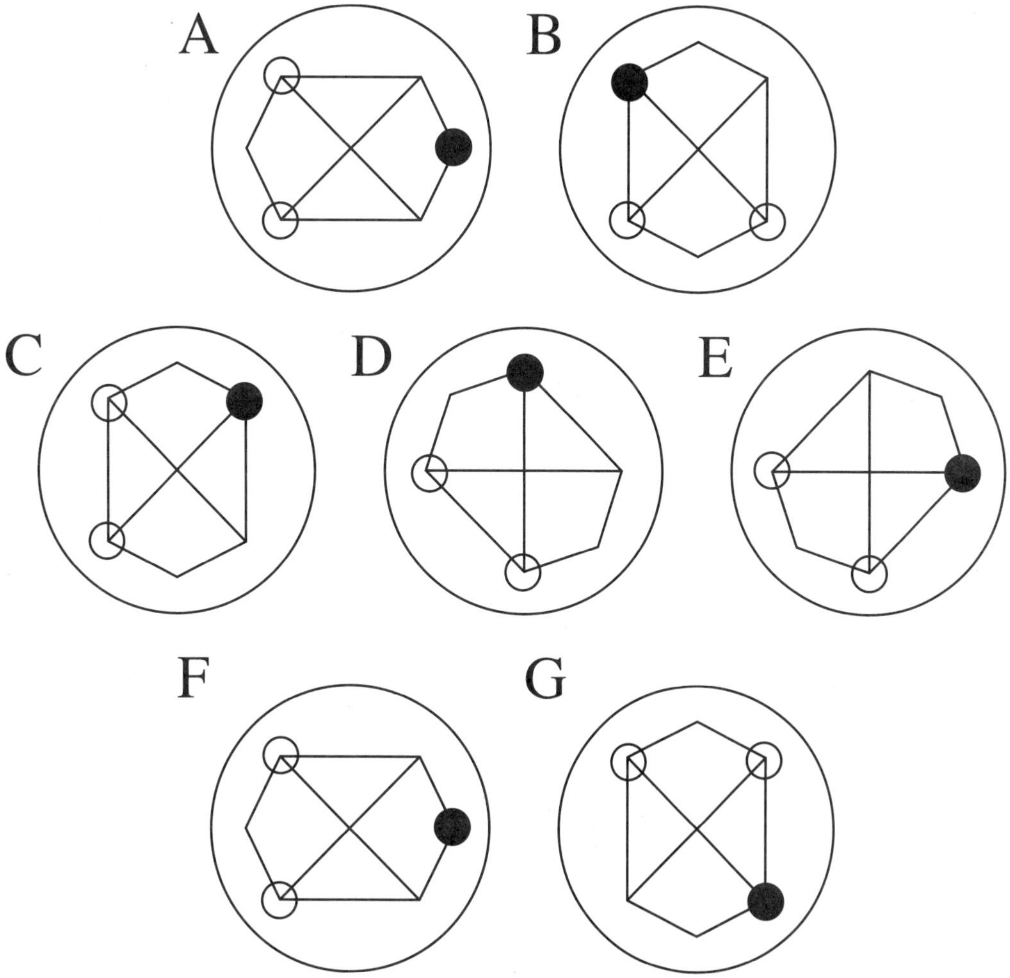

21 PUZZLE

Insert the same number twice
(not the number 1) to make this calculation correct.

6 ÷ 6 = 6

LEVEL 8

PUZZLE 22

Which two words have opposite meanings?

CORPULENT, DAZED, MERITORIOUS, VIRULENT, STANDARD, LEAN, UNCONSCIOUS, END

PUZZLE 23

What number should replace x?

$$14 - (-7) - (-7) = x$$

PUZZLE 24

Out of 10 motors, 3 are defective. Two are chosen at random. What are the chances that both are defective?

PUZZLE 25

How many 4 card permutations (arrangements) can you make in a pack of 52 cards (standard playing cards)?

26 PUZZLE

Which number fits into the empty box?

5	6	8
12	20	36

4	5	7
11	19	35

3	4	6
10	18	

27 PUZZLE

Which letter replaces the blank and completes the sequence?

M	P	S
J	N	R
B	G	L
D	J	

28 PUZZLE

Which number would logically complete this grid?

9	3	4	11
5	17	18	3
3	16	21	8
4	9	6	

29 PUZZLE

What goes in the empty circle?

5	4	S
4	2	Z
2	3	

30 PUZZLE

Which piece fits back into the grid?

I	R	T	W	E	D	B	T	F	O
S	I	R	T	W	E	D	B	T	O
O	W	E	D	B	T	F	O	F	S
O	T	S	I			W	O	O	I
F	R	O					S	O	R
T	I	O					I	S	T
B	S	F	O			B	R	I	W
D	O	T	B	D	E	W	T	R	E
E	O	F	T	B	D	E	W	T	D
W	T	R	I	S	O	O	F	T	B

1

	D	I	
E	O	R	B
D	S	T	T
	I	W	

2

	R	T	
I	E	R	T
W	D	I	F
	B	W	

3

	R	T	
S	I	R	E
O	W	T	D
	F	T	

4

	I	R	
B	T	F	T
W	O	O	W
	D	E	

5

	D	R	
W	I	O	T
E	S	D	B
	I	W	

31 PUZZLE

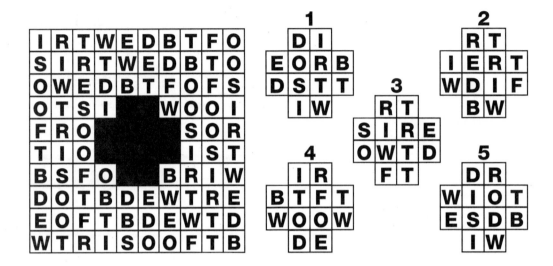

If two men stand back to back, walk in opposite directions for 4 metres, turn to the left and walk another 3 metres, what is the distance between them when they stop?

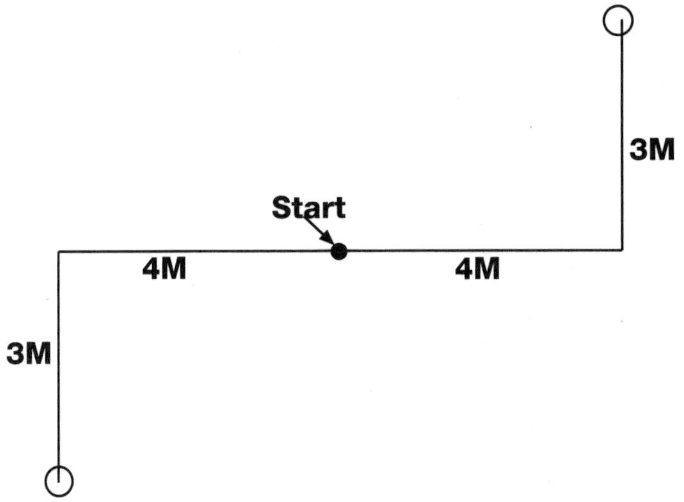

32 PUZZLE

Which of the bottom squares fits logically at the end of this puzzle?

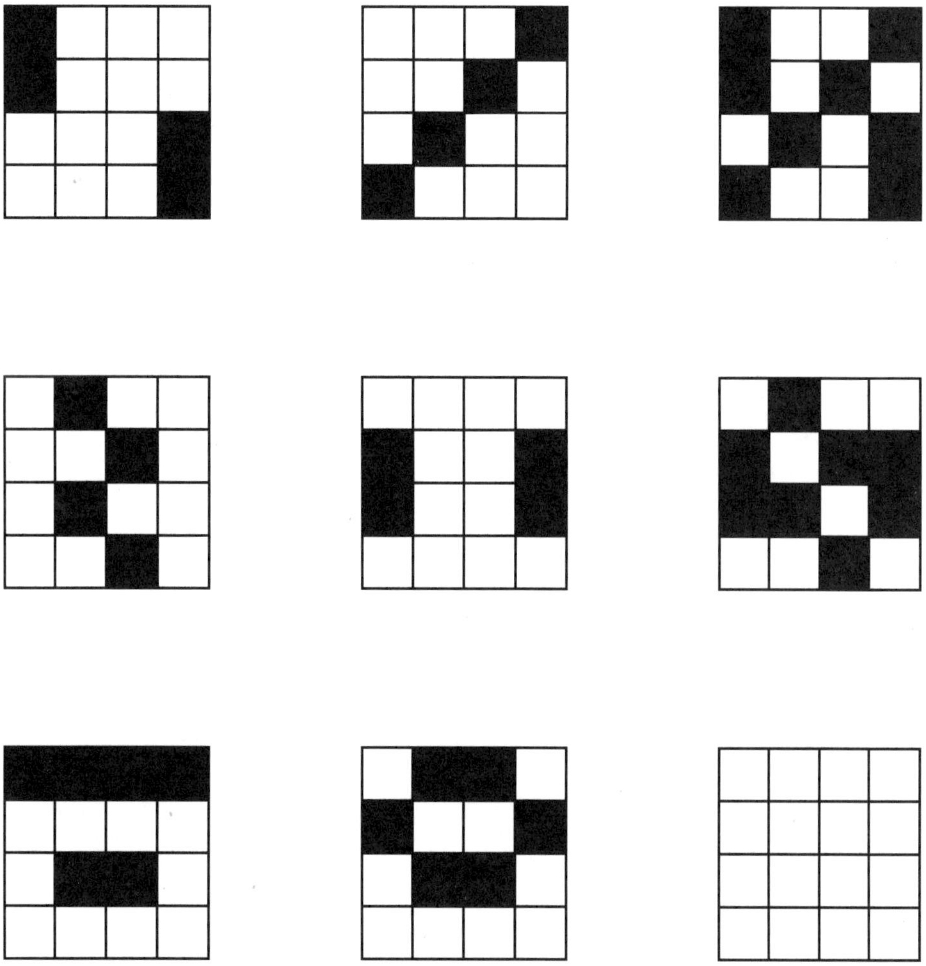

A

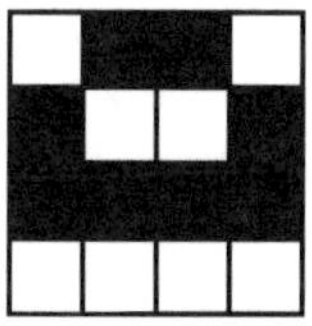

B

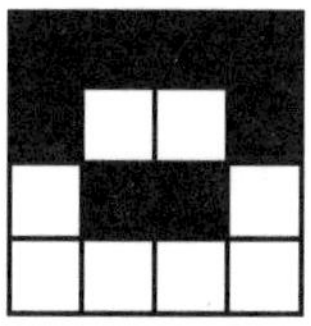

C

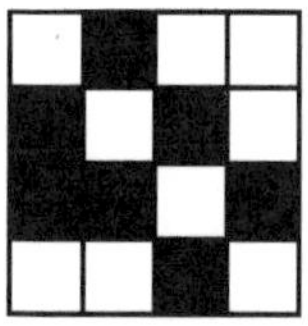

D

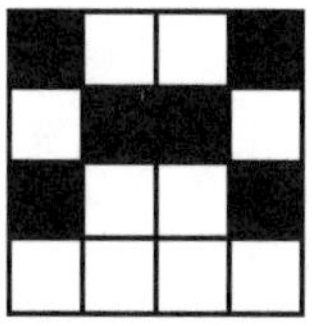

E

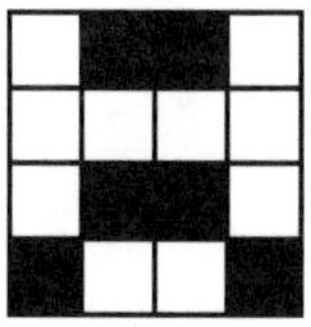

F

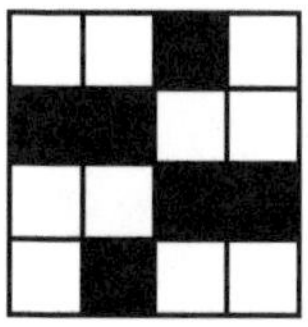

33 PUZZLE

Which number is missing from this sequence?

1	3
2	4
2	6
3	5
4	12
4	

34 PUZZLE

Which number replaces the question mark and completes the puzzle?

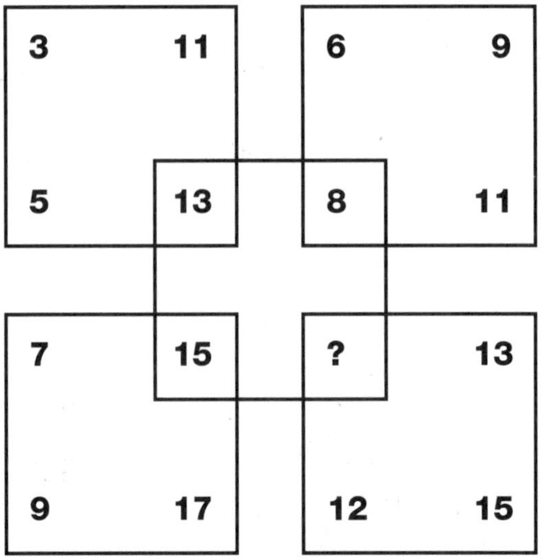

35 PUZZLE

Which two characters go into the empty boxes at the bottom of the table?

3	B
5	C
7	E
11	G
13	K

36 PUZZLE

Joan is extremely fussy about everything, particularly her numbers. She likes 225, but not 224. She prefers 900 to 800, and she absolutely loves 144, but loathes 145.

From this information can you tell if she would like 1600 or 1700?

37 PUZZLE

Luke challenged his twin sister Lucy to remove 8 matches to leave 2 squares whose edges do not touch, can you see how she managed it?

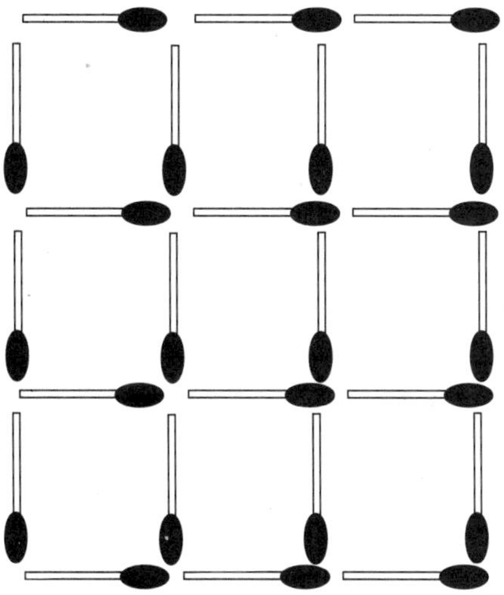

38 PUZZLE

Which number is missing from this puzzle?

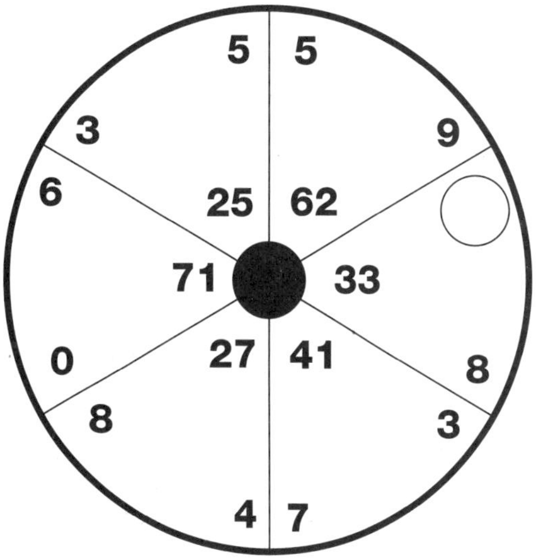

39 PUZZLE

Which number continues the sequence?

40 PUZZLE

Which number replaces the question mark and completes the sequence?

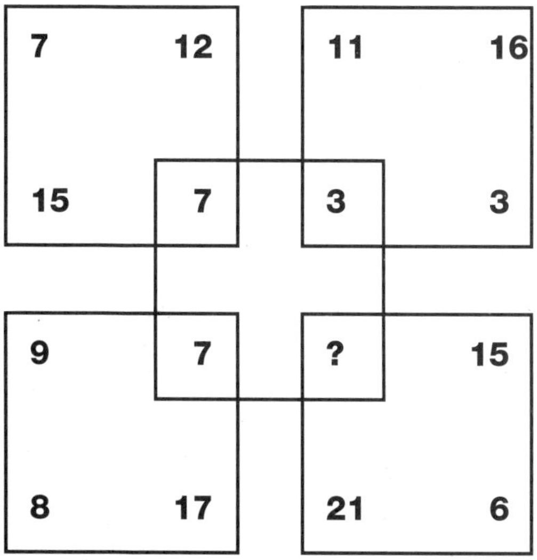

LEVEL 8

41 PUZZLE

Simon showed Jason an arrangement of 9 matches which made 4 identical triangles. Jason then showed Simon how to use only 6 matches to produce the same 4 identical triangles. How is this possible?

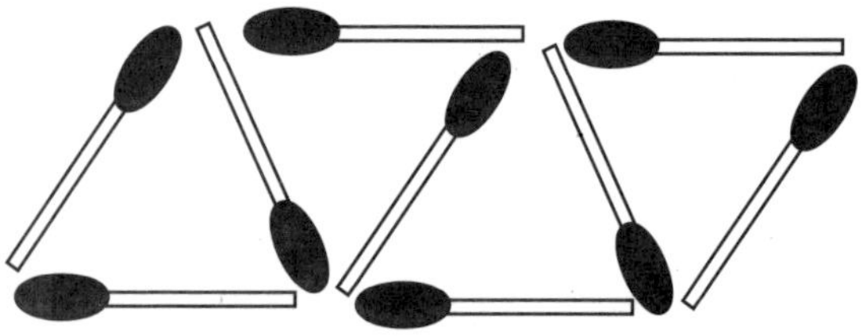

42 PUZZLE

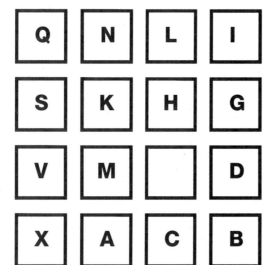

Which number is missing?

6	4	5	3
7	5	4	6
5		7	4
8	7	6	5

43 PUZZLE

Which letter replaces the blank and completes the sequence?

Q	N	L	I
S	K	H	G
V	M		D
X	A	C	B

44 PUZZLE

Complete this puzzle by drawing what you think should appear in the empty box.

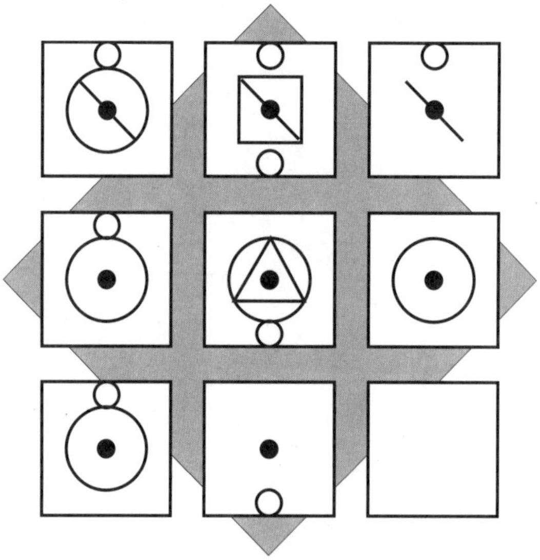

PUZZLE 45

Which number is missing from the middle of the last triangle?

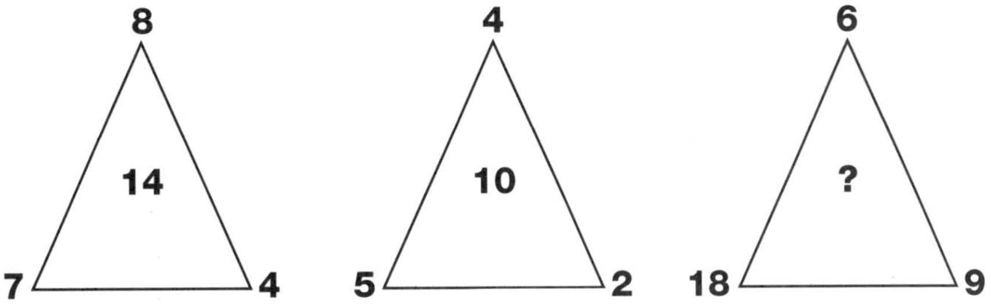

PUZZLE 46

Which number replaces the blank and completes the sequence?

18	25	4
16	20	3
6	15	

PUZZLE 47

Which number is missing from the empty circle?

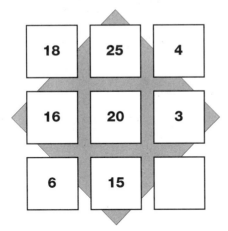

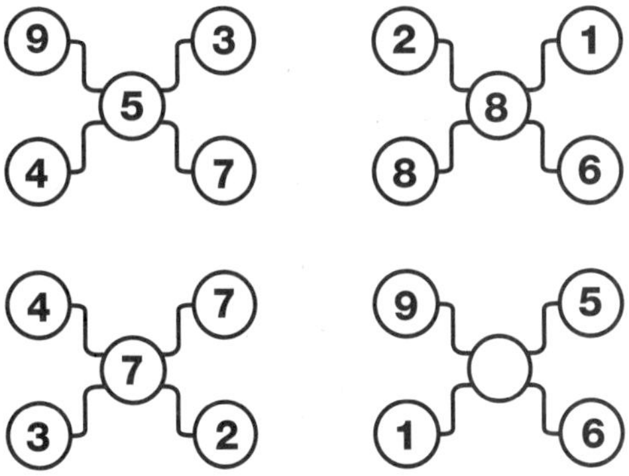

PUZZLE 48

Which number follows next?

LEVEL 8

LEVEL 8

PUZZLE 49

Which box is the odd one out?

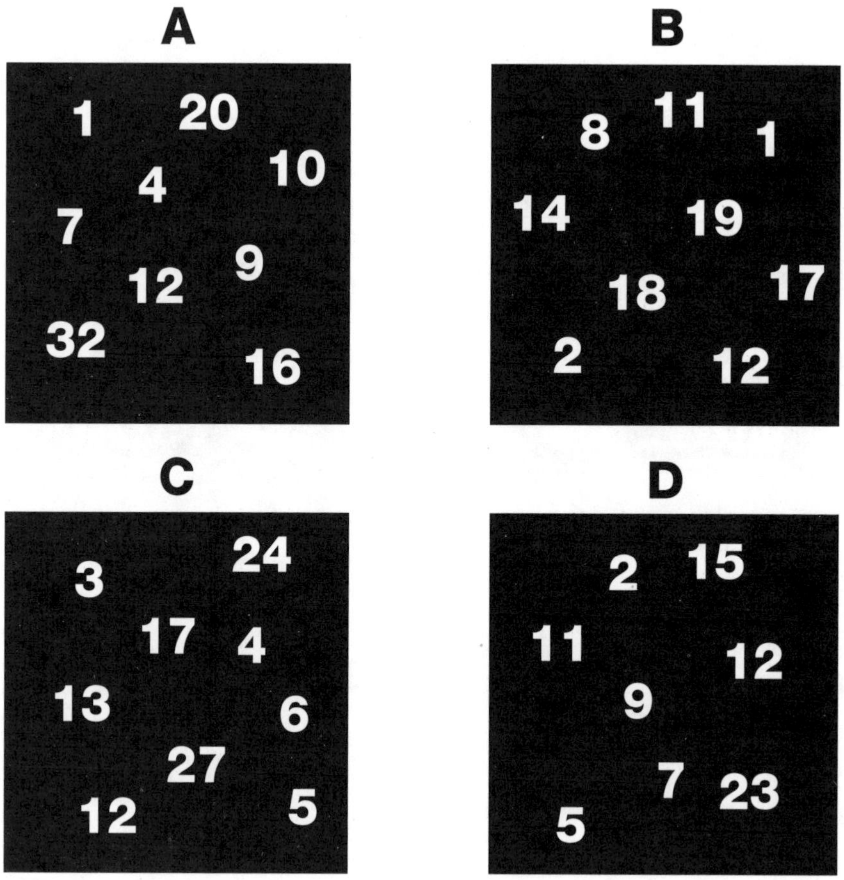

PUZZLE 50

Which letter is missing?

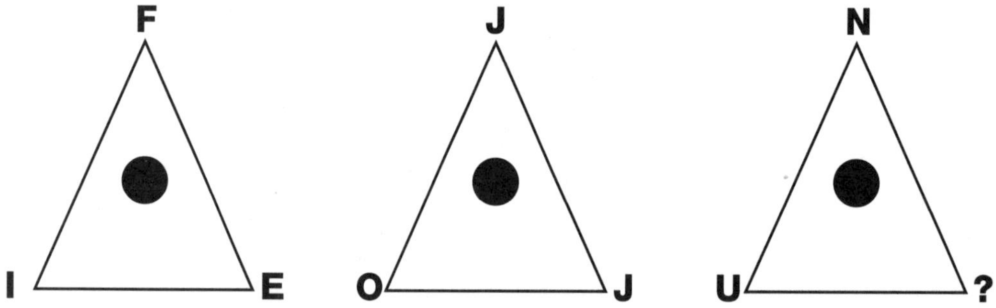

PUZZLE 51

Which letter goes in the empty segment to complete the sequence?

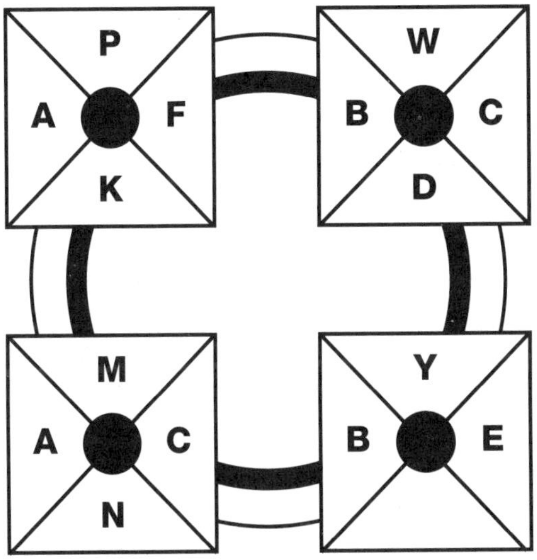

PUZZLE 52

Which number should go in the empty box?

4	7
2	2
6	9
8	12
3	1
7	

PUZZLE 53

Which letter goes in the empty circle?

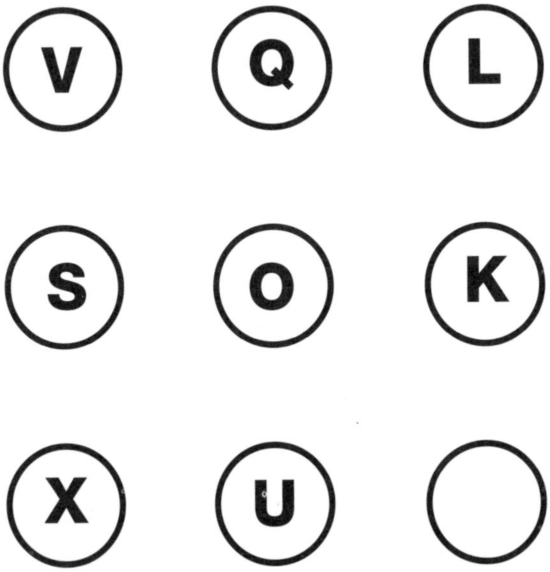

PUZZLE 54

Melinda and her father love puzzles. When Melinda's cousin asked her how old she was she told her:

"If I doubled my age and subtracted 1, it would be the same as my father's age – and if you reverse the digits of his age, you get my age."

Can you work out their ages?

LEVEL 8

55 PUZZLE

Which number goes in the empty segment?

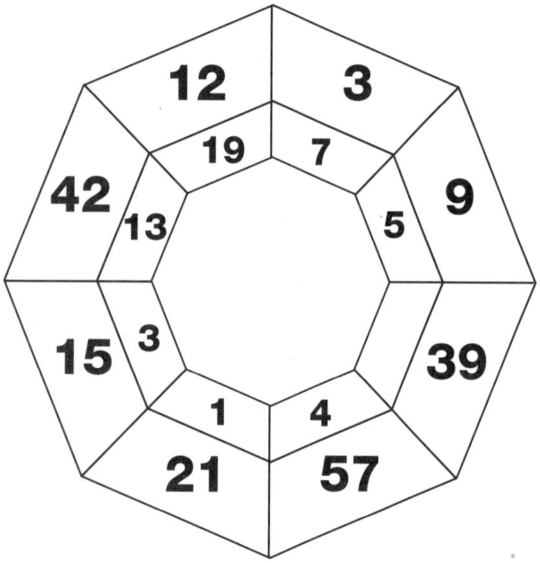

56 PUZZLE

Which number goes in the empty box?

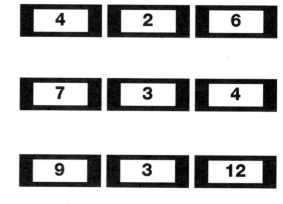

4	2	6
7	3	4
9	3	12
6	1	

57 PUZZLE

Which letter is missing from the bottom triangle?

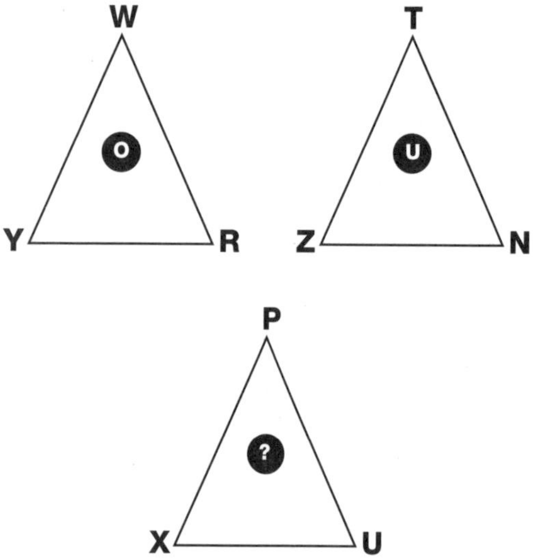

58 PUZZLE

Which number is missing from the last row?

7	8	17
3	11	16
	5	13

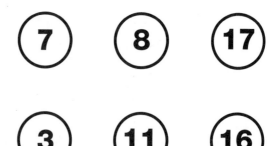

1 PUZZLE

Which is the missing piece?

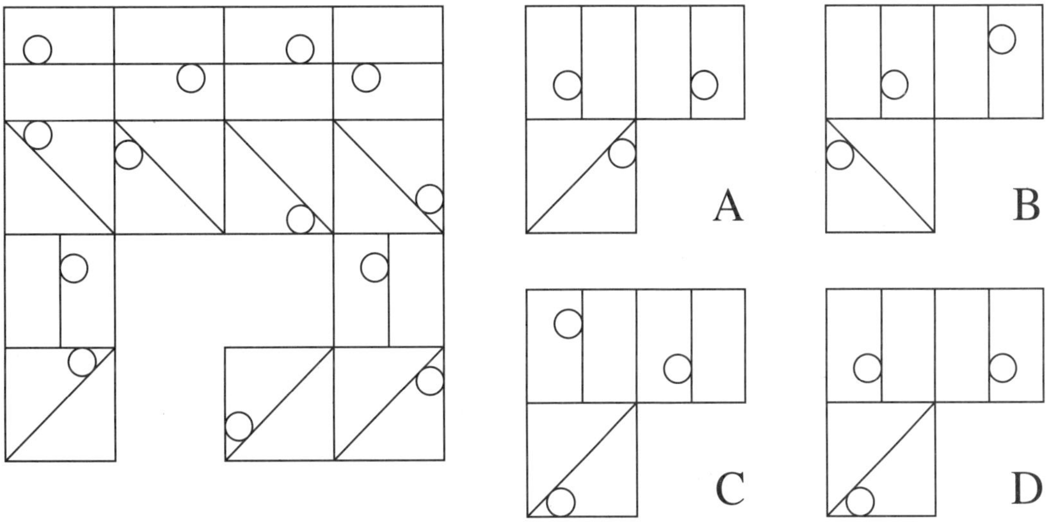

2 PUZZLE

Fill in the two missing numbers.

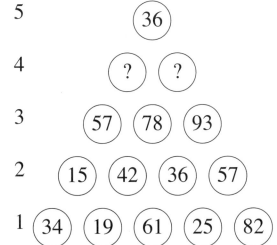

5	36				
4	?	?			
3	57	78	93		
2	15	42	36	57	
1	34	19	61	25	82

3 PUZZLE

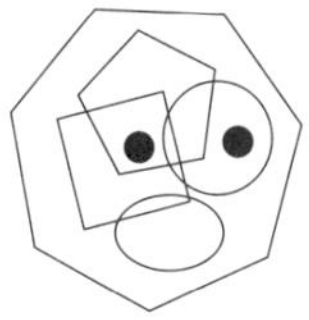

Which heptagon below has most in common with the heptagon above?

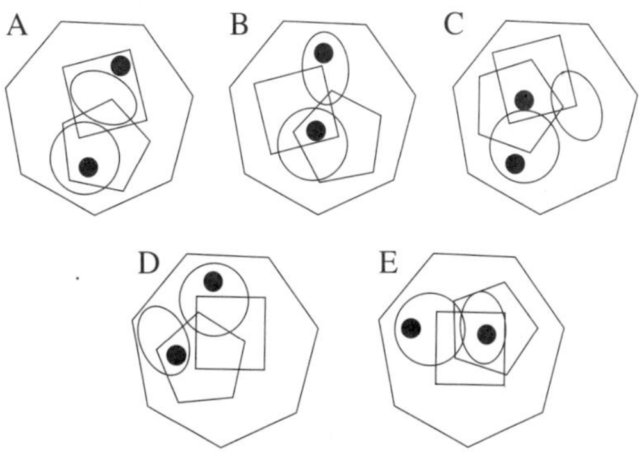

PUZZLE 4

A B C D E F G H

What letter is two letters to the left of the letter immediately to the right of the letter three letters to the left of the letter three letters to the right of the letter C?

PUZZLE 5

How many minutes is it before 12 noon if 132 minutes later it will be 3 times as many minutes before 3.00pm?

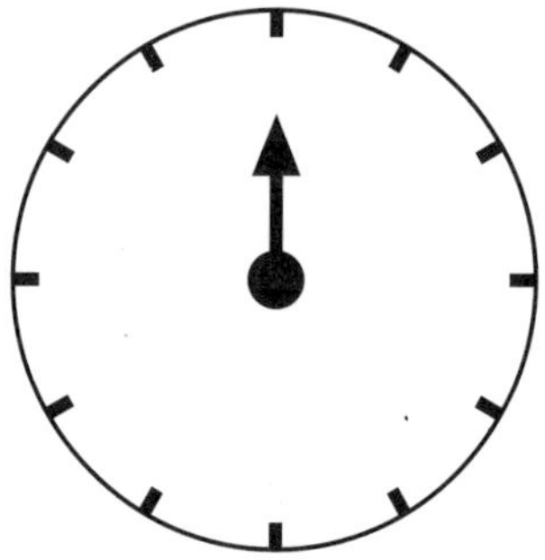

PUZZLE 6

In how many circles does a dot appear?

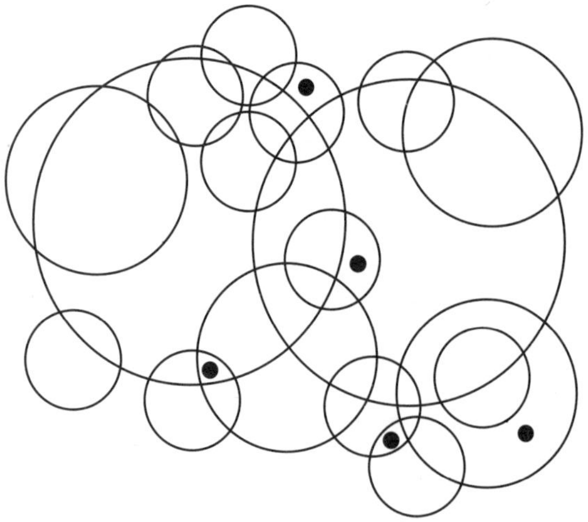

PUZZLE 7

What number should replace the question mark?

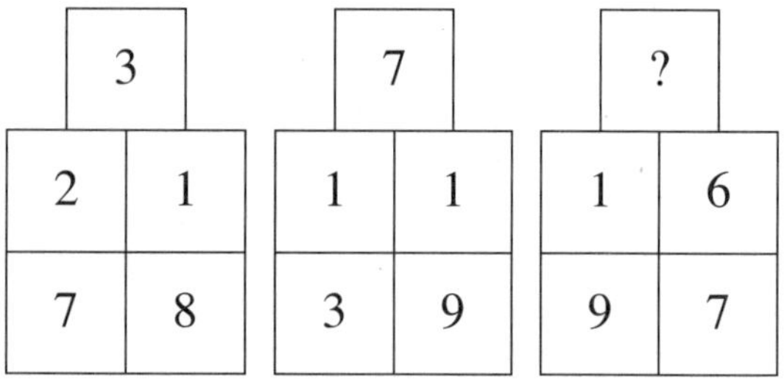

8 PUZZLE

What is the value of the second line?

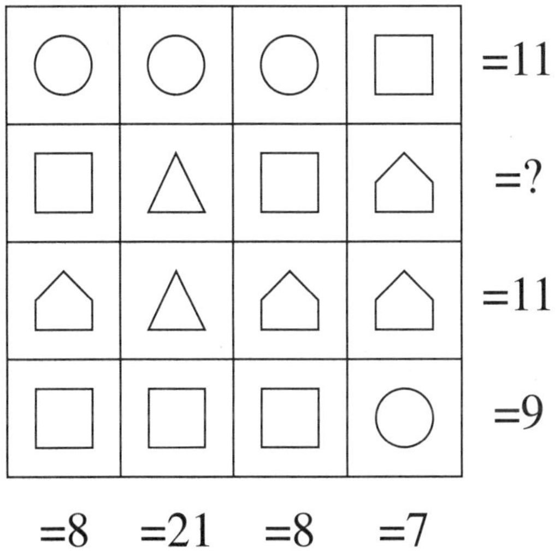

9 PUZZLE

What number should replace the question mark?

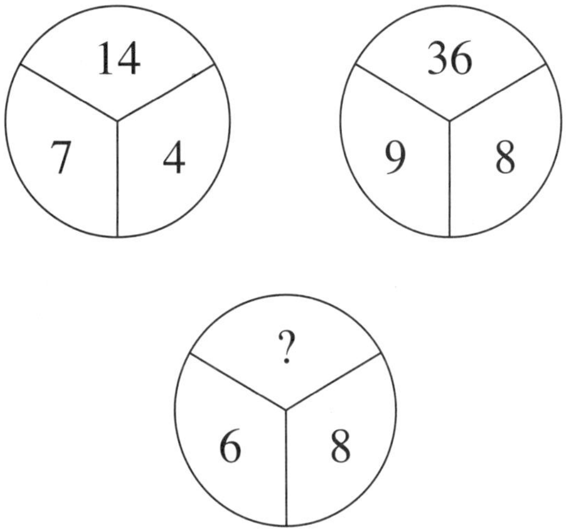

10 PUZZLE

How many lines appear below?

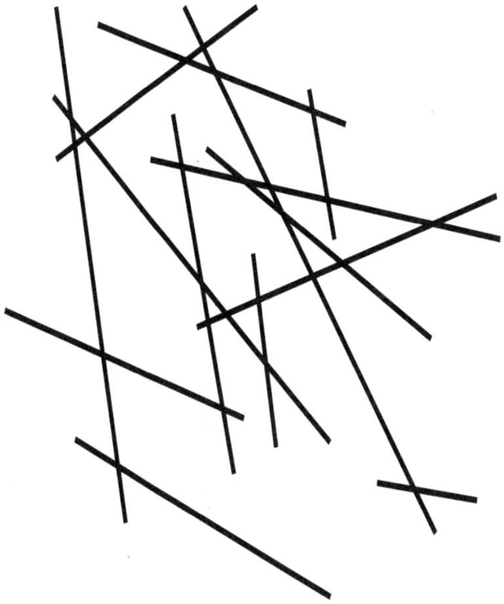

11 PUZZLE

How many triangles in this figure?

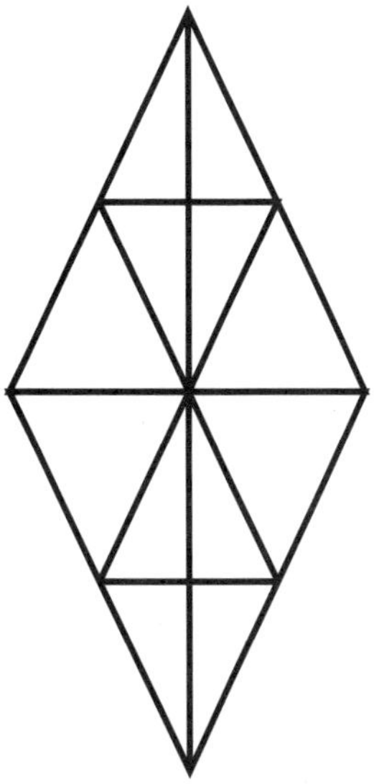

12 PUZZLE

Each line and symbol which appears in the four outer circles, below, is transferred to the centre circle according to these rules: If a line or symbol occurs in the outer circles: once: it is transferred twice: it is possibly transferred 3 times: it is transferred 4 times: it is not transferred. Which of the circles A, B, C, D or E, should appear at the centre of the diagram, below?

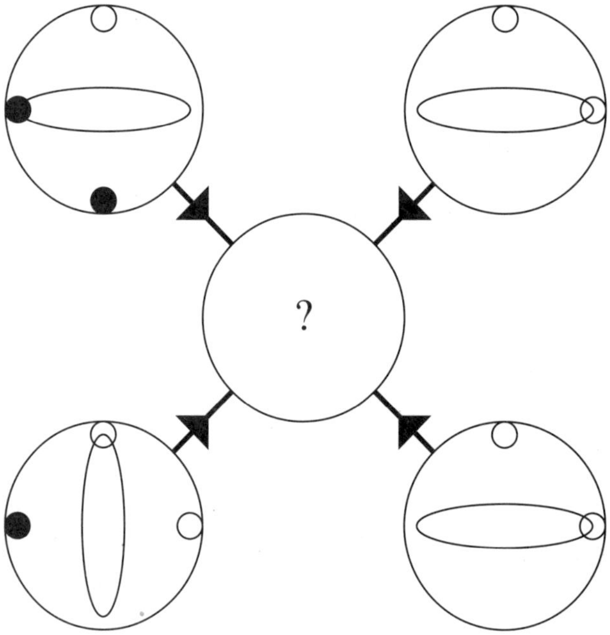

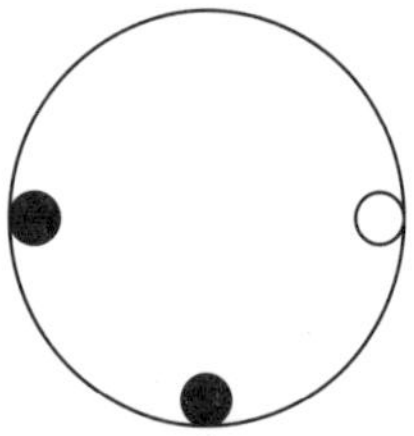
A

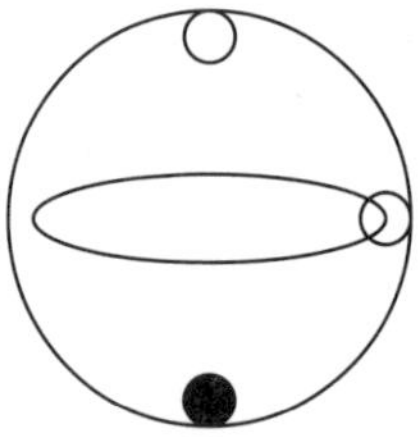
B

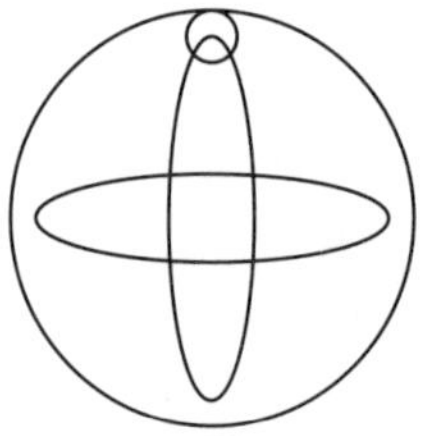
C

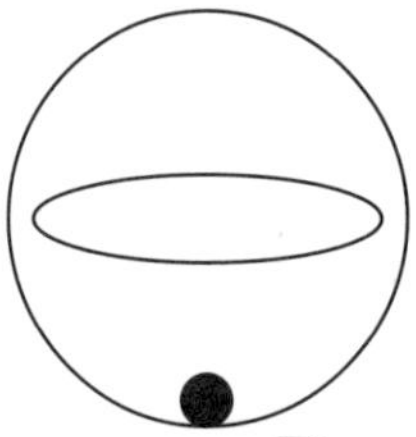
D

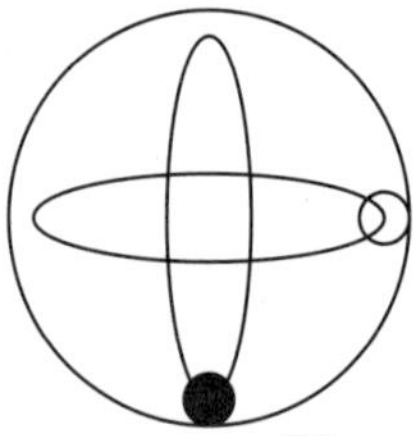
E

13 PUZZLE

This grid consists of 3 squares marked A-B-C and 3 squares marked 1-2-3. The nine inner squares should incorporate the lines and symbols in the letter above and also the lines and symbols in the number to the left. One of the nine squares is incorrect. Which is it?

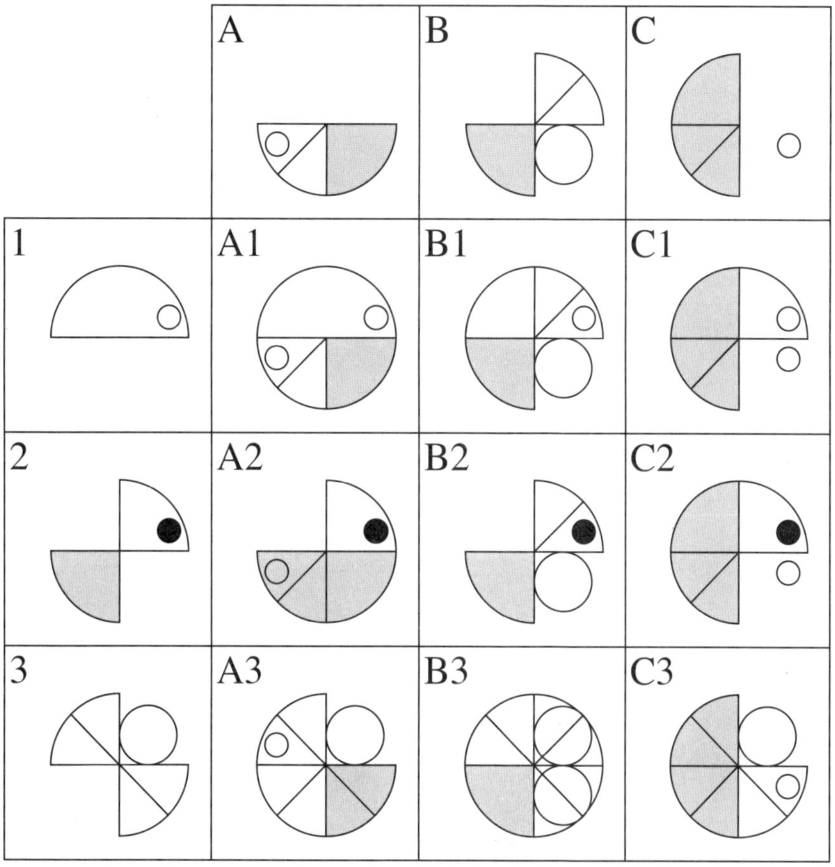

14 PUZZLE

What number replaces the question mark?

17	14	26
18 2 54	19 3 90	19 ? 55
16	9	35

15 PUZZLE

Which hexagon A, B, C, D or E should replace the question mark?

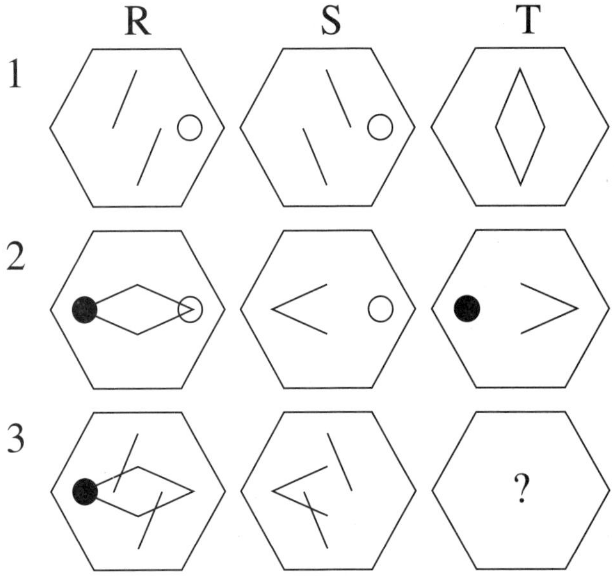

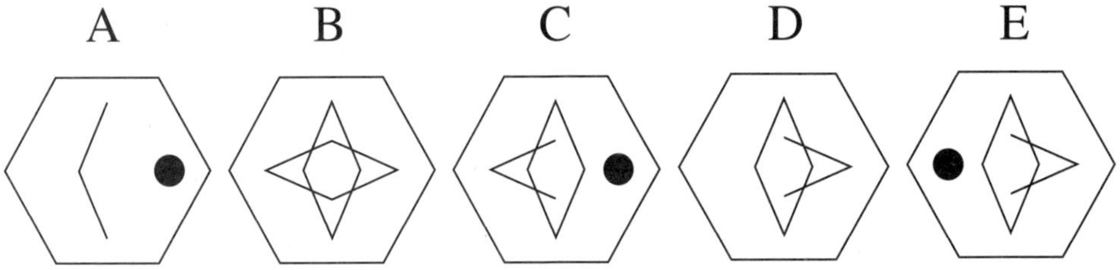

16 PUZZLE

What number should replace the question mark?

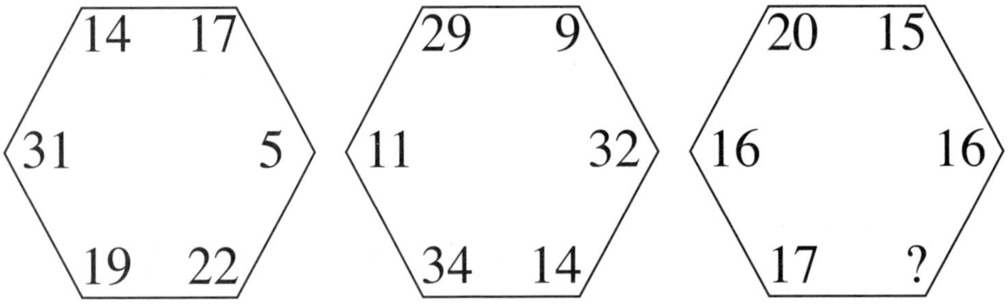

LEVEL 9

17 PUZZLE

Which is the odd one out?

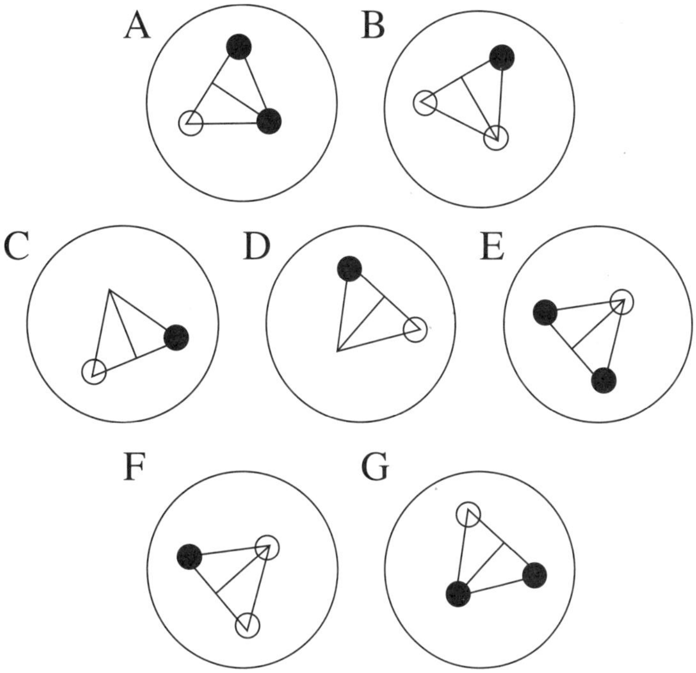

18 PUZZLE

What number should replace the question mark?

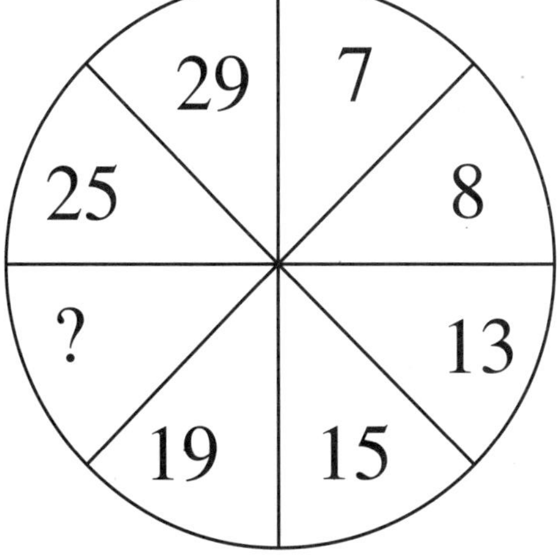

19 PUZZLE

What number will replace the question mark?

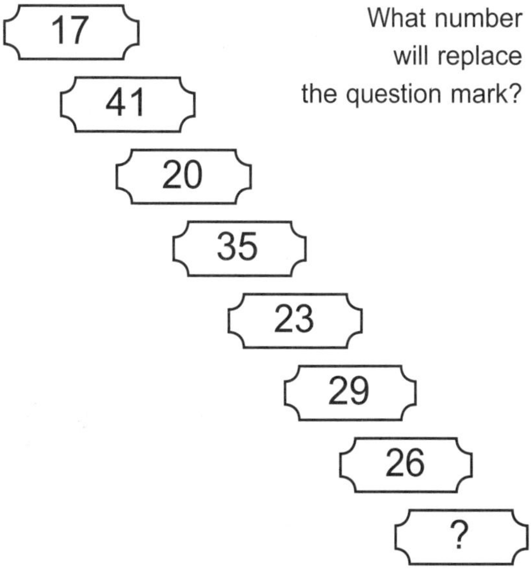

20 PUZZLE

2 stations (A and B) have 4 stations between them. How many tickets must be issued so that a passenger can move from any station to another?

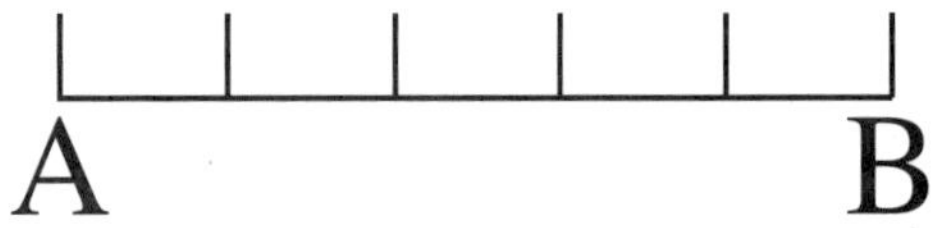

21 PUZZLE

How many different arrangements of the word LONDON can you make?

22 PUZZLE

Simplify and find the value for x.

$$3 \times 7 \times 14 - (8 - 5) - (12 \div 4) = X$$

23 PUZZLE

By which fraction does $^{19}/_{36}$ exceed a $^{1}/_{2}$?

24 PUZZLE

At the State Fair eating contest the winner ate an average of 15 hot dogs at the first 20 sittings. After a further 20 sittings the average increased to 20 hot dogs. What was the average for the last 20 sittings?

25 PUZZLE

Which playing card should replace the question mark?

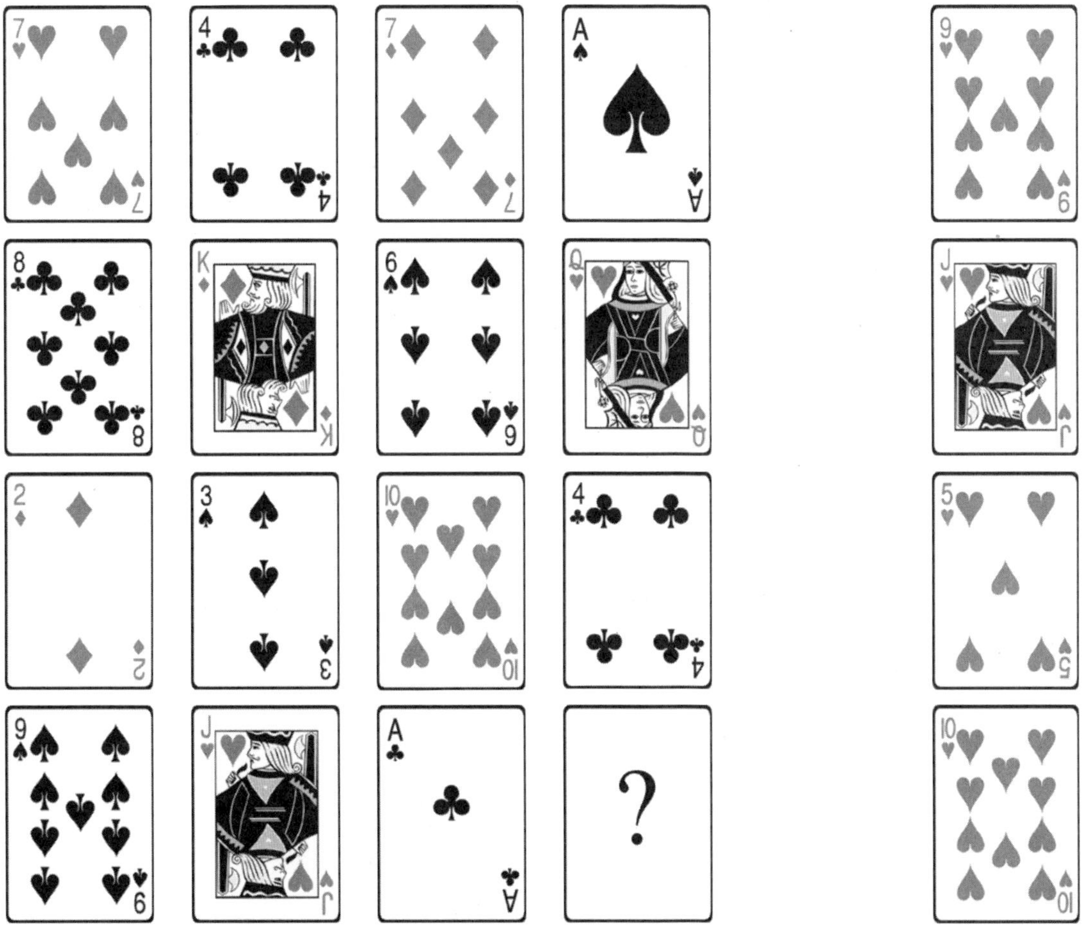

26 PUZZLE

Which number is missing from the centre of the last star?

27 PUZZLE

Which number comes next in this sequence?

9 - 7 - 8 - 6 - 7 - 5 - 6 - ?

28 PUZZLE

Which letter is missing from the blank segment?

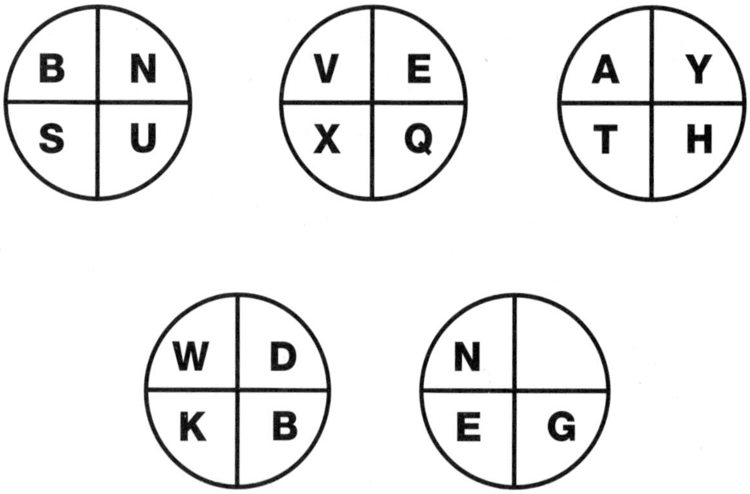

PUZZLE 29

Which number completes this puzzle?

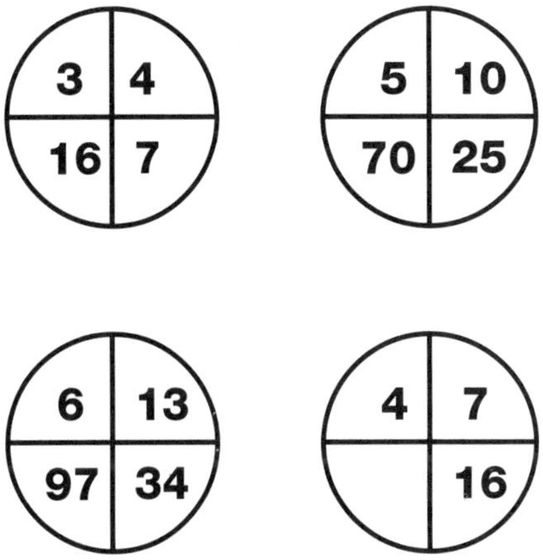

PUZZLE 30

Which number is missing from the last wheel?

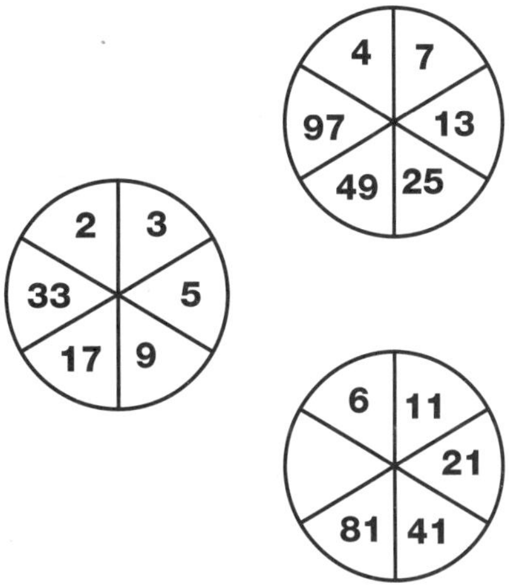

PUZZLE 31

Fill in the blank point of the third star.

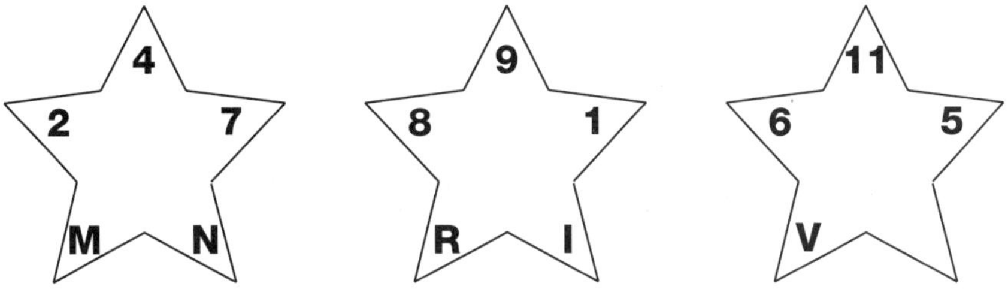

PUZZLE 32

Which number is missing from the last triangle?

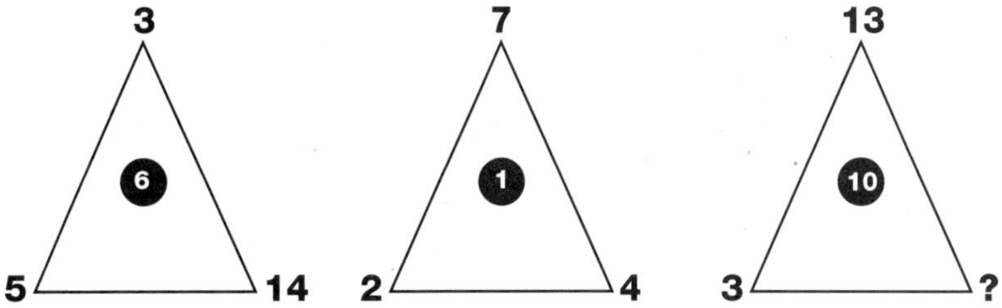

LEVEL

9

33 PUZZLE

Which number goes in the middle of the grid?

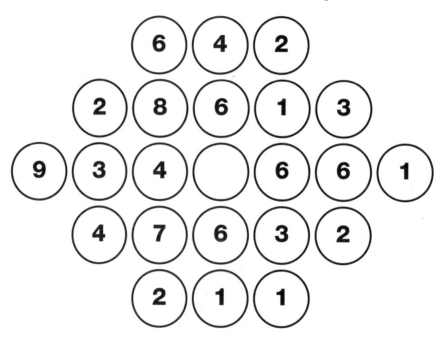

		6	4	2		
	2	8	6	1	3	
9	3	4		6	6	1
	4	7	6	3	2	
		2	1	1		

2 3 4 5 6 7 8 9

34 PUZZLE

Which number is missing?

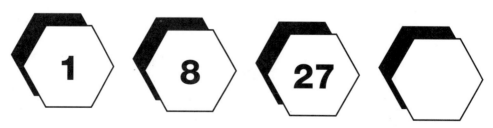

1 8 27

35 PUZZLE

Which letter replaces the blank and completes the sequence?

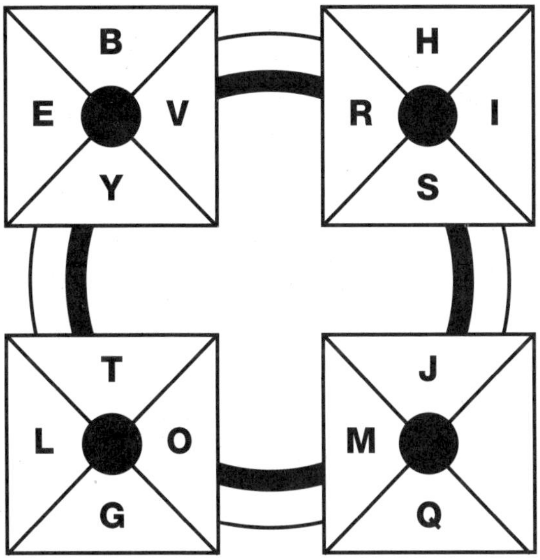

36 PUZZLE

Which number logically completes the grid?

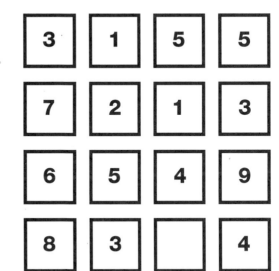

3	1	5	5
7	2	1	3
6	5	4	9
8	3		4

37 PUZZLE

Which letter is missing from around the centre of the wheel?

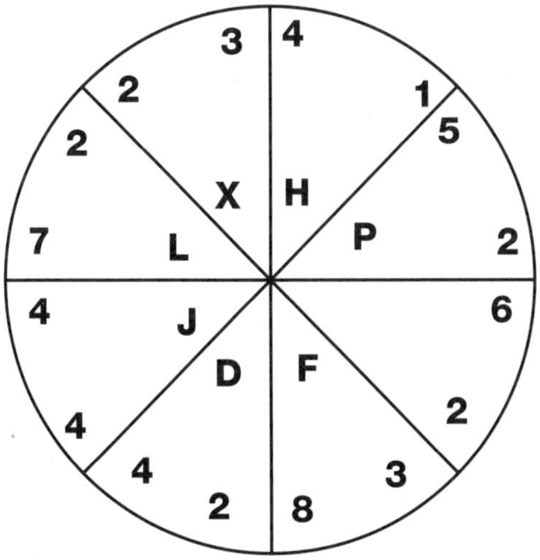

38 PUZZLE

Which letter goes in the empty box?

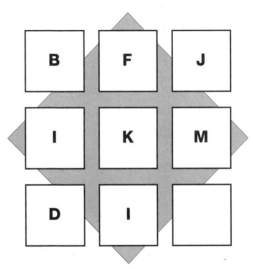

B	F	J
I	K	M
D	I	

39 PUZZLE

Which letter goes in the centre?

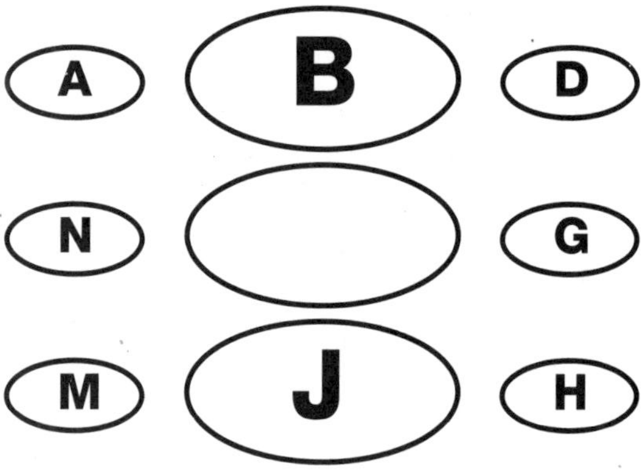

40 PUZZLE

Which number is missing from the wheel?

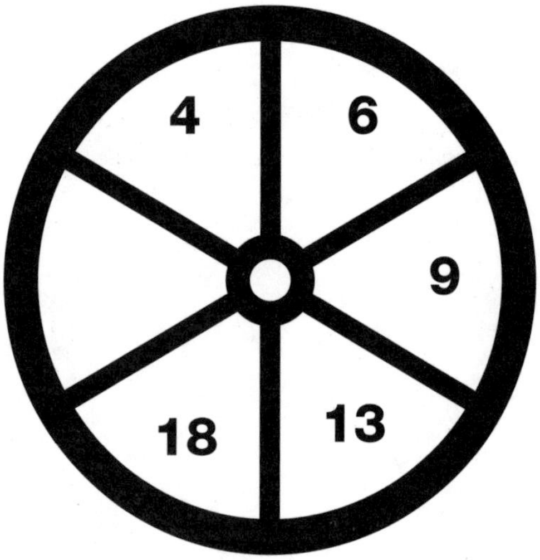

41 PUZZLE

Which of the bottom boxes completes the sequence?

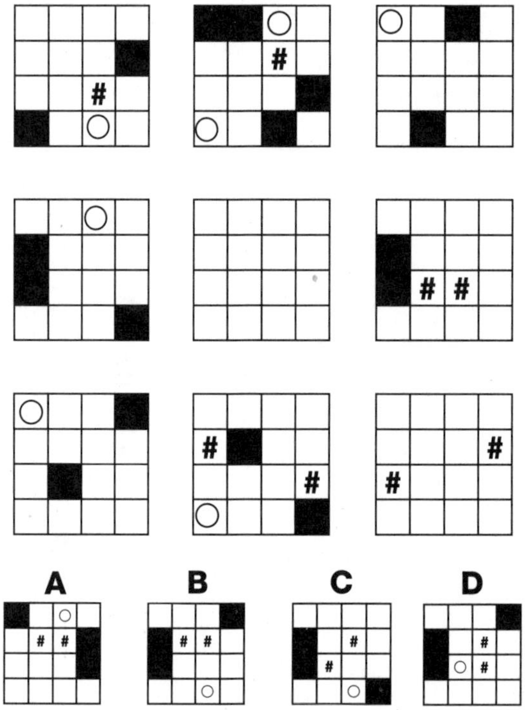

42 PUZZLE

Which playing cards complete the sequence?

43 PUZZLE

Which of the bottom boxes completes this sequence?

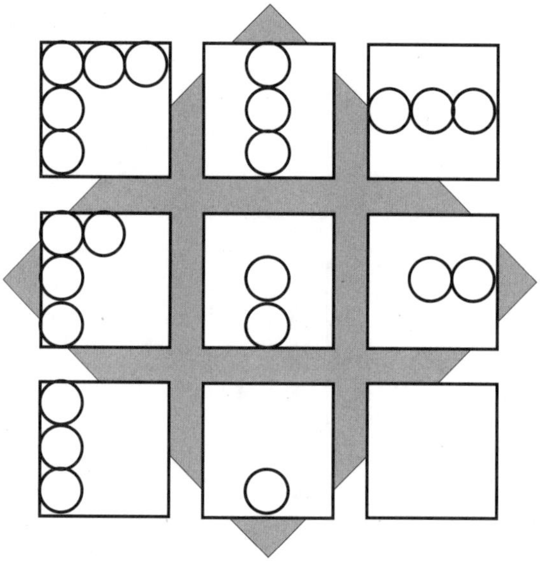

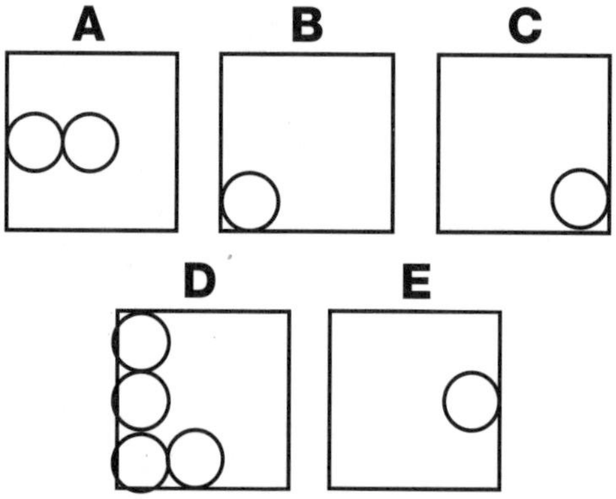

44 PUZZLE

Which number is missing?

45 PUZZLE

Which letter replaces the blank and completes the puzzle?

A	C	F
J	L	O
S	U	

46 PUZZLE

Find the missing value.

24	63	24	21	
@	@	@	!	33
!	Σ	!	Ω	?
Ω	Σ	Ω	Ω	33
!	!	!	@	27

47 PUZZLE

Using these six matches, make three squares all the same size.

48 PUZZLE

Which number is missing from the empty segment?

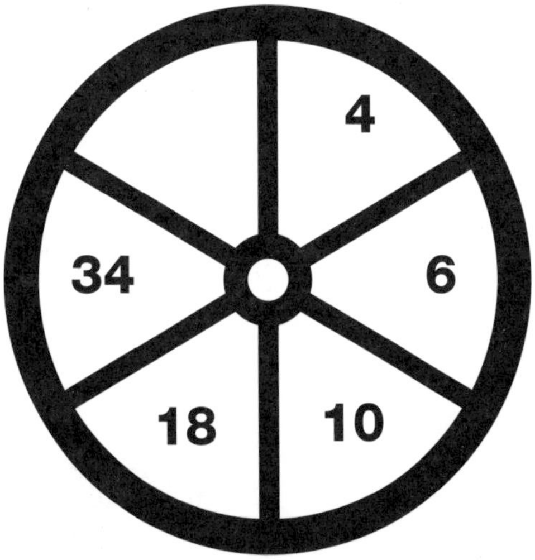

LEVEL 9

PUZZLE 49

Which number is missing?

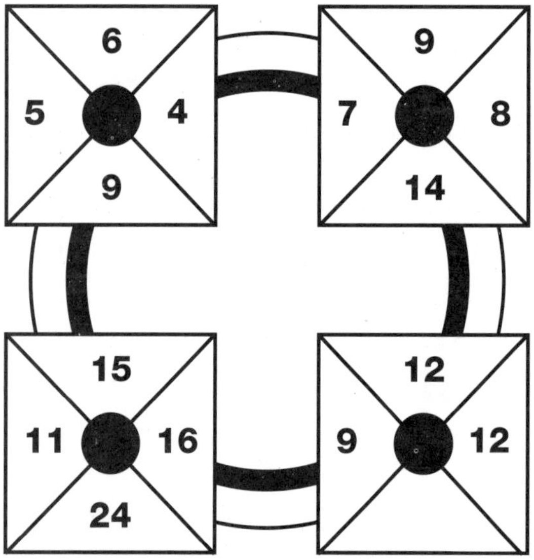

PUZZLE 50

Becky had a large packet of biscuits. After eating the first one she gave half of what she had left to her friend Ella. After eating another one, she gave half of what was left to Chelsea, leaving her with just 5 biscuits.

How many biscuits were in the packet to start with?

PUZZLE 51

Which letter is missing from the last star?

PUZZLE 52

Which letter replaces the question mark?

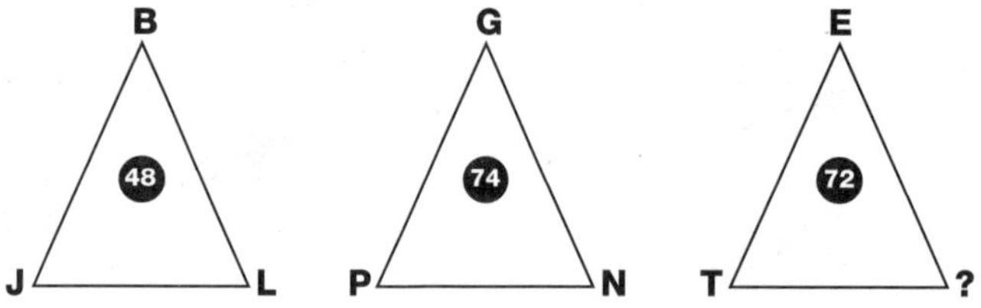

LEVEL 10

1 PUZZLE

How many circles appear below?

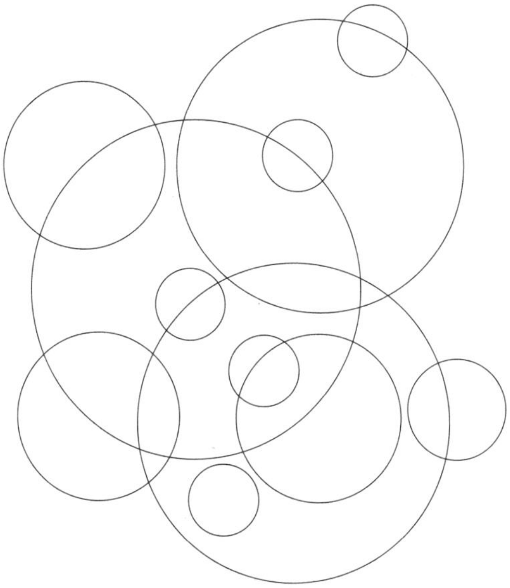

2 PUZZLE

A train travelling at a speed of 80 mph enters a tunnel that is 0.5 miles long. The length of the train is 0.25 miles. How long does it take for all of the train to pass through the tunnel, from the moment the front enters, to the moment the rear emerges?

3 PUZZLE

36 (36) 42

54 (25) 49

72 (?) 61

What number should replace the question mark?

4 PUZZLE

Which is the missing tile?

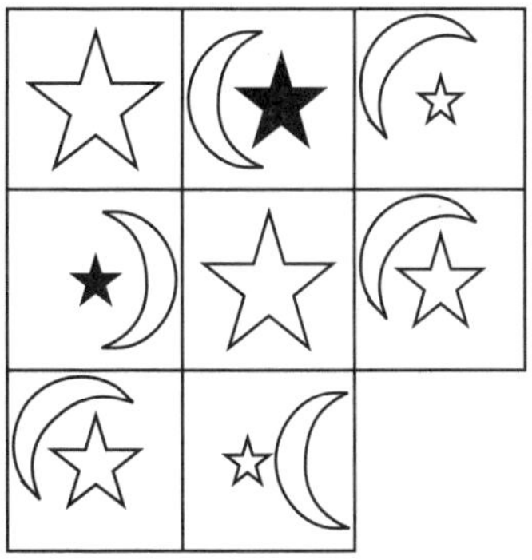

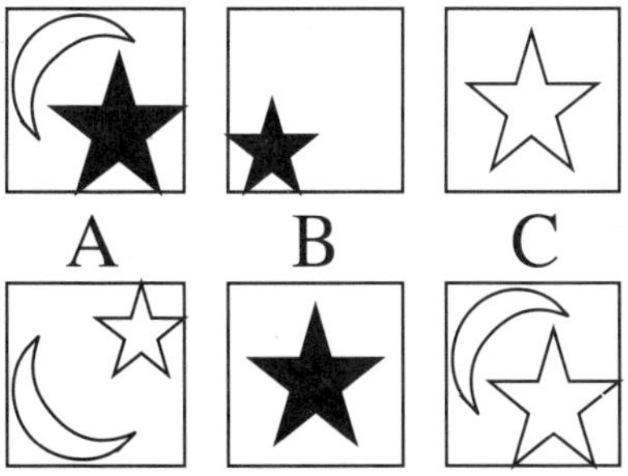

A B C

D E F

PUZZLE 5

In a horse race, the first 5 places were filled by horses 4, 1, 3, 2 and 5 in that order. The jockey of horse 4 wore a green shirt, the jockey of horse 1 wore red, jockey 3 wore yellow and jockey 2 wore orange. Did jockey 5 wear purple, white, blue or black?

PUZZLE 6

A B C D E F G H

What letter is two letters after the letter immediately after the letter four letters before the letter two letters after the letter E?

PUZZLE 7

What is the missing tile?

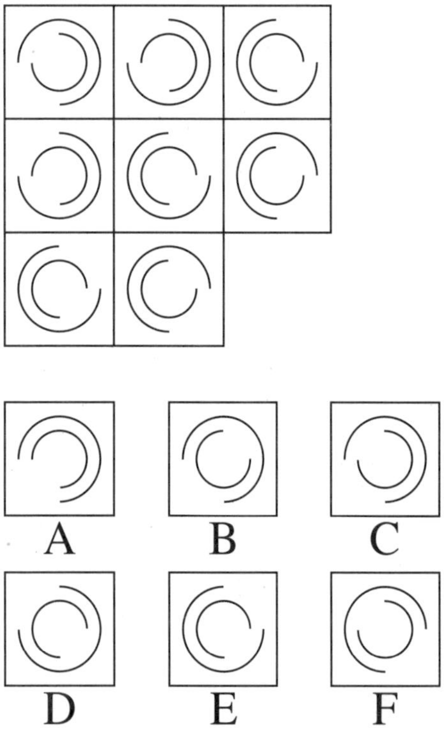

PUZZLE 8

What letter should replace the question mark?

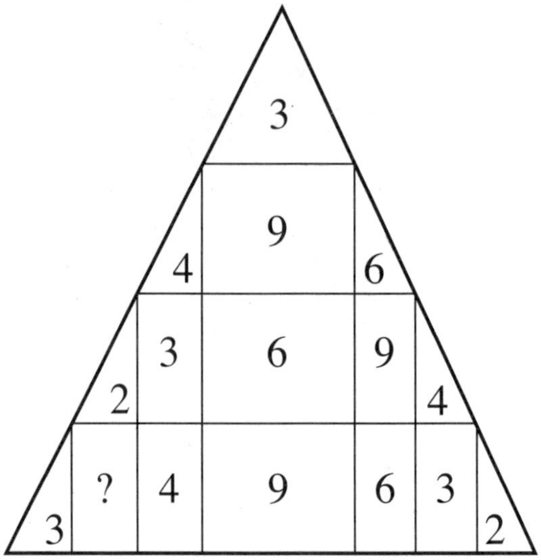

PUZZLE 9

What number is missing?

74286

28674

67428

?

86742

PUZZLE 10

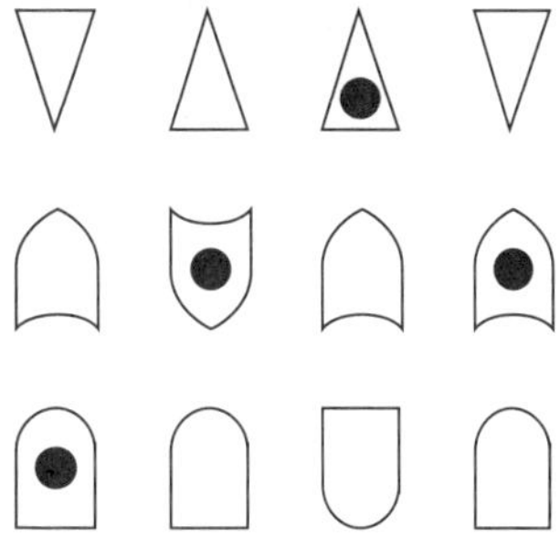

What comes next?

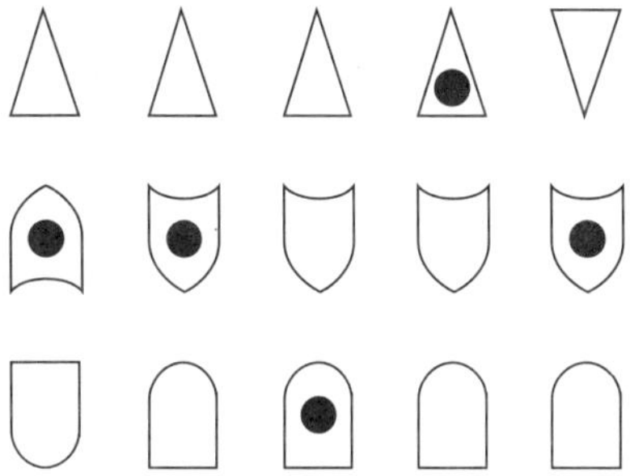

A B C D E

PUZZLE 11

What is the largest rectangle that can be cut from this piece of timber, in one piece?

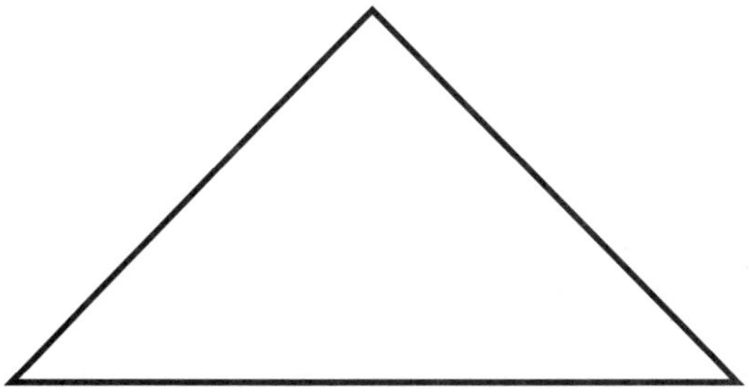

PUZZLE 12

There were 12 runners in the marathon. They lined up as follows.

8 5 4 46 52 61
7 6 9 94 63 ?

What number should the 12th runner have?

13 PUZZLE

Each line and symbol which appears in the four outer circles, below, is transferred to the centre circle according to these rules. If a line or symbol occurs in the outer circles once, it is transferred; if it occurs twice, it is possibly transferred; three times, it is transferred; four times, it is not transferred. Which of the circles A, B, C, D or E, should appear at the centre of the diagram, below?

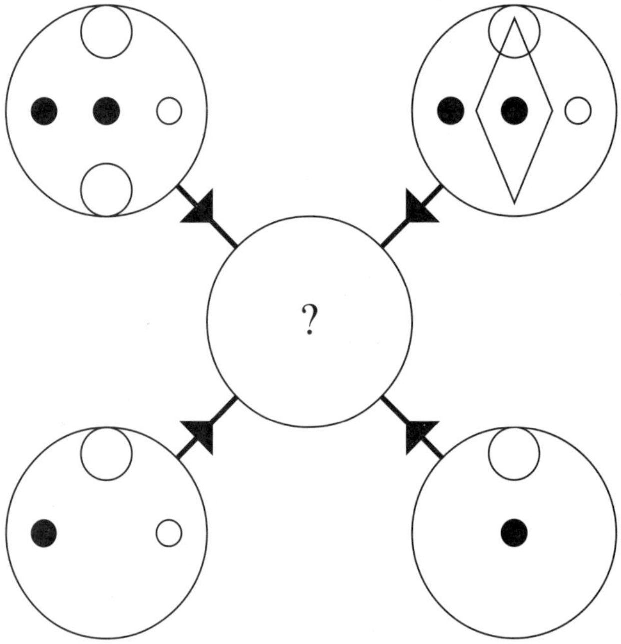

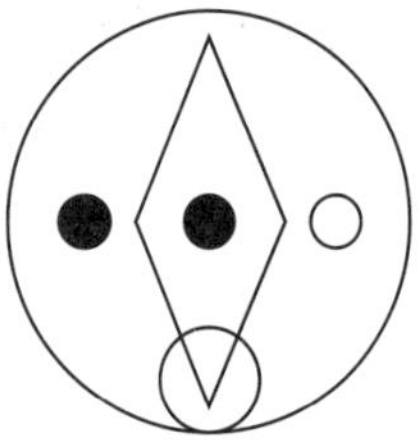
A

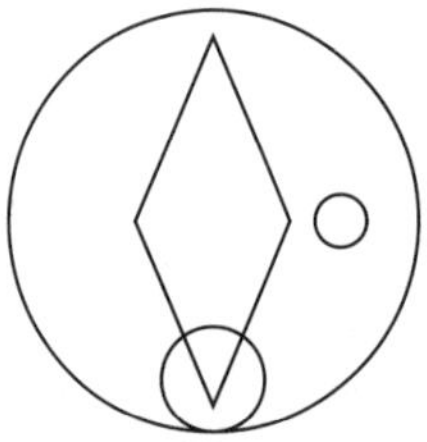
B

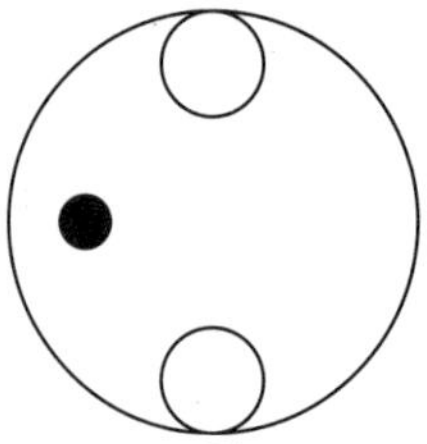
C

D

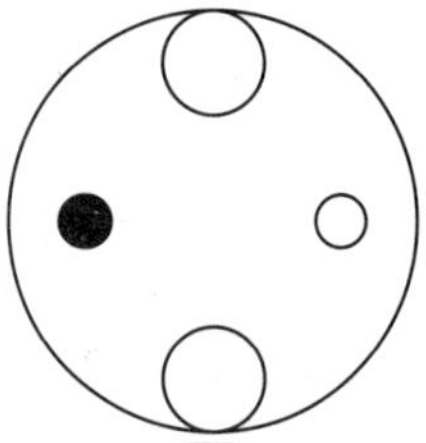
E

14 PUZZLE

Each of the nine squares in the grid marked A1 to C3, should incorporate all the lines and symbols which are shown in the squares of the same letter and number immediately above and to the left. For example, B2 should incorporate all the lines and symbols that are in 2 and B. One of the squares is incorrect. Which one is it?

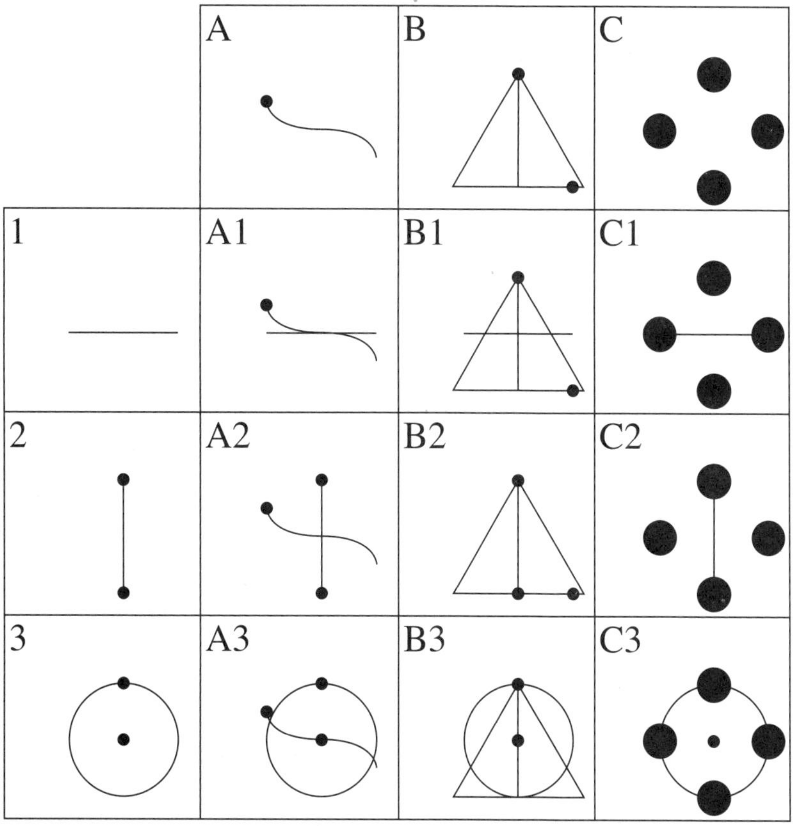

15 PUZZLE

What number should replace the question mark?

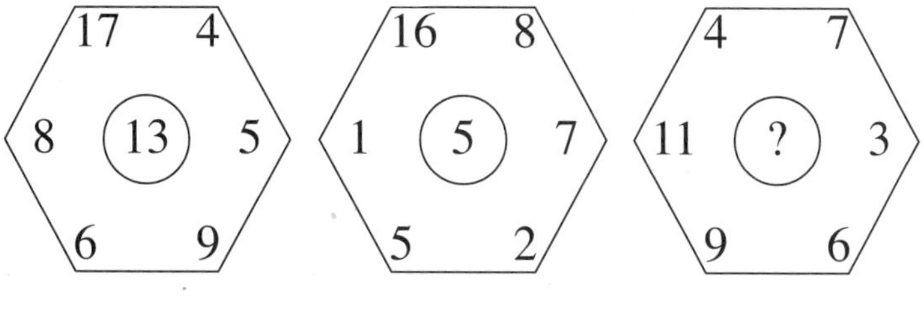

16 PUZZLE

Which hexagon A, B, C, D or E should replace the question mark?

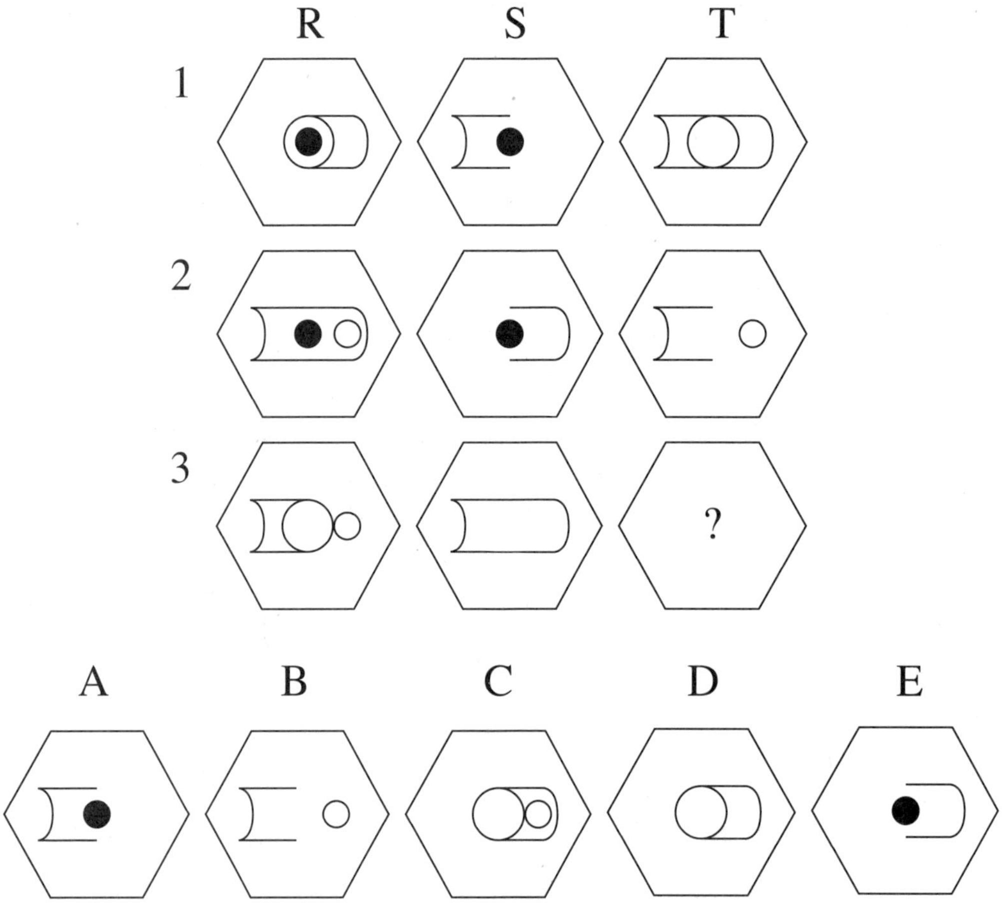

17 PUZZLE

What number should replace the question mark?

16		14	37		15	29		3
	10			6			?	
10		4	8		10	18		10

18 PUZZLE

I went into a furniture shop in order to buy a picture. The salesman told me: "The picture is five times the cost of that ashtray, the chair is 30 times the cost of the ashtray, the table is 4 times the cost of the chair, you can buy the lot for $312." What was the price of the picture?

19 PUZZLE

What number should replace the question mark?

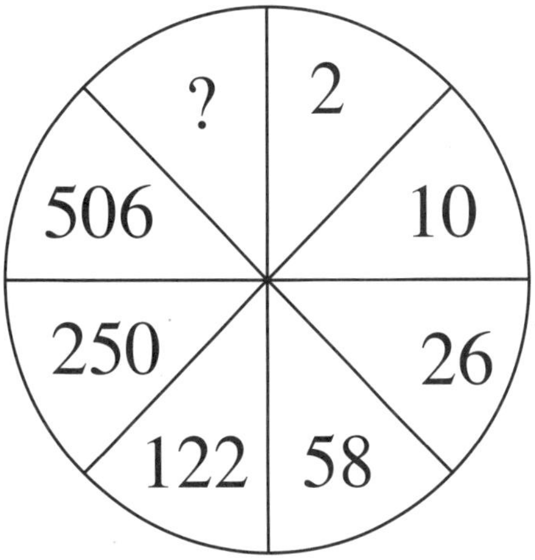

20 PUZZLE

Which is the odd one out?

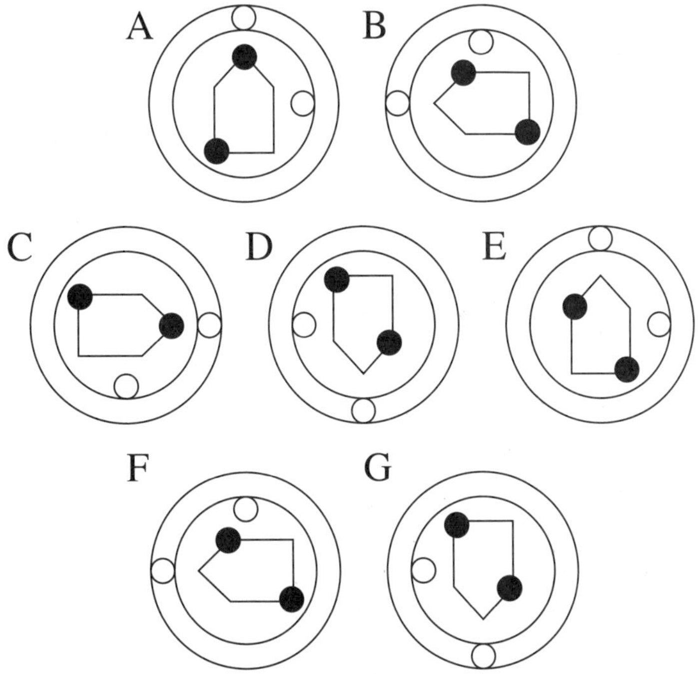

21 PUZZLE

How many squares are there on an 8x8 chess board?

22 PUZZLE

A school challenged a neighbouring school to a hockey match. The team to consist of 6 boys + 5 girls. The squad consisted of 8 boys + 6 girls. How many different teams could they field?

23 PUZZLE

The invoice read "Wine" " - 67.9 - " The first and last digits were missing. There were 72 bottles. How much did each cost? (Each bottle cost the same).

24 PUZZLE

Three women, Mrs Black, Mrs Red, Mrs Brown, met in the hairdresser's. One of them said, "I have black hair and you two have red hair and brown hair, but none of us has the hair colour that matches her name." Mrs Brown responded, "You are quite right." What colour is Mrs Red's hair?

25 PUZZLE

Which playing card should replace the question mark?

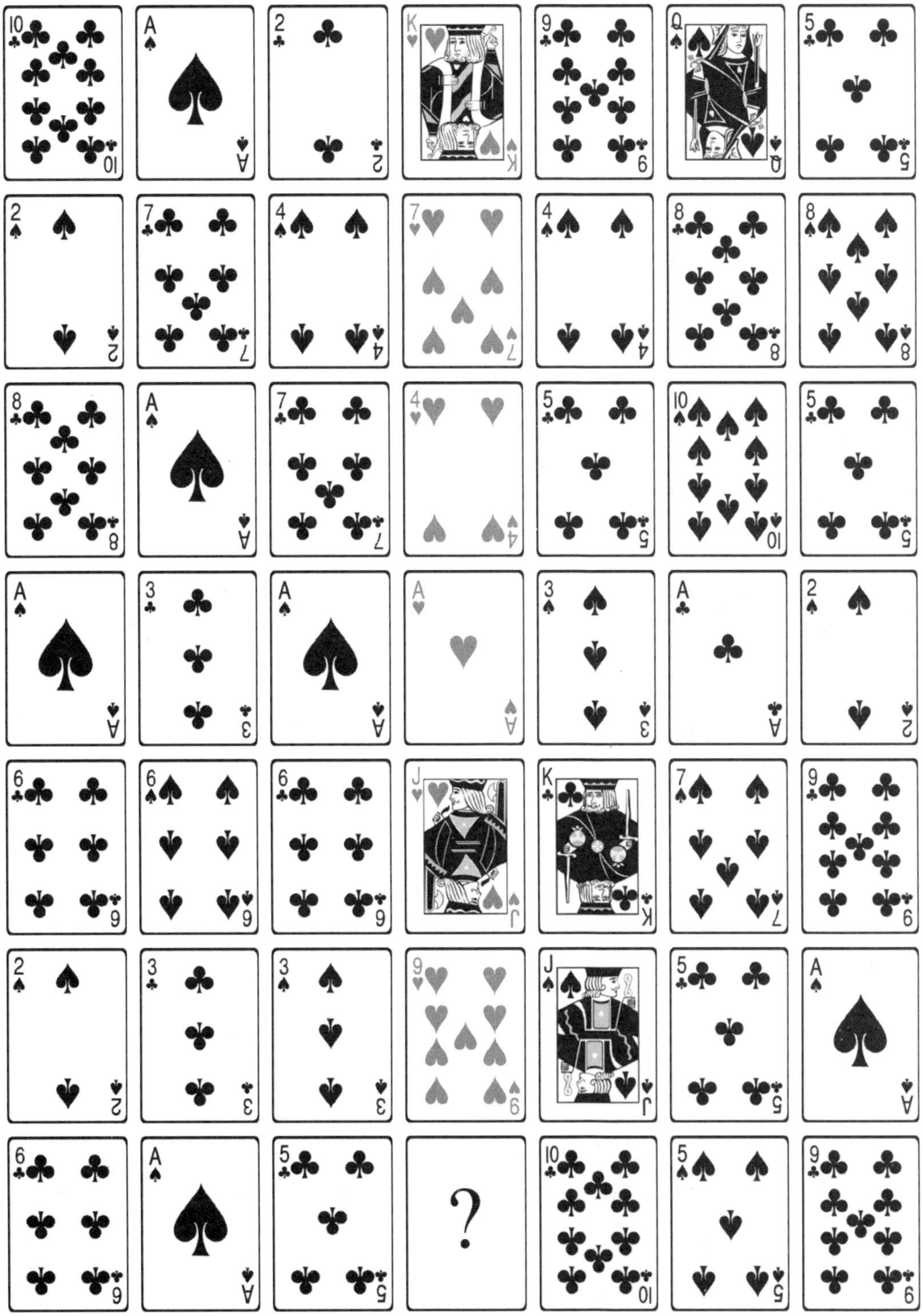

LEVEL 10

LEVEL 10

26 PUZZLE

Which letter goes in the empty circle?

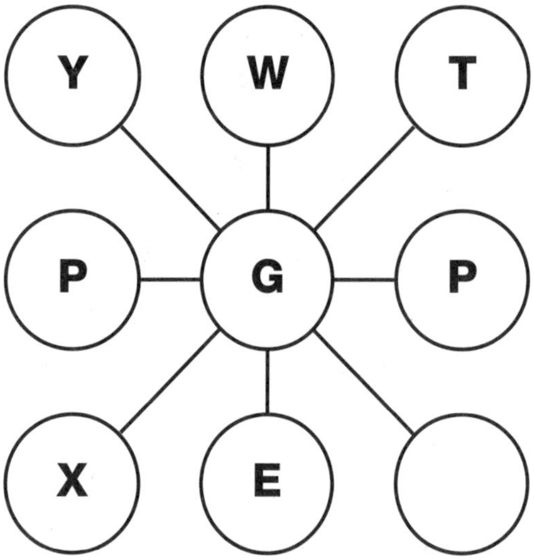

27 PUZZLE

Which letter goes in the empty box at the bottom of the pile?

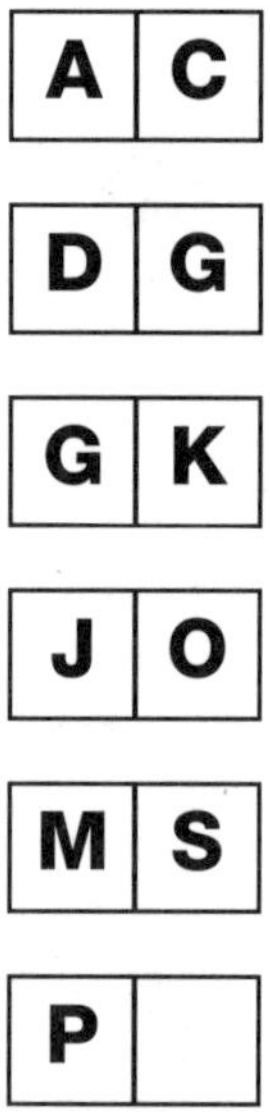

28 PUZZLE

Which number is missing from the empty segment?

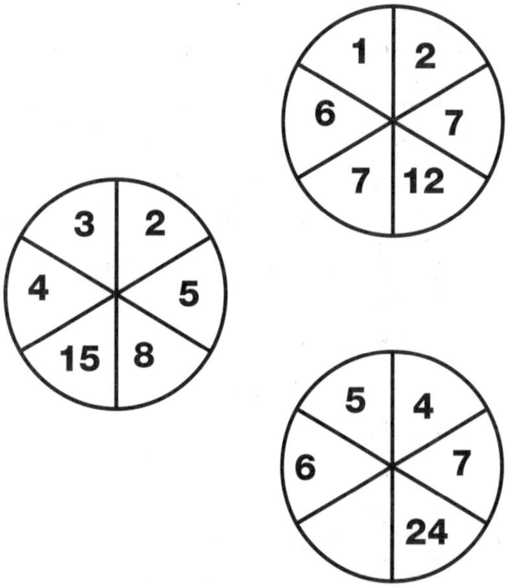

29 PUZZLE

Which number comes next to continue this sequence?

30 PUZZLE

Which letter is missing from the empty segment in the bottom circle?

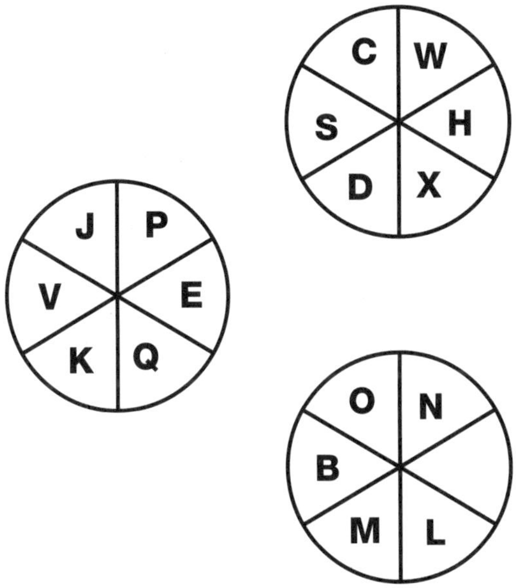

31 PUZZLE

Which number replaces the question mark?

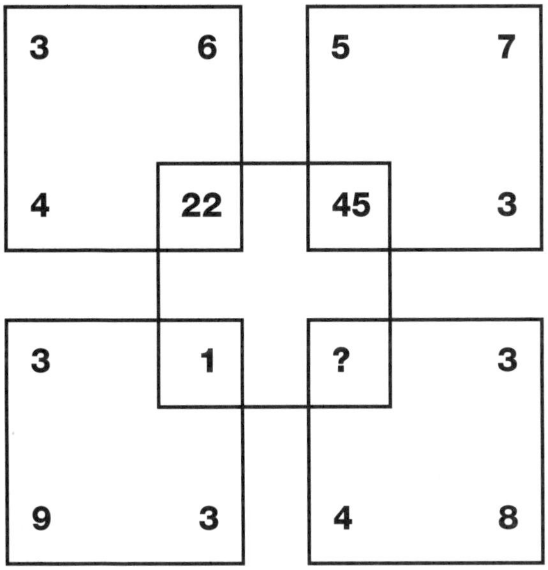

32 PUZZLE

Which number goes in the blank box and completes the puzzle?

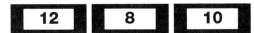

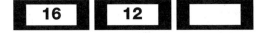

7	3	5
12	8	10
11	7	9
16	12	

33 PUZZLE

Which letter goes in the empty segment?

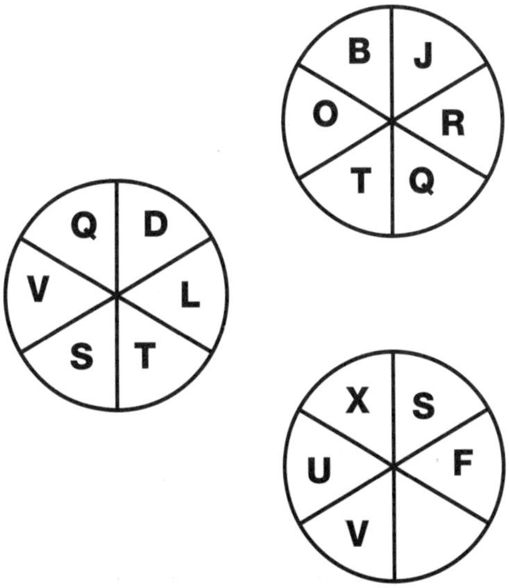

LEVEL 10

34 PUZZLE

Which letter finishes the third circle?

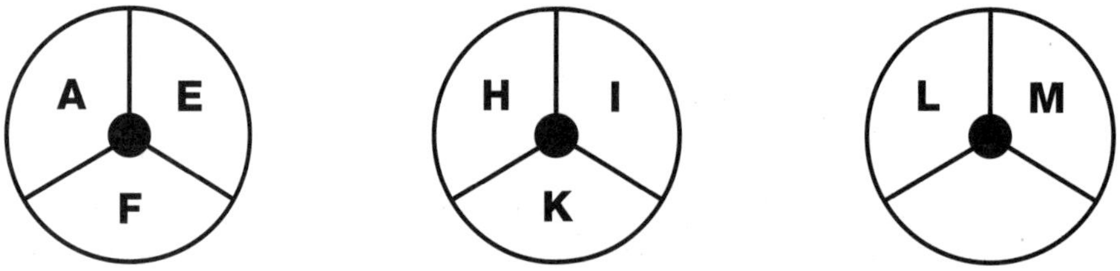

35 PUZZLE

Which number is missing from the last grid?

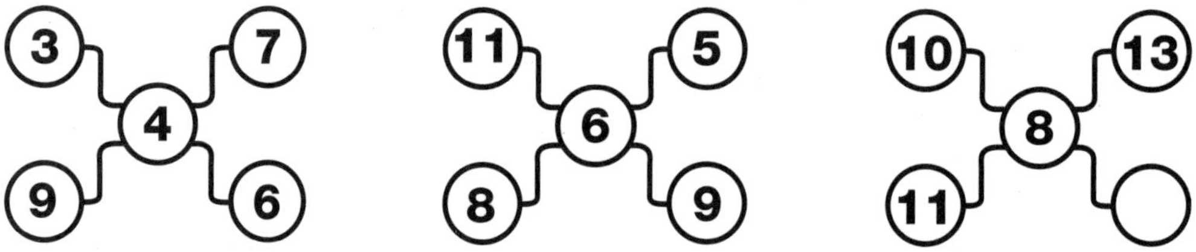

36 PUZZLE

Which number replaces the question mark?

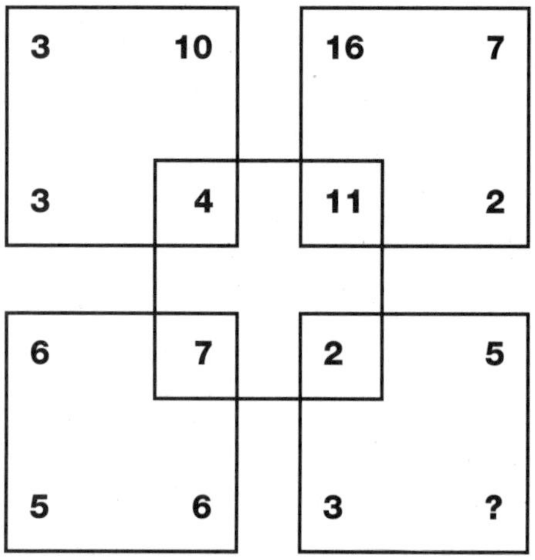

37 PUZZLE

Complete this puzzle.

A	B	B
G	B	E
Q		Y

PUZZLE 38

Which of the bottom boxes completes this sequence?

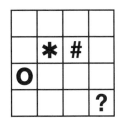

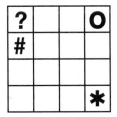

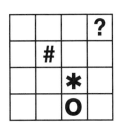

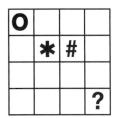

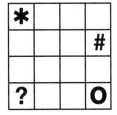

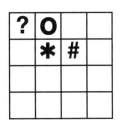

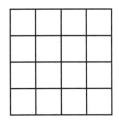

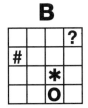

*			?
			#
O			

	*	#	
O			
			?

O			
	#		
		*	
?			

?			O
#			
			*

			?
	#		
		*	
		O	

O			
	*	#	
			?

*			
			#
?			O

?	O		
	*	#	

A

*			
	#		
O			?

B

			?
#			
		*	
		O	

C

?			
	*		#
		O	

D

?			
	*		#
			O

E

			?
	#		
		*	
O			

F

?		O	
	#		
		*	

LEVEL 10

39 PUZZLE

Which letter finishes the third circle?

40 PUZZLE

Which number completes the last grid?

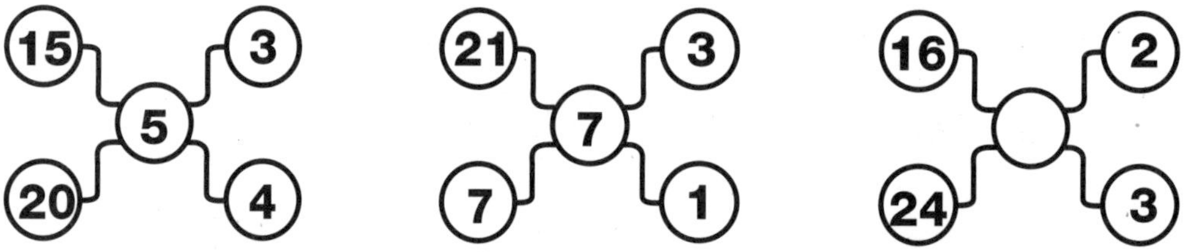

41 PUZZLE

Which number goes in the empty box?

3	11	7
4	14	6
9	7	2
10	62	

42 PUZZLE

Which letter completes this puzzle?

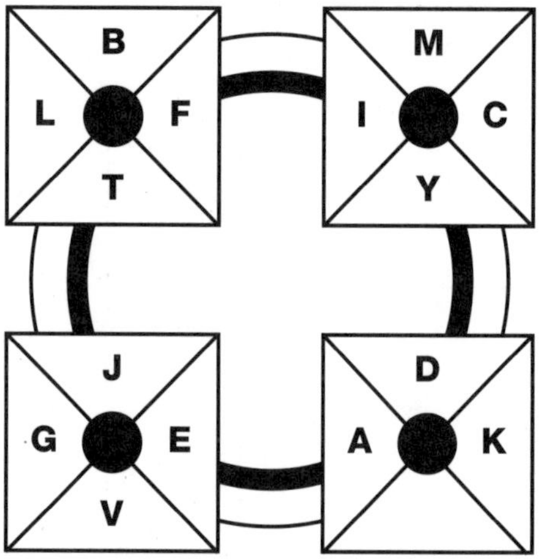

43 PUZZLE

Which letter goes in the empty box?

C	L
H	Q
F	O
K	T
I	R
N	

44 PUZZLE

Which letter completes the wheel?

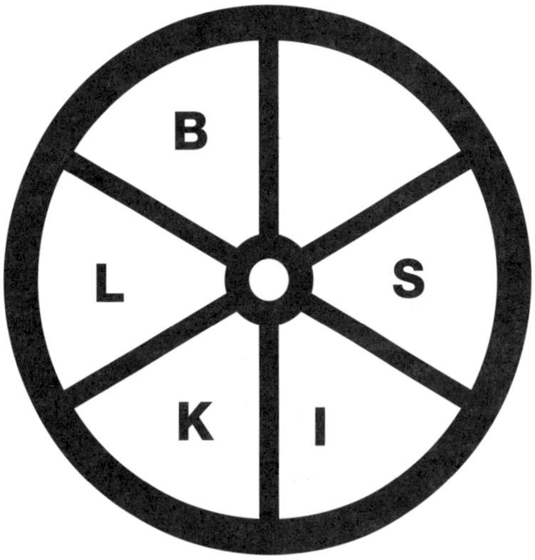

45 PUZZLE

John arranges 4 matches to make an upside down glass and puts a small coin to one side. He promises to buy Gary a drink if he can put the coin inside the glass just by moving two matches and nothing else.

Can you see how he did it?

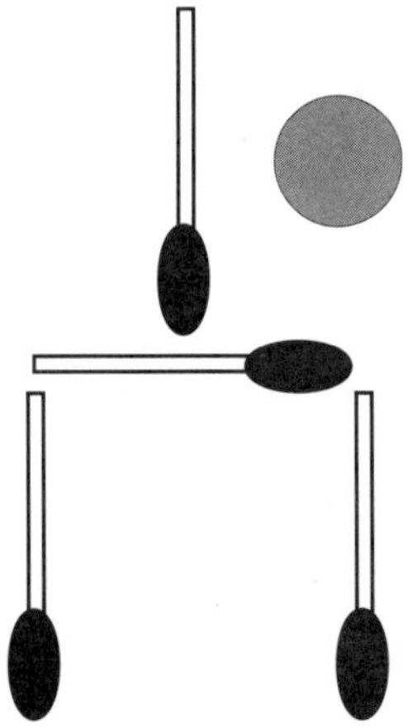

46 PUZZLE

Which number comes next in this sequence?

7
13
24
45

LEVEL 10

47 PUZZLE

Which number is missing from the last grid?

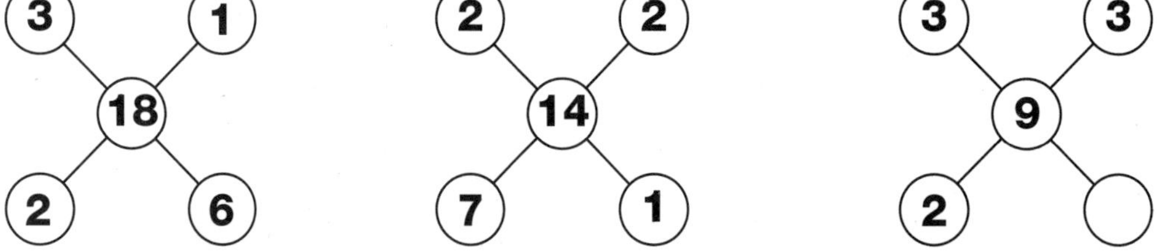

48 PUZZLE

Which number is missing?

3	11	18
33	29	
36	38	39

49 PUZZLE

Fill in the empty ellipse.

5	3	1
8	7	6
11	11	

50 PUZZLE

What shape will replace the question mark?

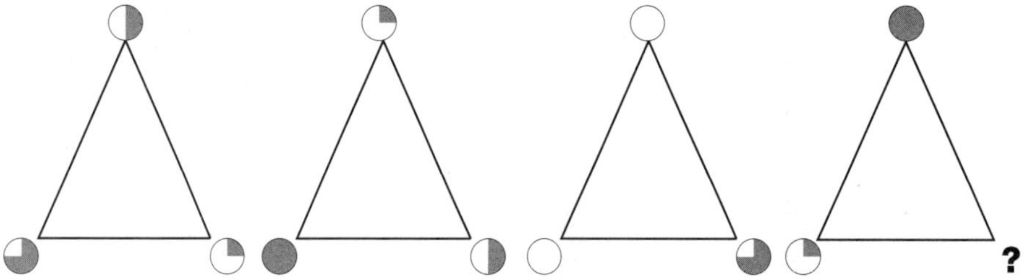

51 PUZZLE

Which letter goes in the empty link and completes the chain?

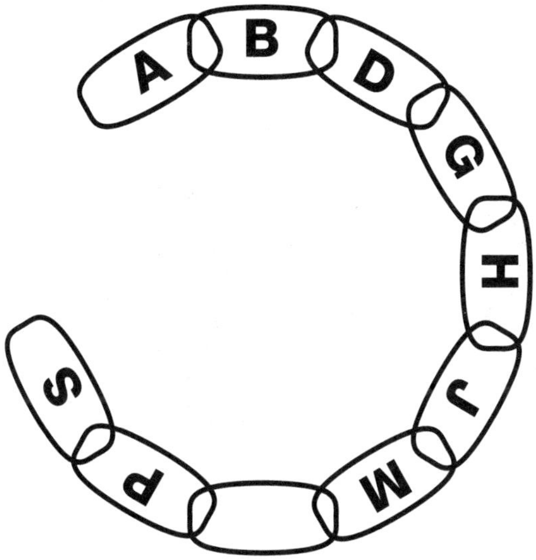

52 PUZZLE

Which number is missing from the middle of the last grid?

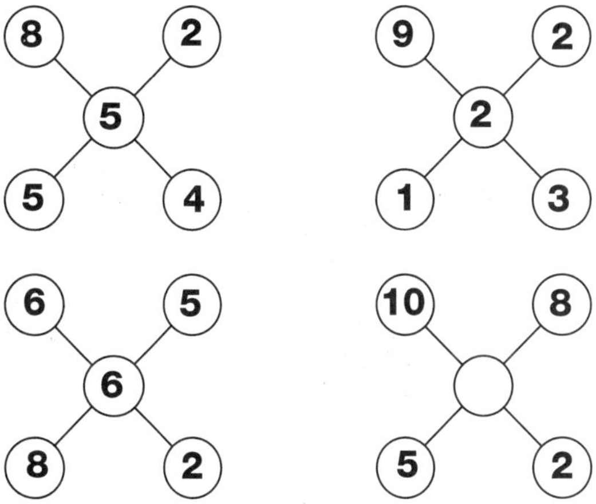

53 PUZZLE

Which number continues the sequence?

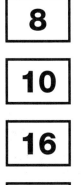

8
10
16
34

54 PUZZLE

Draw the correct markings in the last box.

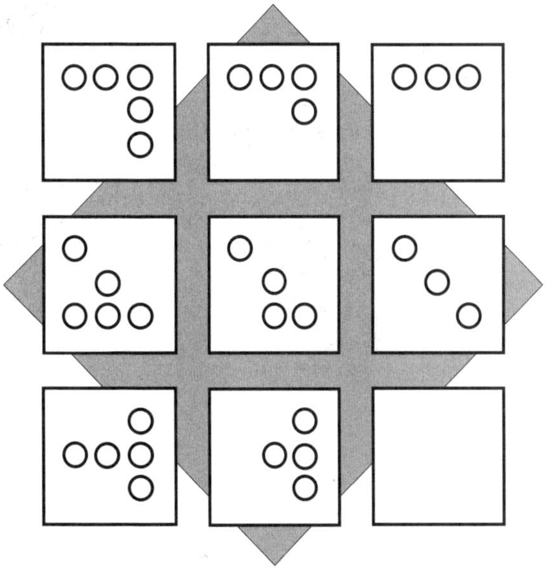

LEVEL 10

LEVEL 10

55 PUZZLE

Which shape is the odd one out and why?

1 PUZZLE

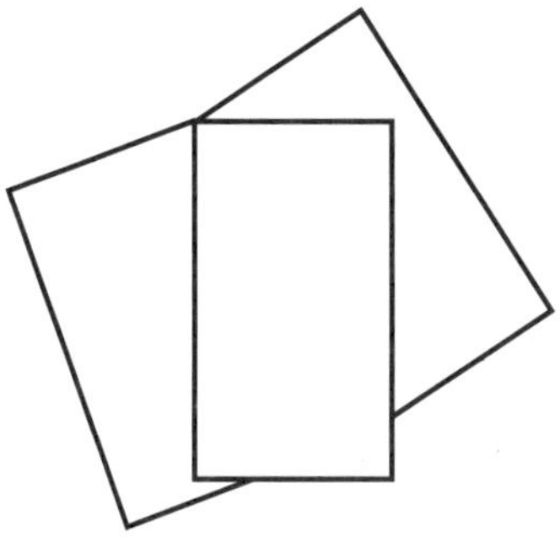

is to:

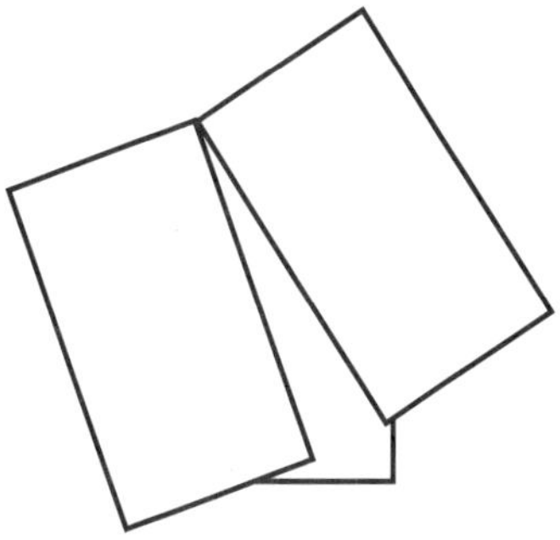

as:

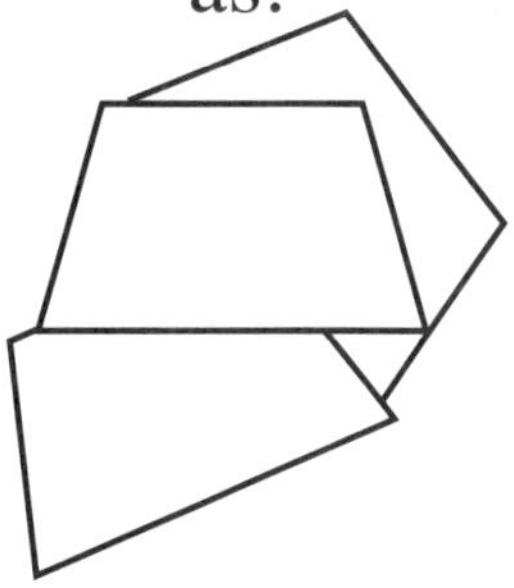

is to:

A

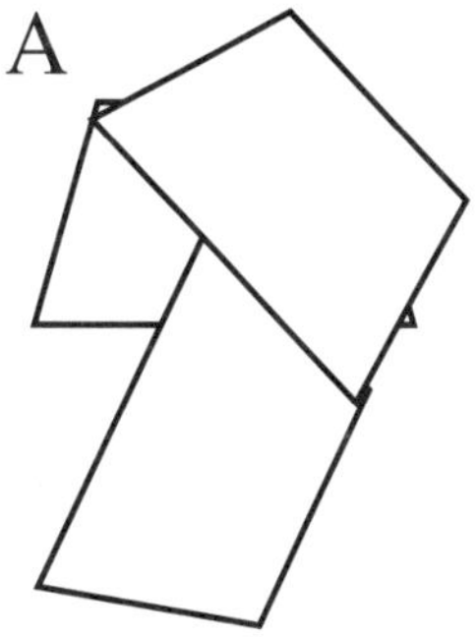

B

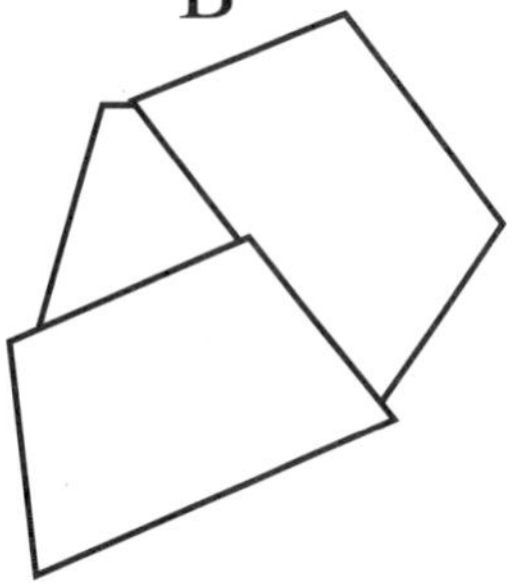

C

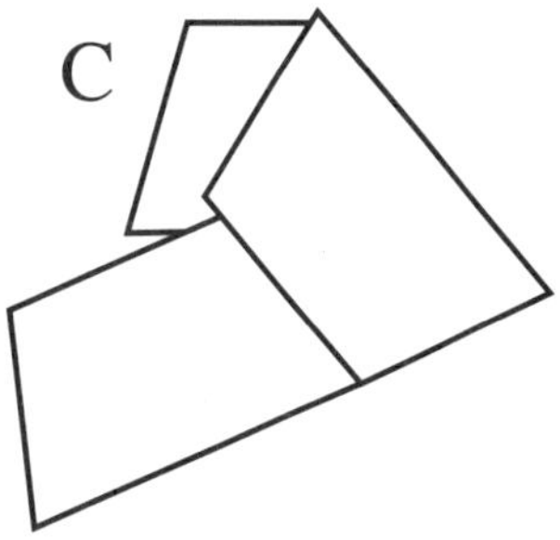

D

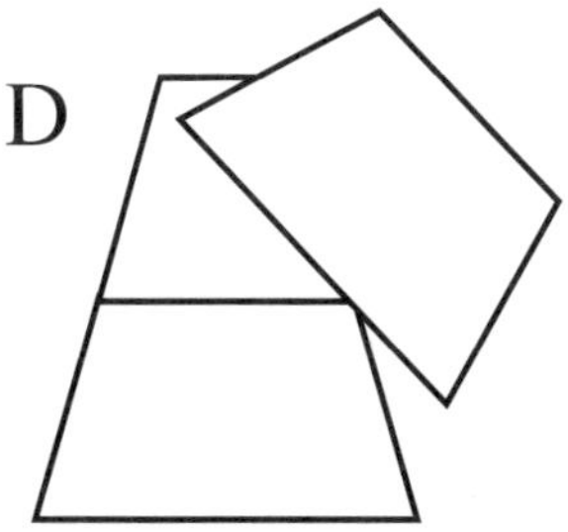

E

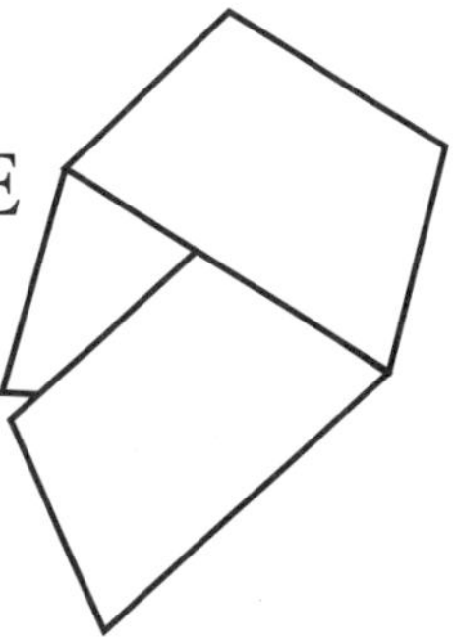

2 PUZZLE

What should replace the question marks?

			A	5	D	11	G	17	J
									23
7									M
?	?	Y	47	V	41	S	34	P	29

3 PUZZLE

What numbers should replace the question marks?

21	23	22	25	27	26
34	35	33	30	31	29
37	39	38	?	43	42
50	51	49	?	47	45
53	55	54	57	59	58
66	67	65	62	63	61

4 PUZZLE

Which is the odd one out?

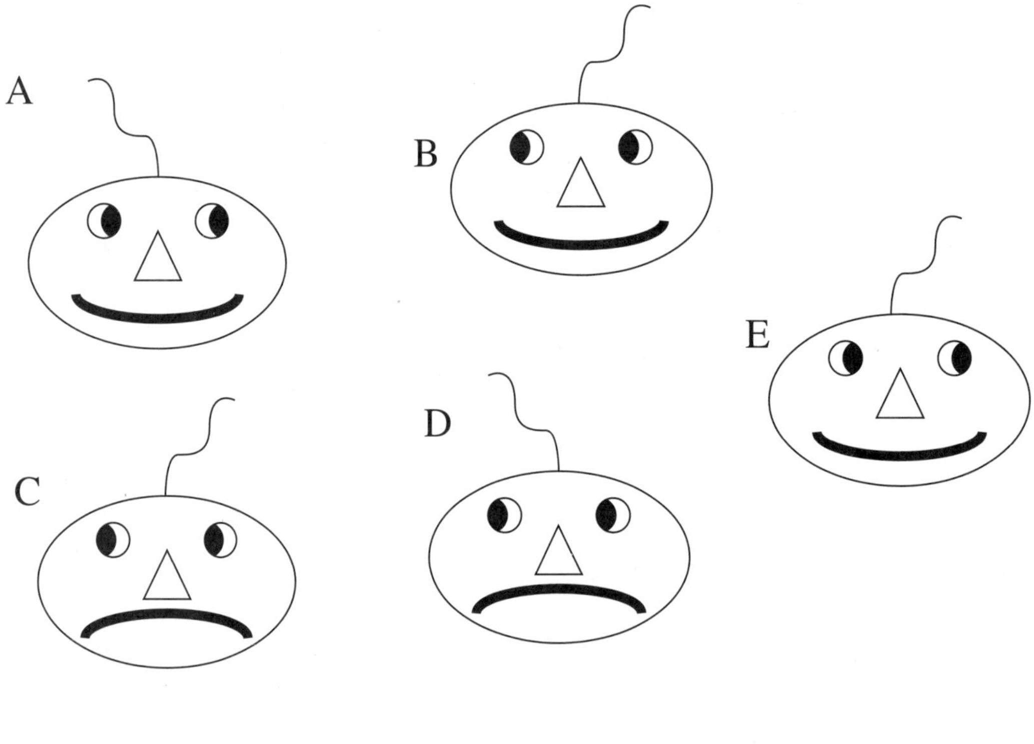

5 PUZZLE

What letters should replace the question marks?

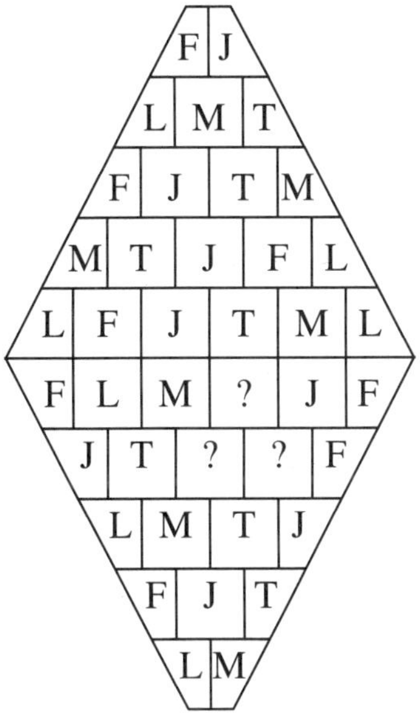

6 PUZZLE

2748 is to **414816**

as

3295 is to **641810**

therefore

6342 is to **?**

7 PUZZLE

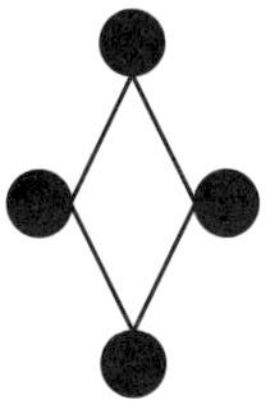

is to:

as:

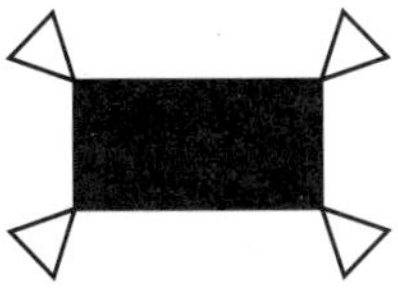

is to:

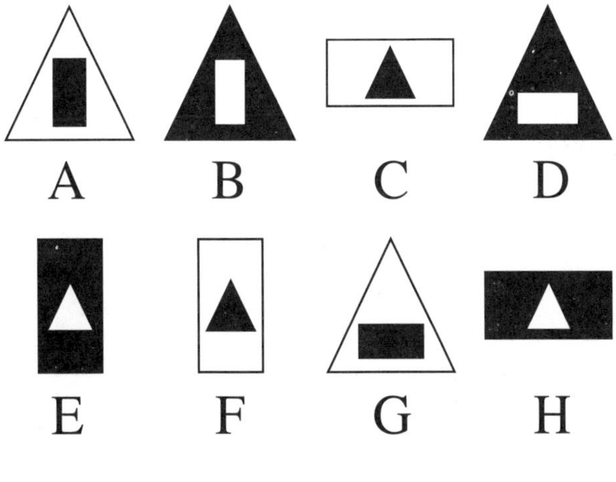

PUZZLE 8

Find the starting square and follow the directions to arrive on the square marked T. Every square must be visited once only.

1N, 3E means 1 North, 3 East.

2S 2E	2E 3S	2W 1S	3W
3E 1S	1E 2S	1W 2S	2S 3W
2N 3E	1N 2E	T	3W
1E 2N	1E 3N	1W 3N	2N 1W

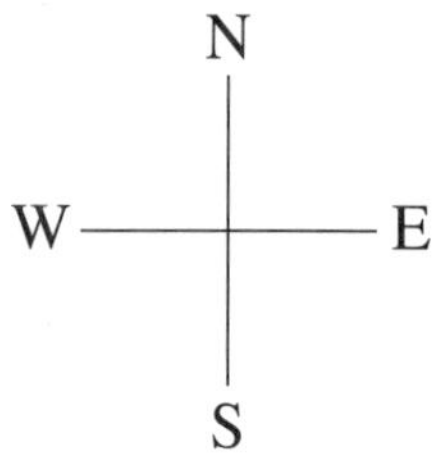

PUZZLE 9

What comes next?

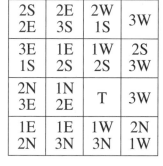

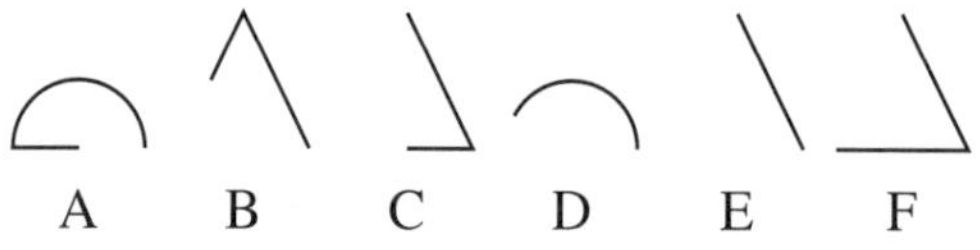

PUZZLE 10

Insert the numbers 1-5 in the circles so that the sum of all the numbers directly connected to each circle equals the sum as indicated in the table shown.

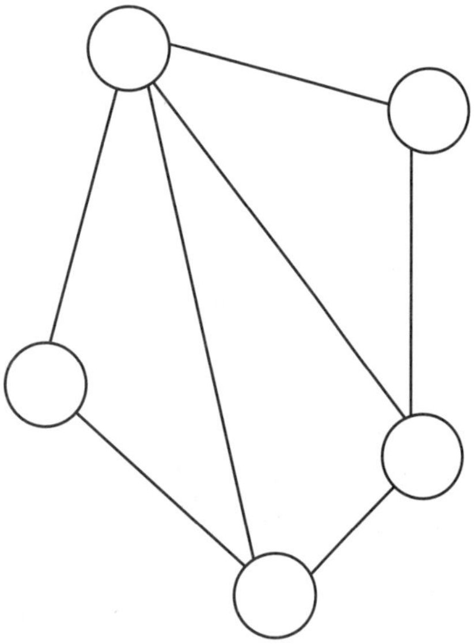

1=11
2=5
3=9
4=11
5=8

for example:

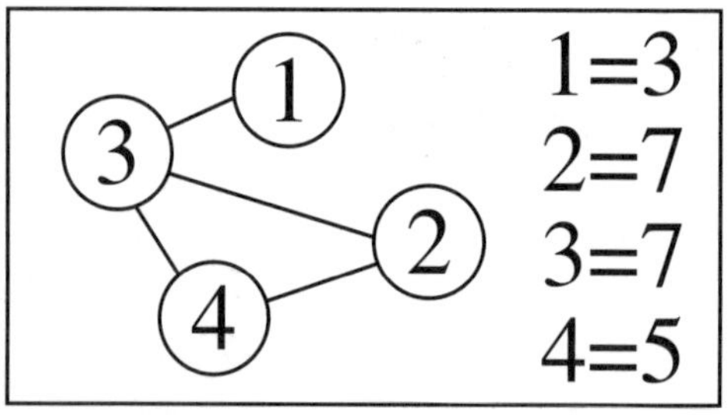

11 PUZZLE

Each line and symbol which appears in the four outer circles, below, is transferred to the centre circle according to these rules: If a line or symbol occurs in the outer circles: once: it is transferred twice: it is possibly transferred 3 times: it is transferred 4 times: it is not transferred. Which of the circles A, B, C, D or E, should appear at the centre of the diagram, below?

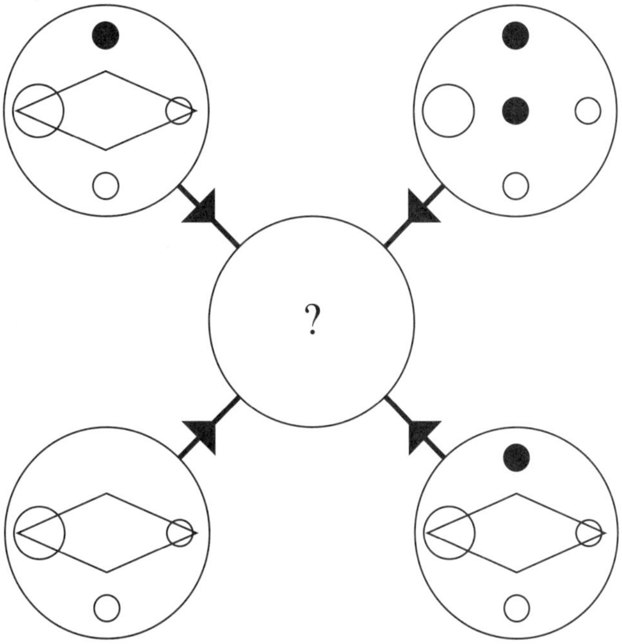

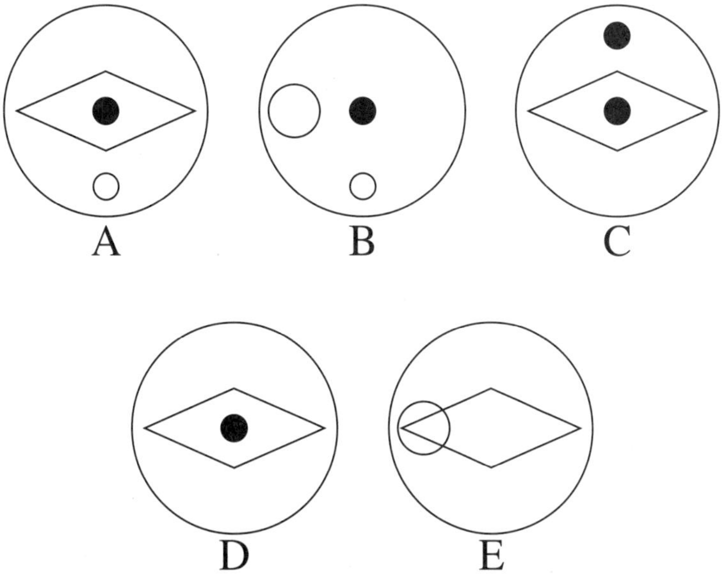

LEVEL

11

12 PUZZLE

Each of the nine squares in the grid marked A1 to C3, should incorporate all the lines and symbols which are shown in the squares of the same letter and number immediately above and to the left. For example, B2 should incorporate all the lines and symbols that are in 2 and B. One of the squares is incorrect. Which one is it?

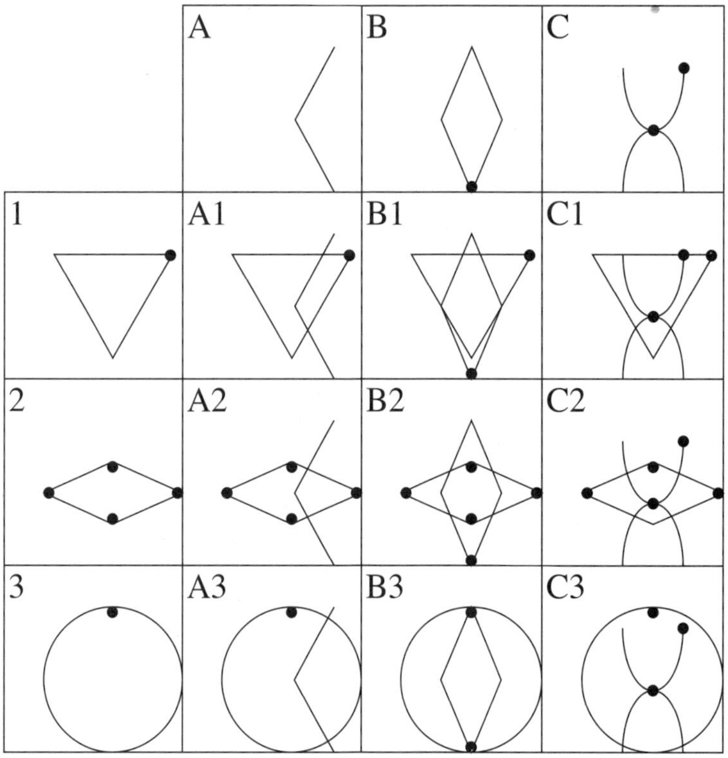

13 PUZZLE

What number should replace the question mark?

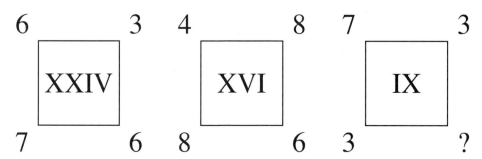

6		3
	XXIV	
7		6

4		8
	XVI	
8		6

7		3
	IX	
3		?

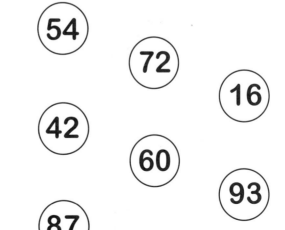

PUZZLE 14

Simplify

$$\frac{7}{11} \div \frac{14}{22} \div \frac{20}{28} = X$$

PUZZLE 15

Which is the odd one out?

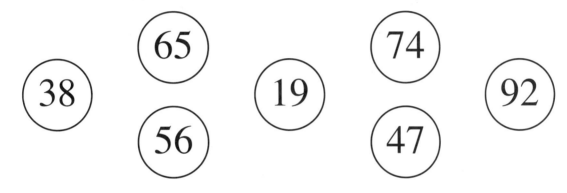

38 65 56 19 74 47 92

PUZZLE 16

What number should replace the question mark?

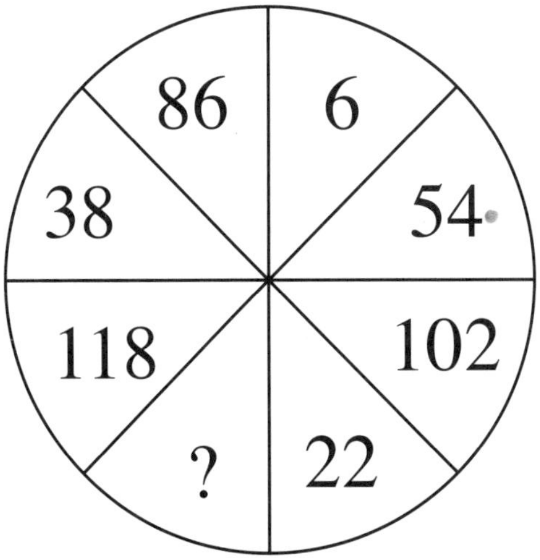

PUZZLE 17

Which is the odd one out?

54 72 16 42 60 93 87

LEVEL

11

PUZZLE 18

What number should replace the question mark?

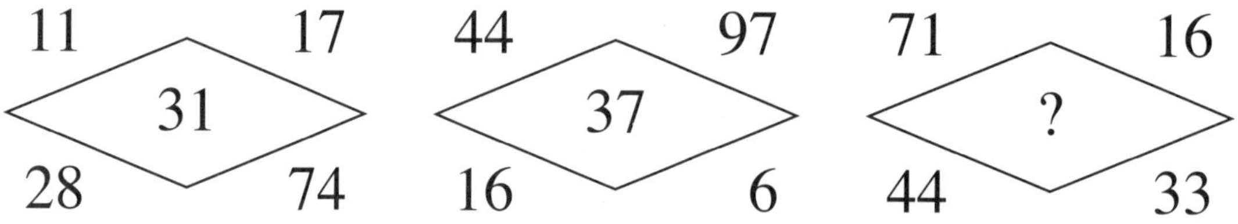

PUZZLE 19

Which is the odd one out?

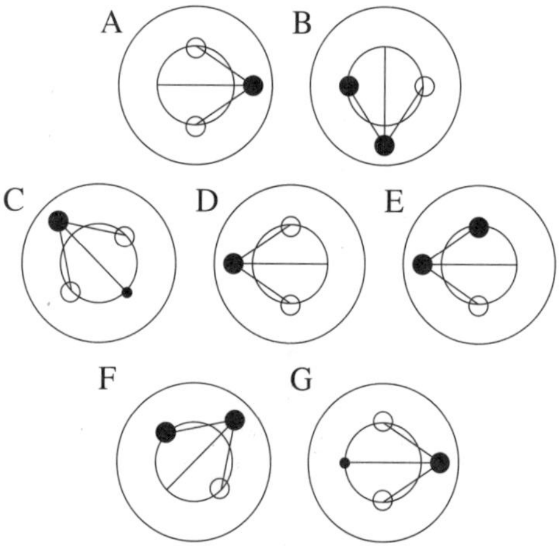

PUZZLE 20

An aircraft flew from A to B at an average speed of 230 m.p.h. It returned from B to A at an average speed of 300 m.p.h. What was its average speed for the two journeys?

PUZZLE 21

There are 12 trees in the orchard, can you connect them with only 5 straight lines?

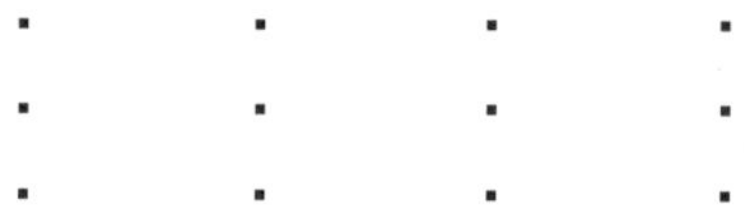

PUZZLE 22

Replace the letters with numbers, so that the sum is correct.

```
   WHAT
x     A
-------
   SHOW
```

23 PUZZLE

In a lottery of 6 winning numbers, how many tickets are there that include every set of 6 numbers out of 30?

24 PUZZLE

A man left a sum of money to his 4 children. Bert received 50% of Cyril's amount. Alan received as much as Bert and John. Cyril received 125% of John's amount. John received $840. How much more did Alan receive than Cyril?

25 PUZZLE

Which hexagon should replace the question mark?

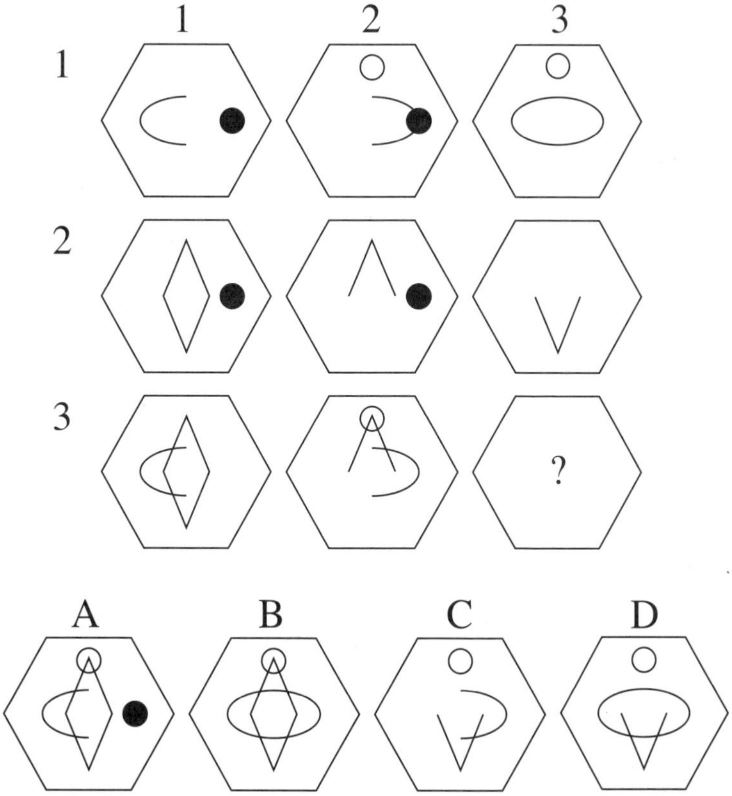

LEVEL

11

26 PUZZLE

Which number goes in the middle of the third triangle?

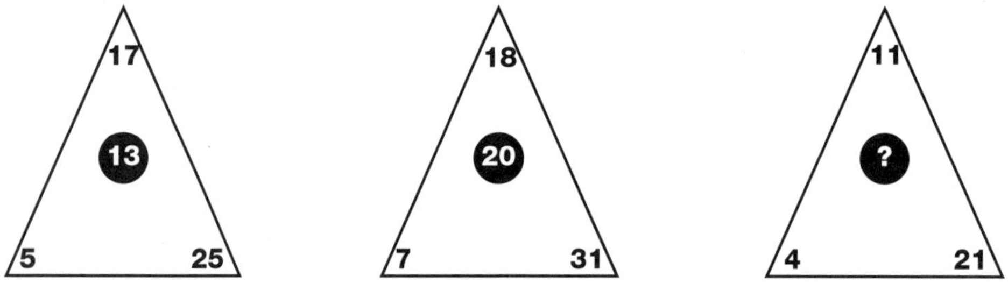

27 PUZZLE

Move one match and make this sum correct.

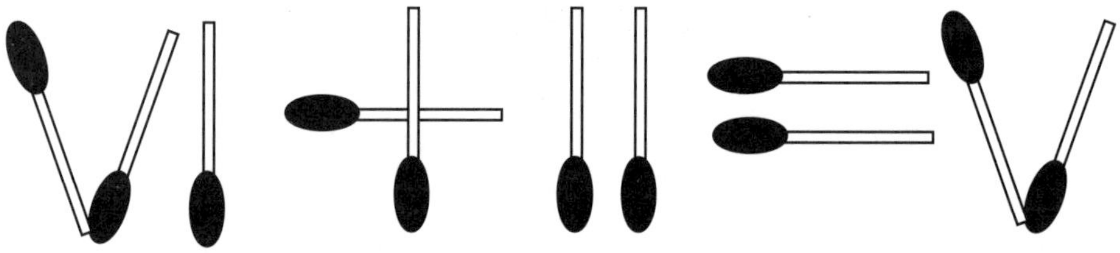

28 PUZZLE

Which number goes in the empty box and completes the puzzle?

3	6	3
10	3	7
8	1	

29 PUZZLE

Which number is missing from the bottom grid?

9	4	6
0	4	3

7	1	3
0	3	1

5	0	4
0	2	

30 PUZZLE

Which number completes the grid?

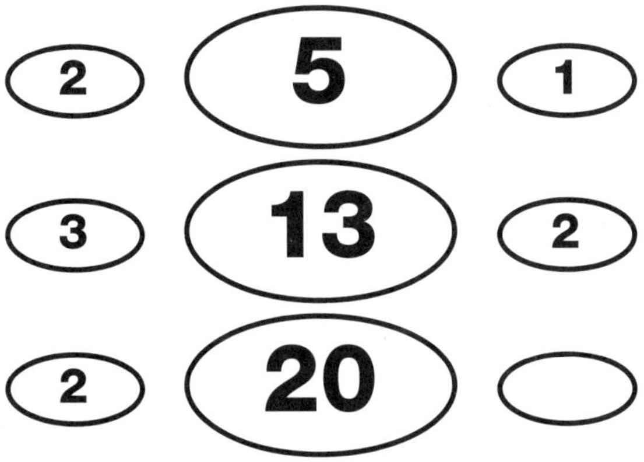

31 PUZZLE

Move just four matches to make seven squares.

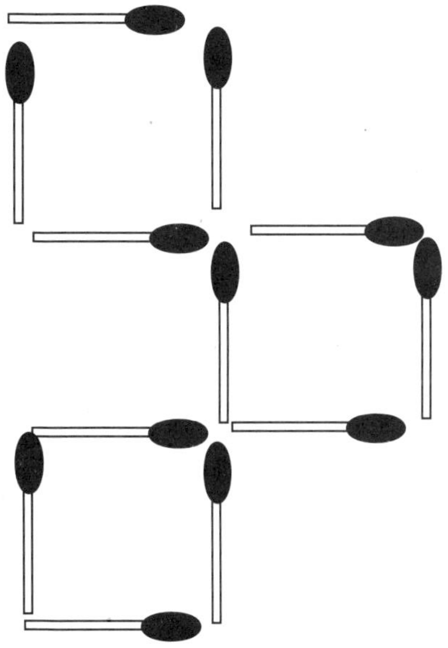

32 PUZZLE

Which number replaces the question mark?

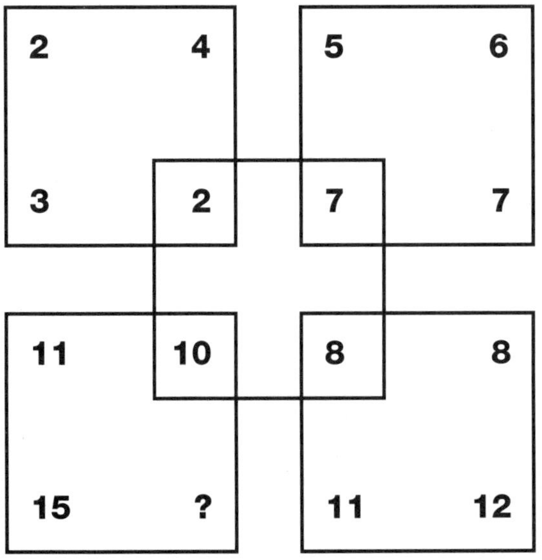

33 PUZZLE

Which letter goes in the bottom box?

PUZZLE 34

What is missing from the empty box?

1	0
J	Q
1	8
R	I
2	4
X	

PUZZLE 35

Which number continues the sequence?

1
5
13
29

PUZZLE 36

What time should the blank watch be showing?

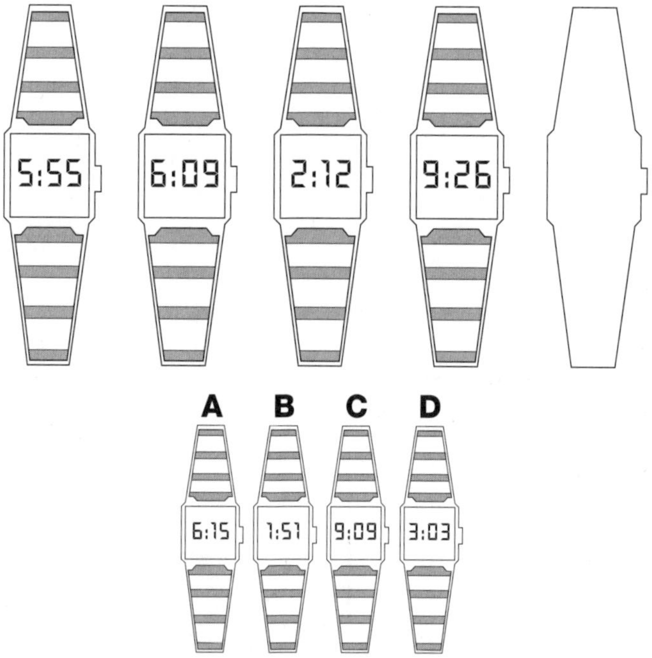

PUZZLE 37

Which letter should go in the empty circle?

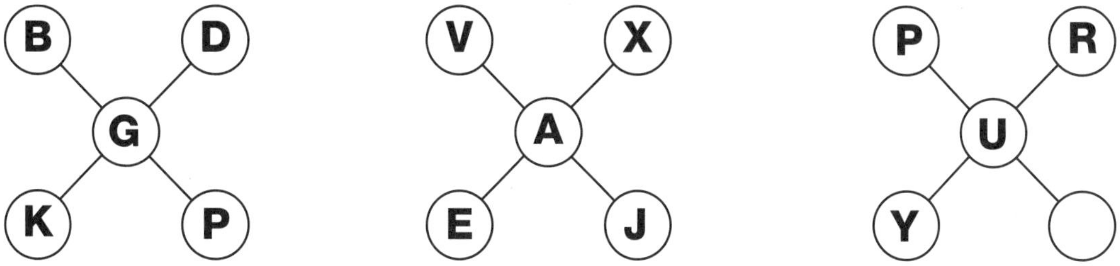

PUZZLE 38

Which number should replace the question mark?

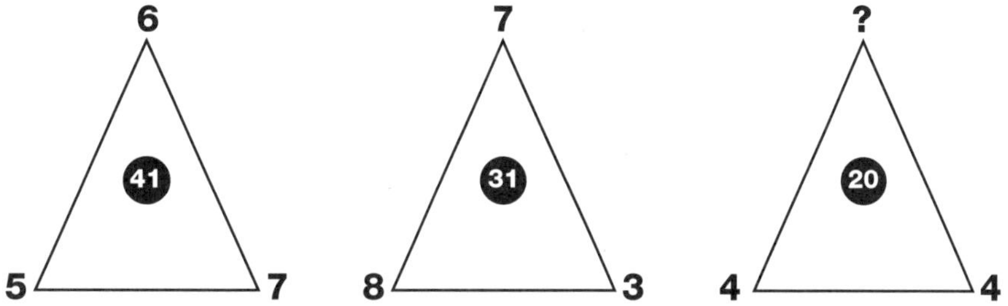

PUZZLE 39

Which of these numbered pieces will fit in the centre of the grid?

5	3	7	9	1	1	9	7	3	5
3	4	2	7	8	8	7	2	4	3
7	2	5	1	2	2	1	5	2	7
9	0	1	6			6	1	0	9
1	8	2					2	8	1
1	8	2					2	8	1
9	0	1	6			6	1	0	9
7	2	5	1	2	2	1	5	2	7
3	4	2	7	8	8	7	2	4	3
5	3	7	9	1	1	9	7	3	5

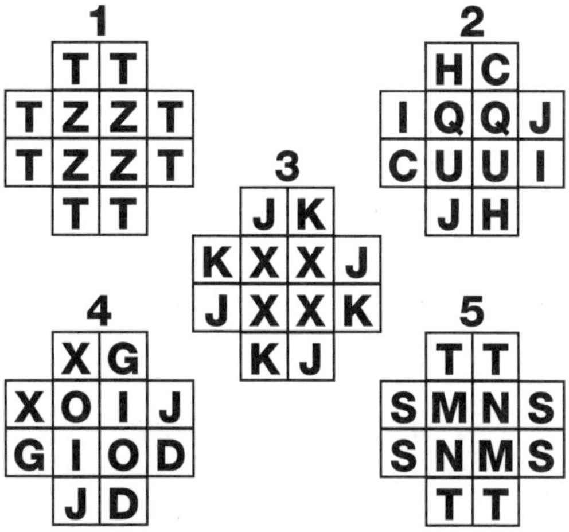

LEVEL 11

40 PUZZLE

Which of the bottom boxes finishes this puzzle?

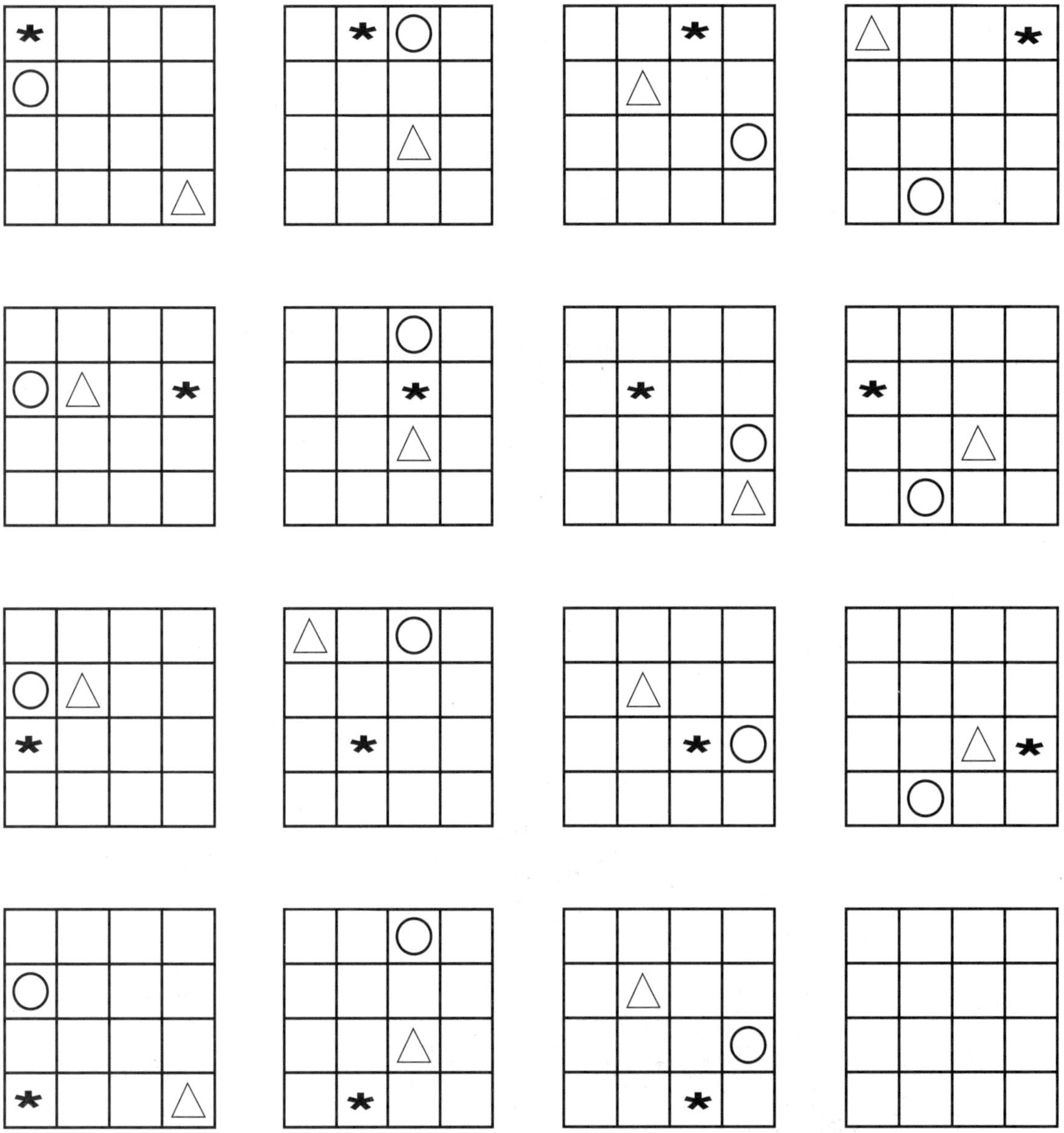

A

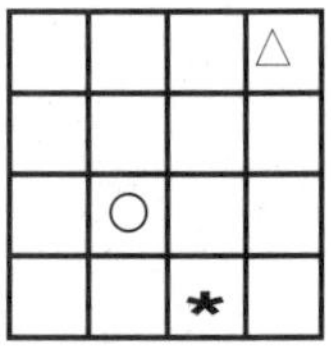

B

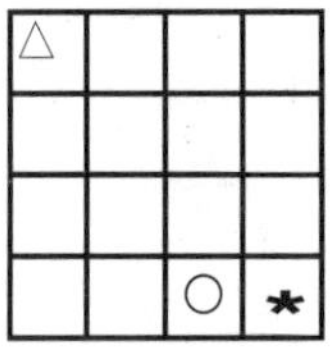

C

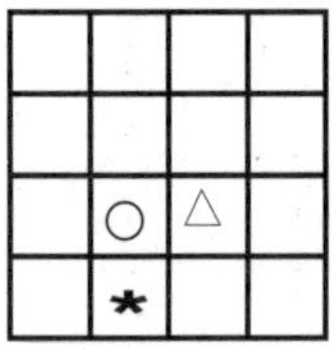

D

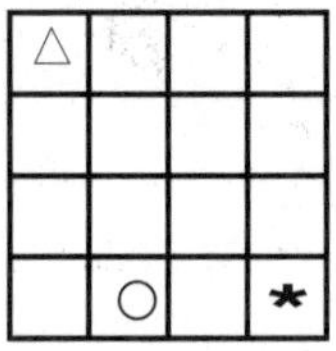

41 PUZZLE

What time should be showing next?

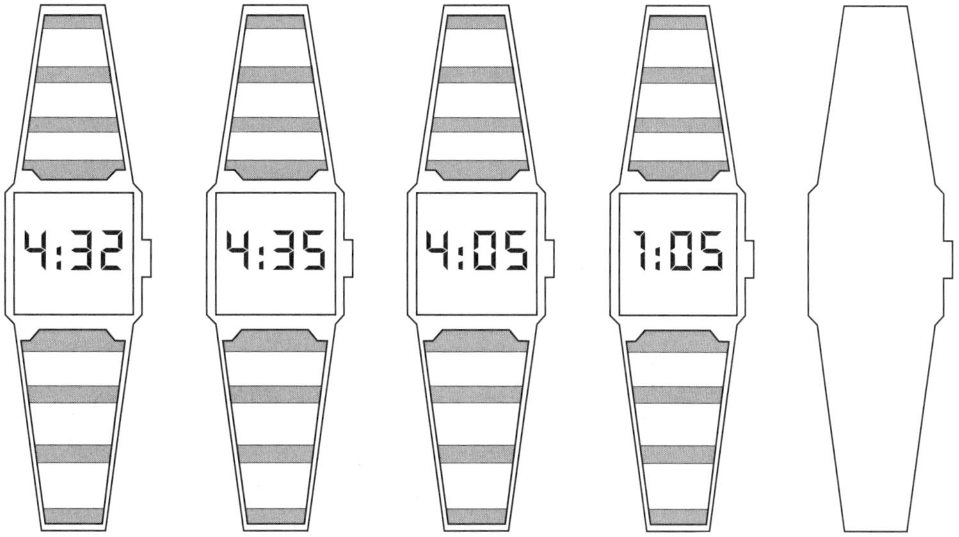

42 PUZZLE

Which letter goes in the empty corner?

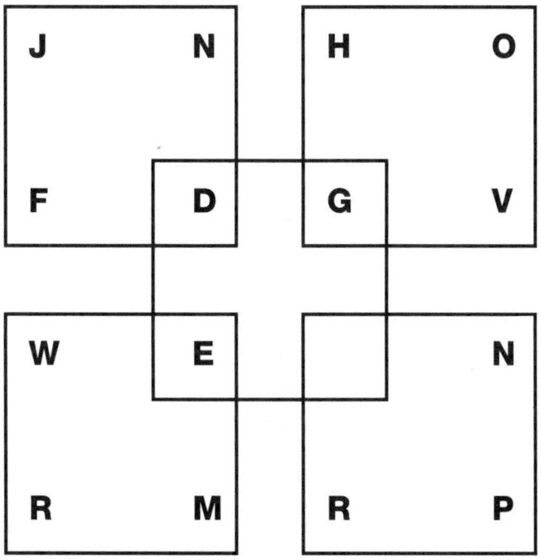

43 PUZZLE

Each number from 1-25 inclusive is to be put in the grid so that each row, column and corner to corner line adds up to 65.

21				1
	8			
		13		
				16
25			2	

44 PUZZLE

Which of the bottom playing cards completes the top line?

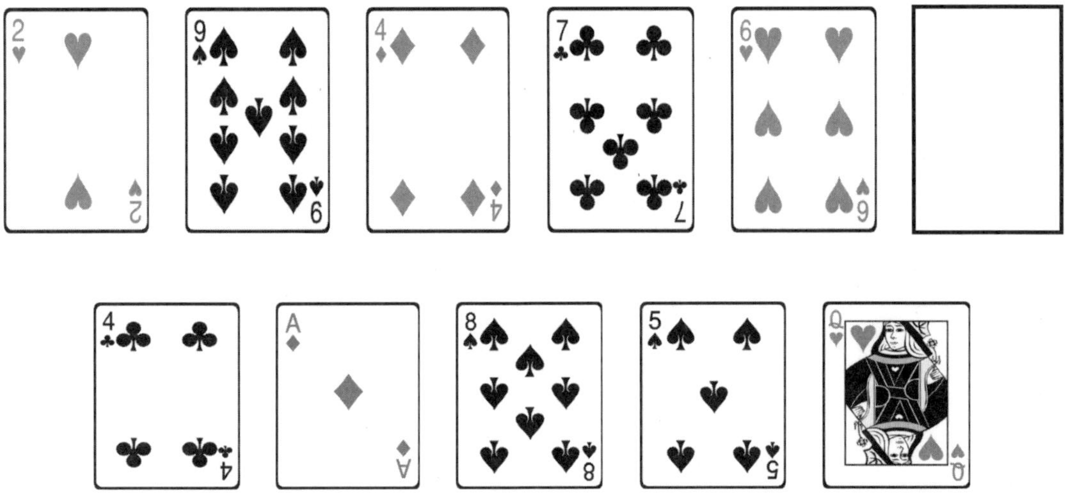

45 PUZZLE

Which number is missing from the empty segment in the web?

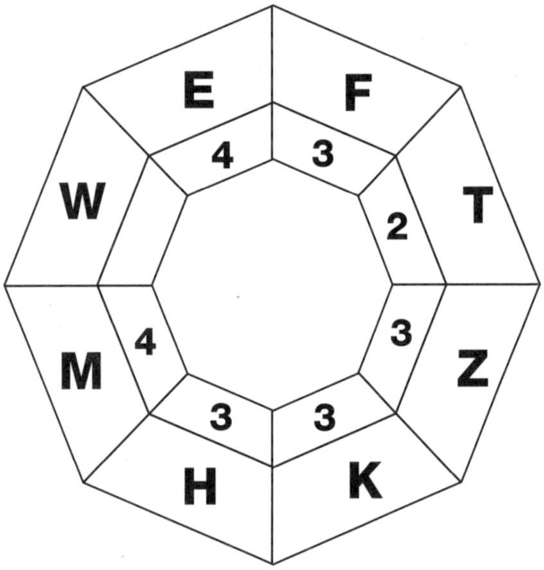

46 PUZZLE

Which number is needed to complete the puzzle?

47 PUZZLE

Which playing card completes the puzzle?

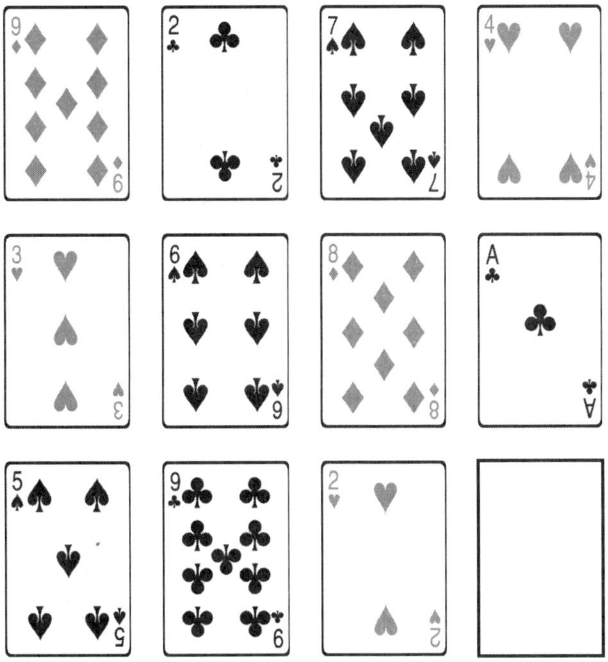

48 PUZZLE

Fill in the empty box.

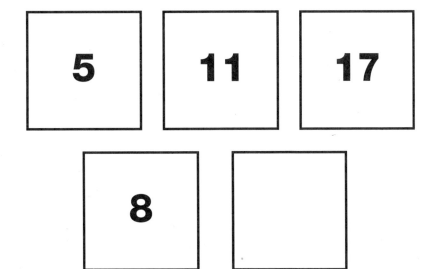

5	11	17
8		

49 PUZZLE

Which number is missing from the bottom circle?

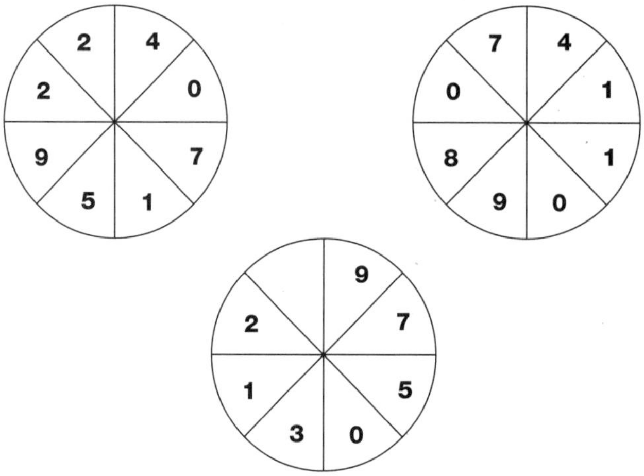

50 PUZZLE

Simon, Steve and Stewart are all apple farmers who pool their crop each year to make cider. For this year's harvest, Steve supplied three times as many apples as Stewart, and Simon supplied twice as many apples as Steve.

If the total weight of apples supplied is 900 tonnes, how much did each man contribute?

51 PUZZLE

Which letter is missing from the empty circle?

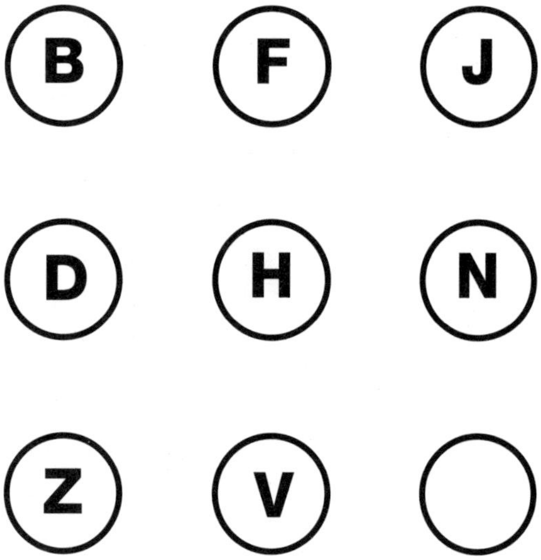

PUZZLE 52

Edward spent $21 on drinks for a party. If the bottle of vodka he purchased was twice the price of the case of beer, and the lemonade was half the price of the beer, how much did Edward spend on the beer?

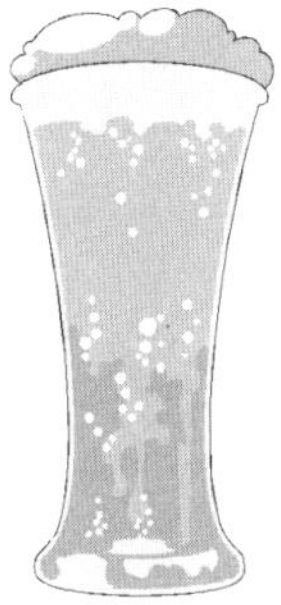

PUZZLE 53

Which number replaces the blank?

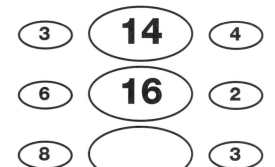

3	14	4
6	16	2
8		3

PUZZLE 54

Which numbers are missing from this puzzle?

14	1	12	7
11	8		2
5	10	3	16
		6	

PUZZLE 55

Move two matches to make seven squares.

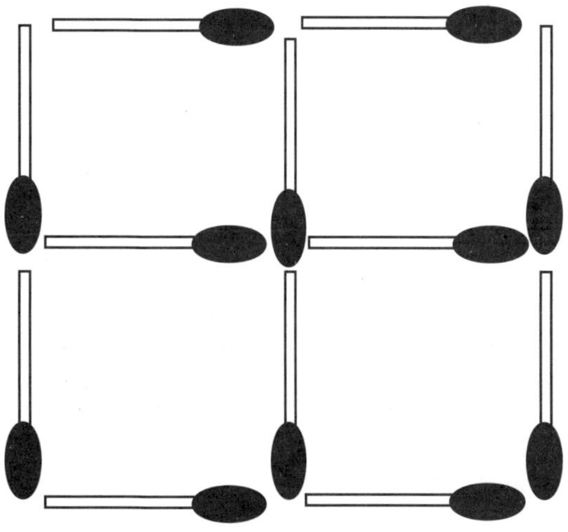

1 PUZZLE

What comes next?

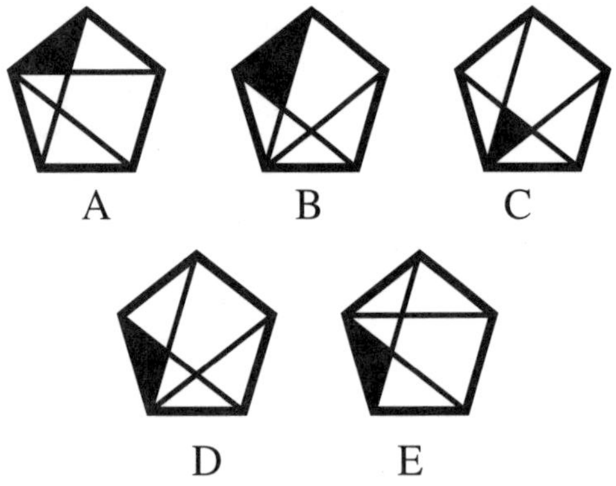

2 PUZZLE

72 (158) 84

33 (126) 92

97 (?) 31

What number is missing?

3 PUZZLE

When the pattern below is folded to form a cube, which is the only one of the following that can be produced?

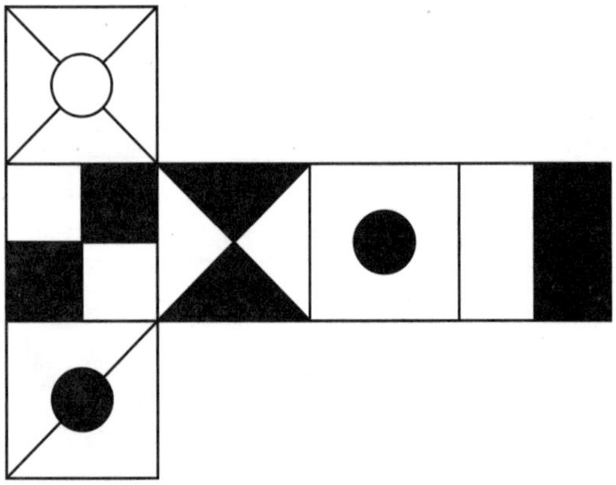

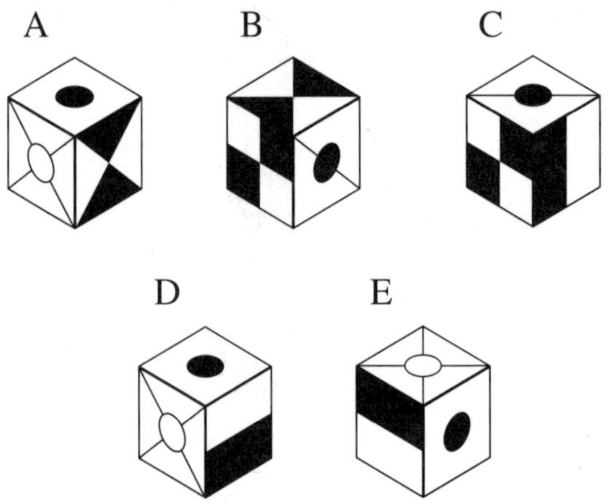

PUZZLE 4

ADF

is to

ZWU

as

GJL

is to

?

PUZZLE 5

Tom and Jerry share out a certain sum of money in the ratio 5:4 respectively, and Tom ends up with $275. How much money was shared out?

PUZZLE 6

When the pattern below is folded to form a cube, which is the only one of the following that can be produced?

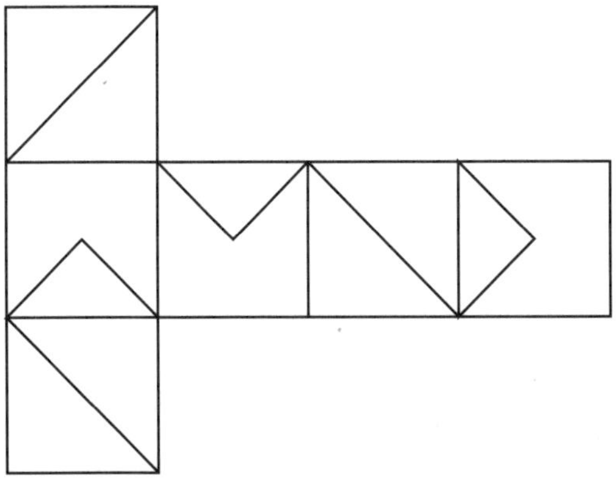

A

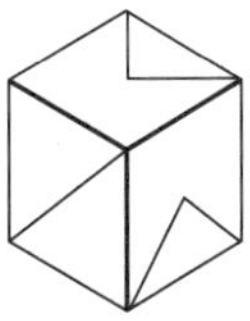

B

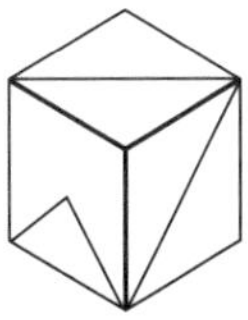

C

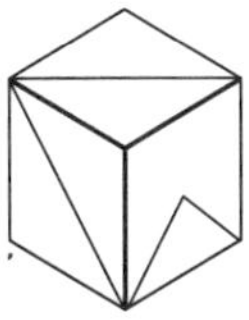

D

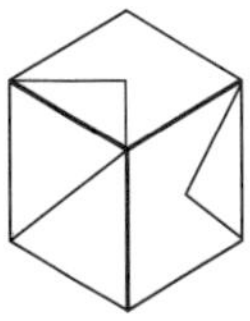

E

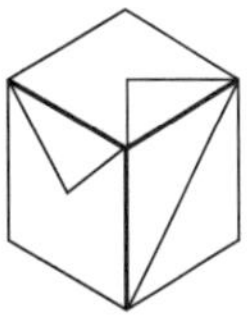

PUZZLE 7

What is the missing number?

2	7	5	9	8	6
3	4	2	7	5	8
6	1	8	7	4	?

PUZZLE 8

What letters should replace the question mark?

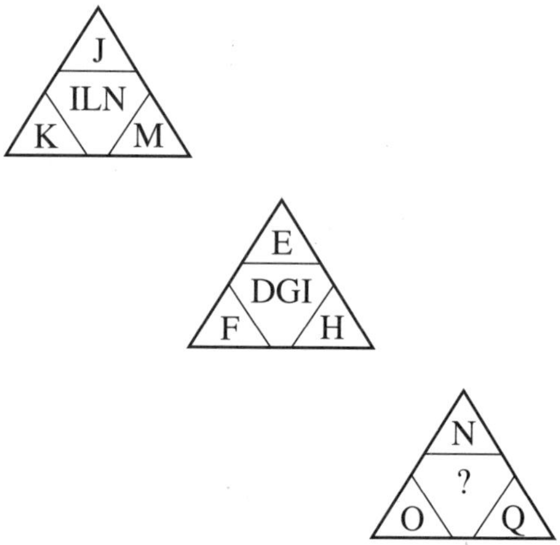

PUZZLE 9

Insert the numbers 1-6 in the circles so that the sum of all the numbers directly connected to each circle equals the sum as indicated in the table shown.

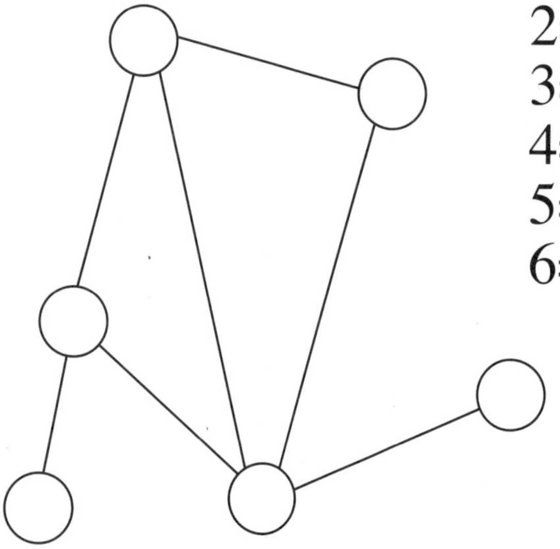

1=6
2=13
3=2
4=8
5=12
6=5

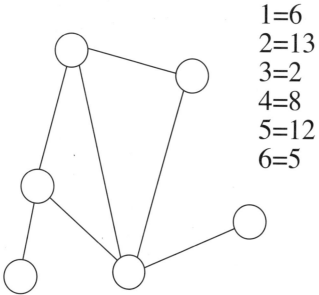

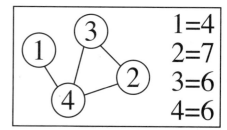

for example:

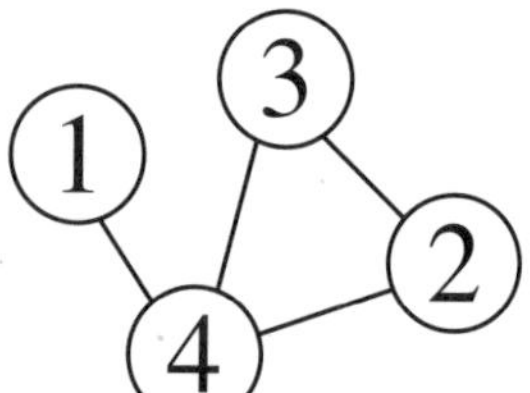

1=4
2=7
3=6
4=6

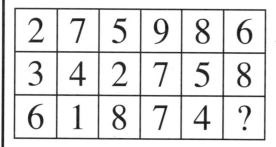

10 PUZZLE

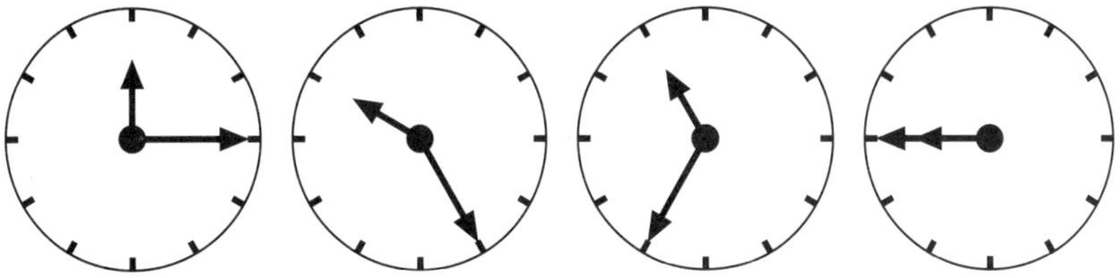

What comes next?

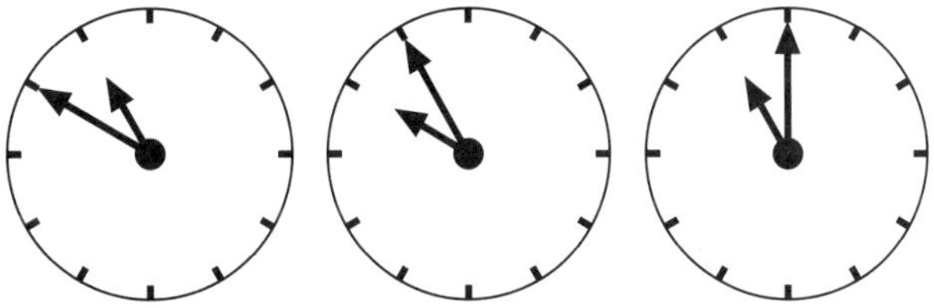

A B C

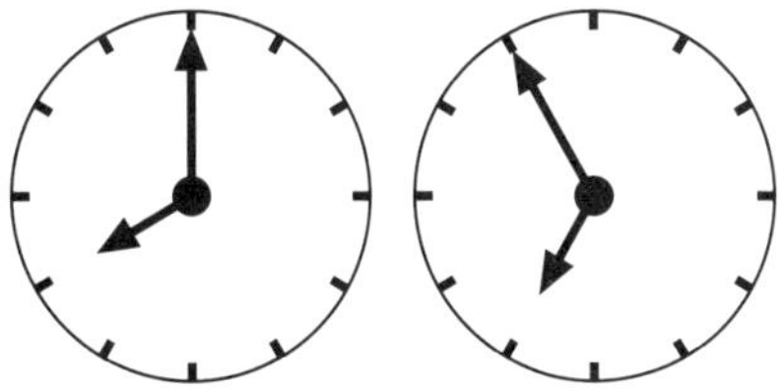

D E

11 PUZZLE

Which of these is not a DRINK?

(a) SILLABUB
(b) MADEIRA
(c) ANISETTE
(d) GRENADA

12 PUZZLE

What number should replace the question mark?

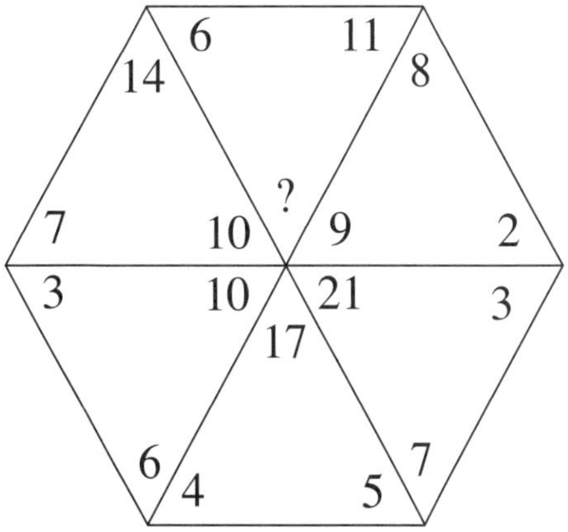

13 PUZZLE

Each line and symbol which appears in the four outer circles below, is transferred to the centre circle according to these rules. If a line or symbol occurs in the outer circles once, it is transferred; if it occurs twice, it is possibly transferred; three times, it is transferred; four times, it is not transferred. Which of the circles A, B, C, D or E, should appear at the centre of the diagram, below?

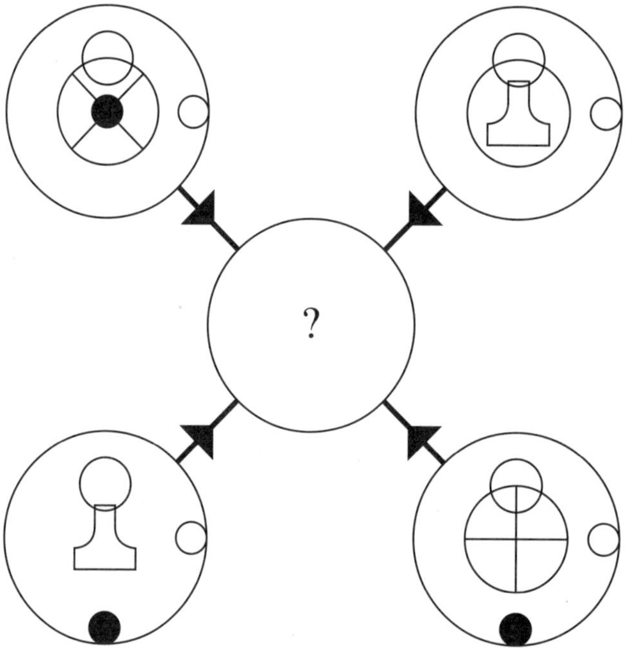

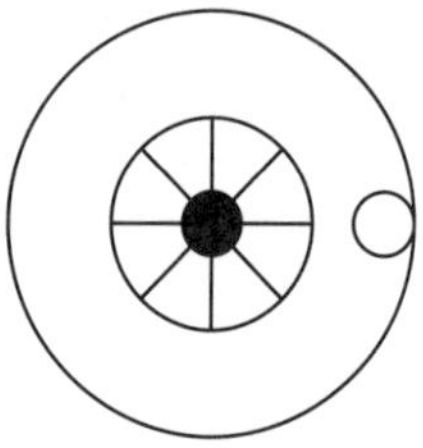

A

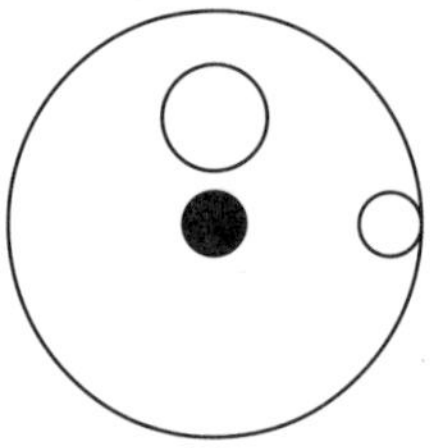

B

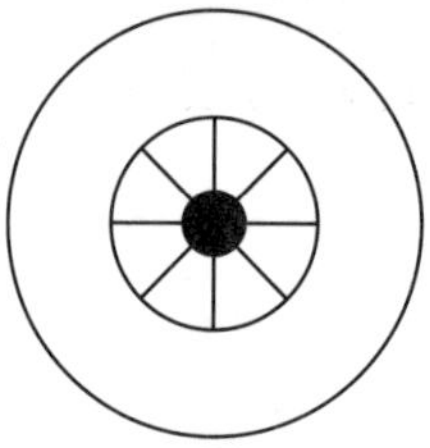

C

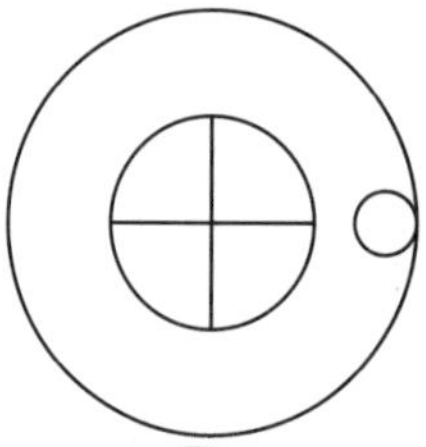

D

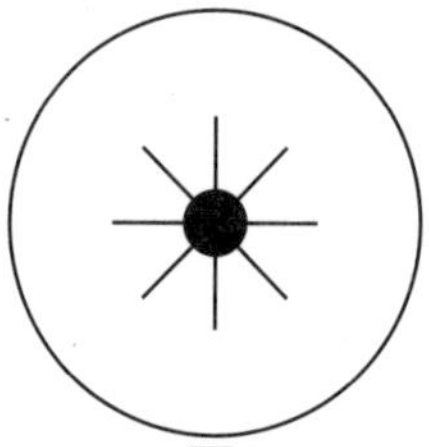

E

14 PUZZLE

Which number will replace the question mark?

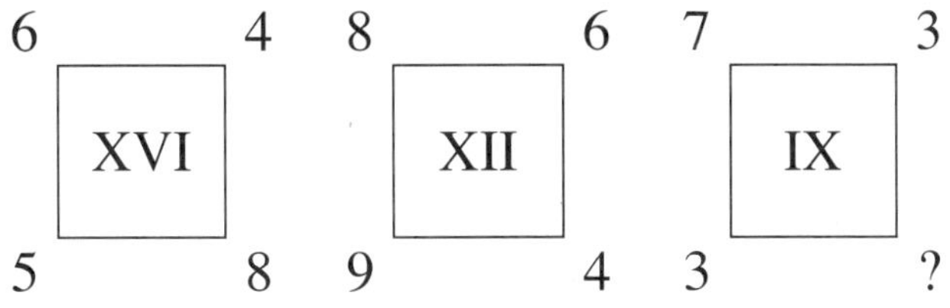

15 PUZZLE

Which is the odd one out?

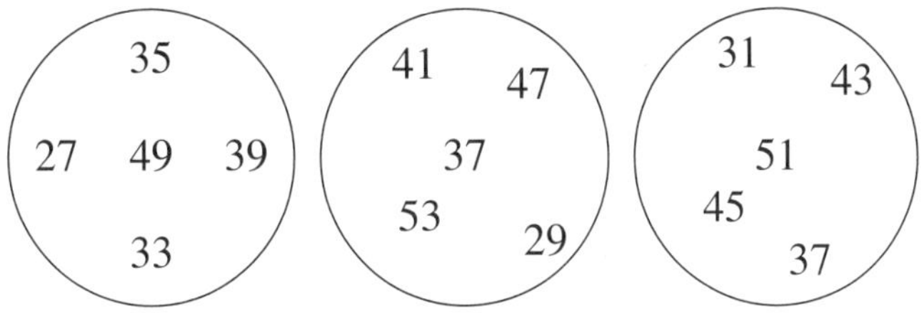

16 PUZZLE

Which circle should replace the question mark?

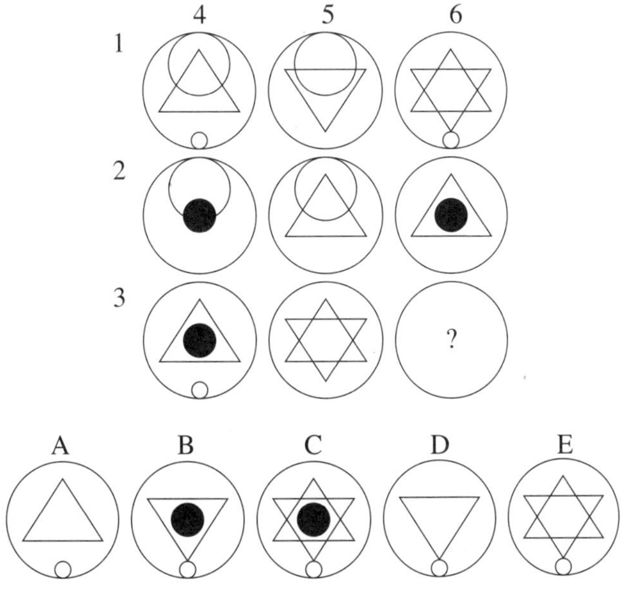

PUZZLE 17

Which two words mean the same?

INORDINATE
CAPRICIOUS
CONTINGENT
REFORMATION
OPULENCE
FANCIFUL

PUZZLE 18

Which number is the odd one?

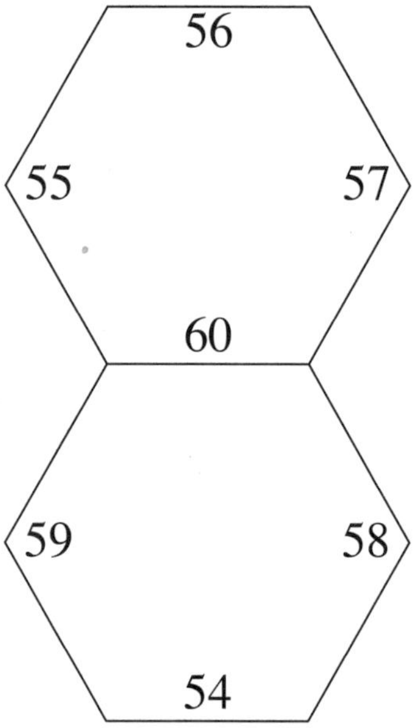

PUZZLE 19

Which is the odd one out?

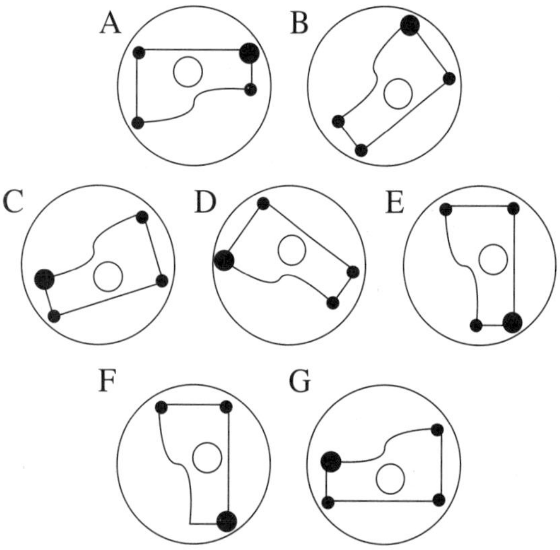

PUZZLE 20

Which is the odd one out?

(a) ENDIVE
(b) FENNEL
(c) MACAQUE
(d) PIMENTO
(e) SEAKALE

21 PUZZLE

What is the name given to a group of MULES?

(a) BARREN
(b) COLONY
(c) CLUTTER
(d) FLUSH
(e) KNOB

22 PUZZLE

If 52 = 64

and

36 = x

What is the value of x?

23 PUZZLE

Which word is the odd word?

(a) HOWLER
(b) CROCODILE
(c) DESTITUTE
(d) DEMURE
(e) CARBON

24 PUZZLE

What is GRAUPEL?

(a) FLOWER
(b) GERMAN SAUSAGE
(c) FROZEN RAIN
(d) INSECT
(e) HINGED FLAP

25 PUZZLE

Each line and symbol which appears in the four outer circles below, is transferred to the centre circle according to these rules. If a line or symbol occurs in the outer circles once, it is transferred; if it occurs twice, it is possibly transferred; three times, it is transferred; four times, it is not transferred. Which of the circles A, B, C, D or E, should appear at the centre of the diagram, below?

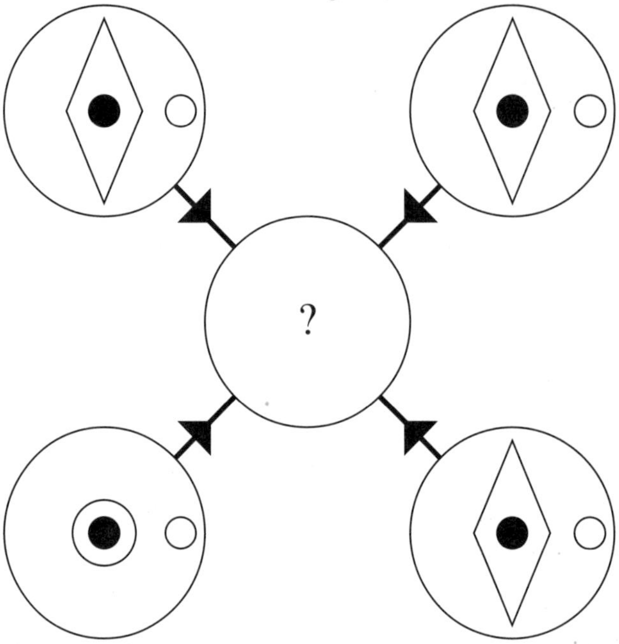

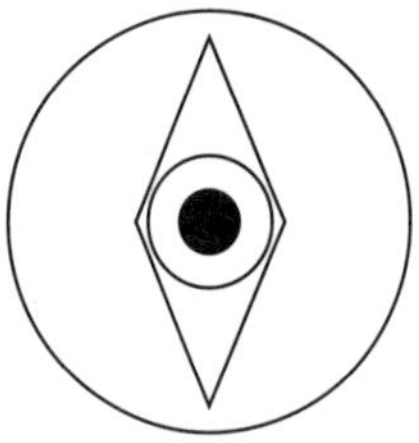
A

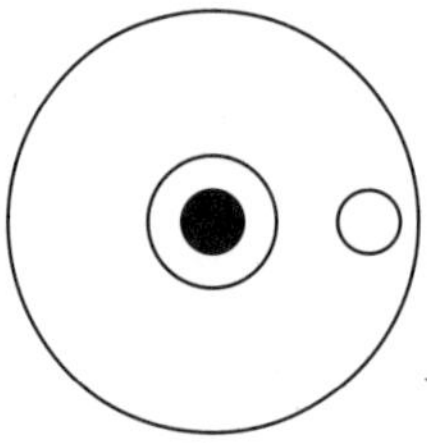
B

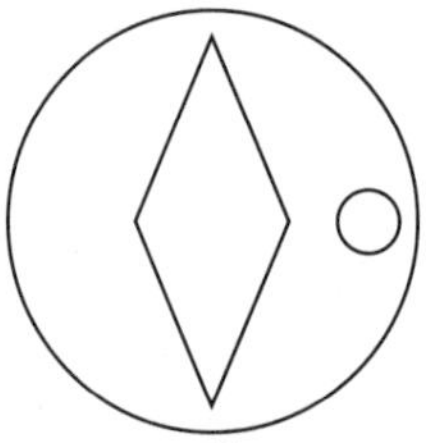
C

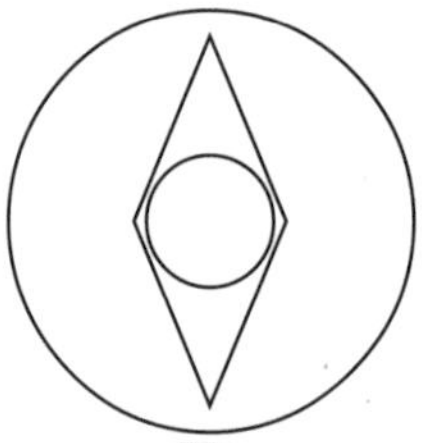
D

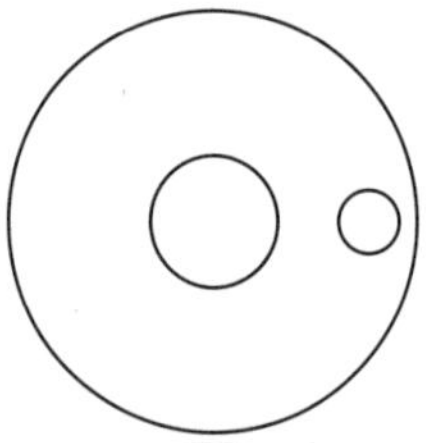
E

26 PUZZLE

Which two playing cards are needed to complete this puzzle?

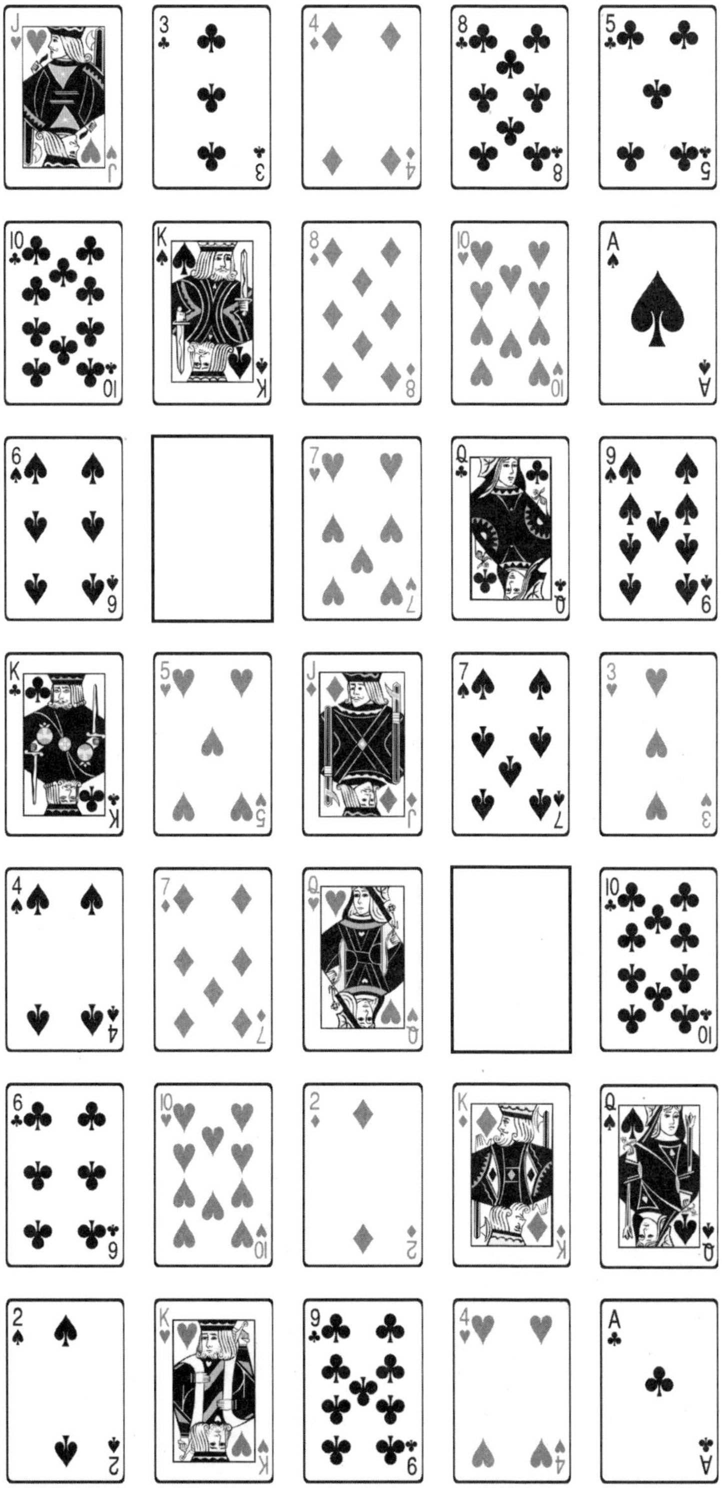

LEVEL 12

27 PUZZLE

Rearrange these coins into a five-line shape, with each line containing 4 coins.

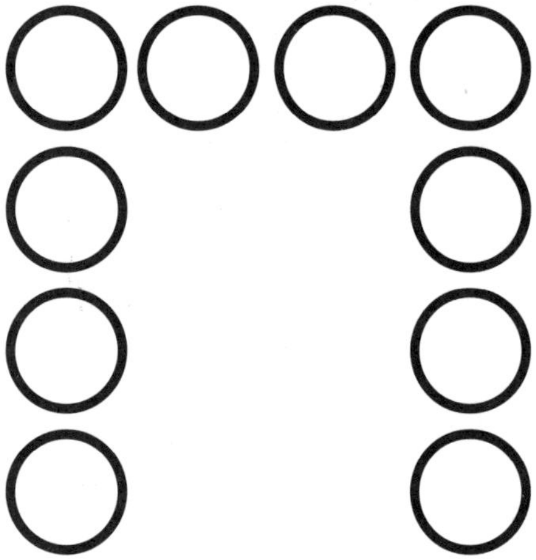

28 PUZZLE

Which number goes in the empty shape?

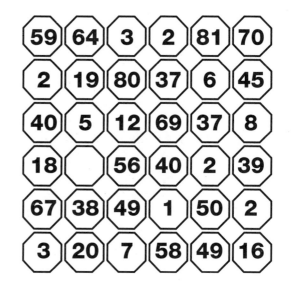

59	64	3	2	81	70
2	19	80	37	6	45
40	5	12	69	37	8
18		56	40	2	39
67	38	49	1	50	2
3	20	7	58	49	16

29 PUZZLE

Which number is the odd one out in each ellipse?

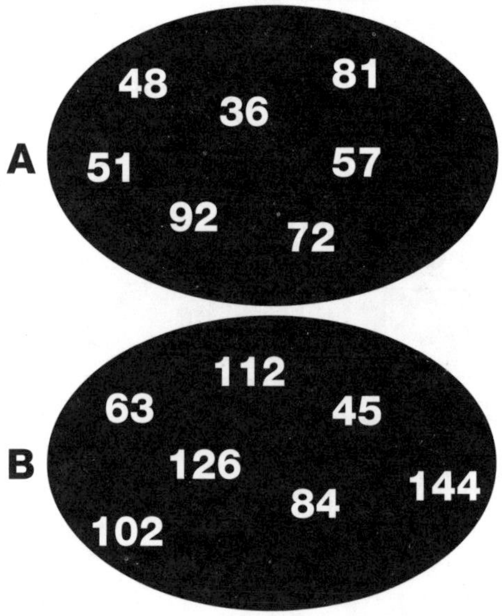

30 PUZZLE

Which number is missing?

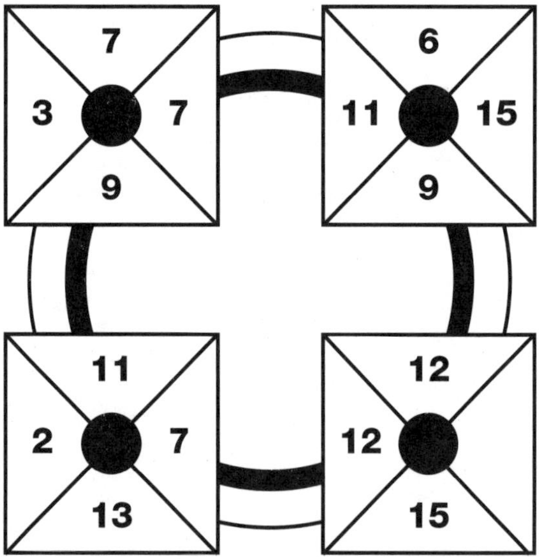

31 PUZZLE

Which of the three letters at the bottom completes the puzzle?

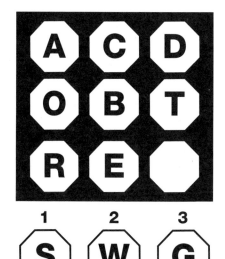

A	C	D
O	B	T
R	E	

1 S
2 W
3 G

32 PUZZLE

Which number is missing?

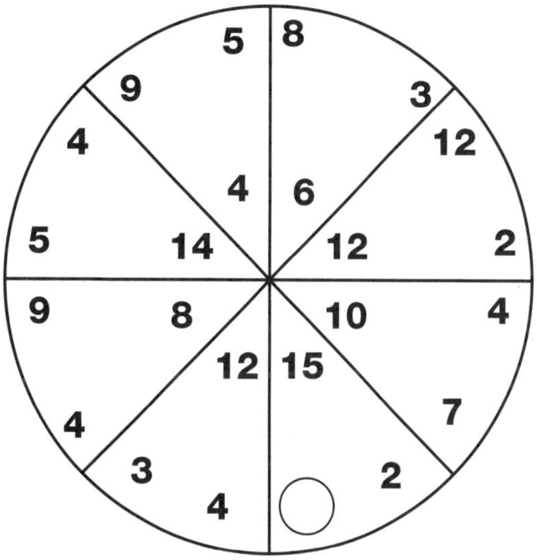

33 PUZZLE

Which number continues the sequence?

3

5

9

15

34 PUZZLE

Which letter replaces the blank and completes the sequence?

J	E	N
O	S	G
A	B	

LEVEL

12

35 PUZZLE

Which playing cards are needed to fill in the blanks?

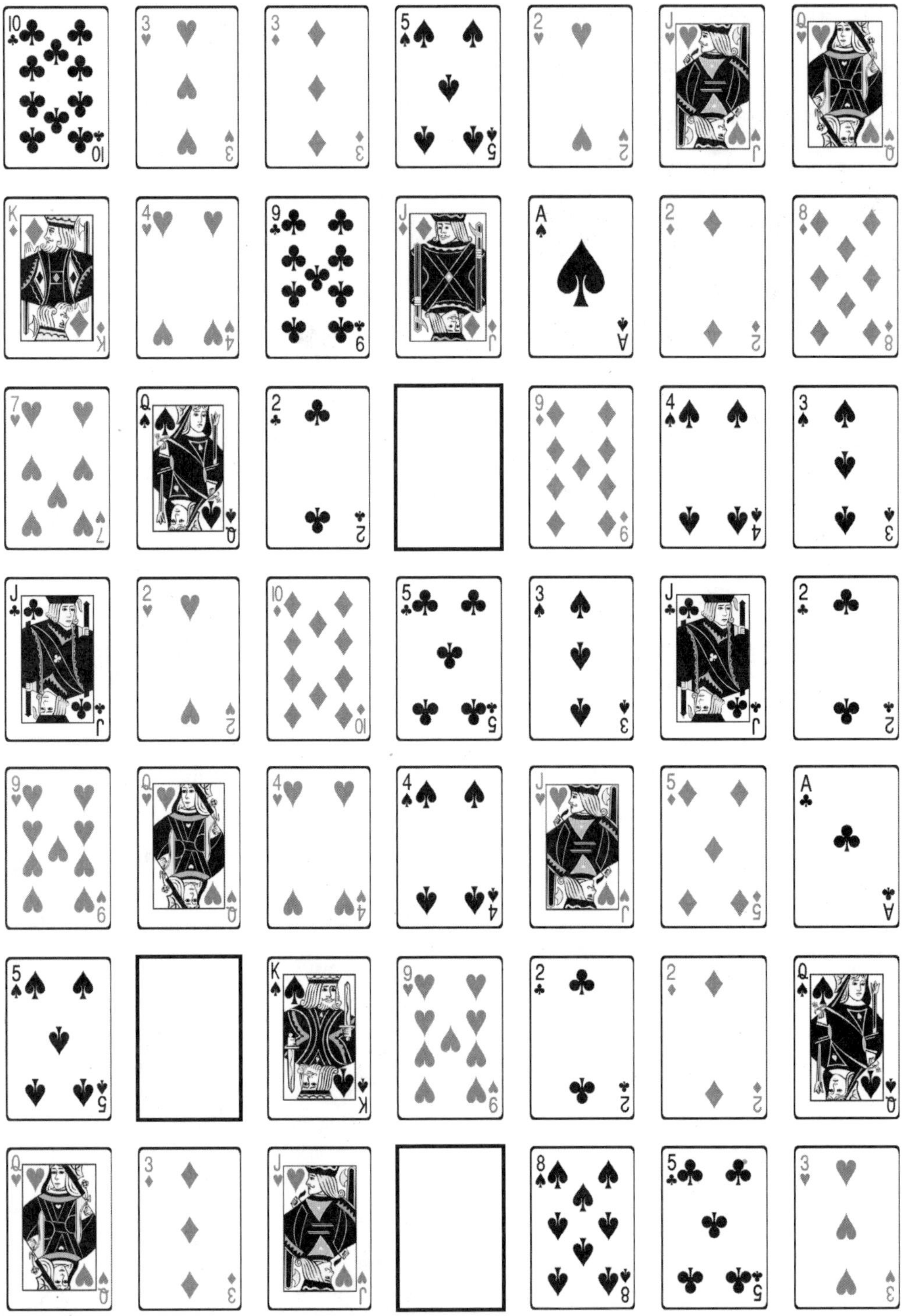

36 PUZZLE

Which number goes in the empty box?

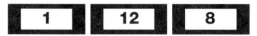

10	5	6
1	12	8
7	9	5
17	1	

37 PUZZLE

What is the missing line value?

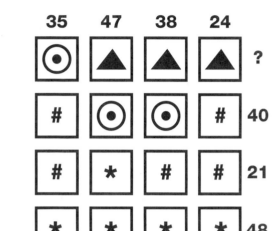

35	47	38	24	
⊙	▲	▲	▲	?
#	⊙	⊙	#	40
#	*	#	#	21
*	*	*	*	48

38 PUZZLE

Which letter goes in the middle?

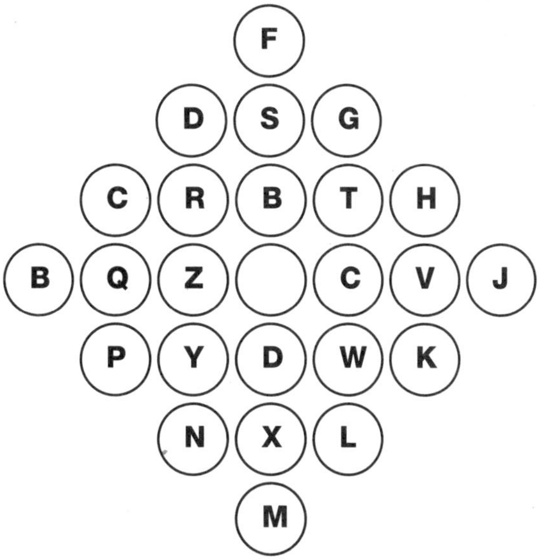

A B C D E F G H

39 PUZZLE

Which number comes next?

1 - 2 - 5 - 10 - 13 - 26 - 29 - ?

40 PUZZLE

Which number goes in the middle of the last star?

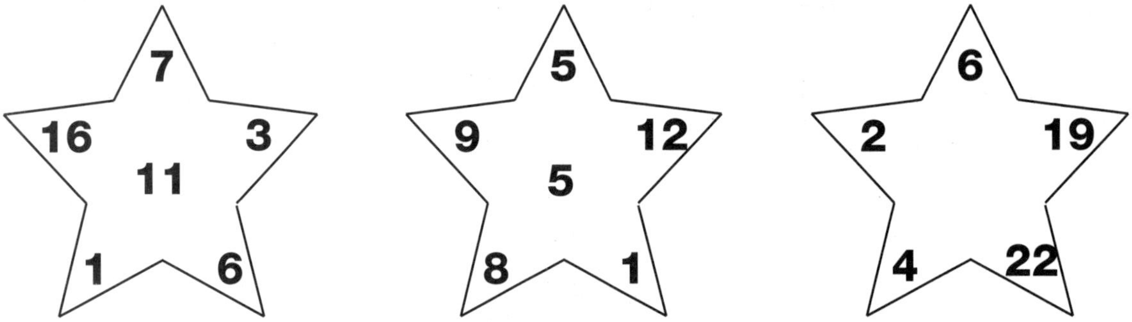

41 PUZZLE

Complete the puzzle.

E	L	Q
H	A	I
D	O	S
S	F	

42 PUZZLE

What is the missing line value?

36	23	24	?	
@	*	#	▲	27
@	▲	▲	#	29
@	*	*	*	24
@	#	#	*	26

43 PUZZLE

Fill in the empty circle.

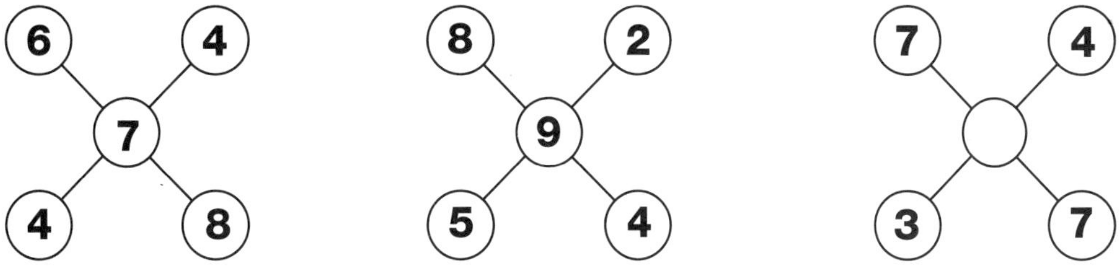

44 PUZZLE

Which letter goes in the empty circle?

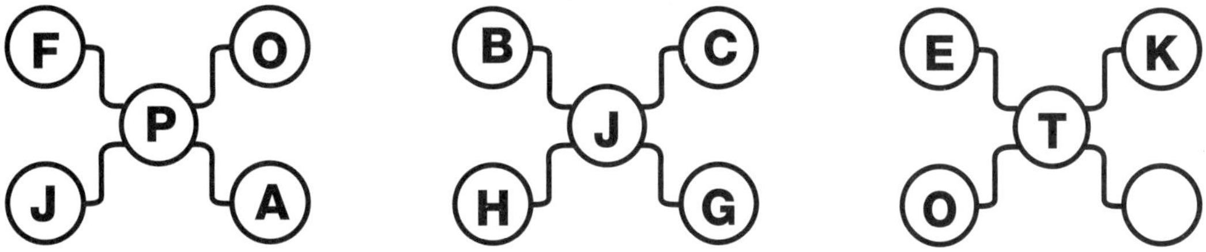

45 PUZZLE

What is the missing line value?

36	40	50	23	
♥	x	#	@	38
x	x	x	@	41
♥	♥	x	@	?
♥	♥	#	♥	37

46 PUZZLE

What goes in the blank corner of the middle square?

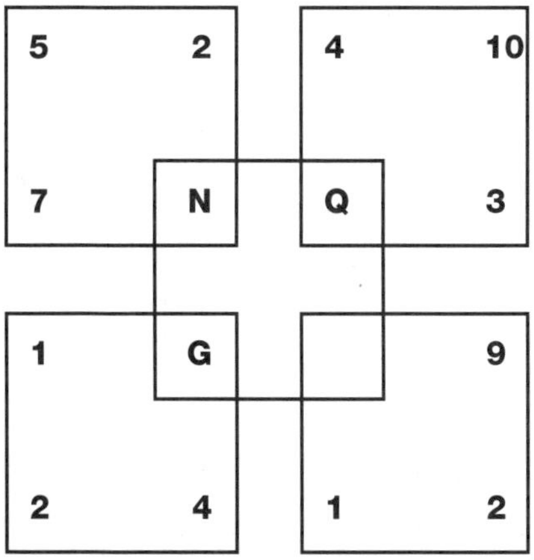

47 PUZZLE

Which number is missing from this column of boxes?

3	1
2	5
8	4
7	12
17	
16	23

48 PUZZLE

Helen's watch needs repairing. She sets it correctly at 4:12pm but three hours later it shows 8:00pm. After a further two hours she notices that it reads 10:32pm.

She goes to bed early and gets up when her watch shows 6:46am.

What time is it really?

49 PUZZLE

What is missing from the blank segment?

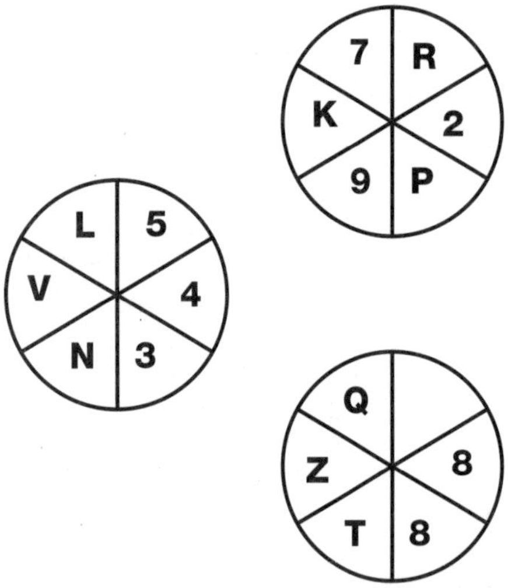

50 PUZZLE

Which number is needed to finish the puzzle correctly?

2	5	3	7
9	8	2	1
4	8	0	8
5	3	4	

51 PUZZLE

Which number needs to be added to the last grid?

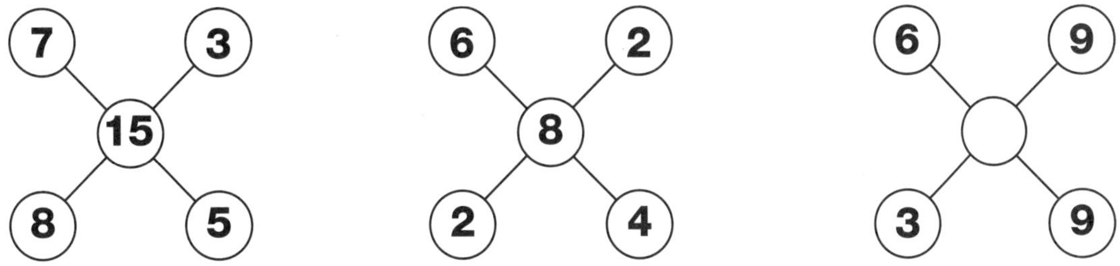

52 PUZZLE

Which number goes in the blank segment?

53 PUZZLE

Which number completes the puzzle?

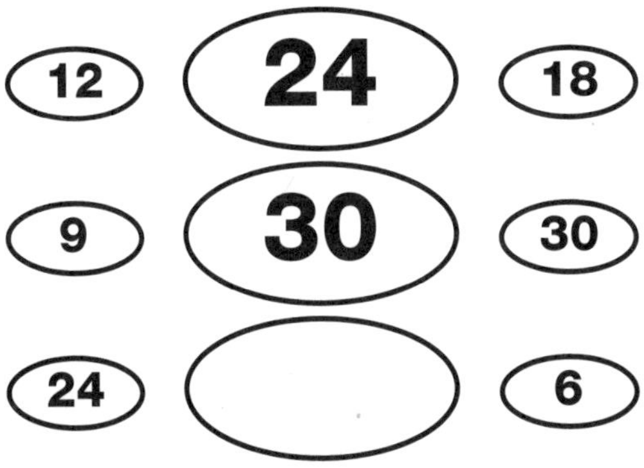

54 PUZZLE

Which number replaces the question mark?

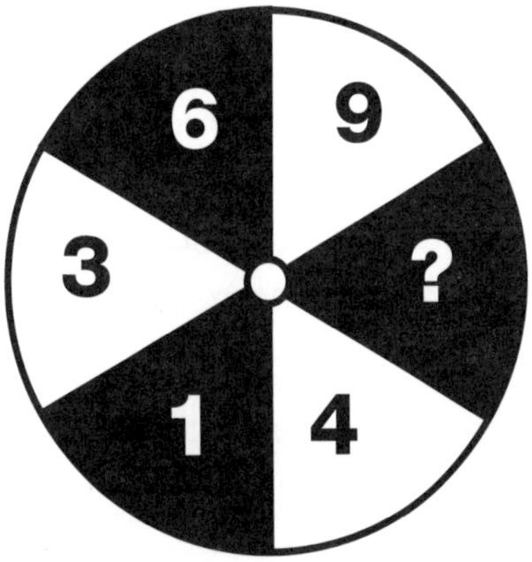

1 PUZZLE

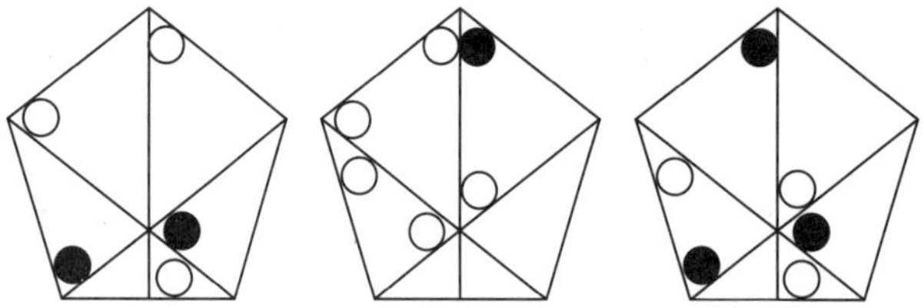

is to:

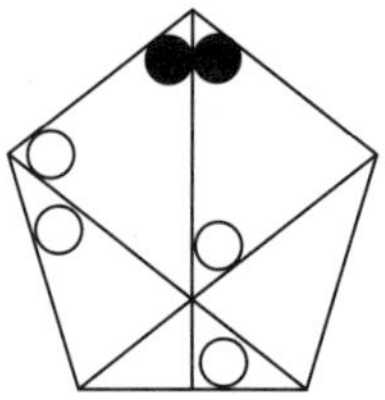

as:

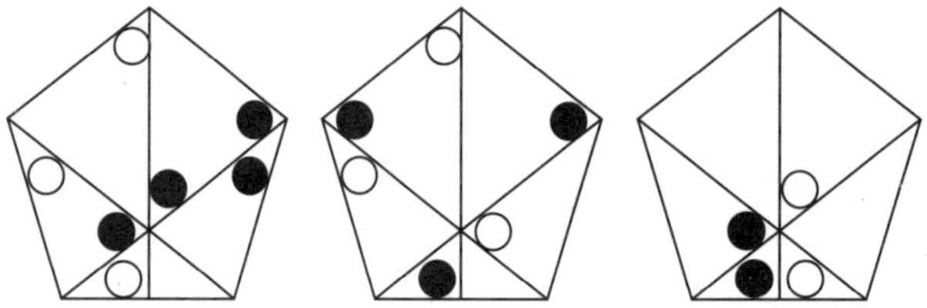

is to:

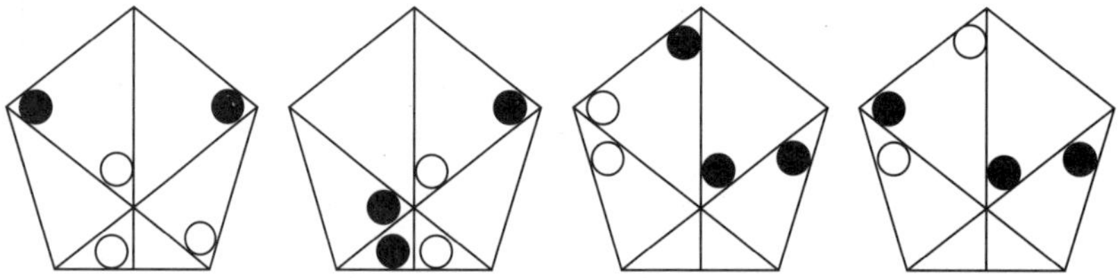

A B C D

2 PUZZLE

Out of 100 people surveyed, 75 percent had a personal computer, 68 percent had a dishwasher, 85 percent had a refrigerator and 80 percent had a video recorder.

How many people had all four items?

3 PUZZLE

Which is the odd one out?

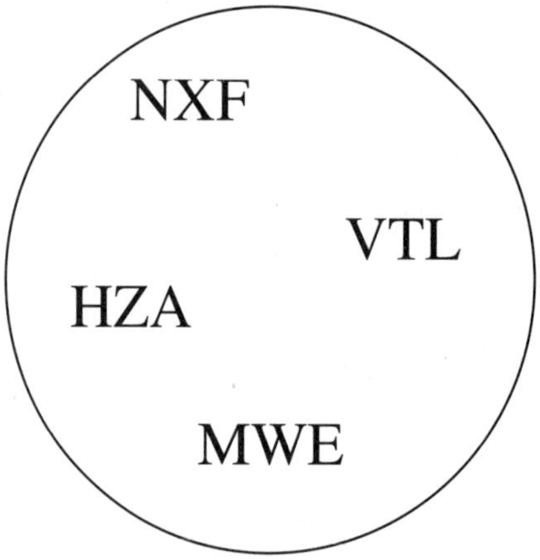

4 PUZZLE

What square should replace the question mark?

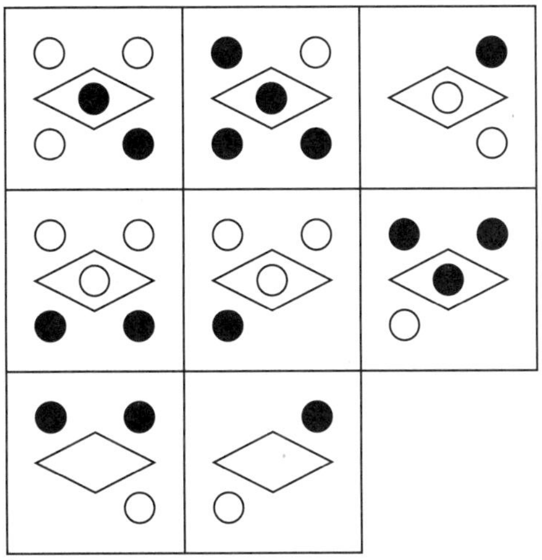

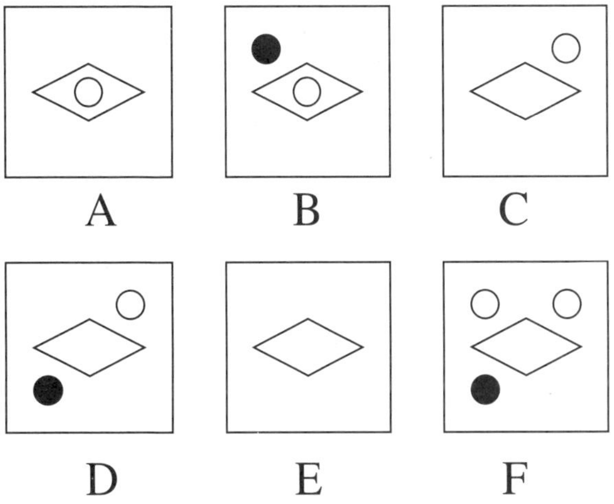

5 PUZZLE

Which is the odd one out?

54	24	17
36	14	51
18	72	12

6 PUZZLE

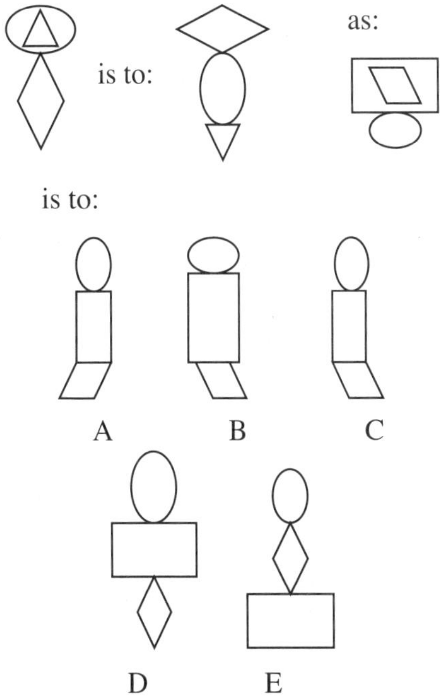

7 PUZZLE

The seventh batsman to be out in the innings has scored 36 runs, which raises the average for all seven batsmen dismissed from 15 to 18. How many would the seventh batsman have needed to score to raise the team average to 20?

8 PUZZLE

6384 is to 183

and

3258 is to 108

and

6191 is to 611

therefore

3194 is to ?

9 PUZZLE

Insert the numbers into the grid, so that all calculations are correct both across and down. 6 and 8 are already placed.

	x		=	6
+		+		÷
	-		=	
=		=		=
8	-		=	

10 PUZZLE

How many lines appear below?

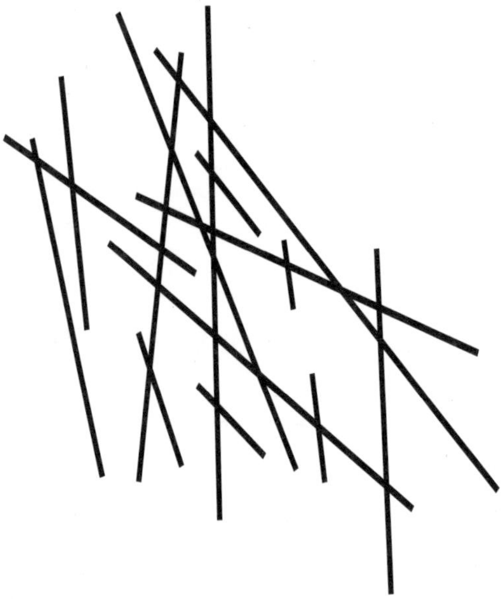

11 PUZZLE

Each line and symbol which appears in the four outer circles, below, is transferred to the centre circle according to these rules. If a line or symbol occurs in the outer circles once, it is transferred; if it occurs twice, it is possibly transferred; three times, it is transferred; four times, it is not transferred. Which of the circles A, B, C, D or E, should appear at the centre of the diagram, below?

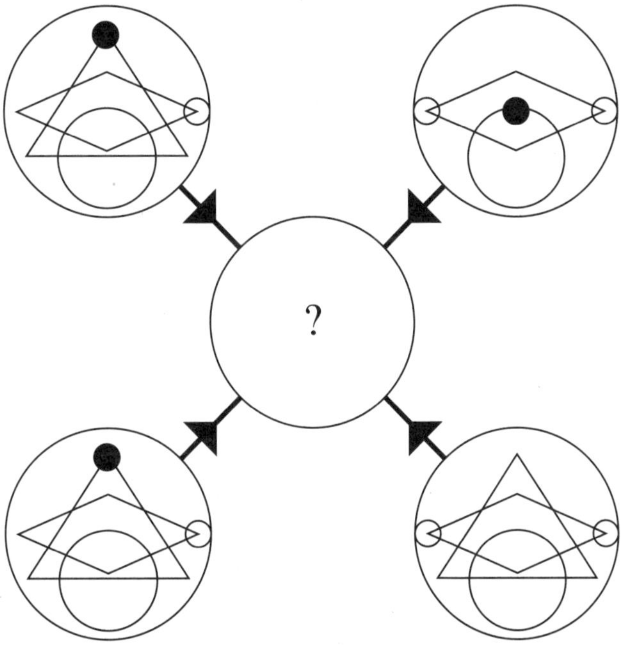

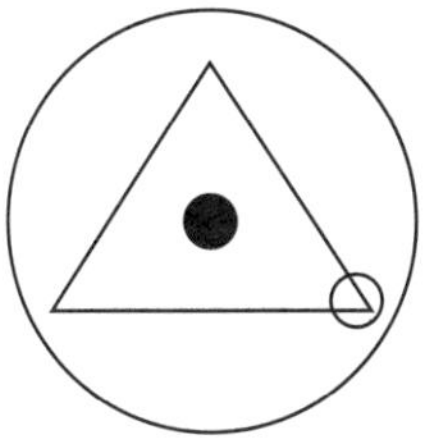
A

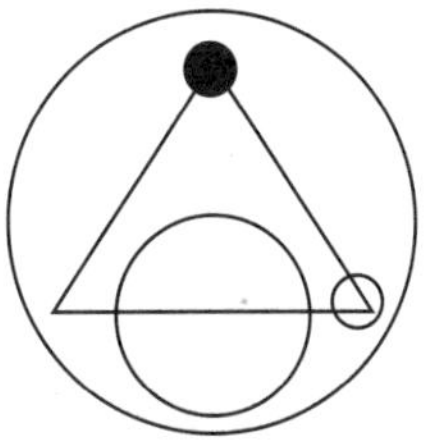
B

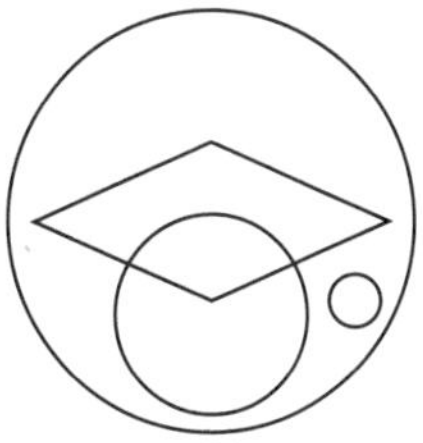
C

D

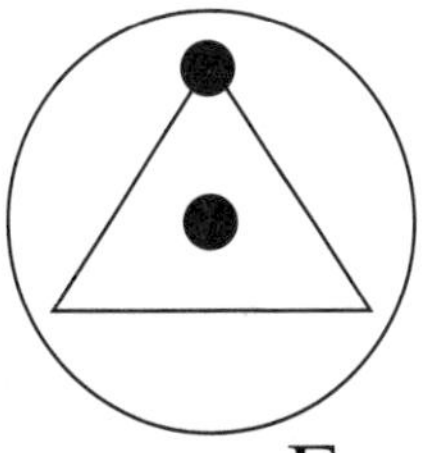
E

12 PUZZLE

Which circle should replace the question mark?

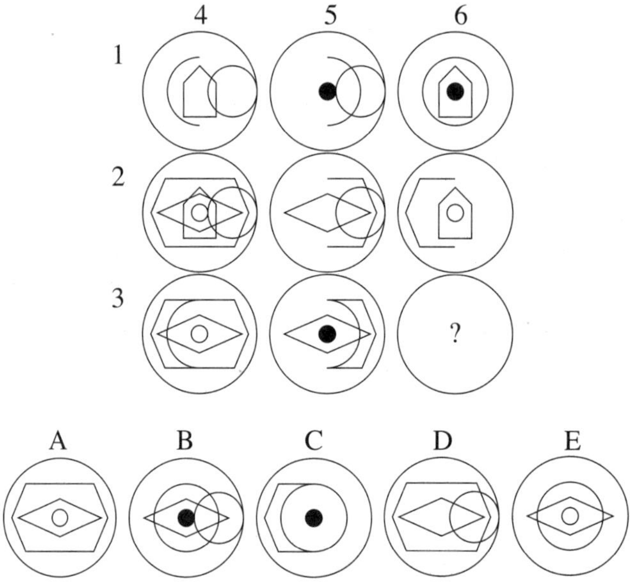

13 PUZZLE

What number should replace the question mark?

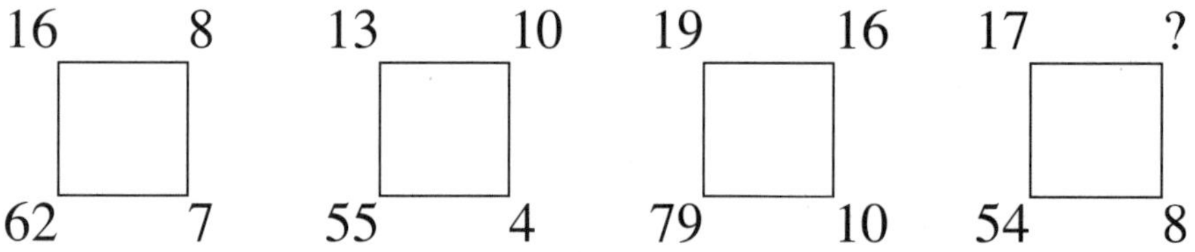

14 PUZZLE

What number should replace the question mark?

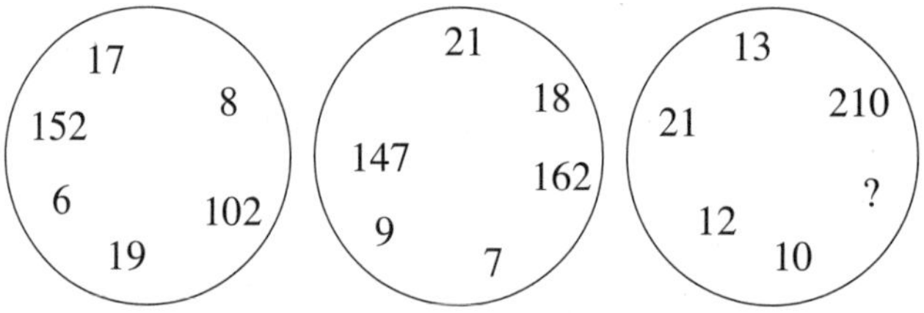

15 PUZZLE

Can you replace the question marks with the signs x or ÷ to make it total 60?

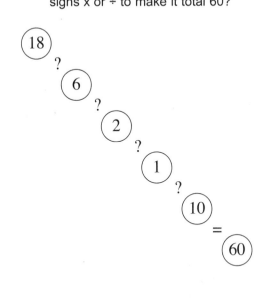

18 ? 6 ? 2 ? 1 ? 10 = 60

16 PUZZLE

What is the name given to a group of TEAL?

(a) MUSTER
(b) MURDER
(c) KNOB
(d) KNOT
(e) GLEAN

17 PUZZLE

Which two words mean the same?

COGITATE
PORTENT
INDIGENCE
INDICATION
INTRACTABLE
SUPERFICIAL

18 PUZZLE

Which letter should replace the question mark?

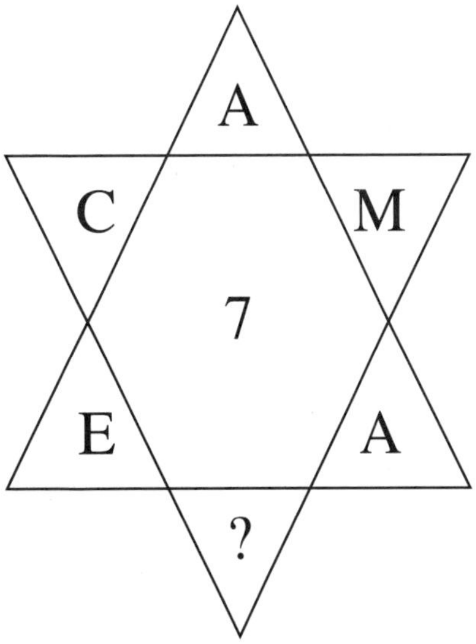

LEVEL

13

19 PUZZLE

Which word is the opposite of ZEPHYR?
(a) JARGON (b) SQUALL (c) TERMAGENT
(d) MANIFESTATION

20 PUZZLE

What number should replace the question mark?

6	4	7	2	1	1	2	7	4
6	6	4	7	2	1	1	2	7
4	6	6	4	7	2	?	1	4

21 PUZZLE

What are GALLIGASKINS?
(a) VEHICLES (b) WARMING PANS
(c) SMALL COLOURED FLAGS (d) TYPE OF HAY
(e) BREECHES

22 PUZZLE

Change 131°F to Celsius.

23 PUZZLE

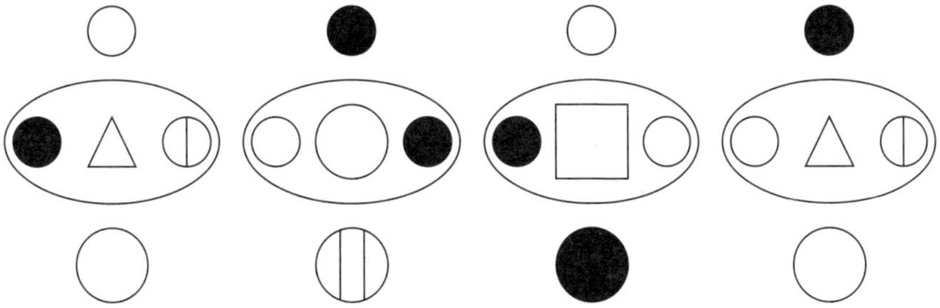

What comes next in the above sequence?

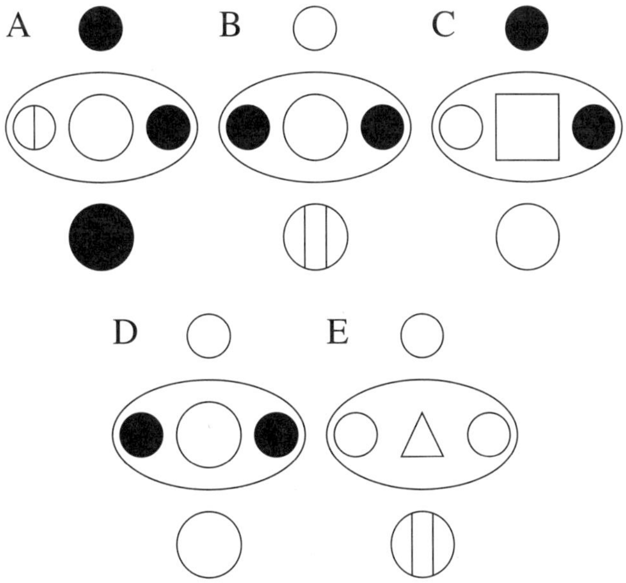

24 PUZZLE

Which word is the opposite of VALOROUS?

(a) UNSULLIED (b) PUNCTILIOUS
(c) TIMID (d) FAWN

LEVEL

13

25 PUZZLE

Each line and symbol which appears in the four outer circles below, is transferred to the centre circle according to these rules. If a line or symbol occurs in the outer circles once, it is transferred; if it occurs twice, it is possibly transferred; three times, it is transferred; four times, it is not transferred. Which of the circles A, B, C, D or E, should appear at the centre of the diagram, below?

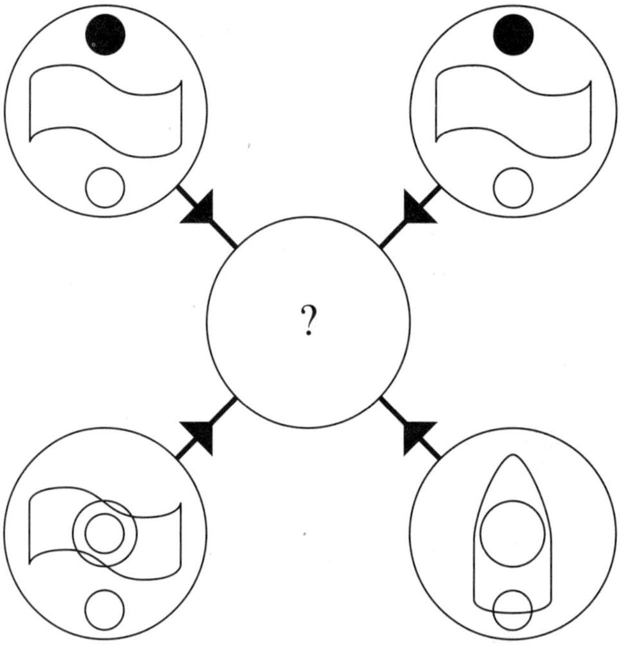

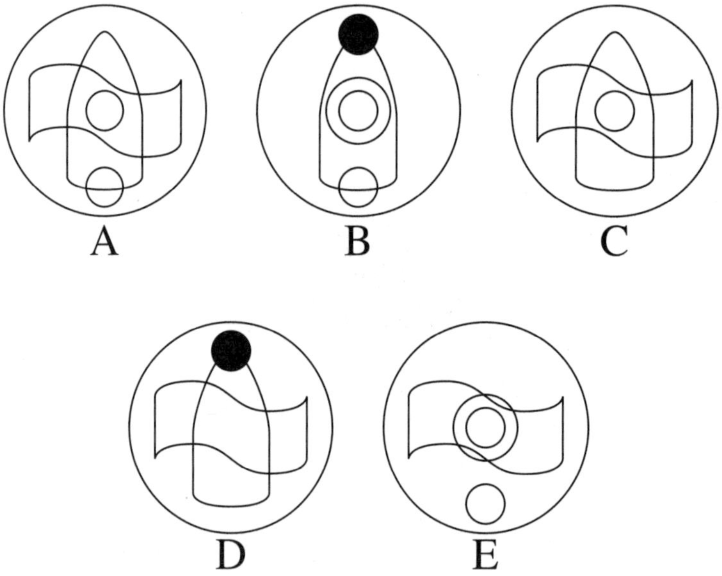

26 PUZZLE

Which of the bottom boxes goes in the middle of this sequence?

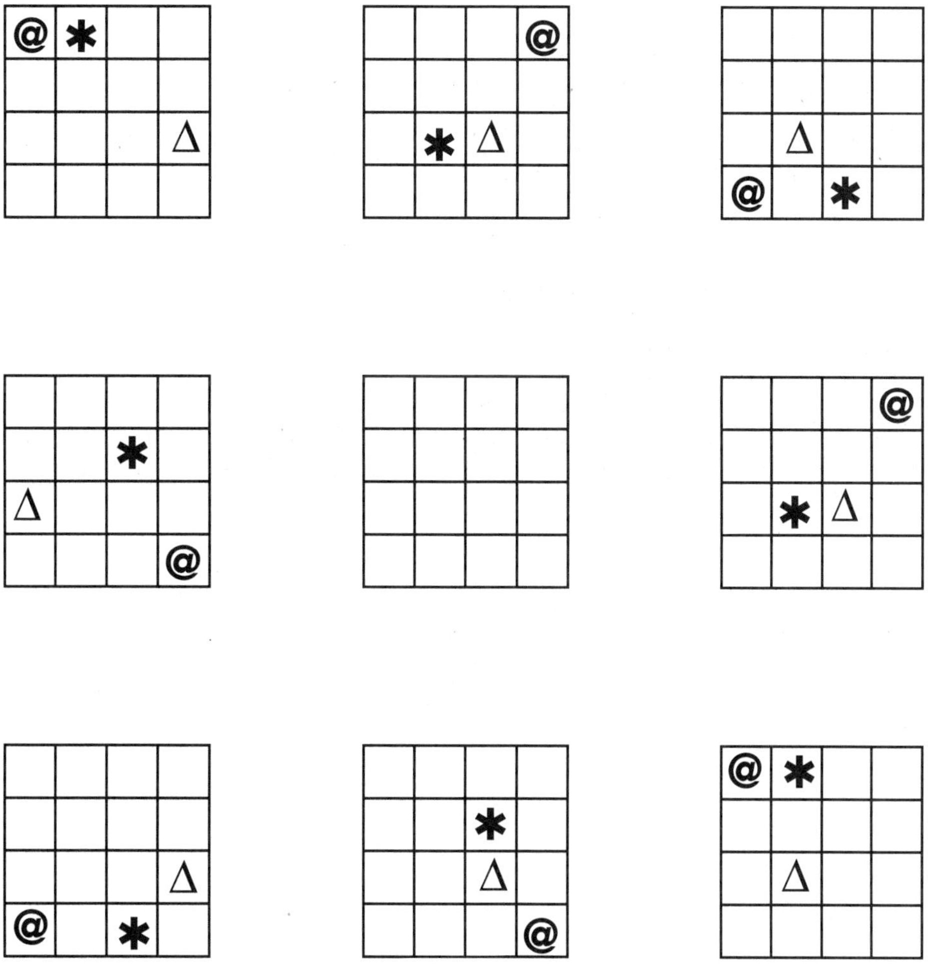

A

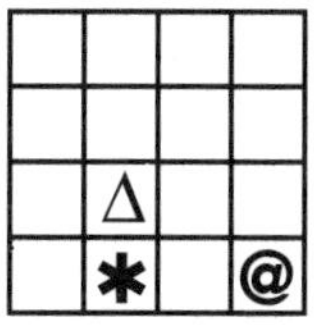

B

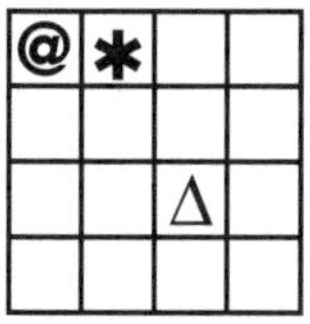

C

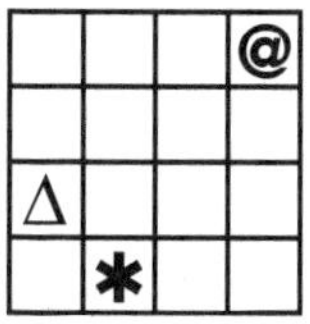

D

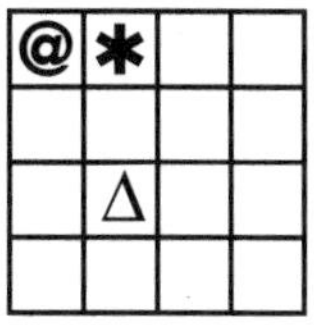

E

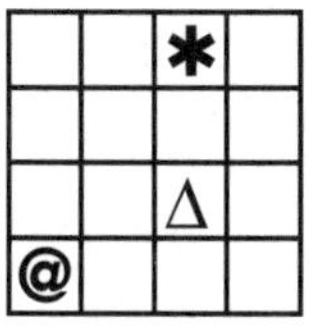

F

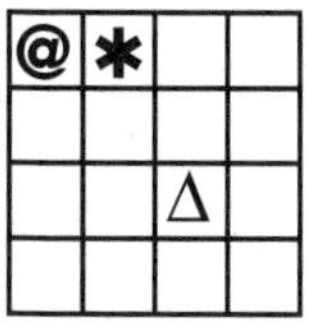

27 PUZZLE

Which domino fits into the empty space in this arrangement?

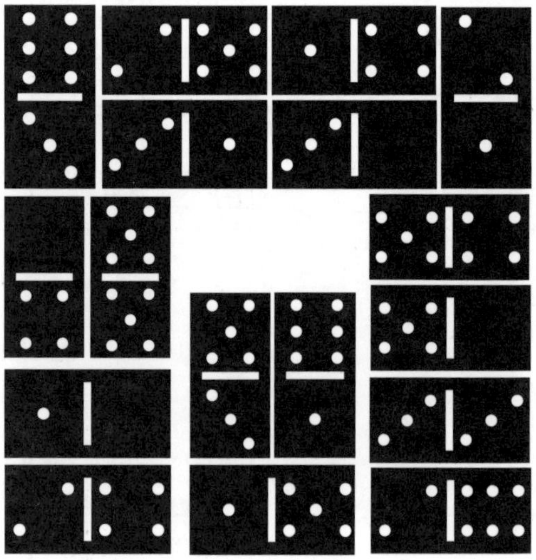

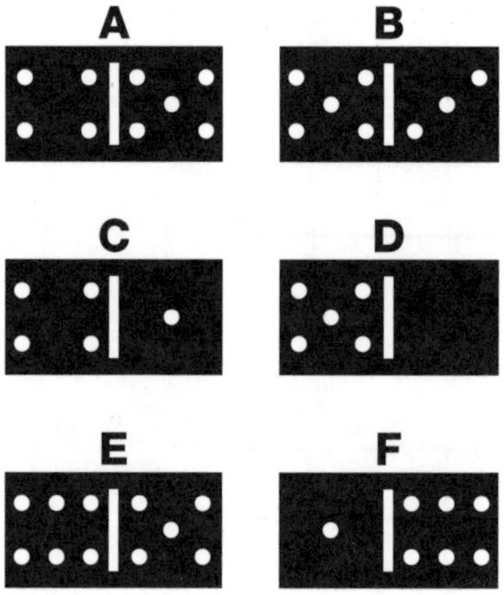

28 PUZZLE

Which number goes in the middle?

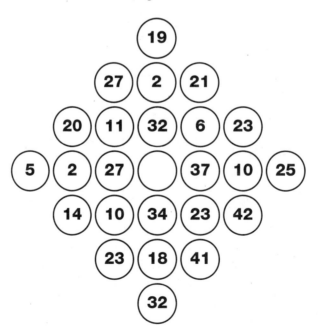

			19			
		27	2	21		
	20	11	32	6	23	
5	2	27		37	10	25
	14	10	34	23	42	
		23	18	41		
			32			

29 PUZZLE

Which number is missing from the web?

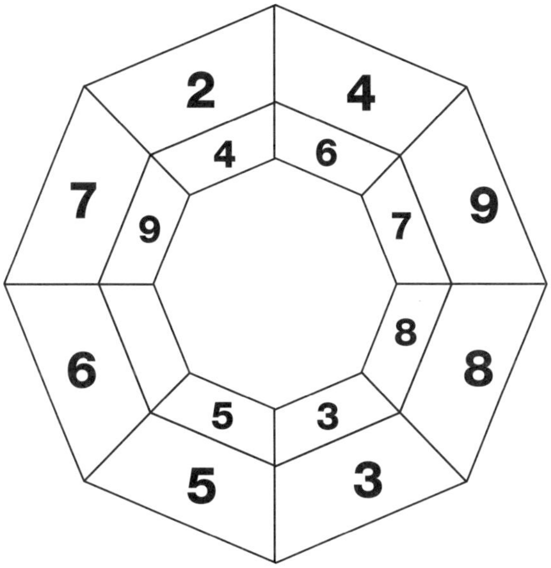

30 PUZZLE

Which number is missing from the wheel?

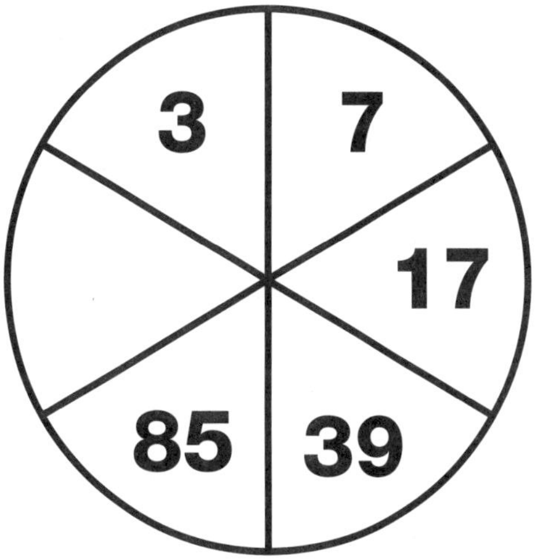

31 PUZZLE

Which watch is the odd one out?

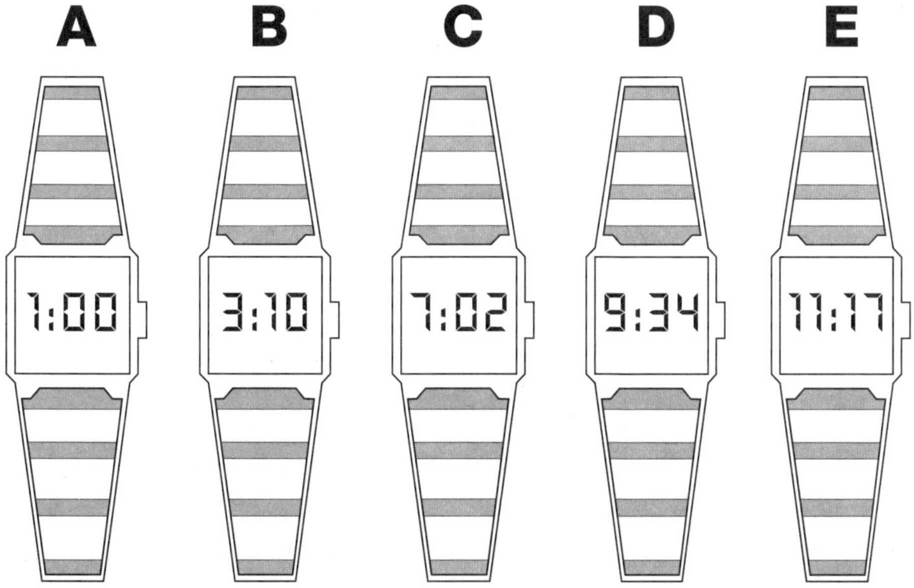

32 PUZZLE

Which playing cards are needed to fill in the blanks?

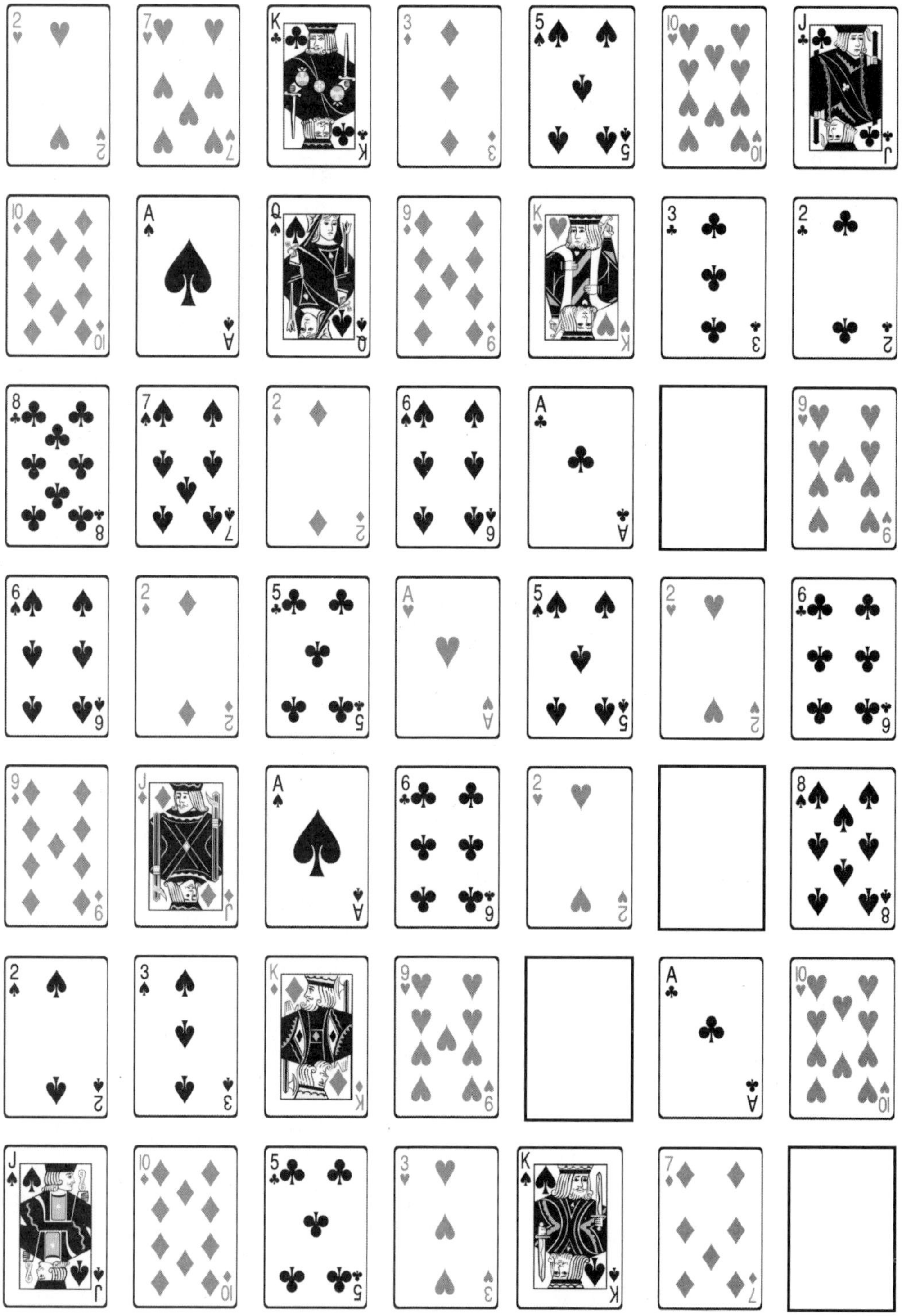

33 PUZZLE

Which number completes the third triangle?

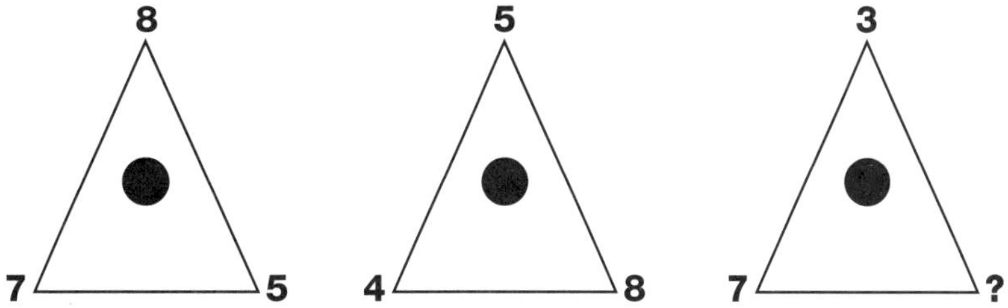

34 PUZZLE

What time should the blank clock show?

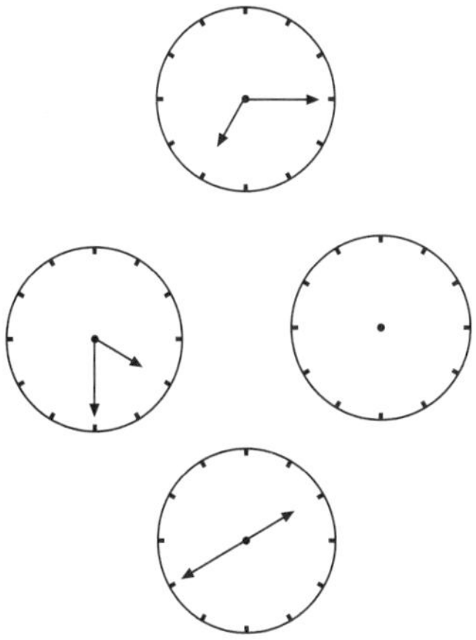

35 PUZZLE

What is missing from the empty segment?

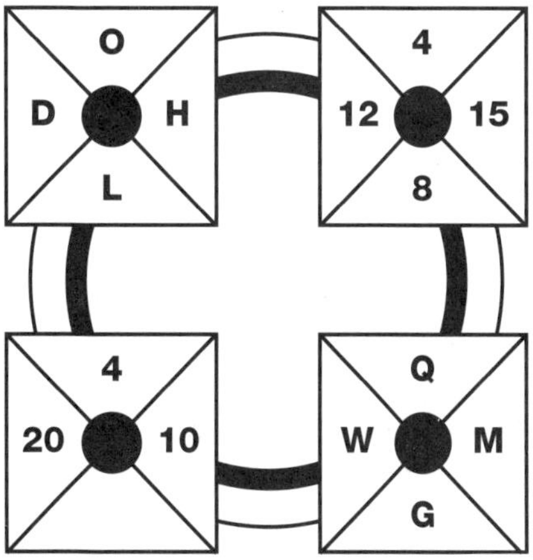

36 PUZZLE

What goes at the bottom of the last triangle?

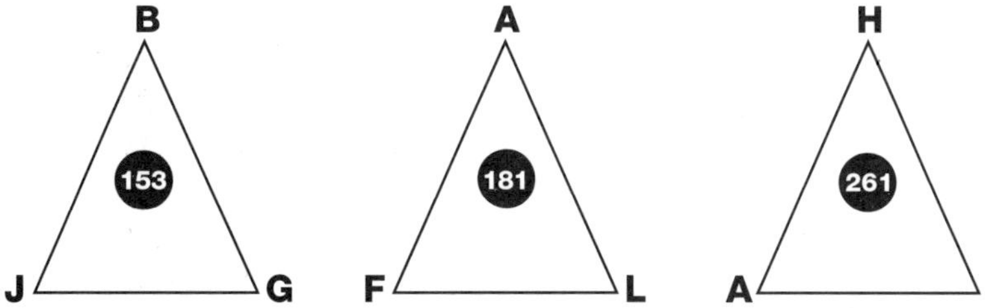

37 PUZZLE

Which letter replaces the blank and completes the sequence?

I	L	O
R	U	X
A		G

38 PUZZLE

Which letters finish the grid?

H	X	J	Z
U	O	D	H
	G	V	P
I	Y	I	

39 PUZZLE

Which number goes in the empty circle?

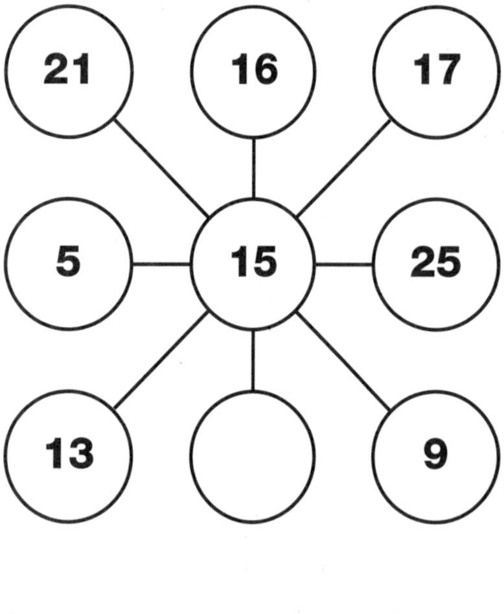

40 PUZZLE

Which letter completes the wheel?

41 PUZZLE

Which two letters are missing from the bottom grids?

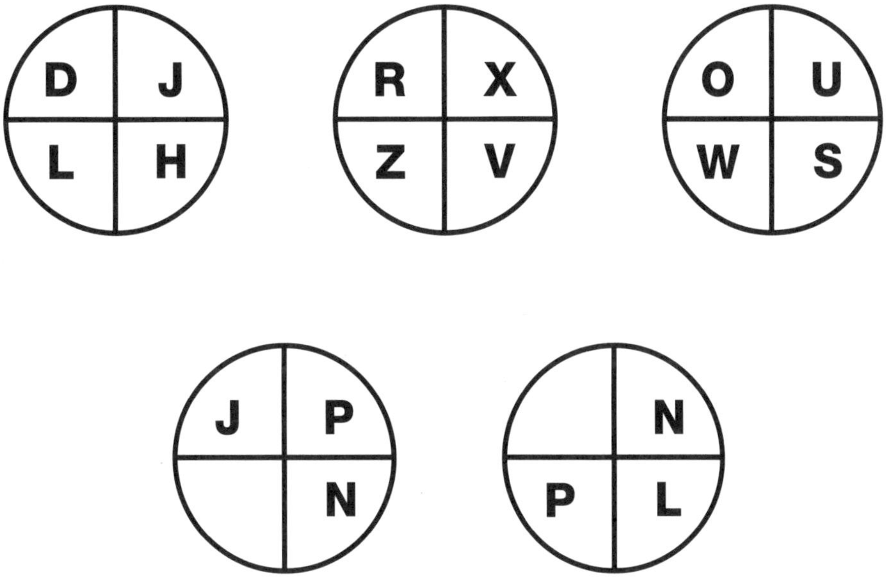

42 PUZZLE

Fill in the correct number.

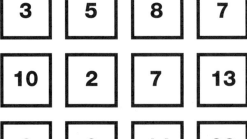

3	5	8	7
10	2	7	13
6	6	14	22
9	2	5	

43 PUZZLE

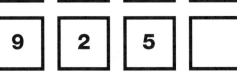

Fill in the empty segment.

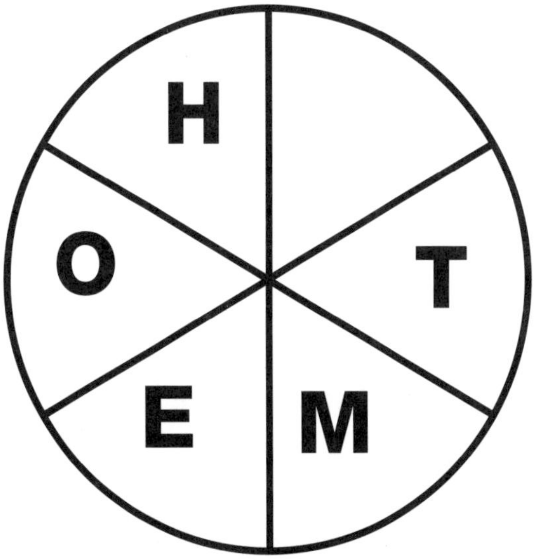

44 PUZZLE

Which number is missing from the last circle?

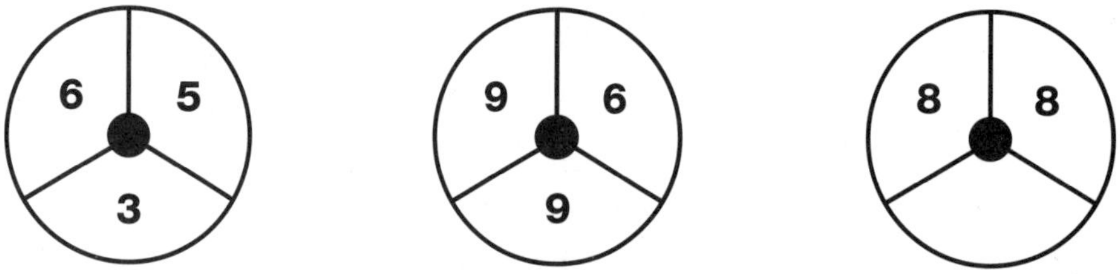

45 PUZZLE

Which number goes at the top of the third star?

46 PUZZLE

Which letter logically goes in the blank segment?

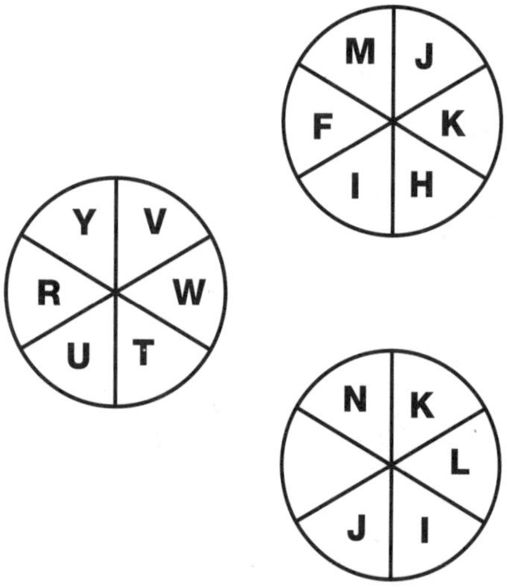

47 PUZZLE

Complete the bottom grid.

3	8	18
5	10	20

4	10	22
6	12	24

7	16	
9	18	

48 PUZZLE

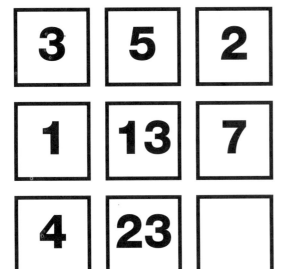

Which number is needed to complete this puzzle?

3	5	2
1	13	7
4	23	

49 PUZZLE

Finish the chain by filling in the blank link.

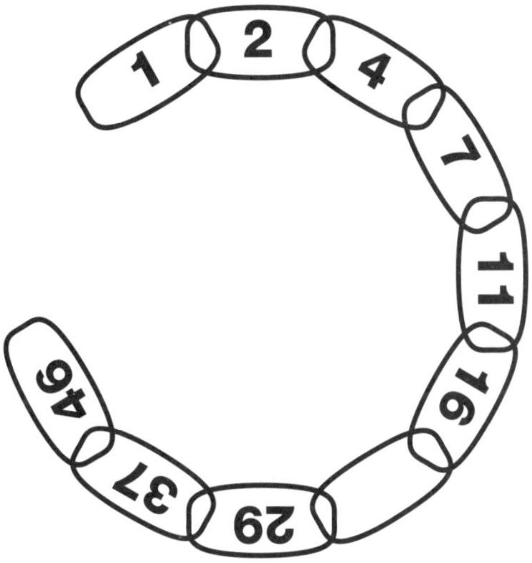

50 PUZZLE

Which letter goes at the bottom?

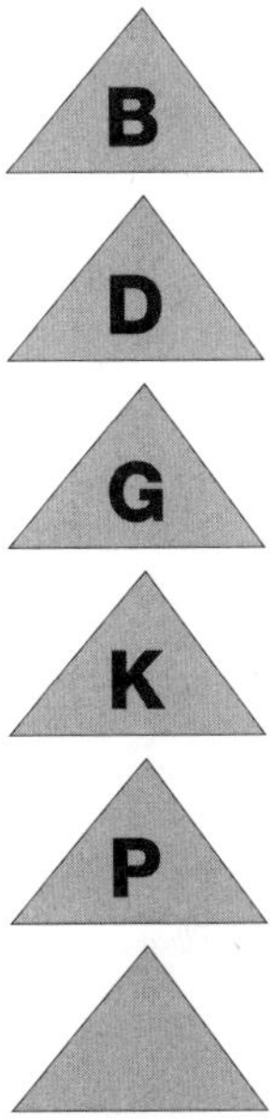

51 PUZZLE

Which number goes in the empty box?

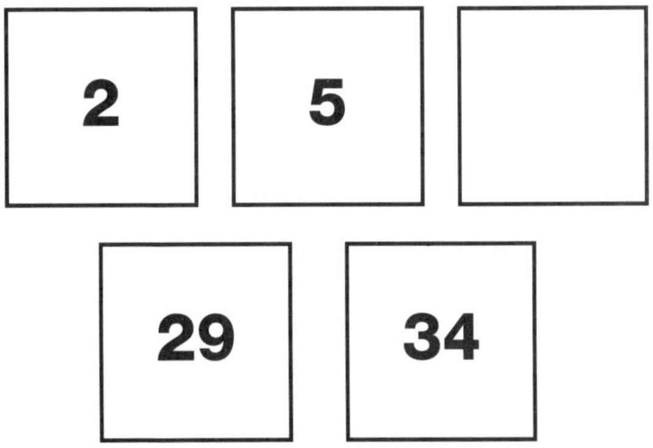

LEVEL 13

52 PUZZLE

Farmer Giles has sent his livestock to market for sale but the farmhand has forgotten how much he was to sell each animal for. The farmer though had drawn him some pictures which showed the equivalent value of each of the animals but didn't finish it. Can you solve the problem for the luckless farmhand?

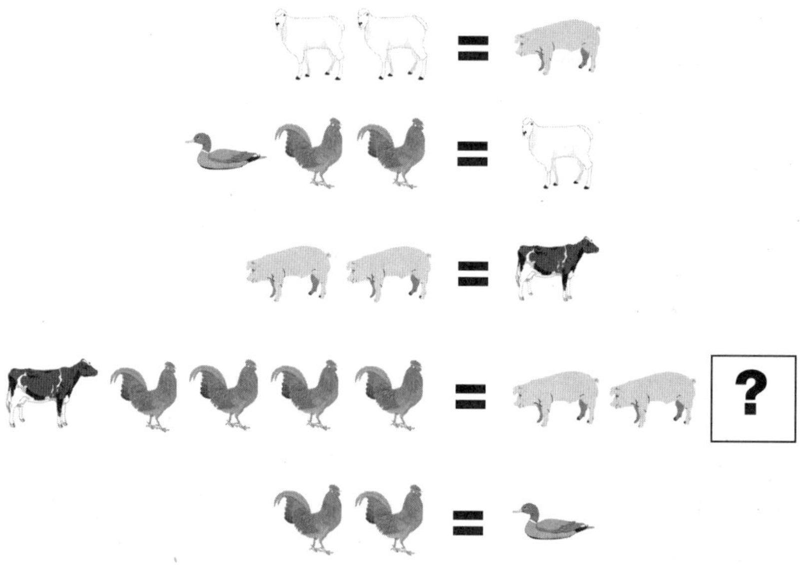

53 PUZZLE

Which letter goes in the empty square and completes the puzzle?

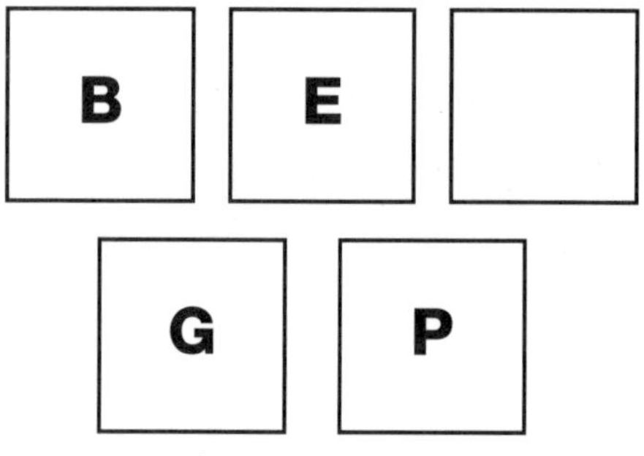

54 PUZZLE

Which letter replaces the blank and completes the sequence?

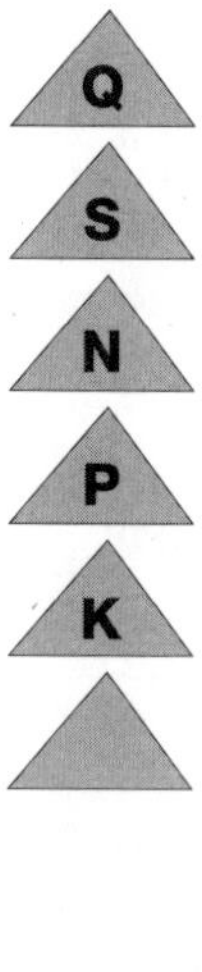

1 PUZZLE

Which cards are missing?

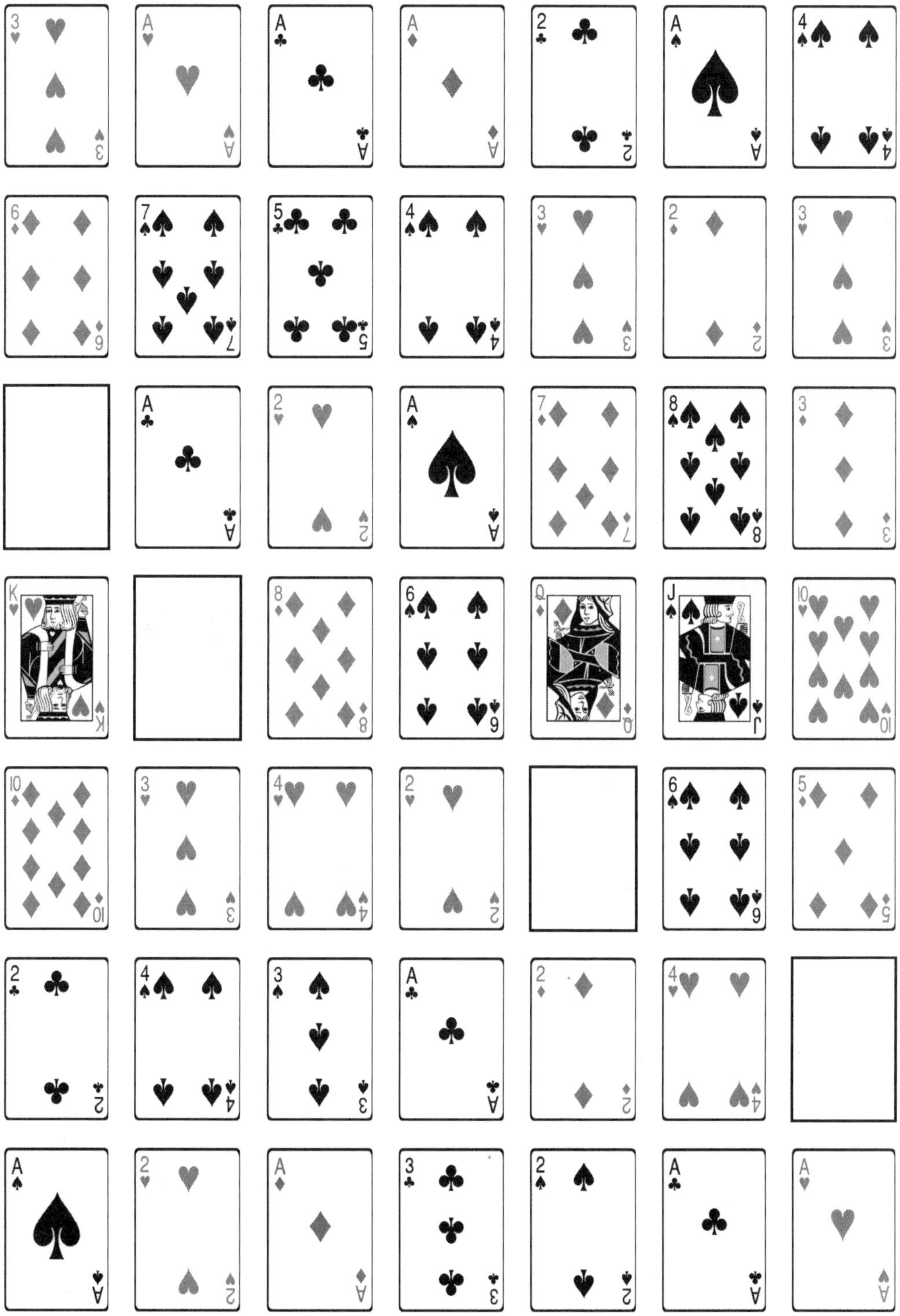

2 PUZZLE

Which is the odd one out?

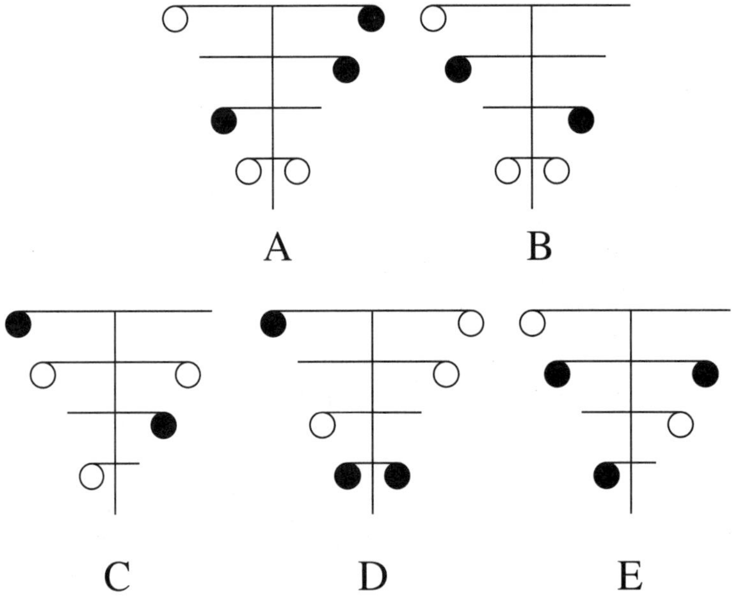

3 PUZZLE

Find the value of x.

18
31
21¼
26¾
24½
22½
27¾
x

4 PUZZLE

Which is the odd one out?

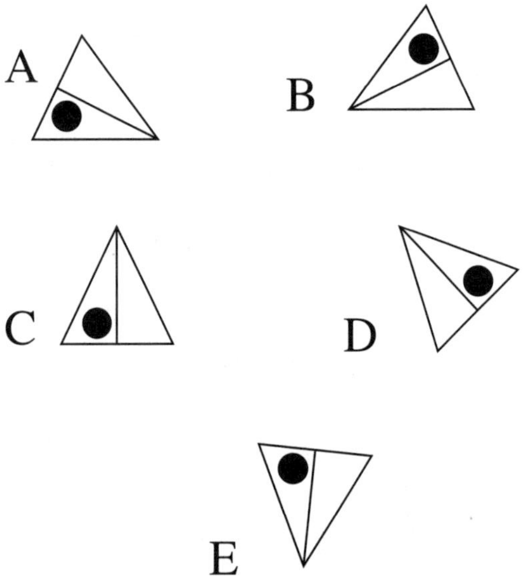

PUZZLE 5

A B C D E F G H

What letter is three to the left of the letter which comes midway between the letter two to the right of the letter A and the letter three to the right of the letter D?

PUZZLE 6

What number should replace the question mark?

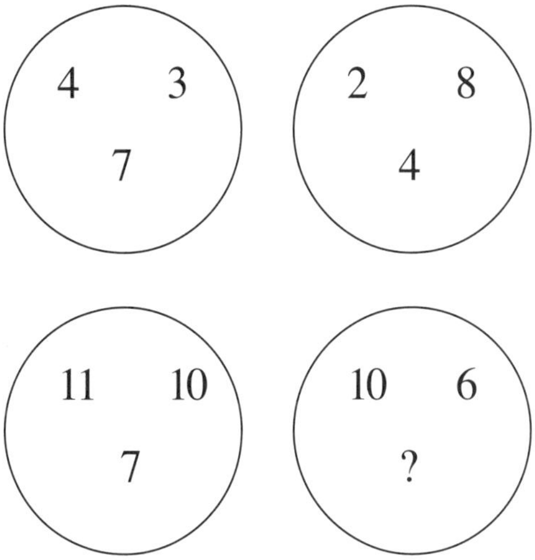

PUZZLE 7

Which is the odd one out?

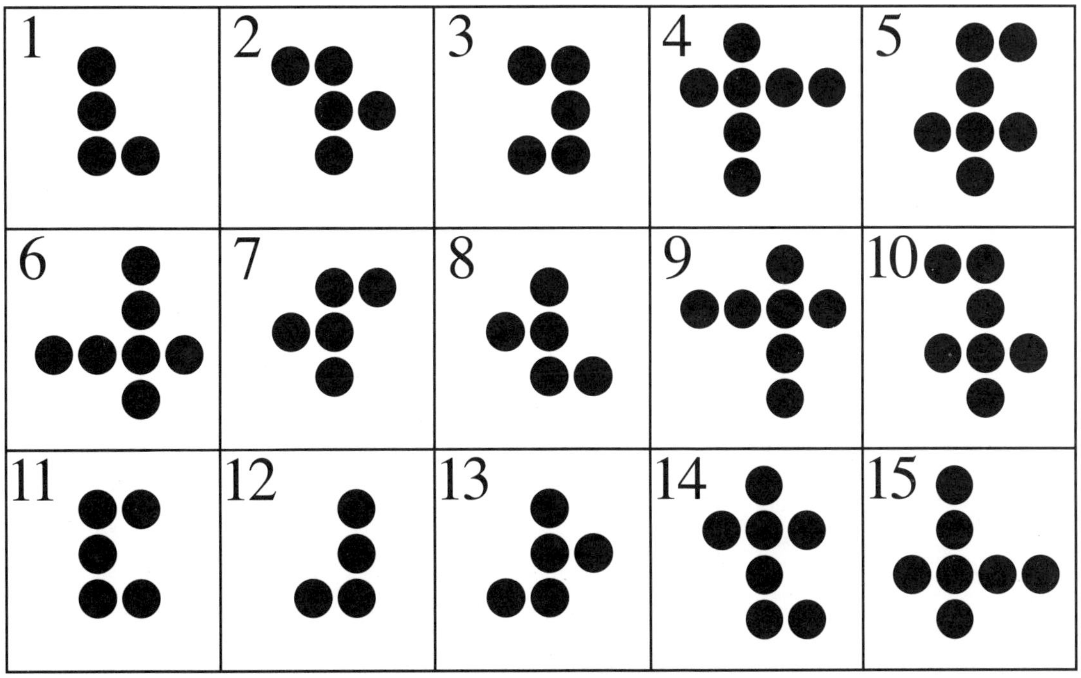

LEVEL 14

PUZZLE 8

What number should replace the question mark?

1		3		6
1	3	4	?	9
6		8		6

PUZZLE 9

What number should replace the question mark?

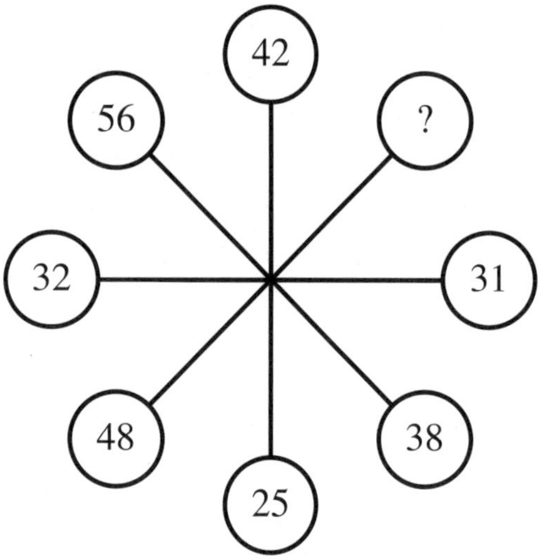

PUZZLE 10

In how many ways can the word TURN be read? Start at the central letter T and move in any direction.

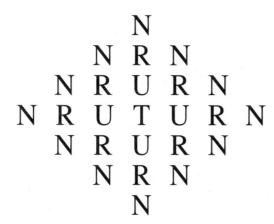

N
N R N
N R U R N
N R U T U R N
N R U R N
N R N
N

PUZZLE 11

Which is the odd one out?

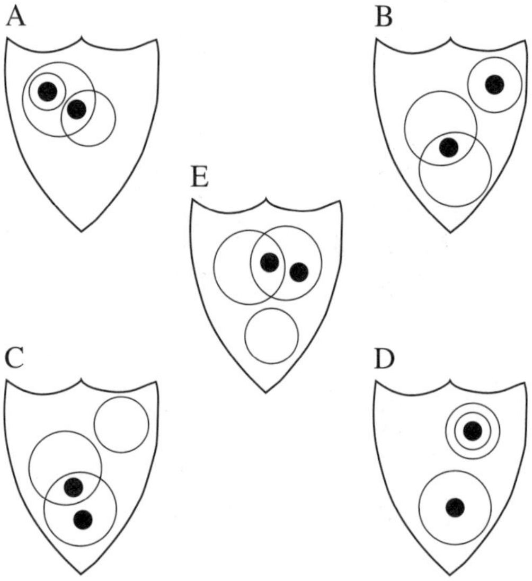

12 PUZZLE

Each line and symbol which appears in the four outer circles, below, is transferred to the centre circle according to these rules. If a line or symbol occurs in the outer circles once, it is transferred; if it occurs twice, it is possibly transferred; three times, it is transferred; four times, it is not transferred. Which of the circles A, B, C, D or E, should appear at the centre of the diagram, below?

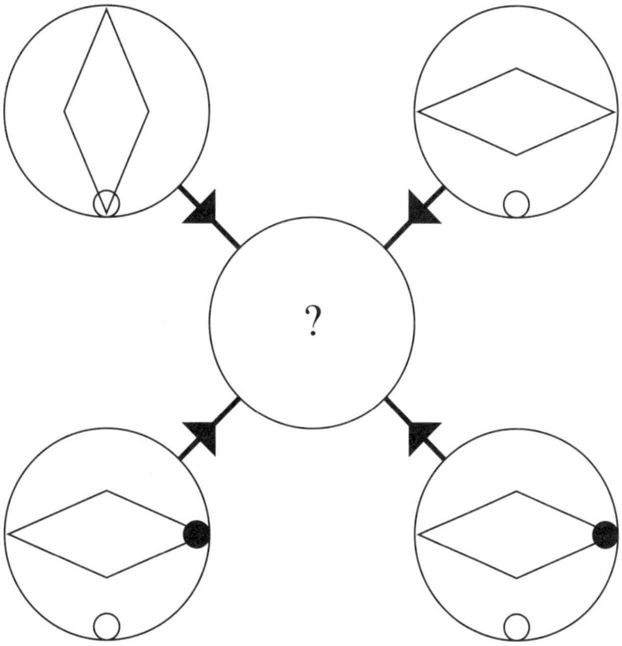

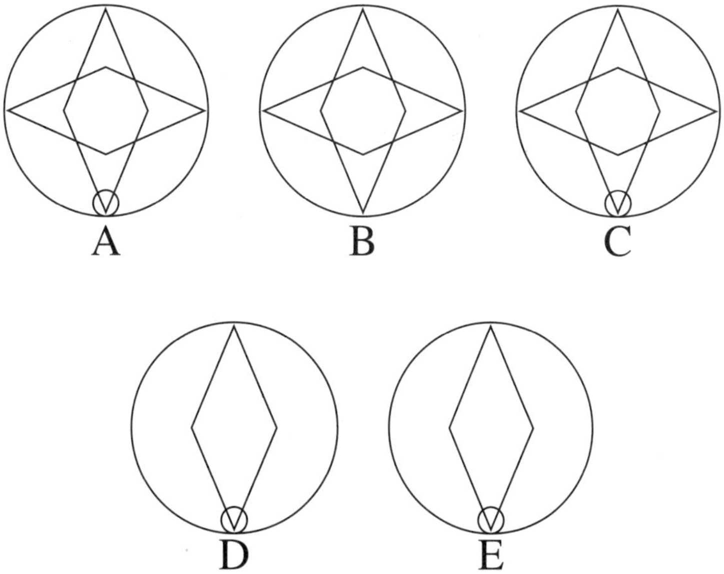

13 PUZZLE

Which pentagons are the odd two out?

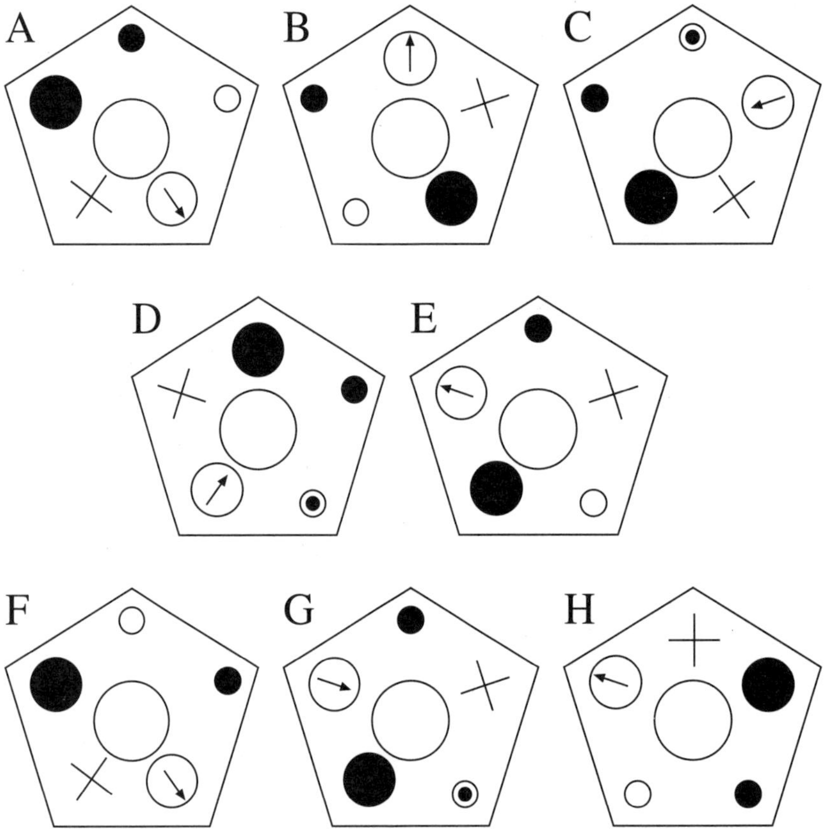

14 PUZZLE

What number should replace the question mark?

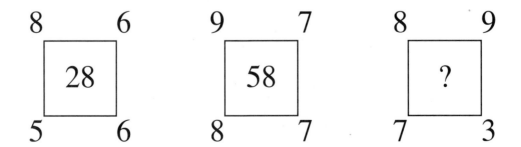

8		6	9		7	8		9
	28			58			?	
5		6	8		7	7		3

15 PUZZLE

Which circle should replace the question mark?

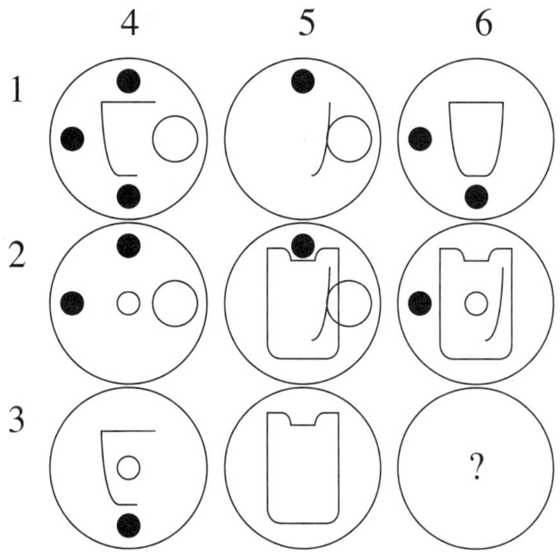

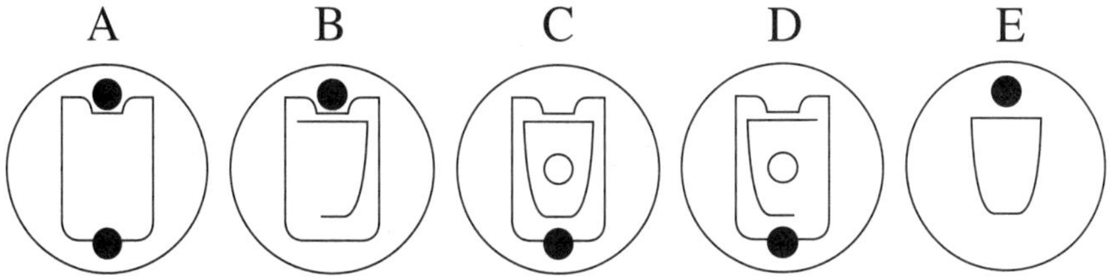

16 PUZZLE

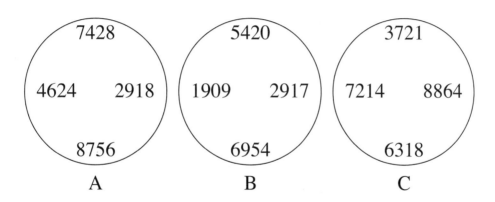

Which is the odd one out?

A: 7428, 4624, 2918, 8756

B: 5420, 1909, 2917, 6954

C: 3721, 7214, 8864, 6318

LEVEL

14

17 PUZZLE

What number should replace the question mark?

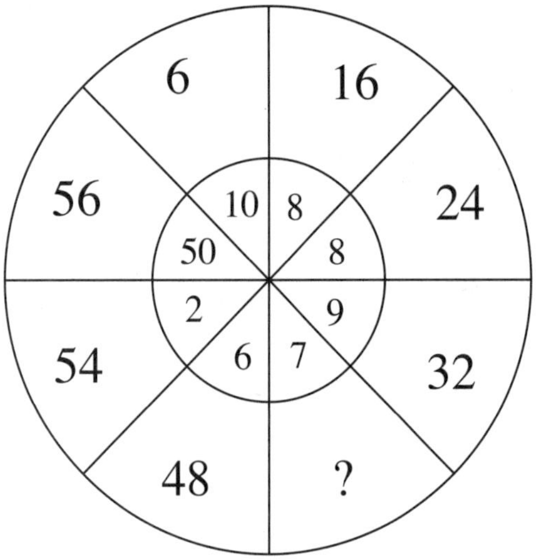

18 PUZZLE

What number should replace the question mark?

7	9	4	64
8	5	5	65
2	4	11	66
5	6	2	?

19 PUZZLE

What number should replace the question mark?

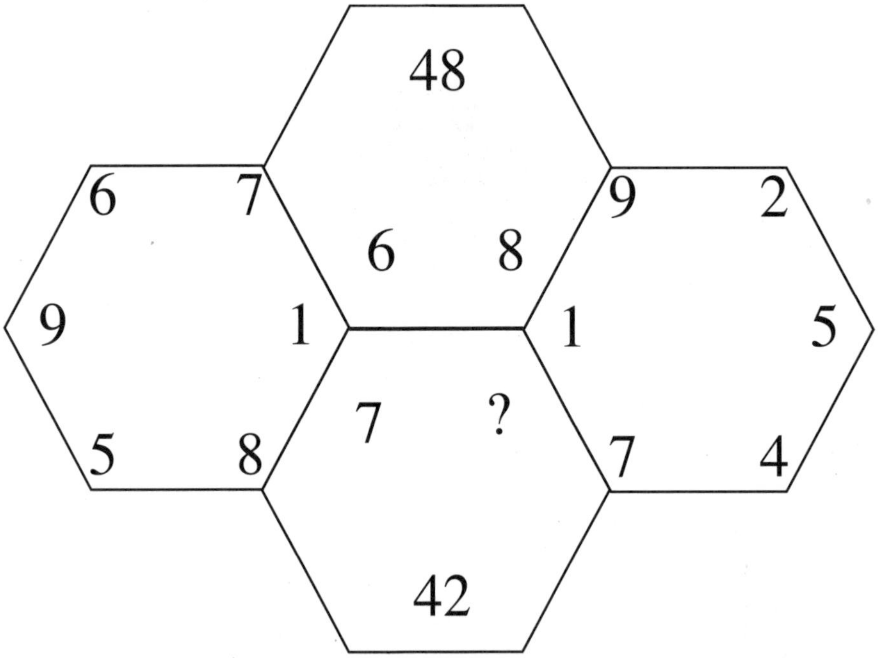

PUZZLE 20

What is a GAUCHO?

(a) MINSTREL
(b) WINE
(c) BOAT
(d) FISH
(e) COWBOY

PUZZLE 21

Which two words mean the opposite?

DELINEATION
DISSIPATE
ILLUSION
DISCONCERT
DERANGE
SAVE

PUZZLE 22

What number should replace the question mark?

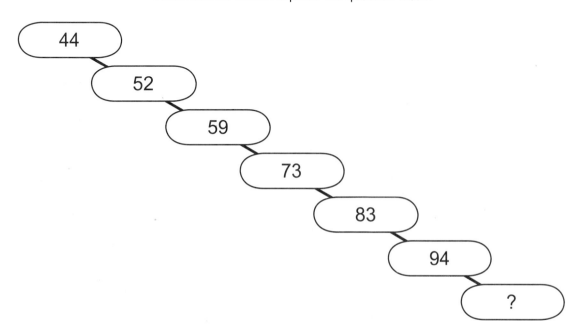

44
52
59
73
83
94
?

LEVEL 14

PUZZLE 23

Find the decimal for

$$\frac{276}{1656}$$

PUZZLE 24

What is always part of a TILBURY?

(a) CLOTH
(b) METAL
(c) TRACERY
(d) LIQUID
(e) WHEELS

PUZZLE 25

What is JACOBUS?

(a) GOLD COIN
(b) CLOTH
(c) PLANT
(d) FISH
(e) SWORD

PUZZLE 26

Which is the odd one out?
Clue: Colours

(a) NORMAO
(b) KINPHIS
(c) SETSUR
(d) DIRIIUM
(e) SHIBLU

27 PUZZLE

Which letter is missing from the chain?

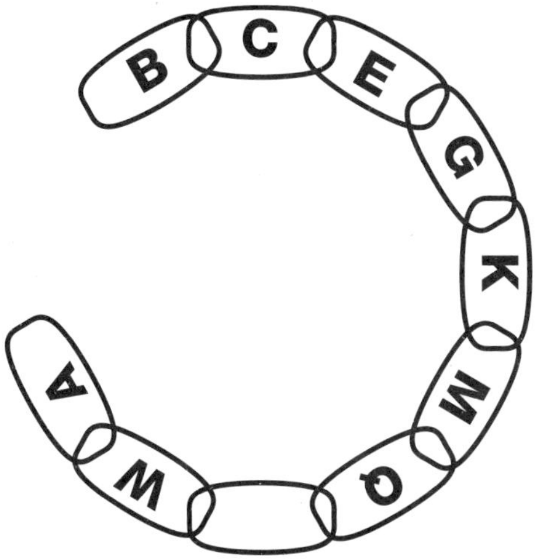

28 PUZZLE

Which number is needed to complete the puzzle?

5	7	10
25	19	
32	40	49

29 PUZZLE

Roy, Molly, Frank and Maude are all keen gardeners. As the diagrams show, they each have room for 10 plants in their plots so they can grow either flowers, trees or vegetables.

Ray grows more flowers than Maude, and Molly has more trees in her garden than Frank. Together Maude and Molly have more vegetables than the men.

Which garden belongs to each gardener?

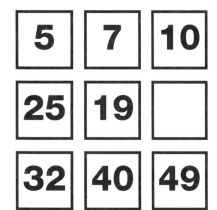

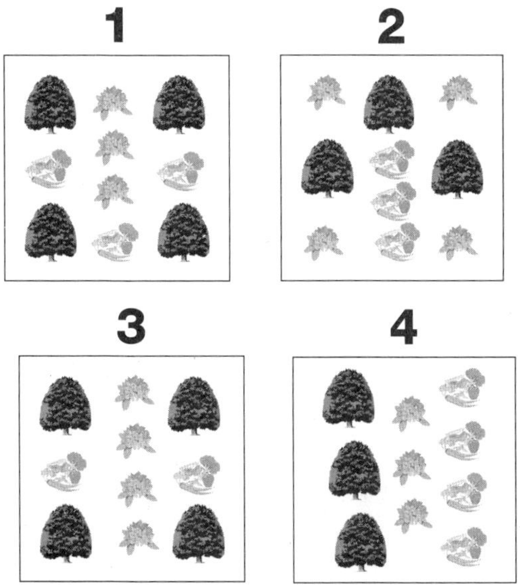

30 PUZZLE

Here is a 4 x 3 grid with twelve matches defining a triangle which takes up half of the area. Move just 4 matches to reduce the area by a half.

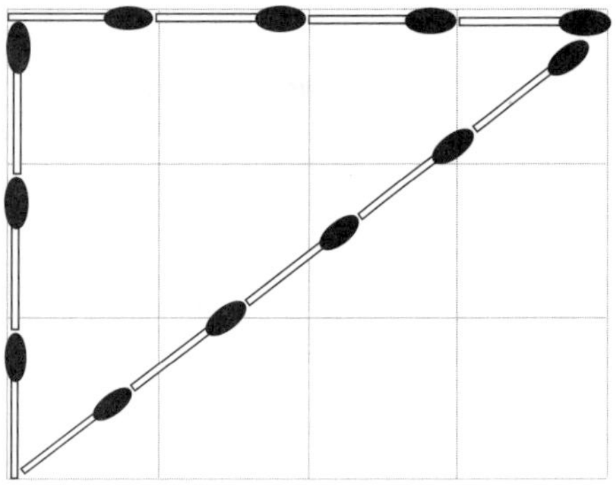

31 PUZZLE

Using the digits 0-5 inclusive, write one number in each small circle so that the values around each large circle add up to ten.

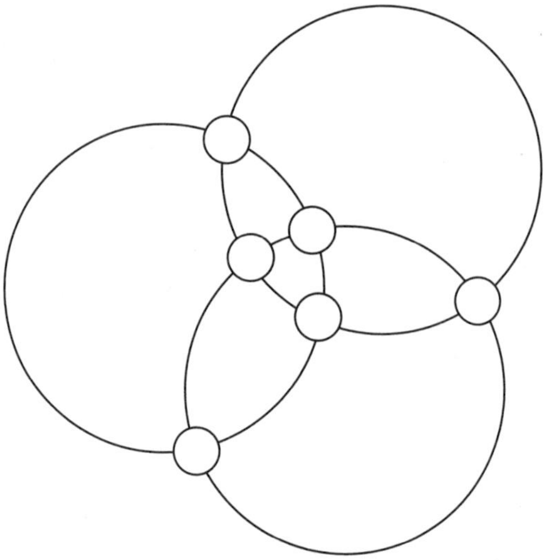

32 PUZZLE

Which letter replaces the blank and completes the sequence?

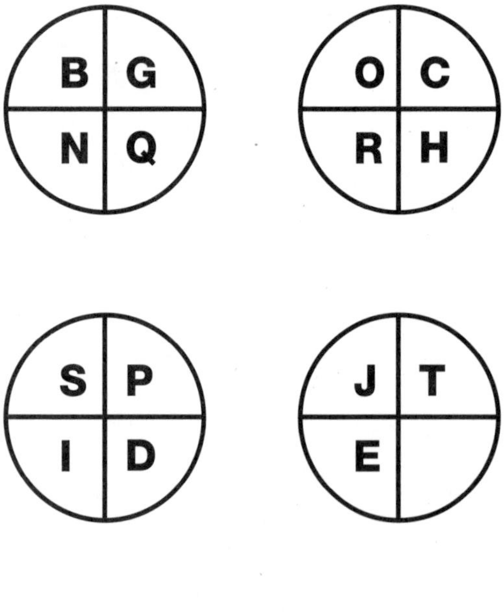

33 PUZZLE

Which letter goes at the bottom of the column?

34 PUZZLE

Which number is missing from the last circle?

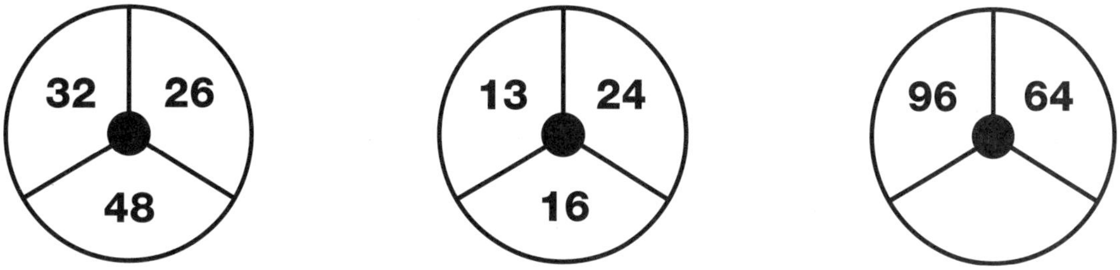

35 PUZZLE

Which playing card completes this puzzle?

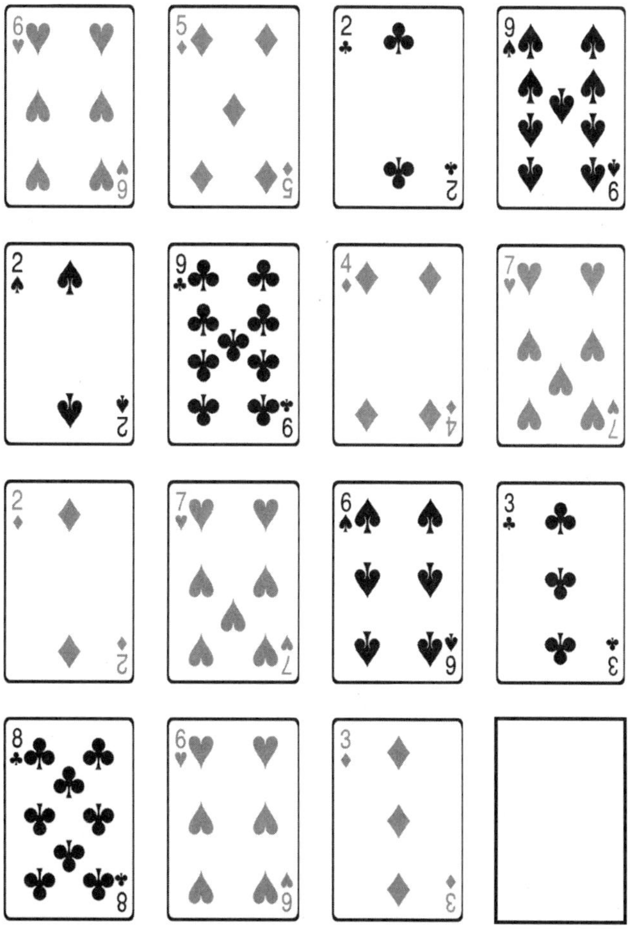

36 PUZZLE

Which watch goes in the blank space?

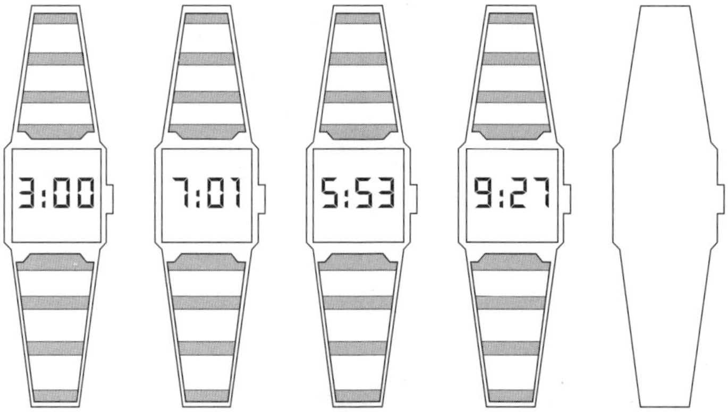

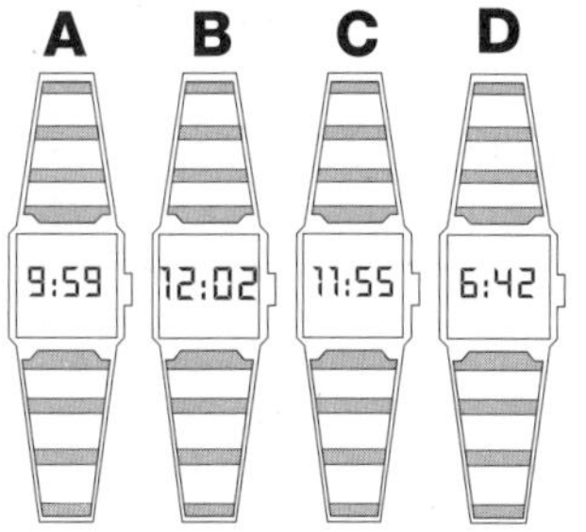

37 PUZZLE

Which number is missing?

1
5
9
15

38 PUZZLE

Complete this puzzle.

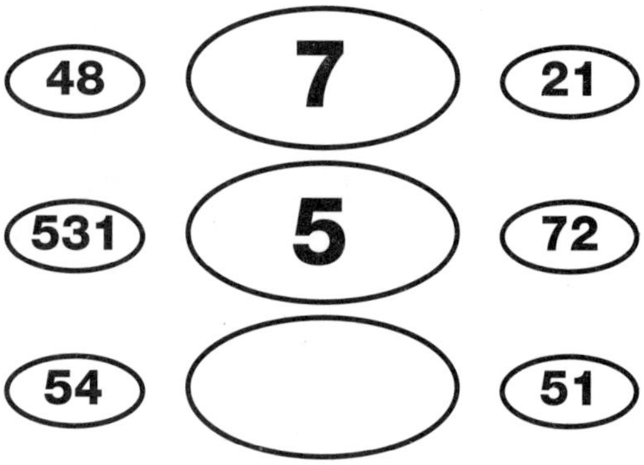

39 PUZZLE

Which playing card finishes the puzzle?

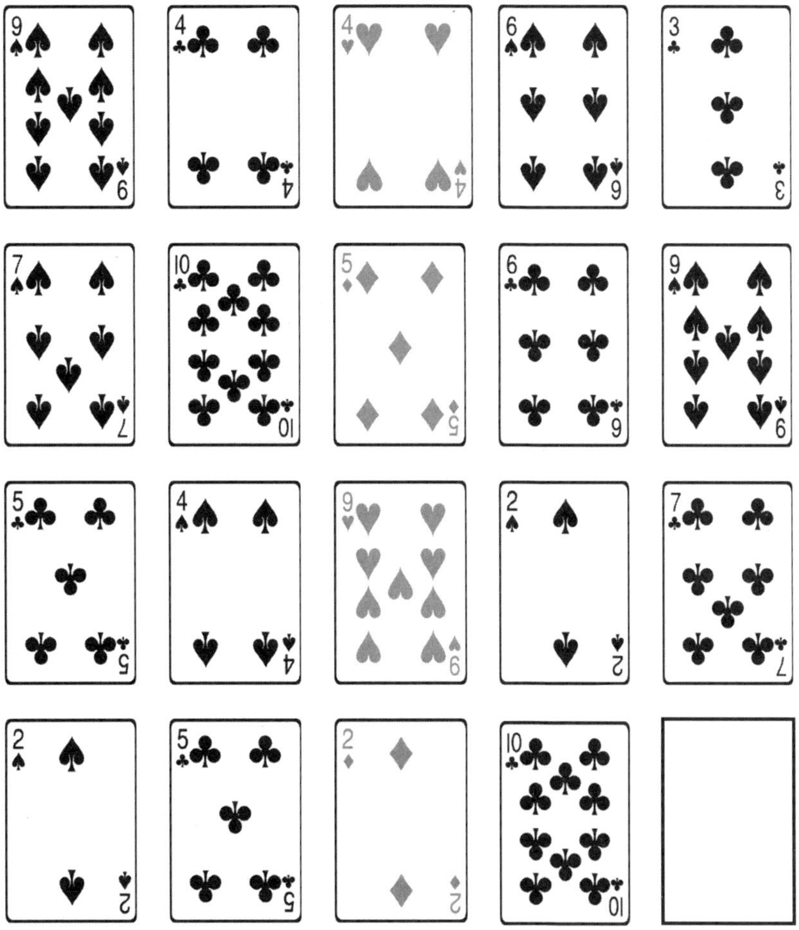

40 PUZZLE

Which letter replaces the blank and completes the sequence?

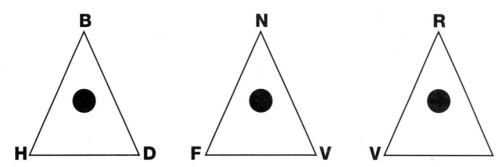

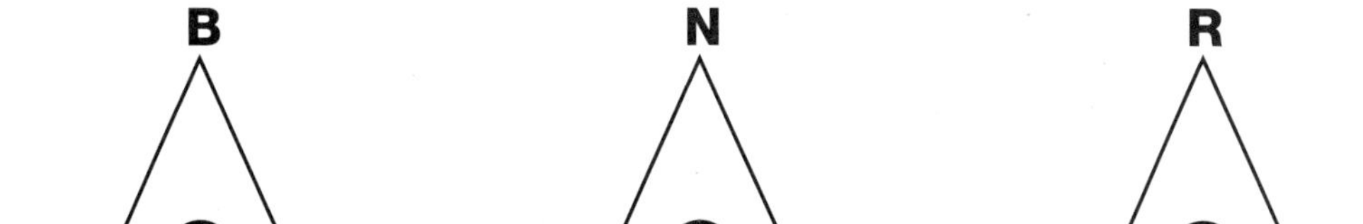

LEVEL

14

PUZZLE 41

Which letter replaces the blank and completes the sequence?

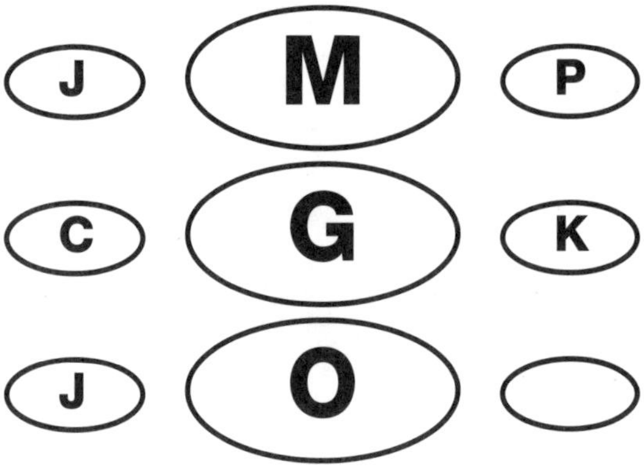

PUZZLE 42

Which number will complete this grid?

2	1	2	7	3	2	4
5	1	4	2	9	2	7
4	1	6	6	2	2	7
1	1	1	6	4	4	2
1	1	4	2	5	0	4
4	1	2	9	3	4	

PUZZLE 43

Which of the numbered pieces fits into the middle of the grid?

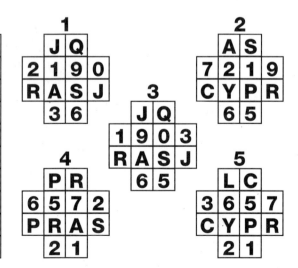

5	7	2	1	9	0	3	6	5	7
J	Q	L	C	Y	P	R	A	S	J
2	1	9	0	3	6	5	7	2	1
Q	L	C	Y			A	S	J	Q
9	0	3					1	9	0
L	C	Y					J	Q	L
3	6	5	7			9	0	3	6
C	Y	P	R	A	S	J	Q	L	C
5	7	2	1	9	0	3	6	5	7
Y	P	R	A	S	J	Q	L	C	Y

1

	J	Q	
2	1	9	0
R	A	S	J
	3	6	

2

	A	S	
7	2	1	9
C	Y	P	R
	6	5	

3

	J	Q	
1	9	0	3
R	A	S	J
	6	5	

4

	P	R	
6	5	7	2
P	R	A	S
	2	1	

5

	L	C	
3	6	5	7
C	Y	P	R
	2	1	

44 PUZZLE

Which playing card is missing?

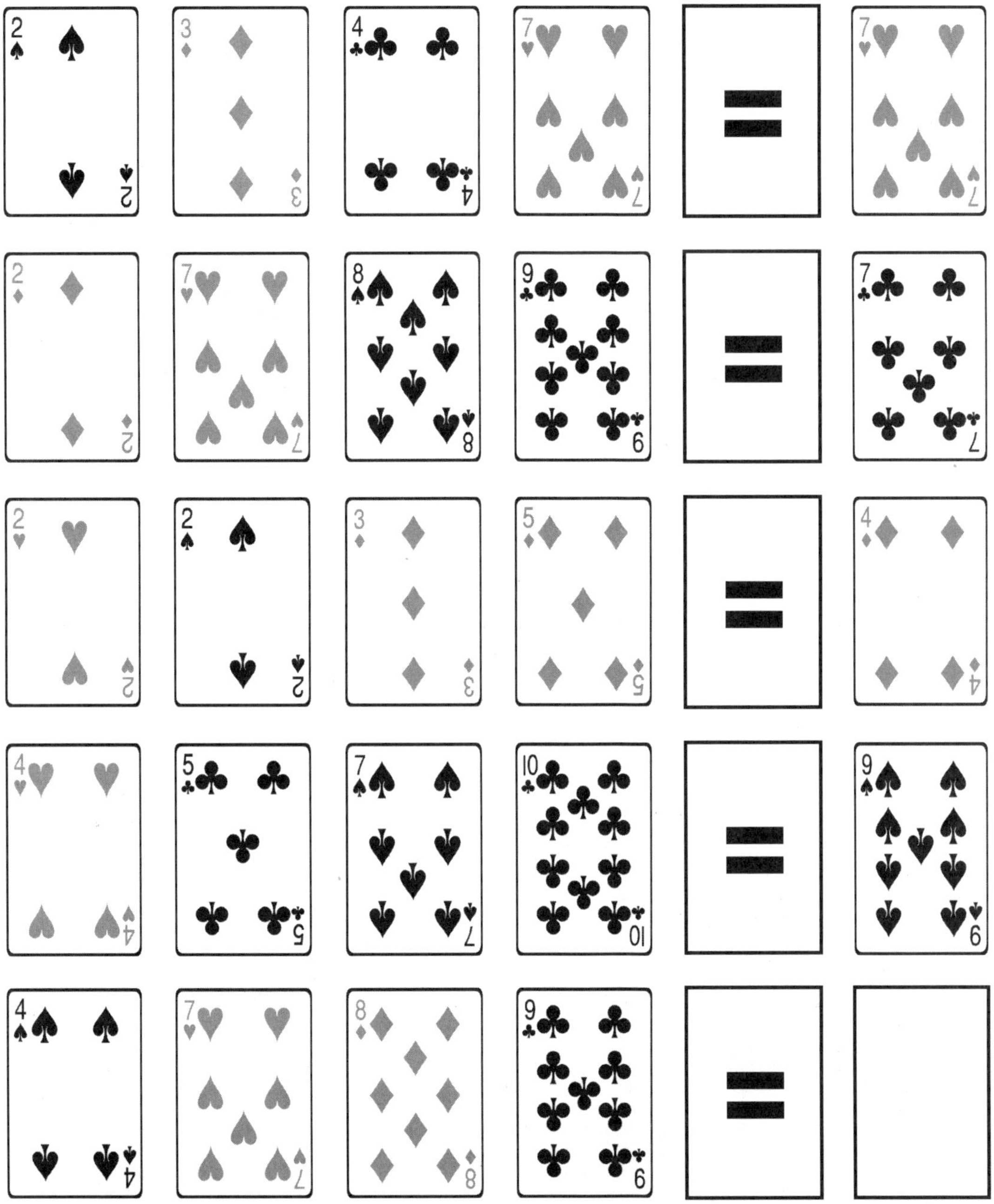

45 PUZZLE

What is the missing value?

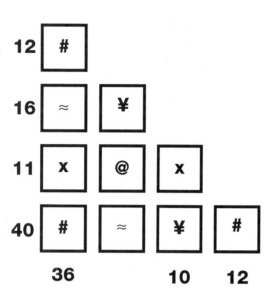

12	#			
16	≈	¥		
11	x	@	x	
40	#	≈	¥	#
	36		10	12

46 PUZZLE

Why is this pyramid correct?

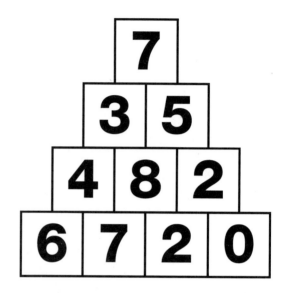

	7		
	3	5	
4	8	2	
6	7	2	0

47 PUZZLE

Which of the numbered pieces fits into the middle of the grid?

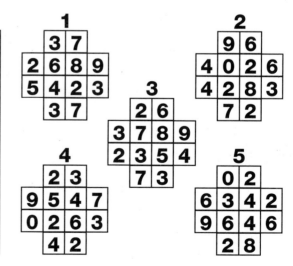

2	3	9	5	4	2	3	9	5	4
7	0	2	6	3	7	0	2	6	3
9	6	4	2	8	9	6	4	2	8
7	2	6	8			2	6	8	3
8	9	1					1	2	6
2	3	9					9	5	4
7	0	2	6			0	2	6	3
9	6	4	2	8	9	6	4	2	8
7	2	6	8	3	7	2	6	8	3
8	9	1	2	6	8	9	1	2	6

1

	3	7	
2	6	8	9
5	4	2	3
	3	7	

2

	9	6	
4	0	2	6
4	2	8	3
	7	2	

3

	2	6	
3	7	8	9
2	3	5	4
	7	3	

4

	2	3	
9	5	4	7
0	2	6	3
	4	2	

5

	0	2	
6	3	4	2
9	6	4	6
	2	8	

48 PUZZLE

Which playing card completes the puzzle?

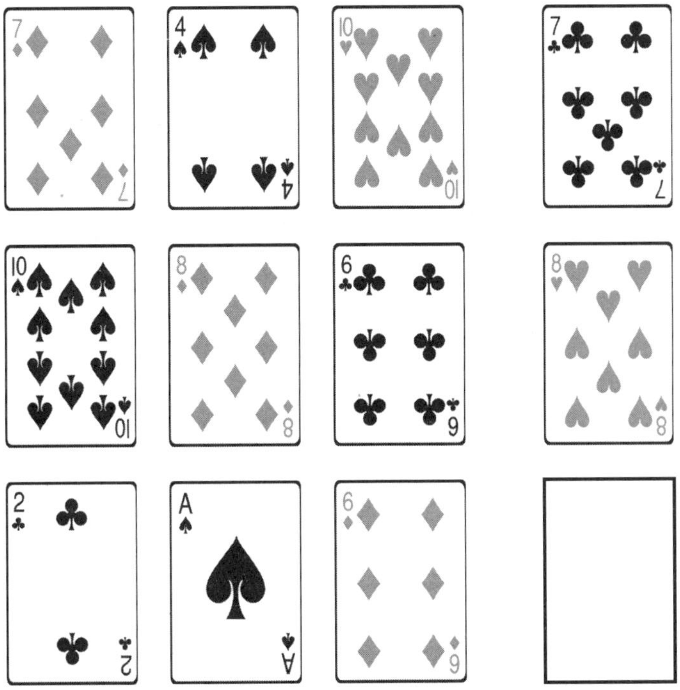

49 PUZZLE

Which number is the odd one out?

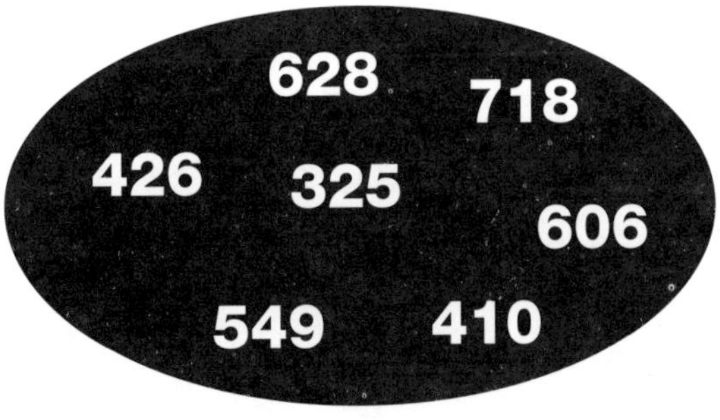

50 PUZZLE

What is the time now if 2 hours later it would be half as long until midnight as it would be if it were an hour later?

1 PUZZLE

Which is the missing piece?

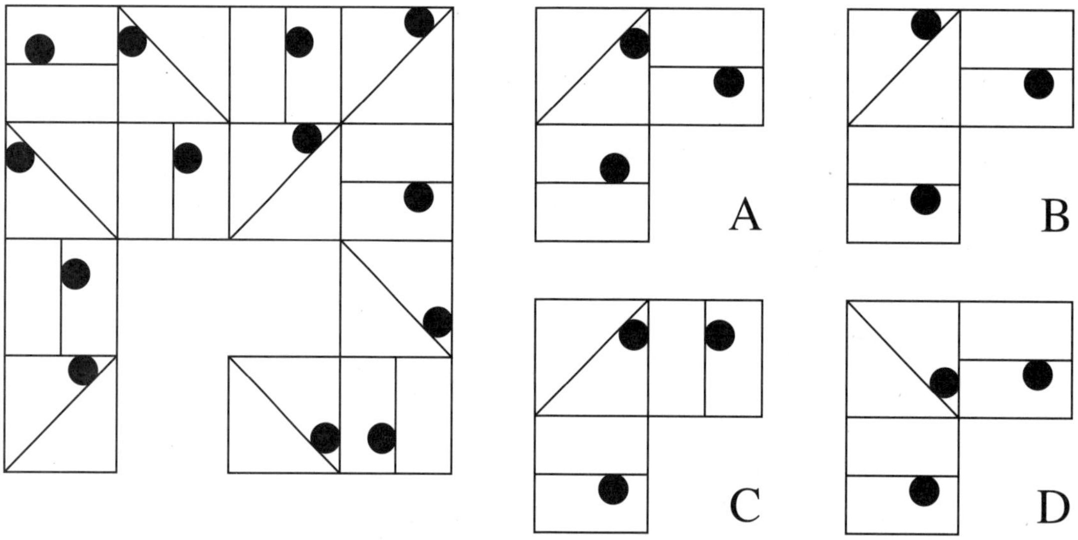

2 PUZZLE

At a recent election, a total of 96347 votes were cast for the four candidates, the winner exceeding his opponents by 10496, 21221 and 34628 votes respectively.

How many votes were cast for each candidate?

3 PUZZLE

A B C D E F G H

What letter is immediately to the right of the letter two to the right of the letter immediately to the left of the letter three to the right of the letter B?

4 PUZZLE

	and	therefore
784329	286913	742163
is to	is to	is to
247983	162389	?

5 PUZZLE

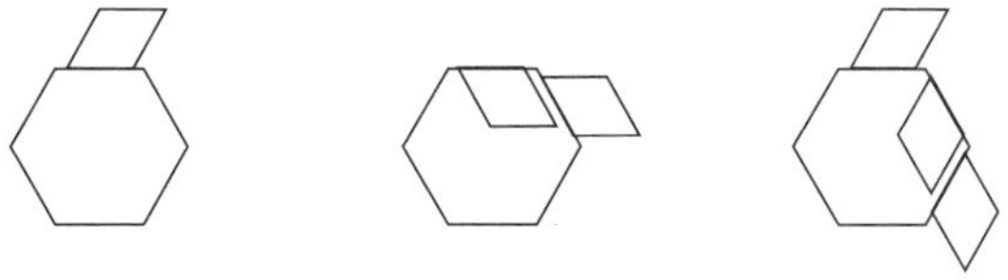

What comes next?

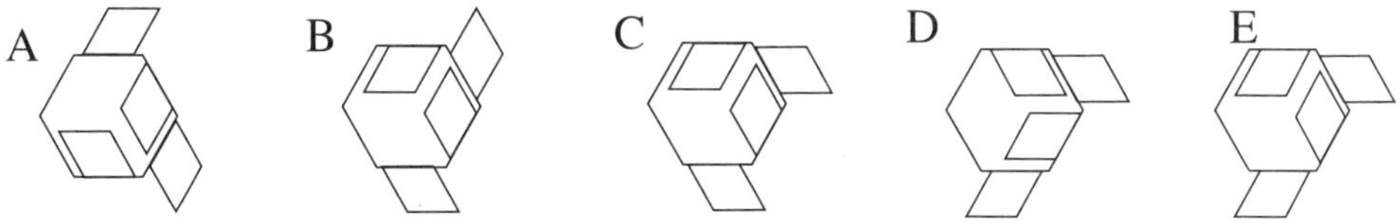

6 PUZZLE

What letters are missing?

ETSFNJDXOK	KOE	ETOK
KODJNFSTE		KONTE
?	KOJNFTE	ETNJOK

7 PUZZLE

101.2 102.4 104.8 109.6 ?

8 PUZZLE

What comes next?

A

B

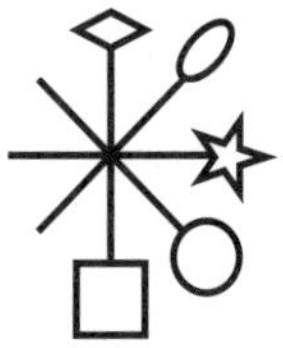

C

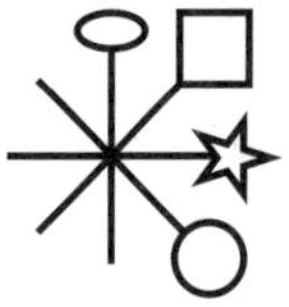

D

E

9 PUZZLE

What numbers should replace the question marks?

A	B	C	D
2	3	5	7
7	8	9	10
16	17	17	18
?	?	?	?

10 PUZZLE

Which is the missing tile?

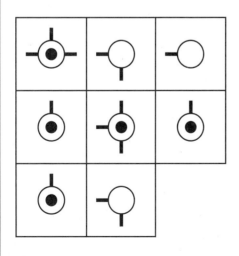

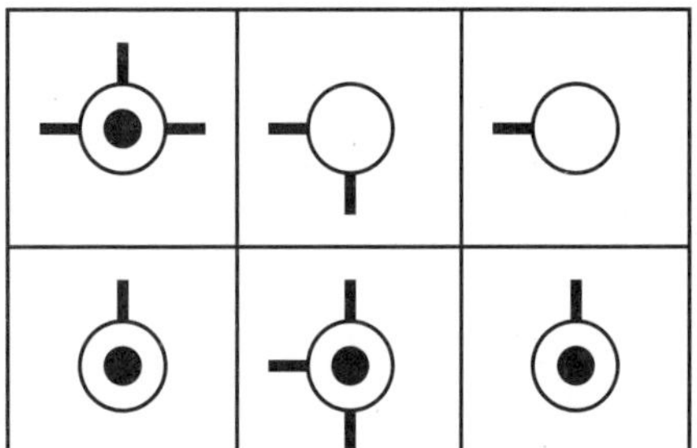

A

B

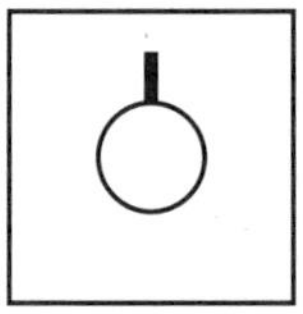

C

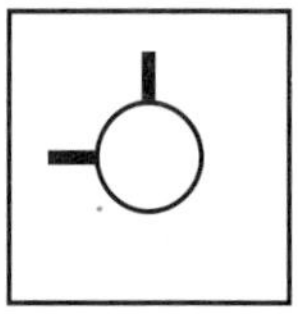

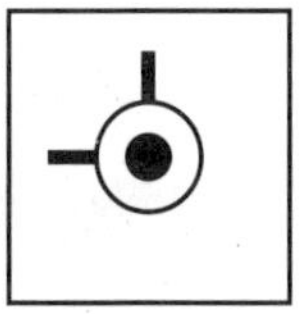

D

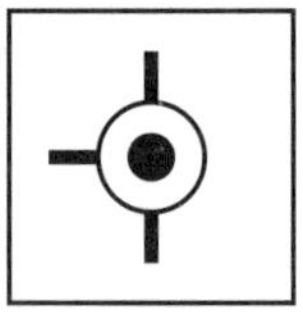

E

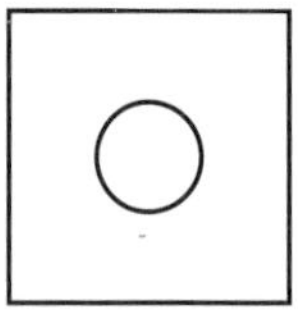

F

11 PUZZLE

Each line and symbol which appears in the four outer circles, below, is transferred to the centre circle according to these rules. If a line or symbol occurs in the outer circles once, it is transferred; if it occurs twice, it is possibly transferred; three times, it is transferred; four times, it is not transferred. Which of the circles A, B, C, D or E, should appear at the centre of the diagram, below?

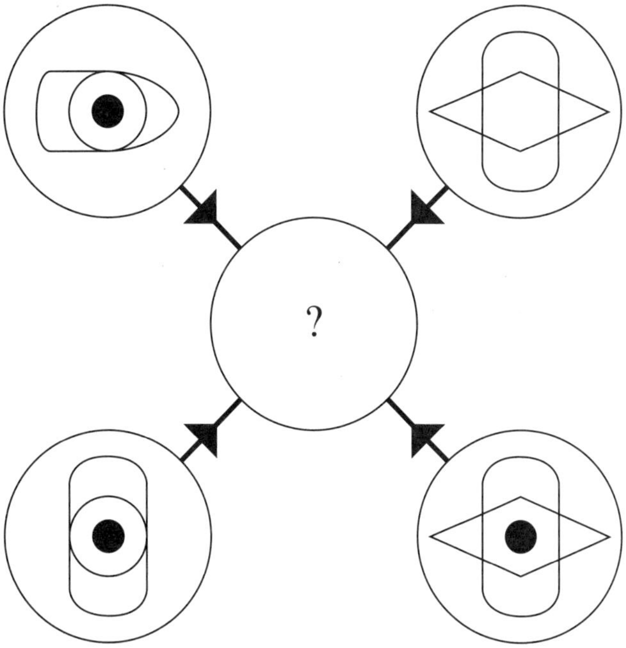

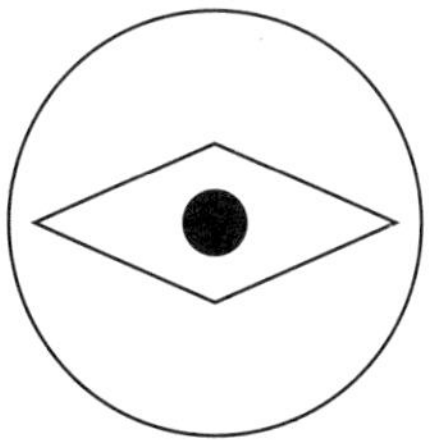

A

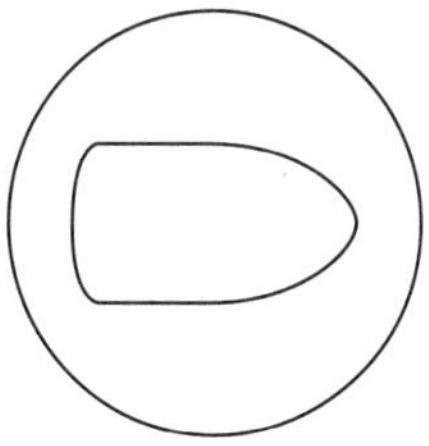

B

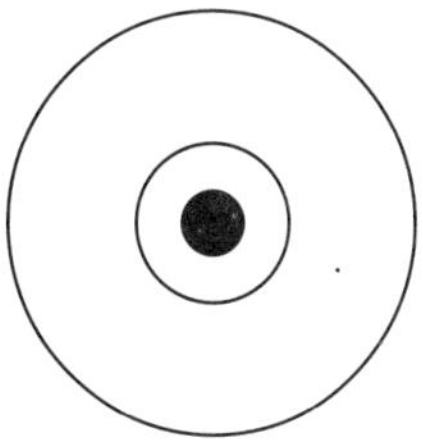

C

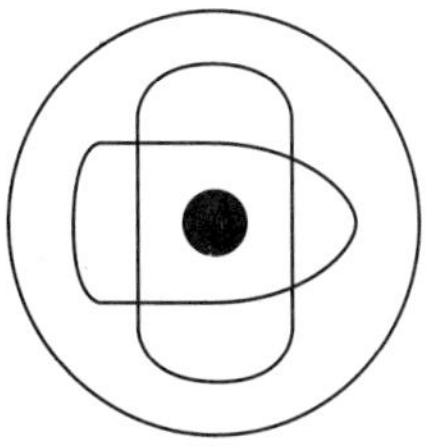

D

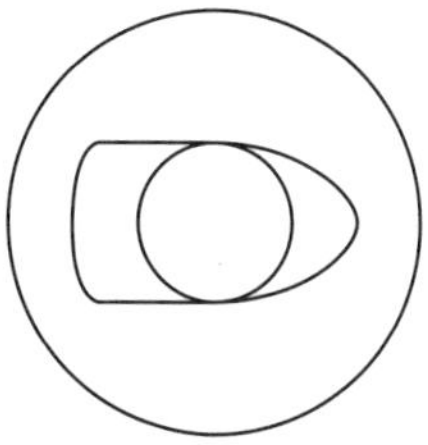

E

12 PUZZLE

Which 2 pentagons are the odd ones out?

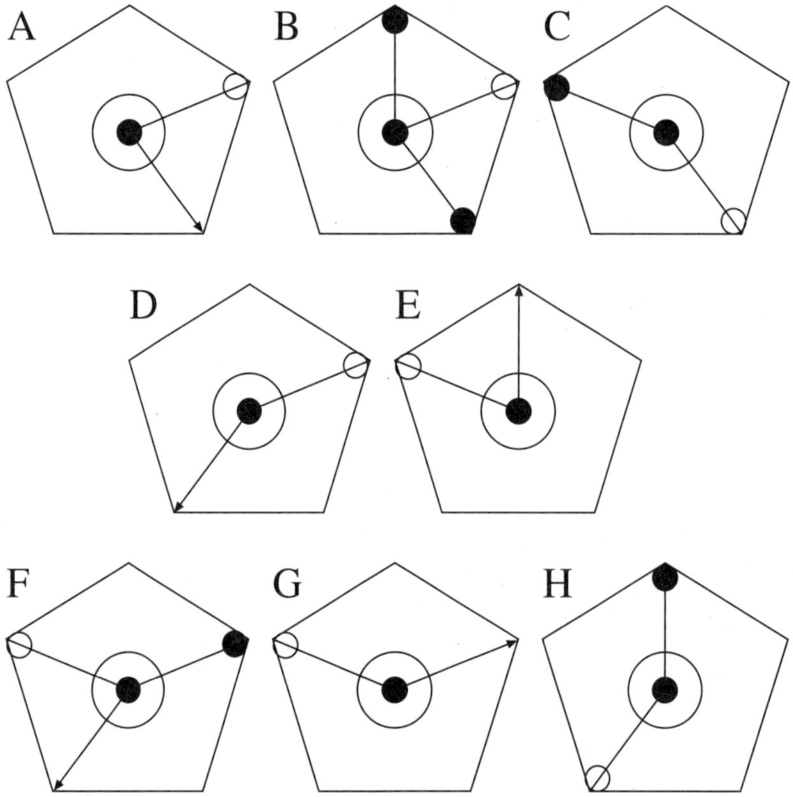

13 PUZZLE

Which number replaces the question mark?

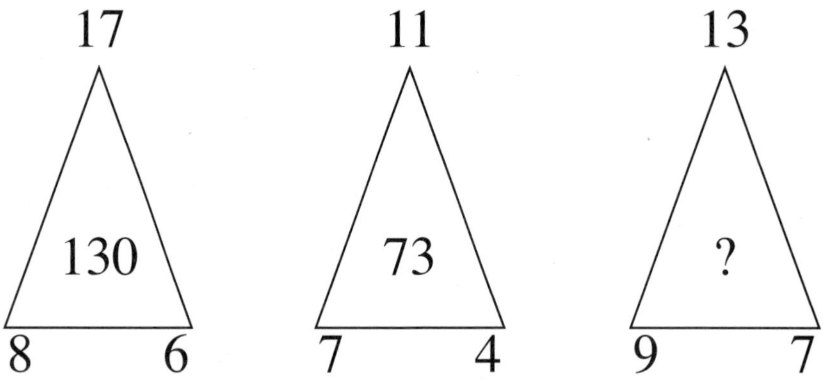

14 PUZZLE

Which hexagon replaces the question mark – A, B, C, D or E?

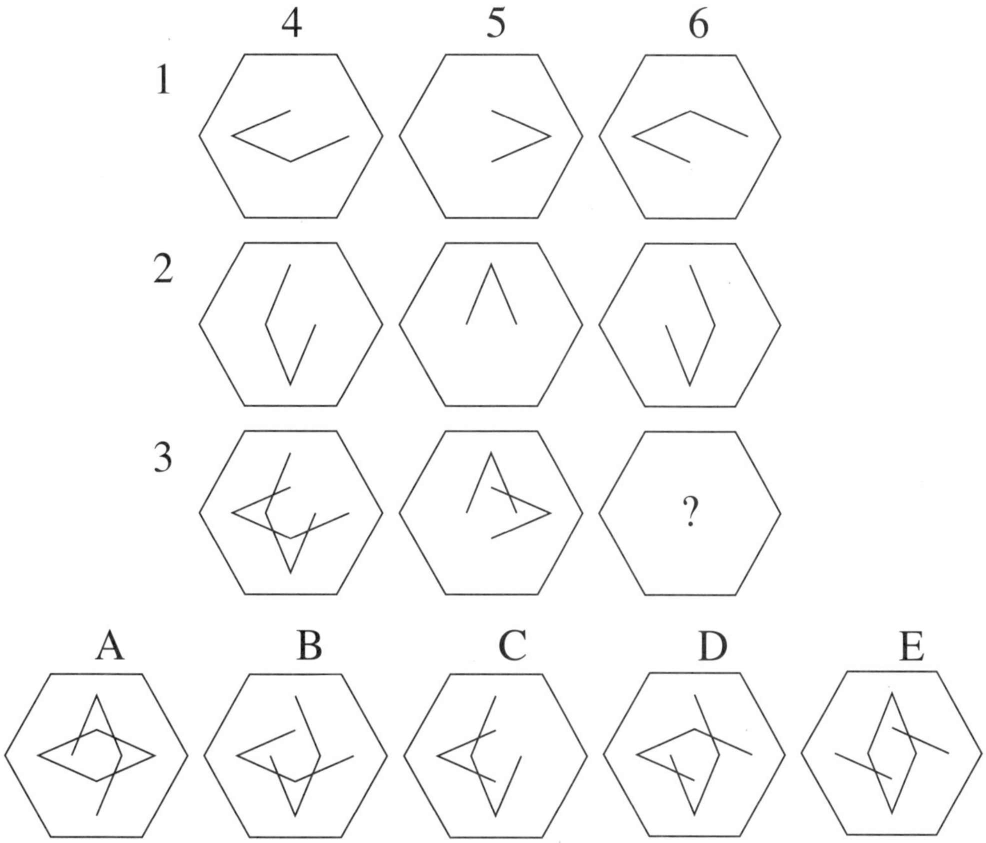

15 PUZZLE

What number should replace the question mark?

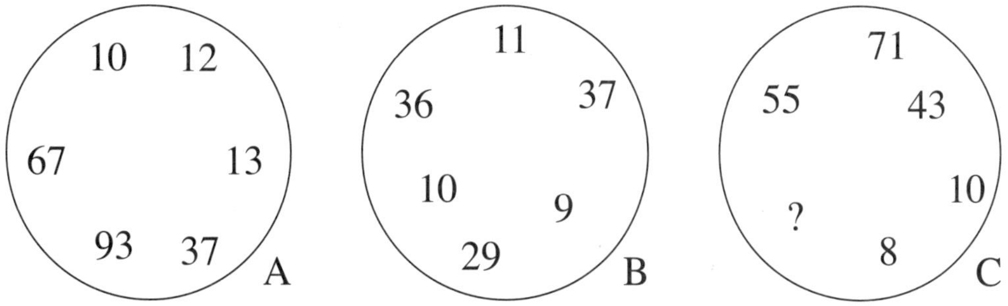

16 PUZZLE

What is the value of this angle?

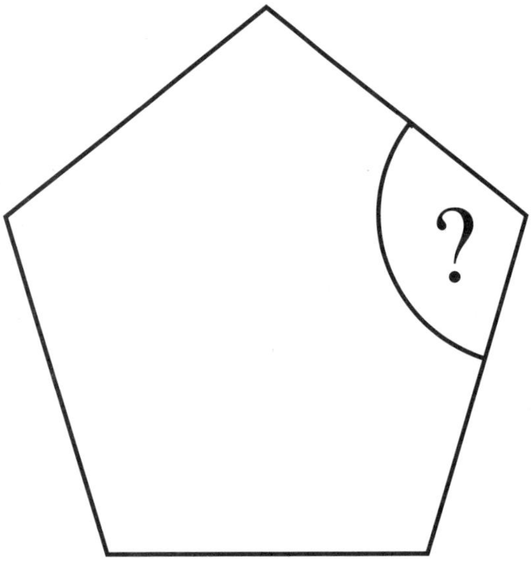

17 PUZZLE

Simplify

$$\frac{3024}{3888}$$

18 PUZZLE

What have these words in common?

DIMENSIONS
GRANDIOSE
REMARKABLE
DESCENT
MATERIAL
RESOUNDED

19 PUZZLE

12 matches are arranged to produce 6 triangles. Can you move 5 matches to produce 3 triangles?

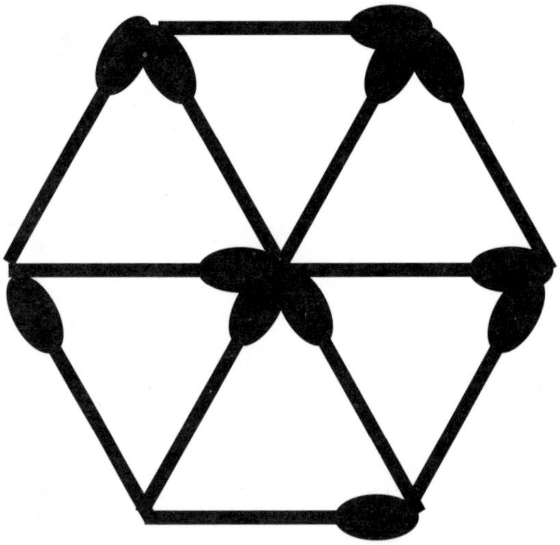

20 PUZZLE

Which playing card replaces the question mark?

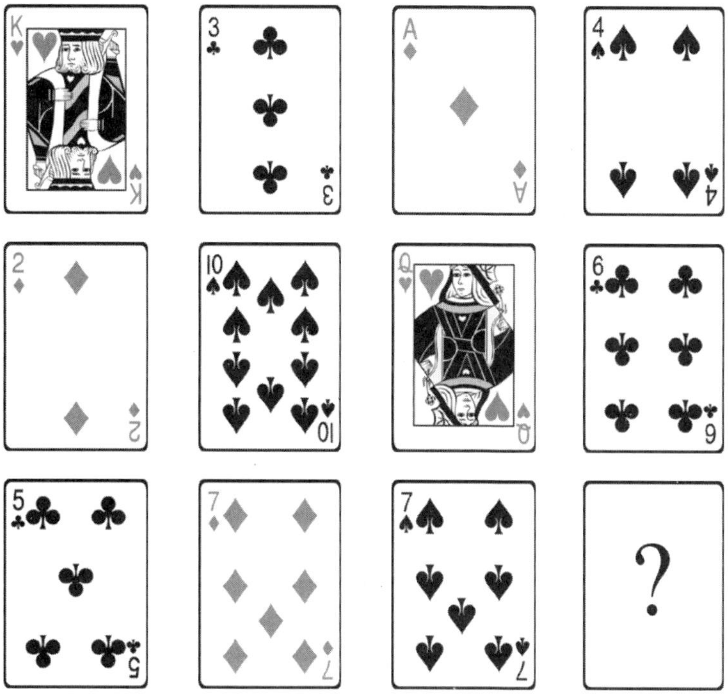

21 PUZZLE

Which watch completes the sequence?

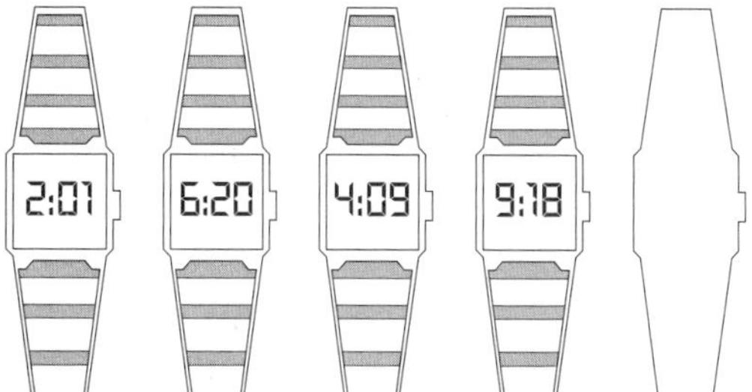

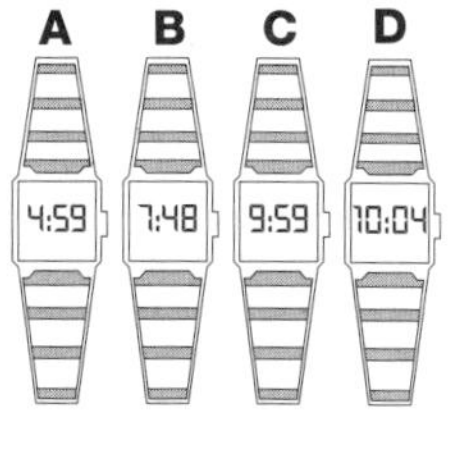

LEVEL 15

22 PUZZLE

What number should replace the question mark?

7	9	6	57
8	6	7	41
9	3	4	23
10	6	11	?

23 PUZZLE

What is a CAPELIN?

(a) A RELIGIOUS PERSON
(b) A WEAPON
(c) A FISH
(d) A BIRD
(e) A CAPE

24 PUZZLE

Which is higher?

19^2

or

7^3

25 PUZZLE

Simplify

$$\frac{99}{16} \div \frac{11}{4} =$$

26 PUZZLE

Which number is missing?

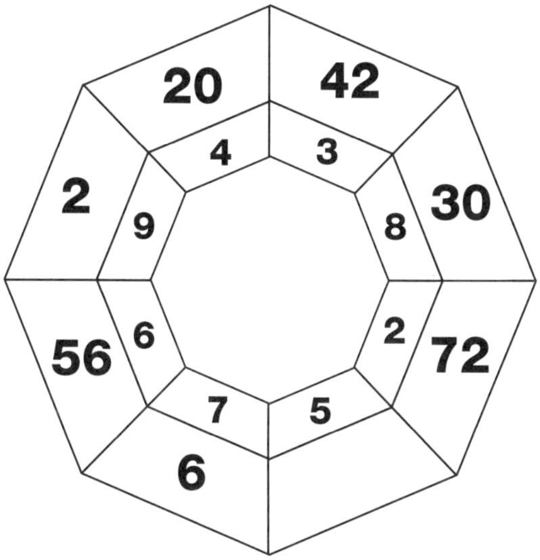

27 PUZZLE

Which number goes in the empty box?

5	6	4
12	2	
7	4	6
8	3	10

28 PUZZLE

Which watch comes next?

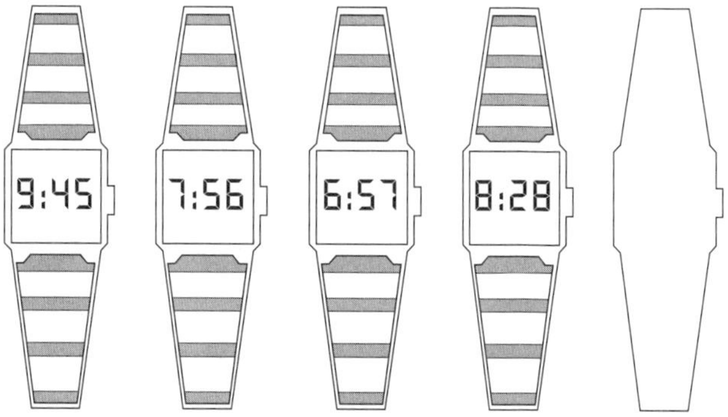

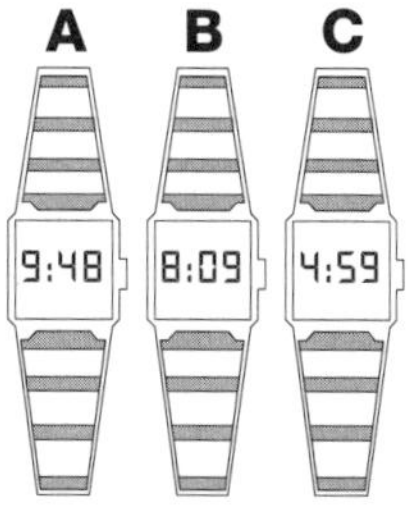

LEVEL 15

29 PUZZLE

Which playing cards are missing?

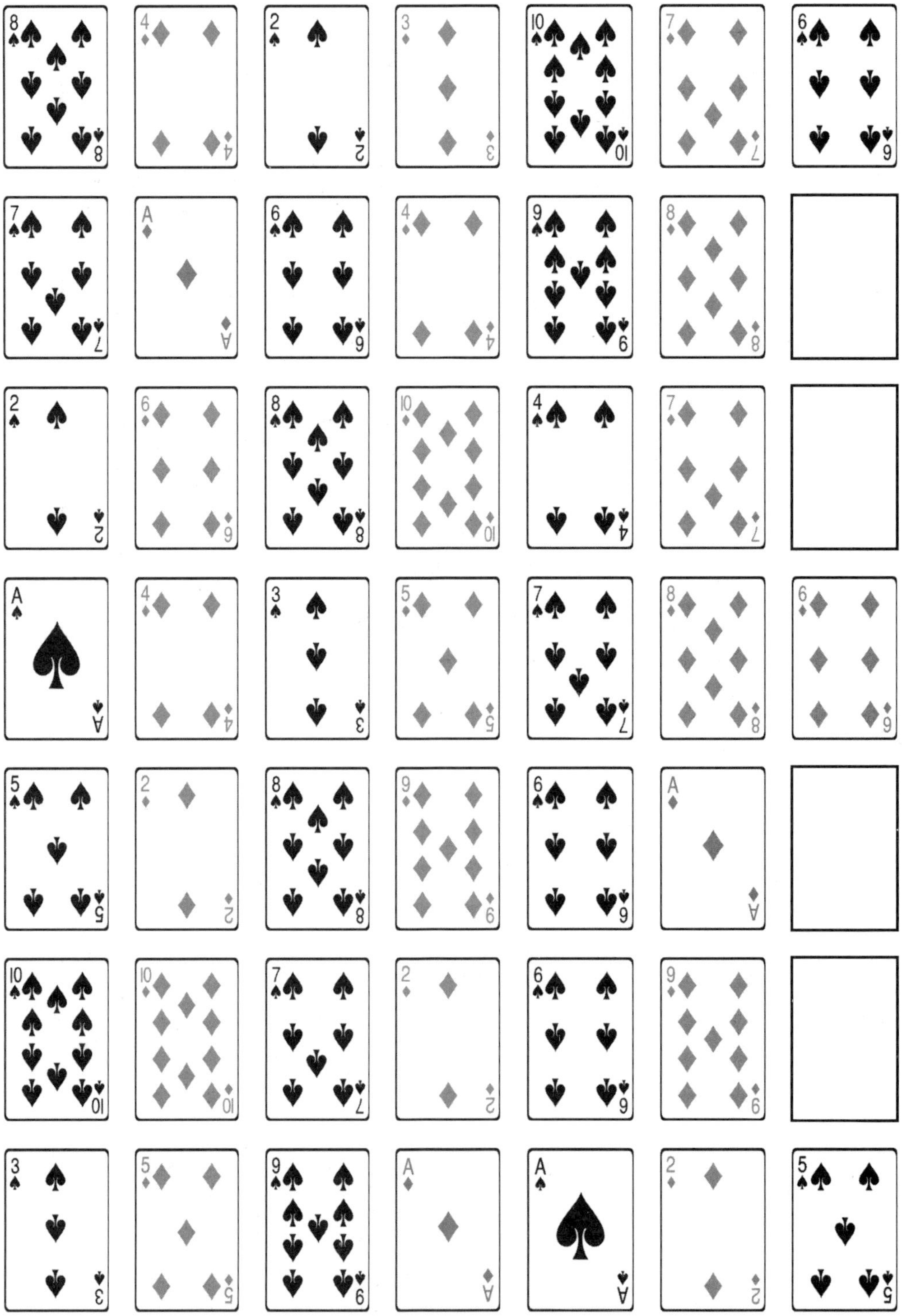

30 PUZZLE

Which number is missing from the last circle?

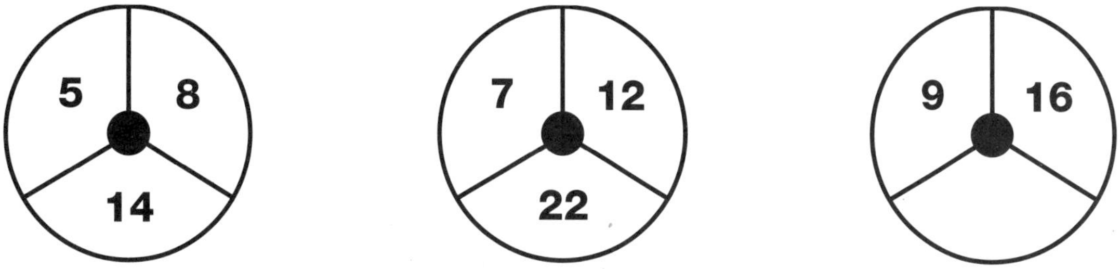

31 PUZZLE

Which of the bottom boxes finishes the sequence?

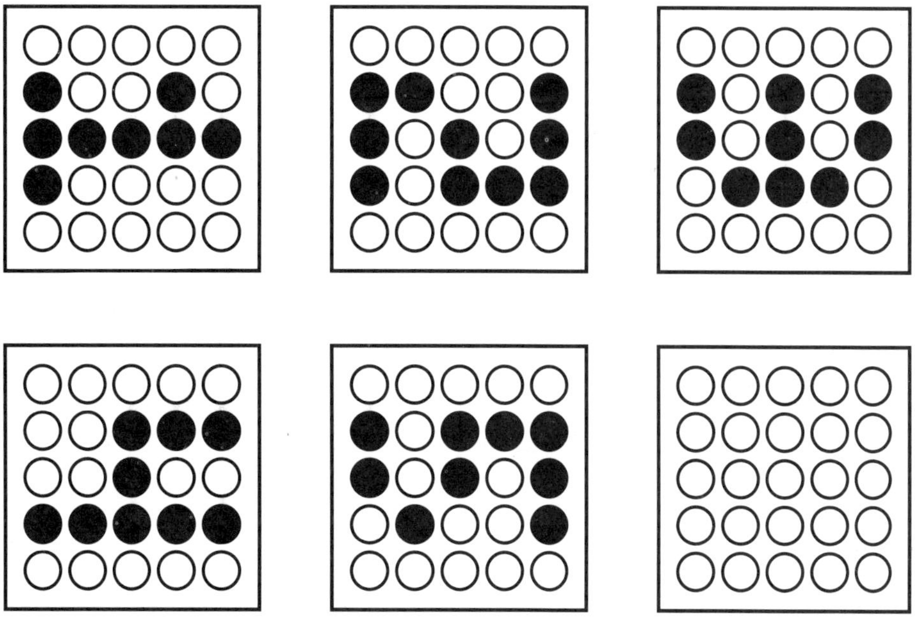

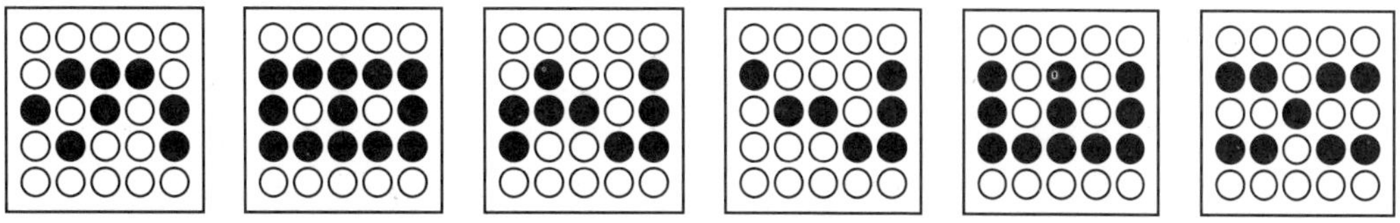

A **B** **C** **D** **E** **F**

PUZZLE 32

Which card is missing?

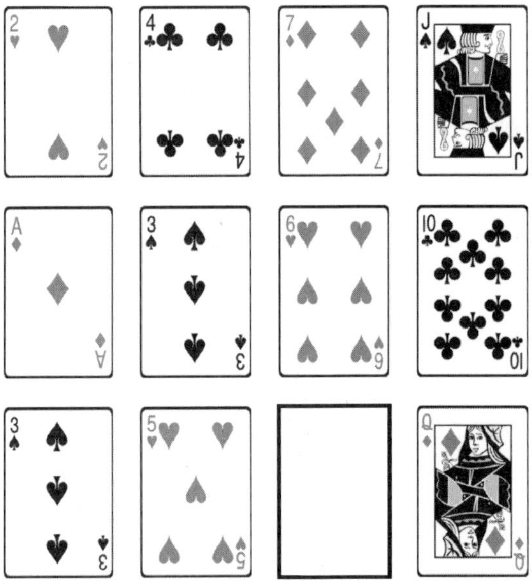

PUZZLE 33

What is the sum of the dots on the hidden faces of these dice?

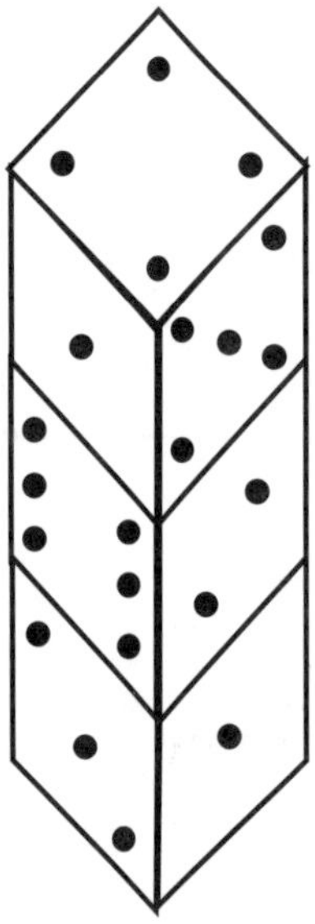

PUZZLE 34

Which number is missing from the chain?

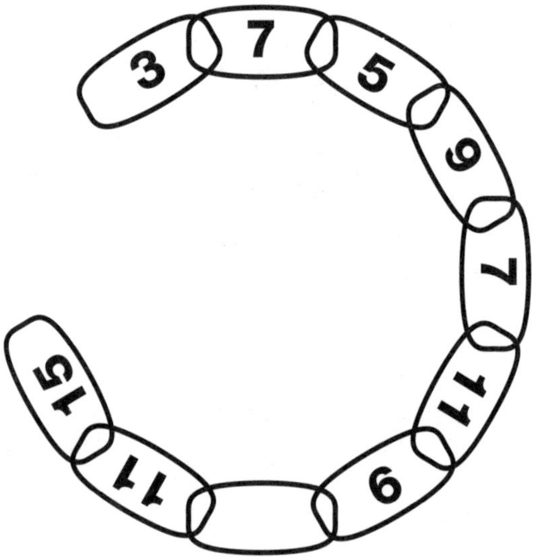

35 PUZZLE

Which numbers need to be placed in the circles in the bottom two boxes?

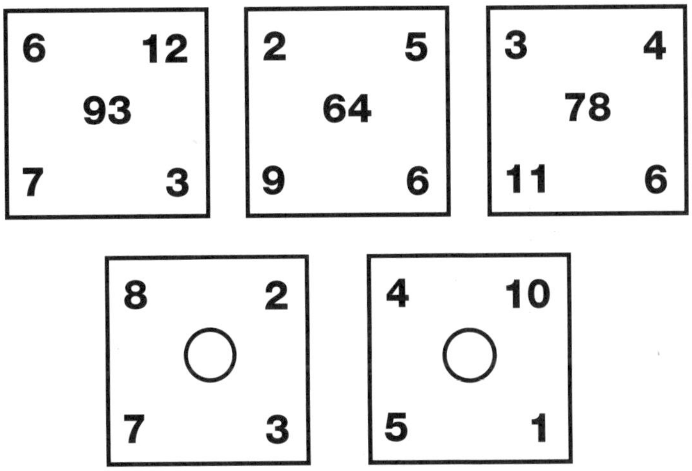

36 PUZZLE

Which number goes in the empty circle?

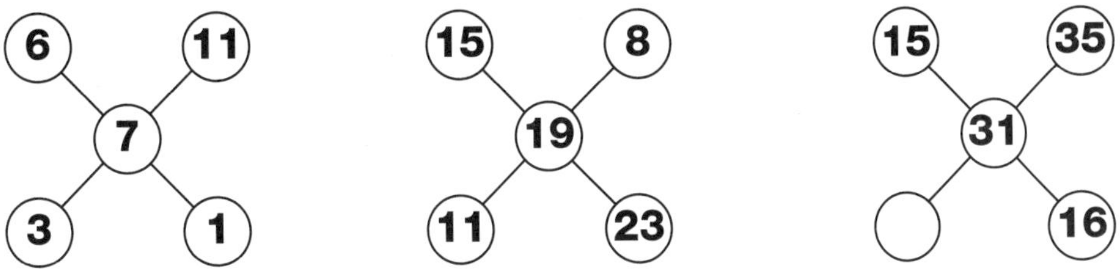

37 PUZZLE

Which number replaces the question mark?

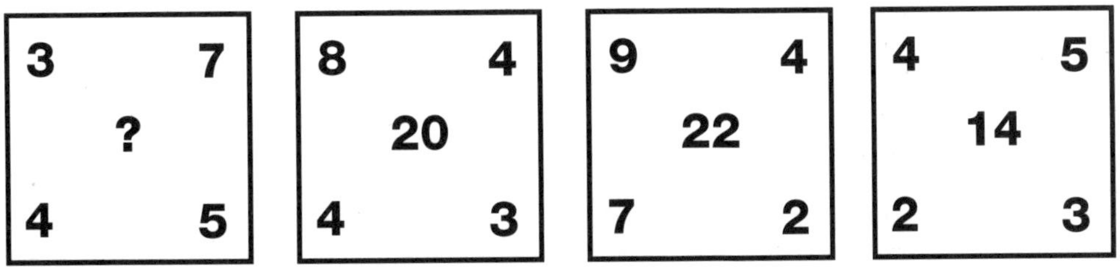

LEVEL 15

38 PUZZLE

Which playing cards are missing from this puzzle?

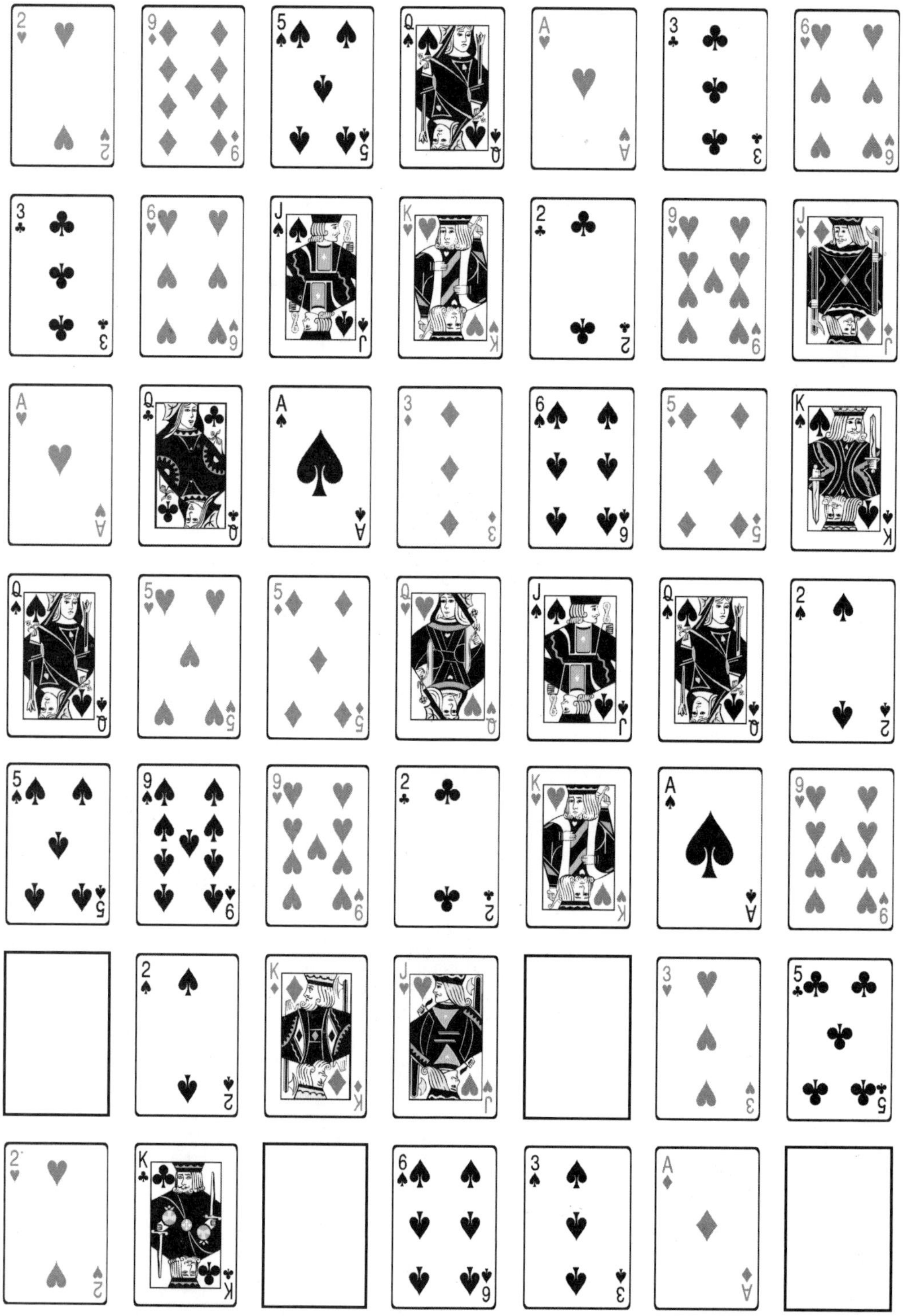

PUZZLE 39

Which letter replaces the blank and completes the sequence?

B	B
F	G
J	L
M	Q
Q	V
T	

PUZZLE 40

Which number goes at the bottom of the column?

5

12

18

23

27

(blank)

PUZZLE 41

What is missing from the empty ellipse?

I	31	E
O	17	Y
	23	O

PUZZLE 42

Fill in the empty box.

5	5	11
3	8	7

6	10	14
7	10	13

2	10	12
6	7	

43 PUZZLE

What is missing from the empty segment?

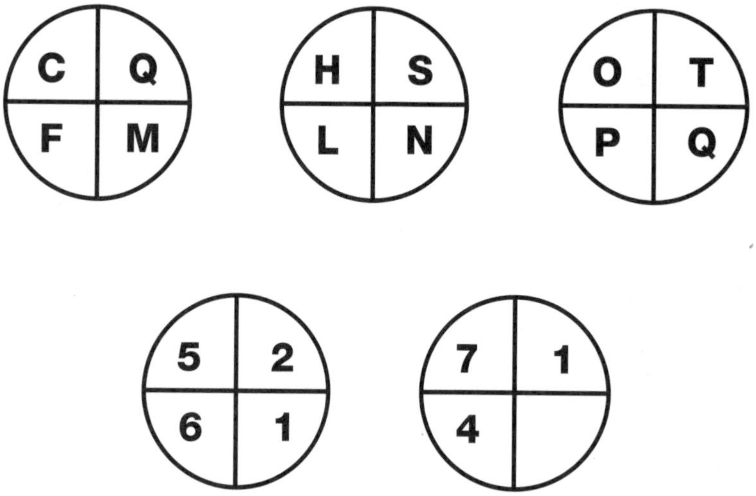

44 PUZZLE

Which letter goes in the middle of the third triangle?

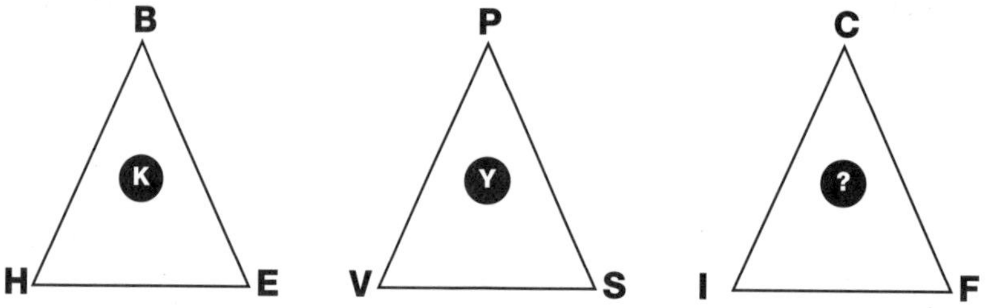

45 PUZZLE

Which letter goes in the empty segment?

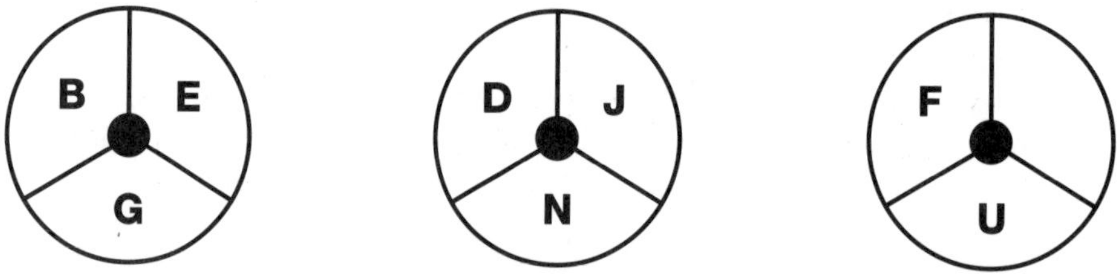

46 PUZZLE

Which letter goes in the empty segment?

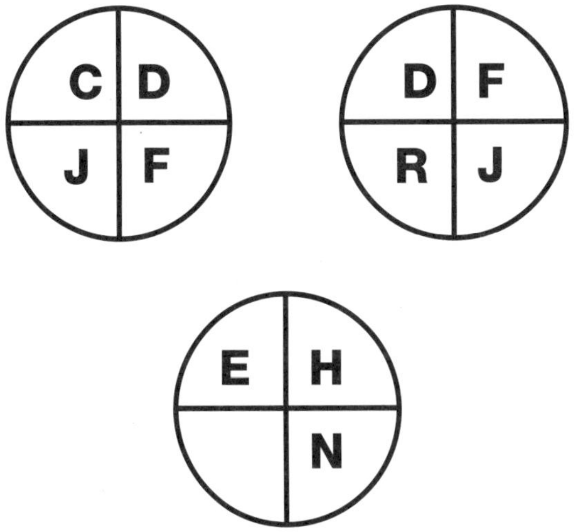

47 PUZZLE

Which number replaces the blank and completes the puzzle?

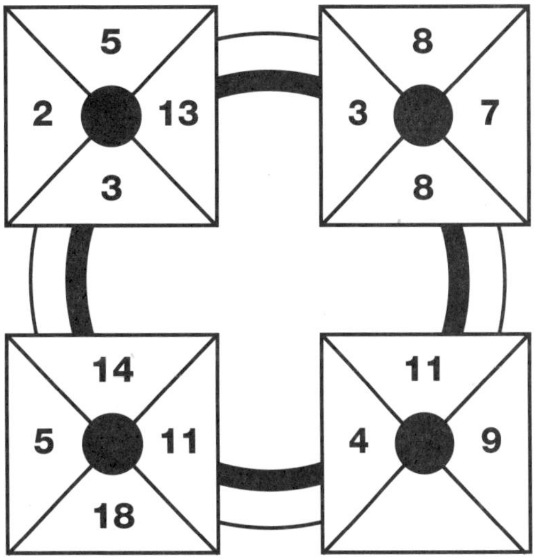

48 PUZZLE

Which of the smaller grids fits into the middle of the larger one?

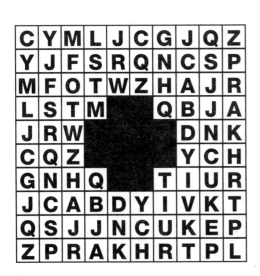

C	Y	M	L	J	C	G	J	Q	Z
Y	J	F	S	R	Q	N	C	S	P
M	F	O	T	W	Z	H	A	J	R
L	S	T	M			Q	B	J	A
J	R	W					D	N	K
C	Q	Z					Y	C	H
G	N	H	Q			T	I	U	R
J	C	A	B	D	Y	I	V	K	T
Q	S	J	J	N	C	U	K	E	P
Z	P	R	A	K	H	R	T	P	L

1

	L	S	
S	K	G	L
L	G	H	E
	E	J	

2

	E	J	
E	K	G	J
S	G	H	E
	J	E	

3

	R	Q	
D	N	K	B
B	K	N	D
	Q	R	

4

	L	S	
L	K	G	J
S	G	H	E
	J	E	

5

	Q	R	
Q	J	C	D
R	C	H	Z
	B	X	

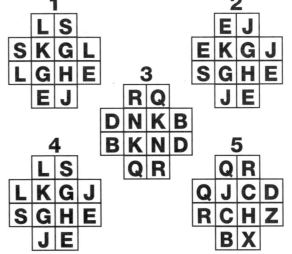

PUZZLE 1

Which is the odd one out?

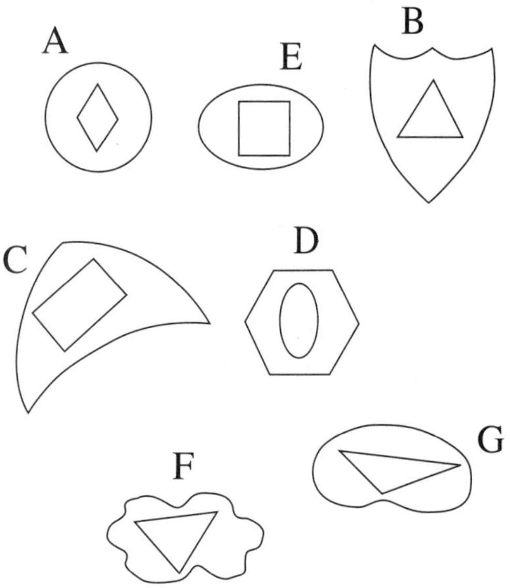

PUZZLE 2

Which is the odd one out?

4789
3568
1458
2479
2548
4679
2378

PUZZLE 3

Which is the meteorological sign for hail?

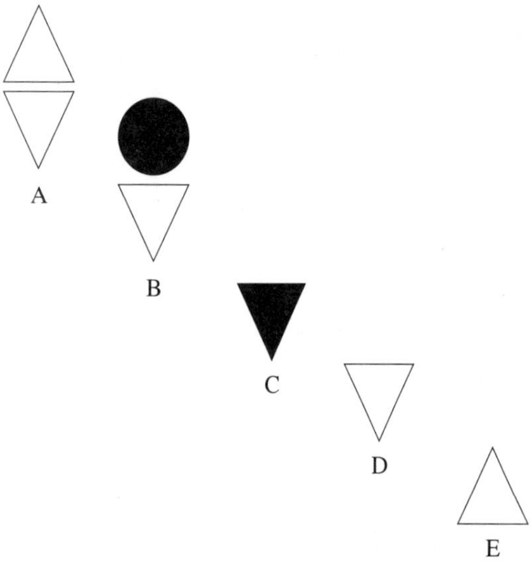

PUZZLE 4

Insert the missing numbers. The connection between each set of numbers in each row is the same.

623	36	?
847	?	16
726	?	?

5 PUZZLE

What letter should replace the question mark?

A	G	C
B	B	H
C	E	?

6 PUZZLE

121

2112

2122

1132

211213

312213

212223

?

7 PUZZLE

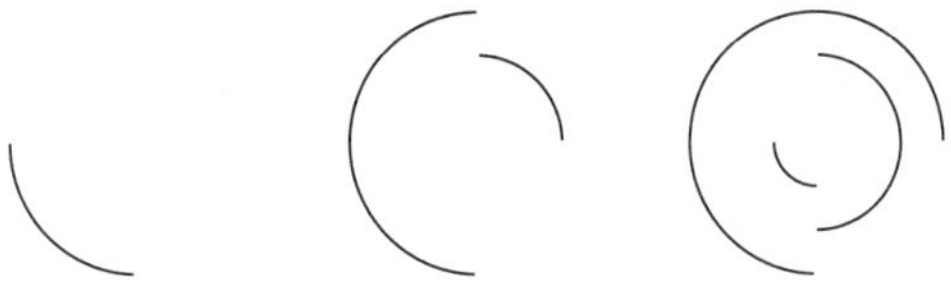

What comes next?

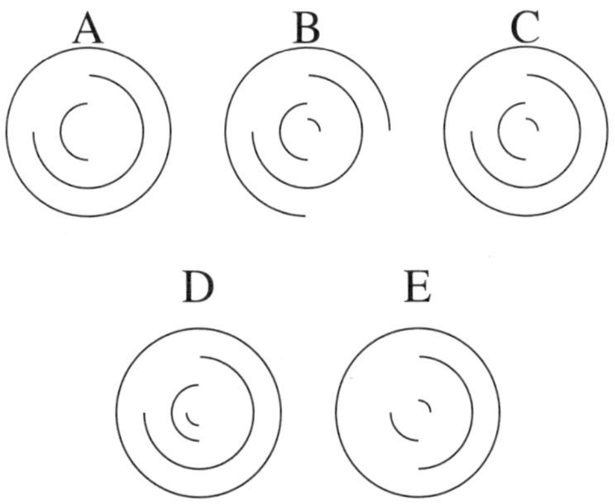

8 PUZZLE

The shapes contain five consecutive numbers (in no particular order) as indicated by the question marks.

When added together:
The numbers in the triangle = 53
The numbers in the circle = 79
The numbers in the square = 50
The total of the five numbers = 130

What numbers should replace the question marks?

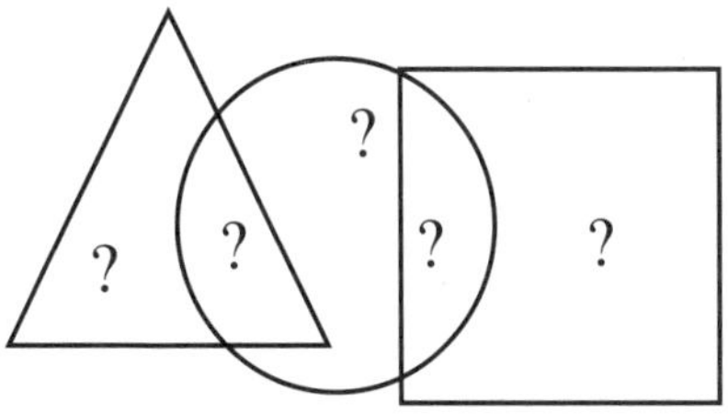

9 PUZZLE

What number should replace the question mark?

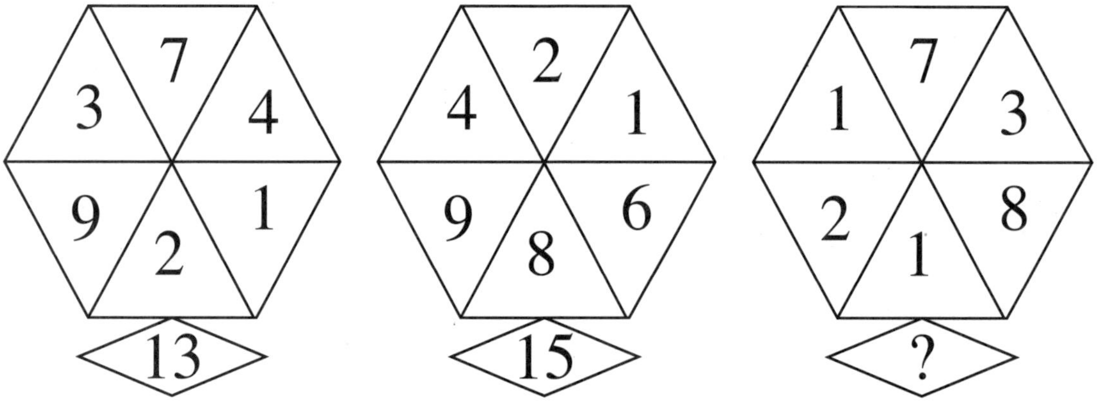

10 PUZZLE

Which is the missing piece?

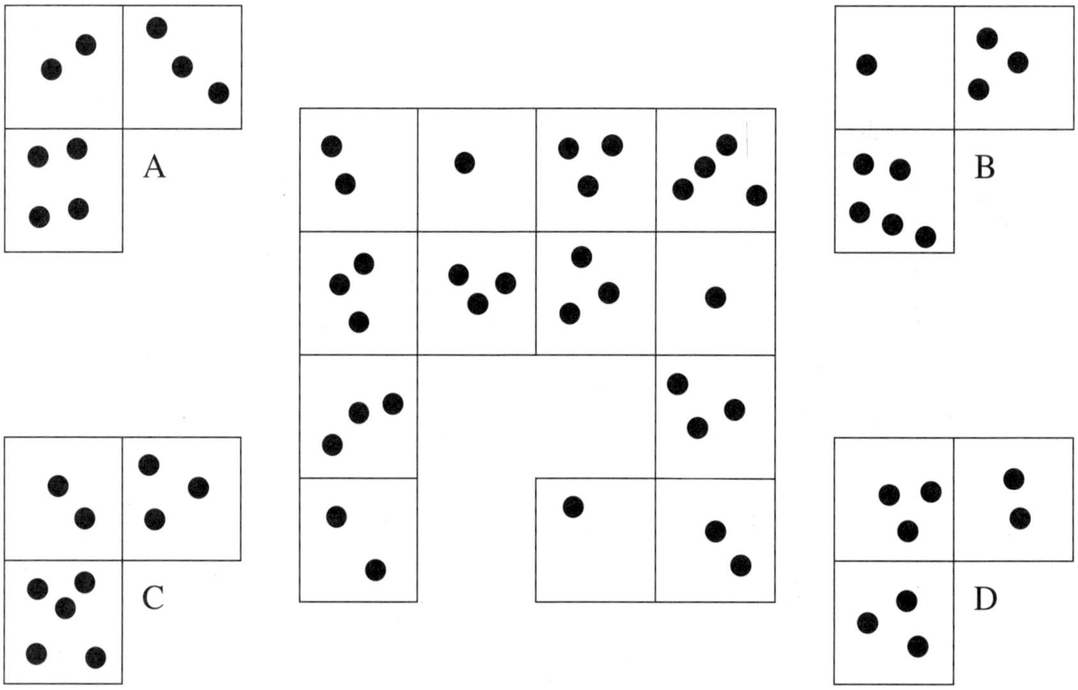

11

PUZZLE

Each line and symbol which appears in the four outer circles, below, is transferred to the centre circle according to these rules: If a line or symbol occurs in the outer circles: once: it is transferred twice: it is possibly transferred 3 times: it is transferred 4 times: it is not transferred. Which of the circles A, B, C, D or E, should appear at the centre of the diagram, below?

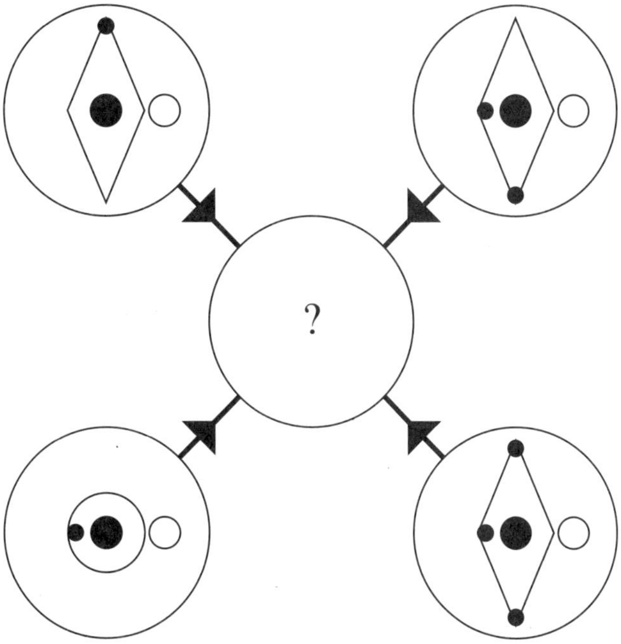

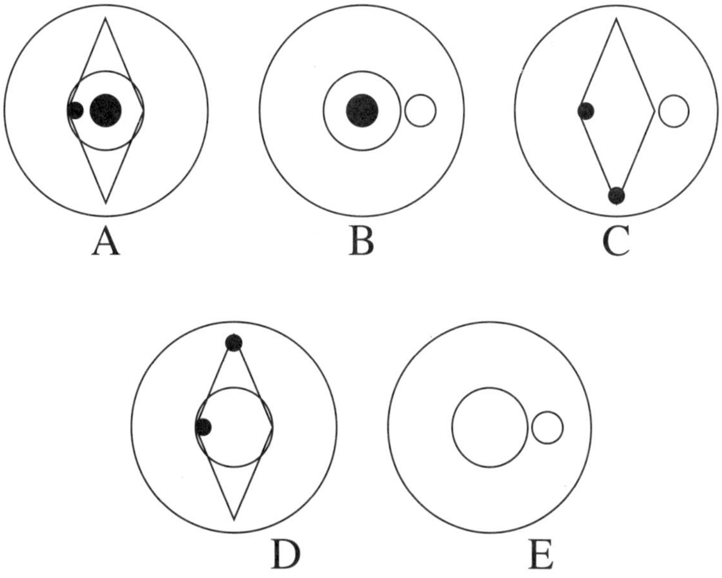

12 PUZZLE

Which playing card replaces the question mark?

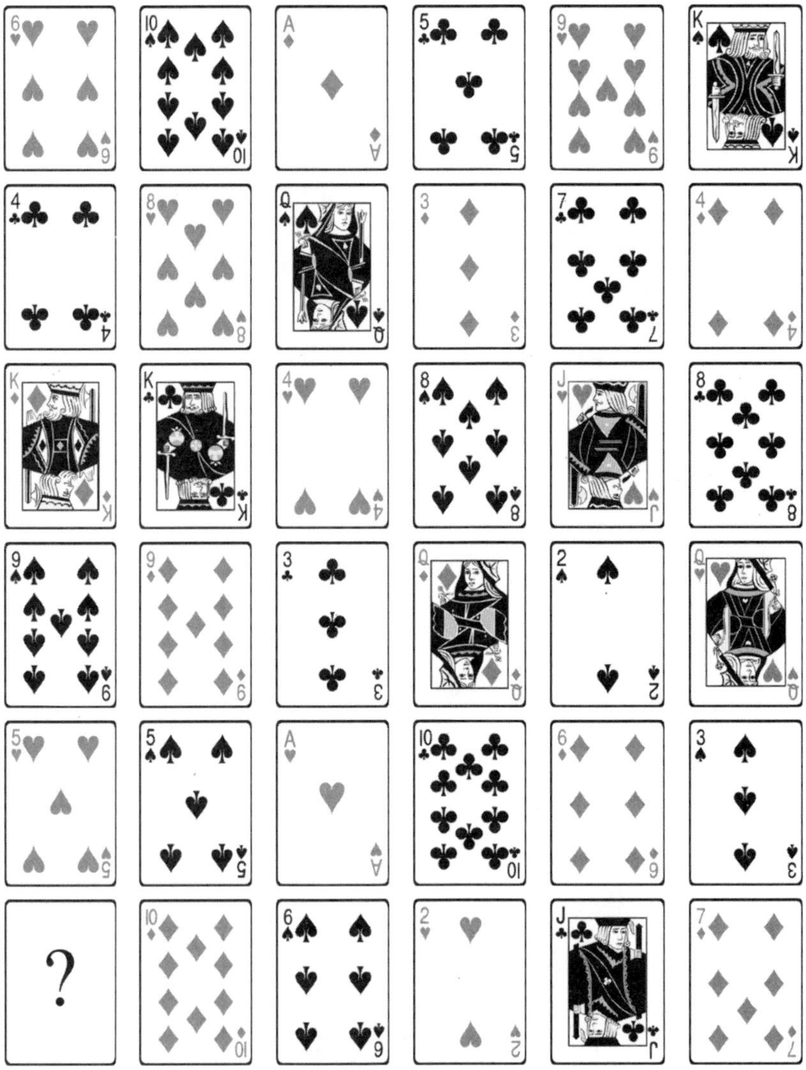

13 PUZZLE

Simplify

$$\frac{1}{2} + \frac{1}{4} \times \frac{3}{8} - \frac{7}{16}$$

14 PUZZLE

Which pentagons are the odd two out?

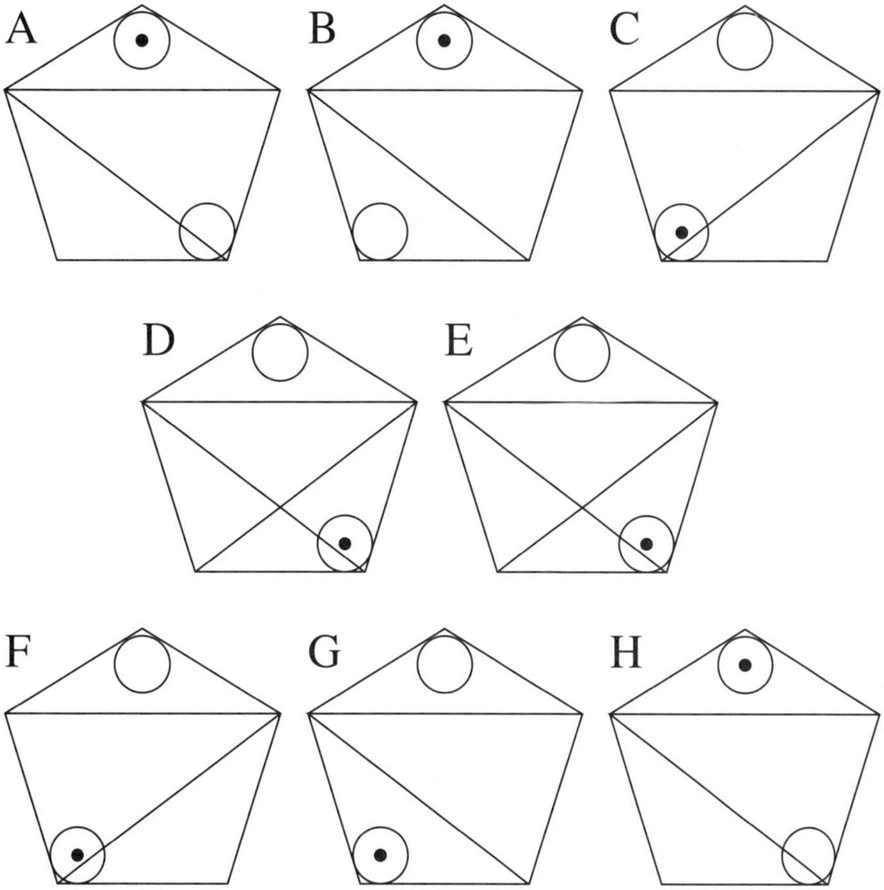

15 PUZZLE

What number should replace the question mark?

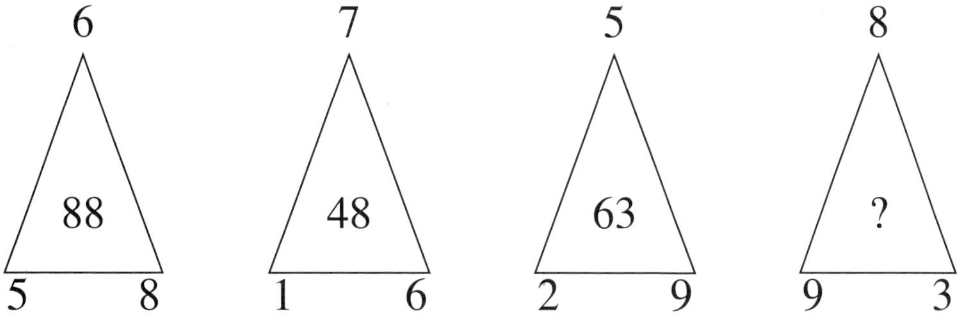

PUZZLE 16

Find which hexagon fills the space to a definite rule.

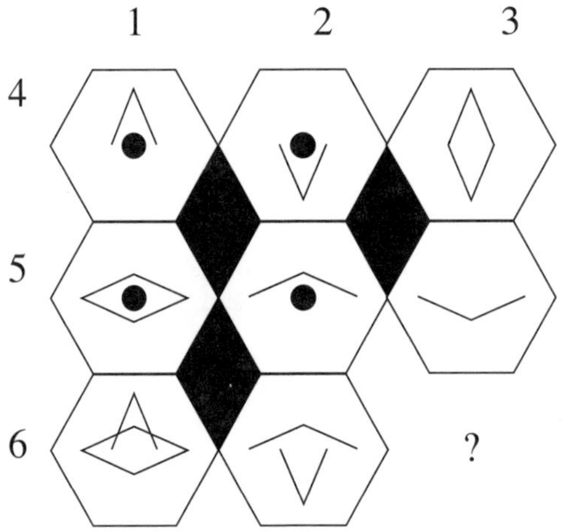

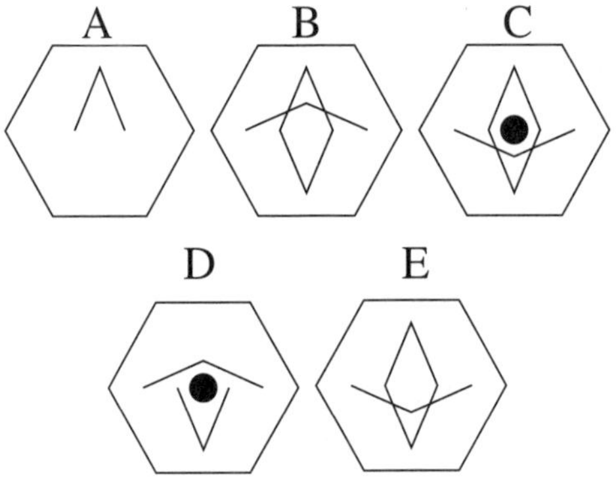

PUZZLE 17

Which is the odd one out, A, B or C?

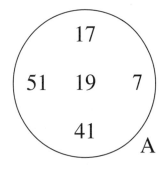

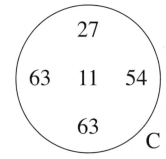

A

	17	
51	19	7
	41	

B

	33	
29	49	35
	79	

C

	27	
63	11	54
	63	

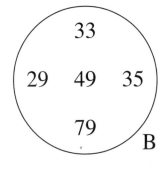

18 PUZZLE

Which letter of the alphabet should replace the question mark?

D F I M ?

19 PUZZLE

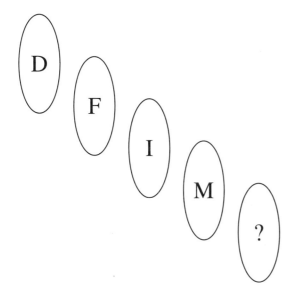

What is the meaning of MILIEU?

(a) DISCORD
(b DISORDER
(c) MARRIAGE
(d) HAPPINESS
(e) ENVIRONMENT

20 PUZZLE

Which word means the opposite of PULCHRITUDE?

(a) UGLINESS
(b) BEAUTY
(c) REALITY
(d) SWEETNESS
(e) ARCHAIC

21 PUZZLE

What number should replace the question mark?

1	80	9
3	40	7
5	?	6

LEVEL 16

22 PUZZLE

What number will replace the question mark?

A	B	C	D
17	18	16	31
23	60	25	37
39	44	36	?
47	28	49	43
81	32	64	47

23 PUZZLE

What is CANASTER?

(a) A TOBACCO
(b) A CARD GAME
(c) A DANCE
(d) A VASE
(e) A BOLD LINE

24 PUZZLE

Which of the following is always part of BANNOCK?

(a) OATMEAL
(b) CELERY
(c) MUSTARD
(d) CHOCOLATE
(e) CARROTS

25 PUZZLE

What numbers should replace the question marks?

78	930	15
29	400	11
37	?	?

26 PUZZLE

Which number is missing from the last grid?

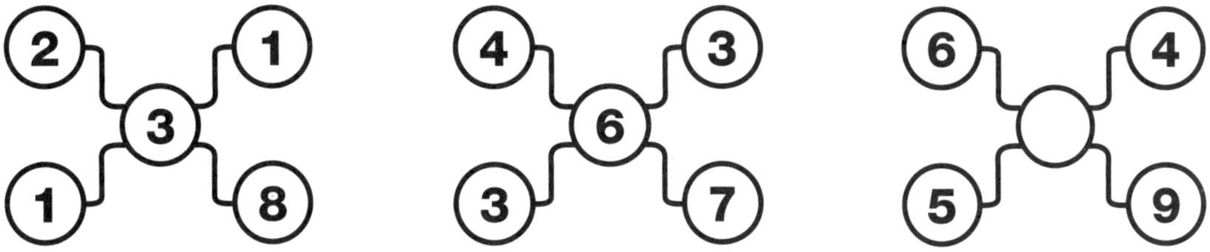

27 PUZZLE

Which card comes next?

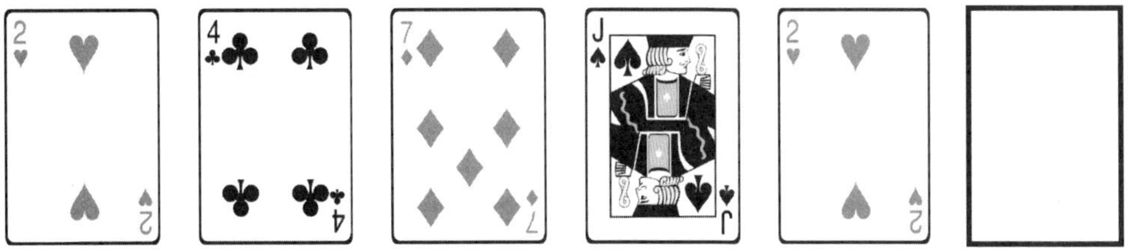

28 PUZZLE

Which number is missing from the last grid?

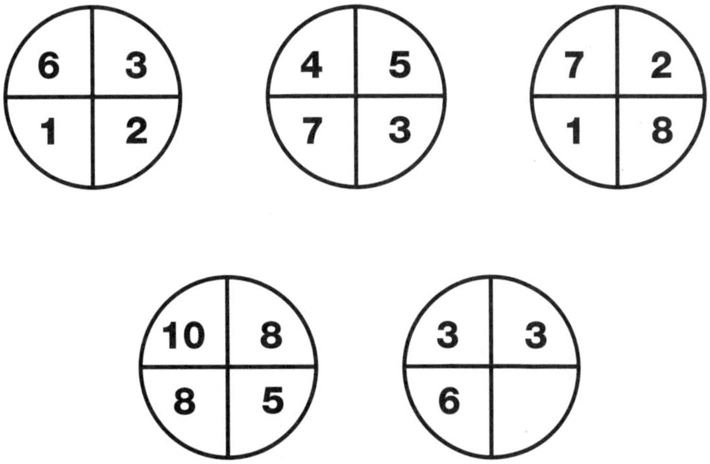

PUZZLE 29

Which number is missing from the empty circle?

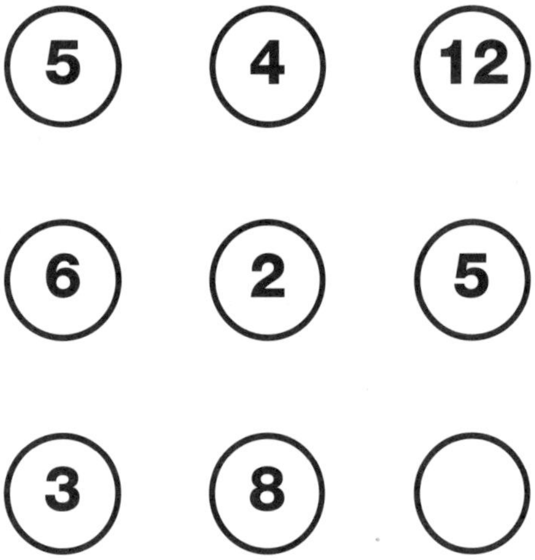

PUZZLE 30

Which numbers replace the blanks?

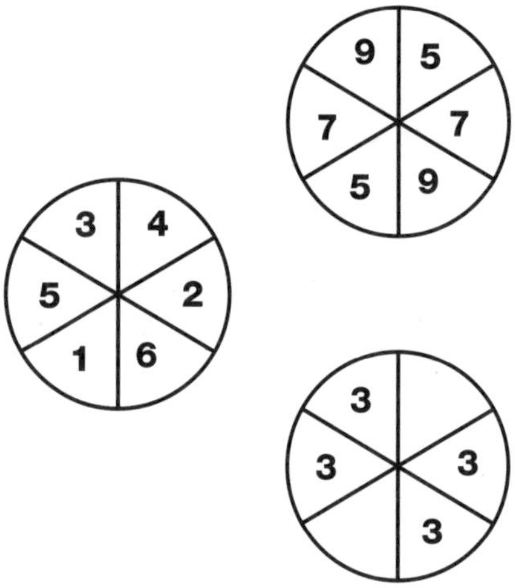

PUZZLE 31

Sisters Janine and Jackie went shopping for new outfits for a wedding. They each bought three items and by coincidence, each spent exactly $222.22.

Janine noticed something else – if you look at the price of each item the value in dollars is the square of the cents value.

If one of Janine's items cost $1.01 and one of Jackie's cost $169.13 what are the prices of the other two items?

PUZZLE 32

Which letter is missing from the wheel?

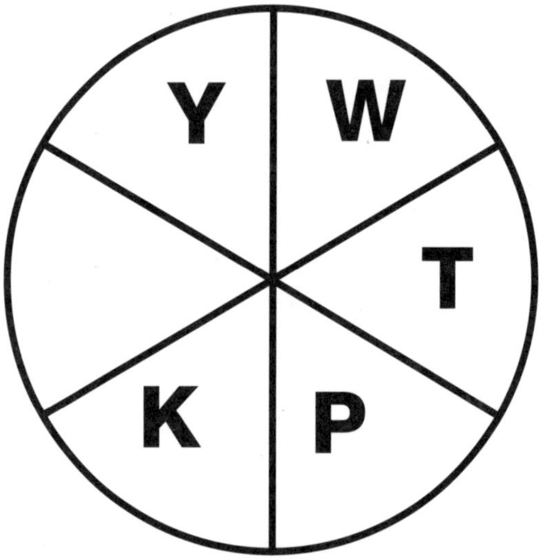

PUZZLE 33

Which of the numbered grids fits into the big one?

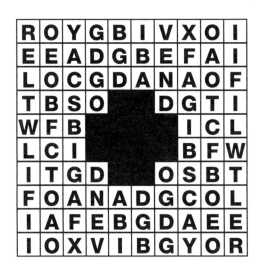

R	O	Y	G	B	I	V	X	O	I
E	E	A	D	G	B	E	F	A	I
L	O	C	G	D	A	N	A	O	F
T	B	S	O			D	G	T	I
W	F	B					I	C	L
L	C	I					B	F	W
I	T	G	D			O	S	B	T
F	O	A	N	A	D	G	C	O	L
I	A	F	E	B	G	D	A	E	E
I	O	X	V	I	B	G	Y	O	R

1

	T	B	
C	Y	L	Y
Y	L	Y	C
	B	T	

2

	Q	Q	
S	L	A	A
C	B	L	S
	Q	Q	

3

	X	Y	
B	S	L	E
E	L	S	B
	X	Y	

4

	O	X	
T	V	V	J
J	T	T	V
	X	O	

5

	T	C	
C	Y	L	Y
Y	L	Y	C
	T	C	

PUZZLE 34

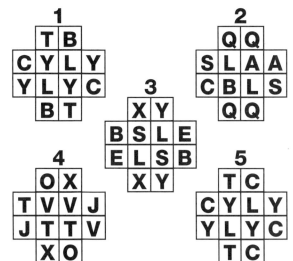

Which number completes the wheel?

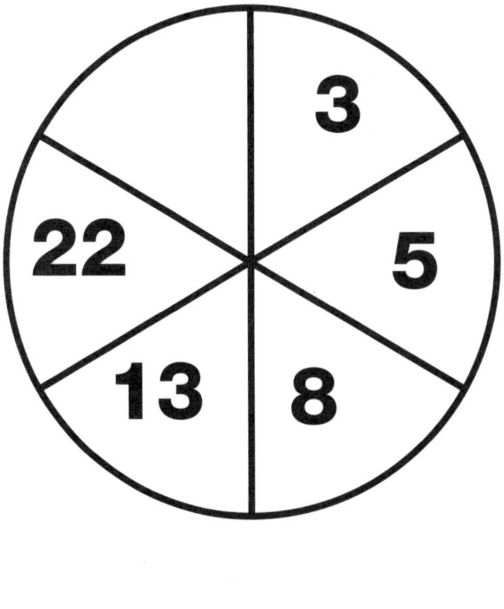

PUZZLE 35

What is missing from the empty square?

M	1	5
O	1	7

V	2	5
I	1	2

T	2	4
L	1	

PUZZLE 36

Which number completes the bottom grid?

1	3	4
5	2	3

6	2	8
7	1	6

4	7	11
11	2	

PUZZLE 37

Which letter goes in the empty square?

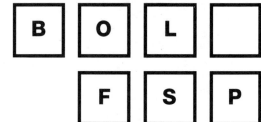

D	R	F	
K	H	V	J
B	O	L	
	F	S	P

PUZZLE 38

Complete the wheel by adding the missing number.

PUZZLE 39

What goes in the empty box to complete the puzzle?

O	V	H
17	10	24

M	E	T
18	26	11

F	N	X
24	16	

40 PUZZLE

Where is the minute hand pointing to in the bottom clock?

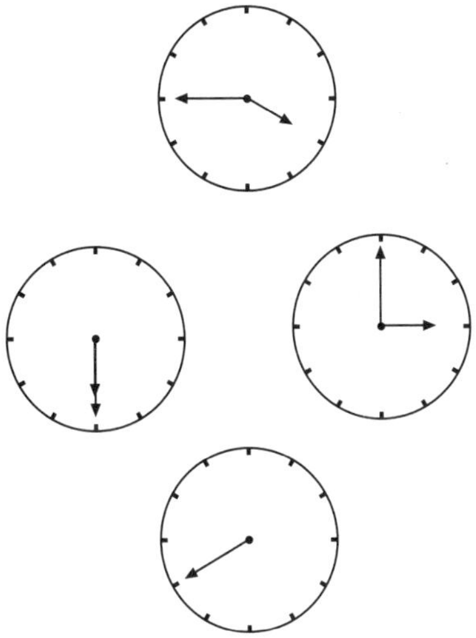

41 PUZZLE

Which number goes in the centre of the bottom right box?

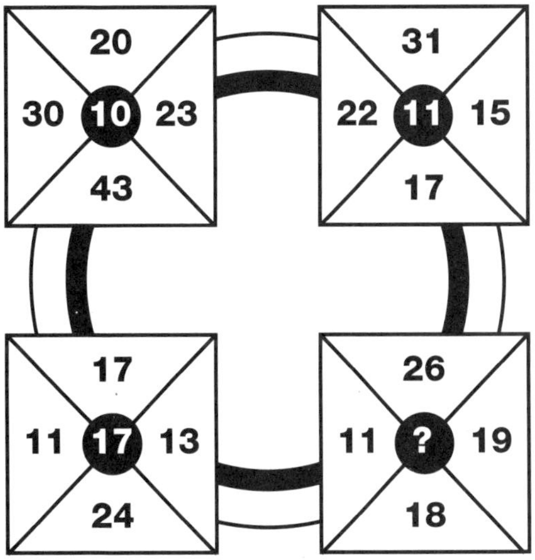

42 PUZZLE

Which of the bottom grids would continue the sequence?

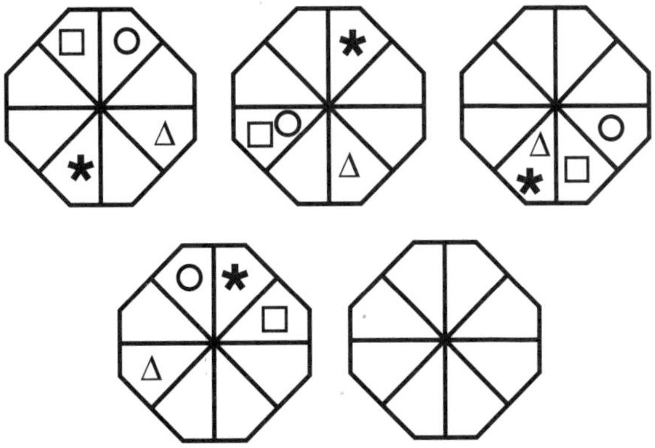

A B C D E

LEVEL 16

43 PUZZLE

Which playing cards will fill in the blanks?

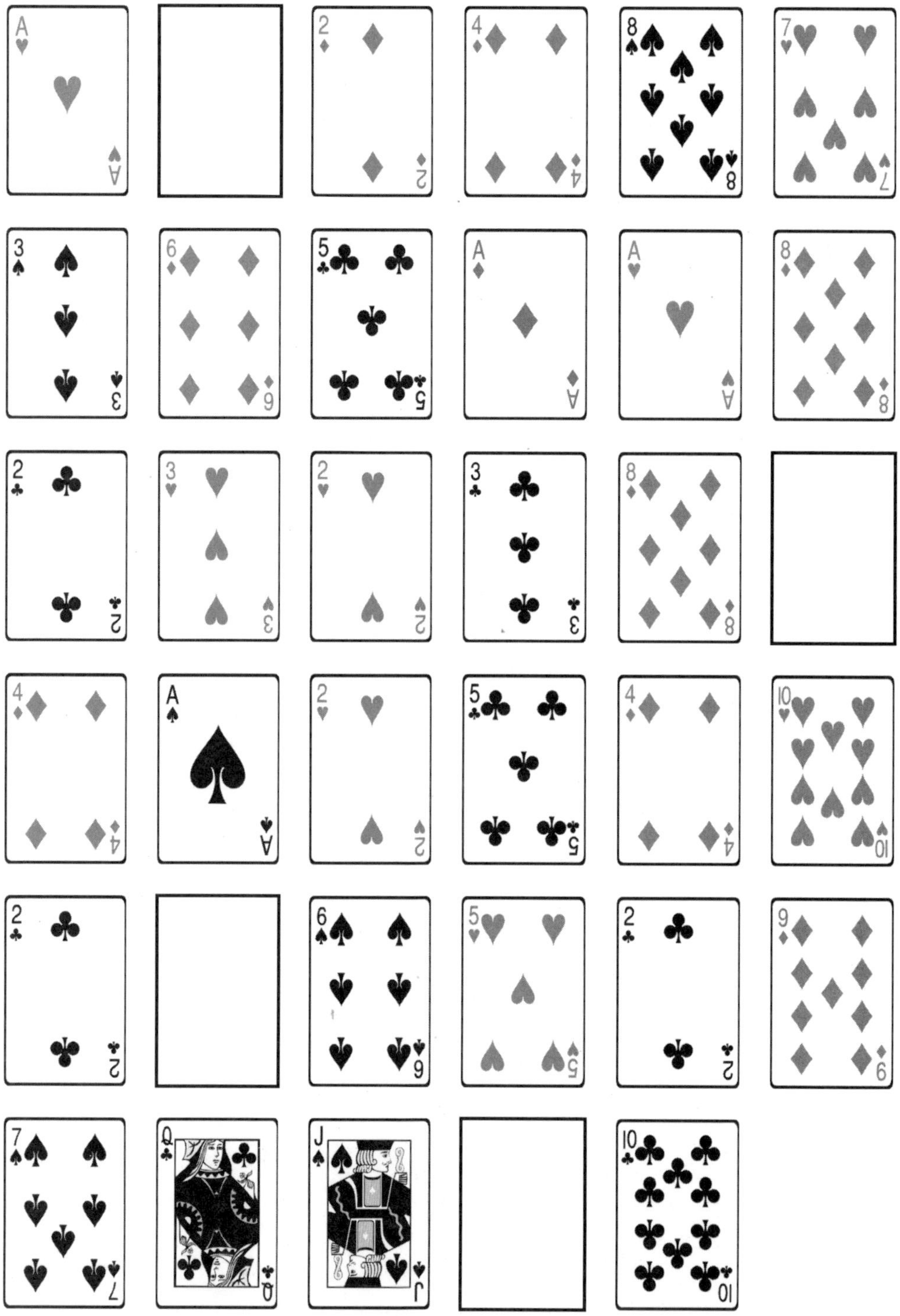

44 PUZZLE

Gary writes out a sum for his girlfriend Selina. Although it was wrong he challenged her to change just one symbol to make the sum correct. Can you see how she did it?

1 + 2 – 3 = 139

45 PUZZLE

Which letter replaces the blank and completes the sequence?

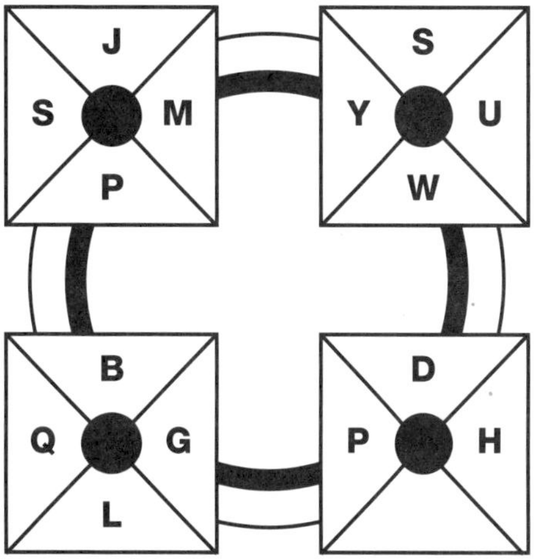

46 PUZZLE

Which figure will come next?

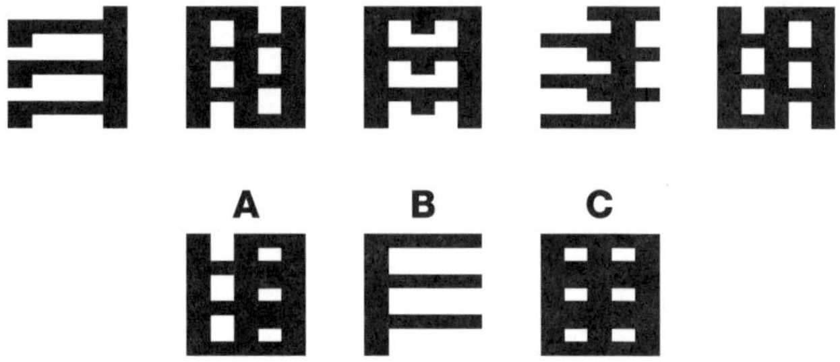

47 PUZZLE

Which number will continue this sequence?

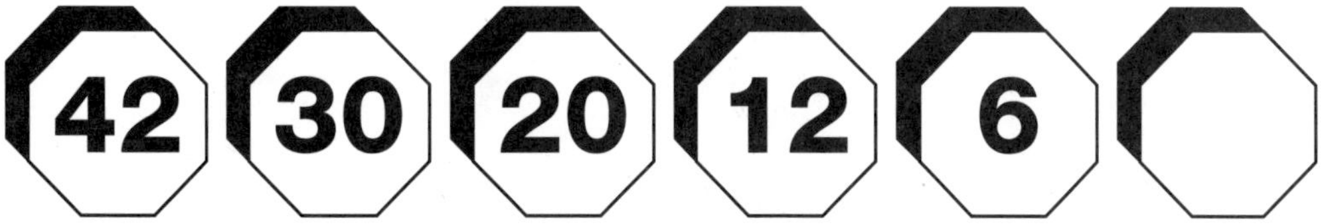

48 PUZZLE

Which number is missing from the last star?

49 PUZZLE

Which shapes are missing?

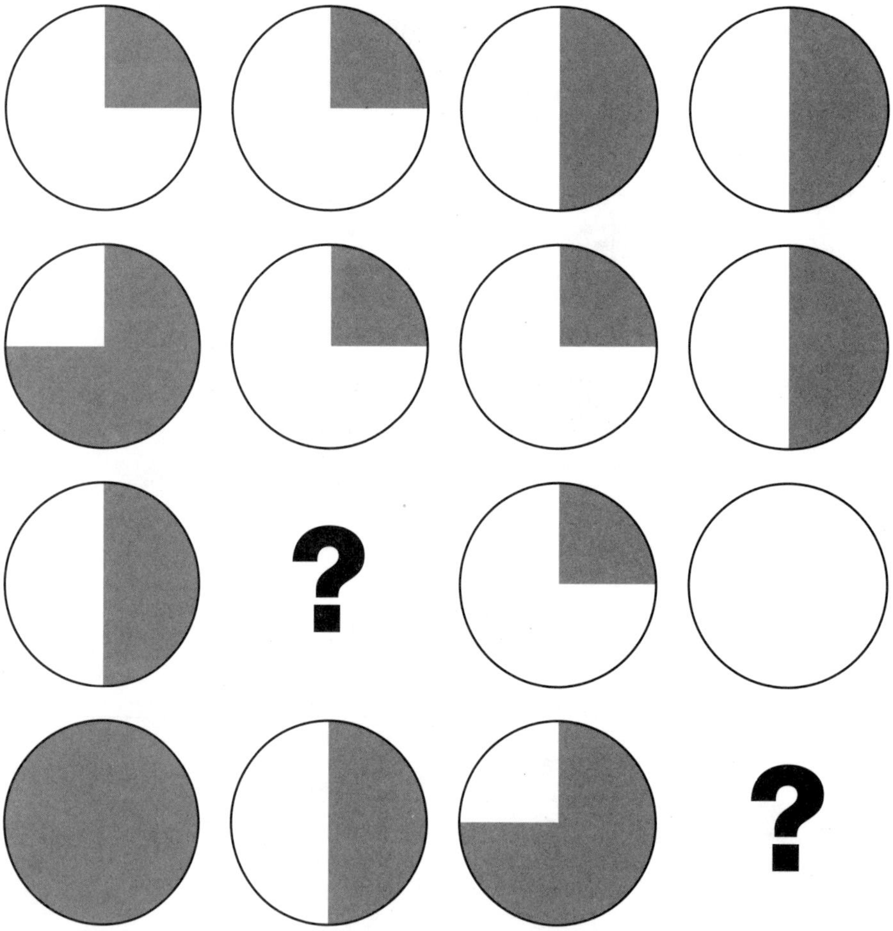

50 PUZZLE

Move three matches to form a pattern containing 8 equilateral triangles.

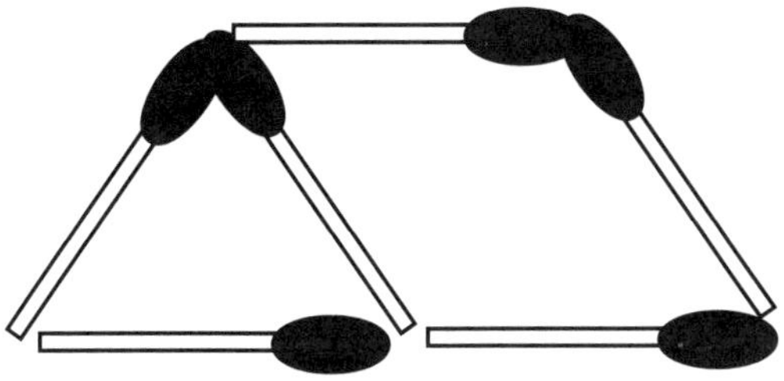

51 PUZZLE

Which number is missing?

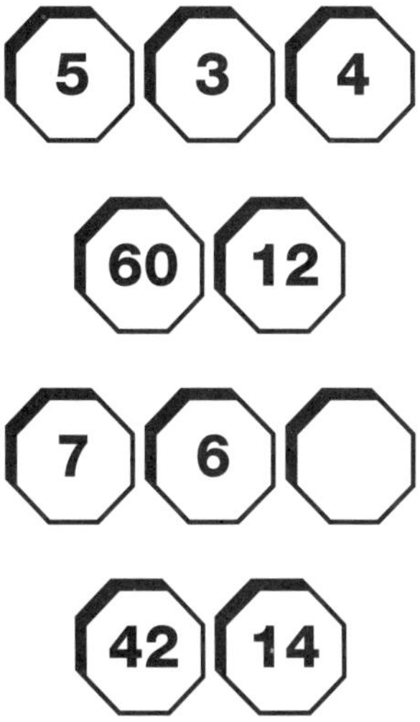

52 PUZZLE

Which numbers are missing from the centre column?

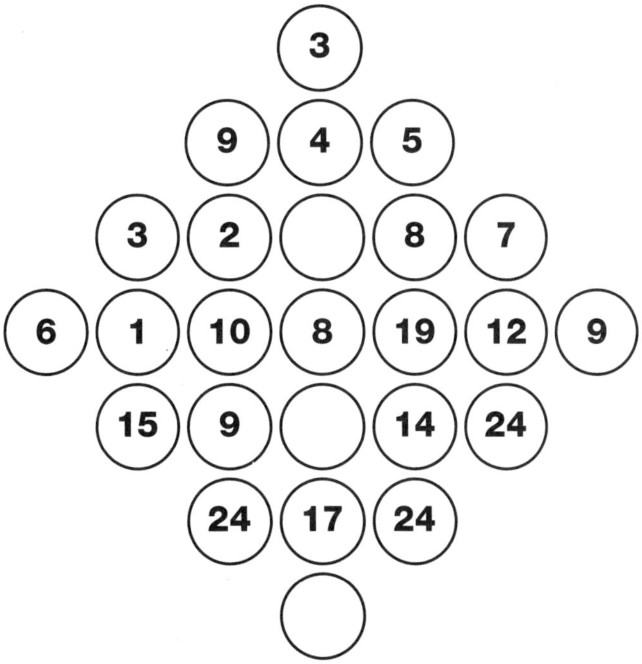

1 PUZZLE

When the pattern below is folded to form a cube which is the only one of the following that can be produced?

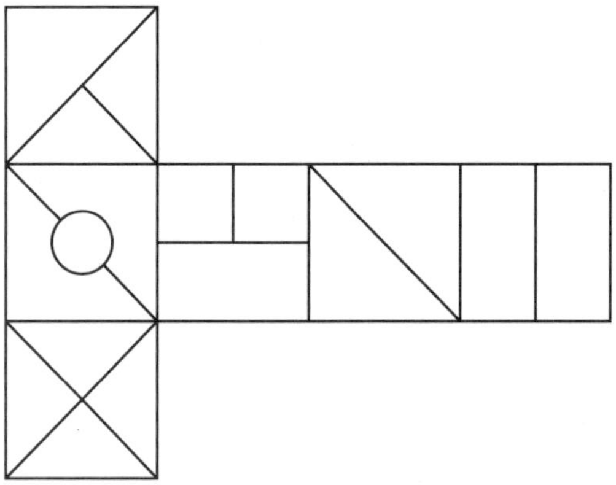

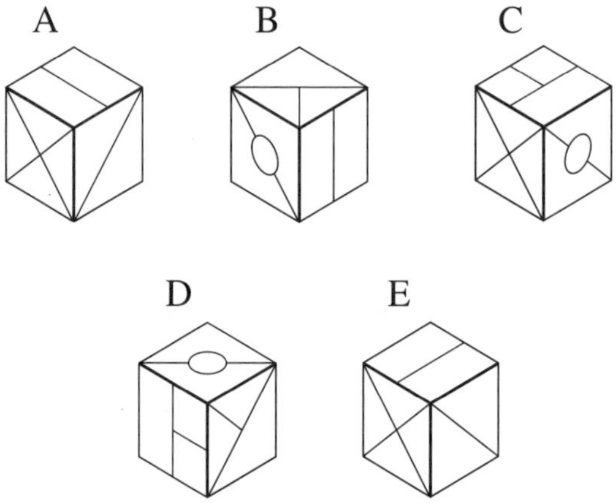

2 PUZZLE

Insert the missing numbers. The connection between each set of numbers in each row is the same.

196	114	?
376	?	44
487	?	?

3 PUZZLE

What should be the missing numbers?

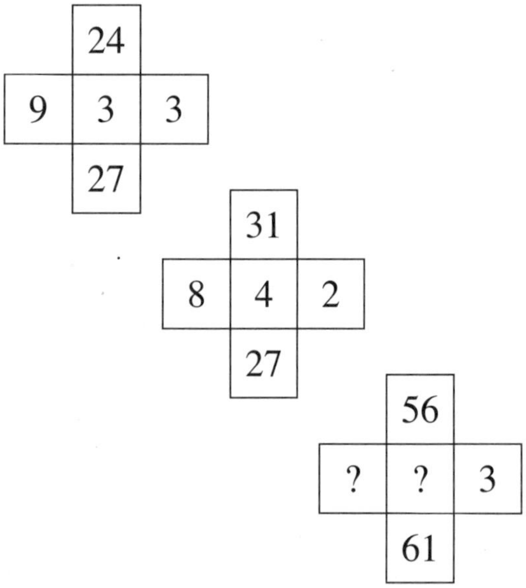

4 PUZZLE

What comes next?

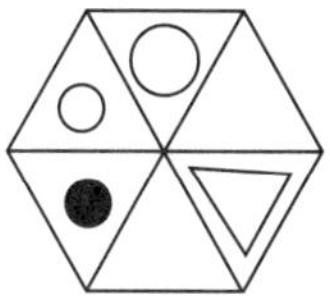

A

B

C

D

5 PUZZLE

What should be the missing number?

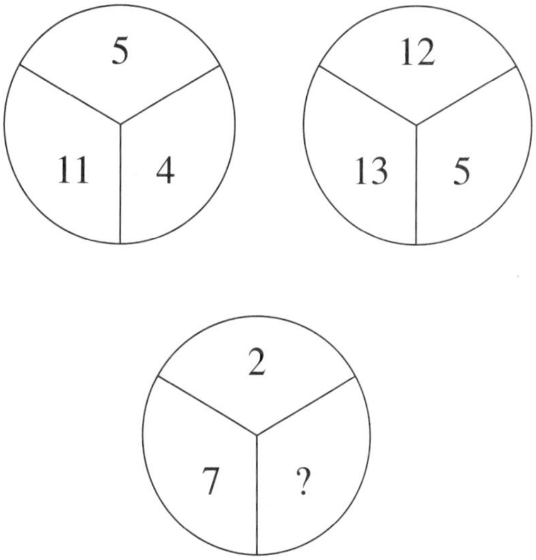

6 PUZZLE

What should be the missing letter?

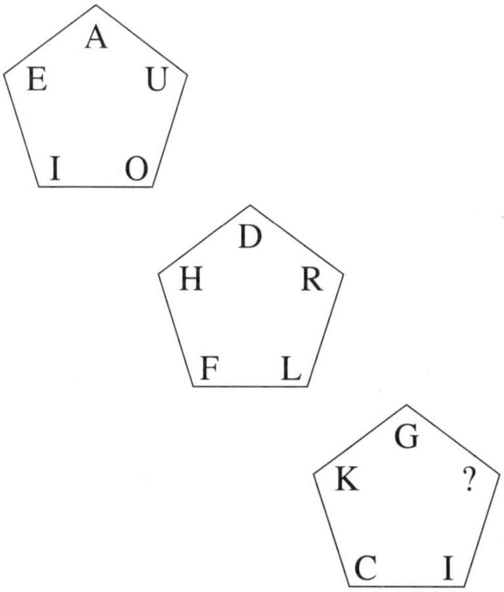

7 PUZZLE

Which is the odd one out?

A

B

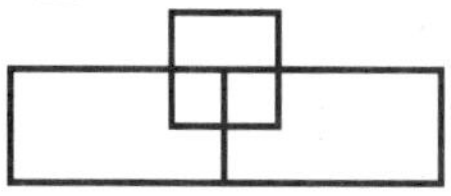

E

C

D

8 PUZZLE

What comes next?

15634

63451

45136

?

9 PUZZLE

What should be the missing number?

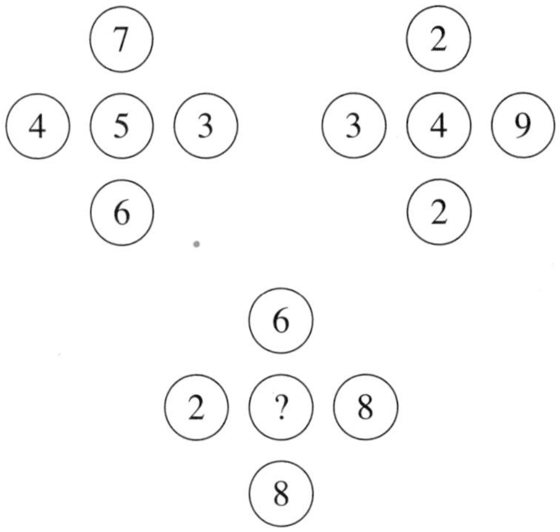

10 PUZZLE

Which is the missing piece?

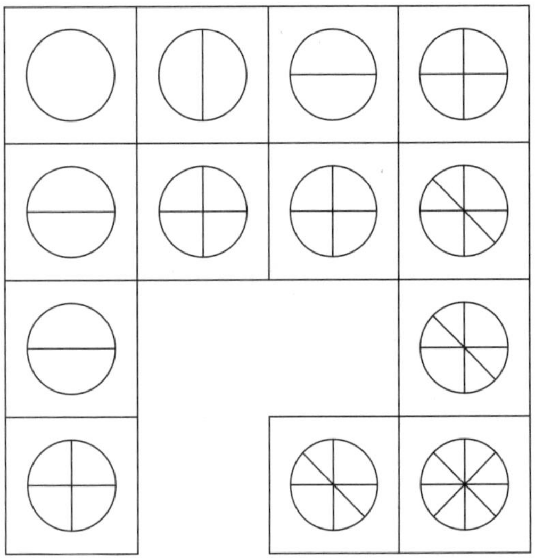

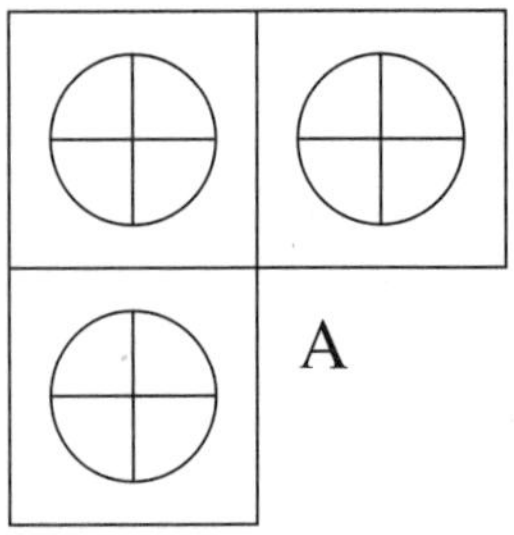

A

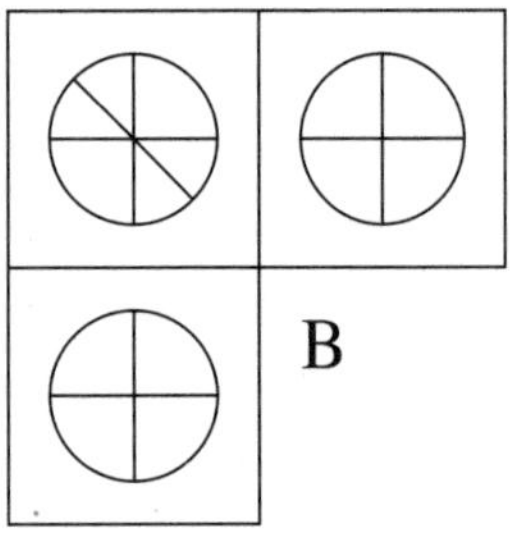

B

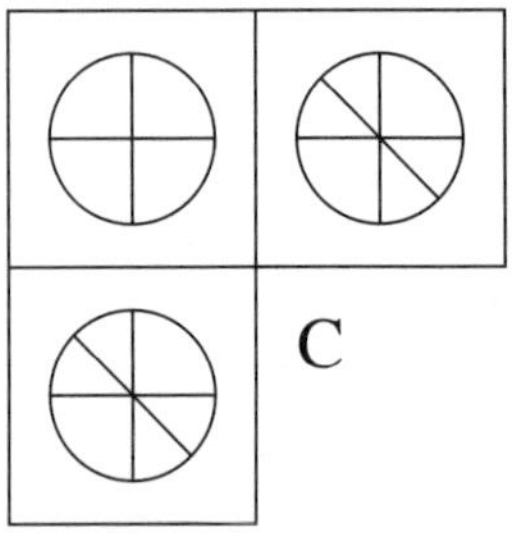

C

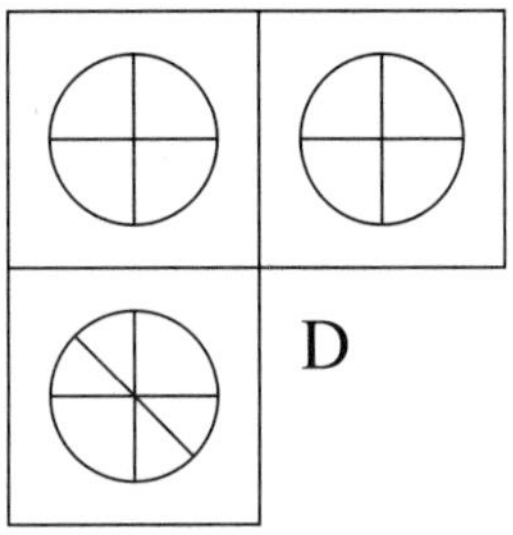

D

11 PUZZLE

Each line and symbol which appears in the four outer circles, below, is transferred to the centre circle according to these rules: If a line or symbol occurs in the outer circles: once: it is transferred twice: it is possibly transferred three times: it is transferred four times: it is not transferred. Which of the circles A, B, C, D or E, should appear at the centre of the diagram, below?

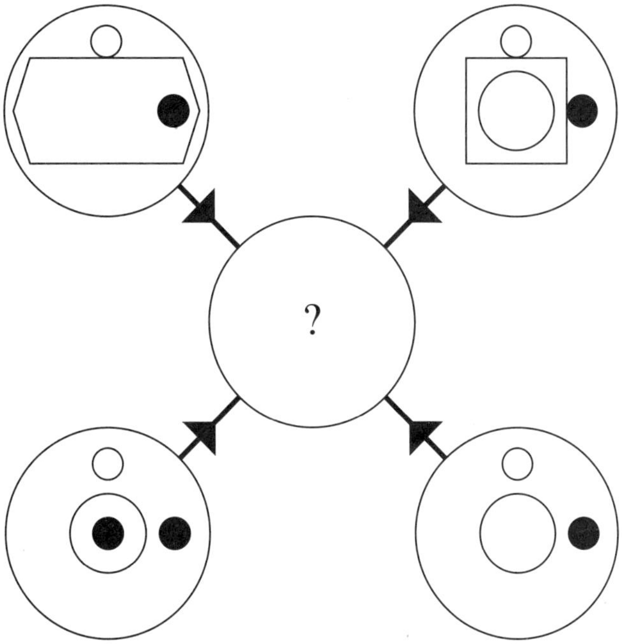

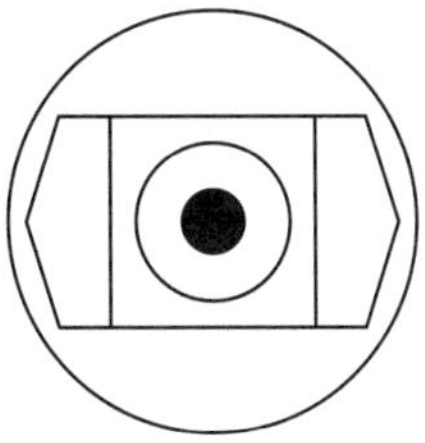
A

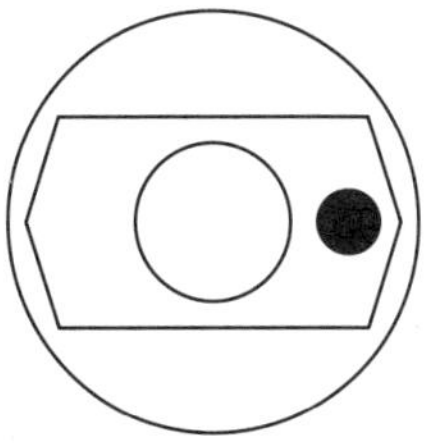
B

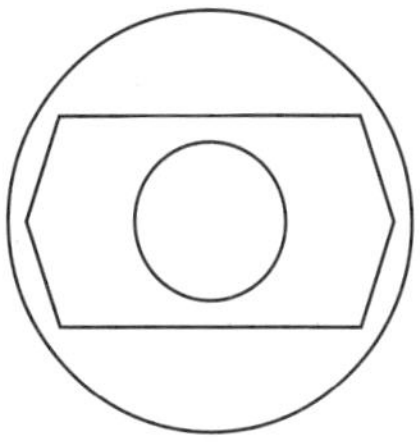
C

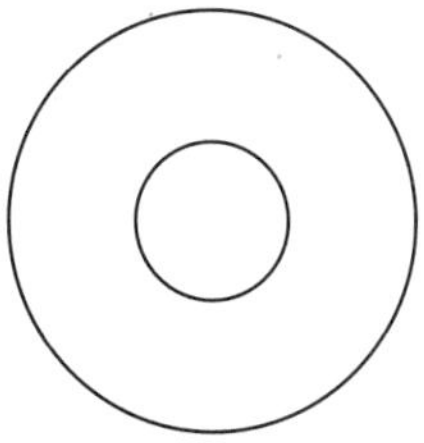
D

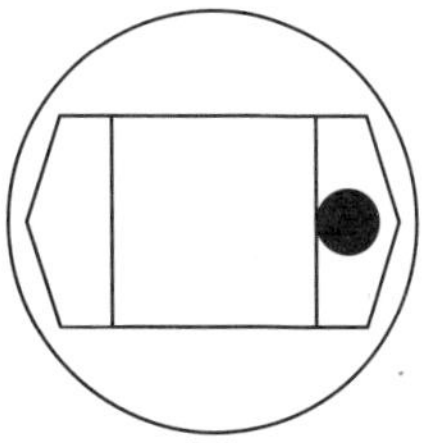
E

12 PUZZLE

What number should replace the question mark?

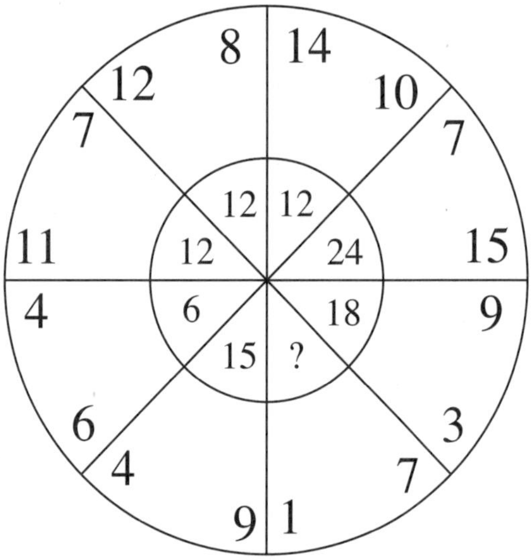

13 PUZZLE

What is the meaning of CAJOLE?

(a) KNOCK
(b) WISH
(c) HESITATE
(d) LEAN
(e) COAX

14 PUZZLE

If (15) (4^2)
= x (2^3)

What does x = ?

(a) 28
(b) 30
(c) 32
(d) 34
(e) 36

15 PUZZLE

What should the drawing for No 6 be?

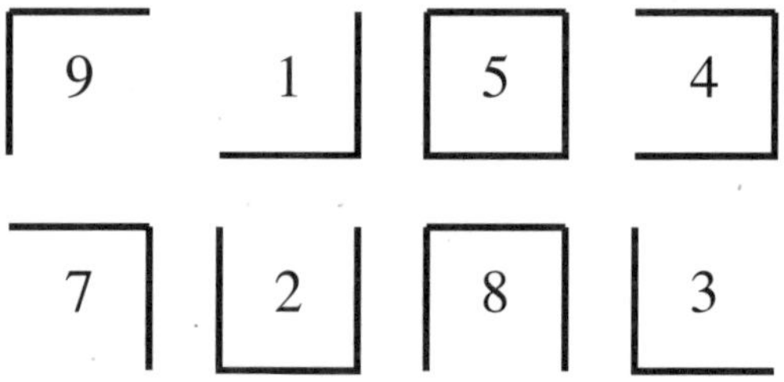

16 PUZZLE

Which hexagonal replaces the question mark
A, B, C, D or E?

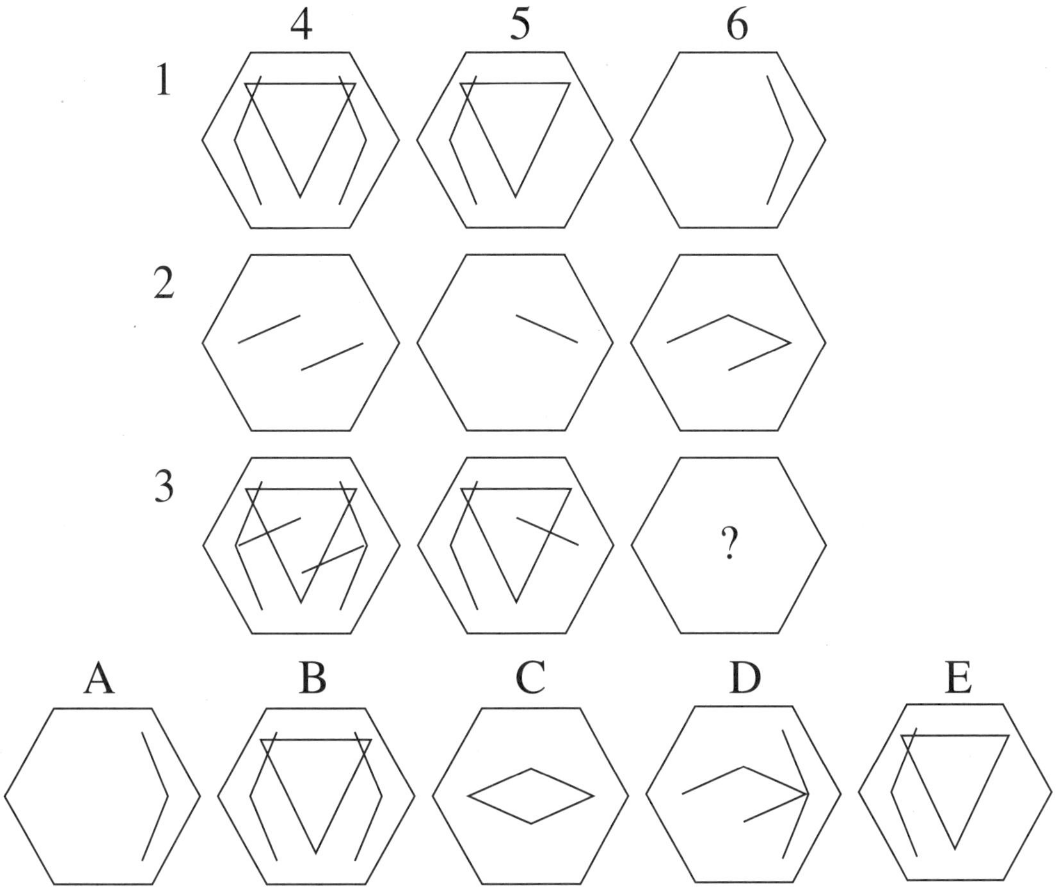

17 PUZZLE

What number should replace the question mark?

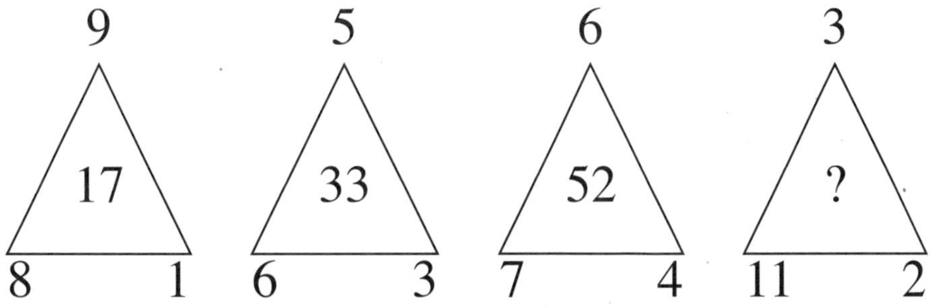

18 PUZZLE

Find the circle to replace the question mark.

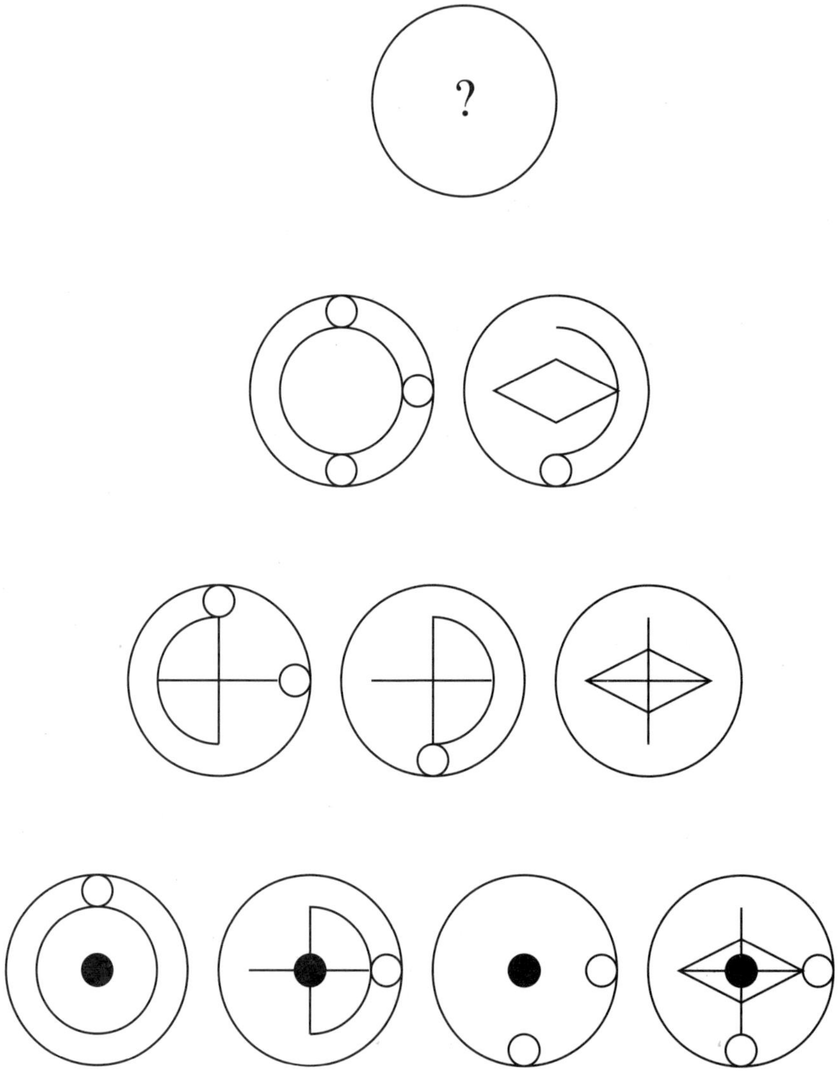

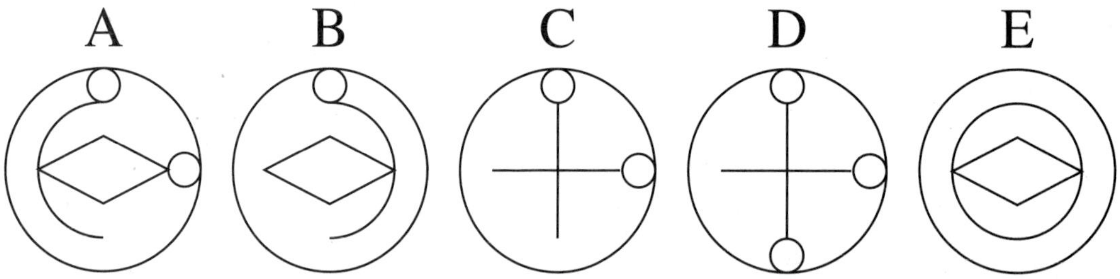

19 PUZZLE

What number should replace the question mark?

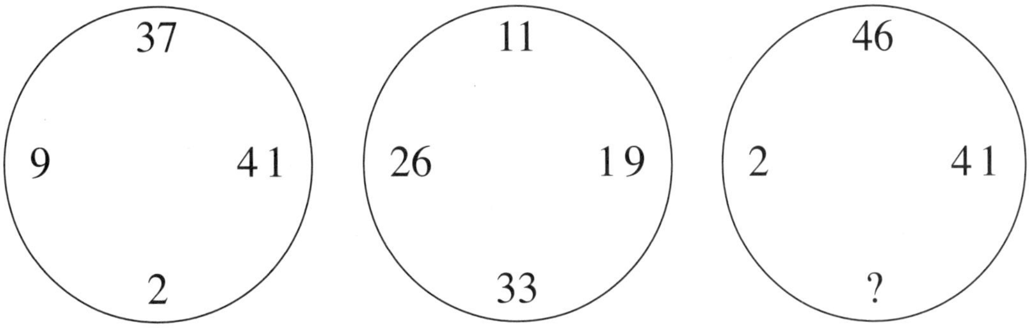

20 PUZZLE

If cola costs 74 cents and
milk costs 63 cents and
beer costs 78 cents,
what does lime cost?

21 PUZZLE

Which number replaces the ? in this sequence?

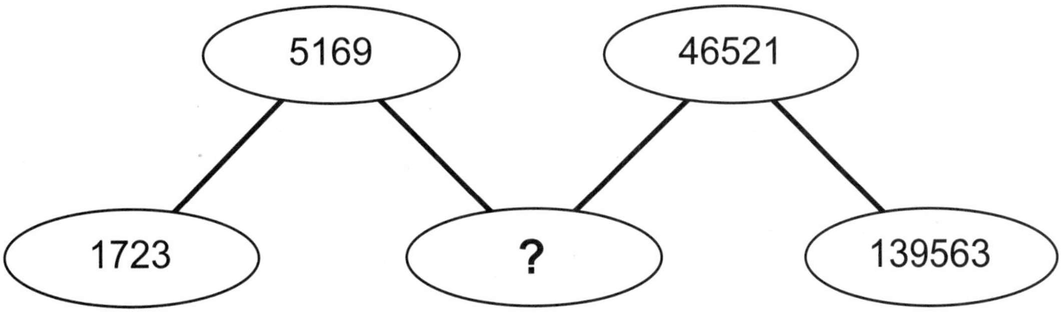

PUZZLE 22

What number should replace the question mark?

5	4	6	2	4	1	7	8	7
6	6	4	2	2	7	8	?	1
5	2	7	1	2	7	6	5	4

PUZZLE 23

What is the square root (√) of 3249?

(a) 47 (b) 53 (c) 57 (d) 63 (e) 67

PUZZLE 24

Which of these is not a SEA?

(a) BERING
(b) WEDDELL
(c) ANNAPURNA
(d) TIMOR

PUZZLE 25

Which number should replace the question mark?

126	3	24
364	4	19
98	?	41

PUZZLE 26

Which of the smaller grids goes in the centre of the large one?

9	4	2	7	6	3	5	6	4	6
1	7	8	6	9	8	4	3	5	1
8	3	5	2	6	7	5	8	1	7
2	4	1	9			7	3	9	5
8	5	3					7	2	8
6	7	2					1	7	6
3	6	4	9			8	7	2	4
8	2	5	1	6	3	9	4	7	7
3	1	9	2	7	8	6	3	9	4
7	3	4	6	9	1	8	5	4	5

1

	3	2	
9	4	6	7
3	1	2	3
	8	9	

2

	9	9	
2	1	6	7
9	3	1	2
	4	4	

3

	6	6	
9	5	3	2
8	7	6	2
	6	3	

4

	4	2	
6	8	3	7
2	1	9	4
	2	4	

5

	2	9	
8	3	7	6
2	1	4	5
	7	3	

PUZZLE 27

Which number goes in the centre of the third triangle?

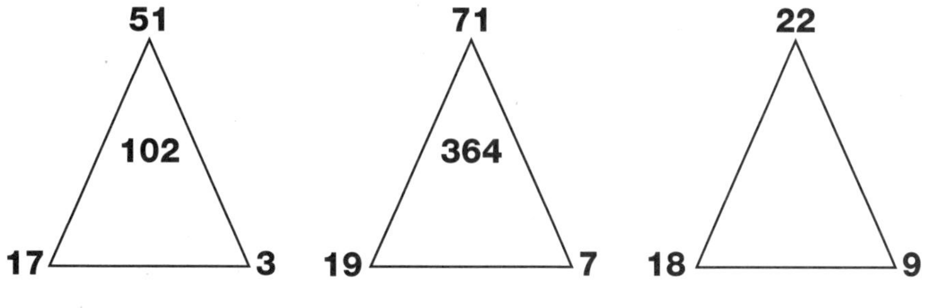

PUZZLE 28

Which number comes next?

PUZZLE 29

Which number is missing?

18	13	26	21
9	266	261	42
14	133	522	37
7		69	74

PUZZLE 30

Which letter completes the chain?

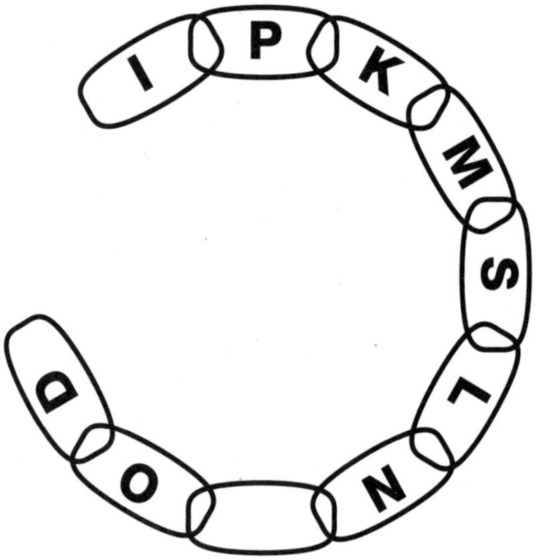

PUZZLE 31

Which letter is missing from the wheel?

PUZZLE 32

Which letter goes in the empty box?

C	I	L
G	M	P

D	Q	S
I	V	X

F	K	R
L	Q	

33 PUZZLE

Which of the smaller pieces will fit into the big grid?

1	7	0	6	3	5	2	4	9	8
9	3	4	2	8	0	7	6	1	5
5	1	8	7	6	2	9	3	0	4
6	9	3	1			5	7	8	0
4	5	6					8	2	9
0	8	2					5	7	3
8	4	5	0			6	9	3	2
7	2	9	4	0	3	8	1	5	6
3	0	1	5	9	8	4	2	6	7
2	6	7	8	5	9	3	0	4	1

1

	6	4	
3	5	7	0
9	4	6	1
	8	2	

2

	2	4	
0	7	1	3
9	4	6	1
	8	2	

3

	2	4	
3	1	7	0
9	4	6	1
	7	1	

4

	2	0	
7	3	8	5
6	1	9	2
	0	7	

5

	4	2	
7	3	8	5
6	1	3	2
	0	7	

34 PUZZLE

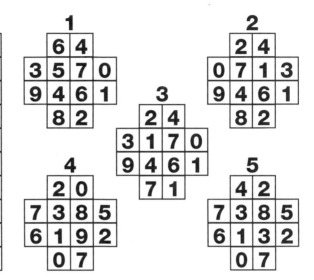

Which number completes the puzzle?

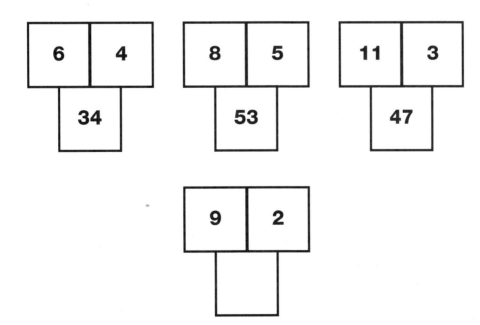

6	4
34	

8	5
53	

11	3
47	

9	2

35 PUZZLE

Which letter is missing from the bottom right hand grid?

E	N
T	O

F	L
S	Q

G	J
R	S

H	H
Q	U

I	F
P	

36 PUZZLE

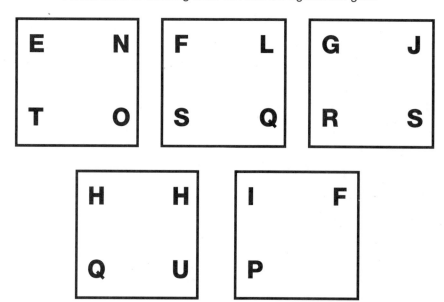

Which of the bottom grids continues the sequence shown on the top line?

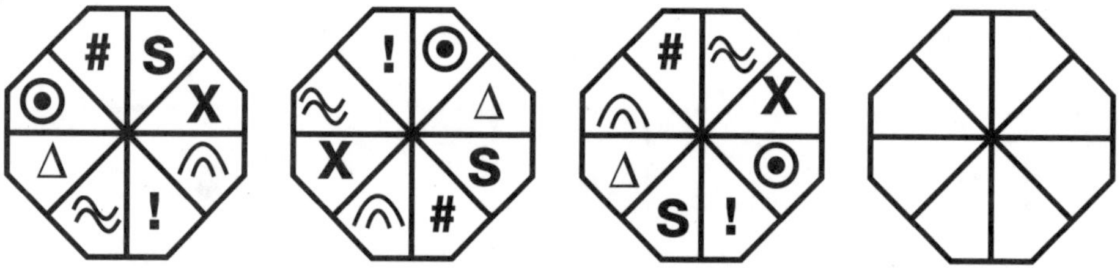

A B C D

PUZZLE 37

Which number goes in the empty circle and completes this puzzle?

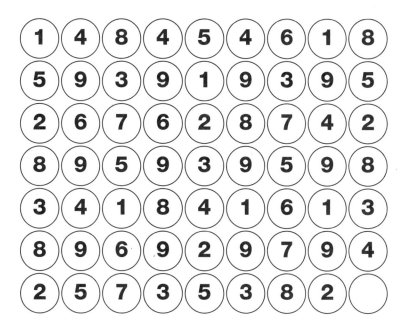

1	4	8	4	5	4	6	1	8
5	9	3	9	1	9	3	9	5
2	6	7	6	2	8	7	4	2
8	9	5	9	3	9	5	9	8
3	4	1	8	4	1	6	1	3
8	9	6	9	2	9	7	9	4
2	5	7	3	5	3	8	2	

PUZZLE 38

What goes in the empty box?

C	R	2	1
Q	W	4	0
L	A	1	3
M	T	3	

PUZZLE 39

Which letter replaces the blank and completes the sequence?

- B
- C
- D
- G
- (blank)

40 PUZZLE

Which of the watches on the bottom row continue the sequence shown on the top?

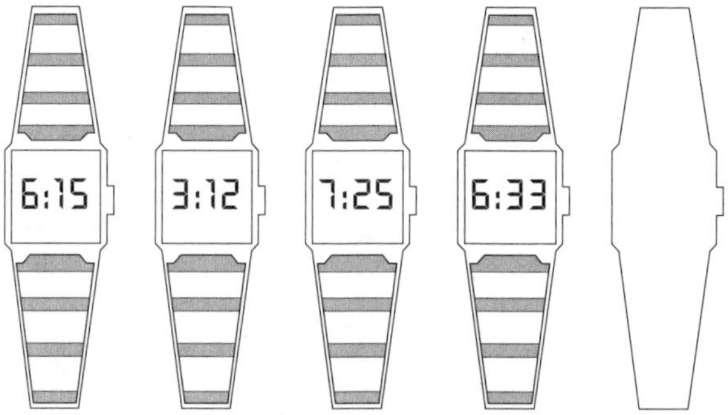

A B C D

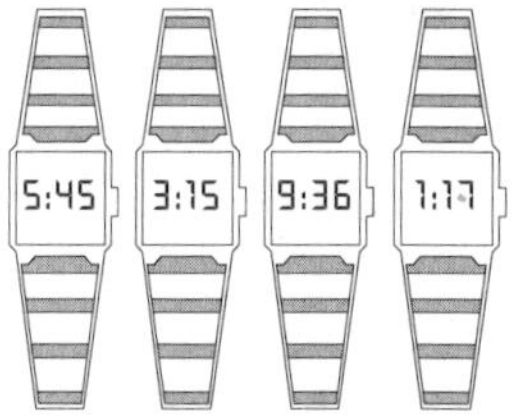

41 PUZZLE

Which of the bottom grids would continue the top sequence?

A B C D

42 PUZZLE

Which numbers are missing?

3	9	1
1		2
7		3
7	2	9

A

1	9	2
3		0
2		6
3	2	

B

2	7	0
5		0
4		5
1	9	

43 PUZZLE

Which letter goes in the blank segment?

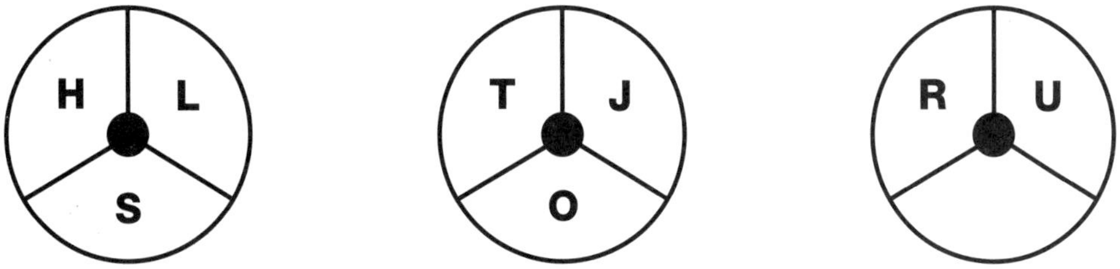

44 PUZZLE

Which number goes in the last circle?

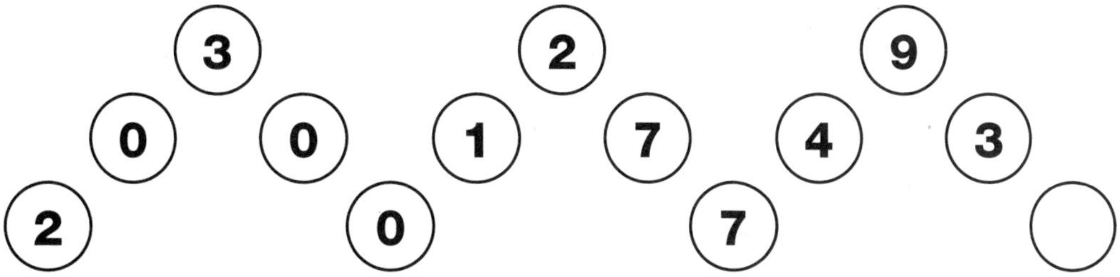

LEVEL

17

LEVEL 17

PUZZLE 45

Which number goes at the bottom of the column?

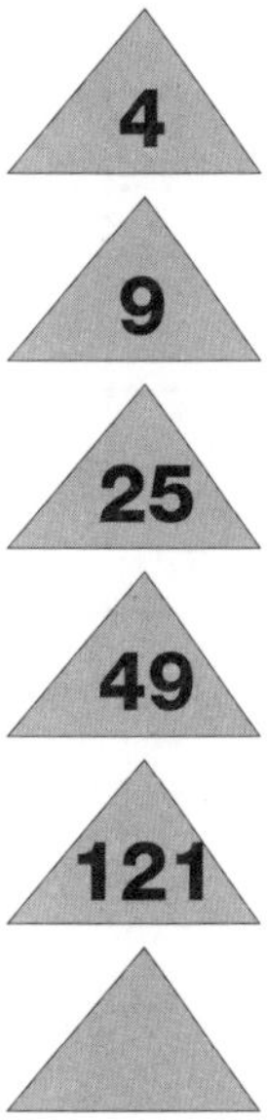

PUZZLE 46

Which number is missing from the empty box?

2	3	5
7	11	13

2	4	8
12	20	24

3	6	12
18	30	

PUZZLE 47

Which number should go in the empty segment of the wheel?

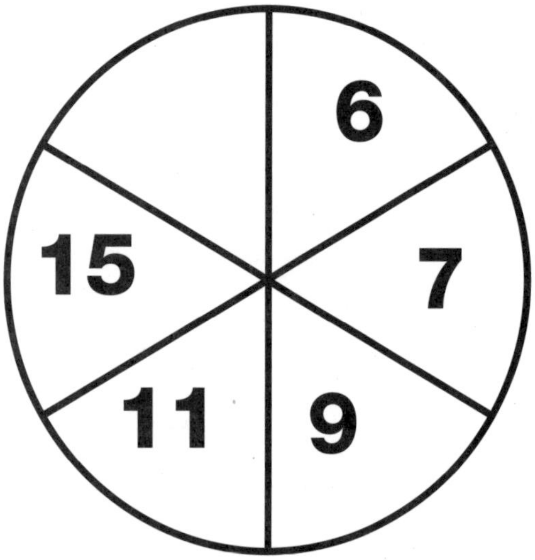

PUZZLE 48

What is missing from the empty ellipse?

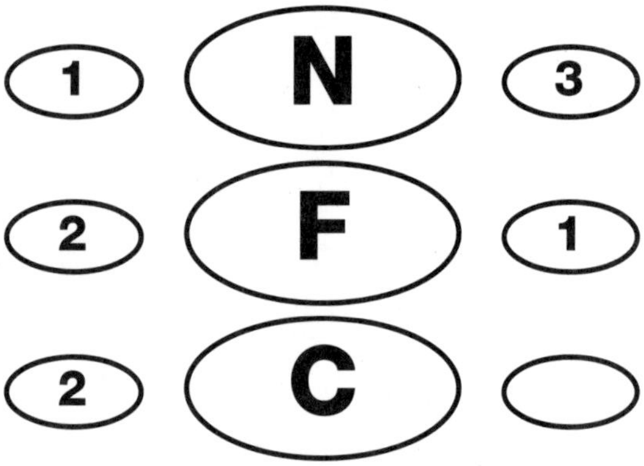

49 PUZZLE

Mr Jones, the local greengrocer, has lost the weights from his shop scales. He sells pineapples, grapes and apples by weight, but bananas cost 20 cents each.

Mrs Brown wants to buy a pineapple, which Mr Jones will sell to her for the price of the same weight in bananas.

He knows that the combinations shown opposite are correct, so how much will the pineapple cost his customer?

50 PUZZLE

Which number is missing from the top of the last star?

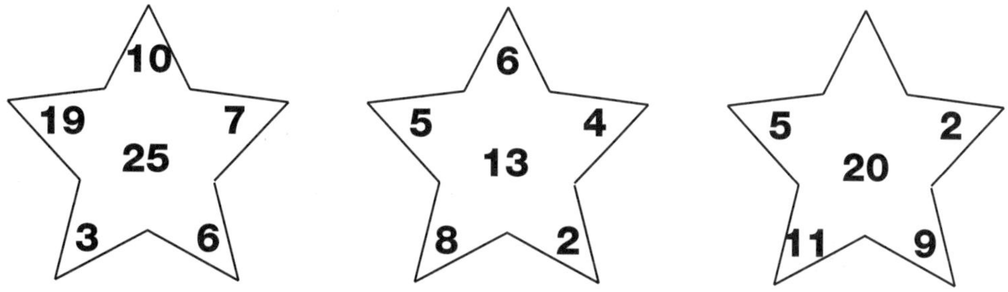

LEVEL 18

[redacted] PUZZLE

Which is the odd one out?

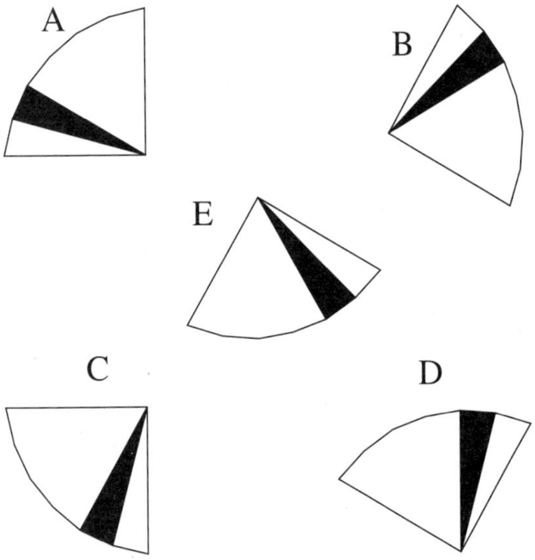

[redacted] PUZZLE

What number should replace the question mark?

4	6	2	3
7	4	3	7
2	8	1	4
5	0	2	?

3 PUZZLE

Which set of letters is the odd one out?

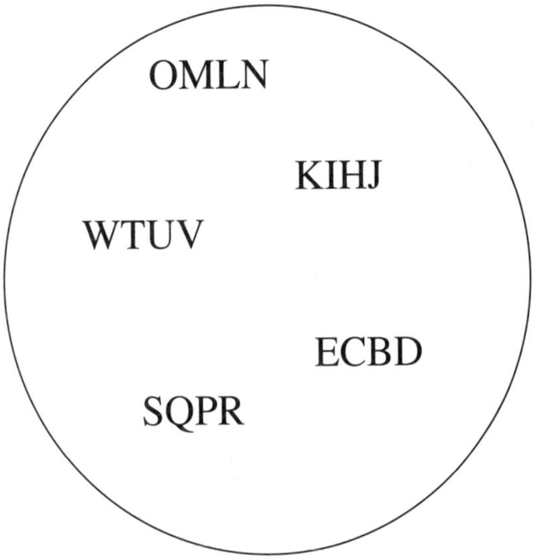

4 PUZZLE

The three cog wheels are in contact with each other. The number of cogs on each is shown on each wheel. How many revolutions must be made by the largest wheel before all of the cogs are returned to their original start positions?

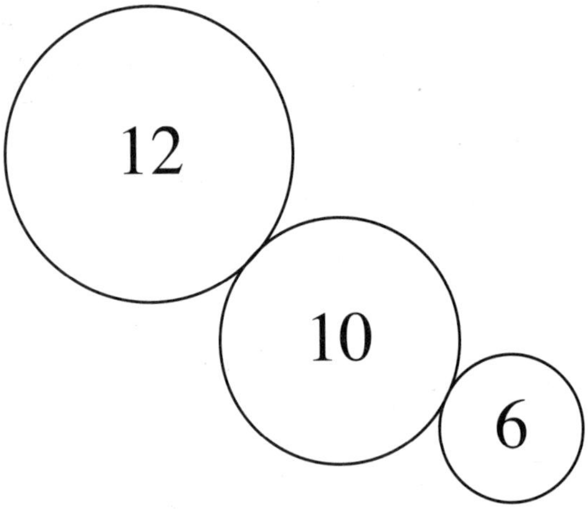

5 PUZZLE

When the pattern below is folded to form a cube,
which is the only one of the following that can be produced?

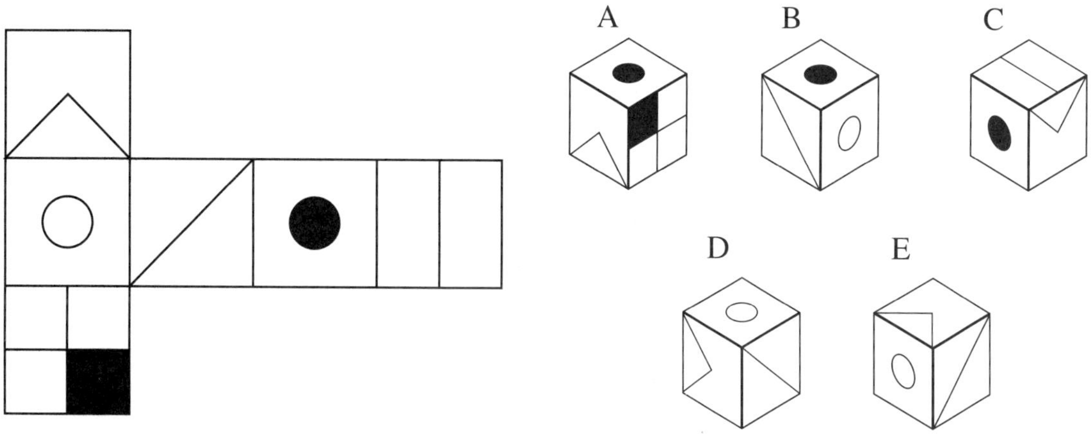

6 PUZZLE

What number should replace the question mark?

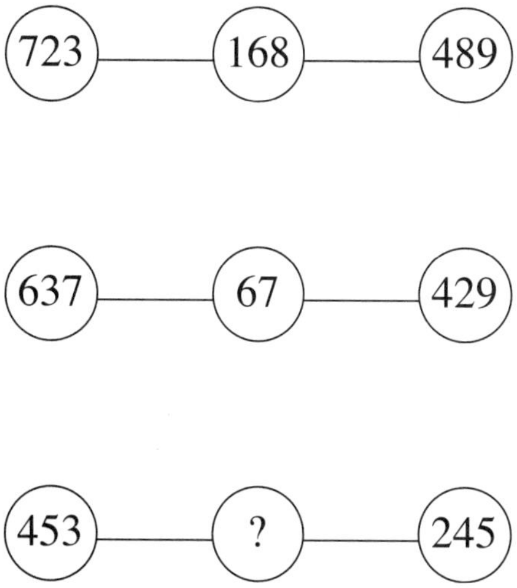

7 PUZZLE

What number comes next?

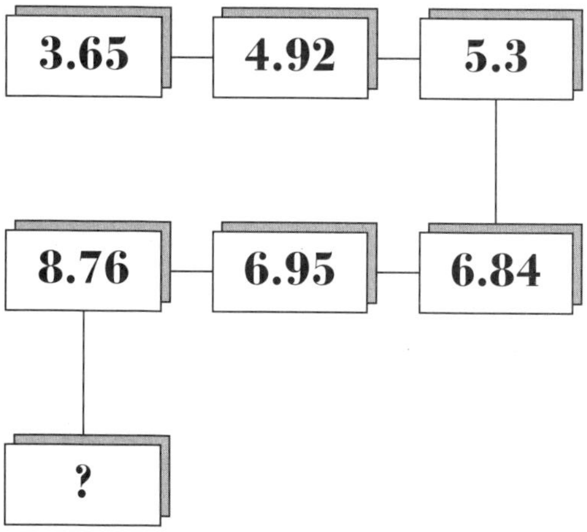

LEVEL 18

8 PUZZLE

Which is the missing tile?

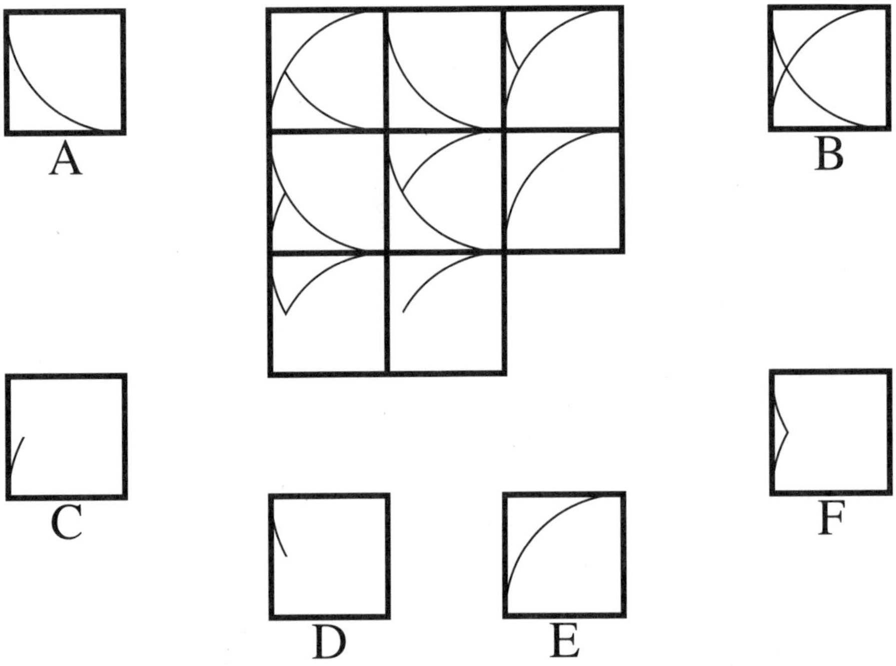

9 PUZZLE

Which is the missing piece?

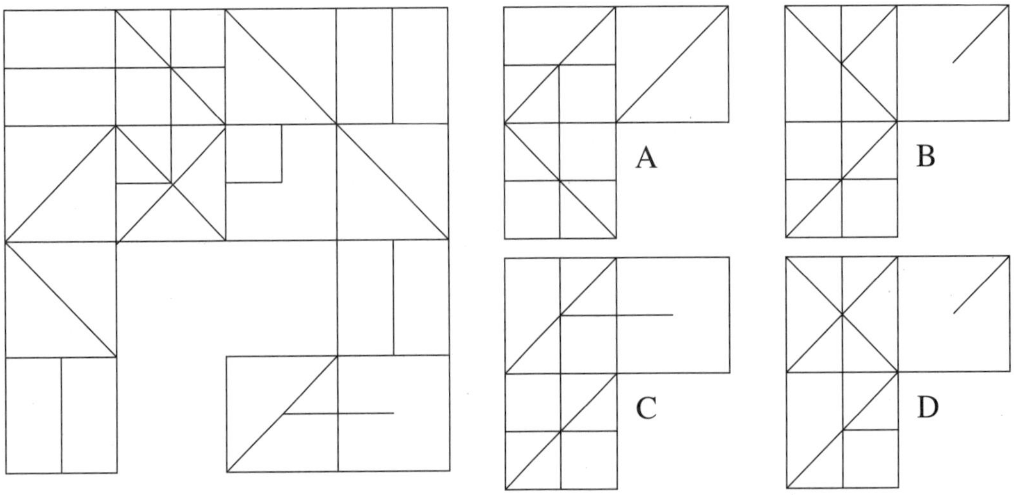

10 PUZZLE

What number comes next?

58, 59.5, 89.25, 87.75, 89.25, 133.875, ?

11 PUZZLE

Which letter should replace the question mark?

C	L	D
F	?	B
E	Y	E

12 PUZZLE

Each of the nine squares in the grid marked A1 to C3, should incorporate all the lines and symbols which are shown in the squares of the same letter and number immediately above and to the left. For example, B2 should incorporate all the lines and symbols that are in 2 and B. One of the squares is incorrect. Which one is it?

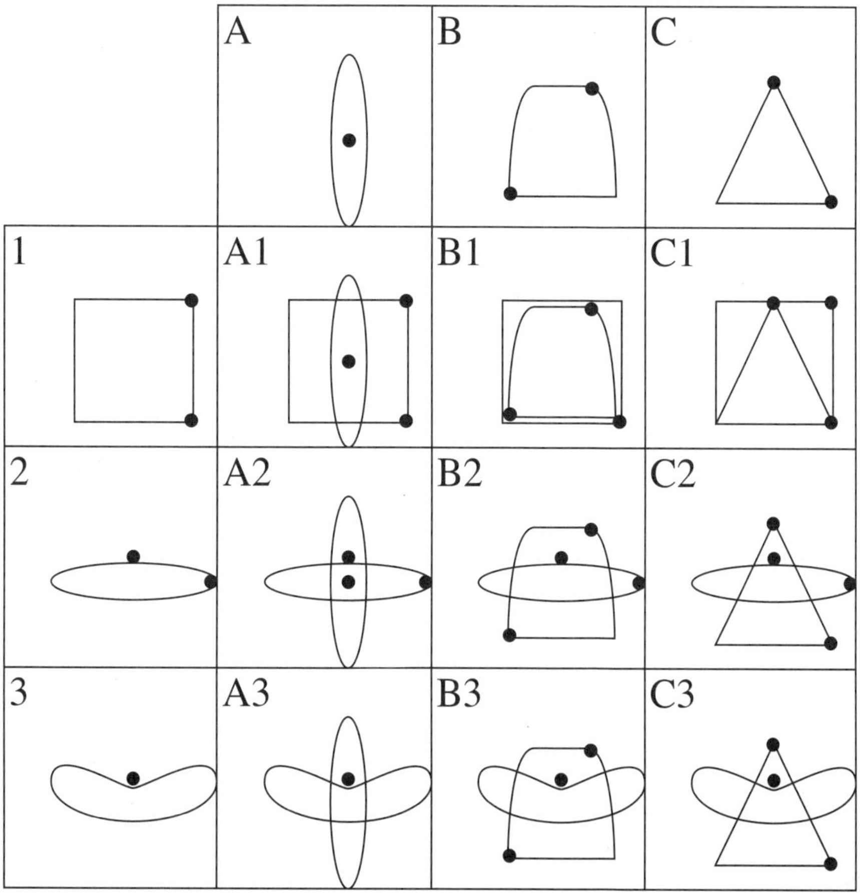

13 PUZZLE

Each line and symbol which appears in the four outer circles below, is transferred to the centre circle according to these rules. If a line or symbol occurs in the outer circles once, it is transferred; if it occurs twice, it is possibly transferred; three times, it is transferred; four times, it is not transferred. Which of the circles A, B, C, D or E, should appear at the centre of the diagram, below?

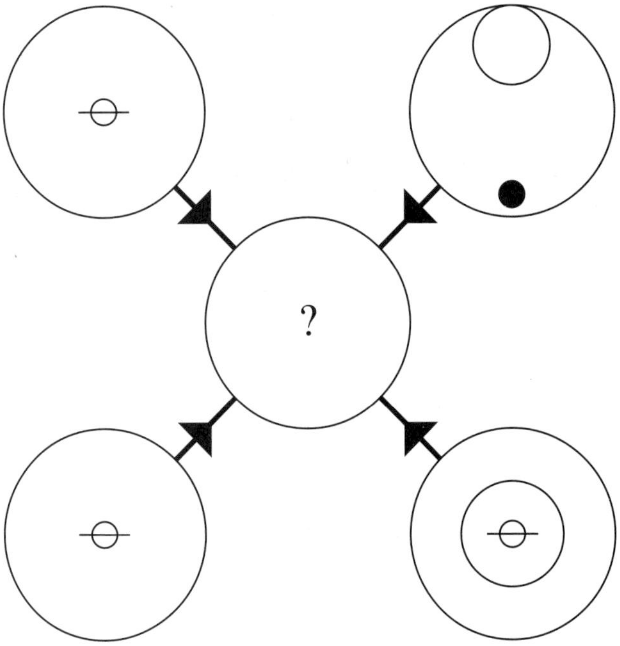

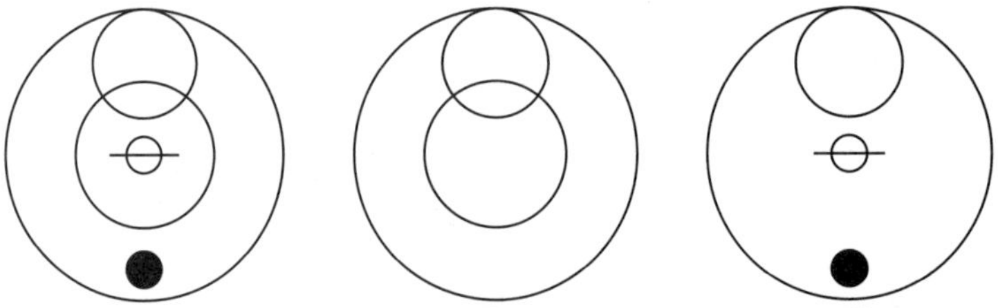

A B C

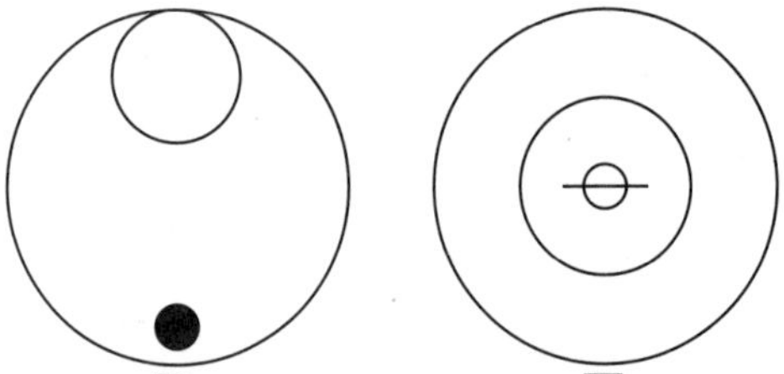

D E

14 PUZZLE

Which pentagon should replace the question mark?
A, B, C, D or E?

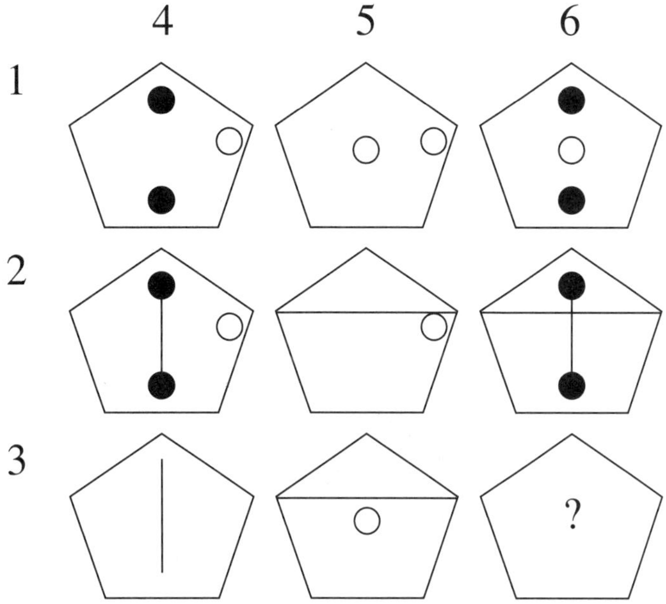

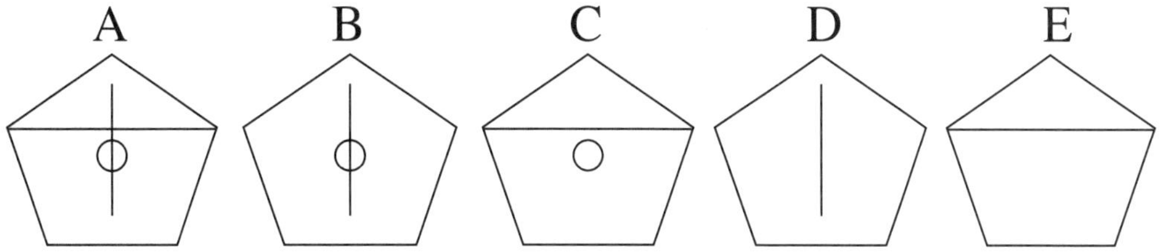

15 PUZZLE

Which number should replace the question mark?

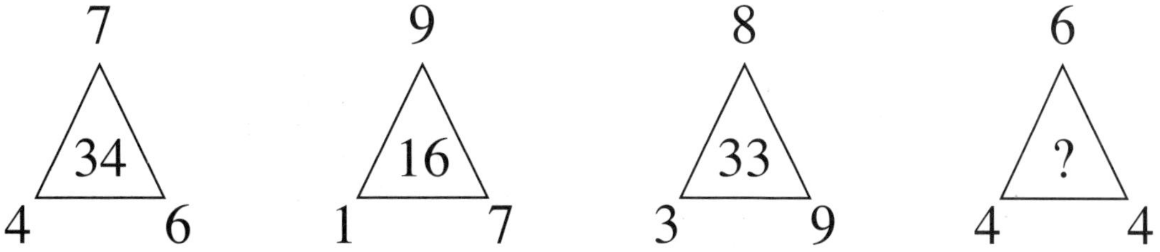

16 PUZZLE

What number should replace the question mark?

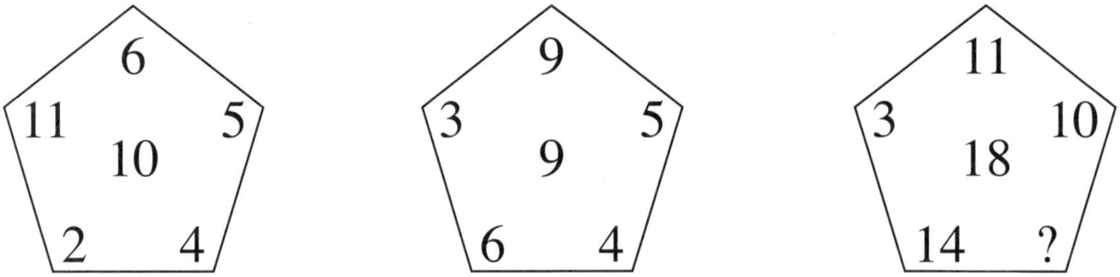

17 PUZZLE

Which two words mean the opposite?

INDOLENT	ERUDITION
IMPOTENCE	ILLITERACY
EPICUREAN	AUDACIOUS

18 PUZZLE

Which playing card replaces the question mark?

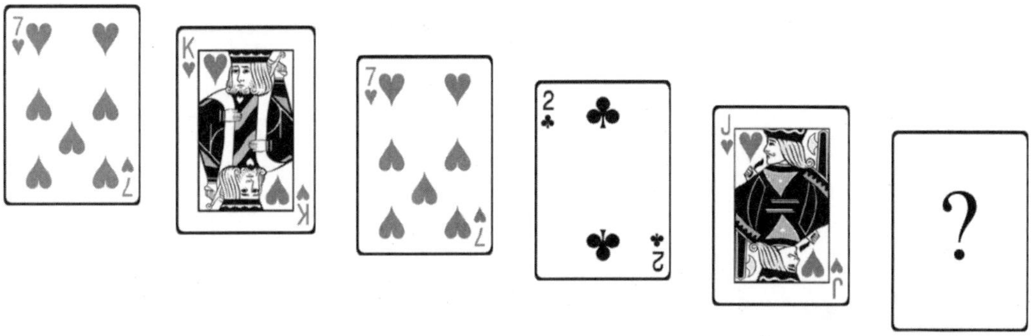

19 PUZZLE

What number replaces the question mark?

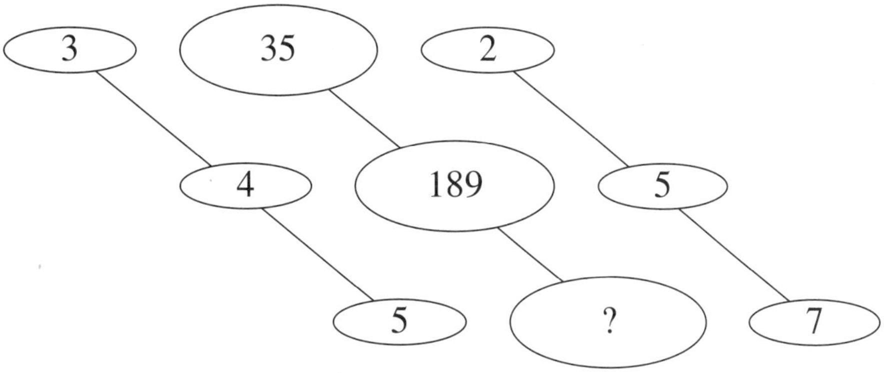

20 PUZZLE

Solve the rebus (one word).

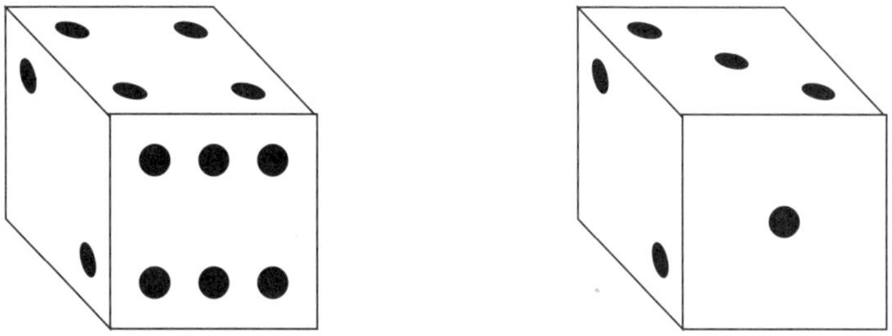

21 PUZZLE

What number should replace the question mark?

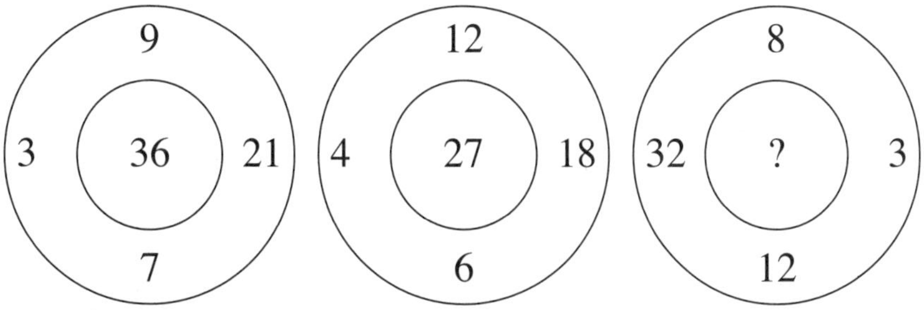

PUZZLE 22

Which is the odd one out?

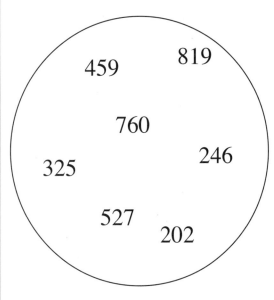

459 819 760 246 325 527 202

PUZZLE 23

What number comes next?

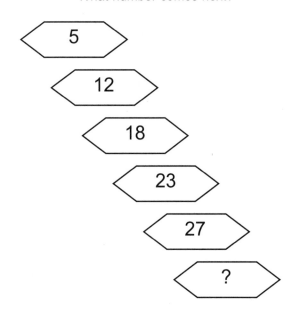

5

12

18

23

27

?

PUZZLE 24

Complete this table.

I	31	E
O	17	Y
?	23	O

PUZZLE 25

Which letter replaces the question mark?

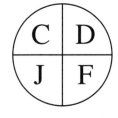

C	D
J	F

E	H
Z	N

D	F
?	J

PUZZLE 26

Which number is missing from the empty box?

3	6	9
14	8	11

2	4	6
12	8	10

4	8	12
19	11	

PUZZLE 27

What goes in the empty square?

C	G	K
12	10	
X	T	P

PUZZLE 28

Which number begins this sequence?

PUZZLE 29

Which letter completes the chain?

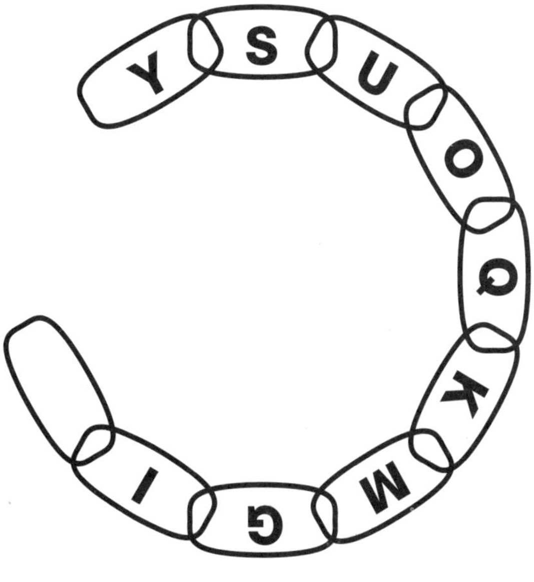

LEVEL

18

LEVEL

18

30 PUZZLE

Which number is missing?

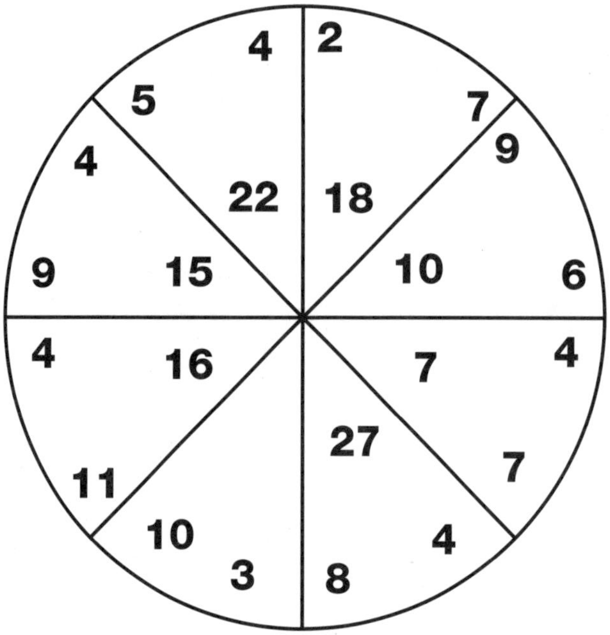

31 PUZZLE

Which two cards from the bottom row continue the sequence shown on the top?

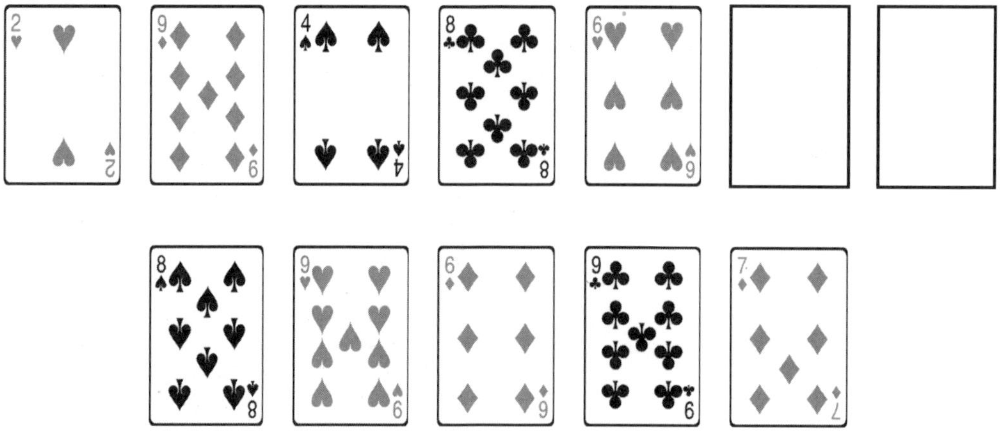

32 PUZZLE

Which two cards complete this sequence?

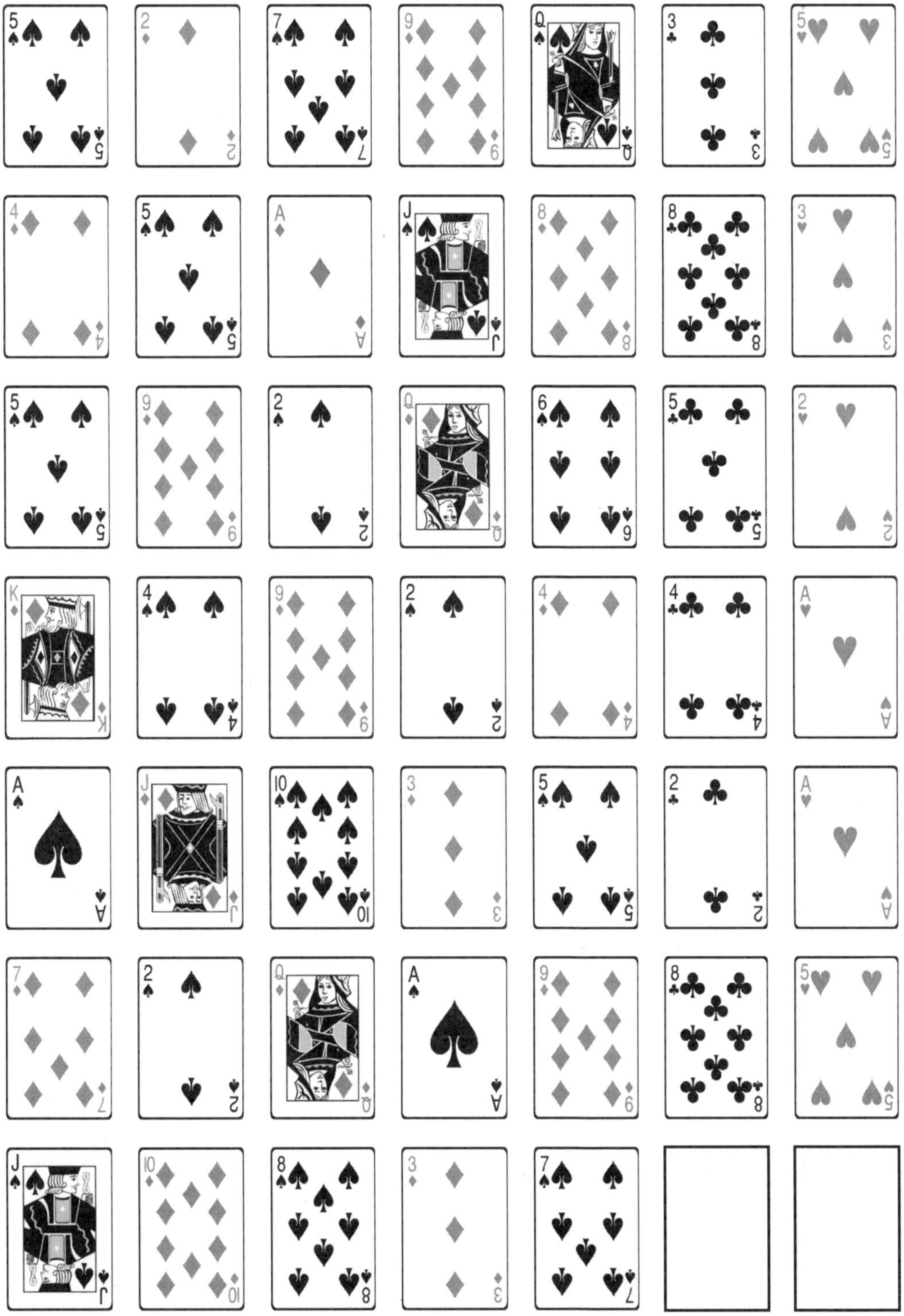

LEVEL 18

33 PUZZLE

Which number is missing?

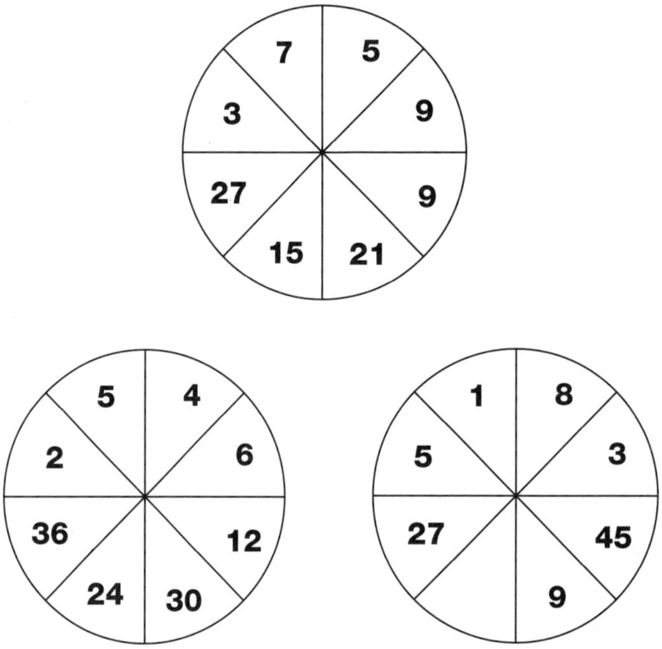

34 PUZZLE

Which of the smaller grids will complete the puzzle?

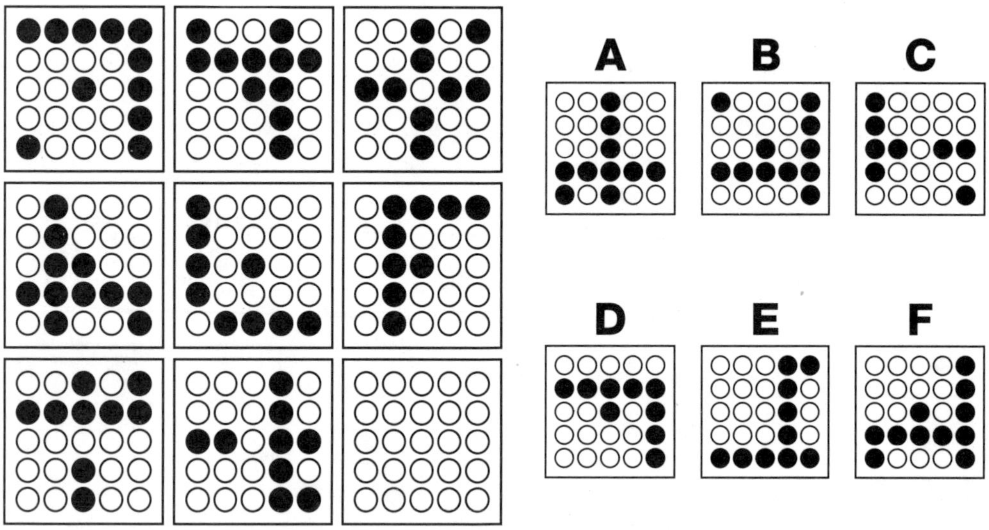

35 PUZZLE

Which number is missing?

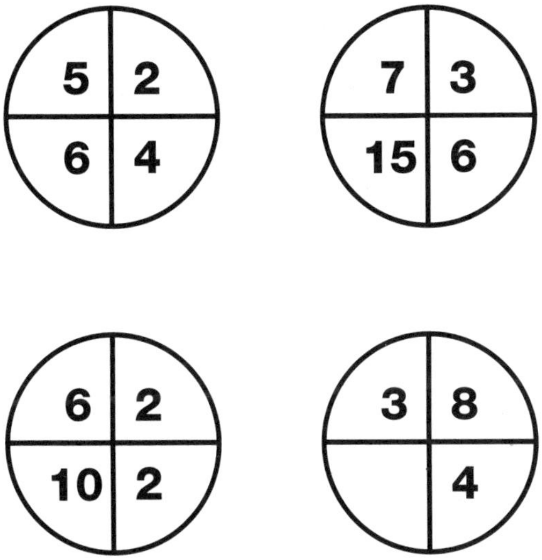

36 PUZZLE

Which number continues the sequence?

37 PUZZLE

Which of the smaller watches would continue the sequence shown on the top line?

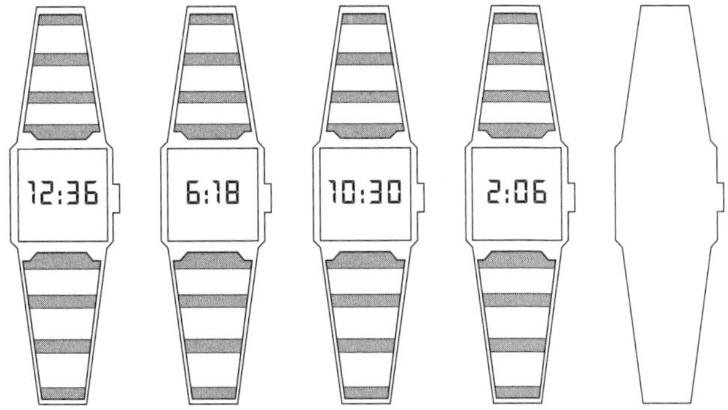

A B C D E

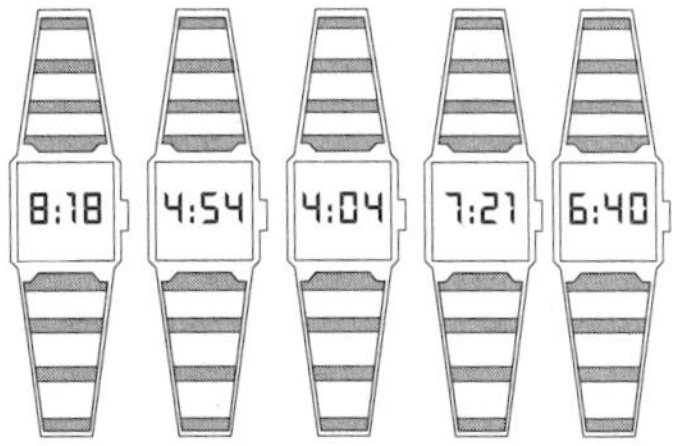

LEVEL 18

PUZZLE 38

Which of the smaller grids goes in the middle?

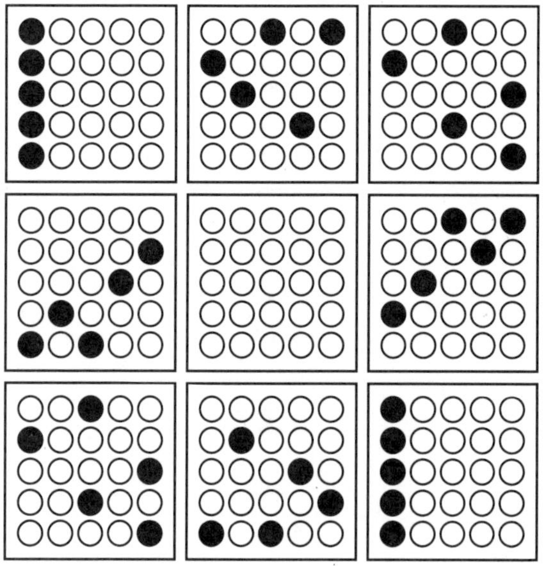

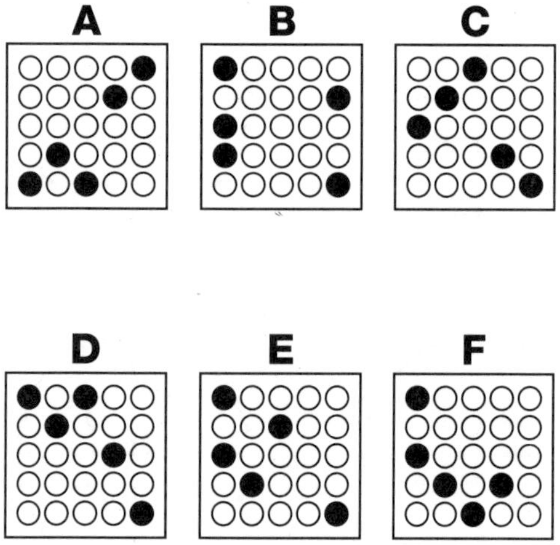

PUZZLE 39

Which number is missing from the empty segment?

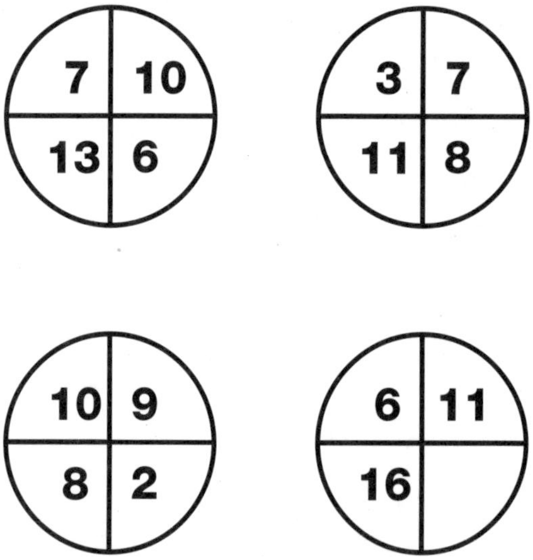

PUZZLE 40

Which letter replaces the blank and completes the sequence?

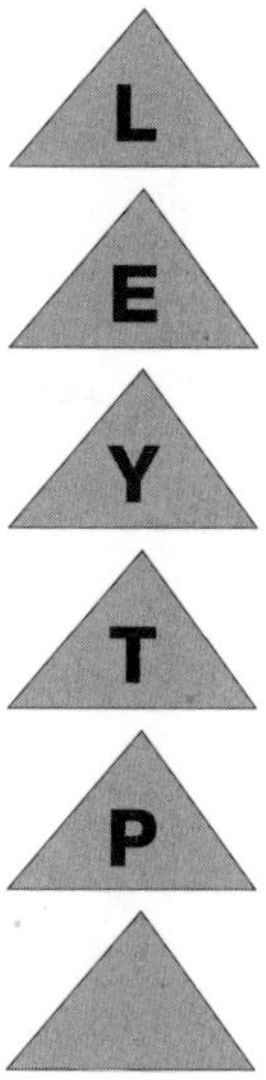

41 PUZZLE

Which number is missing from the last circle?

42 PUZZLE

Which watch continues the sequence?

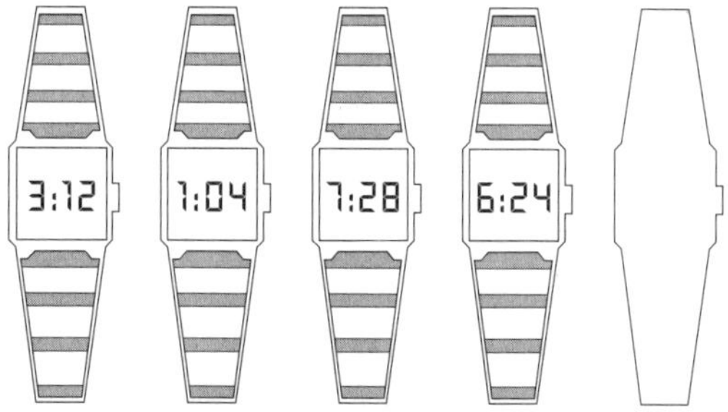

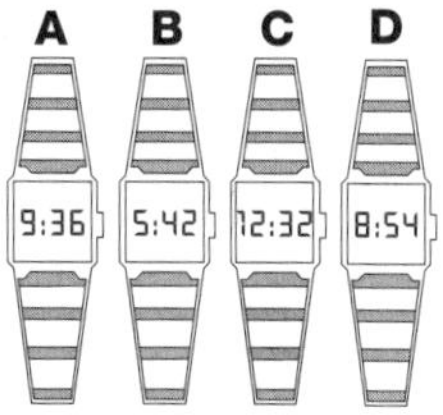

43 PUZZLE

Which number is missing?

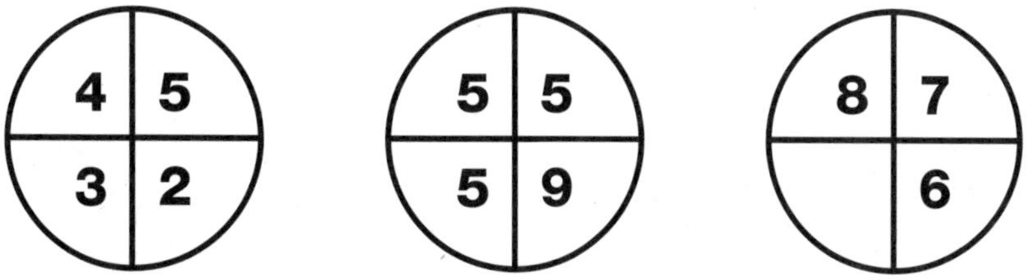

44 PUZZLE

What time will be on the next watch?

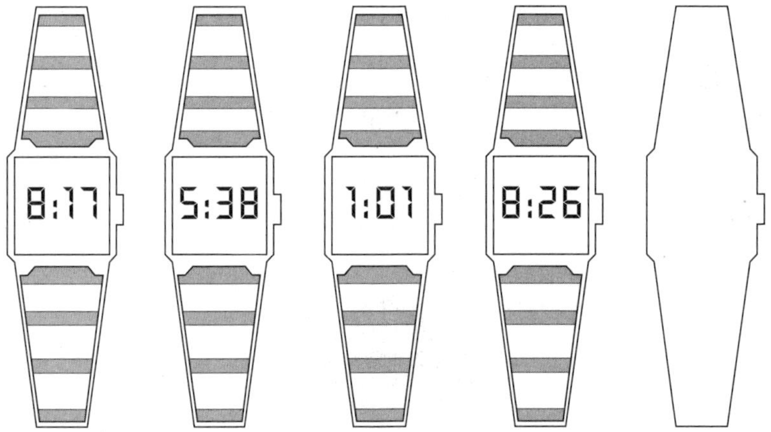

45 PUZZLE

Which number is missing from the third triangle?

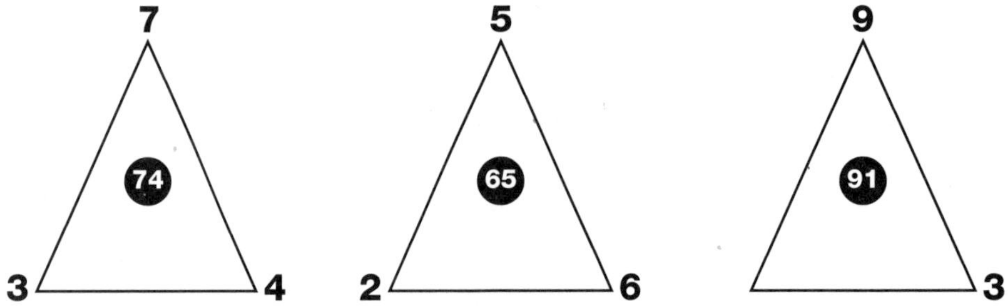

46 PUZZLE

Which number is missing?

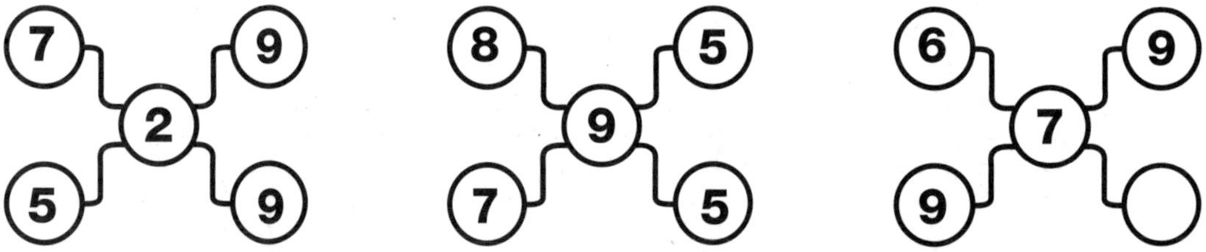

1 PUZZLE

In a box of eggs 6 out of 52 are bad. What are the chances of drawing out 3 and finding them bad?

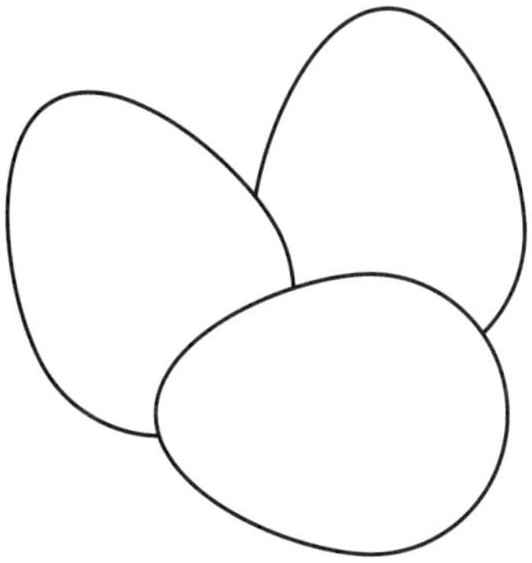

2 PUZZLE

In a single week, each cat in the rat infested village of Catattackya killed the same number of rats as every other cat. The total number of rat fatalities during the week came to 299.

Less than 20 cats achieved this remarkable feat. How many cats were there in Catattackya, and how many rats did each kill?

3 PUZZLE

What number comes next?

100

90

98.25

87.75

96.5

85.5

?

4 PUZZLE

What comes next in this sequence?

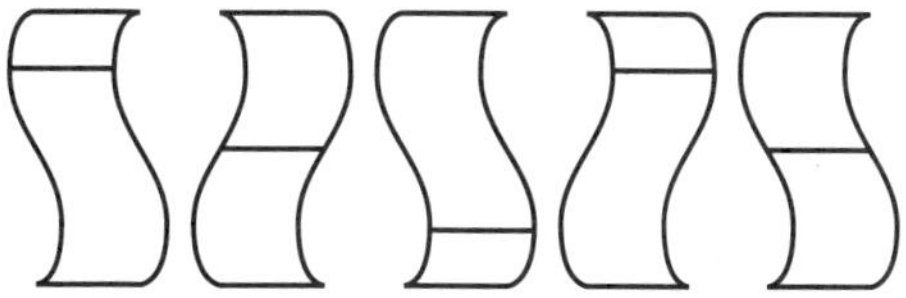

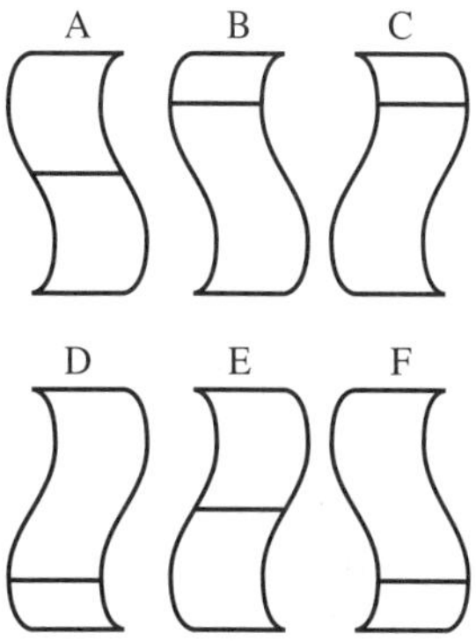

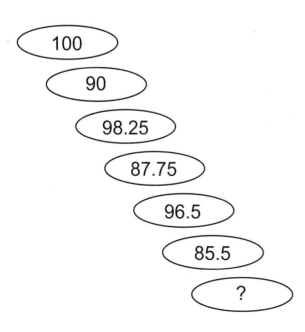

5 PUZZLE

What number comes next?

38

49

62

70

?

6 PUZZLE

In the arrangement below, what is the difference between the sum of the three highest even numbers and the product of the two lowest odd numbers?

14	15	10	3
9	16	21	22
11	8	24	12

7 PUZZLE

Which is the odd one out?

A

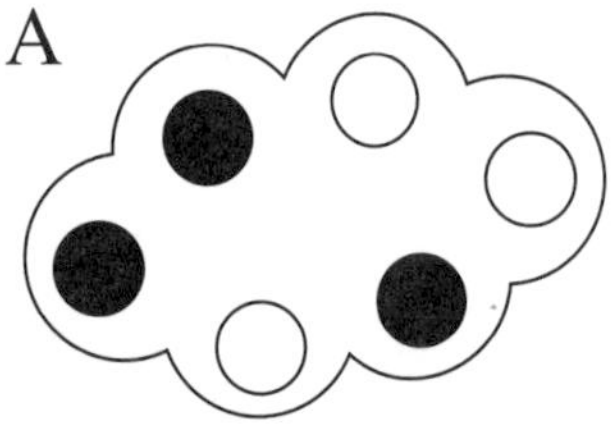

B

C

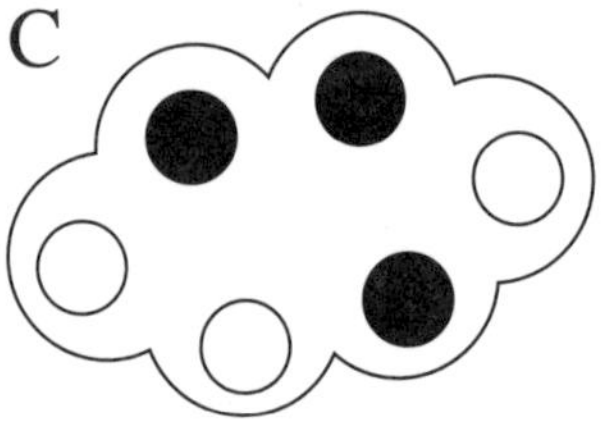

D

E

8 PUZZLE

What letter should replace the question mark?

N	L	O
I	M	K
Q	?	P

9 PUZZLE

The combined ages of Frasier and Niles is 88 years

The combined ages of Niles and Daphne is 76 years

The combined ages of Frasier and Daphne is 80 years

Figure out each person's age.

10 PUZZLE

What is the missing piece?

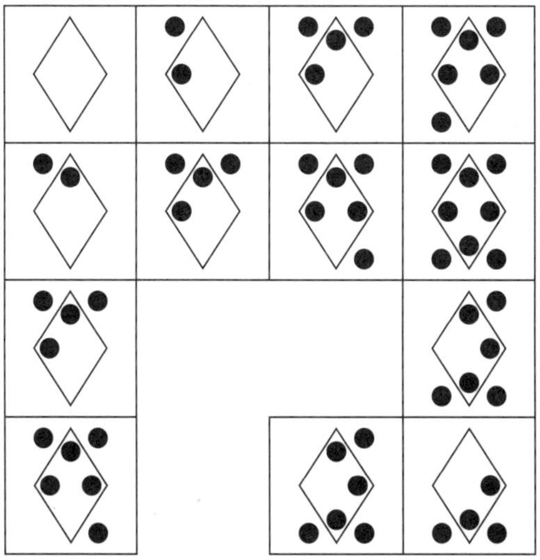

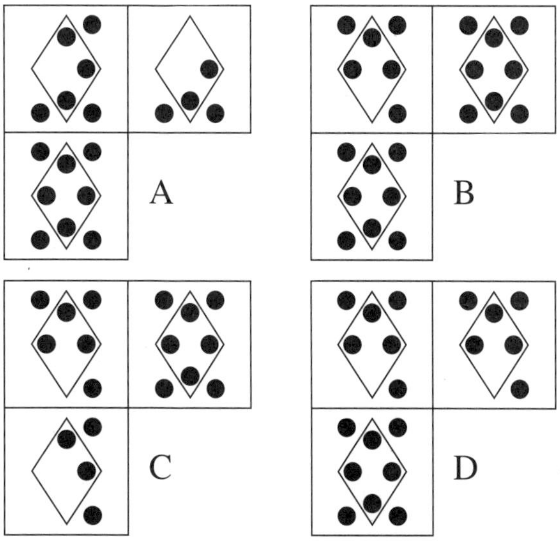

11 PUZZLE

Each line and symbol which appears in the four outer circles below, is transferred to the centre circle according to these rules. If a line or symbol occurs in the outer circles once, it is transferred; if it occurs twice, it is possibly transferred; three times, it is transferred; four times, it is not transferred. Which of the circles A, B, C, D or E, should appear at the centre of the diagram, below?

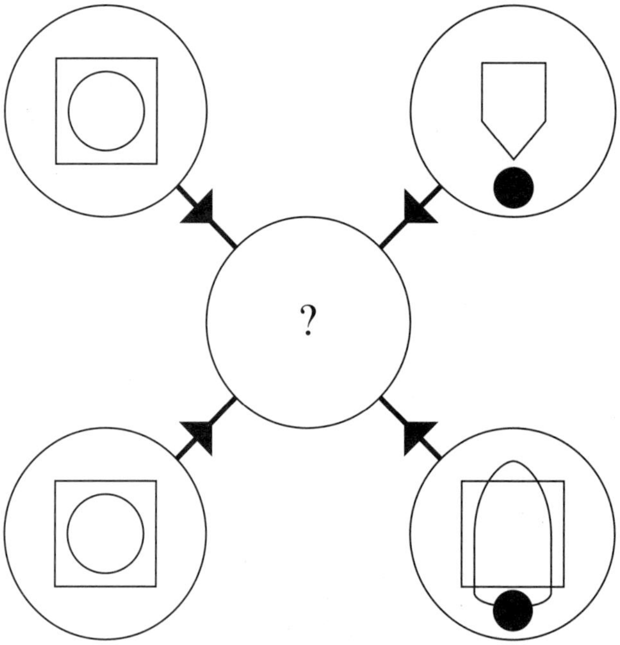

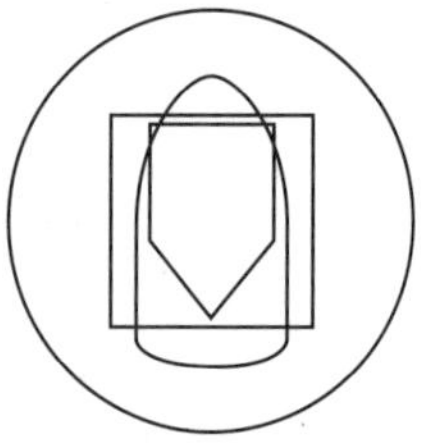
A

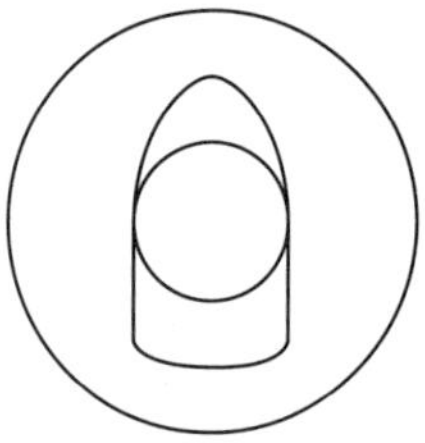
B

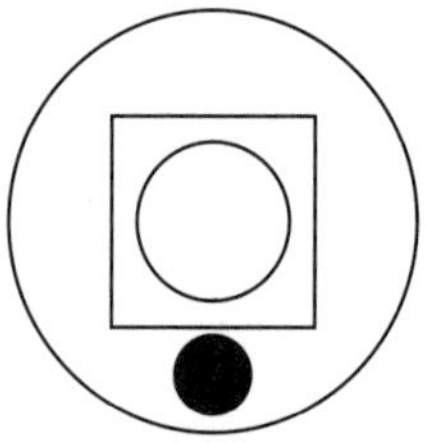
C

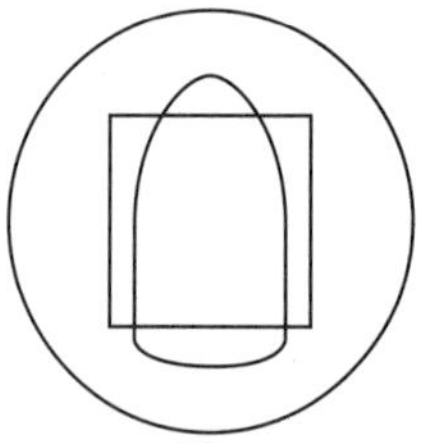
D

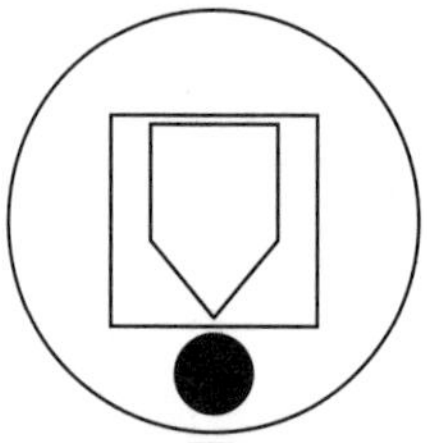
E

PUZZLE 12

What number should replace the question mark?

21	22	26	29
39	36	32	31
41	42	?	49
59	56	52	51

PUZZLE 13

In a sequence

6
-
18
-
54

find the 10th term.

PUZZLE 14

If

60 = 48

then

27 = ?

PUZZLE 15

What number should replace the question mark?

6 | 200 | 4

7 | 318 | 5

8 | ? | 6

16 PUZZLE

Each of the nine squares in the grid marked A1 to C3, should incorporate all the lines and symbols which are shown in the squares of the same letter and number immediately above and to the left. For example, B2 should incorporate all the lines and symbols that are in 2 and B. One of the squares is incorrect. Which one is it?

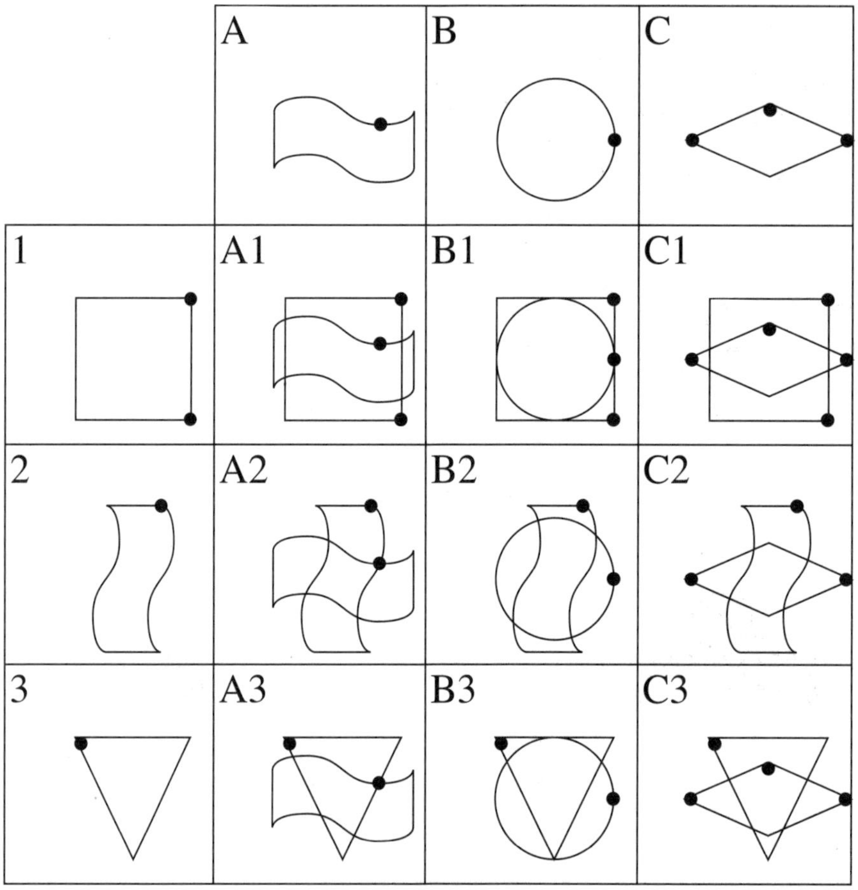

17 PUZZLE

What number will replace the question mark?

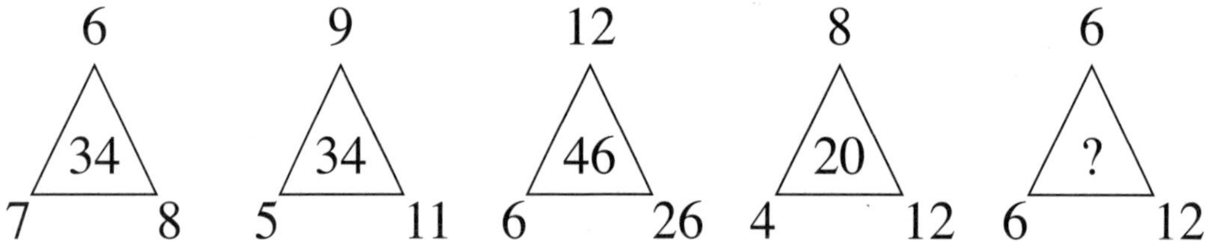

18 PUZZLE

What number should replace the question mark?

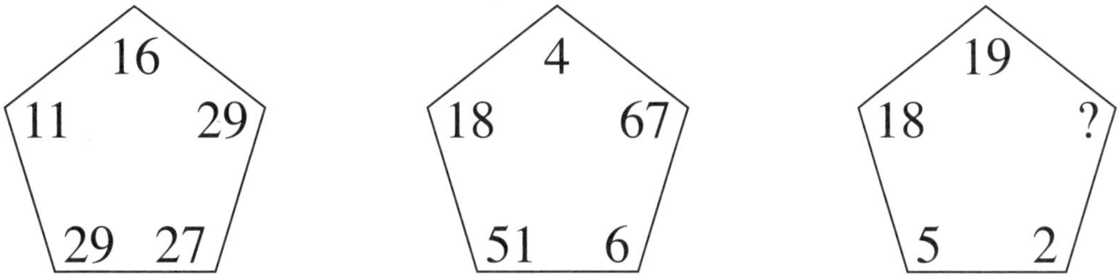

19 PUZZLE

Which pentagon - A, B, C or D - replaces the question mark?

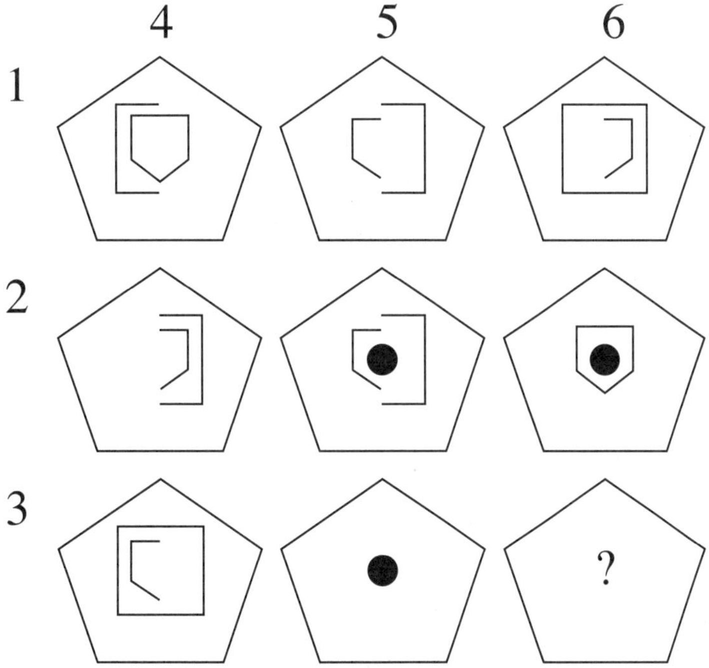

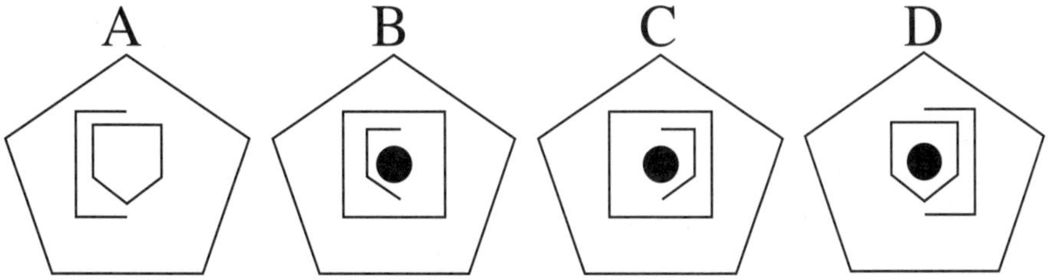

20 PUZZLE

Which triangle should replace the question mark?

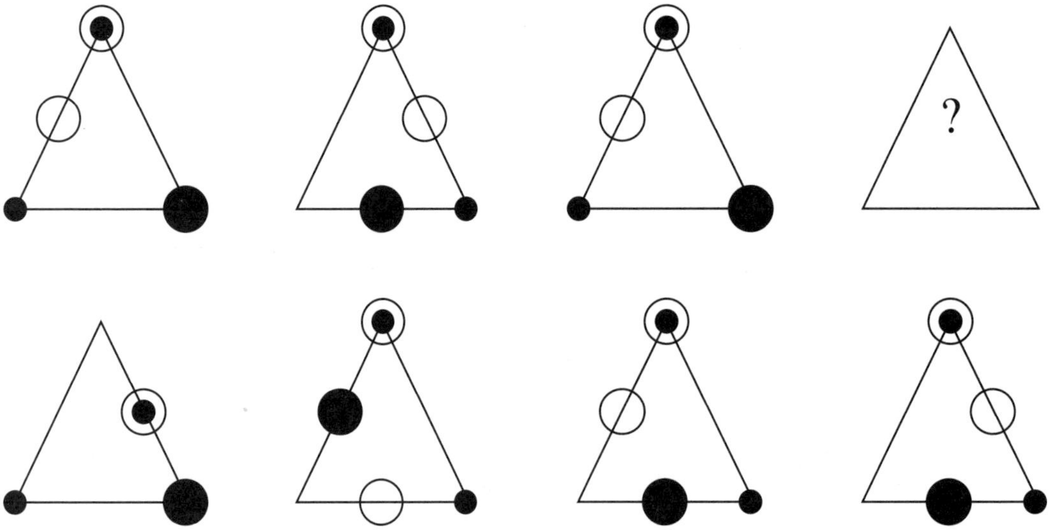

A B C D

21 PUZZLE

Which letter is the odd one out?

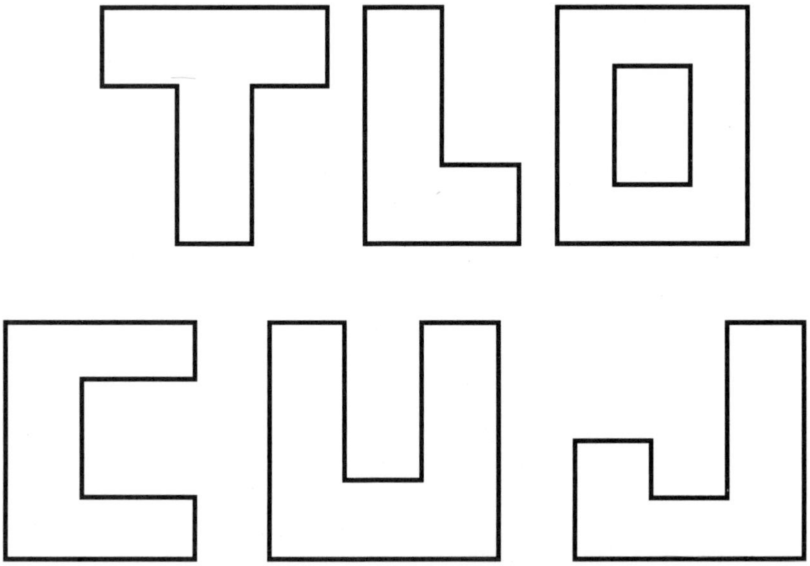

PUZZLE 22

Which number replaces the question mark?

5	4	12
6	2	5
3	8	?

PUZZLE 23

Which letter replaces the question mark?

D	R	F	
K	H	V	J
B	O	L	?
	F	S	P

PUZZLE 24

Which letter replaces the question mark?

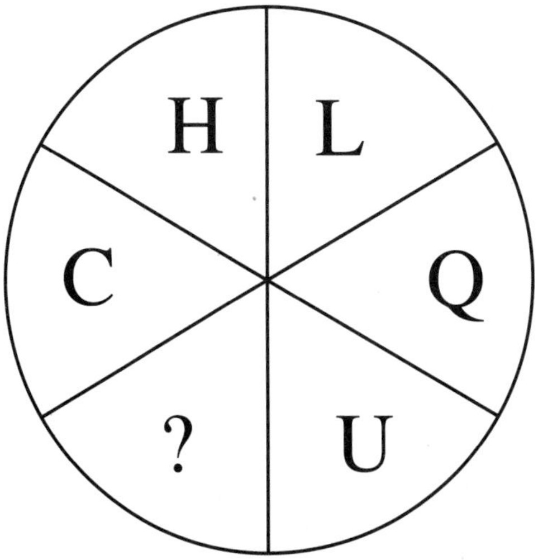

PUZZLE 25

Which number is the odd one out?

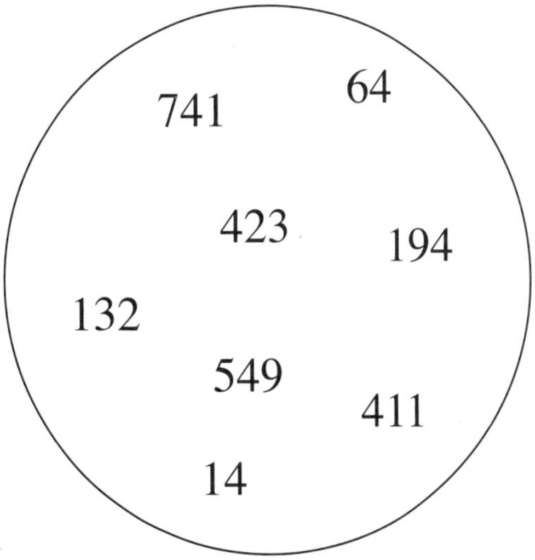

LEVEL

19

26 PUZZLE

Which number is missing from the web?

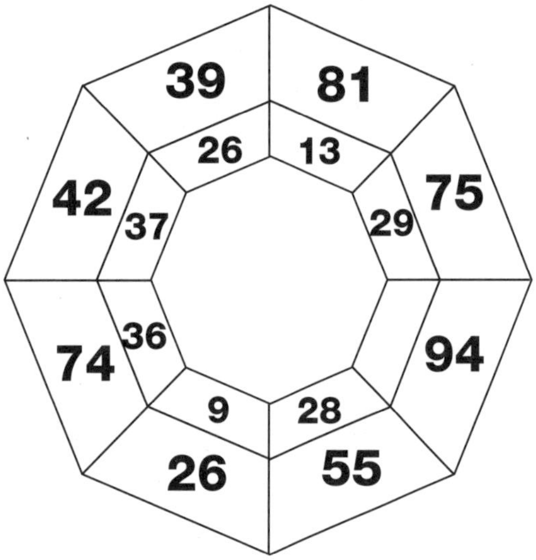

27 PUZZLE

Which number goes in the empty square?

7	3	6
45	5	32

5	8	4
21	60	

28 PUZZLE

Which number goes in the bottom circle?

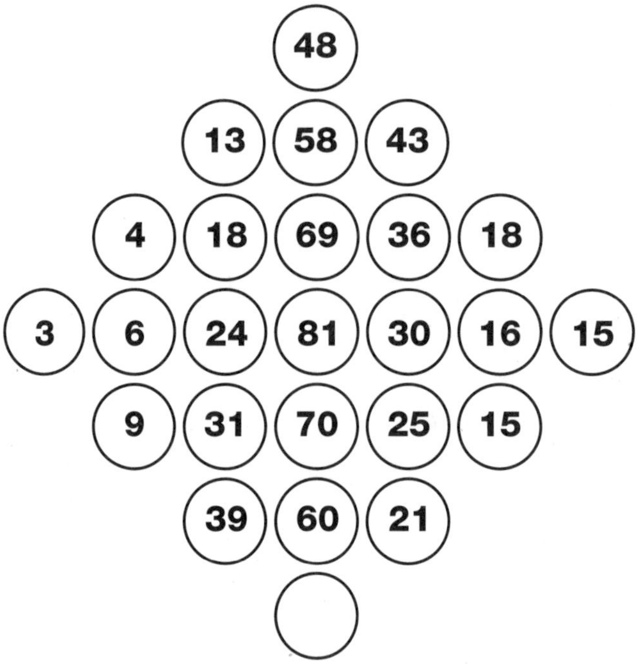

29 PUZZLE

Which number is missing from the bottom grid?

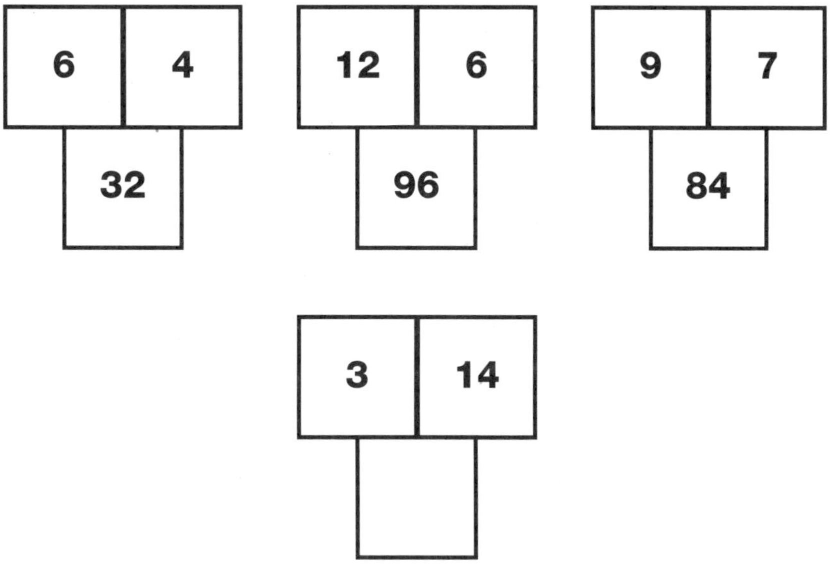

30 PUZZLE

Draw the correct number of circles in the blank square.

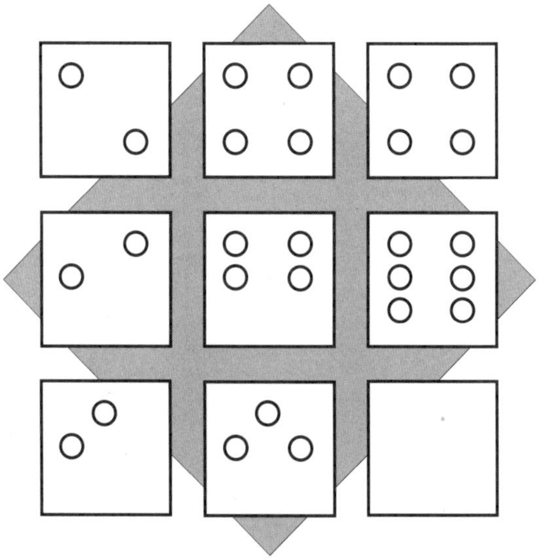

31 PUZZLE

Which number comes next?

32 PUZZLE

What goes in the empty box?

24	W	5
20	S	9
16	O	13
11		18

33 PUZZLE

Which number is missing from the empty circle?

4	10	28
6	16	46
3	7	

34 PUZZLE

Which letter replaces the blank and completes the puzzle?

P	C	H
D	L	K
N		E

35 PUZZLE

Which number comes next?

5
9
17
33

36 PUZZLE

Which letter goes in the empty box?

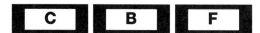

C	B	F
G	G	L
K	L	R
O	Q	

37 PUZZLE

Which number continues this sequence?

3

8

18

38

38 PUZZLE

Which letter goes in the empty circle?

			B			
		T	X	F		
	P	Z	D	B	J	
L	V	P	T	H	F	N
	H	R		J	R	
		D	N	V		
			Z			

I J K L M N O P

39 PUZZLE

What time should the blank watch be showing?

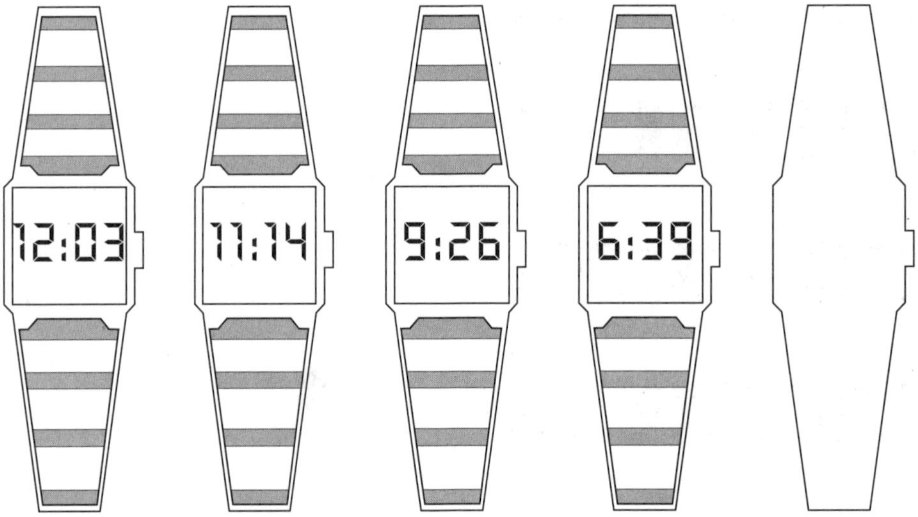

40 PUZZLE

What goes in the empty circle?

1	Q	O
1	H	9
2	C	

41 PUZZLE

Which number is missing?

7	11	3
6	14	4
5	7	3
2	7	

42 PUZZLE

Four men went to the building supplies centre to buy some tools for the workmen on the building sites they were in charge of. Chris buys 3 screwdrivers, 4 hammers and 5 saws for the men on his building site at a total cost of $9.70. Carl buys 4 screwdrivers, 5 hammers and 3 saws for his carpenters at a total cost of $9. Charlie's $8.90 bought 5 screwdrivers, 3 hammers and 4 saws. Colin, who is in charge of a small building site has less money to spend but still needs one screwdriver, one hammer and a saw.

How much did he have to spend?

Chris **Charlie** **Carl**

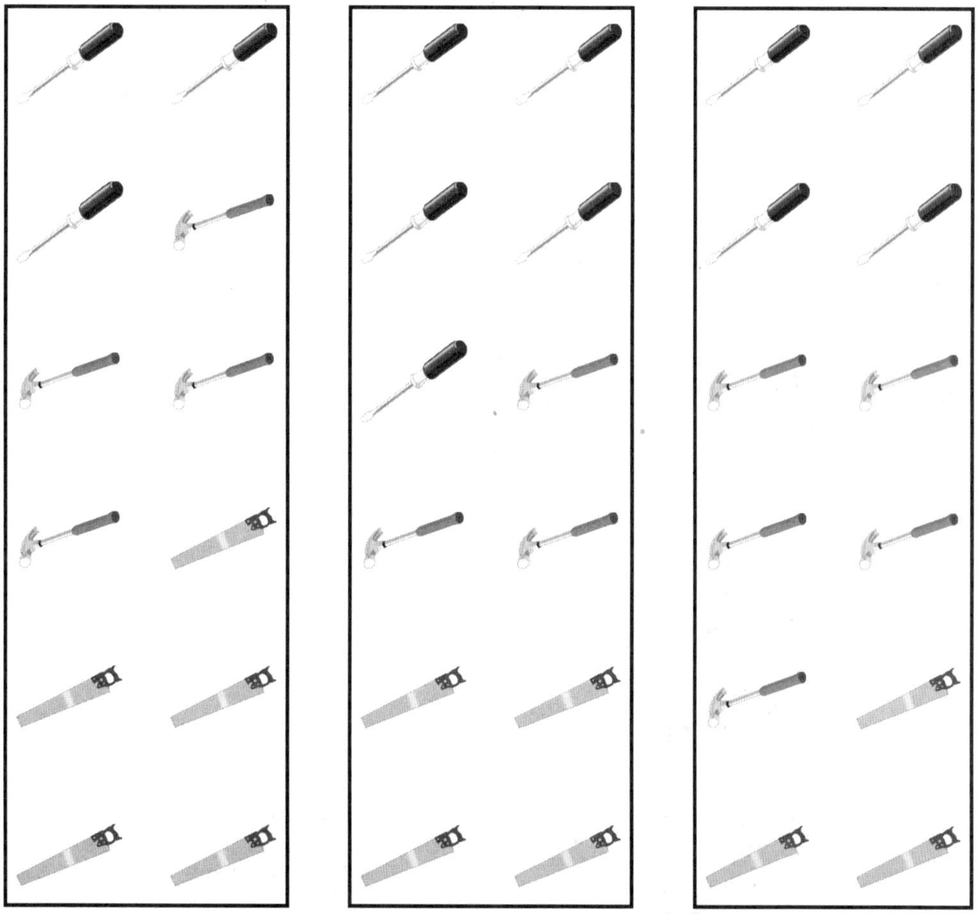

43 PUZZLE

Which of the six smaller boxes finishes this sequence?

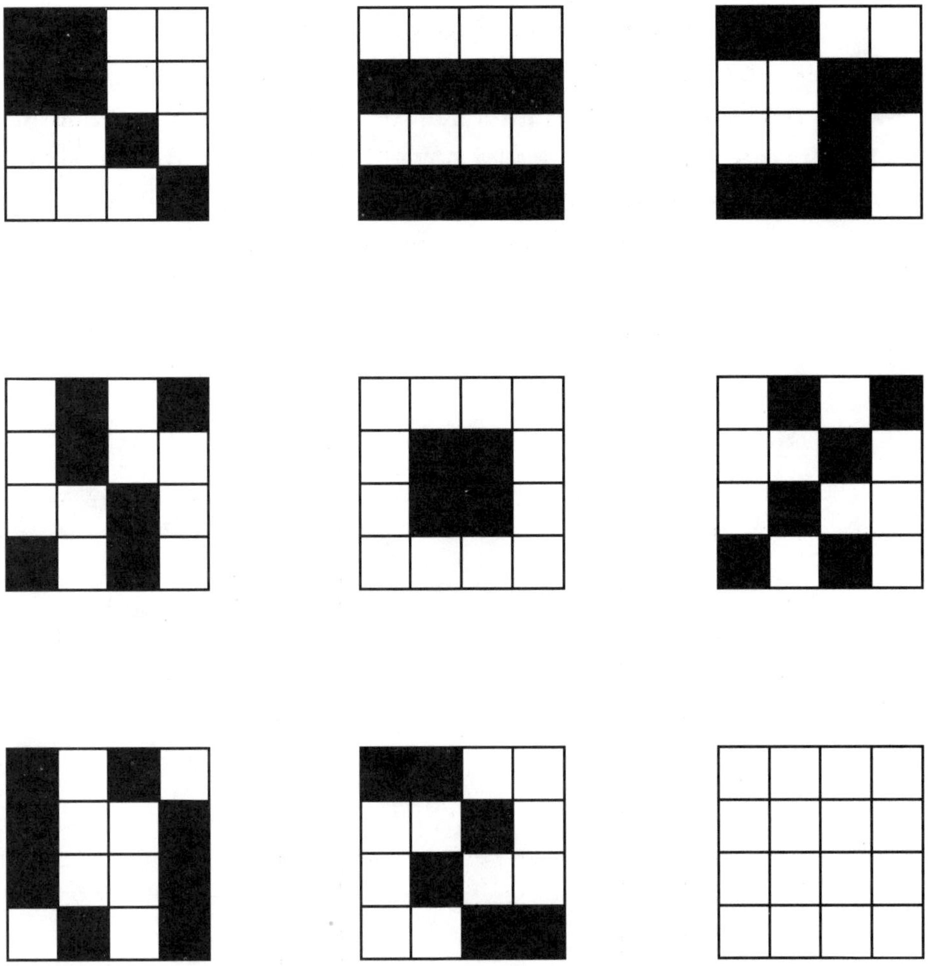

A

B

C

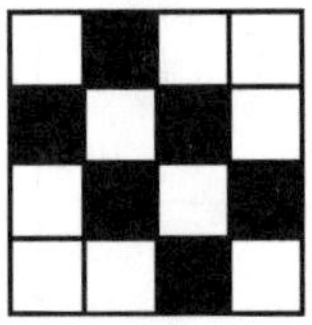

D

E

F

1 PUZZLE

What is the missing tile?

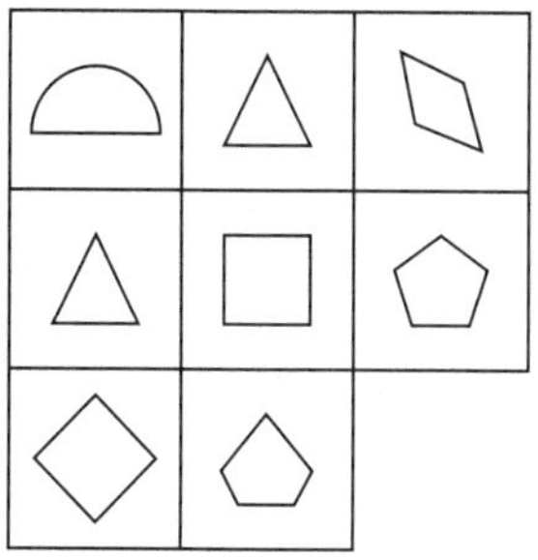

A

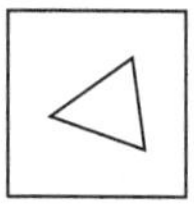

B

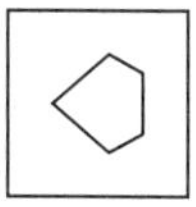

C

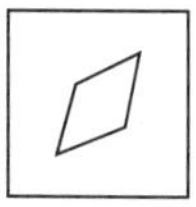

D

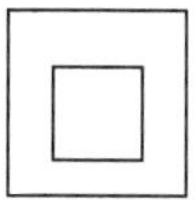

E

F

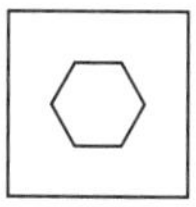

2 PUZZLE

What is the missing letter?

A	D	C
J	I	F
G	?	E

3 PUZZLE

Which is the odd one out?

A

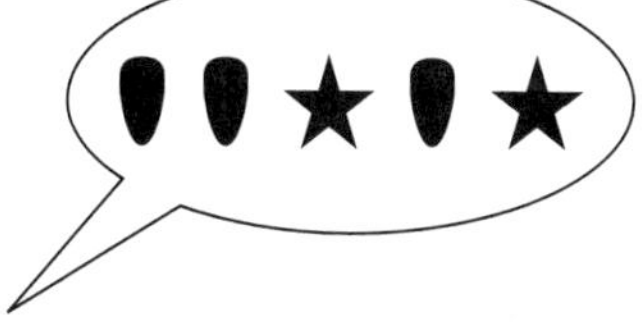

B

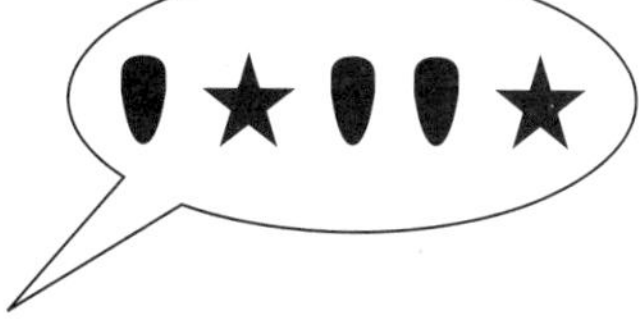

C

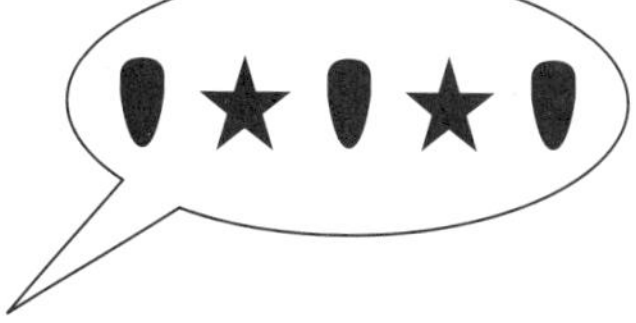

D

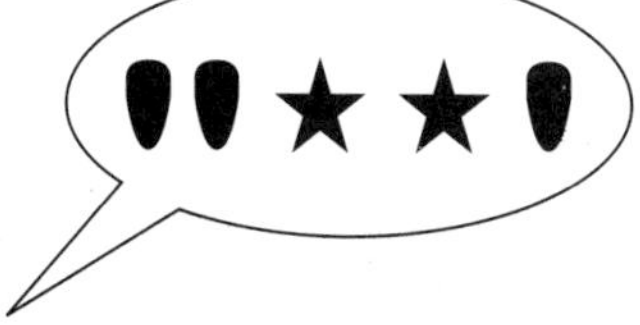

F

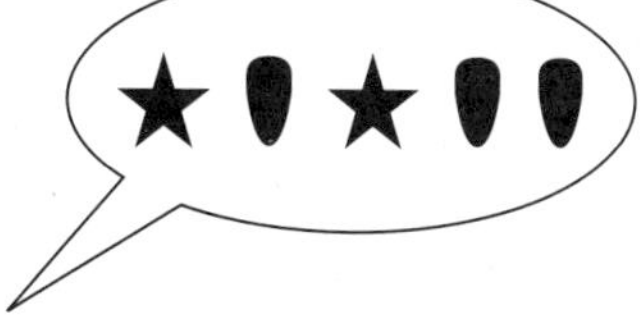

E

PUZZLE 4

What numbers should replace the question marks?

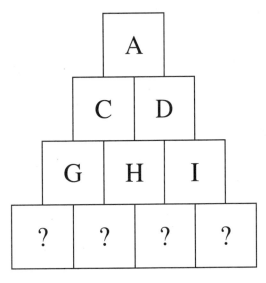

A

C D

G H I

? ? ? ?

PUZZLE 5

What letter should replace the question mark?

A	B	C	D
B	D	F	H
C	F	I	L
D	H	L	?

PUZZLE 6

Which is the missing piece?

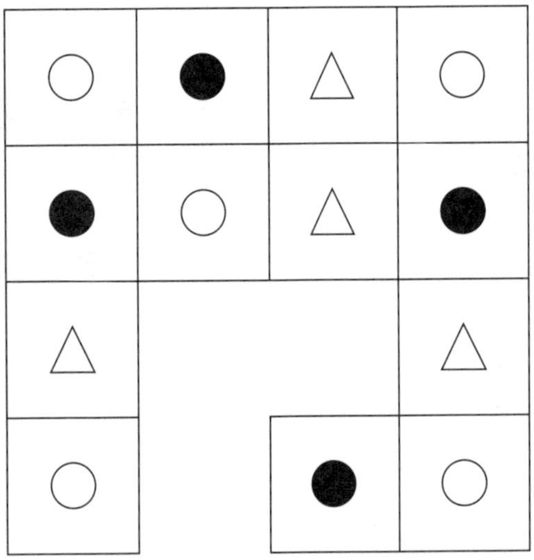

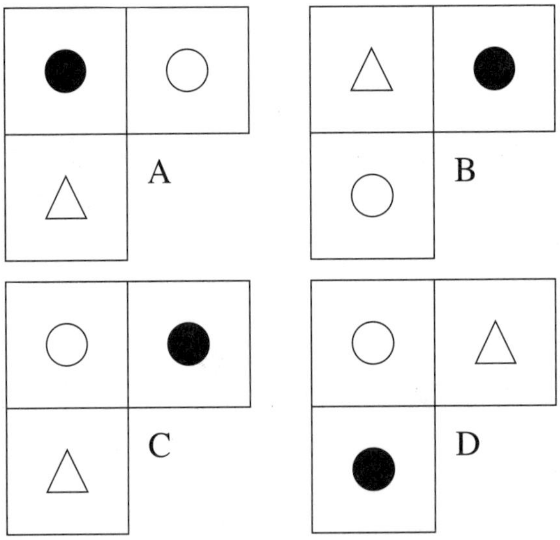

7 PUZZLE

In the arrangement below, what is the difference between the sum of the two highest odd numbers and the product of the two lowest even numbers?

19	4	18	17
16	22	27	10
21	8	15	6

8 PUZZLE

What should be the missing number?

2

5

5.75

7.75

9.5

10.5

?

9 PUZZLE

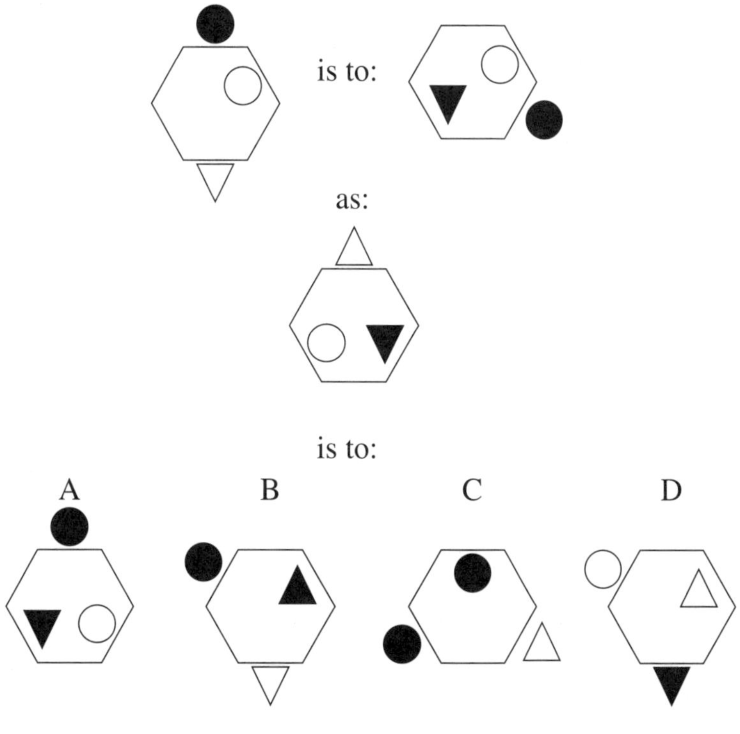

10 PUZZLE

What letter should replace the question mark?

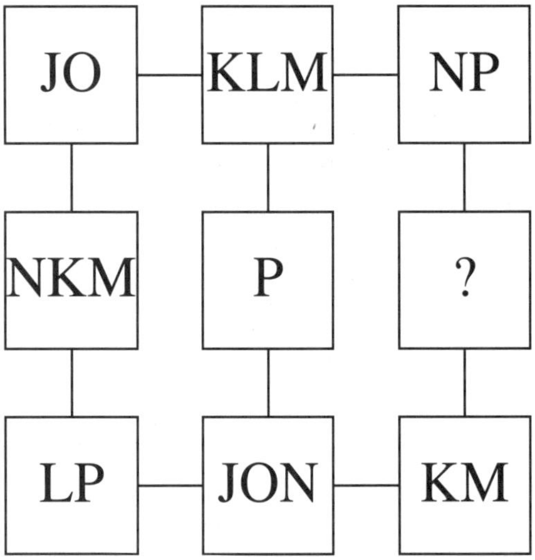

11 PUZZLE

What number should replace the question mark?

?	3	6	1	4	6
6	1	1	1	2	3
1	2	5	0	2	3

12 PUZZLE

Which hexagon should replace the question mark?

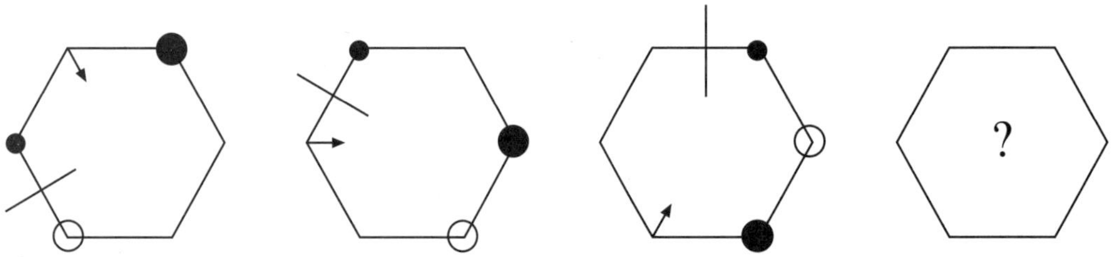

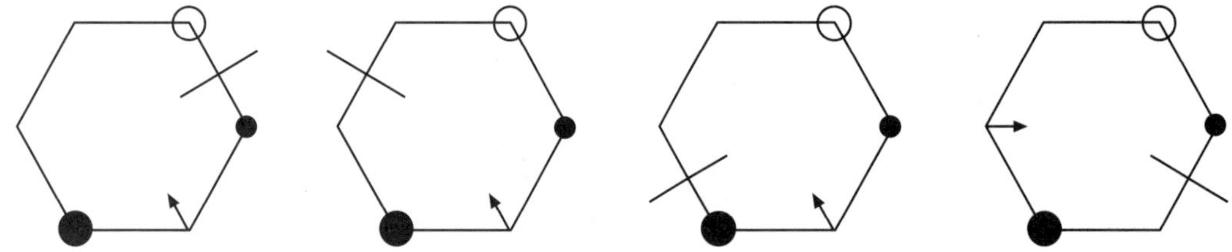

A B C D

13 PUZZLE

What number should replace the question mark?

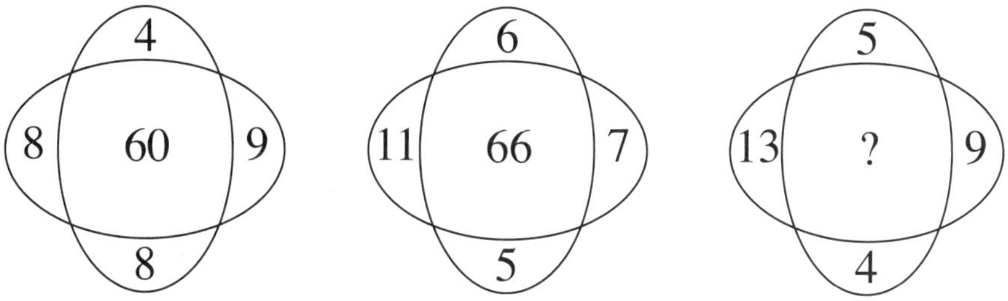

14 PUZZLE

Each of the nine squares in the grid marked A1 to C3, should incorporate all the lines and symbols which are shown in the squares of the same letter and number immediately above and to the left. For example, B2 should incorporate all the lines and symbols that are in 2 and B. One of the squares is incorrect. Which one is it?

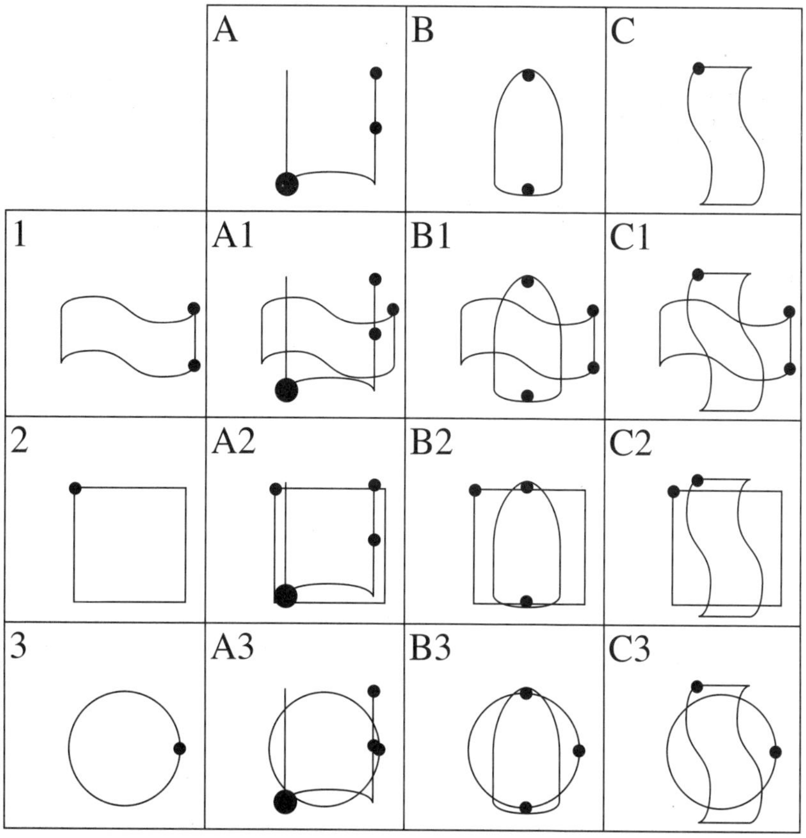

LEVEL 20

15 PUZZLE

Which diagram has the most in common with A?
B, C, D or E.

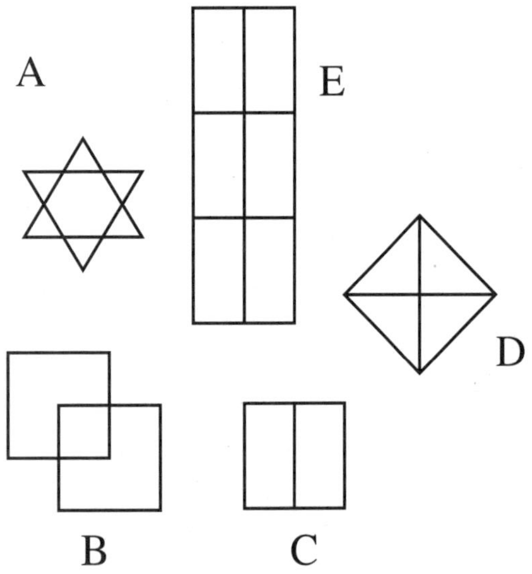

16 PUZZLE

What is always part of a PUCK?

(a) CLOWN'S BOOTS
(b) RUBBER
(c) WOOD
(d) CHAIN MAIL

17 PUZZLE

What have these words in common?

HALF-PENNY
RELIEVED
SHALLOT
PLENTIFUL
OPENED
PATRIOTIC

18 PUZZLE

What number should replace the question mark?

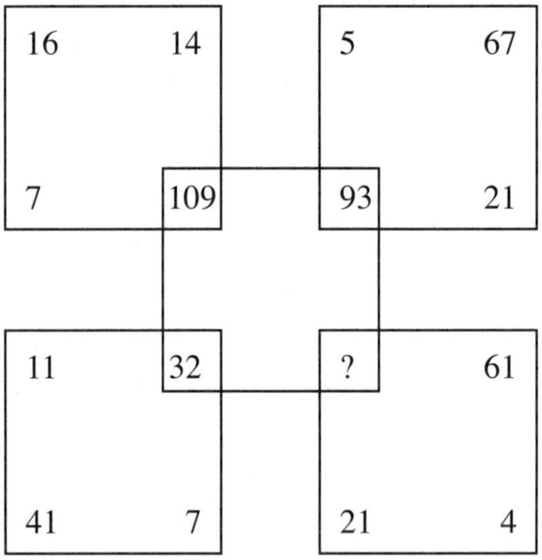

Each line and symbol which appears in the four outer circles, below, is transferred to the centre circle according to these rules: If a line or symbol occurs in the outer circles: once: it is transferred twice: it is possibly transferred 3 times: it is transferred 4 times: it is not transferred. Which of the circles A, B, C, D or E, should appear at the centre of the diagram, below?

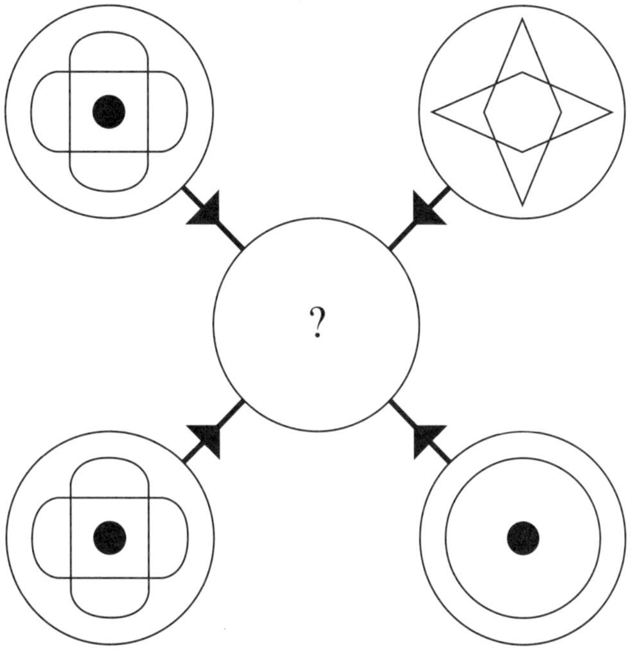

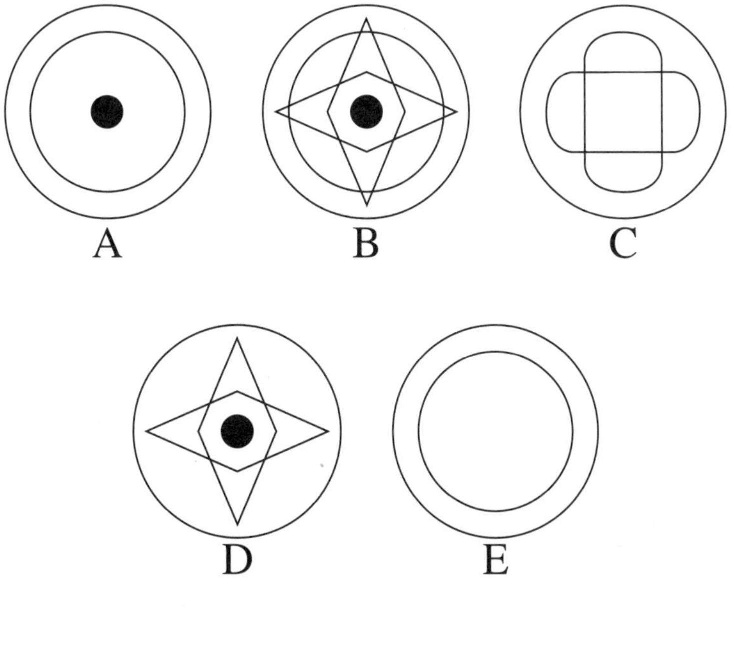

PUZZLE 20

What number should replace the question mark?

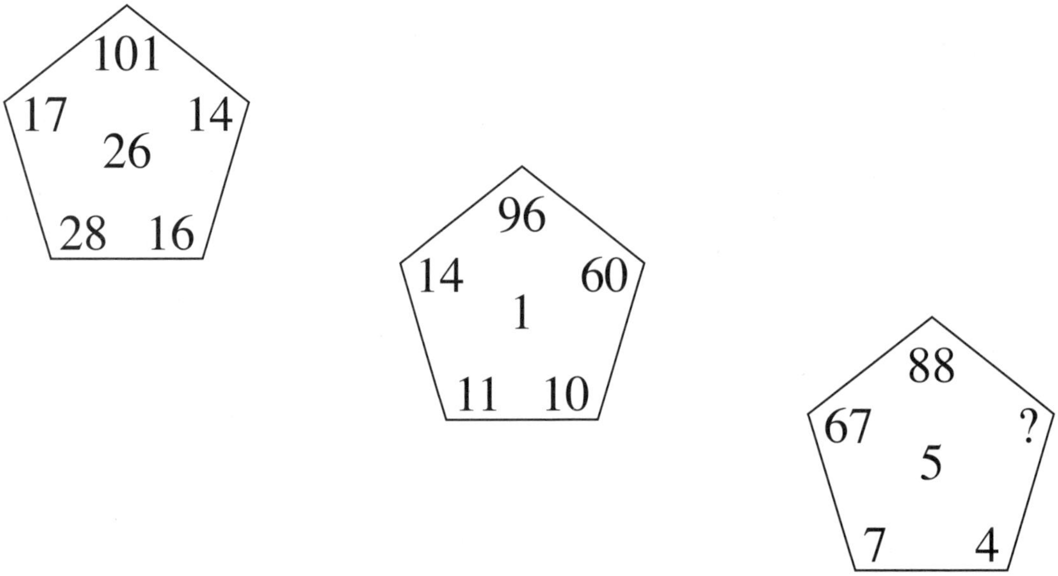

PUZZLE 21

Which number replaces the question mark?

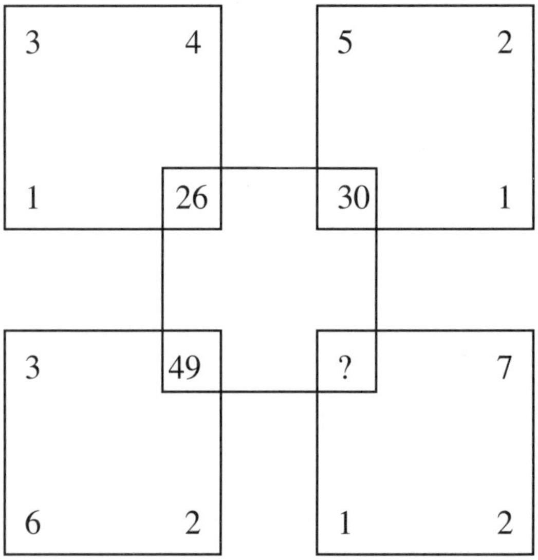

PUZZLE 22

Which letter is the odd one out in each shape?

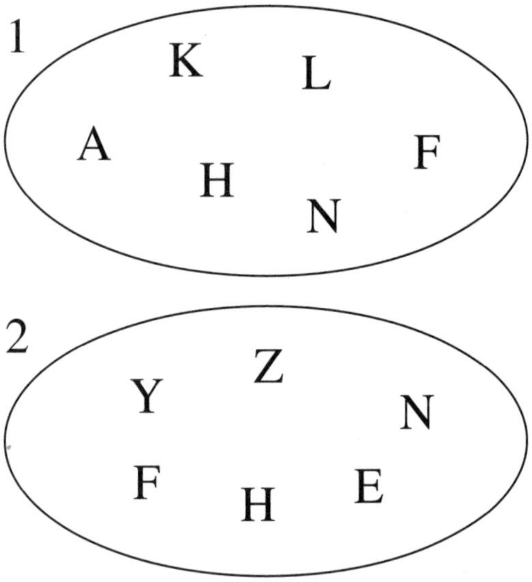

PUZZLE 23

Which letter replaces the question mark?

B	D	G
D	O	K
T	A	P
K	C	?

PUZZLE 24

Which number replaces the question mark?

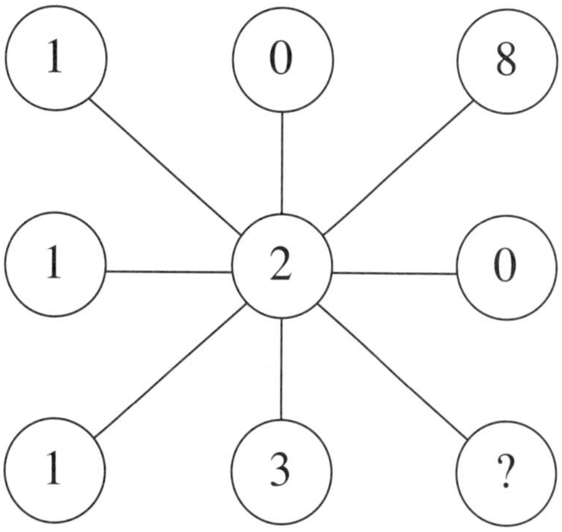

PUZZLE 25

Which number replaces the question mark?

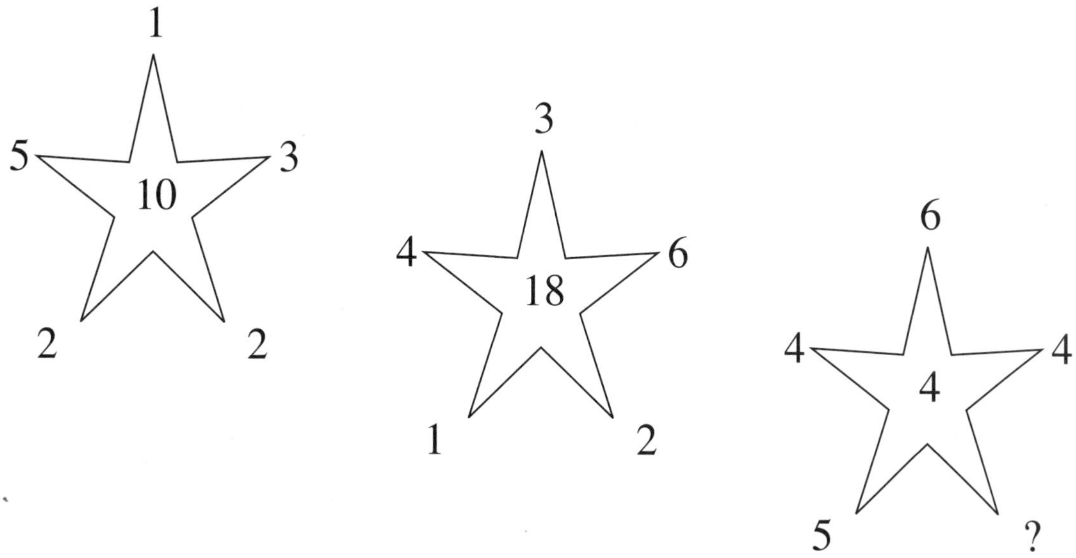

LEVEL 20

PUZZLE 26

Which letters replace the blanks and complete the sequence?

Y	O	V	M
K	B	P	A
M	D	R	
Z	P	W	

PUZZLE 27

Which number goes in the empty box?

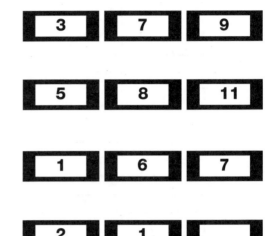

3	7	9
5	8	11
1	6	7
2	1	

PUZZLE 28

Which letter is missing?

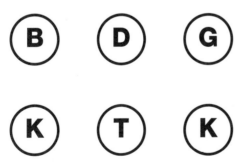

B	D	G
K	T	K
C		P

PUZZLE 29

Which number is missing from the middle of the circle?

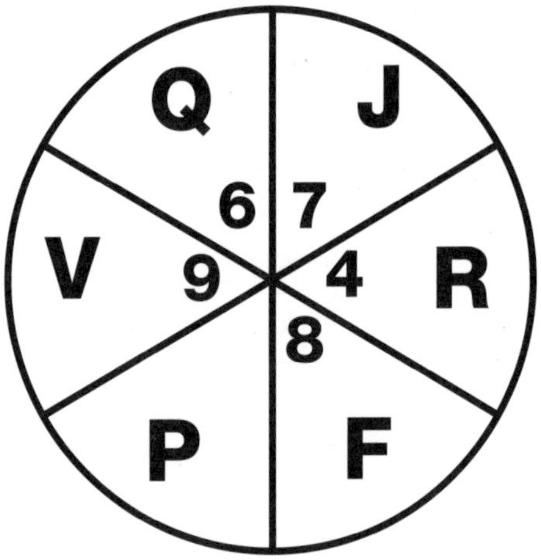

30 PUZZLE

Which number replaces the question mark?

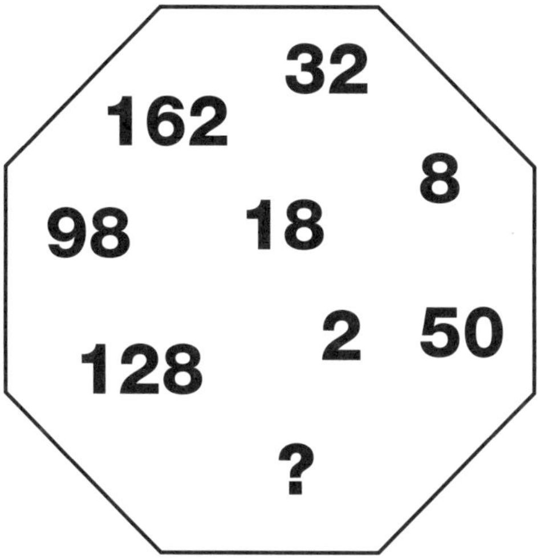

31 PUZZLE

Which number comes next?

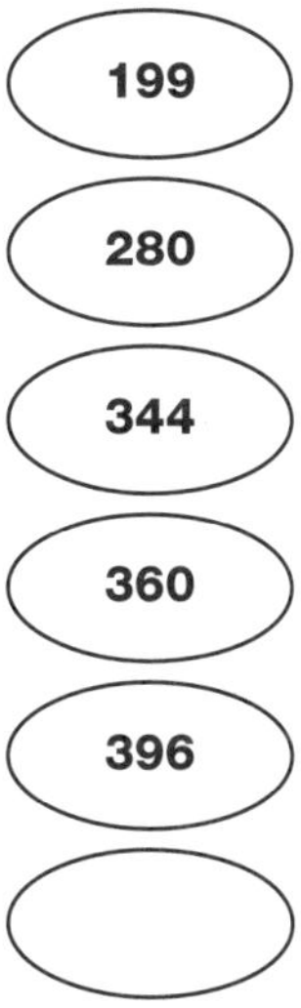

32 PUZZLE

Draw the contents of the empty circle.

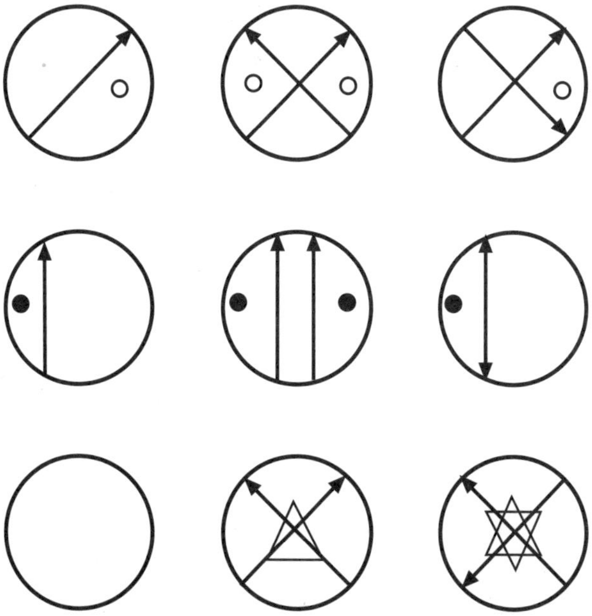

LEVEL 20

33 PUZZLE

Which number goes in the empty circle and completes the puzzle?

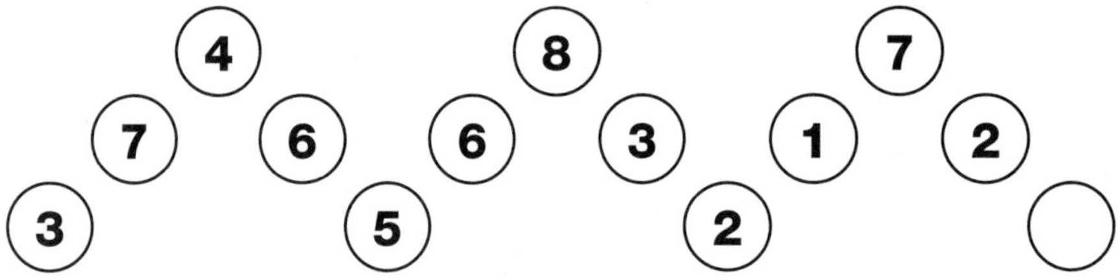

34 PUZZLE

Which numbers complete the last two grids?

7	8	8
9		0
9		8
4	6	0

A

1	9	2
9		0
7		6
2		9

B

8	8	8
2		1
7		8
6		7

35 PUZZLE

Which number is missing?

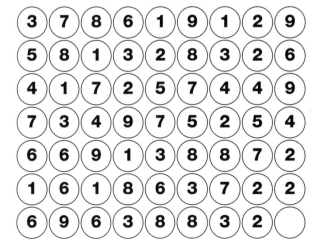

3	7	8	6	1	9	1	2	9
5	8	1	3	2	8	3	2	6
4	1	7	2	5	7	4	4	9
7	3	4	9	7	5	2	5	4
6	6	9	1	3	8	8	7	2
1	6	1	8	6	3	7	2	2
6	9	6	3	8	8	3	2	

36 PUZZLE

Which domino completes the pattern?

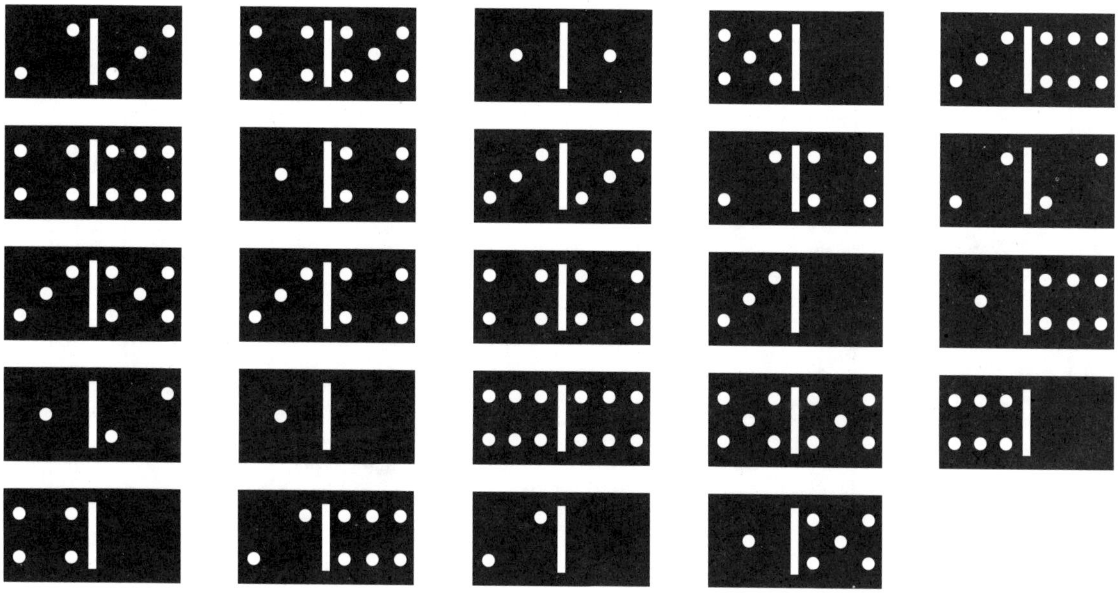

37 PUZZLE

Which of the three letters at the bottom fit into the top grid?

F	C	A
D	L	C
L	D	

1	2	3
G	B	H

38 PUZZLE

Which letter replaces the blank and completes the sequence?

E	H	L	V	E	M
F	K	T	Z	L	X
I	N	Y	K	W	F
M	X	I	V	E	K
W	H	T	Z	I	M
F	N	Y	H	L	

LEVEL

20

39 PUZZLE

Which number logically fits into the empty square?

2	9	3	7	6	8
7	1	5	2	0	7
8	5	4	2	9	3

8	8	2	3	9	8
6	5	1	5	4	8
3	5	6	9	5	

40 PUZZLE

Which letter replaces the blank and completes the sequence?

B	D	G	B	A	F
G	D	C	H	H	D
E	F	G	F	E	B

F	D	C	F	H	H
G	D	A	C	C	H
D	C	G	G	F	

41 PUZZLE

Which shape is the odd one out?

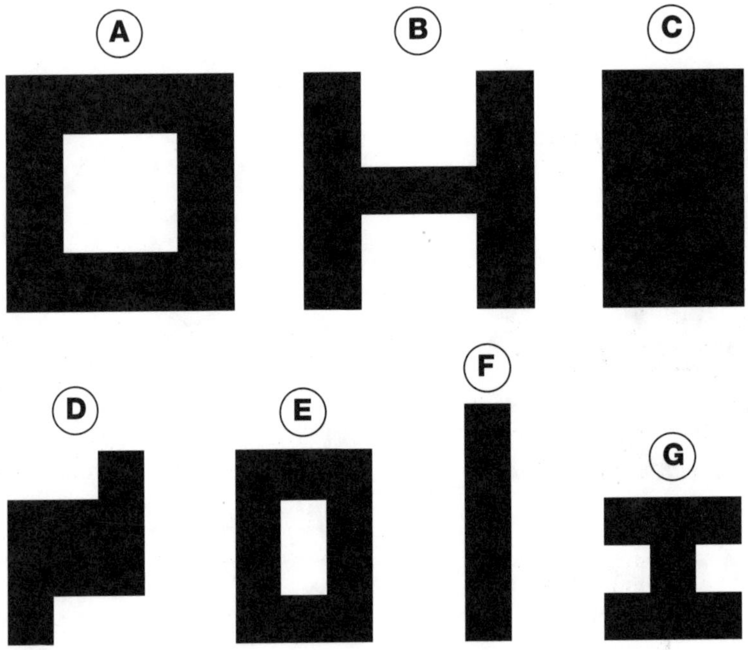

42
PUZZLE

Complete the last row of the puzzle.

B	J	F	F	L	Z	T	R	F
K	D	G	K	A	S	S	D	I
C	H	J	B	R	T	C	J	Q
I	H	C	Q	U	B	K	P	Z
G	D	P	V	Z	L	N	A	B
E	N	W	Y	M	M	B	Z	Q
M	X	X	N	L	C	Y	R	L
Y	W	O	K	D	X	S	K	J
V	P	J	E	W	T	J	K	S
Q	H	F	V	U	H	L	R	E
G	G	T	V	G	M	Q	F	X
H	S	W	F	N	P	G	W	B
R	X	D	O	N	H	V	C	Z

SOLUTIONS

LEVEL 1

1 – A
The figures at both ends move alternately, first the figure originally on the extreme left moves from left to right, then the figure originally on the extreme right moves from right to left.

2 – 36 minutes

3 – 3
So that all lines across and down total 10.

4 –
Mary 44, Sally 66, Frank 99.

5 – 913
The figures 3462891 are being repeated in the same order.

6 – D
The figure on the left moves to the top of the pyramid and the other two figures remain at the bottom but change round.

7 – A
So that in the large circle there are three mirror-image pairs of small circles.

8 – Friday

9 – 4
Looking across and down the middle number is the sum of the two other numbers above and below, divided by 2.

10 – D
The two triangles without the dot remain in the same position. The triangle with the dot moves round clockwise, clamping itself to the nearest side of the remaining two triangles in turn.

11 – 18
The two odd numbers are subtracted from the even number in each square.

12 – 52
6 x 5 = 30 - 7 = 23
2 x 8 = 16 - 9 = 7
14 x 2 = 28 - 6 = 22
8 x 7 = 56 - 4 = 52

13 – B

14 – 0 2 1 8 7 9 6

15 – A
1 is added to 2 to equal 3
4 is added to 5 to equal 6
Like symbols disappear.

16 – B
↗ stays same,
● moves 135° clockwise,
○ moves 135° clockwise,
 moves 180°.

17 – (c) SLUGGISH

18 – 1014
52^2 = 2704, half of 2704 = 1352 and 75% of 1352 = 1014

19 – E nearest to the A contains
• x •

20 – 100
6 x 7 = 42
12 x 3 = 36
11
89

8 x 2 = 16
5 x 21 = 105
2
123

6 x 7 = 42
14 x 4 = 56
2
100

21 – The other shapes are symmetrical

22 – 48

23 – (a)

24 – 1A

25 – (c) QUIBBLING

26 – 6
In each square the bottom segment equals the sum of the other 3 segments.

27 – C
In each row, the sum of the centre letter equals the sum of the left and right hand letters.

28 – 71
Add the first two numbers together to get the third, repeating around the grid.

29 – 23
In columns, add the first three numbers together to get the figure in the bottom box.

30 – P
In each circle, letters move clockwise by increasing steps.

31 – 4
Numbers in each column add up to 9.

32 –

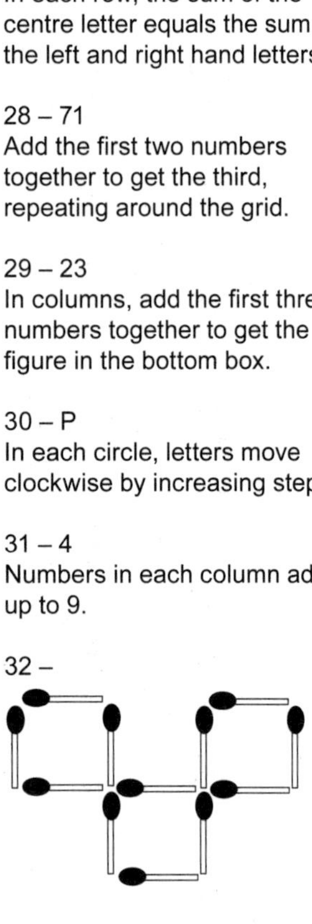

SOLUTIONS

33 – X
Letters advance in the alphabet by 4, 5, 6 and 7.

34 – U
In columns, the value of the bottom letter equals the sum of the values of the other two.

35 – 8
Working in rows, add the left and centre numbers together to give the result on the right.

36 – 9
In rows, add the left and centre figures to get the right hand number.

37 – 3
Working in rows, the figure on the right equals half the difference between the left and central numbers.

38 – 1
Taking the top and bottom lines separately, add the left and centre numbers, then subtract the right hand number to give the figure in the middle.

39 – 4
Numbers in each row add up to 14.

40 –

Working in columns, as you move down, one feature is removed with each step, and the smile alternates with the frown.

41 – 5
In rows, double the left and centre digits and add together to give the right hand figure.

42 – 23
Moving across each row, from top to bottom, the numbers follow the sequence of prime numbers.

43 – 2
In each square, the sum of the 3 outer numbers divided by the central number always equals 6.

44 – 1 = P, 2 = J
All the other letters contain straight lines only.

45 – 36
Segments in the right hand half equal the squares of the diagonally opposing segments on the left.

46 – R
Starting in the top left of each figure and moving clockwise, the letters ascend the alphabet in steps given in the centre value.

47 – M
Each centre letter is the midpoint between the pairs of letters in the diagonal lines.

48 – 11
Working in rows, halve the first number, double the middle number and add them together to give the right hand number.

49 – 5
Working in rows, the first three numbers add up to the right hand number. In the next line, the three numbers to the right add up to the left hand number, etc.

50 – No
As the water level rises the pointer moves towards 'Drought'.

51 – X
The letters in the central column come midway in the alphabet between the left and right hand numbers.

52 – P
The numbers between pairs of letters equal the sum of the values of the letters either side.

53 – Ace (of any suit)
Taking the vertical, horizontal and 2 diagonal lines through the centre of the square, the sum of the values at the ends of the lines equal 12, the value of the centre card.

54 – E & S
Starting on the left and going down, then up the right column, letters advance in steps of two.

55 –

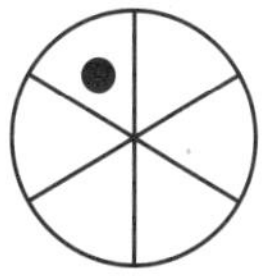

Working in rows left to right, the dot moves anticlockwise by 1, then by 3 segments.

56– 1
In each circle, the bottom number equals the sum of the squares of the top two numbers.

57 – K
In each star, the letters run clockwise in alphabetical order, in steps of 3 for the left hand star, 4 for the centre and 2 for the right hand star.

58 – W & E
In each circle, add 5 to the value of the top left letter to give the bottom left letter, and then add 2 to the top right to give the bottom right.

SOLUTIONS

59 – 7
Working in rows, the central number equals the sum of the left and right hand numbers.

60 – 17
The chain follows the sequence of prime numbers.

61 – J
In rows, the value of the right hand letter equals the difference between the values of the left and centre letters.

62 – 23
Starting in the top left corner and moving clockwise in a spiral, add 3 to get the next value, then 2, then 1, etc.

LEVEL 2

1 – 7
In each circle, the sum of the digits equals 34.

2 – S
The numerical value of the bottom letters equals the sum of the numerical values of the top two letters.

3 – Z
Starting from C and moving clockwise letters advance alternately 5 and 4 places.

4 – M
Working in columns, the bottom letter equals the sum of the top and centre letters.

5 – D
Looking round the octagon there are three pairs which have black/white reversal.

6 –

A	B	C	D	E
C	D	E	A	B
E	A	B	C	D
B	C	D	E	A
D	E	A	B	C

7 – 2.5 minutes

$\frac{1}{5} + \frac{1}{4} - \frac{1}{20} = 0.2 + 0.25 - 0.05 = 0.4$

$\frac{1}{.4} = 2.5$

8 – 16

9 – L
There are two alternate sequences:
AbCdeFghiJklmnO
ZyXwvUtsrQponmL

10 – 106
5 x 2, 1 x 6

11 – 2573
In all the other numbers multiply the first and last digits to obtain the middle two.

12 – B
The bottom figures fold up and across the top figure along the adjoining line.

13 – 41
4 x 8 + 9

14 – B, C, E

15 – C

16 – B

17 – 14

18 – 14
(17 + 11 + 12) - (14 + 19) = 7
(18 + 16 + 15) - (6 + 5) = 38
(19 + 16 + 2) - (15 + 8) = 14

19 – (d) MEDLEY

20 – FUTILE

21 – E
1 is added to 2 to equal 3,
4 is added to 5 to equal 6,
Like symbols disappear.

22 – 4 1/2 "

23 – SCOFF

24 – The pentagon which has only 5 sides (odd number). The others have an even number of sides.

25 – 1A

26 – D = DIAMOND
H = 11
C = 8
D = 5
S = 1

27 – 1½

$\frac{9}{72} \div \frac{36}{144} \div \frac{12}{36} =$

$\frac{1}{8} \div \frac{1}{4} \div \frac{1}{3} =$

$\frac{1}{8} \times \frac{4}{1} \times \frac{3}{1} = 1\ 1/2$

28 –

$\frac{1}{13} \times \frac{1}{12} \times \frac{1}{11} \times \frac{1}{10} = \frac{1}{17160}$

or

17159 to 1

SOLUTIONS

29 – 17 + 6 + 5 + 9 -
(11 + 2 + 4 + 8) = 12

30 –

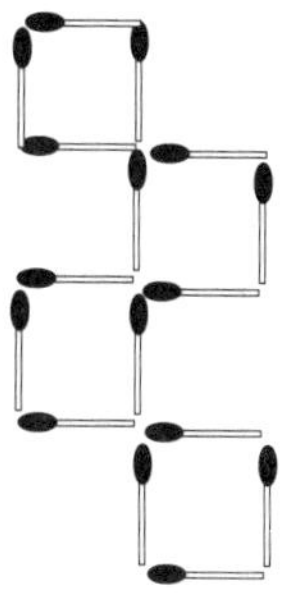

31 – It will rise.

32 – 48
Numbers advance by 2, 4, 8 and 16.

33 – 3
In each row, add the left and the right hand numbers and divide by 2 to get the central value.

34 – U
In each row, add the numerical value of the left hand and centre letters to give the right hand letter.

35 – 9
Each row, column and diagonal adds up to 15.

36 – 2
Add the numerical values of each pair of letters and then write the answer, as two separate digits in the boxes underneath.

37 – G
Working clockwise around each star, the letters increase in steps given by the numerical value of the central figure.

38 – Z
Letters advance in steps of 12, returning to the start of the alphabet after Z.

39 – R
In columns, add the numerical value of the top and middle letters to give the bottom letters.

40 – 2
In each triangle, add the lower two digits and multiply by the top digit to give the value in the centre.

41 – 7
In each line, the central number equals the left hand number and double the right hand number.

42 – H
Going clockwise around each square, the letters increase in value in steps presented by the central square.

43 –

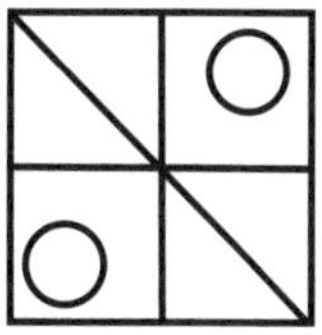

Working in rows, the central figure is made from super-imposing the left and right hand figures.

44 – 81
As you go down, subtract the sum of the separate digits in each number from itself to give the next number.

45 – A
From left to right in each row, the black circle moves clockwise around each corner, the hash moves one place down and the triangle moves anticlockwise around the central 4 squares.

46 – 7
Add the top figures, then the bottom ones. The central figure is the difference between these two answers.

47 – 4

48 – 14
Starting on the left, double each number and add two to give the value in the corresponding segment in the circle to the right.

49 –

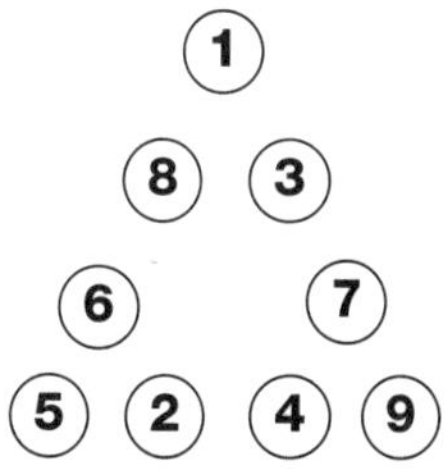

50 – 8
All vertical and diagonal lines through the centre add up to 14.

51 – 8
In each circle, the sum of the odd numbers plus one equals the sum of the even numbers.

52 – 34
Starting at 3 and moving clockwise, double the preceding number and subtract 2.

53 – 72cm

54 – 13
Moving clockwise, each segment equals the sum of the previous two segments.

SOLUTIONS

55 – T
Multiply the numerical value of the left hand letter by the right hand letter to give the central figure.

56 – 13
Going down the columns, moving left to right, numbers follow the sequence of prime numbers.

57 – C
Working in rows from left to right, the @ moves 1 place clockwise in the central 4 squares, the Δ moves 2 places clockwise around the outside of the square, while the ⋆ moves 2 places anticlockwise.

LEVEL 3

1 – C

2 – G
Move five letters forward in the alphabet, then three back, etc.

3 – 3

4 –

3 x 4 = 12   6 x 10 = 60
8 x 6 = 48
60

5 – B
In all the others the top and third segments are the same.

6 – 24 minutes
$40 \times \frac{6}{10}$

7 – D

The dot moves to a different corner at each stage in a clockwise direction, and alternates in and out of the triangle, and also white/black.

8 – 7
Start at 12 and move clockwise. Opposite segments as indicated in the diagram below are plus 1, then plus 2, etc.

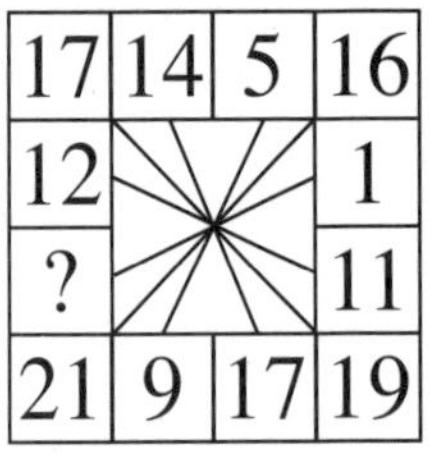

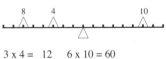

9 – 99
Add the first digit of the previous number, then add the second digit, etc.

10 – C
All segments are divided in half horizontally.

11 – The pentagon has the greatest number by 180°
Diamond 360°
Double triangle 360°
Pentagon 540°

12 –
A 15
B 6
C 3
D 1

13 – (d) CANTAR

14 – 20 & 37 or 3
Opposite segments add to 27
Opposite segments are subtracted = 17

15 – B

16 – 6859
They are cube numbers

16^3	17^3	18^3	19^3
4096	4913	5832	6859

17 – 32
(9 + 8 + 13 + 6 + 10) -
(6 + 7 + 1 + 8 + 4) = 20

(11 + 12 + 6 + 7 + 8) -
(5 + 2 + 4 + 1 + 2) = 30

(17 + 14 + 12 + 9 + 7) -
(11 + 7 + 3 + 2 + 4) = 32

18 – 156
(12x8) + (6x14)
- (2+8 +10+4)

19 – (b) 177

20 – C
1 is added to 2 to equal 3.
4 is added to 5 to equal 6.
Like symbols disappear.

21 – E = 36
Add the number of sides x 3

22 – (e) OBVIOUS

23 – 3C

24 – 133

25 –
Single 1 = 3.50
Pack 1 = 3.25
Saving = .25 $\frac{25}{3.50}$ = 7.1%

26 – G
In each triangle the value of the lower left letter increases by the value of the top letter to give the lower right letter.

27– 29
The sum of the numerical values of the three letters.

SOLUTIONS

28– K
Letters in the left hand column move through the alphabet, skipping letters written without curves, letters in the right hand column skip letters with curves.

29 – 6 Painters.

30 – F
In each circle, the sum of the numerical values of opposite segments adds up to the same: 16 for the left circle, 17 for the top and 18 for the bottom.

31 – 60
Multiply the figures at the opposite ends of the central circle to give the same answer.

32 – 9
The four corners add up to 35, as do the four centre figures on each side of the square.

33 – 6
The numbers in each square, including the middle one, add up to 15.

34 – 3
Working in columns, divide the top value by the centre to give the bottom figure.

35 – 12
As you go down each pair of numbers, the left hand value equals the sum of the numbers above and the right hand value equals the difference of the pair of numbers above.

36 – 2
The figures in each row add up to 11.

37 – W
From left to right each letter represents the numerical value of the first 9 prime numbers.

38 – Ace of Hearts
In each row the sum of the red cards equals the sum of the black cards, with one card from each suit in every line.

39 – 5
The sum of the numerical values of the letters are written on the bottom two points of each star as a 2-digit number.

40 – T
Letters are arranged in alphabetical order, skipping any letters written with curved lines.

41 – 8
The centre value equals the difference between the left and right hand numbers.

42 – 5
The product of the numbers in opposite segments is always 60.

43 – F
Working in columns, subtract the value of the middle letter from the value of the top letter.

44 – 22
The centre number equals the sum of the bottom two digits minus the top digit.

45 – 43
Moving clockwise the numbers increase by 2, 3, 5, 7, 11, etc – the sequence of prime numbers.

46 – F
Moving clockwise, letters decrease in value from U in steps of 1, 2, 3, 4 and 5.

47 – 2
In each circle subtract the right hand digit from the left hand digit, then subtract a further one to give the lower digit.

48 – 6
The sum of the values around the edge of the puzzle add up to the centre number.

49 – 3
The 2-digit numbers in alternate boxes represent the sum of the alphabetical value of the left hand letter in the box above and the reverse alphabetical value of the right hand letter.

50 – T
Letters in opposite segments of the circle are the same distance from the start of the alphabet as the other letter is from the end.

51 – 6
Working in rows, add the first and second numbers, then deduct 1 to give the right hand number.

52 – 8
The sequence follows the formula - double the previous number then add 1, etc.

53 – A = 12, B = 25,
They are the only even number or only odd number in each ellipse.

54 – 4
In each column of three the numbers add up to 16.

55 – 5
In each grid numbers move clockwise in steps given by the central number.

56 – E
In each row, subtract the numerical value of the middle letter from the left hand letter to give the right hand letter.

SOLUTIONS

57 – L
Letters at opposite ends of each line come in pairs: one is the same distance from the start of the alphabet as the other is from the end.

58 – 16 years old.

59 – 26
Going clockwise, numbers represent the sequence of prime numbers multiplied by 2.

60 – O
In each box, multiply the numerical values of the letters, and write the three-figure result in the lower half.

61 – 3
Figures in the centre column equal the sum of the numbers in the right and left.

62 – Q
In each circle the letters move clockwise in increments of 7 for the top left circle through to 3 for the bottom right circle.

LEVEL 4

1 – D
It has two small black circles, two small white circles, one larger black circle, two larger white circles (one with one of the small white circles inside it), and one large white circle (with one small white circle and one larger circle inside it).

2 – Tuesday

3 – 49.5
Add 3, then multiply by 3, etc.

4 – E
Carry forward only lines which appear in the same position in both previous circles, except that the curved lines become straight and vice versa.

5 –
A + E = B,
A + B = D,
D/E = C

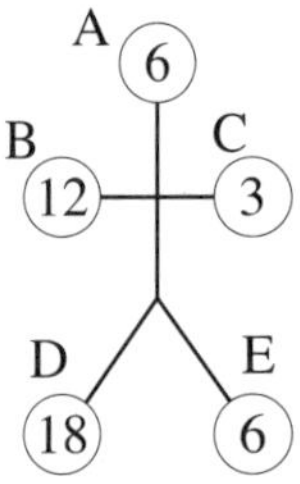

6 – 1 hour
40 miles at 40 mph = 1 hour,
60 miles at 60 mph = 1 hour.

7 – B
Only carry dots forward to the middle circle when they appear in the same position 3 times in the four surrounding circles.

8 – 4
All lines across total 8.

9 – All widgets have a hole in the middle.

10 – B
In lines across multiply the number of circles to obtain the number in the third square. In lines down divide.

11 – C

12 – S
They are the 1st letters of the numbers 1-2-3-4-5-6.

13 – (b) MARCASITE

14 – MANACLE

15 – D
A + C + E = SAME
B + F + G = SAME

16 – 5.50

17 – 5
(7 + 2 + 4) - (6 + 5) = 2
(9 + 1 + 7) - (2 + 2) = 13
(11 + 4 + 2) - (5 + 2) = 10

18 – 152

19 – $18\frac{5}{8}$
There are 2 series
16, $16\frac{7}{8}$, $17\frac{3}{4}$, $18\frac{5}{8}$
(+ $\frac{7}{8}$ and - $\frac{3}{4}$)
21, $20\frac{1}{4}$, $19\frac{1}{2}$

20 – 3C

21 – (c) A TURKISH TITLE

22 – 4
The numbers are the number of letters in the question.

23 – C
1 is added to 2 to equal 3
4 is added to 5 to equal 6
Like symbols disappear.

24 – B

25 – 132

$$\frac{22}{\frac{2}{3}\ \frac{1}{2}} = \frac{22}{\frac{4}{6}\ \frac{3}{6}} = \frac{22}{\frac{1}{6}} = 22 \times 6 = 132$$

26– C

27 – 10
In rows, the centre number equals the difference between the left and right hand numbers.

28 – 3
Add the numerical values of the pairs of letters and write the 2-digit result in the boxes below.

SOLUTIONS

29 –

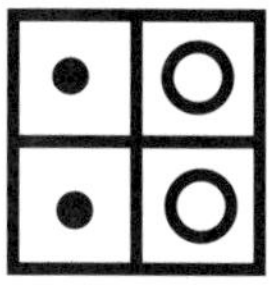

Working in rows, the figure on the right is formed by superimposing the left hand figure rotated 90° clockwise and the centre figure rotated 90° anticlockwise.

30 – 4
In each figure, the sum of the left hand digits divided by the sum of the right hand digits gives the central value.

31 – O
Starting bottom left and moving clockwise in a spiral, letters advance by 9 places, then 8, 7, 6, etc.

32 – 25%

33 – 21
Numbers increase down the row by 5, then 4, 3, etc.

34 – 2 & 0
The digits under each group of letters represent the value of the left hand letter and the reverse alphabetical value of the right hand letter, written as a 2-digit number.

35 – 19
The figures in the central column equal the sum of the numbers in each corresponding row.

36 – O
Working from left to right, letters in corresponding positions on each triangle advance by 7, 6 or 5 places as you move to the right.

37 – 5
Working in rows, multiply the average of the left and right hand numbers by three to give the middle number.

38 – P
In each diagram, the numerical value of each letter plus the numerical value of the letter below it adds up to the same number.

39 – 14
Starting in the top left and moving between circles in a W shape, numbers in corresponding segments increase by 2, 3, 4 and 5.

40 – Y
In each circle, starting with the top left letter, move 10 places forward to give the top right figure, and move another 10 places forward to give the bottom letter.

41 – 2
Working in columns, multiply the top and bottom values to get a 2 figure result, written in the 2 central squares.

42 –

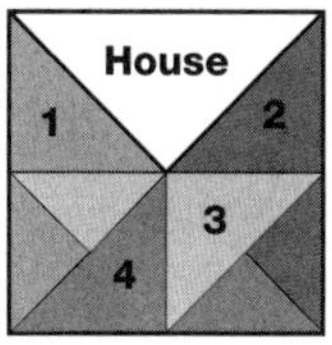

43 – R
Taking rows across each group letters increase by 2, 3, 4, 5 and then 6.

44 – 49
The sum of the digits at corresponding positions on each triangle equals 100.

45 – 54
For each box, the number enclosed by the central box equals the sum of the squares of the other three numbers.

46 – Seven of Hearts
In rows, add the left and central card values to give the value of the right hand card value. The suit of the left card is the same as that of the right hand card.

47 – Q
Starting at the top of each triangle, letters progress clockwise in increments given by the central number plus 2.

48 – 5 mechanics, with a little time left over.

49 – 4

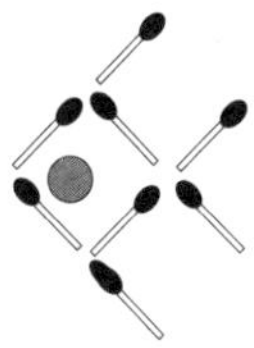

50 – 42
As you go down, double the previous number and subtract 10.

51 – 54 or 6
Segments on the left equal the values in the opposite segments multiplied by three.

52 – 3
In each grid, add the top 6-digit number to the middle number to give the bottom result.

SOLUTIONS

53 –

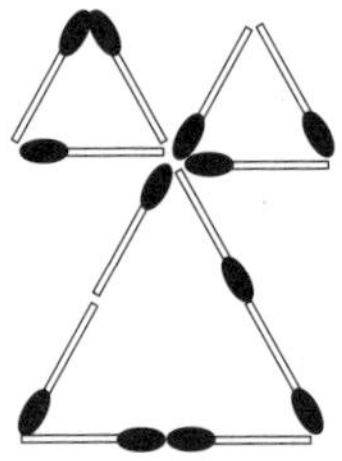

54 – A
Using the numerical values of the letters, each set of four diagonally opposite letters equals 19.

55 – 1 = L, 2 = E
All other letters are written with three lines.

LEVEL 5

1 – B
So that each horizontal and vertical line contains one each of the four different lines.

2 – Q P H
The second set are the same distance from the end of the alphabet as the first set is from the beginning.

3 – D
To complete every possible combination using three of the four different suits.

4 – 630
Multiply by three quarters, one half, one quarter and repeat.

5 – 2
Opposite numbers total 11.

6 – L
Start at T and work down the left side adding 2 letters of the alphabet; move down the right side moving 2 letters back.

7 – B
In all the others rounded figures are black and straight figures are white.

8 – 4
A + D = B + E + C

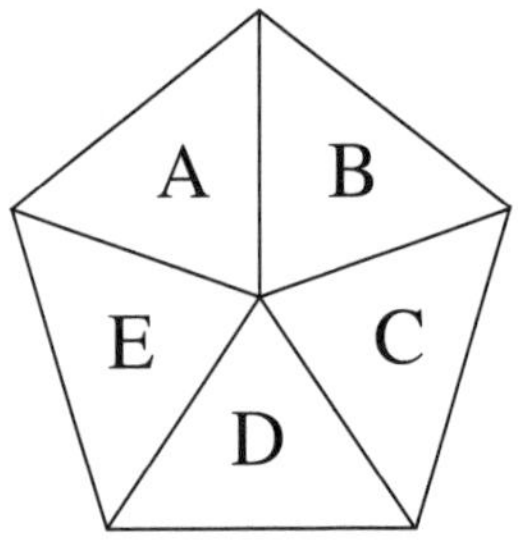

9 – Jack

10 – C
The dot moves from left to right alternating white/black; the triangle moves from right to left.

11 – C

12 – 15

26 - 10 = 16
31 - 9 = 22
38

14 - 7 = 7
12 - 5 = 7
14

21 - 9 = 12
11 - 2 = 9
21

17 - 10 = 7
9 - 1 = 8
15

13 – 16

7+6=13	2+16=18	17+6=23
12+2=14	4+15=19	8+16=24
7+8=15	10+10=20	13+12=25
3+13=16	14+7=21	10+16=26
5+12=17	14+8=22	13+14=27

14 – D
1 is added to 2 to equal 3
4 is added to 5 to cancel 6
Like symbols disappear.

15 – C

16 – DEMODED

17 – ELANCE
(The others are dances)

18 – A
D is the same as G
B is the same as F
C is the same as E

19 – 42

20 – A
Where there is 1 line at a particular angle in (a), there are 2 at this angle in (b) and vice versa.

21 – 29
Prime numbers 6th to 13th.

22 – 1000
The top circle contains the squares of 6-7-8-9-10 (36-49-64-81-100).
The bottom circle contains the cubes of 6-7-8-9 (216-343-512-729-1000).

23 – (c) A COAL MEASURE

24 – (a) PASTA

25 – B
Each circle in the bottom large circle is a 90° rotation clockwise of a circle at the top.

26 – 8 biscuits.

27 – 11 & 5
Alternate numbers increase by 2, the others decrease by 1.

28 – 677
Square each value and add 1 to get the next number.

SOLUTIONS

29 – L
Add the numerical values of the bottom two letters and divide by the value of the top letter to give the value of the centre letter.

30 – 66
Working from left to right, double the previous number and subtract 2.

31 – E
Going clockwise letters increase in value by the value of the centre letter.

32 – 13
Starting at the top, add the two numbers to give the left hand number underneath. The right hand number is the same as the left hand number above.

33 – K
Moving clockwise in alternate sections, letters advance by 6 or 5 places.

34 – 23
Working clockwise, numbers increase by 2, 3 and 4 in a repeating sequence.

35 – 3
The difference in the numbers in each segment equals the numerical value of the letter in the opposite segment.

36 – V
Starting top left and spiralling clockwise, letters advance in steps of 2, 3, 4, 5, etc.

37 – One quarter of the original amount.

38 – 35
Numbers advance in steps of 7, 8, 9 and 10.

39 – 4
In each figure the middle value equals the difference between the products of the top pair of numbers and the bottom pair.

40 – Yes
The bottom left turns anticlockwise, while all the others turn clockwise.

41 – 14
Working in rows, multiply the left and right hand numbers together and add 2 to give the centre value.

42 – 13
In each circle the lower number equals the average of the top two numbers.

43 – D
Working in columns, one cross is removed at each step, first from one side of the pattern, then the opposite side.

44 – D
On each watch the digits add up to 15.

45 – 2
For each circle multiply the top two numbers together to give a 2-digit value, written in the bottom segments.

46 – 4
Starting at the top, the right hand number equals the left hand number plus 6, in the next line add 5, then 4, 3, 2 and 1.

47 – A
Moving from left to right, one dark segment moves 1 place clockwise while the other moves 2 places anticlockwise.

48 – 19
In each circle, going clockwise, alternate even numbers increase in steps of 2, odd numbers increase in steps of 4.

49 – 2
In each row, divide the left hand value by the centre value to get the right hand number.

50 –

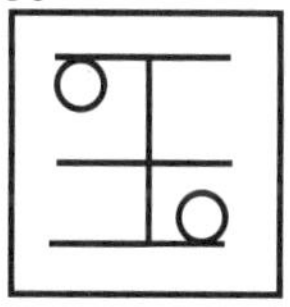

Working in rows from left to right, add the elements of the first two boxes to give the figure on the right.

51 – 8
In each square, multiply the top and bottom numbers then subtract the left and right hand numbers, the result is 40.

52 – 36
In rows, multiply the left and centre numbers then subtract the smaller of the numbers to give the right hand value.

53 – M
Going clockwise move forward 5 places, then back 3, missing out all the vowels.

54 – I
Taking the numerical values of the letters in each figure, subtract the right hand numbers from the left hand numbers on the same line to give the central number.

55 – 15
Each segment in the lower right box equals the sum of the values in the corresponding segments of the other squares.

SOLUTIONS

56 – 2
The numbers in each line of 3 circles, going through the centre, add up to 15.

57 – 10
The values of the points of the central star equal the sums of the values of the corresponding points of the left and right stars.

LEVEL 6

1 – C
The symbols move as in the first analogy, i.e. first to fourth, second to first, third to last, fourth to third, last to second.

2 – 3

3 – A
A new section appears at the beginning then the end alternately.

4 – $48

5 – 8
Add the numbers in the right and left squares to obtain the numbers in the middle square.

6 – 10
There are 8 groups of three numbers round the diamond totalling 15: 10 + 3 + 2 = 15, 8 + 2 + 5 = 15, etc.

7 – P
Jump one letter then two letters etc : AbCdeFgHijKlMnoP

8 – (d) BASKET

9 – B
The circle goes to the top and the triangle flips in to the main figure.

10 – 2
Each side of the triangle contains the numbers 1 - 9.

11 – B
The outer segment moves 90° anti-clockwise at each stage, the middle segment moves 180° and the inner segment moves 90° clockwise.

12 – F
The only one with a line and circle from the shortest side.

13 – F

14 – 207
$72 + 3^2, + 4^2, + 5^2, + 6^2, + 7^2$

15 – 20
(7 + 26 + 17) -
(8 + 12 + 10) = 20

16 – D
1 is added to 2 to equal 3
4 is added to 5 to cancel 6
Like symbols disappear.

17 – (a) TIERCEL
The others are animals.

18 – B
B = 9

No of angles =	1	2	3	4	5
No	1	3	5	7	9

19 – E
A is the same as F
B is the same as G
C is the same as D

20 – CHARNICO (drink)
The remainder are all DANCES.

21 – 90° F

22 – (e) A WHIP

23 – 48
Non-prime numbers between 38 and 48.

24 – 8 KG

LH	RH
8 x 5 = 40	6 x 4 = 24
4 x 2 = 8	8 x 3 = 24
48	48

25 – D

26 – 6
In rows the right hand digit equals double the difference between the left and the centre.

27 – J
Letters move clockwise in steps of 10.

28 – 14
Double the numbers in the top left circle to give the values in the lower left circle. Double the numbers in the top right circle to give the values in the lower right circle. The difference between corresponding values are put in the last remaining circle.

29 – 19
The numbers, starting at 2 and going clockwise around each circle, represent the first 9 prime numbers.

30 –

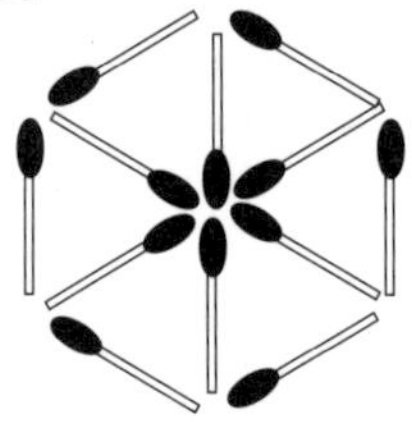

31 – Y
Going clockwise, the letters in alternate segments advance 6.

32 – 6
Numbers in each row add up to 26.

SOLUTIONS

33 – 10
In each circle, add the top 2 numbers and subtract the lower right number to give the lower left number.

34 – 7
Add together the numbers on the outside of each segment and put the result at the centre of the opposite segment.

35 –

	2	
5	8	6
3	1	4
	7	

Other answers may also be correct.

36 – W
Letters on the left descend in steps of 4. The values of the letters on the right equal the values of the letters on the left plus 3, then minus 3, etc.

37 – X
In rows letters in the first line increase by steps of 5 from left to right, the second row in steps of 4, the next by 3 and the bottom line by 2.

38 – 49
Square the values in the segments on the left half, and put the results in the opposite segment on the right.

39 – 24 & 2
Each segment in the lower left circle equals the sum of the corresponding segments in top circles. The numbers in the bottom right circle are the sum of the even numbers in the top circles, minus the odd numbers.

40 – 7
In each circle, multiply the upper left number by 2 and subtract 1 to give the upper right number. Then multiply the original number by 3 and subtract 1 to get the bottom number.

41 – A = 127, B = 56
All other numbers are divisible by 9.

42 – 7
Starting at the top left and working down, and bottom right and working up, add the left hand number to the right hand number and put this answer in the centre column reading downwards.

43 – 14
Numbers on corresponding points of each triangle progress by increasing steps, add 6 then 7 for the top, 5 and 6 for the bottom left and then 7 and 8 for the bottom right.

44 – H
In the first box, starting top left, letters advance by a decreasing amount, starting with 6, then 5, 4, etc. The second box advances by 7, 6, 5, etc, and the third box by 8, 7, 6, etc.

45 – 29
As you go down each block of two, the right hand number is duplicated in the left hand square below, and the right hand number equals the sum of the two squares above.

46 – 15
In each circle, the lower left value equals the sum of the numerical values of the letters and the top right value equals the difference in the letter values.

47 – 8
In each diagram the central value equals the difference between the product of the top two numbers and bottom two numbers.

48 – 75
Each shape contains the same numbers, which are multiplied by 3, 4 and 5.

49 – W
In each circle add the numerical values of the upper two letters to give the numerical value of the bottom letter.

50 – G
In each circle, going clockwise, alternate letters increase in value by 3 steps for the left hand circle, 4 for the upper and 5 for the lower circle.

51 – D
In each row, divide the numerical value of the left hand letter by the number in the centre column to give the numerical value of the right hand letter.

52 – 152
As you move clockwise multiply the previous number by 2 and add 2, 3, 4, 5 and 6.

53 – 3
Working in rows the central figure equals the difference in the squares of the left and right hand numbers.

SOLUTIONS

54 – B
Moving across each row from left to right, the # symbol appears in alternate boxes, rotating one quarter turn around the central 4 squares. The O moves to the right on the top row, then down 1 space and to the left. The * moves to each corner up, down to the left, up then down to the right.

LEVEL 7

1 – B
A is the same as E with black/ white reversal, and C is the same as D.

2 –

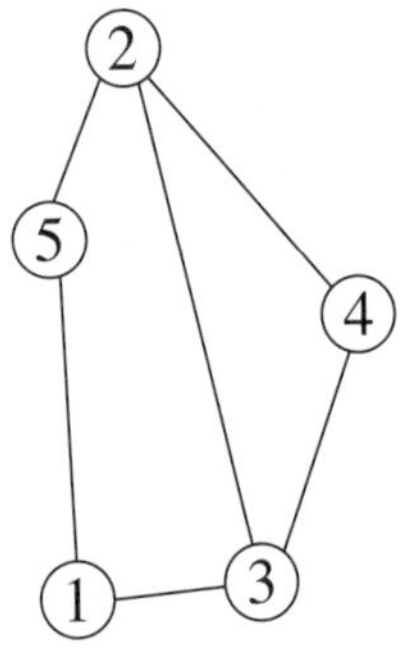

3 – D
It goes anti-clockwise from outer to inner, the others going clockwise from outer to inner.

4 – L M O P
All the others progress in the sequence, for example, K (+1) M (+1) O P.

5 – 8
Numbers in the same shape of geometric figure all total 11.

6 – 2415

7 – 13 seats
37 people each paid $51.

8 –
5
4
6
There are three sequences;
1,2,3,4,5 alternating top second;
0,1,2,3,4 alternating second third, and
2,3,4,5,6 alternating third first.

9 – A
Every third figure is upturned and every fourth has a dot.

10 – B
Every line has one upright diamond and one white star.

11 – E
C is the same as A.
D is the same as G.
B is the same as F.

12 – 89
Moving diagonally left to right each number decreases by the same amount as the one before.

13 – A

14 – 48
(6 + 7) x (5 - 2) = 39
(8 + 6) x (4 - 1) = 42
(10 + 2) x (6 - 2) = 48

15 – A1

16 – 7
Multiply opposite numbers, then add the totals.

6	x	4	=	24
3	x	7	=	21
21	x	9	=	189
				234

11	x	9	=	99
2	x	7	=	14
8	x	8	=	64
				177

31	x	6	=	186
5	x	14	=	70
8	x	7	=	56
				312

17 – B
2nd stack 3 drops out
3rd stack 3 drops out
4th stack 3 drops out

18 – X
They are every 3rd letter in the alphabet with only straight lines.
A miss E, F
H miss I, K
L miss M, N
T miss V, W
X

19 –
ALAN 16
BERTIE 27
CHARLIE 39

20 – PONIARD, DAGGER

21 –
46/27 ÷ 92/9
46/27 x 9/92 = 1/6

SOLUTIONS

22 –
VOWELS = 1
CONSONANTS = 3
ALSATIAN = 16

23 – 7KG

LH	RH
6 x 4 = 24	7 x 4 = 28
8 x 2 = 16	6 x 2 = 12
40	40

24 –
6/100 x 5/99 = 1/330

25 – 8%
81 + 82 + 77 + 68 = 308
Amongst 100 pupils, this gives 3 losses each, and 4 losses to 8 pupils.

26 – 42
Divide each circle into left and right halves. The top right value equals the sum of the left hand numbers, the middle right value equals the product of the left hand numbers and the bottom right hand value equals the sum of the squares of the left hand numbers.

27 – 32
Working downwards, square the numbers 0, 1, 2, 3 and 4 and multiply by 2.

28 – M
Starting from A alternate letters increase in steps of 3, the other letters, starting from G increase in steps of 2.

29 – 10
Going clockwise, the values increase equal increments and move 90° clockwise each step.

30 – D
The lines along each half domino add up to the number of dots shown on the right hand side.

31 – A
Add the reverse alphabetical value of the bottom two letters of each triangle and subtract the reverse alphabetical value of the top letter to give the value of the middle letter in alphabetical order.

32 – 236
Working in columns from top to bottom, on the left, multiply each value by 2 then subtract 2 to give the next number. In the centre column by 3 and the right hand column by 4.

33 – 2
Starting with the digits to the top and left move in lines of 3 digits subtracting the centre digit to give the bottom and right figures.

34 – 2
Add the top 2 digits in each group and multiply the centre, the result is written in the bottom circles.

35 – 6
Starting in the top left of each figure, numbers increase in a clockwise direction by the value given in the central circle.

36 – 4
In each column, the sum of the three smaller figures equals the larger figure.

37 – 6
The centre figure is the product of the left and right numbers, minus 1.

38 – 1 = M, 2 = J
The numerical values of No 1 are divisible by 3, in No 2 the numbers are divisible by 4.

39 – 51
Working in rows, invert the digits in the left and right hand numbers and add them together to give the central figure.

40 – Five of Clubs
In rows, add together the values of the first four cards to get a 2-digit number. Add these together to give the value of the right hand card. The suit of this card is the same as the card to the left with the highest value.

41 – 68
In each circle, divide the difference between the top and right hand numbers by 4 to give the left hand value.

42 – 168
Subtract 4 then multiply each number by 3 to give the next number.

43 – M
Taking the numerical value of the letters each row and column adds up to 27.

44 – U
Taking all 3 groups together, letters increase in value in rows from left to right by 3 for the top row, 4 for the middle and 5 for the bottom row.

45 – F
In columns, the central number equals the sum of the numerical value of the top and bottom letters.

46 – 12
Starting from the top, subtract 2 then add 7 and continue this sequence.

SOLUTIONS

47 – Z
In rows, add the numerical value of left and centre letters to give the value of the right hand letter.

48 – 21
In each grid, add up the 4 numbers at the corners and write the result downwards in the centre column.

49 – 30
In each circle, multiply the two upper numbers and subtract 10 to give the lower value.

50 – B
Divide the numerical value of the left hand letter by the numerical value of the right hand letter to give the value of the lower letter.

51 – 25
The larger numbers are the squares of the numbers in the opposite segments of the circle.

52 – 1
The figures in the right hand column equal the difference between the numbers in the left and centre columns.

53 – M
Starting at the bottom left and moving anticlockwise, letters progress through the alphabet in steps of 2, then 3, etc, returning to the beginning of the alphabet whenever Z is reached.

54 –

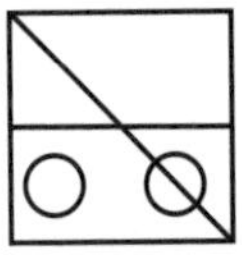

Working in rows, rotate the left figure by a quarter turn clockwise to give the central figure, and a quarter turn anticlockwise to give the right figure.

55 – 2
In each diagram, add the numerical values of the four letters and write the 2-digit answer down the right column.

56 – O
Starting top left and spiralling clockwise, letters follow the alphabetical sequence, missing those written without any curved lines.

LEVEL 8

1 – E
The figure moves through 180°, the black circle becomes a white star, the black diamond a white circle and the white ellipse a black square.

2 – GC, 73
The numbers in the middle indicate the position of the numbers on the left from the beginning of the alphabet and the position of the numbers on the right from the end.

3 – 35 (5 x 7)

4 – J
All the others have one black dot in the vertical line and one white dot on the horizontal.

5 – B
There is at least one black and white of each component in each horizontal and vertical line.

6 – 23
Add 2 to the first 2 numbers, then 3 to the next 3 numbers, etc.

7 – 17
The number in each inner segment is the sum of the digits in the opposite outer segment, ie 9+8=17.

8 – A
So that there is one dot in triangle/circle, and another dot in two triangles and a circle.

9 –

4	6	8
7	T	2
1	3	5

10 – 1.75
There are two alternate sequences, +1.25 and -2.75.

11 – 14

12 – B1

13 – 6
(5 x 6 x 7) ÷ (3 + 7) = 21
(4 x 9 x 2) ÷ (4 + 4) = 9
(6 x 1 x 9) ÷ (4 + 5) = 6

14 – 2
(17+8+9)-(14+11+3)=6
(21+2+9)-(1+17+3)=11
(21+22+4) - (1+17+12)=2

15 – 44
(9 x 5) - (6 - 4)
(8 x 7) - (9 - 3)
(7 x 7) - (10 - 5)

16 – B
1 is added to 2 to equal 3.
4 is added to 5 to equal 6.
Similar symbols disappear.

SOLUTIONS

17 – 2KG
LH = 6KG x 4 = 24
RH = 12KG x 3 = 36
LH = 10KG x 2 = 20/44
RH = 2KG x 4 = 8/44

18 – 88 years

19 – B

20 – E
A is the same as F
B is the same as G
C is the same as D

21 –

$6^3 \div 36 = 6$

22 – CORPULENT, LEAN

23 – 28

24 –

$\frac{3}{10} \times \frac{2}{9} = \frac{6}{90} = \frac{1}{15}$

25 –
52 x 51 x 50 x 49 = 6,497,400

26 – 34
Working with the corresponding numbers in each box the numbers decrease by one each move downwards.

27 – P
In each row letters increase in value from left to right in steps of three for the top row, then 4, 5 and 6 for the other rows.

28 – 7
Splitting the diagram into four smaller squares the value in the box towards the centre equals the sum of the other three numbers.

29 – O
In rows, each letter is represented by a 2-digit figure, the first digit being the difference between the left and centre numbers, the second digit equals the sum of the two numbers.

30 – 3
Starting top left and moving clockwise in a spiral, the sequence of letters I, R, T, W, E, D, B, T, F, O, O, S repeats over and over.

31 – 10 metres

32 – B
In each row, add the black squares from the left hand and centre boxes to give the figure in the right hand box.

33 – 6
For the first sequence, double the top numbers separately and enter the answer in the third box down, repeat this for the fifth line. For the next sequence add one to each figure on the second row and put the answer on the fourth row, repeating again for the last row.

34 – 10
Numbers are arranged in columns of 4, with each one increasing down in steps of 2.

35 – 17 & M
Numbers on the left descend in prime number order, starting with 3. Values of the right hand letters also follow the prime order sequence, this time starting with 2.

36 – 1600
She likes squared numbers.

37 –

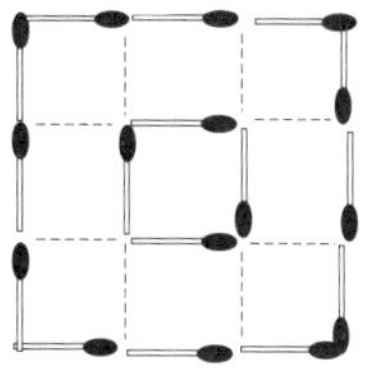

38 – 6
Take the 2-digit number at the centre of each segment putting the sum and the difference of the two digits in the segment opposite.

39 – 37
As you go down, double the previous number and subtract 5.

40 – 6
In each square, add up the outer three numbers, then add the two digits of the result together to give the central number.

41 –

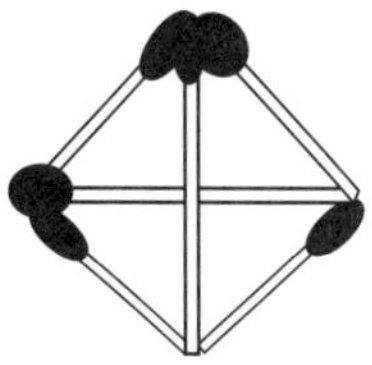

42 – 6
Each row and column contains 4 consecutive numbers in a random order.

43 – F
Starting bottom right and moving in an anticlockwise spiral, letters skip 1 space, then 2, etc, returning to the letter A whenever Z is reached.

SOLUTIONS

44 –

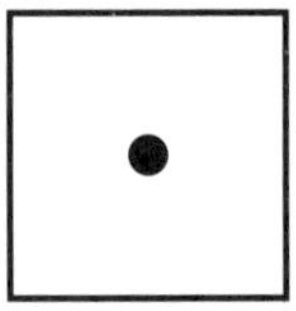

In rows, the right hand box contains only the features common to the two boxes to the left. The columns are calculated the same way, with the bottom box containing only the features common to the boxes above it.

45 – 12
In each triangle, divide the product of the upper and left hand numbers by the right hand number to give the central number.

46 – 3
Working in columns, subtract the middle number from the top number and multiply by 3 to give the bottom value.

47 – 3
In each diagram, add up the 4 outer numbers to give a 2-digit value. Add these 2 digits together to give the central value.

48 – 24
Square the numbers 1, 2, 3, 4 and 5 and subtract 1.

49 – D
The figures in the other three boxes total greater than 100.

50 – O
Moving from left to right, letters on corresponding points of each triangle increase in steps of 4, 5 and 6.

51 – B
In each square take the numerical value of the left and right segments to give the value of the letter in the top segment and the reverse alphabetical value of the letter in the bottom segment.

52 – 8
For each number on the left, starting at the top, double it and subtract 1, then 2, 3, 4, etc, to give the right hand number.

53 – R
Starting on the left in rows, letters ascend in sequence at intervals of 5 for the top row, then 4, then 3.

54 – Melinda is 37 and her father is 73.

55 – 14
The numbers in the inner ring are the same as the numbers in the opposite outer ring, divided by 3.

56 – 5
In rows, the sum of the left and centre value equals the right hand value for the first and third rows, in the second and fourth rows the right hand value equals the difference between the left hand and centre numbers.

57 – T
Add the reverse alphabetical values of the three letters around each triangle to give the middle letter in forwards alphabetical order.

58 – 6
In rows, the right hand figure equals the sum of the left and centre numbers plus 2.

LEVEL 9

1 – D
So that each horizontal line contains the same line, with the dot in each of four positions.

2 – 21 15
Each number is calculated using the two numbers below, In rows 2 and 4, take the difference of the two numbers below, in rows 3 and 5 add it.

3 – C
A dot in a circle and another dot in square/pentagon.

4 – B

5 – 24 minutes

6 – 9

7 – 4
4 x 19 = 76

8 – 13

9 – 24
6 x 8 = 48/2

10 – 14

11 – 28

12 – E

13 – A3

14 – 2
54+16=70÷(18+17)=2
90+9=99÷(19+14)=3
55+35=90÷(26+19)=2

15 – E
R is added to S to equal T
1 is added to 2 to equal 3
Similar symbols disappear.

SOLUTIONS

16 – 12
In the 1st Hexagon opposite numbers add up to 36. In the 2nd, opposite numbers add up to 43. In the 3rd, opposite numbers add up to 32.

17 – E
A is the same as G
B is the same as F
C is the same as D

18 – 22
There are 2 series:
(+6) 7-13-19-25
(+7) 8-15-22-29

19 –
There are 2 series:
(+3) 17, 20, 23, 26,
(-6) 41, 35, 29, 23

20 – 6x5=30

21 – 180 = 6x5x4x3x2x½x2

22 – (21 x 14) - 3 - 3 = 288

23 – $^{1}/_{36}$

24 – 25

25 – 9D
In each row, subtract the sum of the black cards from the sum of the red cards to give the value of the Heart on the right hand side.

26 – 29
In each star the central number equals the difference between the sum of the odd and even numbers.

27 – 4
The sequence is subtract 2, then add 1, etc.

28 – Z
Going from left to right along the top line then the bottom, letter values increase by three while their positions move 90° clockwise.

29 – 43
In each circle, starting top left and moving clockwise, multiply each number by 3 and subtract 5 to give the next number.

30 – 161
In each circle, going clockwise, double the first number and subtract 1 to give the next number.

31 – E
The sum of the numbers gives the left hand letter, and also the right hand letter in reverse order.

32 – 6
The central number of each triangle equals the difference between the sum of the odd and even numbers.

33 – 3
The numbers in the central column equal the sum of the numbers in the same row to the left, minus the numbers on the right.

34 – 64
Each box represents the cube of numbers 1, 2, 3 and 4.

35 – N
In each square letters in opposite segments hold the same position in the alphabet running forwards as they do going backwards.

36 – 2
In rows multiply the far left number by the far right to give the 2-digit result, written in the central squares.

37 – N
The numerical value of each letter equals the product of the two numbers in the opposite segment.

38 – N
Working in rows, letters advance by 4, 2 and 5 places.

39 – P
Starting top left and moving clockwise to end in the centre, the letters increment by a repeating sequence of 1, 2 and 3 places.

40 – 24
Working clockwise, numbers increase by 2, 3, 4, 5 and 6.

41 – B
Working in rows, invert the left and right hand boxes vertically and add the elements together to give the middle box.

42 – 2 and 9 of any suit.
Working in rows the sum of the numerical values of the first 5 cards equals the 2-digit number represented by the last 2.

43 – E
Working in columns, top to bottom, one spot is removed in sequence at each step.

44 – 6
In each diagram, the central number equals the difference between the product of the two right numbers and the product of the two left numbers.

SOLUTIONS

45 – X
Working left to right, starting on the top row, letters increase in value in steps of 2, 3 and 4.

46 – 39

47 –

Break 2 of the matches in half.

48 – 66
Moving in clockwise direction, double the preceding number and subtract 2.

49 – 19
Starting top left and moving clockwise square, numbers in corresponding segments advance by 2, 3, 4 and 5.

50 – 23

51 – Z
Going clockwise around each star increase in numerical values by 6, 7 and 8 spaces.

52 – K
The central number in each triangle equals double the sum of the numerical values of the letters on the triangle's points.

LEVEL 10

1 – 12

2 – 1 minute

$$(0.5 + 0.25) \times \frac{80}{60}$$

3 – 121
72-61 = 11; 11 x 11 = 121

4 – E
Each horizontal and vertical line contains three different shaped stars, one of them is black, and one of them is without a moon.

5 – Blue
The numbered coloured shirts coincide with the colours of the rainbow: blue is the fifth colour of the rainbow.

6 – F

7 – C
Looking across and down, the outer arc moves 90° clockwise at each stage, and the inner arc moves 90° anticlockwise.

8 – 2
Start at the top and move right to left on the second row, then left to right on the third etc, repeating the numbers 36942.

9 – 42867
Each number is the last three digits of the number above followed by the first two digits.

10 – C
At each stage working from top to bottom two figures are inverted, and at each stage the dot moves from bottom to top and down again.

11.

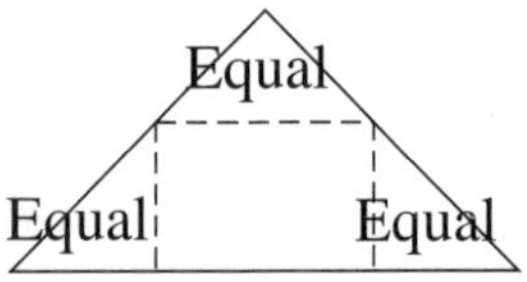

12 – 18
8x8=64 Reversed = 46
5x5=25 Reversed = 52
4x4=16 Reversed = 61
7x7=49 Reversed = 94
6x6=36 Reversed = 63
9x9=81 Reversed = 18

13 – A

14 – B3

15 – 8
(17 + 8 + 6) - (4 + 5 + 9) = 13
(16 + 1 + 5) - (8 + 7 + 2) = 5
(4 + 11 + 9) - (7 + 3 + 6) = 8

16 – C
R is added to S to equal T
1 is added to 2 to equal 3
but similar symbols disappear.

17 – 5
16 + 14 +10/4 = 10
37 + 15 + 8/10 = 6
29 + 18 + 3/10 = 5

18 – $10
Ashtray $2
Chair $60
Table $240

19 – 1018
Moving clockwise, double the previous number and add 6.

20 – E
A is the same as C
B is the same as F
D is the same as G

21 –

$8^2+7^2+6^2+5^2+4^2+3^2+2^2+1^2=$
204

22 – 168

$$\frac{8x7x6x5x4x3}{1x2x3x4x5x6} \times \frac{6x5x4x3x2}{1x2x3x4x5}$$

SOLUTIONS

23 – 72 @ $5.11 each = $367.92

24 – Black

25 – QH
Numbering the cards Ace to King as 1-13, in each row, calculate the sum of the three left hand cards and the three right hand cards, and subtract the left total from the right total to give the value of the heart in the middle of the row.

26 – K
Starting at top left and moving clockwise in a spiral, letters move back through the alphabet in steps of 2, 3, 4, etc.

27 – W
Starting at the top, the value of the right hand letter is two ahead of the left hand letter, then 3 ahead, then 4, etc.

28 – 35
In each circle, multiply the two smallest even numbers and put the answer in the opposite segment, do the same for the odd numbers.

29 – 236
Starting at the top, numbers increase in steps of 25, 35, 45, etc.

30 – Y
In each circle opposite segments contain letters the same number of spaces from the start of the alphabet as from the end of the alphabet.

31 – 26
In each square, multiply the three outer values and subtract the number in the centre. Going clockwise the answers are 50, 60, 70 and 80.

32 – 14
Working in column, alternately add 5 then subtract 1 as you move down.

33 – N
Starting at the upper circle and working downwards, letters in corresponding segments increase in value by 2 each time, while their relative positions rotate 1 segment clockwise.

34 – N
Letters are put in alphabetical order, working clockwise around each circle, and from left to right, missing out letters written with any curved lines.

35 – 7
Working from left to right, all digits increase by 2, with their relative positions rotating a quarter turn clockwise.

36 – 10
In each square, take the sum of the odd numbers and subtract the sum of even numbers to give the number enclosed in the central square.

37 – V
In columns, make a 2-digit number from the numerical values of the top and middle letters to give the numerical value of the bottom letter.

38 – E
Working in rows from left to right, the * moves back and forth along a diagonal line, the ? moves a quarter turn clockwise, the O moves clockwise by 1 space, then 2, then 3, etc, and the # moves left and right along the second row.

39 – F
In each circle add the reverse alphabetical values of the top two letters to give the reverse value of the bottom letter.

40 – 8
In each figure the top left number divided by the centre number gives the top right number, as do the bottom left and right numbers.

41 – 8
Working in rows, the central value equals the product of the left and right hand numbers, minus their sum.

42 – P
The letter in the bottom segment of each square has the numerical value of the sum of the letters in the other three segments.

43 – W
Starting from the top left and going down, then from the top right down, letters advance by 5, then back 2, etc.

44 – R
Letters in the right half of the circle are 7 places in front of the opposite letters.

45 –

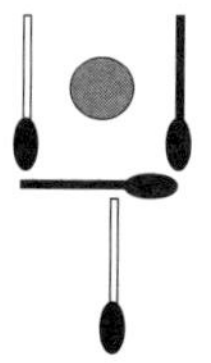

Slide the horizontal match half a length to the right and move the lower left match to the upper right, inverting the glass and enclosing the coin.

SOLUTIONS

46 – 86
Working from top to bottom, double the previous number and subtract 1, 2, 3 and 4.

47 – 1
Multiply the outer 4 numbers together and divide by 2 to give the central figure.

48 – 24
Starting at top left and moving in a uniform pattern, numbers increase by 8, 7, 6, etc.

49 – 11
In each column, numbers increase in steps of 3, 4 and 5.

50 – 

The sequence is as follows:

Working from left to right, circles at the top of each triangle move backwards through this sequence, corresponding circles at the bottom move forwards through the sequence.

51 – N
Going clockwise, letters increase in steps of 1, 2, 3 and back to 1 again.

52 – 2
In each diagram divide the top left by bottom right, add bottom left and subtract top right to get the answer in the middle.

53 – 88
Moving downwards, multiply each number by 3 and then subtract 14.

54 –

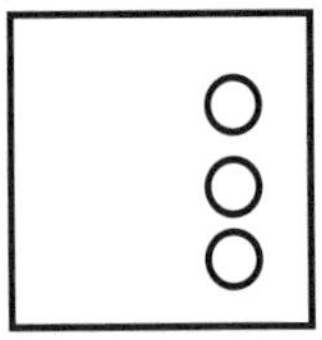

Working in rows starting on the left, one circle is removed in sequence as you move towards the right.

55 – E
The others all cover the same area.

LEVEL 11

1 – B
The figure at the front goes to the back.

2 – B 27
Starting top left, the letters progress through the alphabet, omitting 2 letters each time. The numbers represent the sum of the positions in the alphabet of the missing letters. When the end of the alphabet is reached return to A as if the letters were written in a circle.

3 –
41
46
Start top left and move along the top row, then back along the second etc, in the sequence +2, -1, +3, etc.

4 – B
In all the others left looking faces are frowning and right looking faces are smiling.

5 – T
M L
Start at the top and moving left-right then back right left, repeat the letters F, J, T, L, M.

6 – 12684
Multiply each individual number by 2.

7 – B
The large figure changes to white and rotates 90^0 and goes inside one of the figures on the outside which increases in size and becomes black.

8 –

15	6	10	14
11	4	8	2
13	1	T	12
3	9	5	7

9 – B
There are two alternate sequences, with a piece of each figure disappearing at each stage.

10 –

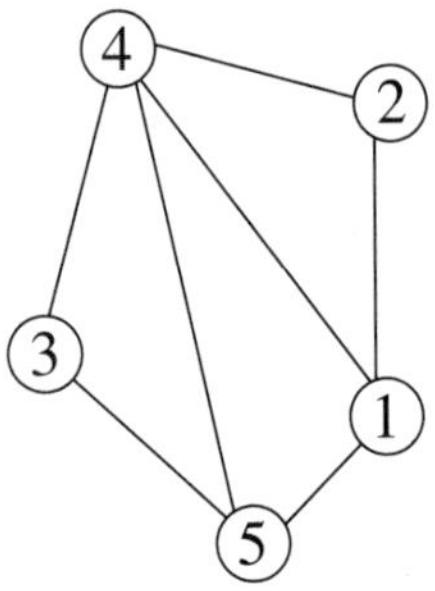

11 – C

12 – C2

SOLUTIONS

13 – 10

$$\begin{array}{r} 7 \times 6 = 42 \\ -\ 6 \times 3 = \underline{18} \\ 24 \end{array} \qquad \begin{array}{r} 8 \times 6 = 48 \\ -\ 4 \times 8 = \underline{32} \\ 16 \end{array}$$

14 – 1 2/5
7/11 ÷ 14/22 ÷ 20/28 = x
7/11 x 22/14 x 28/20 = 28/20 =
7/5 = 1 2/5

15 – 19
Digits add up to 10
Others add up to 11

16 – 70
+ 16 + jump 2 segments

17 – 16
All the other numbers have the first digit larger than the second.

18 – 29
Centre number is total of outside digits.

19 – F
A is the same as D
B is the same as E
C is the same as G

20 – 260 mph.

21 –

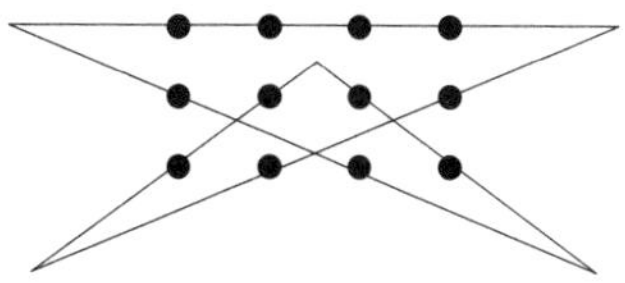

22 –

$$\begin{array}{r} 4027 \\ \times\ \underline{\quad 2} \\ 8054 \end{array}$$

23 – 593,775

24 – $315

25 – D
1 is added to 2 to make 3
4 is added to 5 to make 6
Like symbols disappear.

26 – 14
In each triangle the centre figure equals the sum of the two lower numbers minus the top number.

27 –

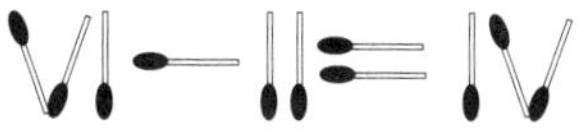

28 – 7
In rows the right hand number equals the difference between the left and centre numbers.

29 – 1
In each box, divide the 3 figure value represented on the upper line by the three figure value on the lower line. The answers are 22, 23 and 24.

30 – 4
Working in rows, the central value equals the sum of the squares of the left and right hand numbers.

31 –

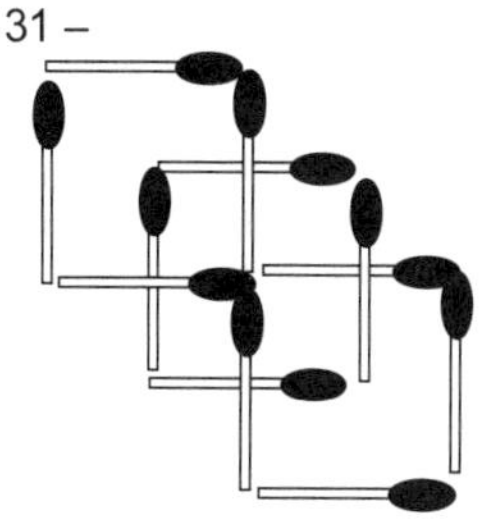

32 – 17
Starting in the top left square and moving clockwise, numbers increase in sequence by 2, 3, 4 and 5, keeping their corresponding positions in each square.

33 – X
Starting at the top, letters increase in value by 5, 4, 3 and 2.

34 – C
From the top, using the first 2-digit figure, the left hand letter below equals the alphabetical value of this figure and the right hand letter below equals the reverse alphabetical value.

35 – 61
Starting at the top, double each number and add 3 to get the next one.

36 – B
If the watches are inverted, the digits read the same.

37 – D
Starting at the top left of the first figure and moving in a Z shape, letter values increase by 2, then 3, then 4, 5, and 6 to reach the top figure in the next diagram.

38 – 4
The number in the centre is the product of the bottom 2 digits, plus the top digit.

39 – 1
The grid is symmetrical around the two diagonal axis.

40 – D
Moving left to right along each row, the circle moves 3 places clockwise around the edge of the square, the triangle moves back and forth along the top left, bottom right diagonal and the star moves from the top to the bottom in a zigzag pattern.

41 – 1:02
Three is taken away from each column in turn.

SOLUTIONS

42 – B
In each square, the outer letters advance the same number of spaces indicated by the numerical value of the centre letter.

43 –

21	4	15	24	1
6	8	17	14	20
3	19	13	7	23
10	12	9	18	16
25	22	11	2	5

44 – Five of Spades
Moving from left to right, cards are placed in alternate colours and suits, the red cards increase by two, the black cards decrease by two.

45 – 4
The numbers in the inner ring correspond to the number of lines used to make the letters in the outer ring.

46 – 24
Each number equals the sum of the two numbers above it.

47 – 2 of any suit.
In each row the sum of the even cards, minus the sum of the odd cards, equals 10.

48 – 14
Starting top left and going to the right, alternatively up and down, add 3 to each number.

49 – 3
In each circle the sum of the digits equals 30.

50 – Steve = 270, Simon = 540 and Stewart = 90.

51 – R
Starting at top left and moving clockwise in a spiral, letters increase by four each time.

52 – $6

53 – 22
In each row, add the left and right hand numbers and double the answer to give the central value.

54 – 13, 4, 15 & 9
All rows columns and diagonals add up to 34.

55 –

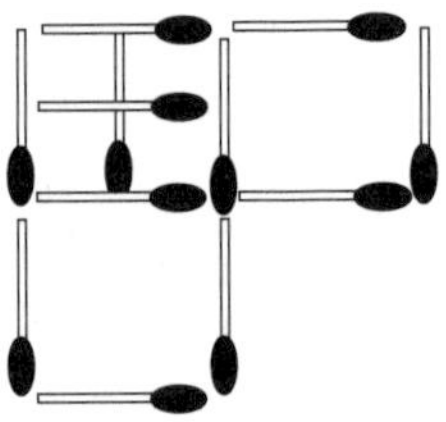

LEVEL 12

1 – D
The figure tumbles over onto a new side clockwise at each stage and also working clockwise a different section is shaded at each stage.

2 – 127
9 + 3 = 12, 7 x 1 = 7

3 – C

4 – T Q O
The first letters skip forward two places then one place from the front of the alphabet, and the second set skips two places then one place back from the end.

5 – $495

6 – A

7 – 4
275986+342758=618744

8 – MPR
Consecutive letters of the alphabet are placed in the same positions as in the two previous triangles.

9 –

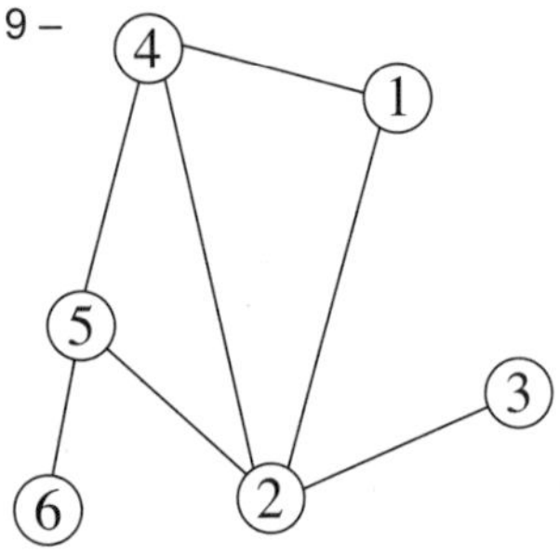

10 – B
The little hand moves alternately two hours back then one hour forward and the big hand moves 10 minutes forward.

11 – (d) GRENADA

12 – 9

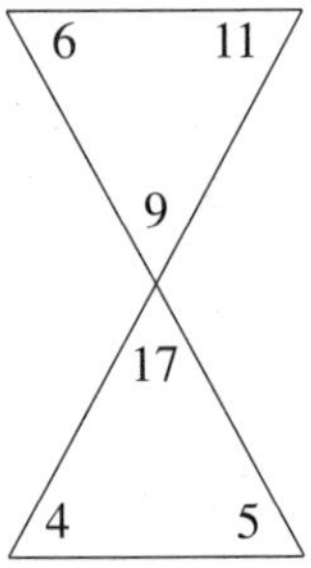

Two outside numbers added together make the opposite inside number.

SOLUTIONS

13 – C

14 – 4
5x8=40
6x4=24
– 16
8x6=48
9x4=36
– 12
7x3=21
3x4=12
– 9

15 – A
It does not contain 37

16 – B

17 – CAPRICIOUS
FANCIFUL

18 – 59 (prime number)

19 – F
A is the same as E.
B is the same as D.
C is the same as G.

20 – (c) MACAQUE (animal)
The rest are vegetables

21 – (a) BARREN

22 – 36 = 44 Modula 8
52 Mod 10 = 5 x 10, 2 x 1
52 Mod 8 = 6 x 8, 4 x 1
36 Mod 10 = 3 x 10, 6 x 1
36 Mod 8 = 4 x 8, 4 x 1

23 – CARBON
All the others contain birds: OWL, ROC, TIT, EMU

24 – (c) FROZEN RAIN

25 – D

26 – From top to bottom Seven of Clubs and Ace of Hearts. Each suit has a value, Hearts = 4, Clubs = 3, Diamonds = 2 and Spades = 1, multiply the cards by its suit value and the sum of each row is 100.

27 –

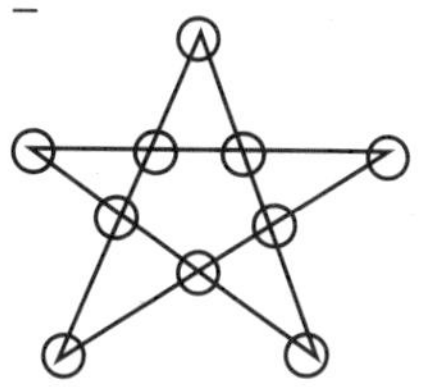

28 – 7
Each row and column contains each digit 0-9 inclusive, sometimes as part of a two digit number, sometimes alone.

29 – A = 92, B = 112
All the other numbers are divisible by 3.

30 – 17
Taking the four segments at a time in vertical and horizontal lines, numbers increase by 2, 3, 4 or 5 for each line.

31 – S
Each line and column contains a letter made up of all straight lines, all curved lines or a combination of both.

32 – 6
Multiply the two outer numbers in each segment and divided by 2 then 3, alternately, putting the result at the centre of the opposite segment.

33 – 23
As you go down, numbers increase by 2, 4, 6 and 8.

34 – E
The numerical values of the letters in each column of 3 add up to 26.

35 – From top to bottom, King of Spades, Seven of Spades and Four of Hearts. The sum of the two court cards equals the sum of the pip cards. There is one pip card of each suit in every row, plus an extra pip card of the same suit as the court cards.

36 – 3
The numbers in each row add up to 21.

37 – 35

38 – F
Starting on the outer left hand circle and going in a clockwise spiral, the letters are written in alphabetical order, missing out the vowels.

39 – 58
The sequence is multiply by 2, then add 3, etc.

40 – 15
In each star the sum of the even numbers, minus the sum of the odd numbers, equals the value of the number in the middle.

41 – Y
In rows, add the numerical values of the left and centre letters to give the value of the right hand letter.

42 – 23

43 – 7
In each diagram, multiply the top two numbers together, then divide by the lower right number and add the lower left number to give the central value.

44 – I
The sum of the numerical values of the left hand letters equals the value of the centre letter, as does the sum of the right hand letters.

SOLUTIONS

45 – 33

46 – L
In each square, the total of the 3 numbers gives the value of the central letter.

47 – 11
Starting at the top left, and moving alternately right and left as you go down, add 2 to get the next value, then 3, then 4, etc. Follow the same pattern with the top right number but add 1, then 2, then 3, etc.

48 – 3:42am
The watch gains 16 minutes per hour.

49 – 2
In each circle, the letter is converted to its 2-digit numerical value. Add these 2 digits together to give the value in the opposite segment.

50 – 3
In each row, the sum of the squares of the far left and right numbers is entered in the middle two boxes.

51 – 18
Starting with the left group, the centre figure equals the sum of the left hand digits, the other groups follow suit but the positions of the outer numbers rotate clockwise 90° as you move to the right.

52 – 18
Add 2, 3 or 4 to the numbers in the left hand circle and rotate their positions one third of a turn clockwise as you move along.

53 – 16
In each row, divide the left and right values by 3 and multiply them to give the centre number.

54 – 5
The numbers in the black segments are the difference between the numbers on either side.

LEVEL 13

1 – D
When white dots appear in the same position twice in the first three pentagons they are transferred to the final pentagon. Black are transferred when they appear just once.

2 – 8 people
Add 75 + 68 + 85 + 80 = 305. This gives three items to all 100 people, and 4 items to five of them.

3 – NXF
The other groups all have letters composed of the same number of lines. NXF has a mixture of 2 and 3.

4 – C
Looking across and down, circles are only transferred to the final square when they appear in the same position in both previous squares, however, they then change from black to white and vice versa.

5 – 14
The rest are all in a 1:3 ratio, 18/54, 24/72, 17/51, 12/36

6 – C
The rectangle turns through 90°, the diamond rotates through 180° and goes below the rectangle, and the ellipse rotates through 90° and goes above the rectangle.

7 – 50
6 x 15 = 90
7 x 18 = 126
7 x 20 = 140

8 – 413
Add the even numbers followed by the odd numbers.

9 –

3	x	2	=	6
+		+		÷
5	–	3	=	2
=		=		=
8	–	5	=	3

10 – 15

11 – E

12 – C
1 is added to 2 to equal 3
4 is added to 5 to equal 6
Similar symbols disappear.

13 – 9
Add digits to equal opposite corner 16 = 7, 62 = 8

16 8

62 7

14 – 156
6x17=102 8x9=152
9x18=162 21x7=147
10x21=210 12x13=156

15 – 18 ÷ 6 x 2 (÷ or x) 1 x 10 = 60

16 – (c) KNOB

17 – PORTENT, INDICATION

SOLUTIONS

18 – R
The word spells camera. Each letter scores its position in the alphabet, ie CAM = 3+1+13=17 and ERA = 5+18+1=24, so the difference = 7.

19 – (b) SQUALL

20 – 1
6-4-7-2-1-1-2-7-4-6
repeats left to right

21 – BREECHES

22 –
131°
$\underline{\quad 32^\circ \quad}$
$99^\circ \times 5 = 55^\circ$
9

23 – B
The dot at the top alternates white black. The large circle at the bottom alternates white/striped/black. The figure right in the centre alternates triangle/circle/square. The dot to the left of it alternates black/white. The dot to the right of it alternates striped/black/white.

24 – (c) TIMID

25 – C

26 – D
Reading from the left, line by line, the @ moves in a figure of 8 around the corners, the * moves anticlockwise in steps of 2 around the 2 central columns, and the Δ symbol moves to and fro along the third row.

27 – E
The dots form a symmetrical pattern from top left to bottom right.

28 – 17
Moving diagonally downwards from left to right, numbers increase by the same amount each line.

29 – 10
The numbers in the top half of the outer ring are written in reverse order plus 1 in the inner ring and vice versa.

30 – 179
Moving clockwise, double the previous number and add 1, 3, 5, 7 and 9.

31 – E
Add all the digits on each watch together. All the others are square numbers.

32 – From top to bottom, Jack of Hearts, Seven of Clubs, Queen of Clubs and Two of Diamonds.
The grid displays rotational symmetry 180° around the central Ace of Hearts, with the cards swapping to the other suit of the same colour.

33 – 3
In each triangle, multiply the bottom numbers to get a 2-digit number, add these together to get the top number.

34 – The figures pointed to by the hands add up to 10, therefore a number of options are available.

35 – 14
In the top pair of boxes the letters are rotated 90° clockwise and the corresponding numerical value is put in the segments on the right. The bottom pair of boxes follows the same rule but the reverse numerical alphabetical value is put on the box on the left.

36 – N
The number in the centre of each triangle equals the sum of the squares of the numerical values around each triangle.

37 – D
In rows, letters increase in numerical value by 3 as you move to the right.

38 – C & Y
Starting at the top of the first 2 columns and working down, each pair of letters is duplicated in the right hand columns from the bottom up with each letter advancing one place alphabetically.

39 – 14
The central value of 15 equals the average of the numbers which are on opposite sides of the diagram.

40 – L
Letters are arranged in pairs in opposite segments of the circle, the lower value letter is the same distance from the start of the alphabet as the other is from the end.

41 – R & H
Starting top left and working clockwise, move forward 6 places, back 2, then forward 4, etc.

42 – 13
In each row, multiply the first and second numbers, then subtract the third to give the value in the right hand box.

43 – J
Take each letter in the left half of the circle and add 5, put the result in the opposite segment on the right.

SOLUTIONS

44 – 1
In each circle, multiply the top 2 numbers together and add the resulting two digits until you get a single figure which goes in the bottom segment of each circle.

45 – 14
The sum of the left and right numbers equals the sum of the other 3 numbers.

46 – G
In each circle, going clockwise, letters move back 3 places, then forward 1, etc.

47 – 34 & 36
From the top left digit add 2 to get the lower number. Add these to get the next top number and continue for each column.

48 – 6
In rows, the centre number equals the sum of the left and right numbers, plus the central number from above.

49 – 22
Clockwise, add 1, then 2, 3, etc.

50 – V
Starting at the top, letters move forward by 2, 3, 4, 5 and 6 places.

51 – 3
The value in each lower box represents the sum of the squares of the two numbers directly above it.

52 – 1 sheep.

53 – K
Add the numerical value of the top left and centre letters to give the lower left letter, similarly with the top right and centre letters to give the lower right letter.

54 – M
Moving down the column, advance 2 letters, then back 5, etc.

LEVEL 14

1 – From left to right - Four, Nine, Eight and Four (of any suit).
In each column the sum of the top three cards and the sum of the bottom three cards equals the value of the central card.

2 – B
A is the same as D with black/white reversal, as is C with E.

3 – 18 1/4
There are 2 series
(+ 3 1/4) (-4 1/4)
18, 21 1/4, 24 1/2, 27 3/4
31, 26 3/4, 22 1/2, 18 1/4

4 – C
The rest are all the same figure.

5 – B

6 – 12
The numbers in the bottom two circles are the sums of each pair of numbers in the top circles.

7 – 14
All the rest have a mirror image pairing.

8 – 2
116 x 3 = 348 x 2 = 696

9 – 55
2 + 3 = 5 and 4 + 1 = 5.
Similarly 1 + 2 = 3 and
5 + 3 = 8.

10 – 28

11 – A
In all the others, one dot is in one circle and the other dot is in two circles. In A both dots are in two circles.

12 – B

13 – E,G
A is the same as H
B is the same as F
C is the same as D

14 – 44
(8 x 5) - (6 + 6) = 28
(9 x 8) - (7 + 7) = 58
(8 x 7) - (9 + 3) = 44

15 – D
1 is added to 2 to equal 3
4 is added to 5 to equal 6
Similar symbols disappear.

16 – 2917 (B)

7x4=28
5x4=20 3x7=21
4x6=24

2x9=18 (17)
7x2=14 8x7=56
6x9=54

6x3=18
2x9=18 1x9=09
8x8=64

17 – 41
6 + 10 = 16, 16 + 8 = 24,
24 + 8 = 32, 32 + 9 = 41,
41 + 7 = 48, 48 + 6 = 54,
54 + 2 = 56, 56 - 50 = 6

18 – 22
(7 + 9) x 4 = 64
(8 + 5) x 5 = 65
(2 + 4) x 11 = 66
(5 + 6) x 2 = 22

SOLUTIONS

19 – 6
7-1=6   6x7=42

20 – (e) COWBOY

21 – DISSIPATE, SAVE

22 – 107
Add digits, ie 44+8=52, 52+7=59, etc.

23 – .1666

24 – (e) WHEELS

25 – (a) GOLD COIN

26 – (d) DIRIIUM
(Iridium, Mineral)
The others relate to colours: Maroon, Pinkish, Russet, Bluish.

27 – S
Numerical values of the letters represent the first 10 prime numbers.

28 – 14
Starting at the top left and moving to the right, then moving down to the left, and finally moving down to the right, the numbers increase by steps of 2, 3, 4, etc.

29 – 1 = Molly, 2 = Frank, 3 = Ray, 4 = Maude.

30 –

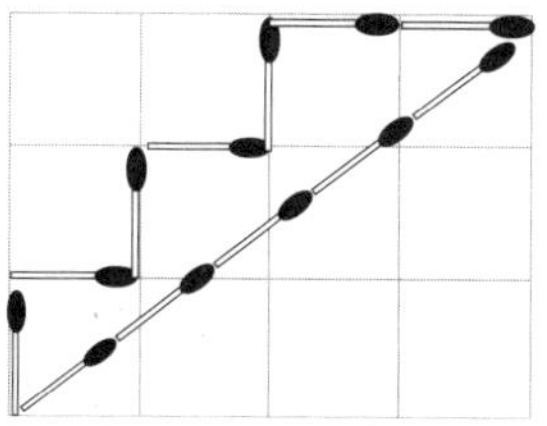

31 –

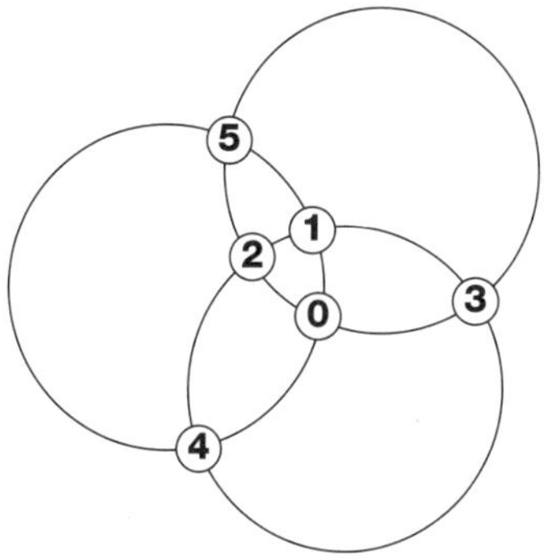

32 – Q
In each circle letters increase in value by 1, while their relative positions move one quarter turn clockwise as you move to the right.

33 – I
Letters are written in alphabetical order, skipping letters written with curved lines.

34 – 52
Divide each number in the first circle by 2 and enter the new figure one place anticlockwise in the second circle. Multiply the first set of numbers by 2 and enter this figure one place clockwise in the third circle.

35 – Ace of Spades
In each row the value of the right hand card equals the difference between the sums of the red cards and black cards to the left. There is always 1 card of each suit on every row.

36 – A
If the separate digits on each watch are added together, the sum increases by 5 each step.

37 – 21
The numbers are the numerical values of the five vowels.

38 – 3
Working in rows, reverse the digits in the left and right hand shapes, then divide the new left hand value by the new right hand value to give the number in the centre.

39 – Three (Spades or Clubs)
In each row, add the values of the black cards to get a 2-digit number. Add these digits together to get the value of the red card in the middle.

40 – F
Starting with the letter at the top left, moving clockwise around each triangle, letters increase in value by 2, 4, 6, 8, etc.

41 – T
In each row, the numerical value of each letter increases by 3 for the first row, 4 for the middle and 5 for the last.

42 – 5
Add the middle three numbers and write the answer, in reverse, in the first two columns. Multiply the same three numbers and write this answer, again in reverse order, in the last two columns.

43 – 4
Working in alternate rows, from left to right, numbers follow a repeating sequence of 5, 7, 2, 1, 9, 0, 3 and 6. The letters follow the sequence J, Q, L, C, Y, P, R, A, S.

44 – Eight of Clubs
In each row, the numerical value of the answer equals the average of the sum of even cards plus the difference of the odd cards. The suit of the answer equals the suit of the highest odd card in each row.

SOLUTIONS

45 – 21

46 – The bottom line is the product of all the other numbers.

47 – 1
The square is divided into four 5 x 5 squares, each with the same pattern of numbers.

48 – Three of Hearts
In each row the average of the 3 cards to the left equals the value of the card on the right. There is one card from each suit on every row.

49 – 410
In all the other numbers, the first two digits added together give the third.

50 – 9:00pm

LEVEL 15

1 – B
Alternating boxes on horizontal and vertical lines rotate by 90°.

2 –
Add 96347, 10496, 21221 and 34628 = 162692.
Divide by 4 = 40673
40673 is the number of votes received by the successful candidate. Thus the second received 30177 (40673-10496), the third received 19452 (40673-21221) and the fourth received 6045 (40673-34628).

3 – G

4 –

A	B	C	D	E	F		E	C	A	F	B	D
7	4	2	1	6	3		6	2	7	3	4	1

5 – D
A new parallelogram is added at each stage, the previous parallelograms flipping outside then inside the hexagon.

6 – ETFNJDOK
The letters in the previous rectangle are reversed, and the one third from last is discarded.

7 – 119.30
Add the last two digits only each time i.e. 109.6 + 9.6 = 119.2

8 – D
The previous figures moves down at each stage and a new symbol is added at the top.

9 –

33	34	34	35
A	B	C	D

A + C = A
B + C = B
A + D = C
B + D = D

10 – F
Only symbols which are common to the first two squares in each horizontal and vertical line are carried forward to the final square.

11 – D

12 – B+F
A same as E.
G same as D.
C same as H.

13 – 110
(17 x 8) - 6 = 130
(11 x 7) - 4 = 73
(13 x 9) - 7 = 110

14 – D
1 is added to 2 to equal 3
4 is added to 5 to cancel 6
Like symbols disappear.

15 – 7
Opposite numbers = total digits
93=12 29=11 71=8
37=10 36=9 55=10
67=13 37=10 43=7
A B C

16 – 108

17 –

$\frac{7}{4}$ x $\frac{7}{9}$ x (6) $\frac{42}{9}$ x (8) $\frac{336}{54}$ x (9) $\frac{302}{432}$

18 –
They all carry coins within the words
DIME, RAND, MARK, CENT, RIAL, SOU

19 –

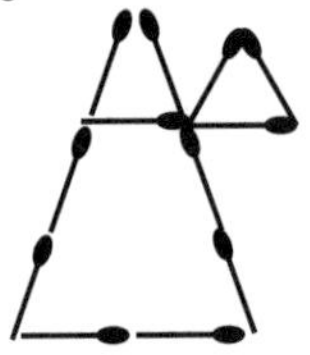

20 – 10H
In each column of the diagram, the sum of the three cards is always 20, and one of each suit is used in each row.

21 – C
Adding up the digits on each watch face, from left to right, the total increases by 5 each time.

22 – 49
(7 x 9) - 6 = 57
(8 x 6) - 7 = 41
(9 x 3) - 4 = 23
(10 x 6) - 11 = 49

23 – (c) A FISH

SOLUTIONS

24 – Square of 19

19	7
19	7
171	49
190	7
361	343

25 –
99/16 ÷ 11/4 = 99/16 x 4/11 =
2 1/4

26 – 12
Square each number in the inner ring and take away the original number. Write the answer in the outer ring opposite.

27 – 14
Taking the first two lines as one group starting top left and the bottom two lines as the second group starting bottom right and moving clockwise, the first number in the top group is doubled to give the corresponding value in the second, the next is halved, etc.

28 – C
The sum of the separate digits on each watch add up to 18.

29 – Nine of Spades, Nine of Diamonds, Seven of Spades and Two of Spades.
In each row, spades represent positive numbers and diamonds negative numbers. The card on the far right represents the sum of the cards to the left.

30 – 30
In each circle starting top left and going clockwise, double the first number and subtract 2 to give the next value.

31 – A
If viewed from the left edge the boxes show numbers 1-6.

32 – Eight of Clubs.
In each row, as you move to the right, the values increase by 2, 3 and 4 with each suit appearing once in each row.

33 – 41
Opposite sides of a die add up to 7, giving 21 dots per die. Multiply this by three and take away the dots you can see.

34 – 13
Going clockwise add 4 to get the next number, then subtract 2, etc.

35 – 37 & 45
In each square the central value equals the sum of the product of the top two numbers and the product of the bottom two.

36 – 27
Starting at the bottom left, move to the right diagonally up, then diagonally down, etc, increasing the numerical value by 4 each step. Additionally the two figures remaining in each group add up to the centre figure.

37 – 1
The centre figure is the difference between the product of the top two numbers and the product of the bottom two.

38 – From left to right – Nine of Diamonds, Jack of Hearts, Six of Clubs and Queen of Hearts.
Starting at the top left, cards move clockwise in a spiral in the repeating sequence 2, 9, 5, Q, A, 3, 6, J, K.
The suits follow the sequence H, C, H, S, S, D in an anticlockwise formation.

39 – Z
Starting at the top letters increase in steps of three for the left hand column and four for the right hand column, whilst missing out all the vowels.

40 – 30
Numbers increase by 7, then 6, 5, 4 and 3.

41 – K
The centre figure equals the sum of the numerical alphabetical value of the left hand letter and the reverse alphabetical value of the right hand letter.

42 – 14
Starting on the left on the first group and moving up and down towards the right, numbers increase by 2 and 3. In the second group by 3 and 4 and in the third group by 4 and 5.

43 – 3
Moving from left to right, letters in the top circles increase in value from one circle to the next by the corresponding numbers in the circles below.

44 – L
Starting at the top of each triangle, letters move forward by three places going clockwise, ending in the centre.

45 – O
Taking the numerical values of the letters in the left hand circle, multiply them by two to give the values of the corresponding letters in the centre circle. Then multiply by three to give the values in the last circle.

SOLUTIONS

46 – Z
In each circle, starting top left and going clockwise multiply the numerical value of each letter by 2 and then subtract 2 to give the next letter.

47 – 13
Going clockwise around the 4 boxes, the values in corresponding segments increase by 1, 2, 3 and 5.

48 – 4
The grid is symmetrical around the bottom axis running from top left to bottom right.

LEVEL 16

1 – D
It is a curved figure in a straight figure. All the others are straight figures inside curved figures.

2 – 2548
The rest have their digits in ascending order.

3 – E

4 –
623 - 36 - 18
847 - 224 - 16
726 - 84 - 32
ie 6 x 2 x 3 = 36, 3 x 6 = 18

5 – K
There are three sequences.
ABC (top/second/top lines)
BEH (second/last/second lines)
CGK (bottom/top/bottom lines)

6 – 114213
Each line describes the numbers in the line above, starting with the lowest numbers first i.e. 212223 has 1 x 1, 4 x 2, 1 x 3.

7 – C
Arcs increase by quarter circles and a new quarter circle starts where the previous arc ends.

8 –
25, 28, 27, 24, 26

9 – 11
Add all the numbers above and divide by 2.

10 – B
So that each line and column contains 10 dots.

11 – D

12 – AC
Start in the top left corner, and move in a clockwise spiral around the diagram, towards the centre. The value of each card increases by 4 each time. To calculate the suits of each card, start at the top left and move in an anti-clockwise spiral towards the centre, following the sequence Hearts, Clubs, Diamonds, Spades.

13 –

$\frac{5}{32}$ $\frac{1}{2} + \frac{1}{4} \times \frac{3}{8} - \frac{7}{16} =$

$\frac{1}{2} + \frac{3}{32} - \frac{7}{16} =$

$\frac{16}{32} + \frac{3}{32} - \frac{14}{32}$

14 – B G
A is the same as H
C is the same as F
D is the same as E

15 –
(9+8) x 3 = 51
(6+5) x 8 = 88
(7+1) x 6 = 48
(5+2) x 9 = 63

16 – E
1 is added to 2 to equal 3
4 is added to 5 to equal 6
Like symbols disappear.

17 – C
All are odd numbers except for C = 54.

18 – R
The sequence is
D E F G H I J K
L M N O P Q R

19 – (e) ENVIRONMENT

20 – (a) UGLINESS

21 – 11
$9^2 - 1^2 = 80$
$7^2 - 3^2 = 40$
$6^2 - 5^2 = 11$

22 – 41
Column A
Odd numbers
Column B
Even numbers
Column C
Square numbers in sequence
Column D
Prime numbers in sequence

23 – (a) TOBACCO

24 – (a) OATMEAL

25 – 470, 10
(7+8=15) 78 + 15 x 10 = 930
(2+9=11) 29 + 11 x 10 = 400
(3+7=10) 37 + 10 x 10 = 470

26 – 5
Taking the top two numbers to form a 2-digit number, subtract the 2-digit number at the bottom to give the central number.

SOLUTIONS

27 – Eight of Clubs
Moving left to right, cards increase in value by 2, 3, 4, 5 and 6, returning to Ace whenever the King is reached and always following the same suit pattern.

28 – 5
Numbers in the bottom left circle equal the sums of the numbers in corresponding segments in the upper left and centre circles. Numbers in the bottom right circle equal the difference between those in the centre and right top circles.

29 – 14
In rows subtract 1 from the left and centre numbers and multiply together to give the right number.

30 – 3 & 3
The values of the segments in the top circle equal the sum of the corresponding opposite segments in the left hand circle. The values in the bottom circle equal the difference between corresponding opposite segments of the left hand circle.

31 –
Janine $1.01, $100.10 & $121.11,
Jackie $4.02, $49.07 & $169.13

32 – E
Starting with Y, letter values decrease by 2, 3, 4, 5 and 6.

33 – 1
The grid displays rotational symmetry of 180° around a central point.

34 – 39
Going clockwise, each number is doubled then subtract 1, then 2, then 3, etc.

35 – 6
Starting with each letter on the left, add 2 to give the number in the next two boxes, for the next groups add 3 and 4.

36 – 9
For each group, add first and second figures on the top row to get the final figure, and the difference between the first and second numbers for the bottom right box.

37 – Z
Working in diagonal lines from top left to bottom right, letters move forward by 4 places.

38 – 1
Numbers in the segments on the right hand half of the circle equal double the value of the numbers in the opposite segments, minus 3.

39 – 6
In each diagram the reverse numerical value of each letter is written in the box below plus 5 for the first diagram, 4 for the second and 3 for the third.

40 – 4:30
Multiply the hour value and minute value to give 36.

41 – 14
In each square the centre figure equals the difference between the sum of the left and right segments and the sum of the top and bottom segments.

42 – B
Working from left to right the square moves 2 segments anticlockwise, the circle 3 anticlockwise, the star by 4 anticlockwise and the triangle 1 segment clockwise.

43 – From top to bottom, Black Jack, Red King, Red Four and Black Eight.
In the first five rows the sum of the red cards equal the value of the right hand card. In the first 5 columns the sum of the black cards equals the value of the bottom card.

44 – 142 - 3 = 139

45 – L
Going clockwise in each square, letters increase in value by the same amount.

46 – A
The figures are groups of three of the same number squashed and rotated 90°.

47 - 2
Moving from left to right each box contains a decreasing square number, minus the root. (7 x 7 = 49 - 7 = 42, etc.)

48 – 16
Starting with the top value and moving clockwise, numbers move around a 24-hour clock, advancing 5 hours for the left star, 6 for the middle and 7 for the right.

49 – From left to right:
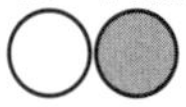
Working in columns add the number of black segments in the first two circles to give the bottom circle. The third circle down is the difference between the first two circles.

50 –
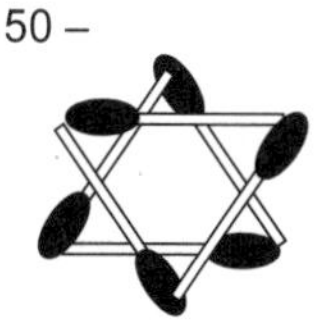

SOLUTIONS

51 – 1
The product of the first row gives the first number in the second row. The sum of the numbers in the top row gives the second number. Repeat this for rows three and four.

52 – From top to bottom, 14, 17 and 33.
Working in diagonal lines from left to right from the top, numbers increase in value by 2, then 4, then 5, etc.

LEVEL 17

1 – D

2 –
196 - 114 - 44
376 - 222- 44
487 - 336 - 198
19 x 6 = 114; 11 x 4 = 44

3 –
15 5
61-56 = 5
15/3 = 5

4 – D
The large circle moves two clockwise, the small white circle moves two anti-clockwise, the triangle moves one anti-clockwise and the black circle moves one anti-clockwise.

5 – 3
5 + 11 = 16; square root of 16 = 4, so 2 + 7 = 9 and square root of 9 = 3.

6 – O
The sequences occur looking across letters in the same position in each pentagon. Two move forward by missing 2 letters in the alphabet and three move by missing 2 back.

7 – B
The others are made up of three identical figures.

8 – 13654:
ABCDE - CDEBA

9 – 6
The number in the middle is the average of those surrounding it.

10 – D
Horizontally and vertically the sequence runs - add one line, keep same number of lines, add one line, etc.

11 – A

12 – 18
The inner numbers are 3 times the difference between the outer numbers.

13 – (e) COAX

14 – (b) 30
$(15)\ (4^2) = x\ (2^3)$
$15 \times 16 = x\ (8)$
$240 = 8x$
$30 = x$

15 –

6

1	2	3
4	5	6
7	8	9

16 – D
1 is added to 2 to equal 3
4 is added to 5 to cancel 6
Like symbols disappear.

17 – 28
(9 + 8) x 1 = 17
(5 + 6) x 3 = 33
(6 + 7) x 4 = 52
(3 + 11) x 2 = 28

18 – A
Each circle is made up by adding together the two circles below, but like symbols disappear.

19 – 0
Each circle adds to 89.

20 – 69 cents
Each letter represents the number of the letter counting from z = 1, y = 2, x = 3, etc.

21 – 15507
Each successive number is multiplied by 3.

22 – 9

546	664	527
+241	+227	+127
787	891	654

23 – 57

24 – (c) ANNAPURNA

25 – 7
98 ÷ 7 = 14 reverse 41

26 – 3
The numbers in each row add up to 52.

27 – 36
The answer in the centre of each triangle equals the difference between the top and left hand values, multiplied by the right hand value.

28 – 63
The sequence follows the cubes of 1, 2, 3 and 4, minus 1.

29 – 138
Starting bottom left and moving in a clockwise spiral, double the last number then subtract 5, etc.

SOLUTIONS

30 – W or E
Moving clockwise, each segment contains an example of a letter written with 1 continuous line, 2 lines, then 3, then 4.

31 – Q
Moving clockwise letters advance in steps of 9, 7 , 5, 3 and 1.

32 – X
Starting top left, add 4 to get the box below, add 5 for the second column and 6 for the third.

33 – 3
Each row contains every digit 0-9 inclusive.

34 – 29
In each diagram multiply the top two values and add their sum to give the bottom value.

35 – W
Moving from left to right, top row then bottom, in each square, letters in the top left corner increase by 1 place, top right letters decrease by 2 spaces, bottom left decrease by 1 place and letters in the bottom right corner increase by 2 spaces.

36 – D
Working from left to right, symbols with curved lines move 2 places clockwise, whilst straight sided symbols move to the segment opposite.

37 – 5
Taking 3 x 3 groups of circles with a 9 in the middle, the figures 1 - 9 appear in every group.

38 – 3
In rows the sum of the numerical values of the two boxes are written as a 2-digit number in the two right hand boxes.

39 – J
The boxes follow the sequence of letters missing out those written with just straight lines.

40 – C
Add the digits in the minutes position to get the hour value.

41 – B
Working from left to right, the X moves clockwise 1 segment, then 2, then 3, etc. The ∆ moves clockwise 4 segments, then 3, then 2, etc. The ○ and □ move to opposite segments and back again. A # and ⋆ fill the first two consecutive empty segments in a clockwise direction, and the • fills any segments left empty.

42 – A = 4, B = 6. Multiply the numbers on the second and third rows and write this answer along the top row, then multiply together the numbers along the top and write their squares along the bottom row.

43 – L
Moving from left to right, letters advance in steps of 1, 2 and 3 with their relative positions moving 1/3 of a turn clockwise each time.

44 – 2
Add the numbers from the top row to the numbers in the second row to get the third.

45 – 169
A descending sequence of the squares of prime numbers.

46 – 36
The first box shows the sequence of prime numbers. The second box multiplies these numbers by 2 minus 2, the third multiplied by 3 minus 3.

47 – 17
Going clockwise the numbers are the first 6 prime numbers plus 4.

48 – 4
The centre letter has the reverse alphabetical value of the corresponding left and right digits in each row when taken as a 2-digit number.

49 – $1

50 – 7
The sum of the 4 lower points minus the number at the top equals the number in the middle.

LEVEL 18

1 – D
The rest are the same figure.

2 – 5
Looking across each row, divide the first two digits (as a number) by two, to give the second two digits, ie:
46 ÷ 2 = 23
74 ÷ 2 = 37
28 ÷ 2 = 14 and
50 ÷ 2 = 25

3 – WTUV
The rest are consecutive letters of the alphabet in the sequence
LMNO OMLN
1 2 3 4 4 2 1 3

SOLUTIONS

4 – 5 revolutions
Take the lowest number (lowest common multiple) that all three cogs will divide into, in this case 60. Then divide by the largest wheel i.e. 60/12 = 5 revolutions.

5 – E

6 – 89
48/3 = 16, 72/9 = 8, so 24/3=8 and 45/5=9

7 – 8.6
There are two alternate sequences, +1.65 and +1.92.

8 – D
Looking across each line and down each column, any lines which are common to the first two squares are not carried forward to the final square.

9 – B
So that one square in each horizontal line contains all the lines in the other three squares.

10 – 132.375
Add, multiply by and subtract 1.5 in turn.

11 – L
Representing each letter by its position in the alphabet, and then multiplying the outside number you obtain the inside numbers.

C L D	3	12 4
F L B	6	12 2
E Y E	5	25 5

12 – B1

13 – A

14 – A
1 is added to 2 to equal 3
4 is added to 5 to equal 6
Similar symbols disappear.

15 – 28
(7 x 4) + 6 = 34
(9 x 1) + 7 = 16
(8 x 3) + 9 = 33
(6 x 4) + 4 = 28

16 – 0
(6 + 11 + 2) - (5 + 4) = 10
(9 + 3 + 6) - (5 + 4) = 9
(11 + 3 + 14) - (10 + 0) = 18

17 – ERUDITION, ILLITERACY

18 – 8C
Starting on the left and moving right, the value of each card increases by 6, 7, 8, 9 and 10, with odd numbered cards as Hearts, and even cards as Clubs.

19 – 468
$3^3 + 2^3 = 35$
$4^3 + 5^3 = 189$
$5^3 + 7^3 = 468$

20 – PARADISE
(pair of dice)

21 – 69
8 x 12 = 96 reverse 69
3 x 32 = 96 reverse 69

22 – 760
In all the other numbers, the sum of the first two digits equals the third.

23 – 30
As you move down, numbers increase by 7, 6, 5, 4 and 3.

24 – K
In each row the central figure equals the sum of the alphabetical value of the left hand letter and the reverse alphabetical value of the right hand letter.

25 – R
Starting in the top left segment of each circle, and moving clockwise, double the value of each letter and subtract 2 to give the value of the next letter around.

26 – 15
Top row follows ascending sequence bottom left to top right, plus 5 for the first group, 6 for the second and 7 for the third. Subtract top middle from bottom left to give bottom middle and add top left to give bottom right.

27 – 8
Letters in the top row are the same distance from the start of the alphabet as the corresponding letters in the bottom row are from the end. The figures in the middle row are half the numerical value of the letters in the bottom row.

28 – 1
Each number equals the square of the odd numbers in descending order from 11.

29 – C
Clockwise, letters move back 6 places, forward 2 places, etc.

30 – 14
Multiply the two outer digits in each segment and divide by 2. This result is put at the centre of the segment 2 places clockwise.

31 – Seven of Diamonds & Eight of Spades
The cards are arranged alternately in two sequences, one increases in steps of 2, the other decreases by 1. The suits follow the order Hearts, Diamonds, Spades Clubs.

SOLUTIONS

32 – Three of Clubs & Nine of Hearts
Taking the first five cards in each row, add the values of the odd cards to give a 2-digit answer. Add these 2 digits together to give the value of the club in that row. Do the same with the even cards to give the value of the Heart in that row.

33 – 72
In the top circle, the numbers in the upper half are multiplied by 3 and the result put in the segment opposite.
In the left hand circle, the numbers are multiplied by 6 and by 9 in the bottom circle.

34 – F
Moving in rows from left to right, the row of dots at the top moves down 1 row each time, returning to the top when it reaches the bottom. The left hand column moves back and forth across the box.
In addition, one dot starts in the bottom left corner and moves clockwise corner to corner and another dot fills the central space each time, however, should a black dot already fill either of these two places as a result of earlier instructions then the dot is left white.

35 – 20
In each circle, multiply the top two numbers together and subtract the lower right number to give the lower left number.

36 – 67
As numbers go down multiply by 2 and subtract 3.

37 – D
On each watch the minutes value equals the hour value multiplied by 3.

38 – B
Starting top left and working to the right in each row, the top and third dot remain stationary, with the dot in between moving to and fro along its line 3 spaces at a time. The lowest dot moves to and fro 1 space at a time and the dot above it 2 spaces. The whole grid rotates 90° clockwise at each step.

39 – 10
In each circle the top right number equals the average of the left hand numbers and the lower right equals the difference between these numbers.

40 – M
Letters descend in reverse alphabetical order in intervals of 7 then 6, 5, 4 and 3.

41 – 21
In each circle, starting top left and moving clockwise, multiply the first number by 3 and subtract 3 to give the next.

42 – A
Divide the minutes on each watch by 4 to give the hour value.

43 – 13
Starting on the left, values in corresponding segments of each circle increase by 1, 2, 3 and 4. The relative positions of the sequence rotate a quarter turn clockwise as you move to the right.

44 – 2:53
Taking the hour and minute values separately, the hours decrease by 3, 4, 5 and 6 hours and the minutes increase by 21, 23, 25 and 27.

45 – 1
The figure in the centre of each triangle equals the sum of the squares on the three corners.

46 – 5
Working from left to right in each figure, the numbers add up to 32, 34 and 36.

LEVEL 19

1 – One chance in 1105 or 1104 to 1
$\frac{6}{52} \times \frac{5}{51} \times \frac{4}{50} = \frac{1}{1105}$

2 – 13 cats killed 23 rats (both factors are prime numbers).

3 – 94.75
There are two alternate sequences, -1.75 and -2.25.

4 – D
The main figure faces the other way at each stage and the line moves down a quarter then back to the top again at each stage.

5 – 77
Add the sum of the digits of the previous number each time.

6 – 35
16 + 22 + 24 = 62;
3 x 9 = 27;
62 - 27 = 35

7 – C
The figures are in the same order but go in the opposite direction as the other options.

8 – J
From the middle letter start at N and work clockwise.
The letters skip +1, -1, +2, -2, +3, -3, +4, -4.

SOLUTIONS

9 –
Frasier 46,
Niles 42,
Daphne 34

10 – B
Horizontally and vertically, add one dot outside and inside the diamond until there are four and then remove one dot.

11 – A

12 – 46
Starting at 21, 1-4-3-2 are added in succession.

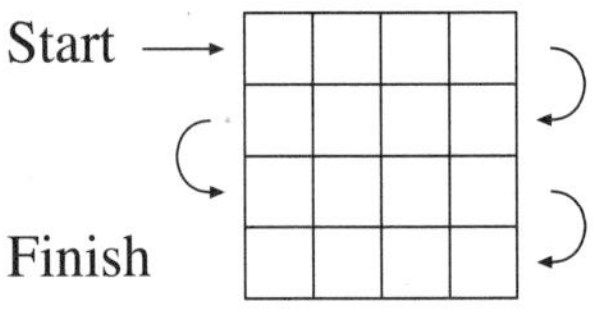

13 –
6x3 (to the power of 9) =
6x19683 = 118098

14 –
60 (MOD 8) = 48 (MOD 10)
33 (MOD 8) = 27 (MOD 10)

15 – 476

$6^3 - 4^2 = 200$
$7^3 - 5^2 = 318$
$8^3 - 6^2 = 476$

16 – C2

17 – 24
(6 x 7) - 8 = 34,
(9 x 5) - 11 = 34,
(12 x 6) - 26 = 46,
(8 x 4) - 12 = 20,
(6 x 6) - 12 = 24

18 – 40
16+11+29=29+27
4x18+51=6+67
18+19+5=40+2

19 – B
1 is added to 2 to equal 3
4 is added to 5 to cancel 6
Like symbols disappear.

20 – (D)
◉ remains,
○ moves opposite,
• moves opposite,
● moves to centre and returns.

21 – L
T has 8 right angles
L has 6 right angles
O has 8 right angles
C has 8 right angles
U has 8 right angles
J has 8 right angles

22 – 14
In each row, subtract 1 from the left and central numbers, and multiply together to give the right hand number.

23 – Z
Moving in diagonal lines, from top left to bottom right, letters increase in value by 4 each time.

24 – Z
Starting at C and moving clockwise, letters increase in value by 5, then 4 alternately.

25 – 132
All other numbers contain the digit 4.

26 – 9
Take each number in the outer ring as a 2-digit number and multiply them together. Write this answer plus 1 in the inner segment opposite.

27 – 12
In each box, square the top numbers and subtract 4 to give the lower number.

28 – 51
Starting from the left circle, working top to bottom in columns, then to the next column to the right, add 1, 2, 3, etc, until the central circle, then subtract 11, 10, 9, etc.

29 – 56
In each diagram, divide the top left value by 3, multiply it by the top right value, then multiply the answer by 4, giving the lower value.

30 –

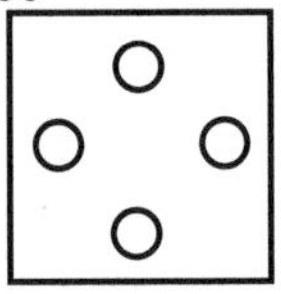

Working in rows, using the left hand figure as a source, reflect around a vertical axis to give the middle figure, and reflect around a horizontal axis to give the right hand figure.

31 – 55
The boxes follow the sequence of prime numbers multiplied by 5.

32 – J
In rows the left hand number equals the numerical value of the centre letter plus 1, the right hand number equals the reverse alphabetical value of the letter plus 1.

33 – 19
In each row, starting on the left, multiply the number by 3 and subtract 2 to give the next number on the right.

34 – H
In each row, add the numerical values of the left and right hand letters to give the reverse alphabetical values of the central letter.

SOLUTIONS

35 – 65
Moving downwards, double each number and subtract 1.

36 – X
Letters increase in value down each column by 4 in the first column, 5 in the middle and 6 in the right hand column.

37 – 78
Moving downwards, add 1 to each number and double it to get the next number.

38 – L
Starting at the top and working inwards in a clockwise spiral, letters increase in value by 4 each time.

39 – 2:53
As you move right the hour value decreases by 1, 2, 3, 4 each step and the minutes increase by 11, 12, 13 and 14.

40 – 4
In each row the first and third numbers when read as a 2-digit number give the reverse alphabetical value of the centre letter.

41 – 9
In rows, the centre value equals the product of the left and right hand numbers minus the sum of the left and right numbers.

42 – $2.30
The first three spend a total of $27.60 on 12 of each item, therefore each tool = $2.30.

43 – F
Working in rows, add together the left and central diagrams to make the diagram on the right. If a black square appears in both of these columns it becomes white in the third box.

LEVEL 20

1 – F
Looking across and down the number of sides in the figures increases by 1 in each square.

2 – H
Start at the top left corner and spiral round the perimeter skipping 2 letters in the alphabet, then going back one letter alternately. Finish in the centre square.

3 – D
It has 2 consecutive stars.

4 – MNOP
Start at A and miss one letter before the next line, then miss two letters then finally three letters i.e. AbCDefGHIjklMNOP

5 – P
Looking across and down omit 1 letter then 2 then 3 in successive rows and columns.

6 – C
Start at the top left-hand square and work along the top and then back along the second row, etc, in the sequence white circle, black circle, triangle.

7 – 24
27 + 21 = 48; 4 x 6 = 24;
48 - 24 = 24

8 – 13.25
There are two sequences, +3.75 and +2.75.

9 – B
All figures move one side clockwise. Then figures outside go inside and black figures become white and vice versa.

10 – J L O
So that all connected lines contain the same letters:
J K L M N O P

11 – 7
The second line is subtracted from the first to obtain the third.

12 – A
● moves 1 corner clockwise
• moves 1 corner clockwise
○ moves 1 corner anti-clockwise
⁄ moves 1 line clockwise
↘ moves 1 corner anti-clockwise

13 – 97

$$\begin{array}{r} 8 \times 9 = 72 \\ -\ 4 + 8 = \underline{12} \\ 60 \end{array}$$

$$\begin{array}{r} 11 \times 7 = 77 \\ -\ 6 + 5 = \underline{11} \\ 66 \end{array}$$

$$\begin{array}{r} 13 \times 9 = 117 \\ -\ 5 + 4 = \underline{\ \ 9} \\ 108 \end{array}$$

14 – A1

15 – D

	No of lines
A	6
B	8
C	5
D	6
E	7

16 – (b) RUBBER

17 –
They all contain a boy's name: ALF, ELI, HAL, LEN, NED, and PAT

18 – 32
Add reversed numbers:

61	76	11	16
41	5	14	12
7	12	7	4
109	93	32	32

SOLUTIONS

19 – B

20 – 5
101-26=17+14+28+16
96-1=14+11+10+60
88-5=67+7+4+5

21 – 54
In each square, the sum of the squares of the three outer numbers equals the number bounded by the central square.

22 – 1=L, 2=E
All other letters in each oval are written with 3 strokes of the pen.

23 – V
Starting in the top left, and moving in a clockwise spiral towards the centre, letters increase in value by 2, 3, 4, 5, etc.

24 – 2
Reading each row as a 3-digit number, rows follow multiples of 123 (108, 120, 132).

25 – 1
In each star, multiply the left and right hand numbers together, then subtract the upper and two lower numbers to give the value in the centre of the star.

26 – C & N
Letters in the bottom row are 1 place lower than the corresponding letters in the top row, letters in the third row are 2 places lower than the second.

27 – 2
The sum of the numbers in the top and bottom rows is put in the corresponding position in the second row, the difference between the top and bottom rows is put in the third row.

28 – V
Starting top left and spiralling clockwise, letters move forward by 2 places, then 3, then 4, etc.

29 – 1
The numbers at the centre equal the numerical value of the letter in the opposite segment, if this value exceeds 9 the digits are added together to give a single digit answer.

30 – 72
Moving in a clockwise spiral, numbers are double the square of the first 9 numbers.

31 – 477
Starting with the top 3-digit number, square the central digit and add this to the original number to give the next number.

32 –

Working from left to right, using the left circle as a source, the middle shows the original and its reflection about a vertical axis, the right shows the original and its reflection about the horizontal axis.

33 – 6
The sum of the numbers in the lines of three going upwards equal the sum of the numbers in the lines of three going downwards.

34 – A = 7, B = 9
The difference between the first and third columns as a 4-digit number going down is written in the central column going down.

35 – 4
The sum of the odd numbers in each column equals the sum of the even numbers.

36 –

30 dots in each column.

37 – 2
Take the numerical value of each letter and multiply by the opposite to get the answer in the middle.

38 – N
Starting top left and moving diagonally upwards from left to right letters are repeated.

39 – 2
Cube the numbers in each column of the top grid and add the answers together. Write this answer going down the columns of the bottom grid.

40 – B
Cube the numerical values of the letters in the top grid and add the answers together. Write this answer in reverse order in the columns in the bottom box.

41 – D
The others are symmetrical.

42 – Y - C - P - M - I - T - D - Y - A
There are two chains of letters. The first chain goes diagonally upwards from left to right starting in the bottom left corner and appears on alternate lines. This chain contains every letter of the alphabet except vowels. The second chain starts bottom right and goes diagonally downwards from right to left and has every letter of the alphabet.